Solidarity in Strategy

Solidarity in Strategy

*Making Business Meaningful in
American Trade Associations*

LYN SPILLMAN

THE UNIVERSITY OF CHICAGO PRESS   CHICAGO AND LONDON

Lyn Spillman is the author of *Nation and Commemoration: Creating National Identities in the United States and Australia*. She teaches sociology at the University of Notre Dame.

The University of Chicago Press, Chicago 60637
The University of Chicago Press, Ltd., London
© 2012 by The University of Chicago
All rights reserved. Published 2012.
Printed in the United States of America

21 20 19 18 17 16 15 14 13 12   1 2 3 4 5

ISBN-13: 978-0-226-76956-1 (cloth)
ISBN-13: 978-0-226-76957-8 (paper)
ISBN-10: 0-226-76956-9 (cloth)
ISBN-10: 0-226-76957-7 (paper)

Library of Congress Cataloging-in-Publication Data

Spillman, Lyn.
    Solidarity in strategy : making business meaningful in American trade associations /
Lyn Spillman.
        pages ; cm
    Includes bibliographical references and index.
    ISBN-13: 978-0-226-76956-1 (cloth : alkaline paper)
    ISBN-10: 0-226-76956-9 (cloth : alkaline paper)
    ISBN-13: 978-0-226-76957-8 (paperback : alkaline paper)
    ISBN-10: 0-226-76957-7 (paperback : alkaline paper)   1. Trade associations—United
States. 2. Business anthropology—United States. 3. Economics—United States—
Sociological aspects. 4. Capitalism—Social aspects—United States.   I. Title.
    HD2425.S65 2012
    381.068'4—dc23

                                                                    2011050359

♾ This paper meets the requirements of ANSI/NISO Z39.48-1992 (Permanence of Paper).

Contents

Acknowledgments

This book explores how economic interests are meaningful by examining American business associations. Both the general question and the specific focus open new territory, and so my arguments—that solidarity is as important as strategy for the pursuit of economic interests, and that business associations' many and various activities are fundamentally about meaning-making—have been built up through many iterations. Clifford Geertz's observation that "every serious cultural analysis starts from a sheer beginning and ends where it manages to get before exhausting its intellectual impulse" captures a truth about this process but elides the support sustaining its ambition.

The sheer beginning of this work was made possible by the John Simon Guggenheim Memorial Foundation. Their reputation for supporting intellectual innovation is well deserved, and as a beneficiary I am grateful. Also important for stimulating the project were extended visits to the Sociology Departments of Northwestern University and the University of Arizona, and the conversation and hospitality of Al Bergesen, Ron Breiger, Bruce Carruthers, Mark Chaves, Lis Clemens, Wendy Espeland, Gary Fine, Joe Galaskiewicz, Wendy Griswold, Kieran Healy, Carol Heimer, Paul Hirsch, Patricia Ledesma Liébana, Peter Levin, Linda Molm, Ami Nagle, William Ocasio, John Sherry, Joel Stillerman, Art Stinchcombe, Susan Thistle, Marc Ventresca, and Katie Zaloom.

The ASA/NSF Fund for the Advancement of the Discipline helped support my census of national business associations, now publically available at the Inter-University Consortium for Political and Social Research. The Institute for Scholarship in the Liberal Arts (ISLA) in the College of Arts and Letters, University of Notre Dame, provided a Research Materials Grant toward that work and also helped in several ways at later stages of the project. I appreciate their support and all the good work ISLA does by offering practical resources for furthering research agendas.

The association census relied heavily on the collaboration of Rui Gao, whose impressive command of the abstract issues and empirical detail involved are evident in the coding protocols she developed. Brian Miller and Georgian Schiopu also contributed smart work on the census data. Xiohong Xu helped complete that work and skillfully prepared the preliminary data analysis. As excellent scholars with their own interesting projects in cultural and historical sociology, they bore with good humor reminders of Weber's admonition that "no sociologist . . . should think himself too good . . . to make tens of thousands of quite trivial computations." Joe Rumbo and Lisa Sustman provided research assistance as the project took shape, and Hyae Jeong Joo, Dan Pasch, and Sarah Shafiq helped with later work. Elizabeth Blakey Martinez provided extensive research that was especially helpful for the new analytical history of American business associations in chapter two. As the work drew to a conclusion, Michael Strand helped with research and analysis, strengthening key arguments, especially in chapters three, four, and seven, and offered smart theoretical reflections on deeper issues they raised.

Midway in what turned out to be the arc of the study, I was welcomed as a Visiting Fellow of the Center for Cultural Sociology in the Sociology Department at Yale University. I want to thank Jeff Alexander for that opportunity and for his patient support of the work from its beginning.

The center's seriousness of purpose and commitment to the power of cultural explanation made welcome space for thinking through and organizing my larger argument. Presentations to responsive audiences at several of the center's conferences and colloquia helped that process. Julia Adams, Ates Altinordu, Scott Boorman, Hannah Brueckner, Phil Gorski, Nadya Jaworsky, Karl Ulrich Meyer, Philip Smith, and Frédéric Vandenberghe were helpful interlocutors there. Lisa McCormick provided a valuable critique, and Isaac Reed and Matthew Norton managed the publication of an early version of what later expanded to become chapters four and five: "A Special Camaraderie with Colleagues: Business Associations and Cultural Production for Economic Action," in *Meaning and Method: The Cultural Approach to Sociology*, ed. Isaac Reed and Jeffrey C. Alexander (Boulder and London: Paradigm Publishers, 2009). (Thanks to Matt Norton, too, for reports of the Fetish Priest and Traditional Healers Association of Ghana.)

Many other scholars offered thoughtful responses to various parts of the work. I'm grateful to participants in the Culture and Society Workshop at Northwestern University; the Georgia Workshop on Culture, Power, and History; the Emory Bogardus Colloquium Series of the Sociology Department at the University of Southern California; and the International Research Conference on Culture and Power at the Institute for Social Research, Oslo. Audiences at several annual meetings of the American Sociological Association as well as meetings of the Eastern Sociological Society, the Society for the Advancement of Socio-Economics, the Social Science History Association, and the International Sociological Association's XVII World Congress of Sociology also helped improve the work. Thanks to Howard Becker, Fredrik Engelstadt, Marion Fourcade, Joan Hermsen, David Johnson, Alexandra Kalev, Terry McDonnell, Aaron Pitluck, Bill Roy, Sheryl Skaggs, and David Smilde for comments and critique.

Ann Swidler helped with important contributions and suggestions at several critical stages of the project, as well as with her friendly, optimistic interest. Nina Eliasoph, Kim Hays, Paul Lichterman, Isaac Reed, and Susan Thistle read and responded to early versions of some chapters, and I'm grateful for both their thoughtful reactions and their friendship.

A long-term project like this inevitably accrues more intellectual debts than are easily remembered, even by some of my helpful creditors. Among those to whom I'm indebted for discussion and help are Mabel Berezin, Gerald Berk, Denise Bielby, Mark Chaves, Paul DiMaggio, Greg Ellis, Christine Ellis, Tiago Fernandes, Bai Gao, Robert Fishman, Roger Friedland, David Hachen, Mark D. Jacobs, Felicia LeClere, Daniel Levy, Michael Lounsbury, John Mohr, Michael Moody, Penny Moore, Calvin Morrill, Chuck Myers, Peggy O'Neill, Lauren Rivera, Abigail Saguy, Marc Schneiberg, Michael Schudson, Barry Schwartz, Abbee Smith, Ken Spillman, Erika Summers-Effler, Richard Swedberg, Jan Thomas, Fred Wherry, and JoAnn Yates. Thank you.

I also want to record with love and sadness a life-long debt to John Spillman for his encouragement of my work. Although he did not live to see it in his hands, I know he would have read this book with interest and understanding.

Toward the end of the project when, as Geertz might say, the work was exhausting its intellectual impulse, Doug Mitchell, renowned editor at the University of Chicago Press, brought to it fresh reserves of energy and enthusiasm, an irreplaceable gift for which I offer my warm thanks. I am also grateful to anonymous reviewers for their thoughtful and detailed readings and critiques. Tim McGovern stepped in with solutions at a critical moment in the manuscript's preparation. Dawn Hall's smart, helpful work as copyeditor significantly improved it.

My husband, Russell Faeges, offered sustained support for this investigation. I thank him not only for the writing session coffee but also for his enthusiasm about the broader theoretical significance of the study. He offered many sociological reflections, quotations, and examples and came to the rescue with some rigorous editing. He also drew my attention to the National Association of Motivation Manufacturers, which "contributes dynamically to the on-going efforts of its members to advance the motivation industry into the 21st Century on a broad front."

This book is dedicated to Neil Smelser in gratitude for his extraordinary support over many years. His contributions to economic sociology long predated its growth in the last decades of the twentieth century, and his influence continues. It's a compliment to his selfless encouragement that although he was always quick with helpful comments it took me some time to realize how much the questions that engaged me in this research emerged on intellectual territory some of his scholarship had mapped. His long career of important writing, generous mentoring, and sustained academic leadership is a remarkable accomplishment.

CHAPTER ONE

Solidarity, Strategy, and the Meaning of Business

Everyone knows that self-interested action in the pursuit of profit is the fundamental dynamo of contemporary economic life. We know that capitalist production and exchange require systematic competitive profit-seeking in markets. We know that firms survive by making money. And so we assume that people in business think of what they are doing to make that happen as rational, self-interested, profit-oriented action.

In this book I challenge this assumption that business is necessarily conducted as self-interested action in the pursuit of profit. I ask an apparently naive question: what makes self-interested action in the pursuit of profit make sense? That is, how do firms and the businesspeople who run them understand their interests? What meaning-making sustains their action? What cultural categories and vocabularies of motive make capitalist understandings of their norms of exchange, objects of exchange, and exchange partners routinely plausible—for capitalists? These questions about business culture and about how profit-seeking actors really understand what they are doing are almost never investigated, because the stereotype of the rational pursuit of economic self-interest has been so powerfully naturalized—even for the most sophisticated observers—in public narratives, in economic models, and in social theory.

To examine how profit-oriented firms and businesspeople make sense of their interested action, I analyze their discourses and strategies of action in contemporary American business associations. Economic sociologists and economists have almost entirely ignored this busy and often surprising arena of American economic activity, so in order to study it I first develop a unique overview of the population of national business associations. Analyzing a new census of these associations and extensive archival data from twenty-five representative groups, I argue that these stable, long-lasting groups are, primarily, institutional settings for routine cultural production—generating categories, networks, industry fields, collective identities, norms, status orders, and camaraderie that orient and motivate economic action.

Then, exploring the meaning-making about business that actually goes on in these settings, I show that businesspeople often understand themselves as disinterested rather than self-interested actors. They often think of what they are doing in terms of technical expertise, professionalism, stewardship of the public good and occupational community, and these vocabularies of motive are a constitutive part of many business identities.

I argue that the pursuit of strategic interest in competitive profit-seeking is conditioned by and relies on institutions and discourses transcending strategic interests, and that such institutions and discourses make capitalist economic action routinely meaningful. Anybody concerned about the power of business needs to understand these important themes in business culture.

This argument expands and adds force to the arguments of scholars who investigate the cultural embeddedness of economic action. Many sociologists now recognize that culture shapes economic action; they show how particular economic "interests" are culturally constructed, and how market and nonmarket relations are profoundly intertwined in everyday life. Looking at how interests are understood in business associations demonstrates that we need to reexamine the very idea of "interests," not only the cultural construction of particular economic interests in particular circumstances. And it shows how market and nonmarket relations are profoundly intertwined even at the heart of capitalist action.

Culture and Economic Interests

The assumption that capitalist production and exchange requires a disciplined orientation to systematic, competitive profit-seeking in markets generates a series of familiar and well-worn contrasts—between market exchange and social redistribution, exploitation and reciprocity, corporations and nonprofits, purchase and intimacy, "market" and "society," and between self-interest and altruism. Positioned by these contrasts, the archetypal capitalist actor will do everything possible to pursue narrow interests in shameless ways at the expense of others, will try to shape state policy to protect profits, and will promote cold and unjust ideologies. Even where welfare states, corporatist regimes, legal regulation, or paternalistic virtue soften the harshness of capitalism, these are only secondary remedies. This profound opposition is epitomized in Charles Dickens's nineteenth-century morality tale of businessman Ebenezer Scrooge's conversion, *A Christmas Carol*.[1]

Certainly, as many sociologists recognize, economic interests are constantly shaped and changed in cultural processes. Certainly, as theorists like Marx and Polanyi suggest, the world has seen other fundamental principles of production and exchange. And certainly, at a more mundane level, business commentators often promote cooperation in teamwork, social responsibility, business ethics, nonprofit management, and so on. Yet even recognizing all this, we surely must admit that in the here and now, in the annual reports and acquisitions, in the outsourcing of labor, the infolding of new technologies, and the marketing excess, economic life in contemporary society requires strategizing about the next statement of earnings or market share, or submitting to the demands of those who must do so. Intermittent public scandals and destructive systemic failures only reinforce the point.

Looking briefly at how classical social theorists understood modern economic exchange clarifies this apparent inevitability and suggests a way forward.

The Classical Origins of the Problem of Capitalist Interests

The easy and compelling familiarity of conceptual oppositions between "market" and "society," "self-interest" and "altruism," and all the other similar and related contrasts (as well as the ways they are sometimes complicated and challenged) is an echo of long centuries of reflection, analysis, and critique by social theorists close to and preoccupied with the development of capitalism in Europe. As any reader of the sociological classics is well aware, modernity is characterized by increasing and increasingly dynamic penetration of market institutions to all arenas of life, the dominance of markets over alternative exchange institutions, and even the transposition of market logics to other institutions and other forms of collective action.

As capitalism became established, in one way or another, across the globe, and as it has changed under the influence of critical challenges, state action, and varying local contexts, the idea that systematic pursuit of particular economic interests in profitable production and exchange is a requirement of modern economic action thus acquired the incontrovertibility of common sense, for both celebrants and critics.

In fact, the large-scale changes in social organization that spread as production came to be organized for market exchange and capitalist business expanded demanded three distinct changes in economic culture. First, traditional views of potential *objects of market exchange* were radically expanded. Most important, labor became a central object of market exchange: but the expansion also ultimately encompassed generalized commodification that, if it was not total, was at least vastly more comprehensive than in precapitalist societies, and was theoretically unlimited in the economists' abstract notion of utility. Second, traditional views of potential *partners and competitors in exchange*—the "imagined community" of the market—were likewise radically expanded in practice and abstracted from particularistic social relations in newly developing economic theory. Third, profit-seeking on markets became the *normative model of exchange relations*, at the expense of exchange relations dominated by reciprocity or redistribution. These cultural conditions for capitalist market exchange could vary independently, but they are often collapsed and reduced to the third, competitive profit-seeking as the dominant normative model of exchange—and the necessity of this normative capitalist culture was least often challenged.[2]

For Adam Smith, of course, removing restrictions on humans' putatively natural inclination to "truck, barter and exchange," and giving competitive profit-seeking free rein as a foundational principle, generated increased commodification and the abstraction of markets from traditional social relations. Objects of exchange proliferated; partners in exchange were no longer restricted. Self-interested exchange could lead to better macrosocial housekeeping, taking care of society's infrastructural chores in a generally more effective way. The power of these ideas is evident in their familiarity even today, not only in popular and scholarly economics but also in commentary on problems ranging from environmental risk to conflicts in developing countries.[3]

Later, Marx retained the political economists' conviction that norms of market exchange in capitalist societies could be nothing other than competitive and self-interested. He deplored the fact that labor increasingly became an object of exchange, and also the "fetishism of commodities," and noted as well the expanded range of potential market relations. His analysis of capitalism, too, still echoes in the contemporary public sphere, in generic critical discussions of such topics as consumerism, social inequality, corporate malfeasance, and economic globalization. Of course, he highlighted the exploitation, loss, and suffering that these abstractions from traditional social relations entailed in much greater depth than Smith and the political economists. But although they differ in their evaluation, both Smith and Marx share the view that the idea of systematic production for competitive, self-interested market exchange lies at the core of capitalist modernity. They set the deep terms of debate about economic processes, generating and regenerating new analyses and applications in new economic circumstances as well as innumerable theoretical addenda.[4]

The originality and significance of Max Weber's economic sociology lies partly in the fact that he did indeed famously highlight the cultural peculiarity of capitalist norms of exchange and wondered how they might have become widely established. He argued that while self-interested profit-seeking was not confined to capitalism, capitalist norms of exchange came to dominate economic life in the West as an unintended consequence of early Protestants' insecurities about their ideal interests in religious salvation, and of the individual disciplines—like systematic planning and record-keeping and limits to consumption—imposed by early Protestantism. His broader theory of economic action in his major works deepened this account by identifying institutional conditions for the contingent success of this historical accident in ways that could illuminate economic development elsewhere. But if economic and religious meanings were intertwined in the origins of capitalism, and that explained how capitalist norms of exchange first came to dominate economic life, Weber saw less need to account for their persistence. They had become the inescapable "iron cage" of modern life. His ideal type of modern, market-oriented economic activity was transient, rationalized, and competitive. He knew that many real economic relationships might fall short of this ideal-typical model, with political institutions shaping interests and "communal" cultural orientations sometimes diluting hardheaded individualistic rationality (e.g., a market relation may "involve emotional values which transcend its utilitarian significance"). But the necessity of a rationalized orientation to production for self-interested, profit-driven market exchange was the inescapable core of modern economic action for Weber, even though he set this norm of exchange in historical and cultural context. Like Smith and Marx, he saw economic action in modern life as a rationalized and expansive systemic orientation to competitive profit-seeking in markets.[5]

Durkheim moved even further beyond Smith's and Marx's concerns, to the extent that he is only rarely understood as a theorist of capitalism.

Yet he speaks directly to the classical problem of capitalist interests in exchange in at least one very important way: in his analysis of the technical and social division of labor. Whereas Weber asked how the self-interested pursuit of market exchange could *emerge* as a dominant economic force, Durkheim begins to raise the usually unasked question about how it could plausibly be *sustained*. For Durkheim, increasing social differentiation and a complex division of labor were fundamental features of modernity (and not only in economic institutions). He was struck by the potential problems for social solidarity posed by increasing differentiation and complexity in modern societies, in contrast with simpler societies in which members shared similar experiences, perceptions, and evaluations. For instance, no society could function simply on the basis of contracts between self-interested individuals: for contracts to be effective there needed to be a shared belief in the legitimacy of contract. More generally, shared meaning was essential even in complex societies in which individuals and their interests were highly differentiated and often conflicting.

By asking how solidarity was possible in complex societies, Durkheim was also asking how society could sustain the vastly widened and potentially unlimited expansion and abstraction of potential *partners* in market exchange, which was one of the major cultural changes brought by capitalism. He rejects the assumption that the *norm* of the systematic, self-interested pursuit of profitable exchange was sufficient to account for the social cohesion of complex capitalist societies (the assumption that was explicit and positive in Smith, more implicit and negative in Marx, and ideal-typical but qualified in Weber). Many subsequent scholars have explored how the sort of solidarity that interested Durkheim is generated in modern societies, for instance, in the political realm. But the radical implications of his theory of solidarity for our understanding of economic life have yet to be fully explored. Critics as well as believers in capitalism have, since Smith and Marx, emphasized that its normative core is the self-interested pursuit of profitable market exchange; so they have not asked— as Durkheim did—how that norm could be meaningfully sustained. By theorizing solidarity in the complex division of labor—which entailed the vast expansion and abstraction of the "imagined community" of partners and competitors in exchange—Durkheim offers leads for answering that question. As many generations of critics have argued, his vision underemphasizes the politics of self-interest in capitalism in general. But Durkheim's project suggests that assuming nothing but self-interest—as Smith and Marx often did—is also naive and shortsighted.[6]

Mostly, though, earlier classical theorists' understanding of self-interested exchange in capitalist economic life are so deeply ingrained in both theory and public discussion that the necessity of an orientation to production for profitable exchange in capitalist modernity has gone almost unquestioned on all sides. This radical essence of capitalism organized the standard dichotomy drawn between market and society and all its variants, setting the terms for most developments and critical debates since. It is easier and more common to investigate and debate changes in the limits and the appropriate objects of commodification—such as the issue of medical care—and the limits and possibilities of expanding inclusion in markets—such as the issue of globalization—than to investigate and discuss capitalist norms of exchange and their alternatives.

Unlike cultural assumptions about commodification and legitimate market actors, the important assumption that market action is necessarily oriented by a norm of self-interested exchange is rarely subjected to empirical investigation. A murmur of dissent did persist throughout the twentieth century, especially among social scientists inclined to demonstrate that ideas about economic interests look more complicated in real life than they do in economic theory. Important general challenges to standard assumptions about market action in capitalist societies were made not only by Polanyi, as noted above, but also by such scholars as Marshall Sahlins, Mary Douglas, Talcott Parsons, and Neil Smelser.[7] But considering that economic analysis dominated scholarly research on markets, that economics treats orientation to self-interested exchange as a primordial constant (even as increasingly sophisticated economic theories accounting for cooperative action have emerged), and that economists have been most interested in markets as price-fixing mechanisms, it is not surprising that the norm of self-interested exchange on markets is still generally taken for granted. Durkheim's concern about how solidarity could work at the heart of economic life in complex societies remained peripheral. Contemporary economic sociology reopens this issue, but has not yet attacked it head on.

Culture and Interests in Contemporary Economic Sociology

For most of the twentieth century, sociology effectively ceded understanding of market action to mainstream economics. Most sociologists focused on human action and institutions that were affected by but analytically distinct from production and exchange. Market norms became an unanalyzed

background to other sociological concerns about the impact of commodification, rationalization, organizational structure and strategy, the organization of labor, and systematic power inequalities. As Viviana Zelizer
among many others pointed out, many sociologically inspired critiques of
market processes tended to take markets (unlike other social structures)
as institutionally undifferentiated and historically invariant, separating
them from broader social and cultural theorizing and reproducing the
economists' sharp separation between "economic" and "social" processes.
The whole idea of particularistic interests in the systematic pursuit of
profitable production and exchange had come to seem so obvious that
only its implementation and its effects seemed worth considering.[8]

The revival of economic sociology in the late twentieth century retrieved
questions about economic life for the closer investigation of sociologists,
challenging these conceptual and ideological oppositions between market
and society. Clifford Geertz's prescription for "incorporation of sociocul-
tural factors into the body of discussion [about economic processes] rather
than relegating them to the status of boundary matters" was fulfilled.
Economic sociologists reiterate that economic action is a form of social
action, that economic action is socially situated, and that economic institutions are social constructions. In doing so, they move beyond broad
assumptions about "market society in general," as well as economists'
assumptions about motivational and microinteractional universals of exchange processes.[9]

Contemporary economic sociologists provide extensive evidence of different ways the systematic pursuit of profitable production and exchange
is shaped by social context. Broadly, they show how capitalist action varies
according to differing national institutions: we now know that we must
speak of cultures, rather than culture, of capitalism. More particularly,
they often examine how changing industry arrangements, diverse organizational forms, and particular network patterns shape real-world economic
action. The findings are important: as Mark Granovetter puts it strongly,
they suggest that "the anonymous market of neoclassical models is virtu-
ally nonexistent in economic life." As this study will show, all these ways
that economic action is "embedded" in social relations are also important
for understanding business associations, because these groups vary by
national context, influence industry formation and transformation, link
different types of organizations, and help create and sustain networks.[10]

But economic sociologists' exploration of the cultural embeddedness of
economic action is especially important for investigating the norm of self-

interested action in markets, and this study builds on the accomplishments of those scholars who have shown how, far from being given, economic interests are actively constituted and reconstituted. Neoinstitutionalist arguments do this by emphasizing the cognitive and normative constitution and change of "industries": they provide a perspective for analyzing the production and reproduction of economic culture, including shaping interests in exchange. Harrison White makes a related point that production markets and industries are constituted in "common discourses"; and for Neil Fligstein, cultural politics is an important determinant of market stability and change. Focusing on everyday business practice, Nicole Biggart and Thomas Beamish highlight how "habits, routines, customs, and standard practices" coordinate perceptions of interests in economic action. Although they differ in many ways, these perspectives all suggest that (changing) discourses affect how economic actors see their interested pursuit of competitive advantage in exchange. However, they do not generally question the underlying assumption that market action demands an orientation to self-interested exchange; rather, they show how the ways this orientation is specified can vary according to social context, how interests get to be defined in different ways. So to some extent they retain too strong a distinction between "economy" and "culture."[11]

Zelizer makes one of the most sustained challenges to a strict separation between "economic action" and culture in a series of studies that show how reductionist views of this relationship are empirically inadequate, and how cultural changes influence economic valuation. Even "money" is not an abstract medium of exchange, but understood in social life through a hedge of cultural categories that shape its uses. In her work on the development of the life insurance industry, Zelizer shows how ideas about the "utility" of life insurance emerged to counter consumer resistance, which at first understood life insurance as an immoral intrusion of economic calculation into the private realm. She repeatedly demonstrates the practical interpenetration of economic and other orientations and activities in fluid cultural repertoires, and she argues that strong distinctions between market relations and other social relations—or the reduction of one to the other—cannot be sustained. However, her empirical support for this claim is based mostly on consumption and private social relations of various sorts, such as household care. Critics can still make the case that however messy the mix of cultural orientations in everyday life, business worlds can demand—and create—a purer, more focused attention to the pursuit of competitive self-interest in exchange at the expense of other activities, orientations, and relations. Thus the impact of her theoretical argument may be quarantined.[12]

So economic sociology demonstrates many ways in which cultural processes affect business interests in particular circumstances. But even if those interests are variable and socially constructed, it usually stops short of challenging the deep naturalization of business interests as normative orientations to competitive profit-seeking market exchange. And while Zelizer makes a strong argument that market orientations are inextricably entwined with other types of orientations, she does not show how this happens in business.[13]

In asking what "business interests" themselves mean to businesspeople, this book builds on and deepens these arguments by recent economic sociologists about culture in economic action. First, in what could be seen as following up a neglected cue from neoinstitutionalist theory, I am focusing on field-level institutions producing meanings for economic action rather than on the particular industries, firms, or consumer practices that are more commonly studied. I first argue that business associations are institutions for cultural production and discuss their standard strategies of action, along neoinstitutionalist lines. Second, while I begin by attending to organized collective action *producing* meanings for economic action, I go on to investigate the cultural conditions for sharing interests. I develop a "thick description" of the cultural *repertoire*, or vocabularies of motive, making business interests meaningful in these settings. In doing this, I show, as Zelizer shows for other settings, that the symbolic repertoires (cognitive, normative, and expressive) that associations and their members use to understand their economic action are more mixed and more fluid than the presumed norm of self-interested orientation to profit-seeking exchange suggests.

But third, and most important, I argue on the basis of this cumulative analysis of vocabularies of motive evident in business associations that disinterested solidarity as well as self-interest structure the underlying *discursive field* making a business orientation to economic interests meaningful—and both poles are constitutive of the cultural grammar of economic claims-making. I show that claims-making about the pursuit of particularistic economic interests carries surprisingly little rhetorical force: economic "interests" are often understood in terms of intrinsic goods transcending self-interested exchange. As we will see, even economic action at the center of capitalist economic life is not understood simply as a matter of a disciplined orientation to systematic, competitive profit-seeking in markets, but of normative solidarity. Different contexts will evoke both particularistic interests, and solidarity transcending them, to different degrees, but the power of business will always be underestimated if this intrinsically solidaristic orientation is neglected.[14]

This is an argument about economic culture, not a claim about social-psychological motivation. I am not asking whether businesspeople are either self-interested or altruistic in what they do. Dispositions can vary: more importantly, social settings vary too in the different ways they evoke and sanction different orientations. (Such variation in the way individuals are selectively encouraged to develop or learn different dispositions can be seen at different scales ranging from the macrohistorical to the interactional.) By focusing on economic culture rather than social-psychological motivation, I emphasize the significance of languages and symbolic repertoires available in contemporary American business culture to make sense of and to communicate strategies of action typically assumed—though rarely demonstrated—to be transparently self-interested. Whether or not the adoption of either self-interested or solidaristic languages is cynical, heartfelt, or unreflective in any particular instance, what is important are the possibilities and limits of plausible meaning-making.[15]

Investigating American Business Associations

To understand what business interests mean, I explore what business-people say and do when they associate at the heart of liberal capitalism. As Adam Smith famously remarked, "people of the same trade seldom meet together, even for merriment and diversion, but the conversation ends in a conspiracy against the public, or in some contrivance to raise prices." Smith's *Homo economicus* might be disciplined and civilized by legally sanctioned cooperation in places where traditional institutions, state corporatism, or strong welfare state settlements soften market pressures. Hapless consumers anywhere may confuse their economic self-interest with messier issues of identity and social connection. But we would expect American businesspeople in the early years of the twenty-first century to be unembarrassed and eloquent speakers of the language of self-interest, and, on Smith's postulate, that business associations would be one important way they might pursue their interests. Durkheim, by contrast, thought such associations could be a potentially crucial basis of solidarity in a complex society, creating meaning for individual action and challenging

anomie with moral regulation. As he saw it, the "amoral character of economic life amounts to a public danger," so the economic group "must become or return to being a well-defined and organized association."[16]

American Business Associations

As we will see, remarkably few scholars have followed up on the intriguing
puzzle presented by this difference of opinion about associations. Nor are
American business associations themselves well understood. Essentially
they are, as Lloyd Warner and Desmond Martin put it—in one of the few
existing attempts to examine them—"nonprofit institutions that operate
cooperatively for and among competitive, profit-making [actors]." The
very existence of such associations is paradoxical in several ways. Most
generally, the fact that profit-oriented businesspeople cooperate in nonprofit associations provides yet more support for economic sociologists'
many arguments that economic action is rarely isolated and anonymous
in the way that neoclassical economic models have assumed. More particularly, as we will see, American associations' power to coordinate economic action in the interests of their members—for instance, by setting
prices—is legally limited by antitrust law, and compared to associations
elsewhere they are weak. "American exceptionalism" is as true of business
as of labor, and American associations are distinctively voluntary—supposedly facing extreme collective action problems in the absence of state
supports. On some accounts, it is hard to explain why they exist at all, and
their healthy persistence is another intriguing puzzle.[17]

Despite the fact that scholars have mostly ignored them, and despite
their apparent weakness, American associations thrive. Their numbers
grew consistently throughout the twentieth century, and they are securely
institutionalized and stable. Over four thousand business associations
operate nationally in the United States (thousands more are regional
or local). They form around an astounding array of economic activities.
Many seem opaque to outsiders—like the Abrasive Grain Association,
the Intelligent Transportation Society of America, the Lignin Institute,
or the Association of Independent Corrugated Converters. Others are
simply unfamiliar, like the Council for Electronic Revenue Communication Enhancement, the Association of Telephone Answering Services, or
the Plasma Protein Therapeutics Association. Only a minority—like the
National Soft Drink Association, the Academy of Motion Picture Arts
and Sciences, and the American Gem Trade Association—are publicly
recognizable.[18]

To take just one example, members of the International Concrete Repair Institute "develop programs and establish precedent to further the quality of concrete repair" and "have the chance to play a vital role in the direction of the repair and restoration industry." They show hundreds of pages of prize-winning concrete repair at their website, and as the institute explains, "the more involved you are with member activities, the more likely you are to be called upon by other members for guidance. It is this recognition that will propel you to the forefront of the concrete repair industry."[19]

Somewhat like religious congregations, business associations seem to have surprisingly diffuse goals and activities. Associations select differently from a range of activities characteristic of the institution as a whole, and they may change their focus over time. In practical terms, most are focused on internal industry issues like education, sharing information, networking, accreditation, developing certification standards, marketing, or research. Others are interested in public influence of some sort, including public relations, monitoring regulations, lobbying, and civic practices (in public settings from the local to the international). Some focus only on one or two such activities; others put energy and resources into a wide variety. Many associations regularly produce newsletters and directories for their members as well as myriad profiles, standards, minutes, histories, initiatives, guides, links, press releases, media centers, member opportunities, time lines, product standards, and so on. They hold conventions, trade shows, and other meetings for their members, and they may offer prizes, develop ethical guidelines, sponsor charity events, and sell t-shirts.[20]

All this busy activity takes place in subcultures that stress normative and expressive meaning for the group as a whole. Associations often dwell on shared identity, admire technical excellence, highlight contributions to the group, and express occupational camaraderie, with little attention to strategic economic purposes. For instance, the International Concrete Repair Institute articulates subcultural boundaries defining their place in a larger "world of concrete"; holds regular talks on topics of arcane subcultural interest like "Structural Stabilization of the Alcatraz Cellhouse," and "Specification vs. Reality"; makes insider jokes about problems like "Rusty Rebar"; makes annual awards in six categories of concrete repair ("Parking Structures," "Historic," etc.); nominates members as ICRI Fellows for "many years of consistent contributions"; and commemorated one dead member—"an energetic and enthusiastic supporter of ICRI and a proponent of improving construction methods" with a college scholarship fund in his name. All this normative and expressive meaning presents yet another intriguing puzzle about American business associations. According to purist Smithian assumptions, they should distill the quintessence of interest-oriented economic action; yet they understand what they do in solidaristic terms, as much as and often more than in terms of strategic and particularistic interests.[21]

The scope and volume of all this little-known but well-established collective action among businesspeople is striking and deserves much closer attention. In the course of the twentieth century, only a few important studies and lone scholarly voices took them seriously, and most of these studies examine particular industries or associations, so we cannot know whether they are representative of the association population.

Census and Archive

This study remedies this glaring omission in our knowledge of American economic life. I developed the first comprehensive overview of the population of national business associations. Based on this new census, I selected a representative focal sample of twenty-five associations and created an extensive archive of all public documents generated by these representative associations. To understand how businesspeople make sense of their interested action, I analyze discourses and strategies of action in these contemporary American business associations.

The population census includes those nonprofit associations composed of members drawn from more than one locality or state who share a common orientation to some sector of industry, trade, business, or commercial activities. I exclude associations composed of "social and cultural specialists"—like museum curators, or sociologists—to focus on those composed of "for-profit" members. This comprehensive data set of 4,465 national business associations tracks basic organizational features and publicly stated goals that have never been mapped before.[22]

This overview offers many resources for other scholars to do more and better sociological investigation of what associations accomplish in American economic and political life than has been done before. In the chapters that follow, I discuss many new observations about national business associations: their organizational features (association membership, staff, organizational differentiation, location, age, and sector); their goals and activities (education, information sharing, standards and accreditation, research, public relations, policy monitoring, lobbying and civic practices); and some of the more notable ways associations vary in these features.

TABLE 1.1 **Sample of national business associations**

Association	Website (2006)
Conference of Consulting Actuaries	www.ccactuaries.com
Aluminum Anodizers Council	www.anodizing.org
Association for Women in Aviation Maintenance	www.awam.org
Automotive Lift Institute	www.autolift.org
Independent Bakers Association	www.mindspring.com/ ~independentbaker
Brick Industry Association	www.bia.org
Closure Manufacturers' Association	www.cmadc.org
International Concrete Repair Institute	www.icri.org
International Society of Certified Electronics Technicians / National Electronics Service Dealers Association	www.iscet.org
Envelope Manufacturers' Association	www.envelope.org
Equipment Service Association	www.2esa.org
Exhibit Designers and Producers Association	www.edpa.com
Firestop Contractors International Association	www.fcia.org
North American Association of Food Equipment Manufacturers	www.nafem.org
International Society of Hospitality Consultants	www.ishc.com
Irrigation Association	www.irrigation.org
American Council of Life Insurance	www.acli.com
United Lightning Protection Association	www.ulpa.org
Mulch and Soil Council	www.mulchandsoilcouncil.org
Pellet Fuels Institute	www.pelletheat.org
American Society for Automation in Pharmacy	www.asapnet.org
Small Publishers Association of North America	www.spannet.org
National Association of Real Estate Brokers	www.nareb.com
International Telecommunications Society	www.itsworld.org
Vacuum Dealers Trade Association	www.vdta.org

However, the most important purpose of the population census in the following investigation is to provide a reliable and comprehensive picture of the organizational features and stated goals of national business associations to ensure that the evidence I develop about business culture is representative and not idiosyncratic. This is important because unexamined assumptions about business culture and about business associations are so powerful that there is strong resistance to empirical investigation questioning and sometimes challenging those assumptions.[23]

But the central interpretive questions demand thick evidence of meaning-making beyond the superficial evidence of the population data. For this I turn to a representative sample of associations that generates the data for qualitative analysis (see table 1.1). This focal sample may look strange to many readers, not only because business associations are quite unfamiliar but also because those we tend to notice are generally not representative. But although they are unfamiliar, and leaving aside some

TABLE 1.2 **Dimensions of variation among American business associations**

Membership Profile	Approximate Percentage of Sample	
	2003 Population ($n = 4,465$)	Purposive Sample ($n = 25$)
Number of Members (Median = 353)		
< 100	23	30
100–1,000	45	46
> 1,000	32	23
Type of Membership		
Firms	50	48
Individuals	36	27
Both	16	27
Industry Sector Representation		
One industry sector	59	34
Crosses sectors	41	65
Industry Sectors Included		
Manufacturing	25	28
Services	25	28
Wholesale and Retail	11	22
Transport and Information	11	6
Finance and Real Estate	8	8
Primary and Construction	16	8

Data set compiled from Kimberly Hunt, ed., *Encyclopedia of Associations*, 39th ed. (Farmington Hills, MI: Gale Group, 2003) by Lyn Spillman, Principal Investigator, with Rui Gao, Xiaohong Xu, Brian Miller, and Georgian Schiopu. Publicly available at ICPSR, www.icpsr.umich.edu. Supported by ASA/NSF Fund for the Advancement of the Discipline, 2003 and the Institute for Scholarship in the Liberal Arts, University of Notre Dame.

minor and unavoidable differences, these associations are mostly typical of the population, as table 1.2 shows. The qualitative data I discuss are drawn from this focal sample, which provides access to a vast, representative body of routine discourse about business.

Adapting the model of archival research, I treated each association website as an archive of documents and made a comprehensive collection. An enormous amount of data was generated: trawled systematically, these websites each included from a minimum of about twenty to more than five hundred pages, with more in the upper ranges. More than thirty sorts of "documents" were available, in many different forms: they included, for example, statements of purpose, committee reports, membership criteria, by-laws, strategic plans, "state of the industry" analyses and prognoses, elaborate technical information, industry and association histories, awards, meeting agendas and convention programs, records of past meetings, archives of newsletters, directories of members, accreditation procedures and standards, information about scholarship and charity programs, safety guides, and promotional information. A surprisingly large proportion of this discourse was oriented to the knowledgeable in-group audience, mostly to the members, rather than to publics or markets (moreover, sites generally displayed few images that might engage outsiders). This sort of evidence is particularly valuable because it is nonreactive—unlike evidence from surveys, interviews, or observations, the evidence is not shaped by the influence of the investigator on the questions asked or in the interactional process. Of course, this is not a full and transparent record of association intentions and activities, much less the interpretations and understandings of their members; clearly there are systematic constraints shaping the nature of the documents available, such as antitrust law, and the organizational imperative of minimizing conflicts between members. However, within such constraints, association documents bring to life previously unknown subcultures and provide rich, lively, and often surprising insights into a world of business often thought to be inaccessible to outsiders.[24]

Evidence and Inference

Beyond their intrinsic importance as a widespread yet neglected feature of the institutional landscape of American capitalism, these national associations offer a new window on the meaning of business. If we see solidaristic language and interpretation even in settings where the pursuit of particularistic interest is considered normative—both theoretically and conventionally—business orientations are unlikely to be entirely particularistic in other settings, either. But—contra Smith—are these national business associations distinctive for their diminution of claims-making about particularistic interests? Are solidary claims entirely absent in firms and corporations? What about peak associations like the National Association of Manufacturers, and what about local business groups? And would associations in other national settings be more rigorous in their orientation to particularistic interests, or less? Generally speaking, what is the scope of generalization possible from these hitherto neglected business subcultures?

Certainly, different settings will generate different variants of business culture. As I show in the following chapters, the cultural repertoire evident in these national business associations does include claims about members' particularistic interests as well as generalized solidaristic orientations like camaraderie, technical expertise, and the public good. Both particularistic interests and solidarity transcending them make business meaningful, and both must be considered fundamental to the cultural grammar of capitalist business. Some settings will be structured so as to reward interpretations in terms of self-interest more than others (as Mitchell Abolafia also found in his study of different Wall Street financial markets). For instance, peak associations will likely draw on languages of business interest more than the national associations here—as political sociologists like William Domhoff assume. Local business groups will likely draw on solidaristic, disinterested rhetorics more, as Terry Besser's important studies of local business suggest (though they will rely much less on solidarity based on shared commitment to technical expertise). Different historical contexts will also encourage different emphases, so solidaristic understandings generated at one time may be turned to the pursuit of particularistic interest at another, as Jeffrey Haydu has argued of business groups in nineteenth-century Cincinnati and San Francisco. But all this contextual variation in the use of a cultural repertoire is entirely predictable and does not change the central point: in order to understand capitalist profit-seeking, we must move beyond theoretical assumptions that presume that business is all about interest-oriented action. As I argue in chapter ten, such assumptions are not only empirically limited but also normatively dangerous. The distinctive business associations I examine offer a broadly applicable lesson about business culture.[25]

A Reader's Guide

Based on this new evidence, I argue that our deeply embedded assumption that modern business calls for a normative model of exchange as disciplined orientation to systematic, competitive profit-seeking is fundamentally flawed. Not only are particular understandings of market actors' interests shaped by their context, as many economic sociologists have argued, the very pursuit of economic interests is often understood as "disinterested" action transcending particularistic interests. Meaning-making about business emerges in a discursive field that is structured by solidarity as well as strategy.

This argument is developed in four parts, each with two chapters.

Part One: A New View of American Business Associations

Part one sets the stage with an analytic history of American business associations, which shows that they are best understood as cultural producers for economic action. In chapter two, "Unstable, Redundant, and Limited: The Puzzle of American Business Associations," I first sketch Max Weber's theory of business associations, highlighting issues of organizational form, cultural orientation, and political process. This perspective shapes social scientists' main assumptions about why and how business associations function, especially for scholars of comparative economic governance. Their comparative approach shows the distinctiveness of American associations, which I demonstrate with brief contrasts to German and Japanese associational history. This Weberian comparative approach generates a major theoretical and empirical anomaly: it cannot explain why American associations thrive. To explore this issue, I reconstruct the history of American business associations before and after the introduction of antitrust law in the late nineteenth century, again considering that history in terms of their organization, orientation, and politics. This history demonstrates that Weberian insights about the pursuit of business interests in associations should be set in a broader Durkheimian framework that attends to issues of cohesion and coordination in an increasingly differentiated division of labor.

Chapter three, "Stable, Diverse, and Minimal: Contemporary Business Associations and Cultural Production," examines the more recent history of associations' political context, organization, and orientations. Against the background of findings from earlier studies, I present a new, comprehensive analysis of the organizational features and major orientations of the contemporary association population. As we will see, they are, overall, well established, multifunctional—and weakly organized. I argue that these features mean they are, first and foremost, cultural producers for economic action.

Part Two: American Business Associations as Cultural Institutions

While part one develops from theoretical and historical foundations a new approach to American business associations as cultural producers that cannot be understood unless we see meaning-making as intrinsic to economic action, part two focuses on meaning-making they actually do, beginning the close interpretation of qualitative data from focal associations.

In chapter four, "'Meet the Movers and Shakers of the Industry': The Social Construction of Business Interests," I build on the insights of neo-institutionalist theory, which has suggested a cultural role for business associations in the production and reproduction of "industry interests."

Arguing that recent neoinstitutionalist analysis has been overly preoccupied with questions about change and relies on unexamined assumptions about how orientations for economic action are reproduced and inculcated, I show how business associations routinely produce and reproduce cognitive categories, networks, and industry fields. This account also shows that recent work by economic sociologists on the importance of cognition, networks, and fields for economic action helps understand mechanisms of institutional production and reproduction.

In chapter five, "'A Special Camaraderie with Colleagues': Presuming and Producing Solidarity," I deepen the standard neoinstitutionalist account further, arguing that it borders on circularity if it relies on the putative prior existence of shared interests and underestimates the degree to which associations treat solidarity as an end in itself. Building on neglected theories of occupational community, I show that a surprisingly widespread theme in business associations' activity and discourse expresses collective identities, normative and status orders, and camaraderie that would make little sense strictly considered as strategic economic action. We enter into subcultures that, with their insider jokes, strange awards, chatty histories, and emotional obituaries, sometimes seem as exotic and arcane as the deviant youth groups or religious cults sociologists (rather oddly) tend to see as more familiar territory. An important part of what American business associations do is produce solidarity in collective identity.

This detailed, theoretically informed qualitative exploration of meaning-making in business associations in part two offers a new and counterintuitive view of American business associations and the cultural embeddedness of capitalist economic action. The picture of the solidarity in business challenges several fundamental assumptions about capitalist economic action. It challenges the broad assumption that all there is to business is strategic, self-interested action. More particularly, it challenges an important corollary of that assumption that has mostly gone unchallenged, the idea that business associations are simply organizational tools for the promotion of business interests. Most students of associations have assumed, like Smith, that they are directly oriented to the promotion of business interests. Sometimes associations are seen as pursuing business interests by coordinating intraindustry collective action, as when they develop standards or dispute the future shape of the industry. More often, scholars assume that associations protect and promote industry interests in conventional political arenas, as lobby groups. (They may also, of course, pursue both intraindustry and public goals, according to context.) From the point of view of these standard assumptions, solidarity is self-evident, and analyzing business associations primarily as cultural institutions seems deliberately obtuse about their strategic pursuit of economic interests. Strategy seems more important than solidarity—even though assumptions about solidarity among businesses also seem particularly dubious from this point of view.

Part Three: American Business Associations and Economic Action

So in part three I examine the ways in which intraindustry associational goals like providing training, sharing information, conducting research, and setting standards are understood. Chapter six, "'To Grow the Industry': Business Associations and Economic Interests," investigates how these strategies of action are connected to profit maximization and industry stability. After outlining standard theoretical assumptions about the pursuit of economic interests in associations, I discuss new findings from the population census and from the focal sample about what exactly national business associations do in this large arena of economic action about which almost nothing is known. I then turn to an analysis of the meanings attributed to these strategies of action. Economistic views that they promote particular members' economic interests are rarely expressed; much more often, economic interests are understood as collective industry interests, regardless of particular interests of members. I analyze how association discourse resolves potential contradictions between particular and collective economic interests, questioning standard solutions scholars have proposed to the Olsonian puzzle of "free riding" in associations. Finally, I discuss cases in the focal sample in which associations pursue tactics oriented to protecting collective "industry" economic interests in the politicized coordination of industry change—at this time, especially, in industries facing technological change and in industries facing problematic changes—such as increasingly powerful concentration—among upstream or downstream partners. The North American Association of Food Equipment Manufacturers (NAFEM) makes a lively illustration of how associations develop and use intraindustry strategies of action to address changing economic circumstances.

But as I go on to analyze in chapter seven, "'The Highest Level of Professional Recognition': Business Associations and Technical Excellence," intraindustry strategies of action are just as frequently seen in a more disinterested way as a matter of technical excellence and "professionalism." I show businesspeople preoccupied with issues generated by the technical division of labor—the intrinsic technical features in an arena of production or line of work. Few scholars have taken account of the fact that business associations are as likely to be oriented to their members' interests in "professionalism" as they are to their collective business interests. I argue that the theoretical distinctions usually made between "professions" and other work worlds cannot be sustained. The argument concludes with an extended illustration from the International Society of Certified Electronics Technicians.

Part Four: American Business Associations in Politics

Whereas part three shows that intraindustry strategies of action usually considered to be transparently self-interested are in fact more often understood collectively and disinterestedly, part four explores the meaning of strategies of action primarily oriented to external audiences—lobbying and monitoring policy, public relations, and civic practices. One of the most common assumptions about American business associations is that they are simply political interest groups. In chapter eight, "'A Voice for the Industry': Business Associations and Political Interests," I discuss sociological arguments for this assumption and show how the evidence of political orientations and activities in the association census and the focal groups challenges these arguments as partial and unrepresentative. Then, focusing on that minority of associations that are indeed active in conventional politics, I examine what exactly they do and the terms in which they understand their political action. I argue that they are mostly involved in routine policy monitoring as peripheral players in policy domains. Then, extending recent arguments about American political discourse, I show how they express their political interests in terms of a democratic code stressing technical reason and stewardship of the common good. These arguments are demonstrated with illustrations drawn from the focal sample and an extended case analysis of the political work of the Irrigation Association.

These findings about associations' political orientations, strategies of action, and vocabularies of motive are amplified in chapter nine, "'A Tense

and Permeable Boundary': Business Associations in the Civil Sphere,"
which examines their publicly oriented languages and strategies of action
beyond conventional politics. First, I assess scholarly assumptions about
associations' interest in public opinion with evidence from the census, and
explore strategies of action and discourse about public relations in the focal sample. Then I point out that although scholars interested in nonprofit
voluntary groups and civil society have ignored business associations,
these groups should also be considered in debates about the strength of
civil society. I assess evidence of orientations to civic goals in the business
association population and explore qualitative evidence of associations'
strategies of action and vocabularies of motive that challenges the distinction between economy and civil society. Attempts to influence public opinion and to participate in civil society are usually understood in languages
of public good, especially stewardship of the public good through technical expertise. Again, an extended case study, of the National Association
of Real Estate Brokers, demonstrates these claims.

Overview

Part one introduces a new overview of American business associations;
part two analyzes their meaning-making work; part three examines their
intraindustry orientations, strategies of action, and vocabularies of motive; and part four does the same for their external orientations. Loosely
stated, the argument moves from historical puzzle to cultural resolution
and then addresses "economic" and "political" counterarguments.

At each step in the argument, assumptions and claims about associations and their members as strategic actors are challenged and modified
with neglected evidence of the significance of disinterested solidarity. In
part one, the inadequacies of historical accounts in terms of strategic economic interest are redressed with a theory of American associations as
cultural producers for economic action. In part two, the neoinstitutionalist
insight that associations supply strategic value in the shape of collective
goods—like shared categories essential to market action—is deepened
to examine the ways they treat solidarity in occupational community as
an end in itself. In part three, languages invoking the pursuit of collective economic interests are balanced against languages that emphasize
the intrinsic professional virtue of technical excellence. And in part four,
associations' framing of their conventional political activities in terms of
the public good and technical expertise is elaborated in their previously

unrecognized participation in civil society. As this outline shows, the argument that business culture is necessarily structured by an orientation to disinterested, generalized solidarity as much as an orientation to strategic interest in competitive profit-seeking is fractal: it applies to business culture in general but also to different variants of business orientations usually considered purely strategic.

In addition to developing this central claim about economic culture, this book also offers extensive new empirical evidence of a field of economically oriented action that economic sociologists have so far mostly ignored. Because little has been known about what American business associations do, this study also contributes new evidence on comparative economic governance; the institutional shaping of cognitive categories, networks, and fields; occupational culture; the politics of industry coordination and change; professions; political interest groups; and nonprofits in civil society. This new evidence adds to our understanding of all these topics and sometimes challenges prevailing understandings of them.[26]

This book weaves two somewhat distinct genres of sociological argument. Theoretically and culturally informed economic sociology often relies on thick description of case studies, so some readers may be surprised to encounter systematic evidence of an organizational population and a cumulative synthesis of qualitative evidence from numerous representative organizations. This strategy is deliberate. I think systematic attention to the entire field from which qualitative evidence is drawn can only strengthen cultural arguments. Such systematic attention is especially important if little is known about the population from which cases are selected or the realm of action to which generalization applies. Moreover, these business associations invite such systemic attention in their own right. For readers less interested in the population-level evidence, I include extended case illustrations after establishing the ways they represent the broader field.

As the outline shows, the book is organized and written so it can be read in different ways, depending on the interests readers bring to it. Readers particularly interested in American economic governance in comparative perspective can attend especially to chapters two and six, and chapter three is most important for readers interested in learning the basic facts about contemporary American associations. Readers most interested in understanding more about the cultural "embeddedness" of economic action can focus especially on the core cultural arguments and evidence in part two. And readers most interested in what business associations do economically or politically can attend especially to part three or part four. Readers with such specific interests can also trace the overall development of the central argument through the conclusions to each chapter.

But it is the cumulative force of the *different* ways we see meaning-making in economic action that supports the central message of this book. And, given persistent scholarly neglect of—indeed, disdain for—business associations, we can only begin to reassess what they mean for our understanding of American economic life if we take seriously the range and depth of their many activities and the many varied voices to be heard speaking of business with passion.

Conclusion

The idea that capitalist business is based on a normative model of exchange that demands a rigorous orientation to systematic, competitive profit-seeking is deeply ingrained in popular culture and in social and economic theory. I question this assumption and investigate what business actually means to the people involved. In doing so, I build on the work of economic sociologists who examine the cultural embeddedness of economic action, and I examine institutionalized cultural production and cultural repertoires making business meaningful. I do so by exploring discourse and strategies of action in American business associations, conventionally understood as quintessential capitalist interest groups. This examination of their meaning-making shows that solidarity and disinterestedness are as important in claims-making about the meaning of business as is the supposedly normative pursuit of particularistic interests. I argue, overall, that business culture is generated in a discursive field shaped as much by solidarity as strategy.

This argument extends economic sociologists' findings about the cultural construction of economic interests because it suggests "interests" themselves are understood in terms of a broader cultural repertoire. It also accounts for the power of business culture better than naive oppositions between transparent "interests" and "altruism." As I will argue in an examination of the normative implications of business culture in the concluding chapter, purely self-interested action is unsustainable for businesspeople, and such naive oppositions are ultimately self-defeating for critics of business, too.

PART I

A New View of American Business Associations

CHAPTER TWO

"Unstable, Redundant, and Limited"

The Puzzle of American Business Associations

A merican business associations today follow in a long tradition. Even among associations still existing at the beginning of the twenty-first century, around 140 (or 3 percent) claim origins before 1900. A hundred of those date themselves to the 1880s or 1890s—associations like the Painting and Decorating Contractors of America (1884), the Outdoor Advertising Association of America (1891), the Pickle Packers International (1893), the Cosmetics, Toiletry, and Fragrance Association (1894), the Maple Flooring Manufacturers' Association (1897), and the National Confectionary Sales Association (1899). Some even trace their lineage earlier—like the Association of Graphic Communications (1865), the American Chemical Council (1872), the Associated Glass and Pottery Manufacturers (1874), and the American Bankers' Association (1875). Of course, the vast majority of such associations would not have survived into the twenty-first century. Older economic activities fade and new ones emerge, and so too particular associations form, merge, and disband. But associating itself has been a standard practice for a long time.[1]

Yet these nonprofit organizations of profit-oriented economic actors often seem to challenge established categories of scholarly analysis. Are they more like cartels, lobby groups, or professional associations? What about their occasional resemblance to community organizations or sports fans? Despite their large numbers, and the enormous field of collective action they represent, we know much less about American business associations than we do, for instance, about corporations, philanthropic groups, social movements, religious congregations, or unions. Nor do we understand them as well. Whereas the main facts and key questions about comparable groups are well-enough established to allow social scientists to conduct research and debate policy against a background of shared assumptions, the few existing studies of business associations are conducted from very different points of view, in very different historical and comparative contexts, at very different levels of analysis and grounded in varying theoretical assumptions. As a result, there is no established field of discourse within which a comprehensive knowledge of American business associations may be built. Even the starting point for a shared scholarly understanding must be clarified.

In this chapter I lay out that field, drawing together theoretical presumptions and historical evidence. Max Weber's socioeconomic theory suggests key analytic questions about business associations: What organizational features do they display? What sorts of purposes orient their activities? And what is their political context? These three questions guide the subsequent historical overview. Developing this framework, more recent theories of economic governance provide a general framework for situating American associations in comparative and historical perspective.

Against this background, illustrative comparisons with stronger associational governance in Germany and Japan begin to highlight an important historical paradox, a puzzle that has been systematically ignored. Comparatively speaking, American associations are considered distinctively voluntary, and they are often considered distinctly ineffective. Yet although specific associations may seem weak, the organizational population as a whole is mature and stable, growing consistently in the course of the twentieth century. The historical record challenges explanations based on theories of comparative economic governance. Why do American business associations persist in large numbers, when they seem rather pointless ways for American business to organize? Why is the American business association population large and well institutionalized?

To begin to answer these questions, I trace business associations' organization, orientations, and political context from their founding into the mid-twentieth century. I explain why American business associations are distinctive compared to those elsewhere, but I also identify neglected features that might account for their persistence and popularity.[2]

I demonstrate that the Weberian account of business associations should be set in a broader Durkheimian framework. Durkheim's concern with the long-term, likely irreversible trend to an increasing division of labor in modern life led him to suggest that occupational groups might help sustain cohesion and coordination. This insight suggests that even though American business associations seem comparatively ineffective in the pursuit of economic and political interests, the historical record will show a sustained orientation to the production of coordinating information that has been mostly neglected in previous accounts and that provides a more plausible starting point for understanding business associations in contemporary American life.

Max Weber and Comparative Economic Governance

Max Weber provides the basis for understanding economic action in business associations as he did for many other forms of economic organization. Beginning with the importance of systematic, self-interested exchange in market societies, he identifies three factors affecting how and why patterns of self-interested exchange will vary.

In Weber's words, associations are a type of "economically regulative organizations," in which the "autocephalous economic activity of the members is directly oriented to the order governing the group; that is, . . . economic action is heteronymous in that respect." In this, business associations contrast with economic organizations such as corporations, cooperatives, and cartels, which involve "*primarily* autocephalous economic action." In associations, members' orientations shift from simple pursuit of their own economic purposes to a collectively understood orientation to shared interests in managing their broader social context.[3]

Here, Weber shares with Adam Smith and with conventional wisdom today the basic idea that economic action in modern societies is self-interested: "all economic activity in a market economy is undertaken and carried out by individuals acting to provide for their own ideal or material interests." For him this principle holds even when such activity is also oriented to local institutional orders (and even if such institutional frameworks are socialist). Economic exchange in a market economy is certainly a social relationship, but in its pure form, that relationship is a transient, rationalized, and competitive one. Contrasted with typically more affective or traditional "communal" relationships, like family or nation, "rational free market exchange" illustrated, for him, one of the purest "associative" relationships.

But for Weber (as for contemporary economic sociologists) this basic idea of economic calculation was merely a starting point for an adequate theory of real economic action. His study of ancient and medieval economic institutions, and of the emergence of capitalist forms, as well as his contemporary policy concerns, led him to explore how institutional environments and worldviews shaped the expression of ideal and material self-interest in exchange. Worldviews and institutional environments affect economic action at different scales, from the very encompassing civilizational level through to the sectoral and the organizational. Three Weberian themes provide an initial framework for understanding how and why economic action varies, and they have implicitly influenced subsequent research on business associations. Organizational forms, cultural orientations, and political processes influence the different ways economic interests might be expressed.[4]

Organizational Forms

Although individual self-interest is his starting point, Weber highlighted the fact that most modern economic activity takes place within organizations, closed or limited social relations in which specific individuals—and usually staffs, too—exercise authority over the group. Indeed, organizations like corporations—rather than individual entrepreneurs or owners—dominate modern economic life even more than during Weber's time. Organizations like American business associations are considered autocephalous because their leaders and staff are "selected according to the autonomous order of the organization itself, not . . . outsiders." Such organizations can be important technologies for the pursuit of self-interested economic action. Indeed, along with free market exchange, voluntary associations based on self-interest provided another important illustration of pure associative relations for Weber. These voluntary associations institutionalize "agreement as to the long-run course of action oriented purely to the promotion of the specific ulterior interests, economic or other, of its members." Members supposedly compromise their own immediate autonomous and likely rival interests; the resulting "heteronymous" economic action, though, promotes long-term autonomous economic action by attempting to shape the "order governing the group." As Weber notes generally of associative relations, however, "outside the area of compromise, the conflict of interests, with its attendant competition for supremacy, remains unchanged." In this view, then, economically regulative organizations like business associations are self-organized groups of self-interested economic actors oriented— intermittently and temporarily—to the joint shaping of their shared action environment.[5]

Cultural Orientations

For Weber, purely rationalized, self-interested exchange in associative relationships is an ideal type, and thus largely an empirical impossibility. Almost every social relationship mixes "communal" and "associative" dimensions to different degrees. As Weber points out, "no matter how calculating and hard-headed the ruling considerations in such a social relationship—as that of a merchant to his customers—may be, it is quite possible for it to involve emotional values which transcend its utilitarian significance." The further implication is that even though voluntary associations based on self-interest are, theoretically, "associative" rather than "communal," in reality they will always mix the two types of social relationship, drawing tradition, affect, and value-rationality into supposedly instrumentally rational self-interested memberships.[6]

Political Processes

The most influential Weberian theme for the understanding of business associations is political. For Weber, all social relationships, both associative and communal, include the potential for conflict, competition, and closure; such processes are clearly intrinsic to business associations, both in their internal organizational relations and in their external relations to other economic actors and the state. Weber includes among economic organizations those which simply "enforce a formal order" among other economic actors, most importantly, the state: "the modern economic order under modern conditions could not continue if its control of resources were not upheld by the legal compulsion of the state." Many subsequent scholars explore the ways political institutions influence business associations.[7]

Weber's dense but precise theory of economic action is an important starting point for a clear understanding of business associations (although, as I will argue, it ultimately obscures the significance of the disinterested solidarity they generate). Beginning with the orientations of self-interested economic actors to the order governing the group, Weber then suggests three dimensions of associational action that may vary in degree and kind according to comparative and historical context: (a) organizational forms (b) the potential combination of "communal" with "associative" orientations, and (c) politics and power relations both internal to associations and in relation to external state politics.

Governance Theory

Governance theory implicitly extends Weberian principles of economic explanation and elaborates how associations are distinctive as a form of economic action.[8] As Udo Staber points out, the simple view that "trade associations are . . . organizations whose function is to aggregate, represent, and promote business interests" begs the question of why self-interested action by business might take this form rather than others. In principle, business interests might be pursued not through association but by relying on pure market exchange. More realistically, business collaboration can take many other organizational forms and strategies besides association—like conglomerates, cartels, informal social networks, interlocking directorates, employer organizations, research and development alliances, joint ventures, market-sharing agreements, and so on. Under what conditions, then, will business associations emerge as an important form of capitalist organization?[9]

Governance theorists help understand associations compared to other types of joint action by business by analyzing ways in which the basic coordination of economic action might be accomplished, and how it might vary. They develop the now well-accepted argument that capitalism is not a generic, globally uniform institution, but varies according to the ways in which it is socially embedded.[10] The transactions of economic actors—especially firms—require frameworks of coordination, which vary in different countries, sectors, and industries. A "governance system" is "the totality of institutional arrangements—including rules and rule-making agents—that regulate transactions inside and across the boundaries of an economic system";

> [it is] the full range of institutional possibilities for deriving collective decisions in an economy. The objectives of economic governance are efficiently and adaptively to co-ordinate the activities of firms and their "relevant environments," that is, customers, suppliers, competitors, labour, technology generators, government agencies, etc.

Governance forms affect the ways economic actors coordinate supply, production, and distribution, and the way they set prices and standards, manage labor and competition, allocate capital, disseminate information, and innovate.[11]

Among the ways forms of governance can vary are in their degree of formal organization and administrative hierarchy, and in the extent to which action is simply self-interested or shaped by obligations or collective identity—observations that develop Weber's themes of organizational forms and cultural orientations. This perspective also follows Weber's intrinsically political vision of economic action.[12]

Economic Governance and Organizational Forms

Economists have mostly focused on governance by (broadly defined) markets or by corporate hierarchies, with some recognition of hybrid forms. But markets and hierarchies do not exhaust the ways economic action may be coordinated. Governance theorists treat different types of associations and networks as significant organizational forms of economic governance, and some scholars also include state and community. Along Weberian lines, many governance scholars also stress that types of economic governance are usually mixed in reality. However, they generally assume that "one particular arrangement is more dominant in a particular configuration."[13]

In this typology associations are relatively high in formal integration and multilateral within a sector, involving "structured negotiations among organizations that mutually recognize each others' status and entitlements and that seek to create formal organizations with charters, bylaws and procedures in order to implement relatively stable and formal agreements in pursuit of some common interests." This formal organization differentiates them from markets, networks, and communities as forms of economic governance. Formal organization is significant because

> association staffs may over time develop a certain autonomy from member firms which facilitates the pursuit of long term strategies for the management of the problems of a sector and stabilizes relationships with the state and other forces in the environment of the sector . . . associations may provide an institutional basis permitting firms to define a set of common interests and develop a sufficient consensus to resolve disputes.[14]

Economic Governance and Cultural Orientations

The second important feature of associational governance is the degree to which it mixes Weberian communal with associative social relations. Speaking generally, there are thought to be more communal social

relations in associations than in ideal typical markets and corporate hierarchies, but fewer than in networks, communities, and state governance
forms. Associations are typically thought to have the capacity to generate
or enforce cooperation among members involved in similar activities; and
although they are usually thought to involve mostly self-interested action—
as Weber suggested—their members are also, as Rogers Hollingsworth
and Robert Boyer put it, "constrained and informed by obligation" or by
members' concern with reputation. As Wolfgang Streeck and Philippe
Schmitter argue, private associations

> must be rooted in the value and interest perceptions of existing social collectivi-
> ties . . . [and] . . . be able to draw on shared norms and collective identities which
> they cannot create . . . [including] . . . some residual commitment to the society
> at large which goes beyond the boundaries of just one interest aggregate . . .
> [such as] . . . professional norms of good performance or to a group's prestige
> and respect with other groups.

And William Coleman suggests that due to associations' close interactions
with states on policy, an association "develops a collective identity that
comes to infuse the consciousness of its members." However, while analysts of economic governance usually recognize a "communal" dimension
of associations, they generally take it for granted and see organizational
and political features as more influential. Their arguments suggest that
communal orientations are too weak to sustain association in the absence
of state supports and in the face of self-interested action.[15]

Economic Governance and Political Context

The third important dimension of variation in economic governance—
and, especially, in associational governance—is the nation-state. Along
with most economic sociology, governance theory assumes that production and exchange are power relations and emphasizes the role of the
state in creating the conditions under which different forms of economic
governance and action are favored with sanctions and regulation. Most
students of associational governance emphasize that it usually depends
on "some kind of state facilitation and authorization" because "associations need to be supplied with more and stronger authority than they can
possibly mobilize by themselves on a voluntary basis." As a result, cross-
national variation is one of the most significant factors influencing the
importance of associational governance. And such cross-national com-

parison helps demonstrate the curious distinctiveness of the American case.[16]

Associations in Comparative Economic Governance

From a comparative point of view, the most significant overarching determinant of the strength of associational governance is the constitutional order, which influences the way property rights are defined and whether the state will encourage associational governance for its own purposes of political stability and resource allocation. As Bai Gao notes, states with continental civil law traditions "give the executive branch of the state more power, and the court and legal profession less power in jurisdiction than is true in the Anglo-Saxon legal systems" and

> since the executive branch of the state . . . has additional concerns (e.g., political stability and resource allocation) other than protecting the liberties of private enterprises, the state in the continental pattern of constitutional order often regards the associational order . . . as a useful tool. . . . By providing the backup by public law, the state can directly designate key posts of trade associations and ensure that trade associations' actions will not violate the state's policy objectives.

At the policy level, Coleman makes a parallel distinction between anticipatory and reactive approaches to policy making about a sector. Research on associational governance shows many different ways that this overarching and deeply embedded distinction makes a difference in particular historical contexts (while also showing that particular sectors may develop as exceptions to the nation-state's constitutional order). For associations, favorable constitutional and policy contexts for associational governance will generate such specific organizational advantages as "professional staffs, compulsory membership, quasi-public status, multiple funding sources, rights to levy fines and regulate access to markets and political bodies, and formal inter-associational linkages," giving associations "the autonomy and capacity to set industry targets, shape investment, assign territories, fix prices, punish violators, and thereby displace market governance."[17]

Strong Associational Governance — Germany and Japan

Because of the strong influence of state authorization on associational governance, most investigations of business associations in political economy and economic governance deal with associations in countries where they have some formal role in state/economy relations—in Western Europe, East Asia, or Latin America. Given the importance of constitutional order, and the influence of the German on the Japanese constitution, associations in Germany and Japan, in particular, have drawn extensive attention.[18]

For instance, Gary Herrigel traces the development of elaborate forms of associational governance beyond market, firm, or state in examples of decentralized industrialization in Germany in the nineteenth and twentieth centuries. During nineteenth-century industrialization, groups of specialized independent regional producers understood industry competitiveness as "a collective, industrial, regional problem, not an individual one." This collective orientation was evident in research institutes, vocational training, cooperative banks, and government-promoted technology policies. Links between industries and governments were embedded in Chambers of Commerce and Industry—"public bodies run by private interests in which membership was compulsory." For most industries, this governance form developed further in the first half of the twentieth century in a variety of cartel forms, and trade associations encouraged the conditions for cooperating about stable nonmarket solutions to changing economic environments:

> First, they provided an essential forum for member firms to meet and negotiate the terms of their mutual specialization. In the machinery industry this took place in what is still today referred to as the Norm Committee. . . . Second, the trade association played a supportive role in a wide range of service areas that could not be covered by individual firms alone . . . [such as] . . . market information . . . [and] . . . legal information. . . . Third, the trade association helped coordinate the relationship between individual member firms and other institutions in the decentralized industrial order.

Alfred Chandler makes a similar point: "strong support given to cartels and other interfirm agreements by the nation's courts reflected a shared belief in the benefits of industrial cooperation. These beliefs were also evident in the larger role played by trade associations in Germany than in the United States."[19]

After 1945 occupying powers encouraged trade associations "as pillars of a renewed civil society" but resisted their influence in creating nonmarket economic governance. Nevertheless, associations, along with other regional governance institutions, reconstructed "the structures and principles of organization that had traditionally governed production and its administration," for instance, in the textile machinery industry in West Germany. Associational governance of this sort continued in many industries throughout the twentieth century. Facing increased competition and technological change after 1970, for instance, the machine tool industry successfully adapted because "the long-standing corporatist network of trade unions, business associations, public law chambers, research institutes, and the state refocused its attention on computerized technology and the problems of microelectronic applications to machine tools."[20]

In Japan, too, elaborate and varied forms of associational governance accompanied nineteenth-century industrialization, and as Herrigel also finds in Germany, local organization of industries was important in establishing it.[21] After guilds were dissolved in the early 1870s, new, local, industry-based associations were rapidly formed to replace them, more than fifteen hundred across the country by 1886. National regulations issued from 1884 onward enjoined compulsory membership, promoted such goals as skill sharing and education of apprentices, and forbade varieties of price competition:

> Local trade associations actually were not only organizations of important industries with compulsory membership for all traders engaged in the same industry in each locality with the capacity to regulate them, but, apart from the government's expectations, they were also organizations that controlled prices, wages, and employment.

Throughout the early twentieth century, the growth of big industry in Japan generated a variety of political cleavages between commerce and industry and between big and small business within this earlier associational system and encouraged the formation of more nationally based and cross-sectoral associations, such as the Chambers of Commerce and Industry, the Industry Club of Japan, the Japan Economic Federation, and the National Federation of Industrial Organizations. New laws from the 1920s onward established broadly based manufacturers, exporters, and merchants' associations and, from 1931, a series of government responses to the Depression and wartime mobilization further strengthened the importance of associational governance and industry regulation or self-regulation as a tool of the state. Both local and general industry associations remained active after the war, and, as in Germany, the tradition of associational governance renewed itself despite brief attempts by occupation forces to change the role of associations. For instance, the Japanese

Printed Circuit Board Association, formed in 1962, was delegated public administrative responsibility from the central government for programs that manage and modernize the industry, and "play[ed] a significant role in sectoral governance." And at least seventeen different but densely connected associations existed even in the highly concentrated steel industry of the 1980s, where more informal business networks and groups are generally considered to be the dominant governance form. Michael Witt reports 11.8 business associations per 100,000 inhabitants in Japan in the mid-1990s, compared to 5.6 for the United States and 9.2 for Germany.[22]

Theories of economic governance, which look comparatively at the way economic action is coordinated, contrast associational governance to other governance forms, like corporate hierarchy. On this view, associational governance is encouraged by formal links between the state and economic actors. These German and Japanese examples illustrate the model most scholars have in mind of strong associational governance—compared to market, corporate hierarchy, or network forms.

Strikingly, American business associations rarely appear in contemporary scholarship on associational governance. If Germany and Japan provided illustrations of associational governance as close to the ideal type as empirically oriented scholars are willing to allow, the United States provides the negative case. Indeed, most studies of associational governance mentioned above routinely invoke brief contrasts with economic governance in the United States. Comparatively speaking, business associations in the United States are considered "multiple, overlapping, competitive"— and thus, the argument goes, ineffective. Voluntary membership and legal restrictions on their activities supposedly create extreme collective action problems. For instance, one study of high-tech associations suggests that compared to German and Japanese counterparts, "U.S. trade associations are unstable, redundant and limited . . . private, voluntary, and flexible." As Schneiberg and Hollingsworth summarize the contrast:

> At the other extreme lie US and Canadian associations—competing voluntary organizations which depend on members for support, resources and staff, which abstain from monopolizing or selectively allocating much of anything, which enjoy little formal authority and which are thus far less able to displace markets with associational control.[23]

Such comparative accounts make it hard to understand why American businesses would associate. Yet as we have already begun to see, the evidence of associations' robust persistence is strong. As Berk and Schneiberg also point out, the "conventional narrative" leaves unexplained the apparent viability of associational governance in the United States. This anomaly demands investigation. How have American associations managed to flourish? What do they do, and how have they developed and responded to their changing political context? How do they pursue collective interests despite their supposedly unfavorable political environment? And what do they teach us about the implicit assumptions of Weberian theories of economic governance? I answer these questions by reassessing their history, before and after the introduction of antitrust legislation.

Historical Perspectives on American Business Associations

In principle, historical conditions discourage business associations in the United States because antitrust law has generally restricted both their formal political authorization and formally coordinated economic action within industries. In the conventional narrative, the earliest national associations were started during the Civil War, accompanying the increasing pace and national scope of industrialization. By the late nineteenth century, they were routinely and publicly making price and production agreements among competitors in efforts at industry stabilization. By the 1880s, however, courts and states were increasingly sensitive to potential restraint of trade. In 1890 the Sherman Antitrust Act "rendered price and output agreements between competitors a *per se* violation of statutory law." Antitrust laws "undermined one of the central goals of trade associations, that of effective industrial governance, especially collective price and output control." In this account, corporate hierarchies became a more powerful and common form of economic governance in the United States than associations. With some historical and sectoral exceptions, antitrust law remained constitutive of American associational "exceptionalism," creating what many scholars see as more serious collective action problems than are faced by business associations elsewhere.[24]

Here I use the Weberian model outlined above and draw on case studies and historical overviews to expand and question this conventional narrative. I examine the development of national associations in the nineteenth century, antitrust law and its consequences from 1890, and associational governance in the first half of the twentieth century. In each period, I pay particular attention to issues of organizational capacity and relations with the state highlighted by governance theory. I also attend to their goals and orientations. What can we learn, through this lens, about the successes and failures of American business associations?

American Business Associations in the Nineteenth Century

The story of national American business associations generally begins in the mid-nineteenth century, at the economic turning point provided by the Civil War, and gathers momentum with the rapid industrialization, organizational rationalization, and nationalization of markets that followed and flowed from the war. Before that time, economic activity was mostly local, and both markets and state involvement in economic development and regulation were also locally focused. Scattered illustrations suggest that *local* business associations may have been quite common; in 1762, for instance, spermaceti candle makers in Rhode Island formed an association and made "a mutual covenant, one with every one, and all together, to raise the price of wax candles and to keep it raised." Twenty merchants founded the New York Chamber of Commerce in 1768, and local chambers of commerce were common in many larger cities. Many local associations were most likely "club associations" of "proprietors and owners working in an informal, ad hoc, 'dinner club' manner to take up specific, relevant problems of business, government and society." However, more formally organized protonational exceptions can also be found, like the American Institute of Marine Underwriters, which was formed in 1820 and investigated shipping disasters for its member insurers, operating with an established structure of formal committees and staff.[25]

National manufacturing associations began to appear in the decade before the end of the Civil War. Some such early associations include the American Brass Association (1853), the National Association of Cotton Manufacturers (1854), and the Writing Paper Manufacturers' Association (1861). Thereafter, the pace of national association formation picked up until by the 1880s associations "became part of the normal way of doing business in most American industries." Associations were frequently formed, disbanded, and reestablished, so it is difficult, if not impossible, to make a reliable assessment of how many there were. However, as a very rough indicator, one study of hardware manufacturers identified at least thirty-eight manufacturers' associations devoted to different types of hardware—nuts and bolts, pumps, locks, and so on—in the 1870s.[26]

As with the simple question of their numbers, we do not know enough about nineteenth-century associations to be more than speculatively confident about their organization and activities. Nevertheless, by combining conventional wisdom, theoretical inference, and case studies, scholars have attempted some brave efforts at generalization. We can think of the standard story in terms of what it says about association organization, orientations, and political context. In the late nineteenth century, the story goes, capitalist *organization*, including in association, was increasingly rationalized; associations' *orientations* and purposes were concerned with managing markets to protect the performance of their members; and the *political context* was laissez-faire. However, I will point out below some observations that significantly qualify this standard story—and may help explain why associations survived the introduction of antitrust restrictions.

EARLY ASSOCIATIONS AS ORGANIZATIONS.   In the broad progressive narrative, national associations emerged fully formed, as rationalized organizations, as a natural consequence of economic development in the second half of the nineteenth century. This is certainly true as a very broad-brush story—and, indeed, Émile Durkheim would have predicted it, although few scholars recognize Durkheim's undoubted influence in shaping that story. But to my knowledge there is almost no systematic information available about early trade associations as *organizations*. How organized were they?

On one hand, Aldrich and Staber contend that trade associations illustrate Weber's association of rationalization with the social differentiation of modernity. And according to William Roy and Rachel Parker-Gwin, the "organizational revolution" of the late nineteenth century, in which "organization became redefined as a necessary means to achieve individual and collective goals of business," was an important theme in a variety of association publications at this time. Case studies also show evidence for rationalized organization; for example, when hardware wholesalers formed the National Hardware Association in 1895, the association they formed was structured with an executive committee and several standing committees. It included grievance committees; forms of accreditation; local organizations responsible for policing national agreements; a permanent full-time, well-paid secretary-treasurer with extensive responsibilities; and the publications of numerous proceedings and reports.[27]

But whether examples like these are representative is an open question. In principle, such elaborate formal organization would seem to protect groups against disbanding at the first external threat or internal conflict, as a group or network of friends or colleagues based only on informal ties might do. Yet anecdotal evidence suggests associations failed or disbanded at greater rates in the nineteenth century than later. So while business probably cooperated in formally organized national associations to an increasing degree, it also seems likely that many late nineteenth-century groups remained "dinner-club associations," as Louis Galambos describes such groups:

> The important function of the trade association . . . was to provide a meeting place, a dinner, a convention, or a luncheon for the members. These meetings enabled the members to coordinate their activities; yet their activities were seldom carried on by the association itself . . . the organization, qua organization, did little more than provide a platform . . . this type of dinner-club association was rather common through American industry during the latter part of the nineteenth century.

If this loose organizational form was common even as many businesses became less local, frequent failures and new foundings would be more likely, as any given association's environment changed or internal conflicts emerged. Indeed, they likely faced more difficulties transcending difference and conflict than earlier "club associations" that were more locally based.[28]

The standard account also directly correlates the emergence of national associations with late nineteenth-century economic development. But a fuller account should highlight the influence of earlier local associations on late nineteenth-century formation of national associations. Although links between earlier local associations and the boom in national associations in the late nineteenth century have not been systematically investigated, hints that such links existed emerge in various case studies drawn from different arenas of economic action and from different decades. For instance, local chambers of commerce federated in the National Board of Trade in 1868, and groups of printers in different cities formed the United Typothetae of America in 1887. Later, milk producer groups formed the National Milk Producers' Federation in 1916, and in 1926 direct selling companies built on earlier more local organizations to form the National Association of Direct Selling Companies, and northern and southern cotton manufacturers' groups formed a national association, the Cotton Textile Institute. As I noted above, more detailed histories of associations elsewhere also demonstrate earlier local traditions of associationalism providing cultural, political, and organizational resources for the growth of associational governance on a larger scale.[29]

For a somewhat more detailed example, from the 1870s, we can return to the hardware wholesalers. They joined first in local, state, and regional groups before these various subnational efforts finally culminated in the formation of the National Hardware Association. Strong subnational associations provided resources and motivation for national associations:

> Merchants prominent in the southern regional association were notable in the founding of the national association. Also taking a leading role in forming the N.H.A. were jobbers from states with especially strong associations like those of upstate New York and Tennessee. The first president of the association was a former president of the Philadelphia jobbers' association, a group with substantial experience in dealing with the problems of the trade. The organizational meeting of the N.H.A was called at the request of Cleveland wholesalers, with the support of other Ohio jobbers.

So accounts of the development and strength of late nineteenth-century associations in terms of industrialization, market expansion, and general social differentiation should be supplemented with inquiries into the influence of earlier, more neglected, local associational activity. Overall, late nineteenth-century business's creation of national organizations for the pursuit of collective interests was both more informal and more embedded in earlier groups than the standard account of industrialization and market expansion has recognized.[30]

EARLY ASSOCIATIONS' ORIENTATIONS. Why did national associations form and what did they do? The answers to these questions in the standard histories are clear: the primary purpose of early associations was to try to manage the depredations of the uncontrolled market, especially for manufacturing industry, with explicit price and production agreements. Schneiberg and Hollingsworth summarize a variety of studies:

> Manufacturing and commercial associations sought to avoid price warfare and mitigate the effects of over-capacity by organizing industry-wide price-fixing; by setting production quotas and arranging for members to produce at some fraction of capacity; and by assigning firms the exclusive right to sell their output in a particular locale.

Association activities like this have a long tradition, as Adam Smith suggested and as the eighteenth-century spermaceti wax candle makers show. The American hardware industry, for instance, faced falling prices and periodic overproduction consistently through the last decades of the nineteenth century, and from the depression of the 1870s onward, they repeatedly formed associations to manage and control markets.[31]

But this stereotype of nineteenth-century association orientations and activities should be qualified in several ways. First, as we saw above, it is likely that most associations were organizationally weak. As a result, typical agreements were probably unsuccessful and short-lived (and as I note below, they also evoked widespread and increasing political resistance):

> Even though cartel-type trade associations became quite pervasive, they generally failed to stabilize output and prices. Cheating inevitably occurred, as members would secretly cut prices, increase output, falsify reports, and/or leave the cartel. In most industries, a number of firms failed to join. Even when cartels met with initial success, this simply provided incentives for other firms to enter the industry, thus destabilizing prices again.

Chandler concluded that "the associations proved to be, in the words of the first president of the Petroleum Refiners' Association, John D. Rockefeller, 'ropes of sand.'" To take the example of the hardware wholesalers, their agreements were usually unsuccessful because they "lacked the power to maintain binding agreements," and manufacturers frequently defected from price and production agreements under the pressures of excess capacity, or because foreign or niche markets protected them against severe price competition. If direct management of the new industrial markets was associations' only goal, they were ineffective.[32]

It is also important to emphasize that the practice of associating was widespread throughout the economy, not confined to the newer, large-scale manufacturing industries at the leading edge of the industrializing economy and the nationalizing market that have received most attention in scholars' accounts of nineteenth-century price and production agreements. It would be a mistake to focus entirely on manufacturing, to the exclusion of finance, transportation, or wholesale and retail sectors. The broader story of associations must include, for instance, the American Bankers' Association (1875), American Transit Association (1882), and the National Wholesale Lumber Dealers Association (1894)—as well as the decorating contractors, outdoor advertisers, pickle packers, and others mentioned above, who formed associations that still exist today. No doubt associations in all arenas of economic activity were sometimes oriented to managing price and production, but associating extended beyond the new, large-scale manufacturing that scholars imply most called for such management.[33]

More importantly, the purposes of associations even at this time were much broader than the standard account of their orientations suggests. The standard story understates the importance of other goals with less direct connections to members' immediate economic interests. Such goals may not have immediate bottom-line consequences, but they are still important ways in which association members are oriented to "the order governing the group." As I will argue below, they provided the historical antecedents for the later development of new association activities.

Associations were explicitly concerned about goals such as information sharing, education, and sociability, as well as price and production agreements. As Joseph Bradley reports of the foundational goals of the American Iron and Steel Institute, for example, it elaborated a detailed program to "provide for the mutual interchange of information and experience, both scientific and practical"—including collecting trade statistics, making collections of books and mineral samples, and encouraging schools for the "proper and thorough scientific training" of young "iron masters." Bradley also quotes a Boston banker who saw the formation of the American Bankers' Association as "a call for better acquaintance, for pleasure, for amusement, to get us away from home for a holiday—for a good time generally." And as Roy and Parker-Gwin elaborate, association publications thematized collective identity, as much as if not more than industry interests: "early trade journals intermingled discourse about business identities, manufacturing identities (republican virtues of productivity), nationality, family, masculinity and Christianity." Industry identities were well established in later journals: for one group, "honor and pride . . . was a common theme at association meetings where speakers frequently raised their collectivity above interest to a calling." Weber's communal and associative orientations seem more mixed in early business associations than the standard story suggests.[34]

EARLY ASSOCIATIONS AND THE STATE.   Finally, the broad-brush story of early national associations as responses to depredations of nationalizing industrial markets through price and production agreements also marginalizes their relationship with the laissez-faire and weak national state. They are usually understood to have been largely independent from and unconcerned with the state and state politics; and they were certainly more focused on market-oriented issues and activities (local associations and other business interest groups were likely more involved in political issues). A more complete picture, however, should "bring the state back in" with several observations usually relegated to the margins of the national association story.[35]

First, the historical truism that wars have an often unintended but large economic policy impact applies to these early associations, as it would to early twentieth-century associations later. Associations' resource-rich environment had been partially generated by the economic impact of the Civil War, especially by innovations in transportation. As Roy notes, the Civil War also "created a national currency, fostered the centralization of production in large companies, [and] spurred technologies to standardize production." The Civil War spurred the trend to national from local associations.[36]

Second, we should note the sociological truism that the wide latitude available to associations to set prices and production levels was conditioned by the state—as its restriction by antitrust law would show later. And more actively, a minority of associations was intermittently concerned with tariff and trade policy. As Roy and Parker-Gwin note, for instance, the American Iron and Steel Institute made "caring for the tariff interest" one of its central purposes, and "advocated protectionism as a general principal." In the depression of the 1890s "business interest in export expansion and protection was intense," especially in such industries as machine tool manufacturing, even though it is likely that less than 30 percent of American firms had export markets. While state/association relationships seem distant in this period, a longer view shows that flourishing associational governance was intertwined with state policy. Given these political conditions, it follows that associations also faced political critique.[37]

In the big picture, then, national business associations emerged in the second half of the nineteenth century as economic development brought industrialization and market expansion. They tried to manage relations among competitors and among transaction partners like manufacturers and wholesalers, largely with price and production agreements, to protect business from unfettered competition. But I have highlighted above some neglected dimensions of this story by considering, as Weberian governance theory would suggest, their organizational form, their orientations, and their relation to the state.

First, although some associations may have been rationalized organizations, their frequent failure in the face of conflicting interests suggests that many remained more informally organized as "dinner-club" associations.

Second, it seems likely that many did not emerge simply as an abstractly logical consequence of nationalizing markets, but rather from established local and regional groups—like the Hardware Association—and were thus always already embedded in thicker, somewhat "communal" social relations. Third, price and production agreements were never the *exclusive* focus of many associations; they were also interested, for instance, in information sharing, education, sociability, and tariffs. Fourth, obviously, their laissez-faire national regulatory environment did not mean that the state did not affect them.

These marginalized aspects of the story of late nineteenth-century associations are important because the standard story implies that when price and production agreements were outlawed, business associations would disappear, whereas, in fact, they continued to thrive. Explanations of this paradox should attend to association features neglected in the standard account.[38]

Antitrust Law and Its Consequences

At the same time as national associations were forming, political resistance to anticompetitive practices and economic concentration was also growing. The major political force behind challenges to monopolistic concentration was agrarian. From the Civil War onward, "hinterland farm families experienced the throes of industrialization more as threat than opportunity. . . . Their discontent was expressed in a number of antimonopoly protests, first against railroads and grain elevators, and then, after the late 1870s, national currency and tariff policies." National antimonopolistic laws were initiated on the strength of farmers' movements and the political clout of unindustrialized states—the Interstate Commerce Act (1887), which regulated railways, and the Sherman Act (1890), which prohibited "every contract, combination . . . or conspiracy in restraint of trade." Their primary target was monopolistic concentration, first in railways and then in other major industries, rather than associating in general.[39]

The consequences of the Sherman Antitrust Act were more ambiguous than its intentions. First, issues of interpretation and enforcement weakened its thrust. Presidential disinterest and Republican resistance put brakes on enforcement, and an 1895 Supreme Court decision in favor of the monopolistic American Sugar Refining Company limited its applicability. Not until more than a decade after the passage of the act did

Roosevelt provide resources to pursue antitrust prosecution with any vigor, and even he had no interest in comprehensive enforcement, distinguishing instead between "good" and "bad" trusts. As the contemporary political satirist "Mr. Dooley," put it, " Th' trusts . . . are heejous monsthers built up be th'enlightened intherprise iv the'men that have done so much to advance progress in our country . . . On wan hand I wud stamp thim undher fut; on th'other hand, not so fast."[40]

Second, the target of antitrust law was mutating quickly. Trusts and pools were replaced by a new species of concentration, corporate hierarchy created through horizontal and vertical mergers, and corporations started to dominate the industrial landscape. For instance, Standard Oil was formed of forty separate companies in 1882 (but broken up by court order in 1911). With innovations in corporate law that created new ways to link finance capital with industry, other giant corporations also became powerful, in industries like sugar, tobacco, and paper. As Hollingsworth puts this point: "Even though many Congressmen voted for the Sherman Act because they wanted to maintain a very decentralized, competitive American economy, a long-term consequence of the Act was to facilitate the development of horizontal and vertical integration in numerous industries and to enhance concentration of the American economy."[41]

Chandler provides the iconic instance of this transition from widespread associational governance to corporate hierarchy. As DuPont grew from family firm to giant corporation in the first decade of the twentieth century, its owners "immediately arranged to consolidate with their largest and normally friendly rival . . . next they brought smaller firms into the consolidation by forming a holding company . . . and then exchanging its stock for that of the smaller companies who were members of the old Gunpowder Trade Association. Next they disbanded this trade association, which had been attempting to set prices and production schedules fairly regularly since 1873."[42]

With weak enforcement and unintended organizational consequences of the antitrust law deflecting its impact on the large, powerful businesses, which were its main targets, the antimonopolistic movements probably had more direct effects for weaker parties in the industrial economy, small capital and labor. Smaller businesses, which did not merge into large corporations, could no longer try to manage price cutting and overproduction through associational agreements. Association announcements about price and production agreements at meetings disappeared after 1890. And in 1914 a Supreme Court ruling confirmed that "trade associations could not attempt to regulate prices, even if the purpose was to assist small businesses in the group." For instance, "cooperatives of dairy producers were relentlessly pursued by the courts on antitrust violations, because they were designed to bargain over fluid-milk prices, and this was seen as a conspiracy in restraint of trade."[43]

With the development of antitrust law and administration, new state-imposed conditions on legitimate forms of industry governance did limit the organizational capacity of associations in some ways. Nevertheless, the institution of the business association survived and, indeed, flourished. As Richard Tedlow puts the paradox: "first, the primary purpose of trade associations in the 19th century has been illegal through most of the twentieth. Second, trade associations have increased in size, budget, and overall activity nevertheless."[44]

American Business Associations in the Early Twentieth Century

Among those associations still existing today, just over a hundred were formed between 1900 and 1909; 183 between 1910 and 1919; and 194 in the 1920s. The Sherman Act did not inhibit the boiler manufacturers or the pickle packers we saw at the beginning of this chapter getting together in new associations. The 1890s also saw the formation of, for instance, the National Hardware Association (1895), the National Wholesale Lumber Dealers Association (1894), and the National Association of Retail Grocers (1896). Even as the Progressive strengthening of antitrust enforcement was being debated early in the twentieth century, organizations such as the American Hotel Association (1910) and the Investment Bankers Association (1912) were forming. In two important arenas, energy and health, most of the important national association developments took place in the first part of the twentieth century. Although corporate hierarchy was becoming a dominant governance form in the United States, and antitrust law and administration was developing, trade associations were still a normal part of the American institutional landscape. Indeed, according to Warner and Martin, "the period 1890–1911 [was] the formative stage of trade associations."[45]

More extended examples from two contrasting arenas of economic activity emphasize the apparent paradox—and begin to suggest a resolution. At the cutting edge of the economy, 1885–1910 saw the emergence and expansion of electricity supply as an arena of market activity, and two associations were active in the process (the Association of Edison Illuminating Companies [AEIC] and the National Electric Light Association [NELA]). As Chi-nien Chung tells the story, these associations worked on a wide variety of lighting companies' "common problems," such as "securing necessary electrodes . . . [and] . . . standardizing diverse illuminating equipment." They also organized relations with workers, suppliers, and the public:

> NELA dealt with the labor strike in 1903 by extending membership to leaders of the worker organization and creating a professional association to oppose striking, agitation, or compulsion. AEIC dealt with the energy-supply problem by proposing a standardized purchase practice. Moreover, both AEIC and NELA handled the problem of negotiating with the generating equipment manufacturers by choosing the type of equipment and standardizing the methods of repair, construction, operation, and even terminology. . . . [NELA] cooperated with educational institutions, distributed pamphlets, established connections with other associations, and even organized women's clubs. . . . All these efforts tried to create a favorable public attitude toward the industry. In general, it is safe to conclude that the trade association was the major intermediary in relations within and outside of the electricity industry during 1885–1910.

The activities of the hardware wholesalers we have encountered before were hardly so new nor so technically glamorous as those of the electricity suppliers. They preceded the formation of national associations, and, like the specialty manufacturing industries discussed by Philip Scranton, remained untouched by the merger movement of the 1890s. Yet associations continued to play an important role:

> In industries like hardware where wholesalers handled a large and various group of products, the multi-functional firm did not generally appear. Nevertheless, hardware manufacturers, wholesalers, and retailers had to deal with problems similar to those confronted by the successful vertically integrated firms. Rapidly improving transportation, enlarging urban markets, and most importantly the increasing productive capacity of American industry were the daily facts of life for all . . . wholesalers of hardware . . . responded to these problems by forming trade associations.

As Berk and Schneiberg argue in their important challenge to the idea that antitrust law wiped out associational governance, "neither the size of the American economy, nor antitrust, nor the great merger wave precluded associations. Instead, actors responded to those conditions by reinventing associations." We can strengthen their claim. Associations did not completely "reinvent" themselves after antitrust. As we saw above, many were likely *already multifunctional*, oriented to collecting and exchanging general industry information, education, and occupational camaraderie. With these antecedents, American associations could shift easily to focus more on a wide range of other purposes and activities.[46]

Available evidence about associations' organization, their orientations, and their political context in the first half of the twentieth century reinforces this more continuous, less episodic view of their history. They did face dramatic swings in their political fortunes, and these swings have preoccupied scholars so far. But at the same time, the business association population continued to grow with the economy. By the Second World War, if not several decades earlier, associations came to look very much like the contemporary associations we will see in chapter three.

EARLY TWENTIETH-CENTURY ASSOCIATIONS AS ORGANIZATIONS. Sixty-eight full-time leaders of trade associations held their first convention in Massachusetts in 1920: they formed the American Trade Association Executives. Some of their concerns included financing associations, management techniques, legal aspects, and government relations. National business associations were becoming more formal organizations with more professionalized managements in the early twentieth century.[47]

Although, as we saw earlier, some scholars see the late nineteenth-century emergence of national business associations as part of an "organizational revolution," Galambos claims that business associations mostly became serious formal organizations in the first quarter of the twentieth century. Before the early twentieth century, he argues, business associations were mostly "dinner-club" associations. But the Progressive movement created a more complex political environment; for instance, "much of the regulatory legislation was entrusted to government commissions" like the Food and Drug Administration. Other relevant market actors, too, became more organized. Manufacturers "needed trade groups that provided more services on a more continuous basis than did the older dinner-club associations" and "needed an alert associational middleman." Compared to dinner club associations, the "service association"

> had a substantial income and a group of full-time, professional staff members—a bureaucracy. These men, selected for their administrative, political, or technical skills, worked for the organization on a continuing basis; no longer was the association allowed to lapse into an inactive state between meetings or sessions of the state legislature. The service association was constantly in touch with the political scene, constantly surveying the industry's economic situation,

constantly watching the actions of other associations. With its staff the service association could perform *for* its members instead of letting the members, through their committees, do all of the work.[48]

The available evidence generally supports Galambos's argument that more professionalized service associations emerged in the early twentieth century—with two qualifications. First, although he emphasizes the relative strength of this new organizational form, it was not complex. In his example—which does not appear unusual—one of the new, revitalized service associations operated four rationalized bureaus and committees with three staff—a secretary-treasurer, one staff member (a Mr. W. F. Garcelon), and, by 1920, another full-time assistant. Second, it seems likely that "dinner-club" associations did not die out. Galambos and subsequent scholars write in a progressive, developmental rhetoric that assumes that one improved organizational form replaces another. But as our examination of contemporary associations will show, both "dinner-club" and "service" associations seem to persist as coexisting organizational forms.

A government survey in the late 1930s provides what is apparently the first full, reliable picture of national trade associations in the United States. It estimates that 1,505 national and regional associations were active by mid-1938, of which around two-thirds, or about a thousand, were national. (There were also an estimated 6,500 state and local trade associations at this time.)[49]

Association memberships were generally small, with the median falling between twenty and forty-nine members. However, membership size varied widely, with around 1 percent of the associations reporting over five thousand members, so the mean membership was 362. Membership size varied by sector; for example, "mining, manufacturing and construction" associations were smaller, with almost half reporting fewer than twenty members, and retail associations were larger, with only 8 percent reporting fewer than twenty members. Some associations linked sectors, joining producers, wholesalers, and/or retailers by extending voting or nonvoting memberships.[50]

Like Galambos's cotton manufacturing groups, these associations were generally small organizations. One in ten had no paid staff; almost a half had only one or two staff members, and three-quarters had fewer than six. (As with membership size, though, the range was wide, with 1 percent reporting more than a hundred staff.) The typical association included an "executive secretary and 1 or 2 stenographers or clerks." A minority of associations, between 10 and 20 percent, also sometimes employed full- or more often part-time experts: lawyers, accountants, engineers, scientists, economists, or statisticians. Although staff was few, wages and salaries made up 50 percent of association expenses, their major outlay.[51]

The key staff member, the executive, was typically a middle-aged man with a background in business, associations, law, or public administration. The language of this rigorously objective government statistical report heightens to describe the apparently heroic requirements of this job:

> In addition to a specialized knowledge of the industry and allied industries, and a wide and friendly acquaintance with most or all of his members and with secretaries of related associations, Government officials, editors of trade journals, and the like . . . the efficient executive is expected by his board of directors to possess most of the following qualifications: Energy; integrity; vision; courage; tact; patience; cheerfulness; resourcefulness; ability to digest quickly and summarize the mass of material of current interest to the members of the industry; ability to speak well in public and effectively guide committee meetings and other conferences; experience in writing; exceptional knowledge of source material; practical experience in Government, labor, and public relations, as well as in trade association techniques; and an extensive knowledge of the antitrust laws. He is often expected to be a statistician and accountant, as well as a lawyer and dues collector.

Galambos, describing the three leaders of his cotton manufacturers' association in the late 1920s, was similarly impressed with their ability, describing them in the same heroic terms.[52]

With this small infrastructure, associations extended their organizational capacity with committees, and some subcontracted particular activities or hired management firms. Although the vast majority reported that staff undertook most of their activities, over half of the associations also involved committees in their work. For instance, information activities like producing trade statistics were more often handled by staff, but committees more often handled standardization activities. A small minority of associations—typically well under 10 percent—contracted particular activities like government relations or trade promotion to businesses. In addition, at least one-fifth of national and regional associations followed a new trend of hiring management firms; these tended to be associations with small, homogeneous memberships that emphasized information services such as trade statistics. Also extending some associations' organizational reach was the practice of federating; 139 national or regional associations, or about one in ten, were members of federations of associations.[53]

As we will see, this picture of the association population—with generally small membership size and staff, but a wide range—still holds true today.

ORIENTATIONS OF EARLY TWENTIETH-CENTURY ASSOCIATIONS. Late nineteenth-century associations, we saw above, probably did a lot more in the way of providing information, education, and camaraderie for their members than has usually been noticed, even if they also tried to manage prices and production (probably unsuccessfully, and in ways that soon became illegal). In the first half of the twentieth century, these neglected antecedents emerged from the shadows and developed as a multifunctional portfolio of institutionally established goals and activities, well-recognized strategies of action across the association population. To understand why American business associations persisted, we need to understand more about all these standard practices and how they developed.[54]

Some of the most important trade association activities in the first decades of the twentieth century were concerned with their expanding scope of information production. In this period, too, associations seem to have developed a more routine political role as national interest groups

TABLE 2.1 **Major trade association activities, 1938**

Activity	% Associations	Illustration
Government relations	58	"information . . . given to government"
Trade promotion	50	cooperative advertising, exhibitions
Standards, simplification	37	"establish . . . quality standards"
Conventions	36	regular meetings (likely understated)
Trade practices	35	standard contracts
Employer-employee relations	30	wage surveys, safety, education
Miscellaneous services	28	insurance, library, patent pooling
Statistics, esp. republication	27	industry economic conditions
Technical research, advice	26	coordinate product improvement
Public relations	26	influence public attitudes, conservation.
Accounting, cost statistics, etc.	22	uniform cost accounting
Credit information services	13	systematic or occasional reporting
Traffic and transportation	12	packaging, shipping, freight rate books
Price and bid information	8	bid filing, open price filing
Commercial arbitration	7	disputes, esp. suppliers or customers
Collection service	4	regular or occasional collection service
Register patents, trademarks	3	"primarily an informational service"

From Pearce, *Trade Association Survey*, 373–75, 22–25. Based on 1,244 national and regional associations active in 1938 (excluding insurance associations). Only associations reporting activity as "major" are included here.

with input in specific policy arenas, and as sources of policy information for their members, a profile still recognizable today. Technical research, standard setting, and collective marketing were other arenas of increasing activity.

The associations surveyed in the 1930s were asked to assess a long list of potential activities as major or minor for them. The length and detail of this list, and the variation in responses (according to sector, staff, membership, etc.) is evidence of the robust multifunctionality of the association population by this time. Summarizing very briefly, and considering only reports of "major" activities, 1,244 associations ranked their activities as shown in table 2.1.

When reports of minor activities are also considered, over 50 percent of the association population was involved in government relations, trade promotion, employer-employee relations, miscellaneous services, standardization and simplification, statistical republication and special studies, conventions, and public relations, in that order. These data both support and qualify existing scholarly understandings of early twentieth-century business associations, because they help set investigations of particular sorts of activities in a broader context. To draw out their implications, we can examine briefly what exactly some of these more common activities involved (apart from government relations, which will be examined below).[55]

- *Trade promotion*, for instance, included cooperative advertising (28 percent) and exhibitions (33 percent), but also a wide variety of other possible activities—technical or commercial publications (37.5 percent), finding new uses (25 percent) or new markets (31 percent) for industry products, market research (34 percent), export promotion (10 percent), or technical merchandising advice (21 percent). It could also include activities like preparing customer directories, handling buyers' inquiries, and promotion of an industry "day." Of all these sorts of activities, publications and exhibitions ranked first—with over a third of the associations reporting them. Clearly, organized information production was central to many of these activities.[56]
- *Employer-employee relations*, in this survey, meant providing "surveys, advice, and assistance" about wages, hours, and working conditions (52 percent of all associations); or about collective bargaining (16 percent); work on "welfare, including safety" (22 percent); employee training (16 percent); or placement service (14 percent). Again, coordinating and distributing information is central in these activities. Although we would expect that labor issues would dominate

association agendas in the heated labor policy climate of the 1930s, providing "surveys, advice, and assistance" relative to collective bargaining was an activity reported by only about one in six associations, and only one in ten considered it a major activity. Many sociologists assume that the main reason firms will cooperate in association is to strengthen their position against labor, but evidence of these national industry associations' preoccupation with labor challenges is usually anecdotal. Certainly, episodes of capitalist cooperation to weaken labor challenges are important, but antilabor cooperation should not be considered the main purpose or consequence of this sort of national association. Rather, local employers' associations were likely the main players in such conflicts. In the bigger picture and the longer historical view, American capitalists seem to have had more issues with other social relationships in their economic environments. As chapter six also discusses, they see and act in a social world in which competitors, suppliers, markets, technical processes, law, administration, and occupational and industry identities typically dominate concerns about labor challenges and conflict. Labor issues should be placed in this larger context. Of course, as Haydu argues about Cincinnati's general-purpose business associations in the late nineteenth century, associations may be important for class formation in ways that are transposed to labor relations. However, the important point is that national business associations in the early twentieth century were not, primarily, "employer associations."[57]

- *Miscellaneous services*, in the late 1930s, included (ranked in order of importance), legal services (34 percent), library service (20 percent), insurance assistance (18 percent), used machinery exchange (8 percent), and "cooperative buying" (4 percent). Each of these was more often minor rather than major to the reporting associations. The careful authors of the report also note that associations reported activities not included elsewhere in the survey here, activities like "an information or educational service too broad and general in scope to be classed under any of the items appearing in the schedule," "directories of industry members or catalogs of industry products," and measures to protect members against fraud—although these activities were not reported by any significant number of associations. Publishing directories was to become a more important association activity later in the century.[58]

- *Standardization and simplification* included "the establishment of uniform product sizes or dimensions and . . . criteria of properties and performance as the basis for grading, certification, or labeling . . . the reduction of the number or variety of product size, dimensions, types, models, patterns, and lines." For instance, Andrew Procassini reports that "standards for automotive products were now being developed, as well as standards of basic material testing." Other standards activities included developing standard contract and business forms, "descriptive labeling," and product certification. Such activities were important to over a third of associations (37 percent) and minor activities of a fifth (22 percent). According to the report, though "it is believed that the frequency with which these items were reported overstates somewhat the extent of activity in this field at the present time."[59]

- *Statistics* "Statistical Republication and Special Studies" referred to information on general economic conditions and involved over half of associations, including more than a quarter for which it was a major activity. But other sorts of statistical information are categorized elsewhere in this report, so compiling statistical information was, overall, an even more important associational activity than this figure indicates. In addition to the information on general economic conditions, 44 percent of associations reported work on "trade statistics"—"the regular collection and dissemination . . . of statistics relating to . . . such subjects as inventories, production, sales, shipments, and orders," and this was a major activity for 34 percent. As noted above, associations sometimes collected information on wages and hours, and another category of sometimes-statistical information was the collection of cost information (45 percent of associations were involved in this activity). Along with the majority of associations involved in "statistical republication and special studies," important minorities were producing statistical information of various sorts on their industries.[60]

- *Conventions* are defined as "regular, annual meetings embracing an association's entire membership," which "in many associations . . . represents a major activity and in some, the principal activity." Over half of these associations reported holding conventions—representing close to seven hundred national meetings of businesspeople held regularly across the United States in the late 1930s. For 36 percent of them, this was rated as a major activity. And according to the authors of the report, this information is likely understated (rather than overstated, as some of the information above); "it is believe[d] that there were some associations which through neglect or misinterpretation failed to report this activity."[61]

Like most scholars of business associations, the authors are not particularly interested in this activity, or socializing more generally, and they mostly focus resolutely on strategically specified activities. However, responses by associations to the one open-ended question they include hint that there might be more to explore here. They asked, "what do you feel have been the significant contributions of this trade association to your industry?" The replies they received were mostly easily categorized and ranked as the sorts of activities listed above. But they found one surprise:

> The chief difference is that the list of significant contributions contains an item that did not appear on the previous list. Somewhat over 200 associations stressed the values of personal acquaintance—characterized above as "fostering the personal association of the members." These values were described in such general terms as "promoting good will among the members," "demonstrating the values of cooperation," "furnishing the industry a forum in which members may discuss their problems," "bringing about an industry consciousness," or "removing unfounded fear and suspicion."

Here again, at the margins of a resolutely strategic analysis, we find hints of what the Boston banker in the nineteenth century had spoken of as "a call for better acquaintance," and the "specialized identities associated with particular industries" Roy and Parker-Gwin found in late nineteenth-century association journals.[62]

- *Public relations* Just over 50 percent of associations reported some sort of public relations activity at this time, and 26 percent saw it as a major activity. However, the meaning of the term was diffuse and understood in different ways. The authors describe it in terms that touch on most of the dimensions we will see in later association activities:

> Broadly speaking, the term applies to all efforts to protect or promote public goodwill towards the industry. As such, it usually is considered to embrace that type of trade promotional activity that is designed to inform the consumer concerning the values and uses of the industry's products or services, and, where there are safety or health hazards involved, to promote the use of proper safeguards in connection with such uses. It also includes the overcoming of prejudices and the influencing of attitudes toward an industry's products or services. Another type of activity is designed to promote legislative aids for or [to] ward off legislative attacks against the industry: in seeking these ends, associations may operate through the molding of public opinion, or more directly through contacting legislative bodies. Affording the general public with statistics and information about the industry, its markets, and business trends, also may be classified in this category of trade association activity, as may efforts by natural resource industries through education and legislation to promote the conservation of their raw materials. Under this

heading have been included 23 associations which reported that they were engaged in promoting the conservation of natural resources.

This diffuse set of public relations activities touches on most of the efforts also made by later associations in the public sphere. (The concluding reference to conservation seems an intriguing historical antecedent to contemporary associations' talk of their environmental activities, discussed in chapter eight.)[63]

This 1930s survey also casts new light on several early twentieth-century association activities that are less common today, but which have attracted some interest from later scholars.

- *Uniform cost accounting* In an important reassessment of early twentieth-century business associations, Berk and Schneiberg argue that after antitrust, they became "developmental associations" and "enhanced members' capacities to experiment, learn, and improve productivity and product quality." In their analysis, a movement for "uniform cost accounting" between about 1910 and 1930 was the most important means to these ends: associations developed a "common language" of cost accounting appropriate to an industry without colluding on actual prices. However, the 1938 survey evidence suggests that this movement was not as widespread as their argument implies. Just over a quarter of associations used it, and for less than half of these was it a major activity. Only one in five saw "accounting, cost statistics and studies" as a major activity, and it ranked eleventh, overall, of seventeen association activities, on the basis of reports that were likely overstated. This suggests that the significance of cost accounting for associations' changing role may be overstated. However, the larger argument about the developmental activities of associations remains important. The evidence suggests that if associations became "developmental associations," they were doing so with wide range of innovative strategies of action oriented to information production.[64]
- *Research* Another arena of early twentieth-century association activity that has drawn scholarly attention is the production of technical information in research laboratories, such as the laboratory established in 1907 in Nela Park, Cleveland, by the National Electric Light Association. But such intensive research was characteristic of only a relatively small minority of associations: according to the 1938 survey, 180 associations, or 14.5 percent, operated research laboratories at this time (and this was a "major" activity for half of them). However, less resource-intensive development of technical information was certainly important: "other forms of technical research" were reported by 30 percent of

respondents, and were major activities for half of those. Overall, research activities were ranked eighth among associations' major activities (although the authors flag the likelihood of overreporting). JoAnne Yates's studies of the insurance industry provide a vivid view of this broader range of associational research strategies. From the 1920s, for example, the Life Office Management Association worked extensively on developing collective knowledge of new office technologies— work that prepared them well for their investigation and promotion of computer technologies after the Second World War.[65]

INFORMATION PRODUCTION.   Common to almost all these activities—and I have outlined only nine of the most important—is the systematic, regularized production of information. Technical and commercial publications; exhibitions; market research; technical merchandising advice; surveys on wages, hours, working conditions, and collective bargaining; employee training and placement advice; libraries; used machinery exchanges; uniform product guidelines; certification standards; standard business forms; and general and industry-specific statistics—regardless of the myriad purposes to which information was put, we can see that its production was a standard strategy of action for these associations. As Francis Sutton and colleagues point out in their study of American business ideology, associations in their time generated "a tremendous stream of print and other public communication . . . both to unite their memberships and to "explain" themselves to the other groups and the public at large." Although we do not have sufficient comprehensive information to assess the extent of information production by earlier associations, this form of association practice had probably expanded significantly in the first decades of the twentieth century. Most of these strategies of action are recognizable among contemporary associations. This suggests that the business association as an institution was established in the early twentieth century.[66]

In the first half of the twentieth century, a strong orientation to collectively produced and shared industry information seems to have become centrally important to associations. In this way they quietly developed a successful and adaptable institutional profile that scholars have only rarely noticed and that, as we will see, they still retain today. But what of the "government relations" over half also rated as important in 1938? The institutionalization of business associations and the overall growth in their population in the first decades of the twentieth century took place against the background of a shifting and somewhat unstable political environment.

ASSOCIATIONS AND THE STATE IN THE EARLY TWENTIETH CENTURY. The interpretation and administration of antitrust law took a long time to settle after 1890. Not until Roosevelt's administration at the beginning of the twentieth century was antitrust enforcement proactive. From that time, antitrust politics gathered new energy, with emergent positions contrasting business-government consultation and oversight of inevitable concentration with nondiscretionary sanctions and stronger enforcement. A decade of Progressive politics eventually consolidated the antitrust regime in 1914 with the Clayton Act and the establishment of the Federal Trade Commission (FTC). The Clayton Act "acknowledged the distinction between constructive and destructive competition," defining some anticompetitive tactics as illegal, and the Federal Trade Commission was intended to enforce competition.[67]

However, the meaning of unfair competition was still open and "conflict over the meaning of the new laws" continued, especially between the stricter Department of Justice and the Courts, on the one hand, and the more proassociation Department of Commerce and FTC, on the other. Overall, Elizabeth Sanders argues that "much of the force of the Clayton and FTC acts was undone by the Supreme Court in the period between its [sic] passage and the arrival of the New Deal." In the two decades after 1914, associations' fortunes swung back and forth, and in the meantime, they developed new political and economic roles and some strong supporters in this period.[68]

In 1914 the Supreme Court ruled against even "well-intended" price setting by associations. But during World War I, the state promoted associationalism as a means of wartime mobilization and coordination of production. Bernard Baruch, chair of the War Industries Board, praised associations and drew on their technical expertise. As secretary of commerce, Herbert Hoover also promoted association activities in numerous ways: in research, statistics, standardization, arbitration, and export development, he wrote, "trade associations have made a most valued contribution to our economic process." Howard Aldrich and his colleagues found that World War I had a significant effect on association formation, and according to one contemporary study, the number of associations more than doubled between 1914 and 1919; moreover, relations between national government and national associations were newly routinized. In another proassociation development, foreign trade was an important exception to the general antitrust prohibition on collective action related to prices: after the Webb-Pomerene Act of 1918, businesses could combine to influence export prices in ways prohibited in the domestic market, provided their "export associations" registered with the FTC.[69]

But the pendulum continued to swing. First, a series of Supreme Court decisions imposed restrictive interpretations of information exchange as price control; for instance, a 1921 court decision "condemned the practice of the American Hardwood Association of exchanging cost and production statistics." The relatively proassociation FTC's ability to organize trade practice conferences was also restricted, and the influence of the Department of Justice outweighed that of the proassociation Department of Commerce.[70] After 1925, however, court decisions were less restrictive; for instance, in 1925 several associations were acquitted of antitrust violations, and information exchange came to be seen as legitimate so long as it was not used in anticompetitive agreements. The Court allowed associations to "gather and publicize statistics on industry conditions." At the same time, Hoover's backing and a generally probusiness policy environment further encouraged association formation and strengthening.[71]

Scholars of associational governance speak of the first New Deal as a golden age. First, in 1931, the Swope Plan—propounded by the president of General Electric and widely discussed—promoted the idea of trade associations (under federal agency supervision) as a mechanism to "match production and consumption." For President Hoover, generally a supporter of associations, this was going too far, and the plan would have required amendment of antitrust law, but President Roosevelt later incorporated aspects of the plan into the National Industrial Recovery Act of 1933. Amid widespread arguments that the Depression discredited market principles and active industrial coordination was now required, antitrust legislation was suspended, and NIRA created the National Recovery Administration (NRA), which would supervise industrywide agreements on price and production. The impact was immediate. The 1938 survey found that "nearly 23 per cent of the associations now extant were organized during the 3-year period, 1933 to 1935." Many more associations were drawn into complex relations with the national government, and within a year hundreds of industries had voluntary written codes. For instance, the National Association of Direct Selling Companies supported the NRA's voluntary code activities, but opposed minimum wage laws at NRA hearings.[72]

However, the "golden age" was also brief and ultimately unimportant. Opposition grew rapidly; a 1934 report questioned the effectiveness of this strategy for industrial recovery; corporations and associations resisted the labor provisions required in the codes; and there were few resources for code enforcement, which was weak. In mid-1934 the NRA began weakening the 1933 program, and the Supreme Court declared the provisions unconstitutional in mid-1935. The late 1930s saw a revival and strengthening of antitrust enforcement, continuing until the United States entered the Second World War. For business associations, NIRA's "effect was short-lived and it did nothing to lengthen the lives of existing associations." On the other hand, as the 1938 report put it, "that the NRA did not, however, exhaust new opportunities for trade association organization is indicated by the formation of some 50 associations from 1936 to June, 1938."[73]

Associations were mobilized by the state again during World War II, when they "participated with varying degrees of responsibility in the allocation of materials to manufacturers, played a critical role in providing statistical information about their industries for national defense purposes, and in other ways facilitat[ed] relations between government and industry." For instance,

> the Association of American Railways managed the movement of 600,000 troops during the first seven weeks of the war. The Council of Machine Tool Equipment Services listed 250,000 pieces of production equipment and cross-indexed all machinery in 450 plants owned by 260 companies.

However, the Second World War did not significantly increase association foundings, as the First World War had done. According to Galambos, this was because "the more mature administrative state of the post–New Deal era had greater capabilities than it had had in 1917 and 1918."[74]

Overall, then, there were some dramatic swings in the political environment of associations in the first half of the twentieth century. What impact did they have on associations' orientations and activities? By the time of the 1938 survey, just after the heady policy days of NIRA, a full 82 percent of associations reported some sort of activity in the general category of "government relations." But only 58 percent considered this a major activity. As the authors of the report point out, "the prominence of this activity in part may be attributed to the unparalleled growth of Federal legislation affecting business in recent years."[75]

The trade association survey canvassed three sorts of government-oriented activity at this time. The first, most passive type of connection, reporting government activities to members, was the most common: two-thirds of associations did so, with a third rating this as a major activity. Second, half of the associations reported "information or assistance given to government," and again just under a third rated this as a major activity. As the report elaborates:

> For current trade statistics the Government has relied to a considerable extent upon data collected by trade associations; it has enlisted the services of trade associations in conducting special statistical and economic surveys and has constantly sought their advice in preparing schedules and mailing lists for its own surveys. It has relied on trade association knowledge of industry conditions in drafting specialized legislation and administration rulings, and has benefitted from the publicity given by trade associations to legislative and administrative acts and their efforts to enlist industry's cooperation in support of them. It has sought the assistance and information of trade associations on technical and engineering surveys and projects and has profited from trade association publicity of its technical findings.

Third, and less passively, associations could "represent members' interests before Government bodies." Forty-five percent had done so before legislative bodies or "other executive and administrative agencies," and smaller percentages had lobbied tariff, taxation, and scientific agencies. However, only between 10 and 23 percent considered any of these lobbying activities major. One in five of these associations had drafted and promoted model laws, although only 7 percent considered this a major activity. (Peak associations such as the National Association of Manufacturers and the Chamber of Commerce were more politically proactive: they "played a leading role in the relations of organized business with the Federal Government" with active legislative and public relations programs.)[76]

Government could also encourage some of the other association activities discussed earlier:

> Through the sponsoring of trade practice conference rules under the auspices of the Federal Trade Commission and the sponsoring of legislation that some associations have attempted to achieve the *control of some types of competitive practice.* In *compiling and disseminating trade statistics* many associations have enlisted the services of agencies of the Federal Government. Most trade associations that are engaged in fundamental *product standardization or simplification* to a greater or less degree have sought the services of the National Bureau of Standards or have engaged in negotiation with Federal, State, and municipal agencies concerned with product certification and, particularly in the fields of construction and food and drugs, with standards of safety and health.

In carrying out programs of *technical research*, trade associations have available the facilities of the National Bureau of Standards and other agencies, which they frequently employ. In a number of industries *cooperative trade promotion* to a considerable extent is a matter of promoting the purchases by Government agencies of members' products or, through contacting *tariff or trade agreement* agencies, of attempting to protect or expand the members' domestic or foreign markets. In the field of *labor relations*, trade associations are actively concerned that legislative and administrative acts shall not encroach upon the interests of their members. But they also find Government agencies a principal source of *information concerning wages, hours, and working conditions* in their industries (emphasis added).[77]

Galambos has suggested that "policy-shaping associations and an association-government alliance" emerged between 1925 and 1935, but that after the NRA period, there was a "revitalization of the service associations." This captures a truth but is probably too absolute a periodization and too blunt a typology. Even in the golden age, 42 percent of associations did not consider government relations a major activity, and the most important way industry associations related to government was passively, by reporting on policy issues to their members. Far fewer were active lobbyists attempting to shape policy.[78]

With a longer-term view, what seems most significant about associations' changing political role is their positioning in policy domains under the apparently bland heading of "information and advice given to government," a model the "service association" could continue. As the quotations above indicate, this realm of activity absorbs the authors of the 1938 report, both for the complex and routinized ways it shows industry influencing government, and for the ways government influences a variety of other associational strategies of action. The turbulent times contributed to the gradual routinization of associations' *political* role in this way, integrating them into particular policy contexts as interest groups, in ways still recognizable today.[79]

Even more important, overall, was the institutionalization of an extensive repertoire of strategies of action oriented to *information production.* As we saw above, this orientation was the common thread in many of the most common activities of associations. We see now that it was also key to associations' political role—since reporting political information to members and providing information to government were their most common political activities.

Conclusion

Max Weber provides the starting point for this account of American
business association history. That history, however, has again and again
exposed buried Durkheimian themes.

For Weber, surrounding institutional environments shaped and organized intrinsically self-interested economic exchange in markets, and
different real-world patterns were characterized in terms of different organizational forms, cultural orientations, and political contexts. Business associations were one among a variety of ways of shaping market exchange.
Likewise, theorists of economic governance understand associations as
one of a variety of possible governance forms, distinguished from others
by a distinctive combination of features (in organizational form and cultural orientation) and influenced by political context. They have generally
argued that associational governance will be most effective where states
authorize and encourage it: the examples of Germany and Japan support
this thesis. From this point of view, American associations are supposedly
"unstable, redundant, and limited" as a governance form.

Superficially, the historical evidence available can support this view.
Even before the implementation of antitrust law, associations were small
and relatively informal organizations. They do not seem to have been
particularly successful in what has been taken to be their major purpose:
stabilizing industries with price and production agreements. They operated in a laissez-faire environment, and the national state was weak. After
the slow, contested implementation of antitrust law, they supposedly lost
their major purpose.

The exceptional times of war and depression when government encouraged economic rationalization and authorized association governance
seem to prove the general rule. For brief periods during the First World
War and between 1933 and 1935, they enjoyed the sort of formal state
authorization of industry coordination usually considered to typify associational governance, and claims about the virtues of this role were probably more common in public discourse than at any other time in American
history. As comparative governance perspectives would suggest, these
episodes of state authorization did increase numbers of associations.
However, these minor episodes of state authorization seem to have had
little direct long-term impact, and they scarcely add up to the sort of strong
industry management that comparative perspectives suggest.

But the evidence also cumulates that this story misses something big, and there is much about American associations that it cannot explain. The nineteenth-century formation of national associations did begin with the nationalization of the economy after the Civil War—but built on earlier local and regional associations more than has previously been recognized. Even in their supposed heyday, associations were multifunctional, with interests in information, education, and camaraderie as well as price and production agreements. The association population continued to grow after antitrust law was implemented; indeed, there is no existing evidence of even short-term population decline after 1890 or after the beginnings of more serious antitrust enforcement with the Progressives. And just as associations persisted after the implementation of antitrust law, the association population continued to grow throughout the twentieth century, almost regardless of political context. As Aldrich and Staber point out, "between 1937 and 1983 the trade association population was growing independently of developments in federal regulatory efforts (at least at the aggregate level)."[80]

Considered in the longer term, antitrust and associations' early twentieth-century political vicissitudes encouraged the expansion and routinization of their range of activities. The specific implications of antitrust law for associations' goals and activities were worked out in several decades of policy shifts and court challenges, but also with innovations in associations themselves. The variable winds of antitrust and FTC politics in the early twentieth century, and the brief episodes of integration in government planning during war and depression, have diverted attention from the concurrent establishment of a robust institution. Associations became more established organizations in the early twentieth century, and associations now look much like early twentieth-century associations in their organizational form. Similarly, associations developed and institutionalized an extensive portfolio of activities in the early twentieth century, an institutional portfolio from which each might adopt a selection of strategies of action according to contingent circumstances. This range of activities and pattern of selection is also still evident today. The common focus of almost all these strategies of action was the coordination of information production.

Weberian governance theory cannot account for this sustained institutional vitality. Without dismissing the value of examining organizational form, cultural orientation, and political context, the consistencies in this picture of American business associations demand that Weberian analysis of business associations be set in a broader Durkheimian framework. The early Durkheim highlighted the increasing division of labor in modern life, and the social differentiation it generated. For him, this was a long-term, likely irreversible trend over and above the vicissitudes of economic interests and political differences. Although he was somewhat deaf to the loud political rumble generated by conflicting economic interests, and indeed to more particular issues of economic coordination, he worried about how social cohesion could be sustained. One of his solutions, of course, was the solidarity and coordination generated in occupational groups like business associations, which offered the possibility that "economic life would . . . be regulated and determined without losing any of its diversity" as the scale of economic action became national. American business associations in the twentieth century might have been following a blueprint developed from the second preface to Durkheim's *Division of Labor*.[81]

The story of American business associations so far suggests a puzzle that Weberian-inspired accounts cannot resolve, a puzzle that calls for Durkheimian attention to the cultural conditions of interested action. I have argued that the neglected importance of information production in American association history accounts for their persistence and development where Weberian accounts cannot do so. In the following chapter, I develop this argument further, with a new overview of contemporary business associations that shows that, like the early twentieth-century associations we have seen so far, they are primarily cultural producers for economic action.

CHAPTER THREE

Stable, Diverse, and Minimal

Contemporary Business Associations and Cultural Production

To the untutored contemporary ear, many of the groups we encountered in chapter two evoke a quaint and somewhat antiquated capitalism, an economic world far distant from the excitement, risk, and complexity of the supposedly globalized, neoliberal information economy that emerged in the late twentieth century. But the National Hardware Association, United Typothetae, Cotton Textile Institute, National Electric Light Association, Cracker and Biscuit Association, Life Office Management Association, and the Council of Machine Tool Equipment Services remain closer to contemporary economic life than either its boosters or critics would like to think.

We saw in chapter two that business associations were institutionalized in the first half of the twentieth century as mostly small, voluntary, multifunctional organizations. Comparatively speaking, their organizational capacities seem weak, and it is often hard for an outsider to see whether and how they are effective in their undertakings, or even to see what the point of devoting energy and resources to associating might be. Nevertheless, while particular associations come and go—emerging, merging, and dissolving—the population of associations continues to grow. Their specific orientations vary quite widely, with no general concerns shared by every business association but with a wide range of practices that might be adopted by any given association. Generally speaking, they sometimes undertake projects aimed at improving their shared economic practices and coordinating their relations with transaction partners, and they sometimes respond to the larger political environment of their members. To do so they adopt and develop a variety of strategies of action that usually involve producing and sharing information of various sorts. This picture—the long-term persistence and growth of the population, and their central concern with information production—suggests that to explain American business associations, Weberian accounts sensitive to shifting political-economic opportunities and constraints need to be supplemented with Durkheim's insight that a long-term expansion in the division of labor called for the development of associations that would allow for practical coordination and cultural solidarity. In contemporary terms, this means that whatever else they might do intermittently or on a short-term basis, business associations should be seen as cultural producers for economic action.

In this chapter I provide a new overview and analysis of contemporary American business associations' organization and orientations, based on a census of national business associations. I also draw on two other sources to fill out the picture of contemporary associations. First, some systematic studies conducted in the 1960s and 1980s tell us more about late twentieth-century business associations. To the extent that this information is comparable, it reinforces the conclusion that the institutional form of the business association remained quite stable throughout the twentieth century. Second, I begin to show what these groups look like in practice, with illustrations from the twenty-five focal associations.

Following the Weberian framework developed in chapter two, I examine associations' political context, organizational features, and orientations. I begin with a brief sketch of the political context within which business associations operated from the Second World War onward. I then turn to examining associations' distinctive organizational features and some of the ways these vary, reviving a neglected typology distinguishing "dinner-club," "service," and "policy-shaping" associations. I go on to argue that their organizational variability and core features reveal them to be best understood as organizations for cultural production. Finally, I explore what can be gleaned of associations' orientations from their statements of goals and activities. This new picture shows an extensive arena of contemporary economic action that has hitherto been largely unknown. Against this background, the following chapters will explore what exactly that economic action means.

Associations and the State in the Late Twentieth Century

Associations' political vicissitudes in the first half of the twentieth century were not repeated after the Second World War.[1] Their national political context remained very different from that generally envisaged by governance theorists to generate strong associational governance, and the experiments of the first part of the century did not result in a strong formal role for associations in state-economy relations. More importantly, their political environment was mostly more routine than in the early twentieth century, and while it generated some adjustments in associational strategies, it did not make significant changes in the institution itself. Cycles in the administrative power of antitrust constraints continued, but for business associations, patterns established in earlier episodic shifts and experiments persisted. The earlier episodes of administrative integration during war and depression did position some associations well as interest groups with expertise in particular policy domains, and there is also some indication that the political climate may have resulted in more (indirect and unnoticed) state support of business association activities like standardization. The potential role of associations as interest groups in national politics was certainly preserved, and many observers claimed it was strengthened, but the evidence for a qualitative change in business associations' political activity is limited.[2]

Although there were no radical changes in the framework for associationalism provided by state law and administration, as there had been in the early part of the century, the political importance of antitrust law continued to shift. There were three different periods: moderate, strong, and weak. At first, antitrust policy in the postwar period was based on the "liberal-pluralist stance," that it "should encompass multiple values"; and "by the end of the 1960s, liberal antitrust policies sustained the New Deal settlement which tied the welfare of American society to maintaining entrepreneurial oligopolistic competition among the nation's largest firms." Policy drew on economic models in which the main target was scale and barriers to entry generating market power against competitors, as for instance in an FTC ruling against Proctor and Gamble's acquisition of Clorox.[3]

This policy regime began to change in the late 1960s, with the political mood of the time generating increasing suspicion of concentrated economic power, and association observers comment on the strength of another episode of heated attention to strengthening antitrust regulation. Fueled by consumer movement coalitions that included prominent politicians and academics, several important reports critical of loose antitrust regulation, increased merger activity, and the oil embargo and recession of 1973, new laws granted the Federal Trade Commission stronger rulemaking and enforcement powers related to consumer product and service industries, and more vigorous monopolization investigations. The FTC Improvements Act (1975) expanded its jurisdiction by changing oversight over "unfair or deceptive acts or practices in commerce," for example, to "unfair or deceptive acts or practices affecting commerce." The agency's proceedings applied to nonprofit trade associations as well as to for-profit organizations. The Magnusen-Moss Warranty Act (1975) streamlined enforcement processes and established stricter penalties by allowing civil court action and penalties in addition to administrative orders. In response to "growing community and state agitation over corporate diversification resulting in the loss of local jobs, taxes and resources," the Hart-Scott-Rodino Antitrust Improvements Act (1976) allowed pursuit of triple damage claims against Sherman-Clayton violations at the state level, made provision for resources to do so, and made a variety of other provisions to strengthen FTC investigation and enforcement, such as the requirement that merger parties prenotify the Antitrust Division of the Justice Department.[4]

However, this flurry of regulatory activity was short-lived. According to Elizabeth Sanders, "growing legislative opposition was sufficient to check the commissions' activism by the end of the decade," and with President Reagan's election in 1980, antitrust enforcement and FTC resources and powers were scaled back. Chicago School economists objected to what Oliver Williamson labeled the "inhospitability tradition" and "entry-barrier reasoning," challenging both the postwar "liberal-pluralist" policy regime and the more recent antitrust activism. The thrust of their argument was that the type of market-entry barriers the old approach confronted did not in fact exist. They led a reassessment of trade-offs between market power and "efficiency" and argued that "to sacrifice economies for reduced market power came at a high cost," especially if, as Williamson argued beyond the Chicago School approach, institutional and organizational forms should be taken into account in assessing efficiency. This reasoning emerged in FTC and Supreme Court cases in the late 1970s and, as Williamson put it, "the 1960s preoccupation with competition, often amounting to no more than a concern over competitors coupled with a naive view of the modern corporation, was thus substantially redressed." From a very different perspective, Leon Lindberg and John Campbell make the same point when they suggest that antitrust enforcement became more lenient in the 1970s and '80s, particularly in declining industries like steel, autos, and nuclear power.[5]

The Reagan administration encouraged the Chicago view of antitrust legislation. Legislatively, the Regulatory Flexibility Act (1980), and the later Small Business Regulatory Enforcement Act (1996) imposed a series of procedural requirements on regulatory agencies before applying regulatory policy to small business. But the main impact came in a more passive approach to enforcement: "The Reagan anti-trust division generally declined to prosecute either price or non-price vertical restraints, a policy the federal courts sanctioned; at the same time these officials took a lenient policy toward mergers. The enforcement attitude at the FTC was similar." This policy regime became well established, and lenient antitrust decisions continued to restrict Sherman's scope. For instance, in 2007, the absolute prohibition of particular practices like resale price maintenance was weakened to a ruling that they should be assessed on a case-by-case basis (according to the "rule of reason").[6]

Business associations were not the leading heroes or villains in these developments, even though antitrust law shapes their organizational limits, and, as noted below, the 1970s and '80s probably saw higher rates of association formation than the 1960s or 1990s. At a more routine level ultimately more relevant to most associations' activities, the administration of antitrust law continued to change in its details. Some court decisions and advisory opinions specified restrictions on such practices as information sharing, standard setting, and membership rules. For instance, in 1967 the FTC specified that certification could not be denied to nonmembers; now, most associations with certification programs simply charge nonmembers more to be certified, tout certification costs as benefits of membership, and, presumably, rely on the fact that certification of obscure products like, for instance, garden mulch, or auto lifts, is not in huge demand from nonmembers. In another 1969 restriction, the Supreme Court further limited the sort of information that could be exchanged about prices in concentrated markets. And in one 1982 case, associations were held accountable for the actions of their volunteer officers: the officer had issued information that a competitor's product did not meet association standards.[7]

Late twentieth-century observers also commented on laws from the 1980s that generally increased the possibilities of associated action by business. One law created new possibilities free of antitrust restrictions for joint action to improve exporting; another created the possibility of research consortia. In general, these seem to have spawned different types of organizations rather than expanded the activities of national business associations. However, such laws may have extended the influence of some business associations indirectly; for instance, consortia founded by business associations were larger and grew more frequently than other consortia, which suggests that associations encourage other collective strategies in industries.[8]

Perhaps more directly beneficial for associations, given their century-long experience with standard setting, was the 1995 National Technology Transfer and Advancement Act (NTTAA), which "requires that all federal agencies use standards developed by voluntary consensus standards bodies instead of government-unique standards whenever possible." According to the Automotive Lift Institute, which received an award from the Standards Engineering Society on the occasion of the law's tenth anniversary, "other benefits of the NTTAA partnership include improving the effectiveness of government and promoting public safety." It seems likely that such explicit privatization of standard setting would provide previously unrecognized indirect state *support* and encouragement for business associations' role in American economic governance, contrasting with the more well-known *constraints* previously imposed on their action by antitrust law.[9]

Contemporary associations do not devote a lot of explicit, regular organizational attention to antitrust considerations; rather, these constraints are assumed in their background operation. Some associations make explicit mention of antitrust rules affecting their members' activities, but many do not. The effects of antitrust are clearest indirectly, in the "safe" activities they do choose to pursue. They may also be explicit in by-laws, and in such practices as assigning a staff member to every committee meeting, or in hiring association counsel (usually in more highly organized associations). Only a few associations in the focal sample discussed regular practices designed to take account of antitrust restrictions in any depth.[10]

But many late twentieth-century observers commented on a more consequential change in the political context of business associations than change in antitrust interpretation and enforcement. Many argued that institutionalized "interest group" politics became increasingly important at the national level. They noted in the 1970s and 1980s a "remarkable explosion in American advocacy groups." According to Louis Galambos the development of the "administrative state" increased the political role of business associations, and in his opinion this was one of the biggest changes in associations in the late twentieth century. These observers saw associations integrated in particular policy domains, blurring the boundary between public and private: "state bureaus fostered stable networks of clientele, funding sources and interorganizational alliances . . . interdependency and reciprocated relations between state bureaus and private associations jointly created the modern organizational state." Interest groups proliferated. As organized sites of specialized industry knowledge, business associations were well positioned for increasing influence as the policy role of interest groups grew in national politics in the late twentieth century. They might influence administrative implementation of broad legislative imperatives and provide expert witnesses and consultants as legislation was developed. One association partisan claimed that "were it not for such industry representation there could be impracticable or even unworkable regulations . . . as quite frequently the authors of legislation are innocent of understanding industry situations."[11]

However, there is no strong evidence that associations were significantly involved in any late twentieth-century "advocacy explosion," nor that it significantly altered them. Business associations' involvement in conventional politics is explored in depth in chapter eight, but here, some initial reasons to be dubious should be mentioned. First, some business associations became systematically organized as "policy-shaping" associations in the late 1920s; and if indeed the late twentieth-century "advocacy explosion" affected business associations, it was probably a replay of earlier episodes. Some political scientists argue, against the "advocacy explosion" thesis, that national interest group politics in the late twentieth century was not qualitatively different than in earlier periods. Second, political scientists have shown that advocacy by corporations became more significant than advocacy by associations (even though firms were also members of associations). Third, the census of associations shows that contemporary associations do not articulate goals and activities oriented to conventional politics like lobbying at much greater rates if they were formed in the 1960s, '70s, and '80s than if they were formed in other decades.[12]

Overall, their late twentieth-century political context was mostly stable for associations, and they generally followed institutional patterns set down in earlier, more tumultuous decades.

Business Associations as Organizations in the Late Twentieth Century

In the late nineteenth century, as we saw in chapter two, the National Hardware Association was a voluntary organization run by a full-time secretary-treasurer and an executive committee with numerous other functionally oriented committees, publications, and affiliations. Association management probably became more professionalized in the early twentieth century, but associations in general remained small organizations, with median membership under fifty. They were run by a handful of staff, and some committees, occasionally hiring experts like lawyers or management organizations. Within the overall governance framework set by antitrust law, and allowing for variations and changes due to shifting political and economic conditions, a flexible organizational form for collective action by business had been institutionalized.

Numbers of business associations expanded steadily throughout the twentieth century. On one estimate, at least 150 to 250 new national associations were founded per decade from 1900 to 1930, and between 400 and 600 were founded each decade from the 1930s to the 1980s. The trend is roughly similar among associations still existing at the time of this study. In the more recent data, between 100 and 200 associations were founded each decade from 1900 to 1930, and between 200 and 500 associations each decade from 1930 to 1970. By the early 1980s, best available estimates put the population at close to 3,500.[13]

So what do these organizations look like? Two studies of national voluntary associations offer a more complete picture for the second half of the twentieth century than is available for earlier periods. In the early 1960s, a neglected study of the increasingly national scale of American social organization by Lloyd Warner and his colleagues included a survey of 334 larger trade and business associations. Roughly twenty years later, David Knoke included sixty large and forty-nine smaller business associations in a phone survey about how national associations mobilized members' collective action. The picture emerging from these snapshots twenty years apart demonstrates notable continuity and shows an established population of mostly small and "minimalist" voluntary organizations not unlike the Hardware Association of almost a century earlier. Depth is added to this simple picture, though, by the fact that organizational size and complexity range very widely.[14]

Size

Even though both samples were biased to larger organizations, they were most notable for their variability and included unexpectedly small and simple groups. For Lloyd Warner and Desmond Martin in the early 1960s, the "number of members varies from the hundreds into the millions," and "the incomes of some trade associations run into the millions, others are relatively small, some no more than a few thousand dollars." Knoke also found that business associations ranged widely in membership size and revenue but noted that the distribution was highly skewed to cluster in lower ranges (for him, fewer than a thousand members and less than ten thousand dollars annual revenue). Compared to other voluntary organizations he studied, business association memberships were smaller, but per-member revenues were higher, and mean association income was also high compared to all other types of voluntary associations except unions.[15]

Organization

Organization size and complexity fell into a similarly broad range skewed to the small and simple. Most associations, even large ones, operated with comparatively few paid staff members. Half of the associations in Warner and Martin's 1962 sample had fewer than fifteen staff, though almost a third reported more than thirty. On a composite measure of bureaucratization (including departments, formal rules, etc.), these authors concluded that seven in ten of their business associations were simple organizations. Knoke found even fewer paid staff than Warner and Martin had done twenty years earlier. He considered only a third of the business associations in his sample to be highly bureaucratized (averaging fifteen staff); the other two-thirds averaged fewer than two staff, so the median would be much lower. Half of all the business associations he studied were rated as small on almost all other indicators of complexity.[16]

Warner and Martin had been concerned about what they saw as increasing organizational dominance of national life in the mid-twentieth century. But their unexpected findings on business association organization evoked the opposite worry: "so simple are the headquarters of most national associations that—rather than concern with the specter of entrenched bureaucracy—questions as to the effectiveness of such small and loosely organized administrative structures might be more in order."[17]

They do suggest several ways the organizational capacity of business associations could extend beyond their typically minimalist formal organization. First, seven in ten trade associations reported affiliates, and affiliation was especially common in wholesale, retail, and manufacturing associations. (As we will see in chapter eight, these loose affiliations may be significant for extending some associations' political capacities.) Second, their members are often firms rather than individuals: in this 1962 study, just under half were composed of firms, a quarter had individual members, and a quarter mixed memberships. Compared to other types of voluntary associations, too, business associations derived more of their income—about three-quarters—directly from membership, as opposed to other public and private foundation sources. And some occasionally extend their capacities by subcontracting associational projects like research or lobbying. These distinctive features of business associations might increase their effectiveness and significance compared to other types of voluntary organization, despite their minimal organization.[18]

Governance

For Warner and Martin in the 1960s, business associations resembled other types of voluntary association in their governance structures, conforming to "the general cultural conception of democratic constitutionalism," with governing bodies, direct election, term limits, and so on. Later, Knoke also found that business associations followed the model of most voluntary associations—noting that this organizational form is "strongly institutionalized in American political culture." Knoke offers the only detailed examination available of factors affecting variation in associations' internal governance structure. Contrary to his expectations, practical organizational contingencies had little influence on association governance; as he concluded, "governance may be less a matter of structural or strategic contingency and more a matter of cultural institutionalization . . . [and] reflect pervasive cultural standards about proper organizational forms and procedures." Again, the institutionalized stability of the association as an organization by the late twentieth century is notable.[19]

Location

One other consistent feature of the population stood out to Warner and Martin. In the early 1960s, almost seven in ten business associations they studied were located in only three cities: New York (24 percent), Washington, DC (25 percent), or Chicago (20 percent). Others were "scattered everywhere in large American cities, but mostly in the East and Midwest"; no other city rated more than 2 percent of business association headquarters. In this feature, too, they were typical of most other types of voluntary associations.[20]

Business Associations as Voluntary Associations

A common theme of these studies is their somewhat unexpected finding that business associations resembled other voluntary associations much more than large corporations or government departments. As we saw in chapter two, theorists of economic governance viewed business associations as one among several ways of structuring economic transactions, like corporate hierarchy, markets, and networks. In the context of that comparison, associations have been considered comparatively high on formal organization, a feature that may, in the right political conditions, "develop a certain autonomy from member firms which facilitates the pursuit of long term strategies . . . and stabilizes relationships with the state and other forces." But in fact, comparisons with other sorts of voluntary organizations—for Warner and Martin, those oriented to religion, sociability, government, recreation, education, science and the arts, and welfare; and for Knoke, professional societies, labor unions, recreational associations, and others—turn out to be more informative about associational governance and organization than the somewhat idealized picture suggested by governance theorists.[21]

Yet scholars concerned with the "third sector" of nonprofit organization have also neglected business associations, in part because they focus more on philanthropic than mutual-benefit organizations. This distinction is sometimes challenged, because mutual-benefit associations sometimes engage in philanthropic activities. But even so they find that considered in the aggregate, business associations are generally more dependent on members, more resource rich, and more organized than, for instance, professional or recreational associations. Moreover, their purposes are usually presumed to be more strategic, more utilitarian, and more political than those of many other types of voluntary associations. And the national business associations considered here constitute only a small fraction of the overall nonprofit field. For instance, Lester Salomon and Helmut Anheier report that "business and professional" associations—a much broader category—make only 5 percent of nonprofit revenue expenditures in the United States.[22]

It is not surprising then that business associations have eluded analysis of both economic sociologists and students of nonprofit organization—and that most of what we know of them emerges in studies focused elsewhere. American business associations' institutionalization in the landscape of American voluntarism suggests that a full account will draw on broader theoretical resources than theories of either economic governance theory or nonprofits can suggest—and requires more focused study of what they look like and what they do.

So far, we have seen that late twentieth-century business associations were predominantly small and simple, but their size and complexity ranged widely. They followed the model of other American voluntary associations in their governance structure. These broad consistencies are striking, especially given the theoretical and methodological differences between the two studies discussed here, which were also separated by twenty years of significant sociopolitical change (change that is neatly reflected by their differing concerns with national organization and with collective action, respectively). But neither study was specifically focused on business associations, and both are based on small samples biased to larger associations. To what extent are these studies of national business associations confirmed by more comprehensive contemporary information? To move beyond these dated glimpses of American business association organization, I develop here more precise information about contemporary associations' organizational features. How big and how complex are they? How do they vary in size, membership, staff, organizational complexity, and sectoral location? How old are they and where are they located? These are obviously rather basic questions. But answering such questions with an analytic picture of the contemporary business association population is important because contemporary scholars understand them so poorly. As a result, a large arena of economic action is usually ignored. When it is not ignored, scholars rely on assumptions about the basic population that, as it turns out, cannot often be sustained.

Organizational Features of Contemporary American Business Associations

I answer these questions with a census of national business associations existing in 2002–3. Several distinctive features of this information should be noted. First, unlike most previous studies, this is not a sample (so tests of statistical significance are not pertinent). Second, sources are more comprehensive than those used for previous studies in several ways, and selection is not biased to larger associations.[23] Third, association goals and activities are coded from association statements, a much more comprehensive and unobtrusive measure of what associations do than in earlier studies, because goals and activities they expressed approximate more closely what is meaningful within associations themselves.[24] Fourth, this information allows a new assessment of one way in which business associations differ from many other voluntary associations—in their inclusion of firms as well as individuals as members. Previous studies have noted this feature, but they have not investigated its implications. Overall, the data provide a comprehensive new map of an essentially unknown feature of the American institutional landscape. Table 3.1 summarizes the main landmarks on this map.

Membership: Size and Type

- Contemporary American associations are *predominantly small*: their median membership size is 353. Memberships of between a hundred and a thousand are most common (45 percent of associations).[25]
- However, an *enormous and skewed range* in membership complicates this picture. A notable minority of associations (14 percent, or just over nine hundred associations) had fewer than fifty members, and almost one in four (23 percent) had fewer than a hundred. On the other hand, 10 percent reported a membership of more than five thousand, and 7 percent—277 associations—had more than ten thousand members. Knoke reported a similarly large though skewed distribution in the 1980s, and William Coleman's study of Canadian associations also shows a similar picture.[26]
- Associations *composed of firms* are most common (48 percent), but 36 percent were composed of *individuals*, and 16 percent included *both* types of members. Warner and Martin also found nearly half of associations were composed of firms, around a quarter were composed of individuals, and a quarter included both types of members. The slight differences in this roughly similar picture may be real historic changes in the population but are more likely due to the more comprehensive census of the contemporary data.[27]
- As one might expect, *associations composed of firms are smaller* than other associations, with a median membership of 152. The median membership of associations composed of individuals is 950, and it is 700 for associations including both firms and individuals. Dichotomizing size around the overall median of 353, over two-thirds of associations of firms (67 percent) were small, but only 22 percent of associations of individuals were of less than median size. However, associations of every membership type spanned the full range of sizes. For instance, 11 percent of associations with fewer than a hundred members were actually composed of individuals, and 14 percent of associations with more than

TABLE 3.1 **National business associations, 2003 ($n = 4{,}465$)**

Features	%	Comments
Membership Size		
< 100	23	
100–999	45	Median = 353
1,000–9,999	25	
10,000+	7	
Membership Type		
Firms	48	Median Membership = 152
Individuals	36	Median Membership = 900
Both	16	Median Membership = 700
Reported Staff		Correlates with size, not type of membership
< 4	42	Median = 4, Mode = 2
4–12	35	
13+	23	
Founding Decade		Size unrelated; > % firms
Before 1940	21	
1940–59	17	
1960–79	29	
1980–99	32	
Location		Mostly stable: See also chapter eight
DC and environs	30	
New York	9	
Chicago/Illinois	9	
Other	52	Widely scattered
Sectoral Focus		See also chapter four
One Sector	59	Some mix industries within sector
Crosses Sectors	41	28% > 2 Sectors
Main Sector		
Manufacturing	25	> since 1960s
Services	25	< since 1960s
Wholesale/Retail	11	> since 1960s
Transport/Information	11	≤ since 1960s
Finance/Real Estate	8	≤ since 1960s
Primary/Construction	16	> since 1960s
Cultural Production		See also chapters two, four, five
Conventions/Trade Shows	76	39% trade shows
Other Meetings	43	
Any Publication	83	Likely underreported
Newsletters	58	See also chapters four, five
Directories	36	See also chapters four, five

Dataset compiled from Kimberly Hunt, ed., *Encyclopedia of Associations*, 39th ed. (Farmington Hills, MI: Gale Group, 2003) with Rui Gao, Xiaohong Xu, Brian Miller, and Georgian Schiopu. Available at ICPSR, www.icpsr .umich.edu. Supported by ASA/NSF Fund for the Advancement of the Discipline, 2003 and the Institute for Scholarship in the Liberal Arts, University of Notre Dame.

10,000 members were composed of firms. Thus, numbers of "exceptional" cases were not negligible.[28]

Staff Numbers and Types of Association

- If *number of staff* is a taken as a basic measure of organizational complexity, most business associations are very simple organizations. The median number of staff for all associations reporting any staff is four, and the mode two. As with size, the range is wide though concentrated at lower levels. More than a third of associations reported fewer than three staff, but almost a quarter (23 percent) reported thirteen or more. As noted in chapter two, almost half of associations in the 1930s had one or two staff members. Warner and Martin's study in the 1960s suggested much higher staff numbers, but Knoke's data from the 1980s also suggest this large staff range concentrated at low levels; so too does that of Coleman in his study of Canadian associations.[29]
- As one would expect, *larger associations* were more likely to have more staff. Two-thirds (66 percent) of associations with fewer than a hundred members also had fewer than four staff, compared to 22 percent of associations with between 1,000 and 9,999 members. More than nine in ten of that minority of associations with more than ten thousand members had more than twelve staff.
- By contrast, and more counterintuitively, *type of membership* made little difference to staff numbers. Around two in five associations of *each* membership type (firms, individuals, or both) reported fewer than four staff, and one in five more than twelve.[30]

Organizational Differentiation, Membership Size, and Membership Type

- Just over a third of associations (37 percent) reported internal organizational differentiation in the form of *committees, divisions, or councils*. These proportions suggest, like the staffing measures, that associational organization is simple, although it is also likely that such organizational differentiation is underreported in these data.[31]
- With this qualification, and judging on the data available, there is a predictable correlation between *organizational differentiation and size*. Committees, divisions, or councils were reported by 46 percent of associations with greater than median size, but by only 35 percent of associations of smaller than median size.
- Association structure, as indicated by reports of committees, divisions, or councils, was also correlated with *membership type*. Two in five, or 40 percent, of

associations that included firms reported committee structure: a third (33 percent) of associations composed only of individuals did so.

- Another type of organizational differentiation is measured by reports of *affiliates*, or of regional or national subgroups or "chapters" within the association.
These are formally recognized connections between associations and other
similar, sometimes subordinate, groups with related concerns. Only 28 percent
of associations reported such connections. As noted above, Warner and Martin
found the majority of their associations (70 percent) reported affiliates and suggested that this extended the capacities of associations. The much lower proportion in this data may be partly a matter of underreporting, but is also likely
attributable to the more comprehensive construction of the data set, and more
representative inclusion of smaller associations.

- Reporting of affiliates and subgroups was highly correlated with association
size. Among *associations of greater than median size*, 47 percent reported affiliates and chapters. Among smaller associations, only 15 percent did so. Almost
two-thirds (64 percent) of that small minority of associations with more than
ten thousand members reported affiliates and subgroups, and slightly over half
(52 percent) of those with more than a thousand members did so.

- Affiliates and subgroups were highly correlated with *type of membership*. Associations with individual members were much more likely to report these connections than associations of firms (40 percent compared to 17 percent). Part of
the explanation of this difference might be inferred by considering associations
with individual members as even more likely to act like other American nonprofit organizations, reproducing what Skocpol and colleagues have identified
as the classic voluntary associational federated structure linking participatory
local groups into national society, although they would not consider business
associations as classic civic groups.[32]

Headquarters Location

- As Warner and Martin had found forty years earlier, business association
headquarters were *concentrated in three cities*. The concentration may have
diminished; only around half (47 percent), rather than seven in ten, association headquarters were located in the DC area (30 percent), New York (9 percent), or Illinois (9 percent). New York and Chicago may have been losing some
ground, though some of the apparent decline may also be an artifact of Warner
and Martin's bias to larger associations. Associations outside these three centers were still widely scattered. However, California (7 percent), Texas (4 percent), Pennsylvania (4 percent), Ohio (3 percent), and New Jersey (3 percent)

now drew a greater proportion than they seem to have done in the 1960s, and Florida, Georgia, Missouri, and Colorado also broke a 2 percent ceiling Warner and Martin used. Associations formed at a much faster rate than the population as a whole in California and Florida in the 1980s, and in California, Florida, Texas and Colorado in the 1990s. These minor shifts make sense, given changes in the American economy in the late twentieth century, but the persistence of the overall pattern is also striking, perhaps another indicator of the long-term stable institutionalization of this population of voluntary associations.[33]

Founding Decades

- Of associations existing in 2003, 21 percent had been *founded before 1940*, and over a third (38 percent) before 1960, another indicator of the stability of the organizational population. The 1970s and '80s probably saw more active association formation: whereas about one in ten currently existing associations were formed in the 1960s, and also in the 1990s, these proportions were doubled for the 1970s and 1980s. The 775 recorded associations formed in the 1970s make up 19 percent of the current population; the 886 recorded associations formed in the 1980s make up 21 percent.[34]
- Their *founding decade made no appreciable difference to size of associations*. For instance, in every decade since 1970 between 22 and 27 percent of associations formed have had less than a hundred members, and 49 percent have had between 100 and 999 members. Considering *type of membership*—firms, individuals, or both—there was a slight tendency for the proportion of associations with firm members to trend down from around 60 percent early in the century to just above 40 percent in the last decades of the century.

Sectoral Location

- Considering associations' broad sectoral location (manufacturing, construction, retail, finance, etc.) 41 percent *straddled more than one sector* (e.g., manufacturers and wholesalers, or even agriculture with "arts, entertainment, and recreation.") Some of these multisectoral associations (28 percent of the population) included members of more than two sectors. This observation of frequent sectoral mixing in associations has not been noticed in most previous work on associations, because scholars have assumed that associations must correlate with economic sectors.
- Considering the *main sector of each association*, manufacturing generates a quarter of all associations. Various kinds of service sectors—professional,

administrative, educational, and such—also generate about a quarter of associations. Between 8 and 11 percent of the association population was generated
in each of four other broad sectoral groupings: "wholesale and retail trade";
"agriculture, mining, and other primary industries"; "finance, insurance, and
real estate"; and "information." To the extent that this information is comparable to information from surveys in the 1930s and 1960s, trends are as one
would expect, with some decrease in the proportion of associations in manufacturing, agriculture, and wholesale and retail, and some increase in associations
in services and information.[35]

To summarize: American business associations are typically small, with
only a handful of staff and relatively little formal organizational differentiation. They resemble other types of voluntary associations. The minority
of larger associations tend to have more staff and to report more organizational differentiation. About half are composed only of firms, and half
include individuals; associations composed of firms are typically smaller,
with a more differentiated committee structure. Associations with individual members are more likely to have affiliates and subgroups. Their headquarters are concentrated in three large cities but otherwise widely spread.
A third were more than forty years old, and 40 percent were formed in the
1970s and '80s. Two in five included members from more than one economic sector. Considering only their main sector locations, one in four associations were in manufacturing, a quarter in services, and the rest were
scattered widely across different types of economic activities.

Stability is the most striking feature of this new analytic overview of
business associations. Not only are a substantial minority of particular
associations long lasting, but also, from all we can glean from previous
studies, business associations as a population have likely persisted in much
the same form for at least a century. Surveys and case studies across the
century find such typically smallish memberships and staffs, with a minority of larger, better-staffed associations. Business associations still draw
on models of organization prevalent in the voluntary sector and in the
American public sphere more generally, often extending their capacities
with committees or affiliates.

New shading is added to this picture in several ways with the additional
information of this census: we see some differentiation between associations composed of firms and associations composed of individuals in their
size and affiliations, and a trend toward individual-based associations (although associations of firms still dominate the picture). We also see minor
shifts in headquarters location over the century, to growing regions (al-

though three cities still dominate the picture), and a rough trend toward more associations in service and information sectors (although manufacturing is still the largest single sector). But this new shading is unremarkable and does not distort the basic picture.

What Do Business Associations Do?

This recent picture—combined with studies from the 1960s and 1980s—adds even more weight to the conclusions emerging from the historical evidence presented in chapter two. We saw there that theories of economic governance did not seem to provide much purchase for understanding business associations as an American institution. While antitrust law made corporate hierarchy the dominant form of American economic organization, business associations developed as a robust, persistent institution. While they lacked any serious organizational capacity to develop agreements among economic actors, their numbers grew. And although they were directly prohibited from enforcing cooperation among self-interested market players, their shared activities and interests proliferated.

Before developing a new account that can make better sense of them for what they are, it is worth reviewing what, according to extant theories, they "should" be. As chapter two showed, economic governance may take a variety of forms, including markets, organizational hierarchies, networks, and associations. Associations are formally integrated (like corporations, and unlike markets and networks) and operate unilaterally within a sector (unlike corporations). They involve "structured negotiations among organizations that mutually recognize each others' status and entitlements and that seek to create formal organizations with charters, bylaws, and procedures in order to implement relatively stable and formal agreements in pursuit of some common interests." Moreover, "association staffs may over time develop a certain autonomy from member firms which facilitates the pursuit of long-term strategies for the management of the problems of a sector and stabilizes relationships with the state and other forces in the environment of the sector." On the information above, this characterization is too idealized for what most real associations can actually do. Most have apparently little organizational capacity to undertake serious structured negotiations or implement stable and formal agreements, and many staffs seem too small and dependent to consistently fulfill a collective long-term policy-making function for their various members.[36]

How are we to understand these organizations, if they are not typically organs of effective industry governance? Answering this question requires, first, a more nuanced typology, and, second, a better understanding of what they all share.

An inductive typology developed in Galambos's case history of early twentieth-century associations illuminates important features of the contemporary population well. As we saw in chapter two, Galambos argued that "dinner-club" associations gave way to "service" associations, which briefly became "policy-shaping" associations but, after the NRA failed in the 1930s, reverted to "service" associations. The bigger picture here and in chapter two suggests the typology captures some truth about the range of variation among associations, but that the periodization is too forced: all three types exist now, and likely could be found at any time throughout the twentieth century.[37]

"Dinner-club" associations, according to Galambos, are weakly organized and do not have much distinct organizational identity apart from their members. They mostly provide an opportunity for members' meeting and discussion: they offer few sustained services, and most of the action they generate is that of the members themselves. Galambos thought such associations were most typical of the late nineteenth century, but they continue today. For instance, the Independent Bakers Association (IBA) seems to offer a healthy example. Formed in the late 1960s and composed of "over 400 mostly family owned wholesale bakeries and allied industry trades," its membership dues ranged from $425 for firms with $1 to 5 million in annual sales, to $2,200 for firms with over $20 million. Eleven members compose an executive committee, and the IBA also maintains a small DC office with three staff members who share responsibility for such duties as meeting planning, press relations, and legislative reports. They also retain counsel. But although it is slightly above average in size, lists some committees and a newsletter, and explicitly expresses goals related to lobbying and monitoring policy, IBA's organizational differentiation is comparatively slight, and the services it offers members are rather minimal and underdeveloped compared to many other associations. It makes little effort in areas like research, public relations, or education, and its major preoccupation appears to be its membership meetings; extensive photo albums include many smiling groups of bakery owners enjoying tennis and golf outings in luxurious Florida resorts.[38]

"Service" associations are more proactive in sustaining long-term, systematic programs and typically involve more differentiated organization and leadership. For instance, the International Concrete Repair Institute (ICRI), formed in 1988 and located in Des Plaines, Illinois, has 1,400 members, both firms and individuals; seven staff; and a relatively elaborate organization of eight administrative committees, seven technical committees (e.g., "grouting," "corrosion"), and active regional chapters. Dues for contractors and manufacturers ranged from $295 for those with gross repair-related income of less than $1 million to $1,590 for more than $5 million; the association also offers company or individual membership to engineers, consultants, architects, distributors, manufacturer's representatives, government agencies, facility owners, unions, educators, and students. It produces numerous publications, including a newsletter, a directory, and a repair manual, and holds several meetings each year. Its aim is "to improve the quality of concrete restoration, repair and protection, through education of, and communication among, the members and those who use their services," and this goal is specified in detail in a nine-point strategic plan. Few of its activities are oriented to the public sphere. Compared to the Independent Bakers, the concrete repair conventions and newsletters are rather serious, and ICRI also offers a wider range of programmatic services for members, including standard setting and education.[39]

Galambos shares the common scholarly nostalgia for the brief flourishing of "policy-shaping associations" in the early twentieth century, with their effective powers of coordination and control. In his example, a "policy-shaping" association was "distinguished by outstanding leaders, a well-defined and carefully articulated ideology, and formidable cooperative programs. It was a semi-autonomous economic institution with an identity clearly distinguished from its members . . . it impinged forcefully upon individual manufacturers, members, and non-members alike." His Cotton Textile Institute allied with government and with "carefully nurtured industry-wide cooperative norms was able to achieve significant changes in the industry's managerial philosophy," although, even under the favorable conditions of the early 1930s, it "failed to stabilize production, prices, or profits." As we have begun to see above, and will explore in more depth in chapter eight, this sort of strong associational governance does not characterize all associations, and even strong associations have little capacity to sanction firms that do not follow their programs. Nevertheless, a minority of associations do come closer to this form than the "dinner-club" or "service" form. For instance, the American Council of Life Insurance is unique among the cases examined because it looks like what most people assume is the stereotypical business association. Formed in 1976, led by a former governor, and composed of 427 firms, it is located in Washington, DC, and reports 184 staff, with numerous committees and interest-based subgroups of members. It "represents the interests of legal reserve life insurance companies in legislative, regulatory and judicial matters at the federal, state and municipal levels of government and at the NAIC [National Association of Insurance Commissioners]. Its member companies hold more than 90 percent of the life insurance force in the United States." Its many publications and meetings support a variety of extensive programs concerning internal industry issues (e.g., financial and accounting, actuarial, health trends), as well as its stated public goals.[40]

This rule-of-thumb typology should not be pressed too far; even dinner-club associations provide some "services" to members, and even the rare policy-strong association often acts as a meeting ground otherwise demanding little of members. But as I noted in chapter one, associations likely change their focus and capacities over time, and the typology helps to specify the sorts of historical shifts that are possible (though certainly not necessary). For instance, in the focal sample, the Firestop Contractors give every indication of making a shift from "dinner-club" to "service" association (see chapter nine); the United Lightning Protection Association seems to have made the reverse shift in the past. And the North American Association of Food Equipment Manufacturers seems to have strengthened its governance capacities in the recent past, becoming a "policy-shaping" association (see chapter six), while the Envelope Manufacturers' Association gives signs of making the reverse shift. Other association case studies also show historically contingent shifts in organizational focus and capacity.[41]

Removed from its forced and teleological periodization, Galambos's typology does help illuminate the range of organizational capacities among American business associations and helps to show why governance theory cannot go far to understand them. Through the lens of governance theory, the majority of American associations here—and many of those we glimpse in studies over the past century—seem, if not inadequate, oddly distorted, perhaps embryonic: tadpoles rather than frogs.

For instance, if we attempted to partition the population, perhaps by selecting associations in manufacturing composed of firms, with large staffs and established organizational differentiation, located in DC, and more than ten years old, we would not learn much that is generally representative of what profit-oriented actors are actually doing in nonprofit association. Such particular investigations need to be conducted against a background understanding of the universe from which the selection is made, and what exactly the selection exemplifies, without taking for granted its significance or representativeness. And contrary to most scholars' assumptions, American business associations are not tadpoles to governance theory's frogs. They are a different species.

What shared features characterize them?

Chapter two showed that early twentieth-century associations selected from a standard repertoire that included a wide range of activities, depending on their circumstances. Beyond the particularities of these strategies of action—which included trade promotion, government relations, employer-employee relations, miscellaneous services, standardization, statistical studies, conventions, and public relations—we saw that all business associations, as an emergent institution, shared an orientation to the production of information. This feature also characterizes other activities that, though less common, have been of interest to scholars of the period—the move for uniform cost accounting, and, more generally, research for technical information. I argued that an overall focus on activities oriented to collectively produced and shared industry information seems to have emerged strongly in the first half of the twentieth century. I also suggested that previous scholars have overemphasized associations' pursuit of economic interests—and its shaping by political context—at the expense of a prior condition that cannot be taken for granted—the production of meaning for economic action, including the meaning of "industry interests."

From this point of view, the apparently weak but variable and well-established organizational form business associations take is easily explained. They are an institutional form—that is, a long-lasting, taken-for-granted model of organizational practice—for cultural production and reproduction. Their typically minimalist organization, their variability, and their persistence pose problems for governance theory, but these institutional features make perfect sense if we see them as meso-level economic organizations routinely producing the constitutive cultural "infrastructure" of industries. Their divisions, committees, promotional activities, publications, and meetings then appear not simply as functional tools for implementing a wide array of "interests" for the economic actor or the industry, but as structures and processes in which an industry exists as collective identity, by which status orders and market niches may be maintained or contested, and broader political and social influence may be articulated or mediated.

General theories of cultural production emphasize the role of specific organizations and interorganizational relations in shaping the availability of ideas, symbols, discourses, and practices. The "production of culture" perspective, developed from the 1970s by Richard Peterson, Paul Hirsch, Diana Crane, Paul DiMaggio, and others, challenges earlier views of culture that assumed that meaning simply emerged as a mirror of macrosocial structures, or else in the process of uncoordinated, actor-level interaction. By contrast, this approach "focuses on how the content of culture is influenced by the milieux in which it is created, distributed, evaluated, taught, and preserved." Influenced in part by earlier approaches in the sociology of organizations, industry, and occupations, production-of-culture scholars are most well known for focusing on dedicated realms of cultural production such as art, popular culture, and science, but the approach applies in principle to more diffuse elements of culture, as is evident, for instance, in Robert Wuthnow's examination of the production of ideological innovation in such large-scale cultural changes as the Enlightenment. With the exception of neoinstitutionalist theory, discussed in chapter four, economic sociologists generally tend to focus more on evidence of firm-level behavior than routinized and institutionalized cultural production; that is, meaning emerges in the process of actor-level interaction in the pursuit of interests. But we can see business associations, like industry media, the business press, and business schools, as field-level cultural production institutions. Just as industry Billboard charts constitute the popular music industry, or the securities analysts' coverage coherence of a stock may affect its volatility, business associations routinize the creation of the cultural infrastructure that constitutes and reconstitutes "industries." For instance, as Michael Lounsbury and Hayagreeva Rao show, industry media like trade magazines and directories constitute and reconstitute product categories.[42]

If we consider the business association population as a whole, and in the long term, in this way, one important implication is that the immediate strategic impact of particular goals and activities of business associations is always contingent and secondary to an understanding of the institution. Cultural producers make the contingent and variable pursuit of particular "interests" possible, but they do not generically express natural or pregiven interests. And, as Hirsch pointed out about "culture industries," organized overproduction of culture is comparatively cheap and easy, but it is also essential when demand—if it can even be characterized that way—is shifting, varied, and unpredictable. In these circumstances, an institutionalized population of "minimalist" organizations makes perfect sense. Considered from a purely strategic point of view, business associations will be overproducing culture—both in instrumental forms, like standards, and expressive forms, like dinner parties (to the extent the instrumental and the expressive can be distinguished). Whether they are the less programmatic "dinner-club" associations, or the "service" associations with sustained programs in such activities as standardization or public relations, or the rarer association with the organizational capacity to shape policy, all business associations are cultural producers.[43]

The most central and widely shared features of American business associations are their activities as cultural producers. Even in the 1930s, at least 54 percent of national and regional associations reported holding conventions, and for a third of them this was a major activity. A third also reported trade exhibitions. The authors of that survey believed this was likely underreporting. Almost all reported other types of meetings as well—executive committee (49 percent), board of directors (63 percent), other committees (66 percent), product groups (16 percent), regional groups (27 percent), or general membership meetings (91 percent). For significant minorities of associations, these meetings were frequent; for example, one in five associations with regional groups reported between twenty-six and fifty meetings of those groups each year. In the 1950s, too, Francis Sutton and his colleagues emphasized the way "associations facilitate and stimulate the production of ideology," with "a tremendous stream of print and other public communication which the voluntary associations generate, both to unite their memberships and to 'explain' themselves to the other groups and the public at large." They saw this as an important part of the institutional infrastructure of American business. And Denise Bielby and Lee Harrington's discussion of the industry events organized for buyers and sellers of television programs by the television distribution industry's associations, such as the national Association of Television Program Executives, provides a vivid contemporary example.[44]

Among contemporary associations, meetings are associations' most commonly shared activity. In the population as a whole, 76 percent—or around 3,200 associations—report holding conventions or trade shows, and 43 percent report meetings apart from or in addition to their conventions or exhibitions. Association size and organizational differentiation make meetings more likely, but even at the minimum, two-thirds of associations report meetings, a major feature of the business association as an institution.[45]

Similarly, business associations are probably the most important producers of industry media, which, beyond their manifest strategic functions, also routinely contribute to the constitution and reconstitution of industry identities, industry fields, and industry relations. Four in five associations report publications of one sort or another. These include newsletters (58 percent of associations); directories (36 percent); and other sorts of publications like guides, magazines, brochures, handbooks, manuals, books, and proceedings (56 percent). One in three associations also report providing libraries or other information services. These proportions probably understate the sheer volume of production and distribution of general information oriented to economic action by associations. At least one in ten associations also reported other types of information production not categorized above. These reports also leave aside, for now, associations' substantive cultural production of standards, statistics, awards, and so on, which may or may not be published. Associations' reporting of any publication was slightly influenced by organizational size, differentiation, and type of membership, but at a minimum, two-thirds of associations reported publications.[46]

Meetings and publications are infrastructure for cultural production. What Howard Aldrich has labeled "minimalist" organizations are well-suited for this sort of purpose, and the flexible variability of the organizational form, evident in the range of sizes, types of membership, and other organizational features, is an advantage for adapting cultural production to the wide range of contingent circumstances that face different sorts of market actors at different times. The American business association as an institution is not a "permanently failing" attempt at the strong coordination demanded of strategically oriented economic governance, but an institution for the production and reproduction of meaning for different sorts of economic action.

Of course, meaning is produced elsewhere—within firms, occupations, educational institutions, various commercial media, and legal institutions, for example—and it also emerges in the process of particularistic interactions among market and other partners. However, at least two features distinguish business associations from other organized sites of cultural production for economic action. First, as I have argued, business associations, as an American institution, cannot be understood *except as* cultural producers, since, as voluntary organizations facing legal restrictions, they have little capacity for sustained, direct economic effectiveness (like corporations) or political effectiveness (like law). Second, unlike many occupations, educational institutions, and media, their organized meaning-making is distinctively specific to particular and obscure market and production contexts that have little significance except for the actors involved. The following chapters will show more of this context-specificity of meaning-making.

But cultural sociologists have frequently argued that meaning-making cannot be understood solely in terms of the features of its organized production.[47] I characterize business associations as organizations for cultural production as a foundation for further investigation of the meanings they actually produce. This step is essential because these associations have been poorly understood by scholars; assumptions about their organizational form are dubious, and their actual organizational features do not match their presumed functions. These puzzles are resolved by theorizing business associations as cultural producers, and we can now turn with more confidence to an analysis of the meanings they actually produce. I conclude this chapter with a brief overview of the goals and activities explicitly articulated by business associations, considering the population as a whole. Subsequent chapters analyze in depth the discourses and the strategies of action these superficial measures only begin to represent.

Orientations of Late Twentieth-Century Business Associations

In chapter two we saw that 1,200 associations surveyed in the 1930s reported a wide range of activities, most commonly related to government relations, trade promotion, employer-employee relations, miscellaneous services, standardization and simplification, statistical republication and special studies, conventions, and public relations. In the 1980s, Knoke asked informants in 109 business associations to rate eight broadly framed goals and consider their importance (see table 3.2). Even though the goals presented were broadly framed, trade associations reported an average of almost four goals each: Knoke concludes that associations have " 'eclectic interests,' contrary to some images of 'single issue' organizations."[48]

Surveys like these are not unobtrusive, and the interests and assumptions of the researchers, as embedded in the options offered in the questionnaire, influence the evidence they provide. For instance, the generality of Knoke's categories, and his categories themselves, relate to his main interest in understanding voluntary groups as sites of collective action. By contrast, the specificity and practical nature of the categories offered in

TABLE 3.2 **Association goals, 1984**

Organization Goals	% Indicating Moderate or Major
Raise members' status or prestige	63
Conduct research or member education	61
Influence policy decisions of government	58
Improve members' economic conditions	57
Affect the lives of nonmembers	55
Change values and beliefs in larger society	38
Develop members' social or recreational lives	18
Enhance members' cultural or artistic lives	13

Based on a telephone survey of a random sample of 109 national associations conducted in early 1984 (Knoke, *Organizing for Collective Action*, 68–70, 80).

the more detailed study of the 1930s come from the contemporary concern of government and associations with issues of economic cooperation, competition, and concentration. Knoke is not concerned with minutiae about strategies of trade promotion, for instance, and the earlier researchers were not concerned with associations' interest in the status of their members. (Researchers' assumptions are reflected even more directly in case studies, which are more common on this topic.)

The results of such surveys should also be handled carefully because respondents' interpretations of what an option might mean in their own context are unknown. Obviously there is likely to be a greater range of interpretation of general purposes like many of those suggested by Knoke than of the more particular activities listed in the 1930s survey. In Knoke's study, even something as apparently concrete as "influencing public-policy decisions of government" is understood very differently in different contexts, as we will see in chapter eight. And even though the authors of the 1930s study were more precise than Knoke in the options they offered respondents, they frequently noted "differences in the construction" of items, or "neglect or misinterpretation" influencing responses to their questions.[49] So although these rare surveys of business associations' activities and orientations are invaluable because they cast spotlights on a dark landscape, the information they provide about trade associations as a population can only be preliminary, because spotlights leave much of any landscape mysterious. Survey data can only be conclusive when much is already known about the discursive field, the orientations, and the strategies of action of the population in question (and even in those circumstances it may produce cultural objects as much as reflect them).

These problems of attempting to access association orientations with surveys are remedied with the comprehensiveness of the current data set, which has not been approached since the 1930s, and its unobtrusiveness, which is new. Association goals and activities were coded from their self-descriptions. These self-descriptions are certainly shaped by the statement of purpose as a genre. So, for instance, they are biased to strategic goals at the expense of expressive purposes. And they may not include all association goals; as we will see in the following chapters, associations sometimes do more than they include in their statement of purpose. But self-descriptions do circumvent the problem of imposition of researchers' own categories.

The goals and activities in the self-descriptions of 4,465 contemporary business associations can be summarized as follows:

TABLE 3.3 **Association goals and activities, 2003**

	Percentage
Internal Goals and Activities (see also chapters six, seven)	
Education (seminars, professional development, other instruction)	40
Sharing information among members	37
Research (surveys, statistics, forecasts, etc.)	35
Standards and accreditation	24
External Goals and Activities (see also chapters eight, nine)	
Public relations (public awareness and status of members/products)	41
Lobbying or monitoring policy	26
Broad civic goals (e.g., minority representation, safety)	13

From Spillman et al., "National Business Associations."

In its broad outlines, this picture both confirms and refines some of the little systematic evidence available from earlier studies. Just over a third of associations in the 1938 survey reported "standardization and simplification" as a major goal, more than in this contemporary study. Around a quarter reported "statistical republication and special studies," "technical research and advisory services," and "accounting, cost statistics, and studies" as major goals, a smaller proportion than we see above. That earlier study did not ask about broader internal goals, like "education" and "sharing information," but many of the particular activities it identified could be seen in this light.[50] Later, in the 1980s, six in ten of Knoke's small sample reported "research or education" to be an important goal, close to the sum of reports of these goals above.

In the 1930s a quarter of associations also reported public relations as a major activity (and over 50 percent were involved in at least some public relations activity). In Knoke's smaller sample in the 1980s, 38 percent agreed that changing "values and beliefs in the larger society" was a goal (and over six in ten were reported concerned to "raise members' status or prestige"). These reports are in the same ballpark as the 41 percent stating public relations goals above.

Some scholars have suggested that public relations became increasingly important in associations after World War II, and a closer look at the connection between founding decade and public relations activities seems to support these impressions.[51]

In the 1930s, 58 percent reported that government relations was a major activity, as (strangely) did exactly the same proportion in Knoke's small 1980s sample. As we see though, far fewer in this census report interest in government relations. This finding is explored further in chapter eight.

Considering the differing purposes and methodologies of these studies, it would be overinterpretation to draw any firm conclusions about trends in associations' orientations over time. What we can note here is the confirmation provided of a general stability in the institution of the business association itself, considered from the point of view of its orientations, as well as, as we saw above, its organization.

We can also note that more narrowly focused internal concerns are at least as important to associations as their stereotypical interest in influencing external audiences, if not more so. There is some indication of this internal orientation even in those earlier studies that were most concerned with associations' public role. Along with the historical evidence, contemporary associations' goals and activities also demonstrate more orientation to narrower industry concerns like education and standardization than to external audiences. Indeed, in 2003, 58 percent of associations expressed *any* external orientation at all (combining measures for lobbying, influencing public opinion, and civic orientations). By contrast, 74 percent of all associations reported one or more intraindustry goals. So intraindustry goals and activities were substantially more interesting to business associations than goals and activities addressing external audiences.[52]

All these goals and activities involve the organized production and reproduction of meaning. I conclude this overview by specifying and illustrating business association orientations drawing on the focal sample of twenty-five associations. The following chapters explore their meaning-making in more depth.[53]

Education

The most popular internal goal, education, mostly unmeasured in previous studies, indicates goals or activities "such as educational programs or projects, seminars, professional development, or any kind of instruction of members by the association." For instance, the Irrigation Association, composed of manufacturers, wholesalers, and contractors of irrigation equipment, reports that it "conducts Educations courses (22) [*sic*]"; similarly, the Exhibit Designers and Producers Association "conducts educational . . . programs" as does the International Concrete Repair Institute. The North American Association of Food Equipment Manufacturers has an Industry Education and Certification committee, the Mulch and Soil Council claims to offer educational programs at its annual meeting, the National Association of Real Estate Brokers "sponsors educational seminars," and the Equipment Service Association "sponsors business and technical workshops." The International Society of Certified Electronics Technicians "offers training programs in new electronics information"; the Vacuum Dealers Trade Association, composed of dealers, manufacturers, and distributors, seeks to "provide a forum for continuing education"; and the Small Publishers Association of North America "offers continuing education." The United Lightning Protection Association says it works to "educate members on the technical and commercial features of . . . [lightning protection] . . . systems."[54]

These associations represent businesses of all sizes and business activity of many types. As we will see in chapter six, their implementation of educational goals also varies widely, from large, ongoing, formal programs to occasional meetings. As chapter six will also show, most educational programs are disconnected from public relations or promotion of particular products and services. What we see here, in these self-descriptions, is the wide significance, for the business association as an institution, of an orientation to the production and dissemination of information specific to the particular context of members' economic activity. This significance is reiterated by the other orientations they expressed.

Sharing Information

Sharing information involves goals or activities such as sharing management, financial, educational, or other information among members understood as a more informal process than organized education programs—in terms of "disseminating" information or "sharing or exchange of ideas and opinions" among members. For example, the Firestop Contractors International Association, a group of building construction contractors, claims to "provide and maintain information for installation of firestop materials and systems"; the International Society of Certified Electronics Technicians "maintains a library of service literature"; the Mulch and Soil Council, composed of producers of soil and bark products and their suppliers, aims to "provide an exchange of business ideas and information"; the Pellet Fuels Institute "acts as an information clearing house among members"; and the Conference of Consulting Actuaries publishes conference proceedings "giving views of specialists in related fields."[55]

Research

Research indicates goals or activities such as conducting surveys, compiling statistics, making forecasts, analyzing trends, or assessing economic impact. For instance, the Brick Industry Association has an active engineering and research committee; the Aluminum Anodizers Council says it "conducts surveys"; the Exhibit Designers and Producers report "research programs"; the Mulch and Soil Council provides a "statistical report of bark product shipments"; and the National Association of Real Estate Brokers claims it "conducts research; compiles statistics on productivity, marketing and development." The Vacuum Dealers Trade Association also reports it "compiles statistics," as does the Irrigation Association.[56]

Standards and Accreditation

Standards and accreditation indicates goals and activities like setting standards, developing measures, standardization, or accreditation of experts. For instance, the Automotive Lift Institute publishes safety standards, the Aluminum Anodizers Council "sets color consistency standards," the Closure Manufacturers' Association "has established industry standards for metal and plastic closures," and the International Concrete Repair Institute "develops guidelines for the concrete repair industry." Certification programs are reported by the Irrigation Association, which "certifies Irrigation Designer, Contractor, & Manager," and the International Society of Certified Electronics Technicians offers certification programs "in the fields of audio, communications, computer, consumer, industrial, medical electronics, radar, radio-television, and video." Similarly, the North American Association of Food Equipment Manufacturers reports a certification program, as does the National Association of Real Estate Brokers.[57]

Public Relations

The most popular external goal, public relations, indicates goals and activities oriented to informing, educating, or increasing the awareness of the general public, or of more specific groups within the general public but beyond the association. It includes indications of a concern with general public reputation, improving the influence or social status of members, or public relations activities, and also includes goals and activities pertaining to advancing members' products, services, and general influence or social status to specified buyers or to other specified groups or audiences. (However, it excludes an orientation to influencing specifically political groups, institutions, or processes.)

In the focal sample, the United Lightning Protection Association "works to increase public interest in and awareness of the lightning protection industry," the Mulch and Soil Council "serves as industry spokesman," and the Small Publishers Association of North America "works to advance the image and profits of independent publishers." The Aluminum Anodizers Council "promotes the anodizing industry," the Closure Manufacturers Association "conducts public relations," and the International Society of Certified Electronics Technicians seeks to "raise their public image." More specifically, the Pellet Fuels Institute "promotes the increased use of pellets, briquettes, chips and other renewable fiber fuels," and the Equipment Service Association "promotes good relations with equipment managers; improves the status and image of the equipment service industry." The Brick Industry Association has a Marketing Promotion committee, the North American Association of Food Equipment Manufacturers has a Sales and Marketing committee, and the Automotive Lift Institute reports a Public Relations committee.[58]

Lobbying or Monitoring Policy

Lobbying or monitoring policy indicates goals or activities oriented to government, law, regulation, or authority, and includes not only explicit lobbying but also other weaker involvement, such as "monitoring policy," "working with local and national government," or "concerned with regulatory matters." For instance, the Independent Bakers Association

"represents independent wholesale bakers on federal legislative and regulatory issues"; the Closure Manufacturers Association "conducts . . . government and congressional liaison activities for member companies"; the
Pellet Fuels Institute "supports lobbying efforts promoting fiber fuels";
and the American Council of Life Insurance "represents the interests of
legal reserve life insurance companies in legislative, regulatory and judicial matters at the federal, state and municipal levels of government." The
International Telecommunications Society includes among its goals "liaison with international government agencies." The Irrigation Association
says it is involved in "Government Relations," the National Association of
Real Estate Brokers has an HUD-VA liaison committee, and the Brick Industry Association and the North American Association of Food Equipment Manufacturers report Government Relations committees.[59]

Broad Civic Goals

Broad civic goals indicate whether or not an association states goals or
activities oriented to general social issues beyond the industry, profession,
or business of members (this category was developed in response to pretesting). Examples are charity, women's issues, minority representation,
environmental protection, or safety issues. In the focal associations, for
instance, the Association for Women in Aviation Maintenance "strives to
help elevate women in the aviation maintenance related fields and finds
ways to network and support each other in this field" and the Firestop
Contractors International Association aims to "promote safety."[60]

Conclusion

The business association as an American institution has persisted in basically the same form created and established in the first half of the twentieth
century. Its political context, organizational features, and orientations all
show remarkable stability. Although the particular, day-to-day concerns
and activities of such groups as the Independent Bakers, the Concrete Repair Institute, or the Council of Life Insurance mentioned above are quite
contemporary, it requires little imagination to project back and see the
bakers, repair contractors, or life insurance companies gathering in 1910,
establishing quality standards and developing cooperative advertising in
1922, or completing government surveys in 1937.

The legal framework of antitrust continues to establish the mostly unremarked parameters of associational activity. Cycles of antitrust enforcement, and the minutiae of its legal implementation, may influence associational activity at the margins: the last decades of the twentieth century were characterized by a generally passive approach to enforcement and some probusiness legislation, which made a comparatively friendly climate for association activity. But this environment did not significantly change existing organizational forms and practices. Late twentieth-century developments in the organization of national politics also likely reinforced some associations' roles as interest groups and policy advocates in specialized legislative and regulatory domains, but these interest-group activities were neither new nor particularly representative.

Business associations follow the template of other voluntary associations in their organizational form, mostly regardless of particular environmental contingencies. The population of national business associations has increased steadily in the course of the twentieth century, mostly regardless of variable political context. Roughly four hundred national associations were formed each decade, and the population reached over four thousand by the early twenty-first century.

The comprehensive census here, and glimpses provided by surveys in the 1960s and 1980s, provides a largely consistent picture of the features of this population. Business associations are mostly small, but their size and staff numbers range widely. They may be composed of firms, of individuals, or both. Committees of members and affiliates of various types extend their organizational capacities. They are concentrated in New York, Washington, DC, and Chicago, but otherwise are widely scattered across the country. Forty percent include members from more than one economic sector; considering main sectoral location only, one in four is based in manufacturing, a quarter in services of various sorts, and the rest scattered widely across other sectors.

On the information available, there may have been some minor changes in membership type, and in geographic and sectoral locations, in the second half of the twentieth century. But overall, the organizational features of the population, like their political context, have remained stable. Galambos's typology of early twentieth-century associations— "dinner-club," "service," and "policy-shaping"—still provides a thumbnail sketch of variation among business associations today. But despite Galambos's belief that these types make an evolutionary series, as well as governance theory's emphasis on the ideal of strong, policy-shaping business associations, the organizational variation itself remains the most notable feature of the business association as an institution.

Business associations are oriented to an established, multifunctional portfolio of goals and activities that, so far as we can tell, have also remained basically stable. No single orientation can be used to characterize business associations in general, and most associations express more than one goal. Their expressed orientations included both intraindustry concerns and concerns with influencing the broader public in some way. Around 40 percent of contemporary associations cite education and public relations goals and activities; just over a third cite sharing information and research; and around a quarter are interested in standards and accreditation, and lobbying and policy monitoring. One in eight includes among their purposes broader civic goals. Previous case studies and surveys have tended to select somewhat unrepresentatively from the range of goals and activities characteristic of the business association as an institution, generally overemphasizing public goals. However, the comprehensive and nonreactive data show that intraindustry goals and programs are probably more important than public goals.

These national business associations are persistent, stable, minimal, and diverse organizations with diffuse goals and activities. I argued in chapter two that early twentieth-century associations were best characterized as information producers. Here, I have extended this characterization by drawing on theorists of cultural production to suggest that business associations are primarily cultural producers for economic action. From this point of view, their puzzling and unruly features make more sense. I have also noted that despite their minimalist organization and diversity of goals, their most characteristic features are their activities as producers of cultural "infrastructure"—of meetings and industry media. This organized infrastructure for meaning-making has been taken for granted, but if we see business associations primarily as cultural producers, it must be highlighted as the core of the institution, around which organizational variability and diverse orientations shift according to contingent circumstances. Minimalist organizations with a potentially diverse portfolio of goals and activities are primarily cultural producers and not (permanently failing) governance institutions.

But what meaning do they actually produce? We have already seen the goals and activities they articulate in a brief statement of purpose. The next chapter begins to dig deeper, by drawing on neoinstitutionalist theory to examine associations' routinized production of meaning in cognitive categories, networks, and industry fields.

PART II

American Business Associations as Cultural Institutions

CHAPTER FOUR

"Meet the Movers and the Shakers of the Industry"

The Social Construction of Business Interests

A merican business associations claim orientations to a variety of established strategies of action, involving both public audiences—such as public relations, monitoring policy, and charity—and intraindustry concerns—such as education, information sharing, research, and standardization. Some associations are strongly focused on one or two of these activities, like the Automotive Lift Institute on certification, or the Independent Bakers Association on monitoring policy, though they also attend to other goals intermittently. A few associations—like the Irrigation Association and the Brick Industry Association—provide an extensive array of established association services. Most develop some selection from the range of established possibilities according to the contingencies of their history and context, which are not generally reducible to simple formulas such as industry type or size. So these associational strategies of action are best understood as an institutional repertoire characteristic of the organizational population.[1]

Casual observers take it for granted that these strategies of action are obviously functional for profit-oriented actors' interests in market stability, efficiency, and profit. But this commonsense view invites many doubts. First, it encourages the stereotype that all associations pursue the same "interests." Second, it assumes that what association members share is transparent to them and to observers: what constitutes "an industry" is a given. Third, it usually presumes a one-to-one correspondence between "industries"—however defined—and the associations that represent them. Fourth, it ignores the comparative powerlessness of American associations, evident both in their limited legal capabilities and in their "minimalist" organizational capacity. Fifth, it tends to explain the survival of business associations teleologically, in terms of the efficiency outcomes imaginatively projected by association goals and activities. The historical and organizational analysis of the American business association population developed in preceding chapters shows that all these assumptions are problematic. But most importantly, a simplistic understanding of business associations in terms of the pursuit of industry interests begs the question raised by economic sociologists I noted in chapter one: where do their interests come from?

So far, this examination of American business associations' history and their organizational features has shown that they are best understood as an institution of cultural production for economic action. In this chapter I begin to examine the cultural embeddedness of interests in associations in more depth, by building on neoinstitutionalist theory, which originally proposed an important role for business associations in the construction and reconstruction of "industry interests." Economic sociologists influenced by neoinstitutionalism provide case studies of the social construction of "industry interests," and associations are often important actors in these accounts. But there is no systematic examination of associational activity in neoinstitutionalist terms. How exactly do associations provide institutional infrastructure for economic activity?

Answers to this question have been sketchy because earlier neoinstitutionalist analysts did not take them up, and subsequent critics and defenders have been more preoccupied with processes of change. In contrast, I emphasize that analysis of change relies on as yet unexplored assumptions about how institutional stability is sustained. What needs more attention is the routine meso-level reproduction and inculcation of categories and social relations—like "industries" themselves—orienting economic action. And only by attending to this routine cultural production—rather than change in specific "industries"—can we explain the thriving, stable population of American business associations as a whole.

Developing neoinstitutionalist insights in this way, we see that American business associations are cultural producers of "industry interests." Although they are comparatively powerless, although taken collectively their actual consequences remain mysterious, although they only rarely represent industry "interests" in a neat one-to-one correspondence, and although their goals and activities are diffuse, this nonprofit sector taken as a whole survives and thrives because it provides important organizational forms, resource infrastructure, and channels of communication for sustaining and changing "industries" and their "interests."

How does this happen? This investigation shows how the work of economic sociologists examining cognition, networks, and fields all helps understand institutional processes understood as cultural production and reproduction. In this chapter, after briefly examining neoinstitutionalist perspectives on business associations, I demonstrate how associations position themselves to produce and reproduce cognitive categories, networks, and industry fields on a routine basis.

The Social Construction of Business Interests

Economic sociologists examining the cultural embeddedness of economic action attend in different ways to the processes of meaning-making that influence how economic actors like firms understand and pursue their interests. As we saw in chapter one, neoinstitutionalists were influential in turning attention to cultural processes in organizations and organizational fields, and thus, also, in economic sociology more generally. As one overview summarizes:

> As firms interact with each other and with their environments, formal or informal rules emerge to govern interaction, and organizational fields are formed . . . they take on an independent status that has a powerful normative effect on subsequent interaction . . . [and] . . . changes in organizational form are driven more by considerations of legitimacy than by concern for rational adaptation or efficiency.

Economic sociologists often focus on the implications of institutional processes for firms, as this statement illustrates. But early statements of the neoinstitutionalist perspective suggested a broader view. By contrast with perspectives that "regarded organizations as both the units that were institutionalized and the key loci of the process . . . neoinstitutionalists view institutionalization as occurring at the sectoral or societal level, and consequently interorganizational in locus."[2]

This focus on a level of analysis beyond organizations led Paul DiMaggio and Walter Powell to theorize an important role for business associations as field-level meaning-makers for economic actors. They suggested that business associations help generate organizational isomorphism. Faced with uncertainty, organizations will adopt models that "may be diffused unintentionally . . . or explicitly by organizations such as consulting firms or industry trade associations," and this leads to mimetic isomorphism. Normative isomorphism, too, may be generated by "professional and trade associations . . . another vehicle for the definition and promulgation of normative rules about organizational and professional behavior," for instance, in workshops and trade magazines. Associations may also help generate status hierarchies in organizational fields: "professional and trade associations provide other arenas in which center organizations are recognized and their personnel given positions of substantive or ceremonial influence." But later scholars did not develop these suggestions about the business association as an institutional site of field-level organization, focusing instead on the consequences of institutional change for firms and industries.[3]

Early neoinstitutionalist theory made a place for business associations because by shifting the level of analysis of economic action from the firm to the field, it suggested that cultural production was an important and neglected process in economic life. Neoinstitutionalism in economic sociology is a special case of the theory of cultural production discussed in chapter three. Whether the outcome is an "industry interest" or a new genre of music, similar social processes are at work. Neoinstitutionalism predicts a cultural infrastructure that constitutes and reconstitutes "industries," and business associations provide such infrastructure, both in their more formalized practices like meetings and newsletters and in the more informal cooperative links and conventions that Howard Becker suggested are characteristic of somewhat more fluid and less structured "art worlds." As we saw in chapter three, if business associations are cultural producers, some of the empirical puzzles they present are dissolved. The apparent contradiction between their secure, sustained proliferation as a population and their legal and organizational weakness as strategic tools can be explained. Their "effects" are systematically constitutive, but their particular, conjunctural political and economic consequences will be unpredictable, only evident over long time spans, if at all, because from a strategic point of view, cultural production is *typically* "over-production."[4]

In this view, business associations do not simply promote interests; they discern, articulate, and sometimes debate them. They may develop common understandings of the objects of their market exchange; for instance, the International Concrete Repair Institute formed when founders attending a more broadly based World of Concrete meeting agreed that concrete repair was a distinct service within that world, "with an industry all its own," and the institute now routinely produces discourses that articulate and refine what good concrete repair means. Associations may also articulate relations with partners in exchange; for instance, the North American Association of Food Equipment Manufacturers (NAFEM) developed programs to identify and respond to new demand from concentrated commercial operators. And they may specify normative frameworks within which their market exchanges occur; for instance, the Firestop Contractors International Association created new standards for their work. As I have argued elsewhere, objects of exchange, partners in exchange, and norms of exchange all frame market actors' understanding of their interests. Business associations provide important settings in which market objects, partners, and norms are defined and redefined.[5]

Certainly, the political and economic significance of associations for producing cultural infrastructure for economic action will be most evident in moments of industry formation and change. Institutionalist scholars and their critics have been preoccupied for some time with the question of change (because neoinstitutionalist theory originally suggested powerful forces for continuity and persistence). Since the 1990s, they have argued that factors exogenous to organizational fields cause some changes, but that endogenous change may emerge when different institutional logics are transposed, when there are multiple inconsistent meanings within institutions, and when institutionalized practices have unintended consequences. Change also relies on institutional meaning-making for its diffusion.[6]

In these circumstances associations as field-level actors will be important sites for struggle and transformation about industry identities and interests. Indeed, a number of studies have examined associations' work in moments of industry change. For instance, Michael Lounsbury and his colleagues identify several associations as key actors in the formation and transformation of solid waste management as an industry field constituted by solid waste haulers, commodity producers, equipment manufacturers, and other businesses, interacting with municipal government officials, state and federal governments, and social movement organizations. In this study industry associations appear as sites of political-cultural struggle and change over cognitive frames defining fields—change in "industry recipes" that articulate firm interests. Similarly, Royston Greenwood and others analyze the role of professional associations in processing, legitimating, and framing accounting industry change in Canada. Case studies like these suggest that associations may constitute "interests"— even "industries"—and are sites of the sort of political-cultural struggle that, according to Neil Fligstein, occurs in markets in formation and markets in which "conceptions of control" are shifting. Indeed, a close reading of many other accounts of industry changes shows business associations in at least walk-on roles, although most of these stories treat the associations as minor research sites, not objects of inquiry.[7]

The more representative focal sample of associations confirms this case study evidence that associations provide organizational and discursive infrastructure addressing or promoting industry change. Association members are often discerning, debating, and addressing industry change in newsletters, committees, and convention panels, and in their routine activities like education, information sharing, research, and standardization. For instance, as chapter six explores further, we can see many associations responding to and working through the implications of technological changes, and for some, like the International Telecommunications Society, the American Society for Automation in Pharmacy (ASAP), and the Food Equipment Manufacturers, this was a major focus (ASAP's mission, for example, was "to assist its members in advancing the application of computer technology in the pharmacist's role"). Some associations were founded in response to changes perceived as threats, like the Independent Bakers fearing mergers and acquisitions or the Concrete Repairers concerned about "unqualified contractors" entering the industry. The Exhibit Designers responded to market weakness following 9/11, the Electronics Service Dealers tried to confront shrinking repair markets and sometimes uncooperative manufacturers, and the Food Equipment Manufacturers and the Mulch and Soil Council responded to demand concentration shifting the balance of power in their markets. We also see numerous examples of associations proactively promoting industry change: the Exhibit Designers sought to connect with and learn about European markets for their services in a "Euroshop" program, the Automotive Lift Institute recounts a history of active implementation of standards, and the Conference of Consulting Actuaries was developing a strategic plan for the industry. Indeed, the Exhibit Designers argued that "associations need to be the sounding board for change."[8]

So in conjunctural moments of industry change, associations' cultural production can provide a set of tools for inventing and challenging "interests" for the economic actor or the industry. They provide a proximate mechanism for the operation of institutional effects on economic actors, and they are likely to be especially significant where change is highly localized in specialized arenas of activity.

But what about continuity? Despite all the scholarly concern about how neoinstitutionalism can account for change, it is continuity, rather than change, that is understudied. Even though Roger Friedland and Robert Alford pointed out that "institutional sources must be found for the stability and routinization of interests, just as much as their transformation," Thomas Lawrence and Roy Suddaby still find more than a decade later that "the institutional work of maintaining institutions is both necessary and overlooked," and they echo Friedland and Alford—and a key concern of this study—in noting that "the real mystery of institutions is how social structures can be made to be self-replicating and persist beyond the lifespan of their creators." Continuity is not necessarily a null hypothesis.[9]

Most accounts of how institutional continuity happens rely on microlevel, social-psychological mechanisms. Cognitive homogeneity and legitimacy imperatives are sometimes seen as sources of continuity. And Lynne Zucker provides a microlevel account of cultural persistence in experiments that show that institutionalization processes affect transmission, maintenance, and resistance to change in cultural understandings. Zucker argues that persistent cultural understandings are not necessarily dependent on internalization, or self-reward, but rather on the fact that "each individual is motivated to comply because otherwise his actions and those of others in the system cannot be understood." Yet while this individual process seems an essential element of any general account of institutional continuity, it does not provide any traction for accounts of the persistence of particular institutions, and nor do appeals to cognitive homogeneity and legitimacy imperatives. What is required is an analysis of active, routine, meso-level cultural production in field-level organizations, and the identification of cultural producers as proximate actors linking macro- and microlevels.[10]

If associations are active in moments of industry formation and change, they must also be important among the active cultural producers reproducing identities and interests in stable industries. Associations' "constitutive" role is a necessary condition for any particular, conjunctural, innovation they may introduce in objects, partners, or norms of exchange. The publications and meetings that are their most widely shared features routinely create and maintain channels of communication and rituals of collective identity.

Some comparative and historical studies of business associations support this view. For instance, Charles Sabel argues that an association can "help create the interests and identity of its members," and even "at the limit . . . dissuade this type of grouping from acting like a conventional interest group at all." He identifies in these "developmental associations" a Habermasian process of discursive revision—for example, of production processes or standards. Unlike Jürgen Habermas, though, he suggests that communicative and strategic action cannot be distinguished in this routine process.[11]

In making this argument, Sabel draws mostly on examples from East Asia and Europe, where the state encourages a formal mediating role for associations. However, some scholars who have examined American associations make similar arguments. Marc Schneiberg traces a process analogous to that Sabel describes in the formation of American fire insurance associations in the late nineteenth and early twentieth century, a process in which "actors can solve otherwise intractable problems of cooperation incrementally by using less costly partial solutions to organize further and address larger issues." In this case, routine processes of cultural production of normative, rationalized standards ultimately reshaped and mediated previously conflicting interests. As we saw in depth in chapter two, this sort of information-producing process characterized the establishment of a new form of American business association in the early twentieth century—associations that "generated individual and collective goods through social, inter-subjective processes of deliberation, joint standard setting, and learning by monitoring."[12]

William Roy and Rachel Parker-Gwin also provide extensive evidence of routine cultural production by associations in stable industries in the late nineteenth century, pointing out that "in associations the organization symbolizes collective interest and collective identity." They argue that organizations like business associations are more likely to shape identity, for instance by generalizing class interests or linking them to other identities, than to represent preexisting identities. The associations they examined emphasized identity and social solidarity; they point out that "capitalist organizations quite possibly were based on particularistic identities that are commonly missed because they are taken as given"—for instance, masculine, white, or rational actor identities.[13]

A few later studies also illustrate the routine constitution of interests and identities in associations. For instance, Anna Lee Saxenian challenges assumptions that groups simply express preexisting interests and argues

rather that because businesspeople "face considerable ambiguity in selecting a course of action" . . . "the appropriate unit of analysis is neither
the individual business or firm, nor is it the entire capitalist class or even
necessarily the sector; rather it is the self-defined group of businessmen
who, through association, develop shared identities and world views." Her
comparison of associations of similar "high tech" producers in two different regions shows that they developed differing identities and "interests."
Like Roy and Parker-Gwin, she argues that interests were defined through
organization, not vice versa: "The divergence in the world views and political demands . . . is not explicable . . . by some individual (or corporate)
calculus of expected costs and benefits . . . these organizations were forums
for the creation of 'high tech' identities and for the definition of the source
and desired solution to common problems."[14]

Such investigations suggest, then, that American business associations
provide routine infrastructure—through periods of stability, as well as
challenge and change—for the social construction of business identities
and interests. How exactly do they do so? What routine discourses and
practices condition particular instances of the production and reproduction of such interests?

Associations in this study routinely provided the constitutive cultural
infrastructure for their members' social construction of their economic
interests in three ways. First, they are an important routine source for the
articulation of cognitive categories and of practices within which members can locate their economic action. Second, they position members in
relation to one another, in part through an explicit discourse focused on
the production of "networking opportunities." Third, they constitute an
extensive and rich field of relations (both imaginary and active) with upstream suppliers; downstream customers; regulatory and standards bodies; similar international groups; academic research units; commercial
industry services; and, importantly, related business associations. Regardless of the actual short-term impact of any given project or discourse at
any particular time, all of their various strategies of action provide routine
resources for the social construction of interests in these three ways.

Producing Categories and Practices

Neoinstitutionalist perspectives "reflect the cognitive turn in contemporary social theory," and "institutions are rules and shared meanings that

define social relations, help define who occupies what position in those relations, and guide interaction by giving actors cognitive frames or sets of meanings to interpret the behavior of others." More generally, and following Mary Douglas's injunction that social behavior is possible only "to the extent that individuals share the categories of their thought," DiMaggio, along with other cultural sociologists, has argued that we should examine the ways universal cognitive processes like attention and classification are embedded in and made meaningful by particular social contexts.[15]

Attention to cognition, its constraints, and its categorical resolution of ambiguities also informs the work of organizational scholars who examine how institutional logics provide cognitive support for "focusing the attention of organizational actors on a limited set of issues and solutions." Harrison White has suggested that a "socially constructed set of cognitive habits"—comparability signals and cost schedules—structure production markets. Gerald Davis discusses a number of studies that show that assessment of firm performance in relation to rivals and peers depends on "cognitive models of industry participants." And Ezra Zuckerman finds that publicly traded corporations' stock performance is influenced by the "industry based category structure" industry analysts produce.[16]

More specifically, the neoinstitutionalist hypothesis that business associations help generate mimetic isomorphism in organizations rests on the assumption that they articulate, systematize, and promote cognitive categories and practices providing models for firms faced with uncertainty, both in times of industry change and in routine circumstances. Supporting this assumption, classification schemas and recommendations about strategies of action are ubiquitous in association discourse.

For instance, most associations routinely present surprisingly detailed systems of classification of their members, their members' products, or both. Membership applications, industry directories, newsletters, certification programs, and committee structures express categories by which members can locate themselves. The Irrigation Association, for instance, includes "common interest groups and committees" on "Aeration and Fountain," "Agricultural Irrigation," "Center Pivot and Lateral Move," "Chemigation," "Drip/Micro Irrigation," and "Turf/Landscape." The yearbook of the Conference of Consulting Actuaries lists members in four categories (Pension, Health, Life, and Casualty); the Closure Manufacturers organize their members not only by product categories (metal, plastic, etc.) but also by subcategories (for instance, there are eight types of metal closures—child-resistant, continuous thread, crown, lug, press-on/twist-off, roll-on, tamper-evident, and vacuum). The Independent Bakers Association offers, in its linked trading exchange, hundreds of options from which members may select in order to complete the statement "I work with the following product types"—options like "Wholesale—Bread/Roll," "Wholesale—Cake/Sweet Goods," "Wholesale—Frozen Dough/Batter," "Wholesale—Pies," and "Wholesale—Snacks." Electronics technicians may be certified in the areas of computers, radar, industrial, communications, consumer, audio, video, and biomedical.[17]

Frequently, applications for membership also ask members to categorize themselves according to the size of their business, measured either by number of employees or income. For instance, the International Concrete Repair Institute structures its dues scale for members according to gross (repair-related) income in categories ranging from fewer than $1 million to more than $5 million. Regular members of the Exhibit Designers and Producers complete a rather detailed form about, for instance, the number of their staff designers, as well as annual gross industry sales volume in categories ranging from under $2.5 million to over $7.5 million. Members of the Independent Bakers are categorized according to bakery sales in categories ranging from $1–5 million to "over 20 million" (at which point members pay dues of $6,000). The Conference of Consulting Actuaries differentiates membership according to "Employment Type," including different categories for small, medium, and large consulting firms (fewer than 20, 20–49, and 50 or more actuaries).[18]

These are only the most obvious ways in which associations articulate and inculcate cognitive categories and classification schemas with which members may situate and model their economic action. Besides categorization, another large part of association discourse articulates "best practices" advice for members, both technical and business related and both formally and informally. As we saw in chapter three, education and information sharing are important goals of associations. As explored further in chapter six, they are implemented in seminars, conferences, scholarships, discussion groups, and publication of training materials like textbooks and videos, online courses, newsletters, and magazines.

For example, the appraisers affiliated with the National Association of Real Estate Brokers offer professional development opportunities in "capitalization methods" and "appraising complex residential properties" as well as loss mitigation training, home inspection, and so on. The Envelope Manufacturers' Association offers "a significant array of in-plant training programs," including "RA and 527 Adjuster Training, five safety programs,

[and] one Inspector/Operator Training program." The American Council of Life Insurance offers such events as "Seminar for Investment Managers" on "trends in the financial, economic and political environment; investment management and portfolio strategy; and current insurance-specific issues," and a "Life Reinsurance Treaty Symposium" with sessions that focus on "best practices in accounting, administration, reserving and actuarial provisions of life reinsurance treaty development."[19]

Somewhat less formally, most associations offer in their conventions and in their newsletters a constant barrage of information on "best practices." For instance, the policy of the editors of the *Concrete Repair Bulletin* is "to give readers information on methods, equipment or materials in order to broaden their general knowledge of the repair industry," and typical articles treat, for instance, "Sealant Replacement: Get Your Money's Worth" or "Cathodic Protection Solutions for Steel-Framed Heritage Buildings." The exclusive Hospitality Consultants do not publish their own newsletter, but they offer links to articles published elsewhere by their members, three to five a month: they treat topics such as "How to Perform a Successful Hotel Turnaround," "Franchise Associations Continue to Proliferate," and "Spring Cleaning: Factors to Consider in a Disposition Analysis."[20]

At conventions, associations vary in the extent to which they emphasize education, discussion, or exhibits, but even those associations more focused on exhibits, or just socializing, include opportunities to reflect on best practices, like the Exhibit Designers and Producers' "variety of educational programs" that "guarantees to cover the gamete [*sic*] of current industry topics." Most conventions present an elaborate menu of heavy fare, like the Aluminum Anodizers' meeting in Atlanta in 2004, where members presented on technical processes and innovations, practical and regulatory environmental topics, and quality assurance procedures, and "explore[d] the latest industry developments . . . benefit[ing] from the opportunity to learn about local and global trends, technical advances, environmental and regulatory affairs, and product development ideas." Among the suggested benefits of membership in the Closure Manufacturers' Association is that "meetings provide resource materials for long term planning and formation of company strategies."[21]

Most of the substantive content of education and information sharing by associations is opaque, unfamiliar if not inaccessible to outsiders (academics are no more prone to jargon than any other occupational group). From an outsiders' point of view, the obscurity of most of the topics, categories, and issues embedded in business association discourse can only evoke a sort of fascinated curiosity. Mostly, the categories and practices they model—and the ways those categories might have been and could be different—could only be understood in any depth through historical case studies such as those mentioned above.

But if we consider the obscurity of much of this discourse from the point of view of members, we can see that these business associations are one of the very few sites where economic actors might see issues that shape their working lives publicly canvassed in knowledgeable ways. Compared to most other sources, like the business press or formal education, business associations' cultural production possesses particular "resonance" for their audiences. Distinctions between different methods of fire prevention may not be recognized, much less understood, by the general public, or even others in similar industries, but the Firestop Contractors International Association finds them compelling and relevant. The associations' cultural production is also characterized by a high degree of "resolution"—"situated at a point of action . . . [or] . . . by nature directives for action." Members of the Mulch and Soil Council can hear about how USDA APHIS quarantines "affect you as a mulch and soil producer," rather than about quarantines in general. Members of the Pellet Fuels Institute can hear about bearing design for pelletizers, rather than bearing design in general. Even where topics of general business know-how like sales techniques are treated, rather than technical topics like aluminum anodizing, the treatments often assume and address particular occupational and industrial contexts. For instance, the Brick Industry Association's "Brick University" for members' sales force ("I'm leaving here a much more knowledgeable brick salesman" ran one endorsement) would not be interchangeable with the Vacuum Dealers Trade Association's sales tips ("Creating New Vac Sales from Scratch"). As Michael Schudson has argued, resonance and resolution are important conditions affecting the influence of particular elements of culture in local processes of what Nicole Biggart and Thomas Beamish call "sensemaking." The very context specificity of most association discourse makes it particularly pertinent for the sort of modeling of economic action—existing or projected—that neoinstitutionalists assume in arguments for mimetic isomorphism.[22]

Producing Networking Opportunities

Economic sociologists have been investigating for some time the significance of networks for economic action, including for firm performance, resource distribution, and diffusion of models. Studies of various industries show network ties influencing outcomes like financing, strategic alliance formation, production economies, entry to new markets, organizational learning, and status hierarchies. However, while the evidence for the importance of network mechanisms is strong, *institutionalized* processes for producing networks within markets are not well understood, with the majority of studies focusing on the aggregated relationships of firms. Marc Schneiberg and Elisabeth Clemens identify networks as important for introducing institutional effects into organizations, but as Laurel Smith-Doerr and Walter Powell point out, "we know a good deal more about the effects of networks than we know about the factors that generate, sustain, and reproduce them."[23]

Several studies suggest that functional demands cannot fully account for network formation. For instance, Gordon Walker and colleagues argue that "social capital" rather than "structural holes" accounts for network formation among biotechnology startups, and Ranjay Gulati and Martin Gargiulo find that in addition to functional interdependence, network embeddedness accounts for strategic alliance formation. If functional requirements do not fully account for network formation, how is it to be explained? Most answers to this question focus on how prior relationships generate new ones: "embedded ties primarily develop out of third-party referral networks and previous personal relations." Overall, such arguments that prior social relationships of one sort or another explain new network formation are well supported. Sometimes, shared membership in business associations is mentioned as one possible type of interorganizational tie, but this possibility has not been explored.[24]

Apart from preexisting ties, Smith-Doerr and Powell also suggest that institutional infrastructure may encourage or discourage network formation. "Supportive intermediary organizations" may "serve as both conduits of resources and as monitoring agents that guide and structure interfirm collaboration." Along the same lines, governance theorists Rogers Hollingsworth and Wolfgang Streeck conclude that networks are "more likely . . . to be present and effective where there is also a facilitating state or association." Another reason institutional infrastructure may be important for network formation is legitimacy. Mostly, such arguments for an institutional grounding of network formation are supported with studies of regional economies. Otherwise, there has been relatively little progress in examining "supportive intermediary organizations" since Joseph Galaskiewicz observed in 1985, of the literature on interorganizational relations, that there had been "scant attention to either the creation of groups [such as trade associations] among horizontally interdependent organizations or the effects of these groups on resource procurement/ allocative processes."[25]

Galaskiewicz supplies one of the few extant studies of association influence in a case study of corporate contributions officers in one city (61.5 percent of the companies in his study had members who were also members of this particular association). He found that the association influenced perceptions of potential recipients of corporate gifts indirectly, by affecting contributions officers' networks. Association membership also muted the effects of job status on network proximity.

> One of the latent functions of professional associations is to put people together in committees, panels, task forces, and study groups who might not otherwise be attracted to one another based on their background characteristics alone. Recruitment to these associations is not based on ascribed criteria.

Association membership, then, could influence access to informal networks and indirectly shape perceptions by shaping networks. Denise Bielby and Lee Harrington also suggest that networking in association conventions is crucial for trust in the global television syndication market.[26]

So we know that network ties influence many dimensions of firms' economic action, and there are also some suggestions that association membership can be one sort of influential tie for industry actors, although the nature of influence of "institutional infrastructure" for network ties, compared to particularistic preexisting relationships, has not yet been fully explored. If networks are so important for economic action, though, it would be surprising if economic actors relied entirely on their spontaneous generation through particularistic connections. One would also expect active, organized attempts to develop and pursue network connections. And, indeed, "networking" is a native concept in association subcultures: associations explicitly see themselves as producing opportunities for networking, especially in conventions and meetings, but also more generally. In the world of business associations, "networking" is a commonly discussed and unassailable good in itself.[27]

Some associations see providing networking opportunities as one of their major purposes. One of the "four major program areas" of the Envelope Manufacturers' Association, for instance, is "networking"—they suggest, "networking opportunities are endless" and members have the "opportunity to meet the movers and shakers of the industry." One of the major incentives the Exhibit Designers and Producers Association offers its members is "NETWORKING . . . to open doors," and it suggests that its convention is the "Most Important NETWORKING EVENT In the Industry." The Closure Manufacturers' Association also offers members the opportunity to "meet industry representatives—improve networking ability by developing contacts which may also be of assistance to customers." The aim of the program committee of the Firestop Contractors International Association is to "provide the membership with professional and social venues to improve the industry through interaction." The International Concrete Repair Institute also identifies "Peer Networking" as a major benefit it offers to members:

> The greatest value in any professional organization is the opportunity to meet others in your industry. The people you meet and build relations with will be the ones you can call upon when in need and will be the ones who may recommend you as a contact for a potential job. . . . The more involved you are with ICRI member activities, the more likely you are to be called upon by other members for guidance. It is this recognition that will propel you and your company to the forefront of the concrete repair industry.

ICRI regional groups, as well as the national association, emphasize networking. The president of ICRI's active Northern California chapter reflected that "we feel this is an important function of ICRI in putting together a great venue for meeting and networking with others in the same industry to exchange ideas and knowledge."[28]

Even where "networking" was not stressed as a major purpose of association, it was often mentioned as an obvious benefit, and as a rationale for social events. Although the Aluminum Anodizers convention is one of the more serious and technical of association meetings, their council ensures, they say, that "there will be several opportunities for delegates to network with others in the anodizing industry scattered throughout the conference," and delegates can "learn from and interact with the industry's most prominent individuals who are available for questions, discussion, and inspiration"—for instance, at a party organized at a bar that offered "a unique networking atmosphere." The American Council of Life Insurance scheduled a "Networking Lunch" at their "Insurance and the Law Seminar," and at their more exclusive Executive Roundtable, they invited senior executives to "examine current and emerging business issues, share managerial experiences, and build long-lasting relationships with each other." The Pellet Fuels Institute's 2004 conference offered a "combination of fantastic educational sessions, networking opportunities and social events." The Small Publishers Association of North America suggests that their member directory is a "wonderful tool for networking . . . so you can 'talk shop.'" A NAFEM conference for service and sales personnel, "Network Today for a Better Business Tomorrow," included, of course, a "Networking Cocktail Party," and an hour of "Networking" was scheduled before a dinner and talk held by the New England chapter of the Concrete Repair Institute.[29]

The association that doesn't claim to offer networking opportunities or "networking events" is more the exception than the rule: both smaller associations, like the Pellet Fuels Institute or the Closure Manufacturers' Association, and large, active groups like the North American Association of Food Equipment Manufacturers, or the American Council of Life Insurance, see themselves offering opportunities, as the Independent Bakers put it, to "renew business relationships" or to make new ones.[30]

Networking could sometimes refer specifically to marketing opportunities and connections to vendors that associations claimed to offer, especially at exhibitions and conventions. However, networking meant much more than that; the illustrations above show that meetings with peers, competitors, and "industry leaders" are often understood as even more important functions of association. A broader portfolio of network ties is assumed to be good for business. So the Food Equipment Manufacturers suggested that "as a professional you know that a significant portion of your business comes through networking. NAFEM seminars, education programs, committees and trade shows provide numerous opportunities to meet your industry peers." A president of the National Electronics Service Dealers tells his members that "the show is the place to network, expand your business . . . if you are going to survive in this business you need to network." Meetings of the Mulch and Soil Council are, among other things, "a forum for new business relationships that can lead to new business opportunities," where "you will meet fellow producers who share your problems and can offer advice on solutions." The Vacuum Dealers are told that "surveys have shown that the most successful dealers attend conventions. Why? Because at conventions they are able to network with other successful dealers. . . . These professionals are willing to share their successful ideas with others, which in turn makes the industry stronger as more dealers find success." Their magazine, the *Floor Care Professional*, offers advice on "Overcoming Stumbling Blocks to Successful Networking."

Like the Vacuum Dealers Trade Association, the Irrigation Association links member benefits with industry development: "networking with competitors, industry leaders, and newcomers to solve challenges and promote the industry is vital to our livelihoods." Their trade show is "*the* show for industry professionals serious about their business—and the industry," and they add that "nothing beats the excitement that a trade show generates." (If their survey of attendees could be trusted, about 30 percent express an interest in general "networking.") As Ezra Zuckerman and Stoyan Sgourev also found, learning and motivation are understood as benefits of peer networking.[31]

As the Irrigation Association's claim that "nothing beats the excitement that a trade show generates" suggests, the strategic connotations of networking do not capture the full meaning of the connections between industry members in association. As we will see in chapter five, association discourse is also full of references to the intrinsic pleasures of sociability. So the opportunity provided at conventions and meetings to "interact in spontaneous ways" (as the rather stolid International Telecommunications Society puts it) is also stressed by the Aluminum Anodizers, who speak of their "evening of camaraderie and networking." The Rocky Mountains chapter of the Concrete Repairers reports that "we are having fun working together, making friends, networking amongst industry peers, and building an organization that is a valuable resource for our industry." Networking quickly becomes a natural alibi for sociability, and strategy is very much intertwined with solidarity here.[32]

National associations' heavy emphasis on networking possibilities has so far fallen on deaf ears among most economic sociologists, but it raises several important topics for further investigation. Is all this association talk merely superficial rhetoric? Do associations typically influence members' networks? If so, how and under what conditions do they do so? What is the character of any ties or opportunities associations generate? Do they encourage formation of ties through third-party referrals, add legitimacy to prospective ties, mute job status effects on network proximity, and widen networks by creating new task-related connections? Other studies of network formation suggest these mechanisms, but the extent to which they work in business associations has yet to be explored systematically. Anecdotal accounts scattered in a variety of case studies provide suggestive hints, and perhaps case study fieldwork and interviews could supplement those anecdotal accounts. But the biggest questions remaining demand more systematic study, more along the lines of the extensive existing literature on institutional conditions for network ties among East Asian business groups.[33]

Certainly, from all we know so far, the conditions associations provide for the ongoing social construction of economic interests include their functioning as a site for the routine production of opportunities for networking, and thus for the potential articulation, development, pursuit, and change of members' economic interests.

Producing Fields

In addition to providing routine infrastructure for their members to make connections with one another, business associations also constitute and reproduce broader fields within which their members' economic activities are situated. A field is formed of "those organizations that, in the aggregate, constitute a recognized area of institutional life: key suppliers, resource and product consumers, regulatory agencies, and other organizations that produce similar services or products." Fields are relational—"situations where organized groups of actors . . . frame their actions vis-à-vis one another." Organizations and other field actors "take each other's actions into account in framing their own actions," and in this sense a field is somewhat analogous to a game. Field theorists differ in the degree to which they see fields as structured by relations of competitive hierarchy between similar actors, or, more broadly, by relations of "dependence and connection" between various types of actors. But whether or not fields are seen as primarily agonistic, they are important because they orient the behavior of the actors composing them.[34]

The social construction of "industries" provides a leading instance of field formation and reproduction. As White argues, "packaging as an industry" provides firms with "long term positions in niches, positions that help to mitigate the vital uncertainties that surround commitment and evaluation in competitive environments." And as Davis shows, "choices of strategy and structure turn out to be decisively shaped by firms' social environment—the choices made by buyers, suppliers, rivals, and peers." "Packaging as an industry" by external analysts may also affect firms' performance in stock markets.[35]

How are fields formed and sustained? DiMaggio and Powell argue that the field formation process involves "an increase in the extent of interaction among organizations in the field; the emergence of sharply defined inter-organizational structures of domination and patterns of coalition; an increase in the information load with which organizations in a field must contend; and the development of mutual awareness among participants . . . that they are involved in a common enterprise." External influences from states, social movements, strong professional organizations, and industry analysts can generate field formation and change. Davis notes that new fields often transpose "templates for organized action" from other domains, usually in the face of economic and political changes in the broader environment.[36]

Still, exactly how field formation and reproduction actually happens remains somewhat obscure—especially considering the myriad ways fields might, in principle, be composed. Perhaps the only appropriate type of account will be a unique narrative, focusing on each field's particular historical trajectory, as Fligstein implies when he argues that "social skill" is the microfoundation of field emergence and change. But it seems likely that the existence and nature of fields also depends on meso-level conditions for systematic cultural production by field participants themselves—independent of their proactive "social skill." The infrastructure for such cultural production cannot be taken for granted. Davis suggests as much—though not in these terms—when he points out that an important part of the process of institutionalizing fields is the development of "a framework to make them comprehensible and to provide a basis for shared understandings, such as norms of exchange"; and that "field-level organizations"—like business associations—can make new models visible and legitimate.[37]

Any answer to the question of how economic actors learn about their relational field must include the collective cultural production of business associations, which provide cognitive maps of imagined connections to relevant others, and often color those connections with active interactional paths created by their projects and strategies of action.

First, we should recall from chapter three that a large minority of associations—40 percent—include members in two different "industry" sectors; just over a quarter include members from more than two sectors. There is also some evidence that associations restricted to one sector sometimes include members of several different but closely related industries. Organizational ecologists have noted that it is difficult to measure growth in the population of associations by industry, because "unfortunately, associations have not limited themselves to clearly defined industries, and their claimed domains often bear little resemblance to Census Bureau SIC codes." But this is not a minor problem of categorization, or an unfortunate research constraint. It is an important and generally unrecognized part of what many associations do, and provides theoretical insight.[38]

Associations' inclusiveness may be consequential for the associations themselves and for their members. Aldrich and his colleagues found that an association's internal diversity, measured by the number of Standard Industrial Classification (SIC) codes it represented, "significantly *lowered* the odds of disbanding, transforming, or merging"—rather than increasing the difficulties associated with merging different member "interests," as Olsonian accounts would suggest. For members, the inclusiveness of their associations may also matter. Examining the influence of executives' external ties on strategic choice and performance, and in particular on how much they conform to industry models, Marta Geletkanycz and Donald Hambrick find that executives' participation as officers in associations limited to *one* industry had a small positive effect on their firms' conformity, but no effect on firm performance measures. However—and in contrast to the neoinstitutionalist focus on strict isomorphism—their participation in associations that crossed industry boundaries had a larger *negative* effect on strategic conformity. Participation in associations that crossed industry boundaries also had some positive effect on firm performance.[39]

These findings are only suggestive, but they do highlight the potential significance of business associations for field formation and reproduction. Associations are as often about crossing boundaries between economic actors as about protecting them. Not only do they frequently include different types of members, as the population data suggest, but they are often explicitly oriented to providing channels of communication, and sometimes coordination, between suppliers, manufacturers, distributors, service providers, consultants, and so on; some also include provision for nonprofit and governmental memberships. Indeed, one important and explicit point of many associations is to create such links and channels of communication. Trade shows do this, but so do other types of meetings and publications—as well as association membership itself. Overall, the boundaries of the typical association are much lower than scholars have recognized.

Many business associations provide routine connections between upstream and downstream actors in an "industry." They frequently include related suppliers or distributors as full or associate members and routinize programmatic connections with customers. Some also have programs for members' employees, and they may expand their boundaries or direct their programs to include other interested parties, such as independent standards bodies and related nonprofit groups, consultants, affiliated groups and "allied associations," and related government staff and organizational units.

For the manufacturers of the Brick Industry Association, for instance, "inclusion of distributors is key" and "just part of BIA's formula for growing wall share." They make much of the fact that they are "the only national association to represent both manufacturers and distributors" and point out that "many manufacturers prefer to utilize the services of our distributor base. They feel more comfortable with people who are involved and who they know from contacts at industry events." And one of their minor projects is the employee training in the "Brick University" mentioned earlier.[40]

The membership of the Closure Manufacturers' Association is formally more restrictive, but they also emphasize the "opportunity to interact with other closure manufacturers, suppliers, equipment suppliers and glass and plastic container manufacturers." The American Council of Life Insurance identifies "Partners" who "bring product and service innovations to our members." The Pellet Fuels Institute sees the "pellet industry" as comprised of "pellet mills, pellet appliance manufacturers, and industry suppliers" and aims to "coordinate and integrate the needs of raw materials sources, pellet equipment suppliers and consultants, fuel producers, appliance manufacturers and distribution entities." The United Lightning Protection Association is composed of "lightning protection installers, manufacturers, engineers, and individuals interested in . . . promoting lightning protection."[41]

The International Concrete Repair Institute makes a big point of their inclusiveness. Since their formation in 1988, they have "grown into a conglomerate of restoration and repair professionals, their suppliers, customers and other interested parties." They draw little distinction between different categories of members:

> The founders also insisted that all classes and categories of membership be treated equally. Initially it was to have been a contractors' organization, but the immediate interest of engineers, manufacturers, and others in its formation and success made it obvious that it should be open to all. Every attempt is made to ensure equitable representation.[42]

Although not all associations are as open to full participation by other interested groups—in other cases they are included only as nonvoting members—most associations do institutionalize some channels of communication among various relevant actors. In 2004, for example, the North

American Association of Food Equipment Manufacturers "expanded its Associate member category to include seven key product and service providers . . . Education and Training Providers, Employment Recruiters, Export Management Companies, Marketing and Communications Service Providers, Systems Technology Providers, Third Party Certification Organizations and Trade Publications," and associate membership was "on the rise." (However, no more than 20 percent of NAFEM's working committees or advisory councils could be associate members.) The Exhibit Designers and Producers Association, with a core membership of designer/producer, transportation, and show services companies, also included member categories for suppliers, freelance/independent designers, government agencies, educators, convention centers, and students. In the focal sample, only a few associations kept strictly to one type of member and did not include various sorts of "industry partners" in their activities.[43]

Not surprisingly, many associations also make systematic efforts to develop links and channels of communication in collective marketing efforts. Most associations mention identifying and connecting with customers and markets, and this is a major focus for some. The Aluminum Anodizers include as associate members "companies that purchase anodized finishes" (along with anodizing companies, their suppliers, and professional members—"architects, academics, specifiers, consultants, and other industry professionals"). Conventions, certification, product information, and so on are sometimes seen as marketing tools. More simply, many associations argue that their membership directories are an important tool for linking customers to members; for instance, some include specific informational and promotional pages on their websites oriented to prospective customers, and some provide the public with a complete list of members and their specialties. The elite International Society of Hospitality Consultants emphasizes up front, in their chairman's letter, that "finding the consultant with the expertise and skills you need has never been easier. The "Consultant Search" Function of our website is user friendly. You can search via a myriad of disciplines or merely search via an alphabetical listing." Associations' marketing efforts sometimes extend beyond routinized marketing tools for members to larger projects. As we will see in chapter six, some have important programs devoted to powerful downstream buyers—such as fast food chains for food equipment manufacturers. And some work systematically to identify and develop new markets; for instance, the Life Insurers were programmatically interested in the privatization of the Japanese life insurance market, and the Exhibit Designers made active attempts to learn about and build connections with European exhibition markets. Among other programs, they held a convention with their European counterparts that they claimed would be "valuable to members who are interested in . . . new working relationships with companies who are exploring global venues."[44]

But the field articulated by the cultural production of many associations also extends much further than upstream and downstream market connections. Many systematic connections to independent standards bodies are built and maintained in associations' work on certification; for instance, this is a major focus of the Automotive Lift Institute, and an important program for the Conference of Consulting Actuaries and the Firestop Contractors. Even the Exhibit Designers, a group that otherwise does not put a programmatic emphasis on standards, reminds its members of a "'must have'" standards document from the third-party standards body Underwriters Laboratory, *UL2305*.[45]

More occasionally, academic teaching and research units are also drawn in to associational fields. The Food Equipment Manufacturers, for example, provided their members with research on the home meal replacement market from the Retail Food Industry Center at the University of Minnesota, and the Brick Industry Association occasionally sponsored and publicized research such as a study conducted by the Wind Science and Engineering Research Center at Texas Tech University on wind-blown debris ("Shelter from the Storm") and a University of Michigan study of masonry ordinances in Chicago suburbs. The Irrigation Association started an "Educational Foundation" because "we feel that it is important to invest time and energy to provide education and networking opportunities for instructors involved in academic institutions who are teaching the future leaders of the irrigation industry"; they also offered information and a scholarship to students. The Association for Women in Aviation Maintenance, too, offered extensive information about relevant educational organizations, and some of these were members. The Johns Hopkins University School of Medicine cosponsored the American Council of Life Insurance's Medical Section's 2004 annual meeting.[46]

Warner and Martin noted decades ago that one of the most consistent features of trade associations was affiliation with other like organizations. Many contemporary associations stress the significance of their links to regional or state affiliates, and to "allied associations," providing extensive listings for their members, and sometimes working with them on common projects and promoting and participating in their meetings. The Conference of Consulting Actuaries

. . . has over 40 liaisons to other actuarial organizations in the United States and abroad and to other organizations of interest to our members. The purpose of this is two-fold [*sic*]):

- Represent the consultants' viewpoint to the other organizations
- Keep Conference members informed of these organizations' activities of interest to consulting actuaries; and
- Have strategic alliances with other actuarial and other professional organizations.

This is one of the more extended statements of a field-monitoring orientation, but many other associations, such as the Food Equipment Manufacturers, do something similar. NAFEM had standing liaison committees with five other upstream and downstream industry groups—the Commercial Food Equipment Service Agencies, the Foodservice Consultants International, the International Food Manufacturers Association, and the Manufacturers' Agents for the Foodservice Industry. The Irrigation Association worked on several projects with a "Green Industry" coalition, listed over fifty regional and international affiliates, and held an "Affiliate Leadership Conference," at which "leaders of affiliate organizations got a chance to network and get more information about running successful associations." The Association for Women in Aviation Maintenance promotes and meets at other aviation industry meetings, like the Professional Aviation Maintenance Association, "Heli-Expo 2005," and the International Women in Aviation Conference. The Firestop Contractors, active in more than a dozen other fire-prevention-related bodies, from the Association of Walls and Ceilings to the National Association of State Fire Marshalls, even defined "the industry" in terms of related associations: "the industry would include FCIA, IFC, The "Alliance for Fire and Smoke Containment and Control—Gypsum manufacturers/Institute, AWCI, Fire Door Manufactures [*sic*]." (The Food Equipment Manufacturers came close to doing this too). The Concrete Repair Institute joined with the American Concrete Institute and the University of Missouri to launch "Fixconcrete.org, a knowledge management site for the repair, protection and upgrade of concrete structures." The Closure Manufacturers' Association is typical in seeing itself as the industry's liaison with "the academic community, allied associations, and others" and aims to "promote academic studies" and "assist allied organizations on projects affecting the closure industry."[47]

Finally, government administrative bodies are part of the field constituted by some associations in their monitoring and occasional lobbying
practices. Some associations occasionally attend to mainstream congressional politics and policy, but more often they monitor regulatory and
administrative agencies like the Environmental Protection Agency or the
Department of Housing and Urban Development. So, for instance, the
Brick Industry Association is interested in "code changes concerning
the most effective uses of brick." The Food Equipment Manufacturers
circulate information on "local regulations," and lobby OSHA on ergonomics regulations. Members of the American Society for Automation in
Pharmacy heard a presentation on "Nuts and Bolts of the Federal Information Security Management Act (FISMA)," at their annual meeting in
Carefree, Arizona, in 2004. Representatives of the Mulch and Soil Council
"met with officials of the U.S. Environmental Protection Agency (EPA)
and the Consumer Product Safety Commission (CPSC) in Washington,
DC . . . to seek . . . assistance by clarifying the prohibition on the grinding
of CCA-treated wood for consumer mulch products from 'should not' to
'shall not' . . . [and] the need for active enforcement against violations in
the interest of public safety." Some associations, like the International Concrete Repair Institute, or the Firestop Contractors, even offer membership
categories for "Government Agency," and "Government Employee."[48]

So associations constitute a field for their members, articulating orientations to and sometimes establishing interactive links with upstream
and downstream market partners, independent standards organizations,
academic researchers, affiliate groups and other related associations, and
regulatory agencies. The links created with other actors in a self-styled "industry" are frequently an important purpose of association, and often this
purpose is built into the structure of the organization itself. Liaison, mediation, and self-promotion with a wide variety of other relevant actors are
certainly crucial in what associations do. Even where active connections are
intermittent or rare, the imagined communities they can create are simultaneously broader fields situating members' day-to-day business concerns.

Conclusion

American business associations make meaning for economic action,
routinely reproducing actors' economic interests and sometimes providing
sites for their creation, challenge, and change. Economic sociologists

who argue for the institutional embeddedness of economic action have provided extensive evidence of the social construction of economic interests in particular changing circumstances. If we see American business associations as cultural producers we can generalize these numerous neoinstitutionalist observations. We can see associations providing ongoing cultural infrastructure on the basis of which particular instances of the social construction of industry interests may emerge. Business associations may develop and pursue a wide variety of specific goals according to particular conjunctural circumstances, but they can do so only because they routinely reproduce "industry" subcultures.

First, they routinely produce cognitive categories and practices that articulate their members' economic action. Many economic sociologists have emphasized the importance of "cognitive habits" for industry outcomes, and the neoinstitutionalist postulate of mimetic isomorphism relies on assumptions about shared categories and practices. We have seen that business association discourse is consistent and explicit in the way it highlights and inculcates classification schemes and strategies of action relevant to members. This discourse is distinctive in what Michael Schudson terms "resolution" and "resonance"—its context-specific pertinence to particular and obscure forms of economic action.

Second, business associations systematically produce opportunities for networking. One of the central findings of economic sociology has been the significance of network ties for many forms of economic action, including their influence on a variety of outcomes for firms. However, institutional conditions for generating network ties have been understudied, especially in the American context. We have seen that business association discourses and strategies of action explicitly and consistently highlight the production of networking opportunities as one of their central benefits for members. Given this focus, social scientists' neglect of American business associations seems particularly unwarranted: no investigation of institutional preconditions for networks can afford to dismiss this busy arena of networking activity.

Third, business associations constitute, monitor, and reproduce industry fields. They are field-level organizations of market peers or competitors, but they also link upstream and downstream actors in a self-defined "industry," standards bodies and academic units, other related associations, and government agencies. Their membership is more likely to be widely inclusive than to be defensively exclusive. Economic sociologists have stressed the importance of fields for orienting economic actors, for instance by "packaging" them as an industry, but again the role of field-level organizations (as opposed to external influences or participants' agency) has been understudied. We have seen many ways in which associations' routine cultural production constitutes fields for their members.

A necessary prior condition of the pursuit of shared interests is the social construction of those particular interests. This process is by no means transparent and should not be taken for granted; a great deal of energetic but routine association activity provides institutional conditions for the ongoing construction and reproduction of members' interests. In this forgotten arena of cultural politics, associations routinely produce cognitive categories and practices, opportunities for networking, and orientations to broader fields of related activities. The evidence of these processes I have examined provides systematic support for neoinstitutionalism's sketchy early claims about the role of business associations in economic life, providing empirical grounding for processes that have hitherto been mostly only presumed. This is all the more important because neoinstitutionalists are among the few economic sociologists who have paid any attention to business associations.

But while neoinstitutionalist approaches are important for understanding associations' cultural production of interests, they often remain too closely tied to a strategic perspective on economic activity. Notably, neoinstitutionalist studies have focused more on the cognitive than the normative and expressive dimensions of institutional influences on economic action, even though DiMaggio and Powell originally pointed out the importance of both cognitive and normative isomorphism. This avoidance of the normative and expressive is even more characteristic of economic sociology in general. Occasionally, some economic sociologists have noted the significance of normative and expressive cultural processes on the margins of their studies, as when Galaskiewicz suggested that "prestige and good fellowship are selective incentives that business people value greatly . . . we might also want to go back and reconsider the role of common values," or when Brian Uzzi pointed out that "the theoretical distinction between instrumental versus expressive interests may be moot because embeddedness changes actors' motives rather than treats them as immutable." Yet generally speaking, economic sociology has lacked the theoretical inclination and analytic tools to pursue the significance of such brief observations about normative and expressive action.[49]

Normative and expressive processes are important because some collective identity and solidarity are preconditions of the collective pursuit of strategic interests, and they cannot be taken for granted. Beyond the social construction of particular economic interests there is another, more profound issue: the cultural conditions for "sharing interests." Before strategies are possible, identities and solidarities are essential.

The next chapter examines the cultural conditions for industry interests rather than the cultural construction of industry interests. As we will see, a major thread of association discourse articulates solidarity as an end in itself; occupational boundaries, codes, status orders, norms, histories, and biographies are often seen in terms of their intrinsic significance, regardless of any connection to strategic value. Neglected theories of occupational community help understand this otherwise unaccountable—because nonstrategic—discourse.

CHAPTER FIVE

"A Special Camaraderie with Colleagues"

Presuming and Producing Solidarity

Economically strategic motives and functions do not exhaust the meanings of association, as this convention-goer seems to have been surprised to learn:

> Ms. Berke, a facility manager for InterContinental Hotels Group, stepped into the lobby where a colleague introduced her to Mr. de Nijs Bik. They talked for 30 minutes. "Though he was cute, frankly I thought nothing more of it than networking," she recalled. . . . A year later he moved to Atlanta to marry her.

Business strategies such as networking are embedded in, reliant on, and generate richer social worlds of nonstrategic normative and expressive action. As another association official commented of her group with more insight, "Yes, it was a good source for networking, but it was more than that. It was a community."[1]

As we have seen, American business associations are cultural producers that help create and sustain institutional conditions for their members' economic action in distinctive ways. Neoinstitutionalist theory's attention to cultural production broadens the usual parameters within which strategic value is assessed. Of course, strategies of action like communicating information, making standards, providing education, doing research, lobbying, and public relations may sometimes provide members with resources for their pursuit of their particular strategic goals. But more immediately (and more verifiably), associations' cultural production—seen from a neoinstitutionalist point of view—provides "strategic" value by providing necessarily collective goods—categories and practices, networking opportunities, and fields.

But this is only part of the story. Theoretically, such a neoinstitutionalist solution to the puzzle of American business associations opens up important new questions. Empirically, this view ignores or sets aside a large and significant part of the meaning attached to association.

The social construction of interests presumes some sort of collective identity and solidarity. Associations' routine formulations and ongoing social construction of interests can only make sense against the background of an understanding that one has an interest shared with other association members in the first place (however incipient or inarticulate). Yet such collective identities and solidarities are not self-evident, even or especially for business. It is circular to argue that members' shared identity and solidarity is grounded in their shared economic interests if associations construct and sustain the ways members understand those interests. As Wolfgang Streeck and Philippe Schmitter have noted, though not explored, "the value systems supporting corporative-associative institutions must include some residual commitment . . . beyond the boundaries of just one interest aggregate . . . for example, to professional norms of good performance."[2]

We need to deepen the typical neoinstitutionalist account of associations with an account of solidarity that does not rely on the putative prior existence of shared economic interests. This suggests that we first need to ask whether or how business associations engage in the sustained production of the cultural conditions for solidarity in collective identity, beyond and conditioning the strategic construction and pursuit of interests.

To understand the social construction of interests is not enough. We need to explore the cultural conditions for sharing an interest. The very possibility of having "an interest" depends on the existence of discourses and practices that transcend strategic language and action. These discourses and practices may define an industry field, articulate collective identities of its members, specify their norms and status relations, and express their shared bonds. Culture is not only an external condition constraining or enabling particularistic strategic action. Culture is also constitutive of identities and solidarities that make "interests" possible.[3]

The question of whether and how business associations engage in the sustained production of the cultural conditions for collective identity and solidarity has been almost totally ignored. But as it turns out, this question sensitizes us to a vast body of associational discourse and practice that makes little sense from an economically strategic point of view. Rather, the technical division of labor seems to generate its own community. In contrast with their stereotype, business associations frequently sound like occupational communities grounded in technical interests. This can be seen in the ways they develop vernacular understandings of their subcultural boundaries, they articulate collective identities, they create normative and status orders, and they express occupational camaraderie.

Solidarity in Occupational Community

In an important but neglected theory of occupational communities, John Van Maanen and Stephen Barley provide a framework for understanding in more depth the solidarity and identity that might derive from the technical division of labor, and they draw attention to the importance of taken-for-granted meanings of work that transcend the pursuit of business interests.[4]

They start with a focus on "some of the existential, everyday reality of the firsthand experience of work," criticizing excessive abstraction by occupations and organizations researchers (and also, by implication, economists and class theorists), who neglect the importance of the fact that "social worlds coalesce around the objects produced and the services rendered by people at work." These worlds are "occupational communities," made up of "people who consider themselves to be engaged in the same sort of work; who identify (more or less positively) with their work; who share a set of values, norms and perspectives that apply to, but extend beyond, work-related matters; and whose social relationships meld the realms of work and leisure." Drawing on ethnographic accounts from a wide range of work settings, from those of fishermen to those of computer programmers, they focus on the subcultural boundaries set, coded, and symbolized by the occupational members themselves, and emphasize the reference group identities they create and sustain for members. They do not discuss corporate executives, business owners, and managers, but there is no reason the scope of their analysis could not be broadened in this way. Indeed, considering David Grusky and Gabriela Galescu's call for class analysts to attend to classlike organization grounded in the technical division of labor at the occupational level, this extension is highly consequential.[5]

Van Maanen and Barley emphasize the importance of the "communal or collegial" as opposed to the "rational or administrative" aspect of work, the community beyond utility. Occupational communities "create and sustain relatively unique work cultures consisting of, among other things, task rituals, standards for proper and improper behavior, work codes which surround relatively routine practices and, for members at least, compelling accounts attesting to the logic and value of these rituals, standards and codes." They emphasize four important and understudied features of occupational communities.[6]

First, "the relevant boundaries of an occupational community are those set by the members themselves"; and these may differ in numerous ways from conventional and analytical job categories and may often be unfamiliar to outsiders. As we have already begun to see, business associations often demonstrate a parallel disregard for conventional and analytical industry categories.[7]

Second, members may identify with their occupational roles based on the sort of work they do, and use a "complex system of codes . . . to communicate to one another an occupationally specific view of their work world":

> Common skills, common risks, and common adventures form the basis for a communal identity by promoting interaction with those others who "know the score" and thereby increase the probability that members of such occupations will consider themselves to be unique.

Garbage collectors, as much as doctors, may develop such a sense of occupational identity.[8]

Third, an occupational community may become an evaluative reference group for members, who share

> a distinct pattern of values, beliefs, norms and interpretations for judging the appropriateness of one another's actions and reactions . . . moral standards surrounding what work is to be considered good and bad, what work is "real work" and therefore, in contrast to "shit work," what formal and contextual rules of conduct are to be enforced, what linguistic categories are to be used in partitioning the world, and so forth.

Such occupational groups may sometimes become primary reference groups, for instance if members share stigma, unusual work demands on time or location, or rigorous socialization.[9]

Finally, occupational communities may encourage "the blurring of the distinction between work and leisure," because they may create tight networks of closer social relationships. Overall, occupational communities are work cultures that often transcend organizational settings and involve work status and skill evaluations that may differ from those of work organizations. For instance, members who are otherwise very different are "able to converse over a wide range of topics indecipherable by outsiders."[10]

In this perspective, associations may form to pursue the economic interests of occupational communities, but "the motive for formation need not always be economic." For instance, they may form simply "to foster communication among members." The benefits of association for members are rarely material rewards or power; rather, they provide "structured paths for attaining centrality or for bestowing prestige on central members within the community."[11]

If business associations form around the occupational communities inhabited by for-profit actors, beyond the white-collar and blue-collar jobs Van Maanen and Barley consider, their pursuit of interests may be secondary and intermittent compared to their institutionalization of occupational community. Supposedly manifest and latent functions reverse their place.

In this view, business associations would draw boundaries, foster identities, and develop relationships that support members' mutual orientations to a line of work. These lines of work may be opaque to outsiders but evident in specialized codes, criteria of evaluation, and status hierarchies with little short-term connection to or utility for reducing transaction costs or defending occupational territory. Their goals and activities would often emerge from solidarities and conflicts generated more by the technical division of labor than by the social division of labor. Their approach to such strategies of action as policy monitoring, public relations, education, information-sharing, research, and standards may be expressed in ways that involve boundary setting irrelevant to outsiders, complexly coded and occupationally specific worldviews and identities, subculturally specific categories and standards of evaluation, and mixing of occupational with nonwork identities, all supporting members' mutual orientation to a line of work. Perhaps the Food Equipment Manufacturers' education committee, the Lightning Protection Association's information sharing, the Envelope Manufacturers' research, and the Closure Manufacturers' standards work are understood as creating intrinsically worthwhile boundaries, identities, categories, and norms in languages and status evaluations that are most important within the association or occupational community itself.

Occupational Community and "Industries"

For Van Maanen and Barley, occupational communities' boundaries depend on how members see them, so they do not necessarily follow official job categories and may be arcane to outsiders. Similarly, business associations are often constituted around obscure, "bottom-up," emergent ideas about what members share, and map poorly onto official industry categories. Indeed, the failure to recognize the significance of this obscure variety has blocked scholars' theoretical perception and understanding of the organizational population.

We often assume that industries are fixed, clearly defined categories, drawing on the economic understanding of industries as composed of firms producing closely substitutable goods, or on official definitions of industries like that of the North American Industry Classification System, which uses a "supply-based, or production-oriented, concept" in which "the lines drawn between industries demarcate, to the extent practicable, differences in production processes."[12]

Typical investigations of American associations have also assumed that they represent formally defined industries in this way, and exemplars are drawn from industries such as printing and brewing where the correspondence between closely substitutable goods or similar production processes, on the one hand, and actors' self-definitions, on the other, is quite strongly instituted. Certainly, the more representative focal sample here does show that some associations understand their industries in ways that resemble such objectivist definitions. So, for instance, the International Concrete Repair Institute is "the only association in the concrete industry devoted solely to repair and restoration." The Aluminum Anodizers Council "represents the interests of aluminum anodizers world wide and is the principal trade organization for the anodizing industry in North America." The Closure Manufacturers' Association claims that membership "illustrates a commitment to the closure industry" and provides a detailed account of the varieties and the history of lids and caps for glass and plastic containers. To outsiders, concrete repair, anodizing, and container closures may not immediately spring to mind as exemplars of industries, but the shared identity expressed in association is linked to related (if not closely substitutable) goods and similar production processes.[13]

But assuming that official and vernacular understanding of "industries" correspond to each other limits our understanding of associations,

encouraging unrepresentative case studies of particular, established industries and their associational politics. Even the idiosyncrasy of the
examples above suggests that regardless of its analytic virtues, the objectivist bundling of economic activities as *industries* is, in fact, rather distant
from most vernacular usages of the term. Overall, there is no one-to-one
correspondence between *industries* and *associations*. Formally defined industries encompass a variety of associations; and associations may include
actors from a variety of formally defined industries (and beyond). The
lack of correspondence between objectively defined industries and associations points to the need for an analysis that puts meaning-making at the
center of our understanding. Just as Van Maanen and Barley suggested
that occupational communities do not necessarily follow conventional
and analytical job categories, many associations do not follow conventional and analytical industry categories. Business association members
are like members of other occupational communities in that "the relevant
boundaries of an occupational community are those set by the members
themselves." They also exhibit distinctive culturally constituted "group
styles" in Nina Eliasoph and Paul Lichterman's sense that they exhibit
"implicit understandings" of their boundaries—"what the group's relationship (imagined and real) to the wider world should be in the group
context." This cultural view accounts for much more about the population
of business associations than an external, objectivist view of industries and
their interests.[14]

First, objectivist views of industries bracket the fact that what constitutes "an industry" is the result of a historically and politically contingent
process of cultural construction.[15] Even cases like those above that do
seem to be clearly defined in terms of goods or production process demonstrate the sort of political-cultural work Neil Fligstein might predict in the
ways they are constituted in contradistinction to other goods or processes
that could be, or have previously been, understood as related. As noted
in chapter four, the International Concrete Repair Institute began when
concrete repair was distinguished from other work involving concrete.
This was, in fact, a politically charged process of cultural construction: as
chapter 7 explores further, ICRI "had its origins in a World of Concrete
seminar in February 1988 during which attendees voiced their frustration
about the lack of standards and guidelines for concrete repair ... [and] ...
expressed their concern over the proliferation of unqualified contractors
entering the industry." In this case, an "industry" was forming by fission
from the larger "world of concrete." The Aluminum Anodizers began as

the Architectural Anodizers Council, but "changed their name . . . reflecting the broader scope of programs targeted to serve anodizers working in additional market sectors." In this case, an industry was changing as new markets developed (e.g., anodizing in industry and automobiles). The Closure Manufacturers "began as a spin-off of the Glass Packaging Institute's Closure Committee" and are still formally constituted under the auspices of the Glass Packaging Institute, although they otherwise act as an independent association and also include a section for manufacturers of closures for plastic containers. This is another case in which one association generated another in a process of fission, constituting a new "industry."[16]

Processes of organizational fission and fusion seem typical of the population as a whole (adding to its analytical intractability, especially for diachronic studies). The *Encyclopedia of Associations* routinely records information about association mergers. Although organizational ecologists have found great stability in the business association population, with very low odds of any given association changing each year, they also find that many associations that appear to fold actually end in merger with other associations. They do not examine foundings by fission, but the qualitative evidence here suggests that this is more common than has previously been recognized.[17]

Many other associations also provide evidence that what is considered a closely substitutable good or similar production process is very flexible, if not a matter of locally heated cultural politics. For instance, outsiders might consider that contractors specializing in fire prevention share an industry identity, but as we will see in chapter nine, members of the Firestop Contractors International Association would be insulted by such an assumption, since they passionately promote "passive," as opposed to "active" fire prevention construction—even though they occasionally speak of "the industry" in more expansive terms too. The Small Publishers Association of North America sees the needs and concerns of small (and self-) publishers as differing from those of publishers in general, and "emerged out of a need for energized, decisive leadership" when another similar group folded. However, and as for most associations, differing identities, interests, and commitments were not mutually exclusive. They reply to one Frequently Asked Question—"Why should I join SPAN if I'm a member of PMA (Publishers Marketing Association)?"—"if you are serious about your publishing business, you should make the investment to join both organizations." In many other instances too, what gets to be considered a closely substitutable good or a similar production process is less transparent than economists or officials might suppose. Distinctions proliferate and boundaries are frequently crossed: what it means to be an industry is fluid, and sometimes contested on the ground, just as Van Maanen and Barley suggest is the case for occupational communities. The many obscure concerns we encounter in the course of examining associations' various activities make more sense as concerns of occupational communities than as concerns of "objectively" defined industries.[18]

But the problem with the objectivist view that associations represent industries runs deeper than the cultural politics of industry formation and change. Even in routine discourse, *industry* is a floating signifier, referring—according to context—to narrower or broader categories of economic action and to groups defined by a multitude of criteria beyond their members' shared orientation to particular production processes or products. The different types of actors drawn in to the fields constituted by associations often include actors who, conventionally and formally, would be considered members of different industries, or even different "sectors" (itself a surprisingly ambiguous term)—for instance, manufacturers and distributors, or suppliers and contractors. In some contexts, these differing members will be seen as sharing an industry identity, as when the Food Equipment Manufacturers includes distributors or engineers in a larger vision of "foodservice professionals"; while at other times, they will be treated as distinct from industry members. Such fluidity of reference is more the rule than the exception.[19]

Some associations are so idiosyncratically inclusive that they are difficult to see as stereotypical trade associations at all, although they certainly involve collective action by business. Some of these are associations with activities including nonmanagerial employees. For instance, one case guaranteed to provoke much classificatory anxiety is the Association for Women in Aviation Maintenance, with organizers and support programs oriented to their eponymous members, but a membership that includes large aviation companies and several top aviation executives among their strongest supporters. Other idiosyncratic associations, like the American Society for Automation in Pharmacy, encompass members from a very wide variety of formally defined industry locations in their activities, while at the same time addressing a narrower set of concerns—the coordination of new technologies—than one might associate with an intuitive "industry" category like pharmacy.[20]

More support for the idea that associations are occupational communities constituted "bottom-up" rather than representatives of "industries" objectively defined in terms of shared products or work processes lies in the observation that many associations are constituted around members' shared relationships with other actors, in addition to their central productive activity. For instance, the Independent Bakers Association we encountered briefly in chapter three—otherwise a rather simple interest group—was "founded in 1968 to protect the interests of independent wholesale bakers from anti-trust and anti-competitive pressures." Here, the association does not represent an industry understood in technical terms but a particular type of business among all those engaged in a form of production (like the Small Publishers). And a surprisingly large minority of associations is constituted around social categories beyond either technical production or business—like gender, industry status, or race. The Association for Women in Aviation Maintenance was "formed for the purpose of championing women's professional growth and enrichment in the aviation maintenance fields." The International Society of Hospitality Consultants is constituted around members' high status in the broader "hospitality industry": its members are 170 "leading consultants" who are leaders in other associations and publish widely on "the industry," and membership is by invitation only. And as we will see in more depth in chapter nine, the National Association of Real Estate Brokers combines racial and "industry" identities (as well as encompassing a variety of work processes and market products—from appraisal to property management) in their understanding of "industry." It is "a national trade association dedicated to bringing together the nation's minority professionals in the real estate industry," and as one president's reflection on the "NAREB family" ran:

> REALTISTS must remember and commit to companies that are owned by people who look like us and not be overly critical but . . . willing to work out any differences. Supporting our own is not being "anti" anything . . . rather I see it as pro Black and there is nothing wrong with that.[21]

Further support for the observation that associations constitute "industries" as occupational communities lies in the fact that the meaning of "industry" is very elastic according to context, even beyond upstream suppliers and downstream distributors of core products and services. As we saw in chapter four, associations often emphatically locate members in fields that include other related associations, technical organizations, important clients, academic researchers, and government bodies. As a result, the notion of "industry" expands and contracts according to context. For instance, the International Society of Certified Electronics Technicians offers "the highest level of professional recognition in the appliance service industry" and is the "leading industry association for certified electronic technicians." Organizationally, though, it is "the technical division of the ... National Electronics Service Dealers Association," and their shared newsletter observes, for example, that "2004 CE [Consumer Electronics] Industry Growth Rate Doubles Earlier Projections." The "industry," then, might be the technicians, the dealers, or consumer electronics, according to context. Similarly, the Irrigation Association "promotes and supports the irrigation industry," yet, in one initiative, joined with other "Green Industry" associations affected by the drought of 2002 (the American Nursery Landscape Association, Associated Landscape Contractors of America, and Turfgrass Producers International). In this case, the signification of "industry" expanded as a coalition was formed. In the same way, the Exhibit Designers and Producers expanded their "industry" identity in their response to the events of 9/11, and in a special report—"Our Industry Reacts to Tragedy"—elaborated the actions and reactions of the various members of the "Convention Industry Council," which was composed of twenty-nine related associations. And as we saw in chapter four, the Firestop Contractors went so far as to define "the industry" itself in terms of a field of related associations—"the industry would include FCIA, IFC, the "Alliance for Fire and Smoke Containment and Control—Gypsum manufacturers/Institute, AWCI, Fire Door Manufactures [sic]."[22]

In a variety of ways, then, a culturally informed model of business associations as occupational communities, with boundaries set by members, fits the association population much better than a model based on objective industry interests. Associations do not simply represent objective industry interests, partly because they are sometimes actors constituting "industries," partly because "industry" itself is a floating signifier, and partly because associations are constituted around categories both within and beyond formal analytic definitions of industries. The political-cultural work we can see even in the constitution of apparently clearly defined "industry" associations; the cultural politics of distinction in what outsiders would consider the same industry; the routine connections and coordination built in to many associations between actors formally located in different industries; the formation of associations according to shared relationships with other actors, beyond shared productive activities; and the shifting contextual usage of the term *industry* by associations themselves—all make associations more like occupational communities than industry representatives.

This observation is consistent with the thrust of neoinstitutionalist arguments about the constitutive politics of industries, but extends it. The social construction and reconstruction of industries performed in association often relies on "occupational" solidarity, which may include but is not confined to solidarity grounded in preconstituted interests, or even to solidarity grounded in shared experience with closely substitutable goods or similar production processes.

Producing Collective Identities

Another important feature of occupational communities is the collective identities they provide their members, who "derive valued identities or self-images directly from their occupational roles"; this is evident in occupationally specific codes and views of their work worlds, solidarity in interaction with "others who 'know the score,'" and a sense of occupational honor. Business associations certainly produce and reproduce discourses and symbols of occupational identities as *collective* identities. Arguably, an important part of what associations do is articulate collective identities closely related to their members' economic action. These identities transcend particular firms or workplaces and are sometimes understood as *industries*, although, as we have seen, they do not always reflect formally defined industries, and they often remain closely tied to the experiential particularities of occupational niches.[23]

Collective identity in occupational community is evident in many of the codes, categories, and practices generated by associations. It is commonly and explicitly cited as a benefit of membership, and it is evident especially in the interactional engagement among peers "in the know," which we can see even in the textual evidence. Moreover, other intermittent features of association discourse and practice—like referring to shared histories and creating collective symbols like coffee mugs—also indicate occupational solidarity and identity.

Collective Identity and Member Benefits

Collective identity—rather than particularistic benefits—is often claimed as a benefit of association membership. The various rationales associations propose to persuade new members to join illustrate this. The "Why Join?" subgenre of association discourse clearly invites answers in terms of selective benefits for prospective members—as the Exhibit Designers and Producers put it, "What Do You Get Beyond the Warm Feeling of Doing Something Wonderful for Your Industry?" But even given that genre constraint, a reified collective identity beyond members' particular interests is also important. The Exhibit Designers and Producers Association answered the question of "why join" with a mix of selective benefits and collective goods: "you and your peers have hundreds of reasons to join. Here are just four . . . VISIBILITY to build your business . . . KNOWLEDGE to keep you ahead of the curve . . . INDUSTRY LEADERSHIP to grow the Exhibition Industry . . . NETWORKS to open doors . . . Become active in EDPA and create additional opportunities for yourself and the entire industry" (emphasis in original). One EDPA president wrote that the association was "committed to providing genuine value to our members and to strengthening our voice to ensure a stronger, safer and more prosperous future for the entire industry." Like most other associations, they could claim particular, if rather intangible, benefits of membership, but they also articulated a collective identity beyond those particular member interests—"the entire industry," "grow the Exhibition Industry." Similarly, the Closure Manufacturers' Association lists ten reasons for joining, mostly (intangible) selective benefits for members, but concluding, *"Being a member of CMA illustrates a commitment to the closure industry, and it also provides an opportunity to give something back to the industry."* It "offers its members the opportunity . . . to more effectively serve the needs of the marketplace by working together as an association rather than by members acting individually."[24]

Many associations place more emphasis on collective identity than selective benefits, to the extent that, to an outsider, membership starts sounding like a rather onerous responsibility. Those who might consider joining the International Concrete Repair Institute can expect "industry recognition," but one of the major incentives offered is "Committee Participation" to "develop programs and establish precedent to further the quality of concrete repair." As a committee member, "you have the chance to play a vital role in the direction of the repair and restoration industry and ICRI as an organization." Similarly, if you join the Aluminum Anodizers Council, which works for "the entire anodizing community," your membership commits you to "support the Council's principle objectives as stated in the by-laws, to comply with the council's anodizing quality standards, [and] to actively participate in council programs designed to improve the industry." The Firestop Contractors International Association understands the benefits it offers almost entirely in collective terms: "FCIA members have the opportunity to help promote the interests of specialty building construction contractors to the market, develop educational programs, recommend association objectives, help expand membership, and direct the focus of the association through their support and participation." Committee membership is "where the action is," and committee members "work together to further our industry through joining together to tackle big jobs." Leaders of the Food Equipment Manufacturers tell their members that "industry leaders who have had a lot of volunteer experience" (including their 252 committee volunteers) would "guarantee you won't find anyone with regrets . . . volunteer efforts were among the most meaningful and fulfilling of their careers," and they all have "a deep passion for our industry." Often it seems that the main benefit of association membership and participation is seen as working for the collective good. Whatever else they do, then, and whether or not they also pursue members' particularistic interests, business associations articulate, produce, and reproduce collective identities—like the occupational communities Van Maanen and Barley theorize.[25]

Occupationally Specific Interactional Engagement

For Van Maanen and Barley, one indicator of collective identity in occupational community is communication of occupationally specific views of the work world and a related solidarity in interaction with similar others. We have already seen in chapter four that associations communicate occupationally specific views of work in their proliferation of arcane cognitive categories and practices, constantly reinforced in typical strategies of action like education, sharing information, doing research, and setting standards. Neoinstitutionalist theory suggests that this cultural production will have an impact as a condition of mimetic isomorphism in industry categories and practices—in the aggregated but particularistic actions of members. Van Maanen and Barley's perspective suggests that whether or not such diffusion is broadly consequential, these occupationally specific worldviews will generate solidary interaction in "shop talk." Indeed, the impact of these occupationally specific worldviews is evident in reports of members' dialogue and interaction.

The occupationally specific problems association members considered and discussed in conferences, committees, and other meetings are often treated as highly engaging. At the 2003 conference of the American Council of Life Insurance, for instance, sessions were offered in which members could "discuss their experiences" of "Surviving a Joint SEC/Insurance Department Privacy Exam" and explore the problem of "Reinsurance: Why Can't We Agree?" The Northern California chapter of the International Concrete Repair Institute met bimonthly to hear talks such as Una Gilmartin's on "Structural Stabilization of the Alcatraz Cellhouse," and they also held an open forum for members to "discuss repair problems they are encountering in the field . . . to exchange information about the "real world" where specifications, installation and repair procedures and contractors collide." At a Firestop Contractors 2003 conference session on contracts, "Bill Munyan, Director, Specifications, Freeman-White Architects, Inc., gave a fact filled and very humorous, presentation about what to look for in standard AIA 201 contracts, from the professional specifier, owner and subcontractor perspective. Substitutions, Shop Drawings, Prime Contract methods were discussed, with much vigor. Lots of notes were being taken at this presentation!"[26]

The Electronics Service Dealers annual convention regularly featured a popular "Best Ideas Contest," with a moderator taking suggestions from the floor and a vote at the end of the hour. Newsletters reported around forty suggestions, some of them rather trivial to an outsider, but all deeply embedded in very particular work processes and certainly evidence of intense dialogue within an occupational worldview. For instance, in 2003 members made suggestions like:

32. Encourage thermal photography maps for major circuit boards and set about a system to require temperature photos for modern component-filled board trouble shooting. Thermal cameras are now readily available.

33. Call-takers should request the owner to supply model/serial/date stamp information when logging a call. Often the client will be made aware of the trinkets and obstructions of getting to the TV. Sometimes if they have to go look at the TV back, they will clean it up a bit before the technician has to waste much time removing statues and flowers.

Photos of the participants in this Best Ideas Contest are textbook illustrations of intense, engaged interactional focus, supporting the writer's comment that the newsletter report did not do full justice to the event, and " 'Being there' is indispensable to effectively utilize this 60 minute idea tossing session."[27]

Similarly, the Baltimore–Washington, DC, chapter of the International Concrete Repair Institute reported an engaging role-playing exercise: "A *Fun* Pre-Bid Meeting"—a "light hearted and entertaining debate of the issues" among members playing engineers, contractors and owners. Perhaps because the "engineer" admitted that "clarification of the bid documents was necessary" for a realistic cost proposal, "chapter members enjoyed the event."[28]

The Brick Industry Association's Western States Clay Products affiliate held a summit in 2002 "to discuss the maximum reinforcement provisions in masonry" ("Rho Max" provisions), which they believed to be too restrictive. An obscure forty-nine-page transcript of that meeting makes the reader a "fly on the wall" observer of engaged shop talk that is both informal and highly technical, as in these (less impenetrable) illustrations:

> If you look at how we want buildings to perform as a system instead of as elements. Terry had kind of broached the subject. Are we looking only at life safety?
>
> . . . But one of the fearful things I heard this morning is allowable stress design (ASD) is better. I mean, we are going backwards, guys, if that is the case.
>
> . . . I question the thought process behind having to tie that compression reinforcement in a section where we have gone to great lengths to insure that there is no toe crush. Can somebody explain to me how that bar is going to buckle out of the center of a wall that can't crush?
>
> . . . Well, the question is, if you go past the design drift there is no guarantee that you are not going to crush a toe?
>
> . . . We are doing that now for autoclave rated concrete to actually get a logical rational procedure for R. But you get into that smoke-filled room where steel starts off with 12, you know how it works.

If "you know how it works" when, in that smoke-filled room, "steel starts off with a 12" you share an occupationally specific view of your work world and related solidarity in interaction with similar others—even if you disagree on the issue at hand.[29]

For some association members, opportunities for peer reflection and discussion are provided in local and regional chapters of national associations, as we have already seen above in the reflections from the Northern Californian chapter of the Concrete Repair Institute, as well as in the brick industry discussion. Typically, active chapters hold regular meetings with talks as well as dinners and social events like golf and holiday parties; some also publish newsletters and conduct other activities resembling those of national associations. For example, the Exhibit Designers report "Chapter News" in their monthly electronic newsletter: in September 2004, for instance, that news included "76 Attendees Show for Southeast Chapter Industry Forum Discussion," and "Las Vegas Holds Annual EDPAF Scholarship Golf Tournament." The Concrete Repair contractors have the most systematic and active chapter system: they index 138 recent chapter meeting topics "for other chapters to use as ideas for their own," related to subjects like "Business of Concrete Repair" and "Special Projects." For example, one of the "business" topics was a panel discussion on "Specification vs. Reality" held by the Florida West Coast chapter. One of the "special projects" topics was a talk on "Chemical Grout Injection of World Trade Center Foundation Walls," held by the Baltimore-Washington chapter. As the president of the active fifty-seven-member Northern California chapter writes, "our chapter keeps the focus on providing interesting, useful, and quality topics each member can appreciate. Our members participate and support our dinner meetings, symposiums, and each other in a very impressive manner."[30]

Conventions, committee meetings, and chapter meetings obviously provide settings for such engaged peer discussions, but collective engagement in topics and issues highly particular to occupationally specific worlds and worldviews is also evident in a number of other formats adopted to one degree or another throughout the association population, like newsletters and Internet discussion groups.

For instance, the Exhibit Designers' newsletter features a regular "Designer Corner" interview. For one designer, employed by a major trade show contractor, her "least favorite aspect of design" was "being asked to create fabulous designs in shorter time frames. Mostly what is lost is the time to meet with the client and the Account Executive to gather all the necessary information to deliver the client's marketing message. This can result in a stab-in-the-dark approach to design that does not always initially meet the intended goal." Another "Designer Tip of the Month" discussed feasibility of installations and the importance of good relations with project managers. This sort of chatty involvement in the technicalities of occupational community is not confined to designers. For instance, the Food Equipment Manufacturers published a newsletter article—"Curing the Installation Blues"—that in its length and concrete experiential detail supported the author's reflection that

> asking industry professionals to talk about where problems exist in the equipment installation process certainly got people's attention. Phone calls to

manufacturers, reps, dealers, distributors and operators alike were returned promptly—as in within minutes—and responses to emails came in what seemed like nanoseconds. Talk about touching a nerve.[31]

So collective identities associated with occupational community are evident in myriad obscure codes, categories, and practices produced in associations and in the interactional engagement they sometimes seem to generate in peer discussion in a variety of settings. It is unnecessary by now to belabor the fact that these subcultures may occasionally become so occupationally specific as to seem incomprehensible to outsiders. Conversely, insiders' complaints about errors and misinterpretations of their occupational world provide indirect evidence of the specificity of occupational subcultures.

For instance, the cover photo of someone installing a piece of commercial kitchen equipment for the Food Equipment Manufacturers' story on "Curing the Installation Blues" drew a quick reaction and apology in the next issue: "we failed to ensure that the image conveyed all of the proper safety measures installers must take on the job, including the use of safety goggles, hearing protection and work gloves. NAFEM strongly encourages safety . . . and regrets our image conveyed any message to the contrary." In another insider's complaint, the secretary of the Electronics Service Dealers debunks at length what he sees as the widespread misapprehension that electronics dealers and technicians are concerned solely with computers: "For several years there seems to have been some kind of quixotic affair associated with the computer," he comments disparagingly, and goes on to list many other essential electronics products. We learn from these insiders' complaints that—in these occupational worlds—"proper" equipment installation attends to safety, and that electronics is about much more than computers. Such complaints are quite rare, because there is usually no need to police the boundaries of the subculture in the sort of intraindustry discourse I am examining, which mostly represents occupational groups talking among themselves. Mostly, outsiders do not engage with most of what goes on in these occupational communities. We can see, though, that the specificity and obscurity of occupational subcultures in associations carries with it the strong likelihood that were outsiders to enter these worlds, their interpretations would quickly evoke many more insider complaints.[32]

Associations' constructions of collective identity around (fluid) categories of economic action are also evident in many other indicators of collective identity—in symbols, discourses, and practices that are entirely predictable from the point of view of the cultural analyst, but rather point-less from the point of view of strategic interest. Several other common indicators of occupational community should be noted briefly in this con-text. Associations sometimes engage their members in discussion of pub-lic projects from an occupationally specific point of view, they sometimes situate occupational collective identities in a shared history, and they sometimes produce for their members totemic symbols like coffee mugs.

Association members sometimes share occupationally specific perspec-tives on subjects of broader public interest with which they may not have any direct business connection. As we will see in more depth in chapter nine, associations can be sites of protocivic reflection on such events as Hurricane Katrina and 9/11, and on national history and future possi-bilities. So, for instance, Concrete Repair Institute chapters meetings on topics like the World Trade Center foundation walls or the Ben Franklin House Cornice Remediation project link occupational preoccupations and the wider society. So too did the Firestop Contractors' 2003 conference session on "The Pentagon Reconstruction"—"a picture tour of the Penta-gon project before and after September 11, 2001." No doubt associational settings also allow more informal connections between occupationally specific language and expertise and members' observations and experi-ences, connections that would have little meaning beyond the occupational community. We get some indication of this in one ICRI president's chatty newsletter message about his vacation trip to Michigan: "Having spent the last 20 years in our industry in a construction supply business in Califor-nia, I could not help looking at obvious concrete repair problems with the bridges and other concrete structures in Michigan, Illinois, and Indiana. . . . Exposed rusty rebar is a common sight even on fairly new structures." In these examples and many others, occupational identities are the basis of shared reflection about broader public issues, often in comments that would have little meaning beyond the occupational community.[33]

Shared History and Symbols

Expressions of collective identity can also be seen in constructions of the occupational community as persisting over time, and reflections on the past and the future (just as Benedict Anderson argued of the imagined community of the nation). We catch a glimpse of this in associations' founding stories mentioned earlier, like the origin of the Small Publish-ers Association of North America in 1996 with the "need for decisive leadership" when another organization folded, and of the International Concrete Repair Institute by fission from the "World of Concrete." Such stories are not essential in business association discourse, but appear officially or informally in about half of the focal associations.

Other examples of occasional, "official" expressions of collective identity through history included, for instance, an obituary for a long-term leader of the Aluminum Anodizers Council noting the organizational changes he guided, "reflecting the broader scope of programs targeted to serve anodizers working in additional market sectors." The 2004 president of the Firestop Contractors devoted a series of detailed newsletters to the theme of "'Where have we been, Where we are, and Where we're going': as FCIA [sic]": "FCIA had an impressive beginning. Each conference brought new programs and new members . . . FCIA's past didn't happen by accident. A passionate 'Charter Member Group,' those who attended the first conference have remained active in FCIA and driven our programs forward." More elaborately, the *Central Vac Professional*, published by the VDTA/SDTA (International Association of Floor Care & Sewing Professionals), included a regular feature on "Historical Perspectives," and another journal of theirs, *Floor Care Professional*, featured an article on "25 Years of VDTA/SDTA Convention Memories."[34]

Older associations sometimes recounted official "founding" stories and celebrated anniversaries. The Automotive Lift Institute (ALI), which devotes much of its attention to standard setting, provides a nine-page history of itself and the industry (written by a past president) starting with its founding:

In 1945, emerging from the industrial chaos of WWII, the need for an association of automotive lift manufacturers was realized. Few lifts had been produced after 1940. The 15 or so manufacturers that survived the war were ready to resume production, but steel and other raw materials used to produce automotive lifts were still under government allocation. High grade steel, required for machined pistons and cylinders and for forming superstructure components, was in short supply, and scrap steel of questionable quality was being used to manufacture some lifts.

Mechanics wanted more than grease pits to work from and the responsible lift manufacturers were worried. The quality of the lifts produced and the safety of the lift operator using that product were of primary concern to this industry in 1945, and that concern continues in the forefront of ALI activities today.

ALI traces in some detail the vicissitudes of the industry and the activities of the association through to the present, treating technological, market, and regulatory changes under headings like "In-Ground Lifts Dominate into the 70s," "Surface Mounted Lift Sales Increase in the '80s," "ALI Membership Grows with Record Lift Sales," and "Third-Party Testing as a Requirement for ALI Membership." Less informatively, another post-war association, the Exhibit Designers and Producers, appealed to collective history in celebration of its fiftieth anniversary—"EDPA is 50 Years Young!"

> The ED & PA, as it was affectionately called, has been going strong for the past 50 years making it one of the oldest exhibition industry trade organizations in the country. In . . . 1978 . . . founding father, Fred Kitzing, wrote, "In 1954, the founding fathers, of which I was one, established our national organization. The year 2004 is 25 years from now, 2004 will be the 50th anniversary of the founding of the Exhibit Designers and Producers Association." . . . President of EDPA Gwen Parsons envisions "2004 will be an exciting year for EDPA to build upon the accomplishments of our past."[35]

More informally, a long letter published in a 2004 issue of *ProService Magazine* reflected on the industry's collective past to interpret the future optimistically:

> I retain my ISCET membership (and certification) dating back to 1973 . . .
>
> I recall talking to Frank Moch, EHF in Chicago in the early 50s. He recognized the need for servicers to unite and form an organization to share wisdom and to have a voice in the industry . . .
>
> In 1953 RCA introduced NTSC color TV, a compatible broadcast system that allowed viewers to watch color programming in black and white on their TV. The system compromised quality to accommodate broadcast change. This will not be the case with digital broadcasting. In effect, we have a new beginning in the industry . . .
>
> Television will once again be a front room experience. A single, large screen, flat panel display, configured in a home entertainment center, will be the center of attention, a full 360 returning television to the front room. TV Dinners, watching Uncle Milty, and the golden years of profit to dealers and servicers are back.[36]

Finally, collective identity in occupational community is also evident in those associations—about 20 percent of the focal sample—which offer badges, caps, coffee mugs, and other paraphernalia for members. As Durkheim might have recognized if he had been writing in the late twentieth century, a souvenir coffee mug can be an important representation of contemporary collective identity. For instance, the Florida West Coast chapter of the Concrete Repair Institute sold a coffee mug with the ICRI logo and a heat-sensitive picture of the Skyway Bridge as a scholarship fundraiser. The Certified Electronics Technicians offer blazer patches, lapel pins, member decals, wallet cards, and framed certificates of membership. The Firestop Contractors "have great promotional items that not only look and feel good, they also make a statement about your commitment to industry excellence and promote the FCIA in the process"—items like shirts and travel mugs with the FCIA logo. Similarly, the Real Estate Brokers offer mugs, folders, mouse pads, umbrellas, and torches signifying membership. And the Association for Women in Aviation Maintenance supports a scholarship fund with sales of an extensive selection of Rosie the Riveter merchandise and occupationally themed jewelry, holiday ornaments, and art, along with the more standard items like clothing and coffee mugs. Holiday decorations in the shape of wrenches surely indicate occupational community.[37]

Occupational collective identities are evident in the codes, categories, and practices of business associations, and particularly in the interactional engagement among peers "in the know" that they can generate. They are also evident on those occasions when association members reflect on public matters from an occupationally specific point of view, when they recount their collective memories, and when they create collective symbols like coffee mugs. Many other association programs and practices, too, are best explained by attending to collective occupational solidarity.

Producing Norms and Status

We learned above that a photo of commercial kitchen equipment installation without proper safety practices may offend members of the North American Association of Food Equipment Manufacturers, and that the reduction of electronics expertise to computer skills pains electronics dealers and technicians. Paul DiMaggio and Walter Powell suggest that associations are "another vehicle for the definition and promulgation of normative rules about organizational and professional behavior," and that they "provide other arenas in which center organizations are recognized and their personnel given positions of substantive or ceremonial influence." Ezra Zuckerman and Stoyan Sgourev analyze the way small peer networks of business owners increase motivation because the owners "identify with a community of peers among whom they wish to be a well-regarded member." More generally, economic sociologists have been analyzing the importance of normative and status orders in other contexts for some time. However, they focus more on the effects of normative orders than on their sources and their production, and to my knowledge, neoinstitutionalist suggestions about the production of norms and status in associations have not been followed up in any systematic way.[38]

Associations do, indeed, routinely propagate normative and status orders. They may do so in standards and certification programs, in codes of ethics, in their awards and prizes, and in more informal languages of recognition.

Making Standards

Standards and certification are cited as major activities by about a quarter of all associations, and as we will see in more depth in chapter six, this probably understates their importance. Standards are not the province of any particular type of industry or activity or business; they can be important in associations focused around a wide variety of economic activities. In the focal sample, the certification program run by the Irrigation Association is about as elaborated and rigorous as that run by the Consulting Actuaries.

Making standards in accreditation and certification programs is often understood in terms of an occupational community's norms and status. The National Appliance Service Technician Certification is said to be "the highest level of professional recognition in the appliance service industry" and, beyond strictly instrumental benefits, offers technicians the opportunity to "gain respect" and helps business owners "show you are a first-class, professional organization." The Certified Food Service Professional Program, run by the North American Association of Food Equipment Manufacturers, lists among its objectives "to award special recognition to those food service professionals who have demonstrated high levels of competence and ethics," and eligibility requirements include "acceptable character, ability, and reputation." The Conference of Consulting Actuaries (CCA) awards membership (and the CCA designation) only on the basis of quite rigorous criteria, including that "the candidate must also have professional and business qualifications, moral character, and ethics that are above reproach."[39]

Codes of Conduct

As Andrew Abbott has argued, the main features of ethics codes may be explained if they are seen as status symbols for various internal and external audiences. In particular, he emphasizes a correlation between ethics codes and intra-"professional" status: "the general correlation of positive attitudes and actions towards professional ethics with high intra-professional status reflects the function of formal colleague obligations, the largest section of most ethics codes, in celebrating personal allegiance to the group." For the purposes here, then, ethics codes provide evidence of normative and status orders within occupational groups. About a quarter of the focal associations develop some formal code of ethics or code of professional conduct.[40]

For instance, certification in one of the six different Irrigation Association programs (earning the designation CIC, CID, CAIS, CGIA, CLIA, or CLIM) requires, among other things, agreement to the following code of ethics:

- To hold inviolate the concepts of free enterprise
- To uphold the integrity of the irrigation industry
- To continually seek to gain respect and recognition for the industry on the local, state, national and international levels
- To improve industry products and services by encouraging research and development
- To subscribe to fair and honest business practices including the legitimate representation of my personal capabilities and experience
- To follow responsible procedure with regard to the design, installation and maintenance of irrigation systems
- To follow ethical business practices in all contractual and warranty obligations
- To promote water, soil, and energy conservation through efficient and cost-effective irrigation systems design, installation, and management

(This is a unique mention of "free enterprise" in the sampled association discourse; it is usually taken for granted.) Apart from this example from the Irrigation Association, which includes manufacturers and some contractors, associations with ethics codes mostly focused on services or sales business.[41]

Many discussions of ethics use a language of professionalism (examined in more depth in chapter seven). For instance, the North American Association of Food Equipment Manufacturers includes a "Service Managers

Group" that provides "public principles of conduct . . . important to the development of a true professional." According to this code, for instance, if you are a good service manager you "will not intentionally downgrade a competitor or a competitor's product in order to benefit [your]self," and you "will maintain [your] personal life to avoid any situations that would jeopardize . . . effectiveness in carrying out . . . professional responsibilities." Other association groups that discuss codes of ethics in professional languages include the Conference of Consulting Actuaries, the International Society of Hospitality Consultants, and the appraisers in the National Association of Real Estate Brokers.[42]

But although a language of professionalism was powerful in this context, codes of ethics were not always understood in "professional" terms. For instance, the Vacuum Dealers do not speak of themselves as "professionals," but they do highlight a code of ethics, and the association has members agree to principles like "to provide quality products and services at fair prices" and "to resolve differences with other members through negotiation, arbitration or mediation." Similarly, the Equipment Service Association (ESA) pledges members to a detailed ten-point code of ethics couched in a strongly moralized language of service and responsibility, addressing relationships with clients, manufacturers, competitors, employees, and peers, and enjoining such virtues as honest advertising, financial responsibility, conformity with regulations, clean and orderly facilities, and honesty with fellow members. For instance, "members shall not perform, or cause to be performed, any act which would tend to reflect adversely on their industry, fellow members, competitors or manufacturers," and "members will be honest and forthright with other members in conversation and dealings. They will not divulge information given to them in confidence. Conflict of interest or personalities will not enter into decisions on members or ESA policies."[43]

The International Society of Hospitality Consultants (ISHC) is notable, among these associations, for its explicit discussion of sanctioning. ISHC members—who own consulting businesses and must be invited to join—are pledged to a lengthy and formal Code of Professional Conduct, with subsections related to "Professional Attitude and Behavior," "Relationships with Clients," and "Professional Relationships." The code is "designed to serve notice to the public that members will assume the obligation of self-discipline above and beyond the requirements of law and that members will maintain a high level of ethics and professional service." It "enforces the Code by receiving and investigating all complaints of violations and by taking disciplinary action, including censure, suspension, or revocation of membership" and specifies procedures for handling alleged violations. But ultimately, they claim,

> It is a desire for the respect and confidence of the hospitality industry and of society that should motivate the consultant or member to maintain the highest possible ethical conduct. The loss of that respect and confidence is the ultimate sanction.

The Consulting Actuaries and the Food Equipment Manufacturers are the only other focal associations that mention sanctioning in by-laws that outline a procedure for handling alleged violations.[44]

These exceptions highlight the general absence of any discussion of or mechanisms for member sanctions in this focal group of business associations. This absence may be surprising, since we might expect heightened boundary maintenance and explicit demonizing around "community" ethics. But these data suggest that we should be careful about generalizing from cultural claims made in heightened moments to those in routine discourse. Polarizing and shunning that we could predict would be occasionally evident in dramatic, behind-the-scenes moments is not thematized in mundane association life. Relatedly, Abbott argues that ethics codes are only infrequently enforced, when offenses are publicly visible; however, informal enforcement occurs in everyday professional routines. Meaning-making in the two types of settings is linked, of course, since mild expressions of shared norms in routine settings and mundane life may occasionally be explicitly invoked for demonizing in dramatic moments, but the discourses operate differently in the two types of settings.[45]

Awards

Beyond standard setting and codes of ethics, another important way associations articulate normative and status orders is by awarding prizes, which get a lot of attention in many associations' websites, newsletters, and conventions. More than half of associations in the focal sample award annual prizes of one sort or another, often for technical excellence or achievement as defined and assessed within the occupational community, but sometimes also for significant volunteer or leadership contributions to "the industry" or the association. Associations in all types of industry locations make awards. While in a few cases the awards seem partly oriented to marketing or public relations for industry products, they are much more often treated as notable and interesting from the point of view of peers sharing concerns, categories, experiences, and norms of little interest to outsiders (if they are even intelligible to others). Prize names can also symbolize associational collective memory, recalling significant founders or leaders. That is, as theorists of social capital might say, awards are mostly understood in terms of "bonding" rather than "bridging."[46]

TECHNICAL AWARDS.   Sometimes the awards are made for technical achievement. Hundreds of pages of the Concrete Repair Institute's website are devoted to their Project Awards Program, describing winners of the Project of the Year award, as well as many winners, past winners, and honorable mentions for Awards of Excellence and Awards of Merit in six categories (like "Parking Structures," "High-Rise," and "Historic"). The 2004 Project of the Year was "Strengthening of a Reinforced Concrete Preheater Tower, Florence, Colorado," a project that was "quite extraordinary as it required precision-drilling horizontal holes up to 87 feet long in the beams of the elevated frame structure, without cutting existing embedded reinforcement." In the particular category of "Longevity" awards that year, the winner was the "Coral World Ocean Park in the U.S. Virgin Islands," and nine awards of merit were also made. In 2003 the Project of the Year was the "Grant Park South Garage Rehabilitation Project, Chicago, Ill." A few of ICRI's chapters also make their own awards—the Carolinas Chapter offers a thousand dollar cash prize and free submission to the national competition—and all promote the national competition with their members. The world of concrete repair comes alive even to the outsider with the accumulated detail of ICRI's award information, but the categories and criteria of assessment are clearly peer generated and internal to the occupational community.[47]

The Irrigation Association suggested that "Peer Recognition is the highest compliment"; their prizes "honor the vision and dedication that are hallmarks of our industry" and "help foster pride in your industry." In their "New Product Contest," in 2004, "the winning entries reflect a growing trend in the industry to save water by efficiently utilizing the latest technology, like "smart" controllers and sensors . . . 'The controller is the brains of the system, and these are sending your irrigation system to Harvard.'" In a completely different occupational world, but still focusing on members' work projects, the Exhibit Designers and Producers' "EDDIE" award goes to "industry companies" for "the most exciting, effective marketing programs."[48]

The Aluminum Anodizers Council presents "Awards of Excellence" for "outstanding achievements by individuals who presented papers at the Anodizing Conference"—winners treat topics like how to understand automakers' specification requirements, or the "Mechanism for Supplementary Organic Coatings on Porous Anodic Films." (Anodizers recall their history in prize names: this prize "is named for Robert [Buzz] Kersman of Lorin Industries in Muskegon, Michigan. Kersman was instrumental to the formation of the Council, helping to fund and organize early meetings.") Similarly, but in a very different occupational world, the Conference of Consulting Actuaries awards the John Hanson Memorial Prize "for the best paper on an employee benefit topic published in *The Proceedings* of the conference."[49]

The importance of awards for technical quality in these associations underlines the significance of the technical division of labor even for business actors, where many sociologists would expect the concerns of their role in the capitalist social division of labor to dominate. As chapter seven explores in more depth, occupational community is strongly associated with shared technical experience.

"INDUSTRY" CONTRIBUTION AWARDS. Expressions of occupational community norms and status with prize giving are not confined to matters of technical quality appreciated within a work world. Many awards are made for broader accomplishments, especially for contributions or leadership in "the industry" (particularly as organized in associations). For instance, the Exhibit Designers and Producers make much of their "Hazel Hays Award"—"the highest honor bestowed by our organization," which is "respected throughout the industry."

> The Award was established in 1976 to honor the memory of Hazel Hays, an industry pioneer who rendered outstanding service to EDPA and the exhibit industry as a whole. Hays, who is known as "the First Lady of the exhibit industry," was the first woman to serve on EDPA's Board of Directors.... The Award Criteria include significant contributions to the knowledge and literature of the exhibit industry; the design or invention of material, equipment, processes or technical services; or outstanding service to associations, companies and other organizations serving the exhibit industry.

EDPA also make an "Ambassador Award" for outstanding service to the association, and a Designer Award, both of which also heavily emphasize contributions to the industry.[50]

Groups like the Exhibit Designers and Producers are oriented to what one might call markets in sociability, so it might seem that they are particularly prone to rewarding contributions to occupational community. But such contributions are also explicitly rewarded in groups whose economic activities and markets do not seem to encourage any special sense that contributions to community are important. The Food Equipment Manufacturers award a "Doctorate of Foodservice" (DFS) to "distinguished foodservice professionals" who "have given their time and energy to the food service industry." Nominees for Women in Aviation Maintenance awards must have demonstrated, among other qualities, their commitment to community service, leadership, responsibility, and professionalism. The Irrigation Association makes a number of awards for "Person of the Year," "Industry Achievement," and so on, as do the Electronics Service Dealers.[51]

Indeed, the Electronics Service Dealers and Technicians institutionalize occupational community norms and status in a genre transposed from popular culture sports and entertainment—the National Electronics Hall of Fame. Categories of accomplishment for nomination to their Hall of Fame are instructive: "Scientists, Inventors, and Engineers," "Business and Industry," "Communications," "Association Executives and Industry Association Members," and "outstanding individuals who do not clearly fit any of the other groups." Manufacturers and dealers of floor care products also have a chance to earn a place in a Hall of Fame, but only if they make exceptional community contributions. Nominees

1. must have a minimum of 20 years in the industry
2. must have made considerable contributions to the industry
3. must have been involved with the association in ways to help others in the industry, i.e., taught classes at the shows, association member, helping others with marketing ideas and customer service ideas, etc.
4. must have been involved within his or her community
5. must have made a difference in someone's life associated with the industry and/or their community
6. must have worked toward maintaining a positive public image of the independent vacuum and sewing dealer
7. must be dedicated to making the industry better for all.

Since nominators were restricted to hundred-word submissions, though, the bar for induction may have been lower than this list suggests.[52]

"Industry" Standing

Finally, associations more or less explicitly articulate status orders in a language of "industry visibility," "industry leaders," "supporting members," and "industry peers." Associations often see themselves as creating opportunities for increasing members' "industry visibility," either indirectly or directly. Indirectly, as the Concrete Repair Institute explains to its members, "the more involved you are with member activities the more likely you are to be called upon by other members for guidance. It is this recognition that will propel you and your company to the forefront of the concrete repair industry." Similarly, membership of the Closure Manufacturers' Association is said to "increase the company's visibility . . . within the closure marketplace."[53]

Many direct opportunities for increasing industry "visibility" are created at conventions and in newsletters. For instance, members attending the Independent Bakers Association convention are invited to be among those making one of the "increasingly popular" company profile presentations. Association newsletters sometimes note news from particular firms or individuals, as the Mulch and Soil Council did in its November 2005 newsletter with stories like "Smith Promoted at Becker Underwood" and "Oldcastle Buys Jolly Gardener." The Concrete Repair Institute sometimes did stories on member firms, and their *Chicago Tri-States Chapter Newsletter* reported at length, with photos, "Jeff Carlson named as ICRI Fellow at National Meeting in Orlando," detailing his "many years of consistent contributions on both national and chapter levels."[54]

Many associations also offer special opportunities for sponsorship of association activities and events, or offer "premium" memberships. Among the benefits members can receive in exchange are more chances to flaunt their logo and more newsletter exposure. For instance, large member companies of the Women in Aviation Maintenance sponsor awards and "benefit from promotional exposure and community recognition. Plus supporting women in the aviation maintenance industry." "Supporting Members" of the Concrete Repair Institute make larger contributions, and in turn are "recognized as strong supporters of ICRI and the concrete repair industry." More locally, their Baltimore–Washington, DC, chapter held a golf outing that was said to be a "tremendous success" thanks to a long list of members who sponsored meals, balls, and foursomes.[55]

Occupational communities possess normative and status orders peculiar to self-defined work worlds. As we see here, associations provide

cultural infrastructure for such normative and status orders in their certification and accreditation, codes of ethics and professional conduct, awards
for technical excellence and "community" contributions, and the ways
they speak of and provide opportunities for extra-credit "visibility" and
"support." While the meaning of such common association features is occasionally understood in terms of members' market interests, they mostly
seem to offer rather few strategic benefits and make little immediate business sense except as status generators, or as expressions of affiliation with
a collective identity. "Disinterested" affiliation with the collective identity
provided by associations as occupational communities can also be seen in
many direct expressions of solidarity.

Producing Camaraderie

Recall the Boston banker mentioned in chapter two for whom the
nineteenth-century formation of the American Bankers' Association was
"a call for better acquaintance, for pleasure, for amusement, to get us away
from home for a holiday—for a good time generally." The point of view
might seem somewhat naive and idiosyncratic, but we also saw in chapter
two that respondents to an extensive 1938 survey repeatedly pointed out
that sociability was important to them, when researchers had asked them
about everything but sociability. Like those researchers, most conventional analysts of business associations have usually bracketed or ignored
camaraderie. But if we set aside the theoretical blinders of interest-based
analysis, we see immediately that the woman quoted at the beginning of
the chapter who commented of her association that "yes, it was a good
source for networking, but it was more than that. It was a community," was
highlighting a routine feature of associational meaning-making.

For Van Maanen and Barley, occupational communities consolidate
groups around shared work interests beyond the firm or the job, drawing
distinctions with others who lack the work experience that would enable
them to recognize and communicate about boundaries, categorical distinctions, norms, and status judgments that are emergent in the particularities of the work process. They also suggest that this sort of shared work
experience may generate solidarity beyond work, for instance by creating
friendships and involving activities that blur the boundaries between work
and leisure. If business associations share many of the features of occupational communities, we should see some evidence of solidaristic con-

nections and practices that relate to members' concerns and experiences beyond the world of work and industry.

Indeed, many contemporary associations demonstrate camaraderie well above and beyond the pursuit of shared interests. This is particularly evident in reported experiences of conventions and other association meetings. Insider jokes, charity programs, scholarships, and obituaries are all further evidence of a blurring of boundaries between work worlds and the rest of life in occupational communities sustained by associations. As the rather serious International Concrete Repair Institute claims, "membership brings with it a special camaraderie with colleagues and a high level of responsibility to serve the industry."[56]

Sociability in Meetings

A major activity for almost all associations is their meetings. As we saw in chapter three, at least three-quarters of the population holds annual conventions. These are not simply trade shows; only just over a third include exhibits at their meetings. For larger and more active associations, the annual or (occasionally) biennial convention is only one in a busy calendar of meetings. In addition to their annual conference, the American Council of Life Insurance held eleven other conference meetings in 2004 for groups within the association, such as the "Seminar for Investment Managers," "Compliance Section Annual Meeting," and "Forum 500 Leadership Retreat." The Food Equipment Manufacturers hold a major trade show but also several other meetings each year, like the "Sales and Marketing Conference" and the "Service Managers and Engineering Conference," and also provided a calendar of related events in the United States and worldwide, as do many other associations. Smaller associations encourage their members to meet at other related events. The Association for Women in Aviation Maintenance listed ten events of interest to members, such as the "Professional Aviation Maintenance Association" conference, and the "Maintenance, Repair, and Overhaul" conference, reporting members' activities at these events.[57]

To different degrees, conventions and meetings frequently blur for members the boundaries between work and leisure. Certainly, many of the programs include serious business, with an impressive array of educational and technical sessions. The small Pellet Fuels Institute conference at Niagara Falls in 2004 included sessions like "Is Safety & Health a top priority where you work?" "Lawmakers Do Listen," and "Bearing

Lubrication." The American Society for Automation in Pharmacy, which included chain, independent, and hospital pharmacists and senior management of software companies, held their 2005 "Industry and Technology Issues" conference at the Ritz Carlton on Amelia Island, Florida. It was intended to be "the one meeting that will take you to the heart of the industry and technology issues facing the pharmacy market today" and offered sixteen sessions on obscure topics like "Update on the Schering Report XXV: Community Solutions to Pharmacy Issues" and "Putting CSOS into Practice: EDI, Process Flows, and the Pilot." The 2006 meeting in Las Vegas of the Vacuum Dealers Trade Association (VDTA) offered, along with its exhibits and product training, a full program of sixteen concurrent sessions on topics like "Retaining Good Employees through Competitive Employee Benefit Packages" and "Troubleshooting Commercial Equipment."[58]

But as the vacation locations suggest, even the associations that present their meetings in the most technical or strategic terms also hint at life beyond work. As we would expect, there are also tours, dinners, and parties. The Pellet Fuels Institute held a Vineyard Tour and Dinner. Amelia Island was supposedly "an ASAP favorite, set among barrier island dunes, backwater marshes and maritime forest on miles of beach off the North Florida coast." The Vacuum Dealers emphasize the golf, water sports, entertainment, and restaurants at Myrtle Beach, South Carolina, the location of their next convention: it "will be the perfect place to mix business with pleasure," and "there should be something for everyone to enjoy." Another association that usually speaks mostly in more strategic terms, the Irrigation Association, noted that their twenty-fifth International Irrigation Show in Tampa, Florida, in 2004 offered "a sunny, warm, climate, beautiful, white-sand beaches, a rich cultural heritage, and a host of dining establishments for every taste . . . out-of-the-ordinary entertainment choices . . . a slice of paradise for fishing and golfing" (although members might justify the trip with shop talk about the local setting—"in the midst of a heavily irrigated market with unique challenges"). And the highly technical and well-organized meeting of the Consulting Actuaries offers, at least, a trip to Hawaii, and

> irrespective of the packed program, attendees and their guests will have ample time to enjoy themselves . . . treated to a casual outdoor luau—meander around the pools, dance, or sit back and enjoy the music while dining . . . a good time to meet old friends, make new friends and relax.[59]

While many associations do stress the value of the substantive content of their meetings more than the leisure, they are also quite explicit about emphasizing the pleasure in what the Independent Bakers' Association called the "mix of business and pleasure" in meetings: "We look forward to seeing you at The Breakers [Palm Beach, Florida] for some important policy decisions and a great vacation!" The Independent Bakers, like some other associations, left extensive time free from industry-related sessions for golf, tennis, and sightseeing. The leisure was emphasized in their extensive album of conference photos; eighty-three showed groups of mostly middle-aged men and women happily engaged at dinners, social events, and tennis, about the same number as the eighty-five photos of speakers and session audiences. Similarly, the Firestop Contractors were careful to note of their 2004 conference that "the FCIA Program Committee has scheduled free time for touring, a golf & fishing tournament, and fun. Bring your spouse, and don't miss this event!" Their 2003 meeting in Orlando, Florida, ran from Wednesday to Saturday, but Friday afternoon and Saturday were free of "Education Events" while members focused on their important "Annual Golf Tournament." And the Exhibit Designers and Producers, while they begin by highlighting their "challenging program" and featured speakers, also stress leisure and social events:

> In keeping with tradition, our meeting starts with the Annual Van Lines Golf Tournament. . . . This year we are starting a new tradition with our 1st Annual International Tennis Tournament. From there it's three nights and two days of pleasantly paced educational programs, exhibits, and of course plenty of food, and entertainment.[60]

Associations' provision of leisure opportunities in a vacation setting in their various conventions and meetings routinely blurs the boundaries between work and leisure, as Van Maanen and Barley suggest is common for occupational communities. Importantly, this blurring is not usually understood in particularistic ways. The vacation and leisure activities may of course be attractions for members as individuals. But leisure is also typically seen as providing opportunities to socialize with others in "the industry" or work world. For instance, a joint conference of the Service Managers and Engineers in the Food Equipment Manufacturers Association with an association of Manufacturers' Agents provides "opportunities to relax and rejuvenate your mind and your body" because it offers "fun-filled social and networking events, including beach volleyball and Miami tours."[61]

"Social and networking events" blur strategy and solidarity as well as work and leisure. They are important features of association meetings. Of course, if the meeting links members with upstream or downstream exchange partners, socializing may be mostly business, just as gifts, lunches, and golf are often sales strategies. For example, the food equipment manufacturers, who were working on globalizing their business, held a "Global Networking Event" at the Marconi Automotive Museum—a museum, they said, that "exudes an international flair": "let the museum stimulate the senses while you get in the fast lane . . . by mingling with international customers." But even if the socializing involves networking with customers—which is not true of most association meetings—meetings with peers are also important. The Food Equipment Manufacturers' main event was an "All-Industry Celebration," not only "the perfect opportunity to entertain clients" but also "a first-class reception" in "the ultimate venue for honoring some of the industry's leaders and networking with your peers." Similarly, the Mulch and Soil Council includes its "Annual Membership Meeting" among the benefits of association, because it offers recreation and peer networking (as well as supplier contacts and education): "while combining comfortable surroundings with recreational opportunities . . . You will meet fellow producers who share your problems and can offer advice on solutions." The Exhibit Designers, who make a lot of what they title their "Networking Events," offer, for instance, a "Welcoming Reception Featuring Havana Nights" at which members can "network with more than 250 industry colleagues overlooking the beautiful bay of Florida." Contact with colleagues, rather than industry partners, was also important at the Firestop Contractors' Education and Committee Action Conference: "we all attended the education sessions, worked together at committee meetings while having a bit of fun in Las Vegas at shows, casinos, and just relaxing by the pool."[62]

As we saw in chapter four, talk of "networking" is a cliché in association discourse. As this image of the Firestop Contractors around the pool in Las Vegas illustrates, "networking" with peers is often understood in terms of camaraderie. The term is often used as an alibi for socializing. For instance, the ICRI's active New England chapter claims to offer a "superior technical and social calendar" with golf outings, dinner cruises, and other such events. As their president explains, "in addition to the high end technical aspect of the organization we also feel a strong social component is a key element in producing a group which individual members want to involve themselves with."[63]

Thinking of interactions with those with whom one shares experience, problems, and specialized languages as "networking"—as the hotel facilities manager quoted at the beginning of the chapter also did—constructs sociability as strategic action, but the referent of the term frequently shifts between strategy and sociability, as it did for her. When the delegates to the Anodizers' convention "enjoyed an evening of camaraderie and networking," they could indeed "maximize this opportunity to build contacts" but were also provided with "additional opportunities to meet and greet friends." As we also saw with the otherwise very technically serious Consulting Actuaries, above, meetings are often understood as "a good time to meet old friends, make new friends and relax." The Exhibit Designers' 50th Annual Presidents' Ball "begins with the President's Reception and provides free flowing cocktails followed by the President's Dinner.... It's an occasion to take pleasure in the company of colleagues and a chance to dance to the electrifying sounds of live entertainment." Their 2003 president, at least, claimed to "truly enjoy the formal atmosphere, the awards presentations, and the general feeling of saying goodbye and thanks to the old, and hello and welcome to the new. It sort of reminds me of a New Years celebration."[64]

The Electronics Service Dealers were particularly warm in their reports of the camaraderie of their National Professional Service Convention (NPSC):

NPSC! Wow!

Maybe it was the record registration (822 registered attendees)... or maybe it was the feeling that the economy was finally turning around. Or maybe it was the feeling that the training offered was just what was needed in this pressurized atmosphere of "what do we do now to make things better?" Maybe it was the feeling of family that always pervades NPSC. Old friendships rekindled once a year as a whole. Whatever it was, this year seemed to especially shine in eyes of NESDA and ISCET leaders who are meeting challenges never dreamed of just a few short years ago, eyes that reflect the positive attitude they all project... not to ignore the very beautiful and functional surroundings of the Renaissance Hotel and Nashville Convention Center, and especially the fun and good times had at the third floor "Bridge Bar & Games."

A year earlier, the report was similar: "something special and important was happening... old friends who meet all too seldom allowed their exuberance to invade the otherwise tranquil sense of being with their warmth toward each other and the laughter combined with the dedication to leaving better prepared for tomorrow than they were when they arrived." At the same time, one leader recalled that "the path that led me to the ISCET presidency" began with a convention:

> Although I've been in the electronics industry for 40 something years (the exact number is a secret), I didn't become really aware of NESDA [National Electronics Service Dealers' Association] until sometime in the 80s. . . . After attending my first convention, I became immediately addicted, and haven't missed one since.[65]

The Firestop Contractors were another such group with a strong and explicit discourse of occupational community, frequently making solidaristic claims about relationships and activities that blurred the boundaries between work and leisure. The meeting in Las Vegas, when they socialized around the pool, was only one of a regular series of events that always seemed to evoke a discourse of camaraderie as well as of technical excellence. For instance, their highly technical 2004 conference on "International Effective Compartmentation" also promised that "we'll finish early each day for some fun activity, and provide opportunities for spouses/significant others to be included as well." As a result, they said, "technical and industry knowledge was gained while relationships were formed amongst FCIA Member families. If you missed this one, you really missed some great exchanges." The previous year, a former president, who was "leaving the board to spend more time with her business," was " 'honored with song,' for her attendance at her own expense at countless ICC and NFPA code hearings over the past 4 years." Some of her work is evident in an earlier report that also mixes concerns with technical excellence, political engagement, and camaraderie: "the Technical and code committees met in Colorado [sic] . . . (25+ people traveled at their own expense to Kathy's . . . even slept at her bunkhouse vacation home . . . real FCIA fellowship!)."[66]

"Fellowship" in technical tasks was also evident in other smaller groups. The Rocky Mountains chapter of the Concrete Repair Institute claimed ten active committees in which "we are having fun working together, making friends, networking amongst industry peers, and building an organization that is a valuable resource for our industry." The president of the Association for Women in Aviation Maintenance reflected that "aviation for us is not a 'big fat pay check' . . . It is a passion and a fascination and for some a cause. A cause that speaks of freedom," and one AWAM chapter reported a small meeting where

> as those in attendance introduced themselves and told their stories, we found common bonds and even some networking opportunities.
>
> As pilot Joyce Samuelson spoke of flying, and PAMA scholarship winner Cathy Soper related her soaring hot air balloon exploits, you can't miss the gleam in the eye and the catch in the voice of people who love aviation.[67]

Such sociability is quite fragile, of course, and even in these typically dry or promotional sources we can see occasional evidence that camaraderie is fleeting and emotional energy evaporates. The Western New York chapter of the Concrete Repair Institute expressed such a concern. Although "since the Chapter's inception in 1994, dinner meetings have introduced the latest technology in concrete repair materials, techniques and have featured marquise projects by local contractors [*sic*]" the chapter was languishing. By 2004 its president called for change in "sometimes-dour e-mails" and complained, "my concern is that the core group (myself included) is tired and shrinking in number."[68]

Drawing on a survey of disparate literatures touching on sociability, Charles Potts points out that sociability involves a noninstrumental approach to association, smooths over social differences, and creates an affective inducement to interaction: as a result, forms of sociability can "create a sense of community or solidarity outside of and apart from communities based in formal or otherwise institutionalized organizations or groups." And as Ailsa Craig has argued, after Georg Simmel, "sociability can create tenacious ties and salient effects despite its lack of intimacy . . . sociability is social interaction for the sake of interaction and its pleasures . . . it is sociability that can make one feel a sense of belonging in a gathering where no one there is a friend. Sociability is surely part of the draw and necessity of our annual meetings." Yet the idea that business associations always involve essentially strategic action has been so powerful that the sociability in occupational community we see here has been almost entirely ignored.[69]

Insider Jokes

Camaraderie brings with it insider jokes, too, and even in typically dry or promotional sources it is possible to find knowing nudges. The president's messages to the San Diego chapter of the Concrete Repair Institute run under the heading "Message from the Rusty Rebar," and at their New Year's gathering "anyone who's walked on cracked concrete is welcome." The Baltimore–Washington, DC, chapter of the Concrete Repair Institute reported that third place in their Annual Golf Outing went to "the team of Rob Pusheck, Rick Edelson, Adam Berkle and an Elvis sighting." The Firestop Contractors' "Las Vegas Photalbum [sic]," with its typical images of members presenting, listening, chatting, and touring, includes one member in Mickey Mouse ears who "models his Fall Conference golf hat" and two others "dueling" with cell phones. Their "Nashville Photoalbum [sic]" shows a golf course group with a dig-in-the-ribs caption: "Rumor has it, that Bob Meister, 3M, Matt McKenzie, McKenzie Insulation, Salt Lake City, UT, and Ray Usher, SUPERL, Inc., Fridley MN know how to play golf in the dark!! Ask them about it." Similarly, the United Lightning Protection Association's newsletter included a photo of three cheerful, bald, fortyish men socializing over a beer at their conference with the caption "ULPA's own Blunt Air Terminals . . . Smooth dudes . . . are living proof of recent research that suggests lightning rods sporting smooth round tops are the most attractive."[70]

Collective Responsibility: Charity and Scholarships

The camaraderie of occupational community is also explicit in association talk about charity and scholarships. Strong claims about "industry" collective identity can be associated with a collective responsibility for caring for needy or young group members. Occupational community sometimes generates collective responsibility, although considering association discourse overall, this is a minor thread.

Charity and scholarship programs are sometimes supported in tax-exempt foundations supported by associations' fund-raising events. For instance, the Manufacturers' Agents for the Food Service Industry "continues its tradition of giving back to the industry" with a silent auction ("a popular and exciting event") at a NAFEM conference. And the Irrigation Association runs an Education Foundation (IAEF) devoted to "Building a Legacy . . . Creating a Future," which "will create lasting relationships and build generations of irrigation professionals for years to come" by developing educational opportunities.[71]

The Exhibit Designers provide a vivid illustration of how occupational camaraderie is expressed in intra-"industry" charity and educational programs. They discuss at length their charitable activities and scholarships, and in particular the camaraderie generated by their annual fundraiser, the Randy Smith Memorial Golf Classic—a "best ball scramble format that welcomes all golfers" with "cart decorating contest, on course prizes . . . [and] a dinner banquet in which the recipient families address the attendees to express their gratitude and appreciation." They repeatedly remark on the significance of helping others "in the industry" (or occupational community):

> All proceeds are donated to designated industry families who have suffered severe tragedies or are facing insurmountable medical expenses. . . . As always, we are reminded that what has happened to all of our recipients could have happened to any one of us," said co founder and event director, Rich Johnson, of Renaissance Management. "This event puts life into its proper perspective," added Norm Friedrich, national EDPA president of Octanorm USA. "We will continue to support this event with all the resources we have at our disposal."

Recipients' stories are recounted each year in person and in print. In 2002, for example,

> Representatives of the five families, who were selected as 2002 recipients, attended the evening banquet and spoke about their loved ones. Several of the family testimonies moved the audience to tears.
>
> The family of the late Mike Witt, a bench carpenter for ten years with H. B. Stubbs Company in Michigan . . . Witt was killed in suburban Detroit by a group of thugs in a senseless act of violence in November 2001. Only 41 years old, Witt left behind a wife and four children.
>
> . . . Reynolds, 41, was a longtime Nth Degree employee who was tragically killed in an automobile accident while working a show in Las Vegas in April 2002. A 20-year veteran in the industry, Reynolds was the single mother of a 16-year-old daughter and an adult son.
>
> . . . Brendon Koshoshek family . . . Brendon, who is employed by United Audiovisuals, a huge supporter of the RSMGC, lost his 8-year-old daughter Alexandria to Leukemia last march. After enduring 18 months of cancer treatments, Alex was finally removed from life support shortly before her 9th birthday.

They also return continually to the experience of camaraderie in the event: "the spirit of cooperation and unity for a common purpose generated for this event is truly inspirational" and helps "your industry brothers and sisters." They report that "many experienced the palpable camradery [*sic*] that set this event afire. . . . 'This event is like no other. You can feel the excitement and pride of everyone participating in this great event.' "[72]

The Exhibit Designers were also concerned with education, which they understood as intergenerational transmission within the community:

> Think back for a moment. Remember when you were up at 3 a.m. in your dorm room trying to finish for a jury review the next morning? . . . Here is your chance, to help shape the minds of young design talent just like you once were!

Like helping the unfortunate, looking toward the future in the young was a way of expressing occupational community. Indeed, the " 'excitement of imagining these fresh young talents entering our industry brought every judge together for the sake of the students and the future of our industry,' reflected judge Alan Cordial."[73]

Other associations, too, wrote of some of their education activities— especially student prizes, student chapters, and partnerships with colleges and universities—in terms of intergenerational transmission and "building a legacy." For instance, the International Concrete Repair Institute began a scholarship program "to increase awareness of ICRI and its membership among college students," and their Rocky Mountain Chapter established its own award "in an effort to promote the development of future professionals." The Food Equipment Manufacturers' undergraduate program aimed to "build a better tomorrow." The Irrigation Association Education Foundation would "create lasting relationships and build generations of irrigation professionals for years to come." For the Certified Electronics Technicians, "the Student Chapter program is one of the most rewarding for ISCET members. To have a hand in the molding of young minds is one of the most exciting activities ISCET undertakes."[74]

Remembering the Dead

Camaraderie in occupational communities is sometimes expressed in concern with the young. It is also expressed in memory of the dead. Earlier, we saw collective history being told in the obituary of a former leader of Aluminum Anodizers; we also saw stories of the Exhibit Designers' "unknown soldiers" recounted during the emotional dinner following their charity golf tournament. More generally, obituaries of association members are common, even in associations that rarely blur the boundaries between work and the rest of life.

The otherwise very technical journal of the International Telecommunications Society, for instance, published a lengthy tribute "in memory of the late Jean-Jacques Laffont . . . an exceptional figure, both as a man and an economist." And the Mulch and Soil Council published an obituary, with a photo, for

> Horace Hagedorn, founder of the Miracle-Gro line of garden products. . . . Horace began his career in advertising in Manhattan where, more than 50 years ago, he conceived the idea of selling a water soluble fertilizer to the public. Since then, the Miracle-Gro brand became the most recognized consumer garden product in history with its unique green and yellow packaging . . . [and] the largest consumer fertilizer and organic products company in the lawn & garden industry. . . . In addition to his hard-driving business sense, Horace Hagedorn . . . supported numerous charities within and outside the gardening industry and sponsored the "Give Back to Grow" awards program to recognize the many accomplishments of gardeners across the U.S.

More commonly, obituaries added emotion to the formality. The heart attack victim of one brief obituary in the Exhibit Designers and Producers' monthly newsletter was "one of the best friends and colleagues anyone could ever hope to have. . . . It will be difficult to replace him professionally, and impossible as a friend."[75]

This tribute mixes business skills with friendship, but most obituaries emphasize contributions to associational life or to the occupational community more generally. The Electronics Service Dealers (NESDA) were particularly attentive to contributions to their occupational world:

> Bob was a charter member of NESDA of Ohio and a long-time NESDA member. He served as President of NESDA from 1993 to 1995 and had also held many other local, state and national titles. He was a CSM as well as an instructor and administrator for the CSM program. . . . He will be missed throughout the NESDA community.

Another NESDA member was noted because he "donated so much of his time for nothing more than the chance to improve the service industry for all of us."[76]

There is some evidence that such deaths could strike a real chord. One ICRI newsletter eulogized John Ward as "an inspiration and an energetic and enthusiastic supporter of ICRI and a proponent of improving construction methods" and established a scholarship fund in his name. Later, they printed an announcement from his widow, thanking ICRI members "for all of the cards, notes and flowers she received after John passed away" and "such a huge, heartfelt response." And one NESDA member's death evoked an inventive tribute at the Electronics Service Dealers' next convention:

> Also new this year was Hawaiian Shirt Day, held on Saturday in memory of Rich Mildenberger CET, former NESDA Region 2 Director and ISCET member who passed away suddenly in April. Rich loved brightly colored shirts, and after the Hitachi crew announced that they would wear Hawaiian shirts at their Saturday breakfast in his memory, other attendees followed. (*Photos showing some of the Hawaiian attire at the bottom of page 12.*)[77]

Conclusion: Interest as Totem and Alibi

We saw in chapter two that the long-standing institutional vitality of American business associations cannot be explained by simple assumptions about the pursuit of transparent economic interests, and we noted there that a Durkheimian account in terms of social cohesion in complex societies made more long-term sense. Building on the observation that early associations coordinated information production, our examination of contemporary associations in chapter three suggested that they should be seen primarily as cultural producers, making meaning for economic action. In chapter four we saw how American business associations provided infrastructure for "industry" categories and practices, networks, and fields, as neoinstitutionalists have suggested. In doing so, they make meaning for economic action, routinely reproducing actors' economic interests and sometimes providing sites for their creation, challenge, and change.

We had already moved well beyond a simple Smithian vision of conspiracies over shared interests. This commonsense view captures some truth, but it also misses large and important arenas of association discourse and action. As economic sociologists have sometimes argued, the pursuit of shared interests involves, as a prior condition, the social construction of those particular interests, a process that is by no means transparent. Much routine association activity can be seen as providing the institutional conditions for the ongoing construction and reproduction of members' interests, an arena of cultural politics. Culturally informed neoinstitutionalist approaches to understanding business associations suggested that we need to expand our understanding of what is strategic for business to include the production of collective cognitive goods.

But we have now seen that there is, in fact, much more to business associations than their production of collective cognitive goods fulfilling strategic functions for business. A large realm of business association activity and discourse is normative and expressive: business associations are often occupational communities. First, the boundaries of association are set by members and do not conform to objectively defined "industries." Second, association discourse emphasizes and articulates collective identities, which are also evident in occupationally specific interactional engagement, insider complaints, occupationally specific perspectives on public matters, collective memory, and collective symbols. Third, associations articulate occupationally specific normative and status orders, evident in standards making, ethics codes, technical awards, awards for "industry" contributions, and languages of "industry" standing. Fourth, association discourse expresses occupational camaraderie blurring the boundary between strategic interests and sociability, in reports of meetings, insider jokes, charity, provision for the young, and in obituaries. Here, as elsewhere, "economic life is permeated by expressive interests that are not tradable and which cannot be rated as commensurable choices on a single schedule of preferences."[78]

The accumulation of this various evidence suggests a more radical development of the Smithian vision of interest-based business conspiracy than the standard neoinstitutionalist account of the necessary cultural production and reproduction of industry interests we explored in chapter four. Collective identity and solidarity are necessary conditions for the production and reproduction of industry interests. Moreover, the neoinstitutionalist account of associations as latently strategic cultural producers is ultimately incoherent if it suggests *both* that business associations create cultural conditions for the pursuit of (preexisting, transparent) business interests, *and* that they are institutions for the social construction of business interests. Both the social construction and the pursuit of business interests ultimately rely on collective identity and solidarity. So, normative and expressive discourse and action—discourse and action that is primarily nonstrategic—is fundamental to associational life.

But to give the normative and expressive meaning-making of business associations more weight than their cognitive and strategic cultural production seems to challenge common sense. It suggests that what has been ignored or treated as incidental to our understanding of business associations is, in fact, their main point. Whereas strategic accounts essentially reproduce the (presumed) folk belief of economic actors themselves that associations are simply means to specific strategic ends, this view challenges us to situate actors' (presumed) self-understandings in terms of a broader sociological explanation that recognizes the significance of unintended consequences, the importance of latent functions, and the explanatory limits of common sense. Given some of the observations in this chapter, it is tempting to reverse Marx and argue that the language of strategic economic interest can be ideological camouflage for "real" wishes for sociability. Expressing "an interest" sometimes seems to be a totem for a particular sort of social membership.

But how can this textual evidence tell us anything about solidarity and identity? Surely systematic observation of face-to-face interaction in association would reveal the textual evidence of collective identity and solidarity I have assembled to be minor sentimental lapses, if not bald-faced front-stage maneuvering for backstage strategic ends. But this suspicion is based on an unwarranted faith in the validity and significance of the evidence of face-to-face interaction, compared to textually mediated communication, as a primary site of meaning-making. If this faith were ever justified, it is increasingly hard to justify when one considers meaning-making in public organizations in the modern world. Meaning-making in copresent interaction differs from textually mediated meaning-making in significant and interesting ways, but neither one is a more valid indicator of cultural processes than the other.

In fact it is unlikely that the conference-goers and obituary writers we have encountered would seem more focused on strategic interests and less concerned with solidarity if we had observational rather than textual data. The fact that we find so much apparently expressive talk even in genres and settings where one might expect hard-nosed, rational discourse suggests, rather, that we have only seen a fraction of hitherto unplumbed occupational community.

It is certainly true that all association discourse involves strategy as well as solidarity, interests as well as identity. It is also true that associations, and association texts, differ in the degree to which interests or solidarity dominate their claims—associations have different "group styles," and their texts may be written in different genres. But the point is that it may ultimately be more naive to see solidarity claims as a suspicious beard for the pursuit of interests, than to see interest articulation as a (sometimes destructive) rationalization of the search for solidarity. In fact, neither view fully captures the ways economic action is understood.[79]

Because this argument may seem counterintuitive, the following chapters examine in more depth the ways business associations understand their economic and political interests. As we will see, the pursuit of business interests—whether economic or political—relies to a surprising degree on the cultural articulation of nonstrategic meaning.

PART III

American Business Associations and Economic Action

CHAPTER SIX

"To Grow the Industry"

Business Associations and Economic Interests

If conventional accounts of business associations were correct, then all associations would sound like the Small Publishers Association of North America (SPAN):

> *Our purpose is to bring success to small publishers, self-publishers, and authors!*
>
> We are your one-stop online resource for book publishing know-how. We work to advance the image and profits of self publishers and independent publishers through education and marketing opportunities.
>
> *We help our members sell more books and make greater profits.*
>
> The Small Publishers Association of North America (SPAN) is the premier voice of independent publishing and the second largest such association in the world. We concentrate on your need to sell more books.
>
> Faster. Smarter. Easier.

With 1,300 members, both firms and individuals, SPAN constantly and almost exclusively emphasizes its members' particular economic interests. The goal of their annual conference is "to send you home with a customized book marketing plan." SPAN also emphasizes such member benefits as a health benefits program through which "the combined buying power of SPAN allows us to . . . keep health insurance affordable"; discounts on publishing books, services, supplies, and promotional items; credit card merchant status; access to publishers' liability insurance; freight discounts; and marketing tips. And they highlight their extreme attentiveness to members' direct economic benefits through endorsements like the following from a business called Soft Skull Press—"I was a Writing and Literature major at the New School, but now I feel . . . [I'm] . . . taking the marketing class never offered at the academy. Taking it? Heck, I'm living it."[1]

However, few associations appeal to members' particularist, strategic economic interests in this way. In fact, SPAN is an exception, and particularistic economic assumptions are a weak basis for plausible claims in this world, even though our baseline assumptions about economic action suggest that they should be the most important rationale for associations' activities and goals. The belief that business associations exist to promote particular, strategic economic interests is an "article of faith" without empirical basis.

Instead, most associations are more concerned about "growing the industry," a way of appealing generically to the collective good, as in a Pellet Fuels Institute conference about a "variety of ways to grow the marketplace," and the Food Equipment Manufacturers sessions "designed to help . . . grow all aspects of the global foodservice industry." Even SPAN resorts to an occasional, hesitant appeal to occupational solidarity, their online discussion group being "a wonderful way to participate in 'community.' "[2]

We have seen so far that American business associations have flourished long term as stable, diverse, minimal, and multifunctional producers of cultural infrastructure—of cognitive categories, networking opportunities, fields, "industries," collective identities, normative and status orders, and camaraderie—an infrastructure within which capitalist economic action is located.

I do not argue that American business associations are irrelevant to particular interests and strategic action—far from it. Rather, I argue that they are cultural producers of "interested" identities that are *necessarily* communal *as well as* strategic, solidaristic *as well as* cognitive. This multidimensional theorization challenges conventional assumptions that associations are transparently strategic actors pursuing collective business interests, or simple organizational tools for the promotion of members' particularistic interests.

In this chapter I analyze how, exactly, the pursuit of strategic interest is understood in the context of associations' cultural production of collective identity and solidarity. I show that the cultural account of business associations and their "disinterest" developed so far cannot be quarantined from an account of their supposedly more strategic and practical pursuit of economic interests. Rather than being mutually exclusive, as conventional views would have it, these two dimensions of business associations are inextricably linked.

I explore how business associations orient their actions to intra-"industry" concerns of members about profit maximization, survival, and industry performance. After an overview of assumptions about the economically strategic purpose of association, I examine strategies of action oriented to intraindustry concerns like organizing education, producing research, coordinating standards and certification, and sharing information. This is an energetic but little-known arena of collective action in American economic life that seems to institutionalize settings for and processes of collective economic coordination and episodic economic change.

I examine what these intra-"industry" strategies of action mean, and how intra-"industry" economic interests are understood. This close analysis of meanings attributed to strategies of action, such as providing training, sharing information, doing research, and setting standards, shows that the pursuit of particularistic economic interests—members' profit and economic stability—is only rarely discussed. When economic interests are explicit, they are usually understood as collective, to the extent that members are encouraged to sacrifice their particular interests out of responsibility to the good of the (self-defined) group.

I also ask how association discourse handles potential contradictions between particularistic and collective understandings of economic interests, and I assess alternative proposals about the way business associations survive given the Olsonian puzzle of "free riding."

Finally, I show how associations articulate and pursue collective "industry" interests in changing industry circumstances, including an extended illustration based on the work of the North American Association of Food Equipment Manufacturers to update technological coordination and please powerful buyers like McDonalds.

Economic Purposes of Association

Associations' pursuit of economic interests may be understood in two ways. First, conventional assumptions imply they are primarily oriented to improving particular association members' business situation, by providing information or services inaccessible or too costly to member firms, as SPAN presents itself. Second, sociologists and historians of economic governance focus more on the ways economic interests might be collective "industry interests," and inherently political, rather than functional. In this second view, even if specific members do not usually derive specifiable benefits from association activities, the "industry" in general—however understood—thrives better when collective governance takes care of co-ordination and defense.

It is difficult to prove that the national associations studied here consistently achieve either of these purposes, but they set a baseline for exploring how economic purposes of association *are* understood.

The "Paradox" of Particularistic Economic Benefits and Theories of Transaction Costs

The assumption that associations are oriented to improving particular members' business situation actually presents a paradox. A stereotypical view of capitalist production, distribution, and exchange suggests that each economic actor pursues profit in competition, not collaboration, with others. Cooperative collective action with other market actors in association contradicts this stereotype, and economic sociologists have adduced extensive evidence against the simplistic individualism of many economic models. To this I am adding an account of some of the cultural conditions for collective coordination of market action.[3] Nevertheless, associations' intra-"industry" strategies of action are typically assumed to be economically strategic benefits for members. So how can the particularism of economistic models and the collective action of associations be reconciled?

An analogous problem once faced economists regarding economic behavior in firms, whose bureaucratic hierarchy contradicts anonymous organization of the pure market through the price mechanism. One influential resolution of this puzzle pointed out that transactions vary in costs, such as costs of finding information about exchange partners, or costs of monitoring quality. Oliver Williamson and other new institutional economists theorize the impact of variations in transaction costs on economic organization, for instance, whether manufacturers will sell their product to distributors, or integrate distribution within the firm to ensure more control of the exchange. New institutional economists also analyze how varying institutional conditions, such as property rights, might frame and motivate economic action.[4]

Although American business associations are rendered invisible by standard perspectives on economic action, a few scholars have applied principles of new institutional economics to account for them. Even if transactions organized in markets and within firms are considered the major types of economic organization, "hybrids"—like franchise arrangements—can be important ways of combining the transaction cost advantages of markets and hierarchies. On this view, business associations seem like "hybrid" forms of organization. For Ben Schneider and Richard Doner, for instance, associations may operate within an industry to "reduce transaction costs, promote or restrain competition, extend or restrain rent-seeking" (as well as "lean on the state to protect property rights," see chapter eight). Search, bargaining, and enforcement and monitoring costs of transactions within and beyond industry boundaries may encourage collective action in associations to improve firm-level efficiency.[5]

Some economic sociologists have drawn loosely on transaction cost principles propounded by economists. For instance, some suggest that associations may offer particular advantages to economic actors in industries where organizing interfirm compacts is difficult, because of large numbers, spatial dispersion, and heterogeneity, as well as high fixed costs, ease of entry, and substitutability of goods. Similarly, Kim Weeden conceptualizes associations of individuals in business as potentially increasing and channeling diffuse market demand and signaling quality of service. Even in their critique of a transaction costs theory of associations, Marc Schneiberg and Rogers Hollingsworth argue that transaction cost theorizing can account for how associations are *routinely* organized and operated. In such arguments sociologists are suggesting that organization in associations can, in some circumstances, provide for members' economic interests in stability and profit by reducing costs that would be associated with unorganized competition, or worker training, or with accessing diffuse markets.[6]

The idea that particularistic strategic interests in reducing transaction costs explain associations' strategies of action may seem self-evident, or self-evidently necessary. However, we might also expect that rational, strategic business owners and managers would demand some evidence-based cost/benefit assessment of this assumption, at least occasionally, whereas there is no sign that associations are asked to provide such evidence or see any other reason to address such questions. As one association partisan complains, "many businesses take their trade associations for granted," and "have no way to evaluate whether they are getting true value," perhaps because they treat associations like any other nonprofit and "regard their association as they would some caregiver pleading for time." Equally important, not only do members themselves seem to need no evidence of associations' benefits, scholars have ignored the question too, conduct-ing almost no systematic investigation of whether associations really do reduce transaction costs or improve efficiency of members.[7]

As Mark Granovetter and many other economic sociologists have argued, transaction cost theories tend to hold the principle that different organizational forms like firms, markets, or associations are selected according to their relative efficiency simply as "an article of faith." In the absence of research-generated evidence the idea that association mem-bership usually reduces transaction costs for members seems just such an article of scholarly faith.[8]

Collective Economic Interests and Political Conditions of Economic Action

Many economic sociologists have argued that new institutional econom-ics is flawed by "just so" stories and post-hoc functionalism, and empha-size political conditions of economic action. They understand interests as political-economic rather than simply economic, and often distinguish between outcomes for particular economic actors, like associations' con-stituent firms, on one hand, and industry-level, collective interests and outcomes on the other.

Granovetter, among others, suggests that new institutional econom-ics makes implausible assumptions about how markets *and* firms actually operate, because markets are less anonymous and firms less internally authoritative than economists assume. Hence he argues for more detailed empirical attention to the actual interrelationships within which economic action is "embedded." However, regarding business groups, he confines his discussion to groups like Korean *chaebol*, Japanese *keiretsu*, and similar Latin American and Southeast Asian groups, explicitly excluding trade *associations* from his analysis because "their activity has less to do with operations and more with negotiating and affecting the institutional and governance arrangements under which their industry proceeds." So this approach leaves unexamined American associations' actions and consequences for industry-level performance.[9]

Schneiberg and Hollingsworth assess more directly whether transac-tion cost principles explain business association activity, but focus on the unrepresentative minority of American business associations that set price and production levels. They argue that the emergence and longer-term survival of even these sorts of associations depends on factors miss-ing from the transaction cost paradigm.

While firms mobilize this associative strategy in order to regulate relations in which they find themselves vulnerable to the strategic behaviour of others, the relations at issue do not involve prior transfers of goods and service, and the extent to which firms find themselves vulnerable does not depend on the nature or properties of exchange relations. Instead, the principal object of the price and production association is to regulate horizontal relations among non-transacting competitors, and the shift from market to collective self-regulation is far more sensitive to industry and political factors than it is to characteristics of transactions.

This argument shifts questions about how associations pursue economic interests from the level of the individual economic actor to the collective level. Leaving aside the question of individual benefits, associations respond to political conditions, and to intraindustry power relations with upstream suppliers and downstream markets, to protect economic interests of "industries" identified and considered collectively. They note that associations may be "a reaction to the market power or organizational efforts of an industry's transaction partners" or to "potential or actual state regulation." For these collective interests, association activities like cooperative creation of standards, or education, may minimize "industry" costs or promote efficiency. Collective economic benefits in association are also implied and sometimes examined in the governance theory of Hollingsworth and others discussed in chapter two.[10]

Whether business associations actually produce collective economic benefits for their "industries" is almost as understudied as their putative production of particularistic benefits for their members, and for similar reasons. There is little solid evidence for consistent and generalized economic benefits of business associations for the groups they represent. Gerald Berk and Marc Schneiberg find that some 1920s associations improved the performance of their industries when they helped develop strategies of uniform cost accounting and benchmarking. Scattered hints in other research on other questions imply more indirectly that associations sometimes improve industry-level economic performance. For instance, some economic sociologists argue that associations could affect collective-level economic performance when interorganizational networks are important for firms. Associations may encourage other collective strategies in industries; for instance, consortia founded by business associations "started larger and experienced more frequent but smaller multiple member growth events" than other consortia. One study finds participation on technical committees links firms to potential allies. Another model hypothesizes that given explicit conflict over industry technical standards, standardization committees are likely to produce more efficient outcomes than market competition (even leaving aside other committee functions like sharing information, active product design, negotiating compromises, and testing standards).[11]

These hints about potential economic influence of associations are supplemented with evidence of a variety of industry case studies that, like Berk and Schneiberg's study, show associations active in moments of industry conflict and change. For instance, Michael Lounsbury and his colleagues show associations involved in solid-waste industry changes in the late twentieth century. Many other case studies mention associations taking at least walk-on parts in industry change—including, for instance, in electricity production, news, television, book publishing, finance, insurance, and agriculture. Such particular historical investigations do not establish widespread, consistent associational influence, but do suggest that associations' cultural production can be an important condition for occasional episodes of economic conflict and change.[12]

However, any isolated successes associations may achieve or claim along the preceding lines are vastly disproportionate to the proliferation of associations' routine programs of education, information sharing, standard setting, and research, and the energy and resources they routinely absorb.

Thus for most association members, and most "industries" most of the time, association contributions to their economic profit and stability are "articles of faith," and it is unknown, at best, whether there would be any great strategic or tactical loss to members if most of their programs vanished. *This is typical of institutions oriented to cultural production.* As Paul Hirsch points out (of culture industries), cultural "production" is often necessarily "overproduction" if viewed from a strategic point of view. Some meaning-making will turn out to be consequential in strategic games, but it is difficult to know a priori what will be consequential and what not, and when.[13]

How, then, are associations' economic purposes understood? What exactly do associations do to promote members' businesses and industry growth? Do different sorts of associations pursue different strategies of action? Most importantly, what meanings are developed to sustain routine belief in the power of business associations as an article of faith among economic actors who are, putatively, narrowly self-interested and strategic?

Intra-"Industry" Strategies of Action

However much business associations act as political interest groups, they actually focus far more on arcane topics that industry outsiders never consider and may barely understand. Easy as it may be for the average reader to bracket these concerns as obscure shoptalk, it is important to make the effort to grasp them, because they generate an enormous amount of collective action by business. This collective action is typically oriented to (1) education and training, (2) sharing information, (3) doing research, and (4) setting standards.

Education and Training

Forty percent of all business associations in the population—over 1,800—indicate goals and activities oriented to education and training. Most likely, this significantly understates the organized instruction business associations conduct. Over half of the associations examined in depth turned out to manage some educational activity. For example, the Firestop Contractors did not mention education as a primary purpose, but had an educational committee whose goals were:

- Create Installer Education Program and training standard.
- Maintain Educational Programs and Training Standard developed by FCIA.
- Start building material content for videos and CD Production.
- Create a training or educational session at each FCIA conference.
- Coordinate with and support other committees to include new industry information in educational programs.[14]

Many associations claim that "education" is a goal, a member benefit, or a reason to join. They include not only businesses involving "professionalized" services, like the Conference of Consulting Actuaries, which stresses "a diverse array" of continuing education, but also associations of manufacturers. Members of the Aluminum Anodizers Council are said to "gain a better understanding of anodizers theory and practice at . . . periodic 'mini-conferences.'" The Mulch and Soil Council offers a "Plant Managers Training Course on Weights and Measures." Even the Brick Industry Association, which does not emphasize education, offers a Brick Online Training Center with "highest quality training materials" as well as their "Brick University," with classes for "professional development."[15]

Such education may be oriented to owners and managers, their employees, or, occasionally, to students who might become members of "the industry." Some associations oriented to education make it a major focus and develop and maintain systematic, resource-rich educational strategies of action, like foundations and continuing education programs; others offer occasional seminars and conference presentations; and some simply count informational links and small scholarships among their offerings. As discussed in chapter four, the cognitive categories and practices of these educational activities embrace topics with distinctively high resolution and resonance for association members' economic action.

Sharing Information

Thirty-seven percent of all associations—almost 1,700—indicated goals and activities oriented to sharing management, financial, technical, or other information among members. Again, the real rate is likely higher: among associations examined in depth, 60 percent spoke of sharing information, with systematic and sometimes resource-intensive programs for doing so.

In a very general sense associations' cultural production is *all* about sharing information. However, information sharing is frequently articulated as a distinct purpose by associations and involves distinct strategies of action. Such programs included both top-down processes like "disseminating" or "providing" information and more horizontal processes like "discussion" or "exchange of ideas among members." For example, the United Lightning Protection Association "collects and disseminates information related to the industry," while the Association for Women in Aviation Maintenance sees itself as "providing opportunities for sharing information." The International Concrete Repair Institute cites as a member benefit its role as a "clearinghouse of information" providing "full access to the information you need to improve your knowledge and status in the industry"; the Irrigation Association claims to be "acting as a source of technical and public policy information within the industry"; and the Vacuum Dealers Trade Association publishes a magazine "dedicated to keeping the independent floorcare/cleaning retail dealer updated with current industry news, business tips, and new product development."[16]

Business associations see themselves as "sharing information" in their newsletters and magazines, their conventions, their many publications, their websites, and occasionally through direct consultations. For example, the North American Association of Food Equipment Manufacturers publishes a monthly magazine, *NAFEM in print*, which "corrals information from every corner of the foodservice equipment and supplies market and presents it to NAFEM members and industry constituents in a timely, comprehensive and focused manner." The Concrete Repair Institute chapter in Western New York held dinner meetings that "enhanced our understanding of the mechanisms behind concrete deterioration and what repair is most appropriate." The Brick Industry Association's "Brick Bookstore" offered over a hundred publications and videos, including "an abundance of free resources" on multiple technical topics. The Aluminum Anodizers offered a web forum for "exchange of information pertinent to the industry in a timely fashion." And members of a few technically focused and relatively resource-rich associations—like the Concrete Repair Institute and the Brick Industry Association—were invited to contact association engineers or technical committees directly with questions.[17]

This shared information is sometimes business related, but most often technical. Among their functions, informational channels serve to develop the sort of organized instruction discussed above. And sometimes—though not commonly—the shared information draws on another organized strategy of action common in business associations: research.

Research

Thirty-five percent of all associations indicate in the *Encyclopedia* census goals and activities generally oriented to research, such as surveys, compiling statistics, forecasting, analyzing trends, or assessing economic impact. This measure captures organized "primary" research (sponsored or conducted by the association), in contrast with routine "secondary" research associations do in assembling and sharing information (above). Again, it is a low estimate: 44 percent of associations examined more closely do or sponsor some "primary" research.

Associations' research is sometimes systematic and institutionalized, though more often occasional. A small minority of associations has dedicated staff and committees routinely producing technical and business research. One of the International Society of Hospitality Consultants main activities, for instance, is the "ISHC CapEx Report," a survey of five hundred hotels they claim is the "most comprehensive summary of capital expenditures" and "excellent resource data" for the hospitality industry. More commonly, associations produce occasional or intermittent research reports. For instance, the Food Equipment Manufacturers conducted a biennial "Size and Shape of the Industry Study" in nine volumes, on topics like "Refrigeration and Ice Machines" and "Serving Equipment." They also issued the occasional "Wage and Benefit Study" and generated reports like the "Handbook of Steam Equipment." And some associations sponsor research only occasionally for particular purposes. For example, the Mulch and Soil Council conducted "a month-long investigation into the differences between the numerous Spanish language dialects spoken in the U.S." before adopting a Spanish translation of their certification logo.[18]

Overall, associations' research activities are less common than their strategies of action oriented to education and to sharing information. The immediate purposes of research vary, but research questions usually address intraindustry concerns, which may be business related or technical. The quality of the research varies as much as its purpose and frequency. Nevertheless, we can estimate that somewhere between fifteen hundred and two thousand associations do some research, a significant volume of neglected cultural production oriented to economic action.

Certification and Accreditation

In the overall population, 24 percent of associations indicated goals and activities oriented to collective endorsement by setting standards for certification of products—for example, automotive lifts—or accreditation of expert skills—for example, property management—in the industry, occupation, or business represented. Many associations have programs of both types, like the Food Equipment Manufacturers, which develops multiple industry standards and runs a highly developed Certified Food Service Professional accreditation program. Looking beyond the thin data of the association census, setting standards is even more common. Seventy-two percent of associations examined in depth included a certification or accreditation program among their offerings. Many were a minor activity. But at least 44 percent of the focal group conducted institutionalized, systematic certification or accreditation programs. For example, the Firestop Contractors were very proud of the elaborate work that resulted in their FM4991 Approved Contractors accreditation and certification standards like the "ASTM E 2174 inspection standard draft for joints." These associations operate between one thousand and two thousand serious national standards-setting programs. Although most do not result in elaborate rankings, they suggest that associational life is an important arena for exploring further some of the basic social processes underlying commensuration.[19]

While both certification and accreditation involve collective, rationalized processes for establishing and maintaining standards intended to orient economic action, the organizational strategies of action they entail for associations differ.

Certification usually involves working with one of a number of independent standards bodies, like the American National Standards Institute. For example, the Mulch and Soil Council conducts a detailed, legalistic, and expensive certification program for different categories of mulch, and newsletters routinely list newly certified and recertified products. "Products must pass stringent screening at the time of application and will be subject to random field testing directly from the market place." Four types of products may be certified (e.g., "Landscape Soils and Soil Amendments"), and they are formally licensed to bear the MSC logo. Applicants are provided with detailed instructions, complete a three-page application form, and pay application and renewal fees. The program description includes a complex flow chart involving a program administrator, an external laboratory, certification committee, standards committee, an appeals board, the association's executive director, and their board of directors.[20]

Internal skills accreditation programs are even more elaborate, but do not usually involve independent third parties. For example, the Irrigation Association conducts an accreditation program, involving a board of directors; continuing education and biennial renewal; twenty-seven courses on topics such as "Landscape Drainage Design" and "Job Site Leadership Skills"; six certification areas (earning for successful irrigators the respective designations CIC, CID, CAIS, CGIA, CLIA, and CLIM); three-hour closed-book exams scheduled frequently every month in different locations; numerous textbooks; and a newsletter with information on topics like supporting documentation and lists of those who had recently achieved certification. They certified 1,200 people in 2003. The Electronics Service Dealers support an even more prolific and long-standing certification program.[21]

Even in this severely abbreviated overview of associations' intra-"industry" strategies of action, their scope and volume is striking. One need not be interested in garden mulch to be impressed by the organizational effort that has gone into certifying good mulch; the technicalities of golf course irrigation may be abstruse, but the energy that goes into education on the subject is intriguing. The scope and volume of this sort of collective action in each of these social worlds is extraordinary given their vast number and seeming distance from generic social life.

Variations in Intra-"Industry" Activities and Types of Associations

Do different types of associations pursue different strategies of action? Do some focus more on intraindustry goals and activities? Do some favor the different intraindustry goals to different degrees? The association census provides some answers to these questions.

First, stronger formal organization was associated with orientations to the four intraindustry goals:

- Larger associations expressed all four intraindustry goals more than smaller associations, especially educational goals. Two-thirds of associations below median size expressed at least one internally oriented goal, compared to four in five associations above median size.[22]
- Associations reporting committees, or other affiliated groups, were more likely to express internal goals, regardless of the type.[23]
- Better-staffed associations were more often interested in research, and in education, with the tipping point at around four staff. However, there was no significant relationship between staff numbers and claims about standards and accreditation, and sharing information.[24]

Second, and highly significant, internally oriented strategies of action were rarely associated with interest in political claims-making (see chapter eight). This (unusual) absence supports differentiation between external and internal orientations of associations and suggests that internally oriented activities are not undertaken to strengthen industries' political claims.

- Location in the DC area was either negatively or unrelated to intraindustry goals. Associations interested in sharing information, and in research, were slightly less likely to be located in the DC area; associations doing education, or standards and accreditation, were equally likely to be in DC as those uninterested in these goals. Overall, seven in ten associations in the DC area expressed some internally oriented goal, compared to three-quarters not located in DC.[25]

Third, there were some minor differences in types of associations favoring different intraindustry goals and activities:

- Associations with individual members, versus firms, were much more likely to claim an interest in education, and somewhat more likely to claim an interest in sharing information and standards and accreditation. Associations composed of firms were very slightly more likely to claim research as a goal. More generally, 69 percent of associations composed of firms, but 78 percent composed of individuals, expressed at least one internally oriented goal.[26]

- Ongoing associations founded in the 1970s/'80s were more likely to claim education and sharing information as goals than the population as a whole or than associations formed in the two preceding decades. However, founding decade little affected interest in research, or in standards and accreditation.[27]

- Although many associations in all sectors were oriented to each intraindustry goal, there was some patterning of goals by sector. Associations primarily located in agriculture and in manufacturing well exceeded the population average in their interest in research, and in standards, but fell below average regarding education and sharing information. Associations primarily located in services exceeded the population average in all four intraindustry goals, particularly in education. More generally, interest in any intraindustry goal correlated with sector: in some, like wholesale, or information, fewer than 70 percent of associations expressed one or more intraindustry goals, while in others, like utilities, and "professional, scientific, and technical services," over 80 percent did.[28]

Overall, more recently formed associations of individuals in service-oriented companies would be more likely to express interests in goals internal to "industry" activities, especially education and sharing information. An association of manufacturing firms would likely be interested in research, but not so much in education and generally sharing information. Those associations located in the DC area, smaller, and composed of firms were somewhat less likely to express any intraindustry orientation.

But this is a matter of minor shading. Too many associations of every type are interested in intra-"industry" goals and activities to strictly partition the population, and the large majority of associations in every measured category expressed some intraindustry goals. For instance, among the focal associations, the Aluminum Anodizers and the Envelope Manufacturers did education, the Closure Manufacturers and the Pellet Fuels manufacturers shared information, and the Hospitality Consultants and the Real Estate Brokers did research—all counter to the minor correlations noted above. These intraindustry strategies of action are a repertoire of organizational practices, a repertoire best seen as a cultural property of the business association as an institution, rather than as a set of particular activities conducted by particular types of associations, or particular types of economic actors.[29]

However, the widespread flourishing of practices oriented to education, information sharing, research, and standardizing, as well as their obscure variety, demands further explanation. Why do business associations bother? Why do members go along when the North American Association of Food Equipment Manufacturers offers a "Certified Food Service Professional" (CFSP) accreditation, when the Automotive Lift Institute spends years researching safety labels, when the Concrete Repair Institute offers a discussion list, or the Envelope Manufacturers start an educational foundation?[30] We have explored in previous chapters many of the latent functions of such group activities. We can now examine more closely how these activities are meaningful as strategies oriented to the pursuit of economic interests.

Strategic Vocabularies of Motive and Intra-"Industry" Strategies of Action

What vocabularies of motive make association activities meaningful in association subcultures? Do discourses about economic interests provide rationales? If so, are they interests of specific members, or collective interests of the "industry"? To what extent are different types of interests distinguished in associations' operations and the ways they are understood and reconciled?

Particularistic Rationales for Intraindustry Strategies of Action

Claims about direct economic advantage accruing to members compose a subordinate vocabulary of motive for association activities in which association members' particular economic interests are supposedly promoted by educational, informational, research, and standardizing activities. Sometimes networking, collective marketing, and discounts were also understood as selective benefits of association membership.

Deliberately isolated for analysis, these claims echo a classical economist's assumptions about isolated, self-interested economic actors. Why do businesspeople associate? Because, the Irrigation Association suggests at one point, membership "rewards your *business* . . . and your career."[31]

Educational activities were sometimes seen benefiting members' economic performance. For the Vacuum Dealers Trade Association, an association of 2,200 independent dealers "providing avenues to increase sales, communication, service, market share and profit for all independent vacuum and sewing retailers," "educational seminars are just one of the tools the association uses to reach its main goal." At their Convention and Show in Las Vegas, members could brush up on topics like "Competing with Mass Merchandisers" and "New Central Vacuum Technologies." Information, too, was sometimes treated as a direct member benefit. For the seven-hundred-member North American Association of Food Equipment Manufacturers, the mission of their lively and well-produced quarterly magazine, *NAFEM in print*, is to keep "NAFEM members, as well as many equipment and supplies channel readers . . . up to date on the issues that affect their success in the foodservice industry."[32]

Research could occasionally be tied directly to members' particular economic interests. The Food Equipment Manufacturers industry study was presented as a "tool for strategic planning, goal setting, product development, category rationalization, manufacturing investments, acquisition strategies, distributional analysis and more," and the "ability to accurately define our market share is a tool most of us have not enjoyed."

The often-arduous processes of certification or accreditation also offer particularistic member benefits. According to the Mulch and Soil Council, certification is a means of product differentiation and "protects your product name from being identified with poor quality products . . . [in] . . . sensitive times when we are all only one headline away from disaster."[33]

Several other types of association activities were sometimes understood as oriented directly to the particular economic interests of members: networking, collective marketing, and member discounts. Although "networking" was often seen as intrinsically pleasurable (chapter five), some groups understood it strategically, as a particularistic economic benefit for members. For example, face-to-face meetings with potential or actual suppliers and customers were sometimes seen as a direct benefit of exhibits. The Food Equipment Manufacturers argued that "this age of email and cyber catalogs provides you with immediate access to plenty of information. But it can't replace the need to come face to face with your business partners—those individuals that equip your business for success—and experience the latest products they have brought to market." NAFEM's survey reported that over 80 percent of their exhibit attendees claimed interest in seeing new equipment and visiting specific manufacturers, and "to spark new ideas and foster profitable business partnerships."[34]

Services oriented to collective marketing are perhaps the most common basis of association claims that they provide members with particularistic business benefits. Some provide product and service information for pro-spective customers, some provide member directories explicitly oriented to marketing, certification and accreditation is sometimes seen as a mar-keting tool, and some suggest that membership itself is a marketing tool signaling "quality of service." For instance, although the International Concrete Repair Institute seems primarily interested in technical issues, it also suggests that "ICRI offers many marketing opportunities to . . . ICRI member companies," opportunities including advertising discounts, a "who's who," an online directory, and regional marketing through chapters. The president of their Rocky Mountains chapter suggests to members an "underlying perception" among potential customers

> that companies that belong to such organizations are committed to ongoing education, process improvement, quality and reliability. . . . Consider using your affiliation and designation as an ICRI member as a competitive advantage in the marketplace . . . the fact that your firm is a standing member of a profes-sional organization whose purpose is to improve the quality of repair, restora-tion, and protection of concrete . . . [M]y affiliation with ICRI has helped me to enhance my companies [*sic*] reputation and build confidence with a client which eventually helped to close a sale.[35]

Ironically, however, the most obvious economic benefit members might derive from association is also the least emphasized. Association mem-bership can provide access to "preferred pricing" (Aluminum Anodizers Council), "reduced rates" (Exhibit Designers and Producers Association), "special programs" (Vacuum Dealers Trade Association), or "affinity pro-grams" (Brick Industry Association). For most associations, these cost advantages applied only to the association's seminars, reports, conventions, and so on. The very few associations in the focal sample to elaborate on direct cost-saving benefits for members—small business groups like the Vacuum Dealers, the Equipment Service Association, and, as we saw earlier, the Small Publishers—emphasized their collective purchasing power for products and services like insurance, freight, and publications.[36]

The point of business associations is conventionally understood to be economic benefits they offer to their members, and associations do sometimes commit to this "article of faith" as they account for and pro-mote their activities, but they do so relatively rarely. This discourse of particularistic interests emerges in small islands within an ocean of more solidaristic communication about *collective* interests and technical matters among people committed to and absorbed by "lines of work." Considered in context, particularistic strategic claims are deeply fused with more broadly grounded, more collective, and less economistic discourses (see chapter five), just as we might see in any mutual-interest volunteer group.[37]

"Our Industry": Collective Rationales for Intraindustry Strategies of Action

Business associations usually express the *meanings* of their intraindustry strategies of action in terms of collective identities and collective benefits, rather than particularistic benefits. Moreover, these collective goods can sometimes be understood as responding to or protecting the industry from actions of industry partners—like organized buyers—or state regulation.

As we saw in chapter five, collective identity, over selective benefits, provides a vocabulary of motive even when associations answer the question "why join," which would seem to invite an answer in terms of particularistic strategic benefits. For instance, recall that the Closure Manufacturers' Association claims to provide nine informational and promotional benefits for members but sums up, emphatically: "Being a member of CMA illustrates a commitment to the closure industry, and it also provides an opportunity to give back to the industry." This is not an isolated instance. The Brick Industry Association lists marketing, research, informational, and discount benefits for members but also that members can "make a contribution to the association and industry through your participation." Another reason for becoming a member is to

> show your support for your industry and contribute to industry efforts in building market share. Let your customers know that you are involved in your national association with superior industry standards. The personal satisfaction in knowing that you and your company make a difference.[38]

These sorts of claims about collective identity are articulated in many ways that position the group and its members in relation to others (see, again, chapter five), and specify the cognitive, normative, and affective meaning of group membership. To reiterate, collective identity provides rationalizations for intra-"industry" strategies of action. Associations' collective action is usually oriented, implicitly or explicitly, to the benefit of "our industry."

For instance, the Brick Industry Association points to its Brick Show as "the only national exhibition for our industry." The Los Angeles–Orange County chapter of the International Concrete Repair Institute is a "committed group of individuals dedicated to improving our industry," and the members of their Rocky Mountains chapter are "building an organization dedicated to improving our Industry." The Envelope Manufacturers' Association is "THE premier organization united to support the paper-based communications industry," and its educational, informational, research, and political activities are all linked directly to this collective identity. They "speak with one voice when addressing the realities of the industry in terms of an electronic age." The Exhibit Designers and Producers Association is "the only organization that unites all segments of the exhibition industry," and "your support continues to fuel positive growth in our industry." As the Food Equipment Manufacturers articulates their core values, "we" are "dedicated to engaging our members in moving our industry ever forward" and will "provide leadership to improve the global foodservice industry." The Irrigation Association, like many others, makes awards to those who "contribute to the growth of our industry" to "honor the vision and dedication that are hallmarks of our industry"—and is, like many other associations (see chapter eight), "the voice of the industry." The United Lightning Protection Association "promotes National Safety Standards regulating our industry." The Pellet Fuels Institute "serves the pellet industry." The Mulch and Soil Council "promotes industry growth," provides "a voice for the industry," and honors members who "contribute to the improvement of the industry through ongoing training and education." The Vacuum Dealers Trade Association aims to "improve the industry as a whole."[39]

Intraindustry strategies of action oriented to education, information sharing, research, and standards are understood in terms of the collective advancement of the "industry"—like the Envelope Manufacturers' education, information, and research; and the Lightning Protection Association and the Firestop Contractors work on standards. Collective identity and collective performance are much more likely than particularistic benefits to provide a generic rationale for associations' work, and once articulated, the collective good then provides an assumed and implicit way of understanding particular association activities.

Particular Interests, Collective Interests, and the "Paradox" of Collective Action

This language about benefits to "our industry" would be senseless without the sustained construction of collective interests and collective identities we have seen in previous chapters. But how are the potentially contradictory languages of particularistic interests and collective identity reconciled?

What if members' (putatively preexisting) economic interests differ from the group's, or conflict with those of other members, or members could receive supposed benefits of association by "free riding"? Since these are voluntary groups some prospective members will surely never join, for this sort of reason. Moreover, more than one group is often associated with any given arena of economic activity. Unlike in national-legal settings where associational governance is stronger, American national associations rarely monopolize their fields. But if particularistic economic interests always trumped collective identity, these national business associations would not be the long-lasting, stable institutions that they are, and the initial puzzle of their existence examined in chapter two would be reprised here.

Reconciling Particularistic and Collective Interests

In practice connections between collective industry benefits and members' particularistic benefits are usually left vague and unexplored, with little attempt to claim any logical connection, nor to articulate any empirical "trickle-down" effect, from the advancement of the "industry" to the particular performance of members. Sometimes this creates glaring textual tensions as writers make ambivalent appeals to members' self-interests before dropping them for appeals to the pleasures and responsibilities of collective identity and occupational community.

Calls for active participation, not simply nominal membership, most clearly illustrate this sort of unresolved ambivalence. As one president of the Food Equipment Manufacturers wrote:

> These association commitments take up a lot of time. We spend money and ignore our real job responsibilities. We really can't justify these volunteer activities and social time. Right? Wrong! This time commitment is incredibly valuable. How often have you heard "business is all about relationships?" A few leading volunteers in the industry want to make industry-leading movements (and they do). But most association activists are involved for selfish reasons . . . who you get to know, what you can learn and maybe even, what you can sell. . . . What are the most important activities during association meetings? . . . The most important events: the morning coffee break, the evening cocktail hour, your foursome. . . . It sounds like fun and games. These are all reasons why your boss wouldn't let you go . . . besides, the resort location. It doesn't matter. You should be there. . . . The commitment to the association and events is really a commitment to continuous improvement, personal development, industry leadership, networking, increasing knowledge, and helping to clarify marketplace complexities. . . . You

should approach industry leaders. . . . Ask them if they regret spending their time
becoming more involved. . . . I can pretty much guarantee you won't find anyone
with regrets. As a matter of fact, they'll tell you that their volunteer efforts were
among the most meaningful and fulfilling of their careers.[40]

He starts with "selfish" reasons for active membership (which are
rather immaterial, certainly compared to pursuing direct strategic interests in firm stability and profit by reducing costs or improving efficiency),
but by the end he has shifted to active membership based on meaning and
fulfillment in collective identity.

Occasionally, the two vocabularies of motive are connected by specifying the basis of collective action as particularistic interests shared by
members, that is, the Tocquevillian solution of self-interest properly understood. For example, the Aluminum Anodizers Council aims, not exactly to pursue collective industry interests, nor entirely to serve members'
interests, but to promote "the common interests of our members." Similarly, the Independent Bakers Association was founded to "protect the
interests of independent wholesale bakers." Such formulations—aggregating some particular interests of members—are a logical compromise
between fully formed appeals to collective identity, which are common,
and full commitment to members' particularistic interests, which is rare.
This compromise formation is associated with explicit claims explaining
the power of collective action (an explanation unnecessary in a stronger
language of collective identity). As the Aluminum Anodizers explain,
"members together accomplish more," and "merging many individual
voices into a single greater voice, AAC can accomplish things individual
companies could never dream of." The Exhibit Designers, who speak of
both particularistic interests and collective identity, emphasize that "*there
is strength in numbers and that is Power with EDPA.*" Closure Manufacturers can "more effectively serve the needs of the marketplace by working
together as an association rather than by members acting individually."[41]

Alternatively, rhetorical ambivalence is avoidable by emphasizing one
or the other vocabulary of motive. It is possible but rare that particularistic interests exclude any expression of collective identity, as we saw above
with SPAN. More often, associations pay little attention to particularistic
member benefits, emphasizing collective identity instead.

This highlights even more the significance of chapter five's evidence
that associations often articulated membership in terms of collective responsibility, of reciprocity or redistribution for the collective good of the

"industry." Particularistic benefits fade out of the picture. In this paradoxical rhetoric, the supposedly classic connection between particularistic
strategic interest and collective action is reversed. Members are called to
"show your support for your industry" (Brick Industry Association), "give
something back to the industry" (Closure Manufacturers' Association),
"play a vital role in the direction of the repair and restoration industry"
(International Concrete Repair Institute), and "ensure a healthy and
strong industry for everyone" (Exhibit Designers and Producers Association). One of the first things the International Concrete Repair Institute
notes when they talk of member benefits is that "the greatest rewards you
can reap as an ICRI member match the effort you put forth in the organization and grow exponentially from there." The Firestop Contractors are
emphatic about the responsibilities, as opposed to the benefits, of membership: members are offered the "chance to be part of a collective voice
in the growing firestop industry," and one president, in a distorted echo of
President Kennedy, exhorted members to "give back to the industry . . .
and expect nothing in return. . . . Ask not what your association can do for
you. . . . Let's get together, help shape our industry and grow."[42]

So a collective identity around shared orientation to a realm of economic action—to an "industry"—can create a rhetorical distance from
members' particularistic interests that even makes it possible to ask,
rather, how members contribute to the collective good. A large majority of associations adopted this vocabulary of motive. In so doing they
resolve putative collective action problems by attributing status to group
contributions.[43]

Of course, we cannot systematically assess here how members themselves understand and respond to the cultural work done by associations.
David Knoke's careful study of this question for members of other types
of national voluntary associations finds that "occupational and altruistic
motivations carry considerable weight in members' affiliation decisions,"
and, against Olson's theory of selective incentives, "public goods, in the
form of normative inducements, are among the strongest factors motivating member contributions," such that "the centrality of noneconomic,
public-good incentives cannot be denied." Unfortunately his survey did
not include members of business associations.[44]

No doubt, as with collective identities such as nationality or race or religion, collective occupational identity is central to the self-understanding
and self-presentation of some members, for others it is one among many
identities, while some view association membership in terms of particular

incentives. We can expect that the salience of such collective identities (by contrast to others) will vary with context, ranging from strong and intense expressions by core members during convention rituals, to minor appeals to shared identity of peripheral members when appropriate to a conversational interaction. We can also expect that members will vary in their evaluative attachment to occupational collective identities asserted in association, from committed to critical to cynical.

Business Associations and the "Paradox" of Collective Action

Conventional assumptions that social life is fundamentally the strategic pursuit of particularistic interests immediately raise the puzzle Olson famously framed: how to motivate collective action when "free riding" is possible? And the problem seems acute when dealing with supposedly strategic economic actors. Some scholars follow Olson in asking when and how collective action in business associations is possible when members' goals are supposed to be inherently competitive.[45]

Those concerned with this question typically respond by differentiating types of organizations. Generally, they suggest that voluntary business associations may be small, homogeneous, exclusive, and undifferentiated—providing nonrival, excludable goods to all members—or larger, more inclusive, and differentiated in membership and organizational structure—mobilizing members with selective incentives. In the former, members' goals are "isomorphic with the group." Small, narrowly based memberships might increase the plausibility of "shared interests" and decrease internal governance problems. Alternatively, larger and more diverse associations, where "transaction costs" of linking members might be higher, may survive through the provision of "selective benefits" only to members, such as discounts, joint marketing, or employment information. Members are thought to have a more instrumental relation with such associations, and the management role is more differentiated.[46] The implication is that some associations are collectivistic, some particularistic.

In support of this distinction, one organizational study of manufacturers' associations found they were normally distributed between small and homogeneous ones, with implicitly shared interests, or large and differentiated ones, offering "particularistic goods as an instrumental basis for membership." However, other research on associations of manufacturers concludes that they tend to be *both* small and focused on providing selective services to members: "while the primary activities of associations tend to be oriented to providing 'collective goods' . . . benefitting their industry as a whole, 'selective services' are relied upon to attract members who otherwise might choose to free-ride on the efforts of industry leaders." As we have seen, while most associations describe themselves in terms of collective purposes rather than selective benefits, many also provide a standard package of membership benefits, such as otherwise unavailable information or discounts. Most, in fact, simultaneously adopt both strategies—collective identity and selective benefits—that putatively resolve the problem of collective action by business.[47]

Closer examination of the evidence suggests other reasons that the "two-track" solution to Olson's puzzle is implausible. If we take Olsonian assumptions seriously, (potential) interest diversity could be irreconcilable even in small associations. Contrary to conventional wisdom, associations often include members from more than one sector or "industry," this internal diversity was often considered an important feature, and there is some evidence that internal diversity helped associations survive (see chapter three). Even associations drawn from only one "industry" often include both large and small members, whose interests may differ due to associations' reliance on member contributions, and we have seen illustrations of this in examples of stratified contributions categories.[48]

The evidence of association discourse also challenges the "two-track" solution to the Olsonian puzzle. If different sorts of associations resolved the supposed problem of motivating collective action differently, then their discourses should vary accordingly. Small, homogeneous groups would generate discourses of collective identity along the lines of the Electronics Service Dealers' newsletter, which claimed "there is great personal satisfaction in belonging to a society of better-than-average professionals. There is also pride in supporting projects that improve conditions within, and elevate the status of, the electronics profession—as well as boosting the image of the technician," while large, diverse groups would stress particularistic benefits, as when the Food Equipment Manufacturers claim that their accreditation program helps "assist you as an individual in furthering . . . knowledge and standing in the industry." But smaller, supposedly more homogeneous associations and larger, more diverse associations *both* combine particularistic and collective vocabularies of motive and emphasize the latter. Both the Electronics Service Dealers and the Food Equipment Manufacturers mixed particularistic claims with claims about collective identity, and in this resembled the population generally.[49]

Thus analysis of business associations using theories emphasizing pursuit of particularistic economic interests explains little about their organization or their discourse and creates more puzzles than it solves. As Neil

Smelser puts this point more generally, the "individualistic-utilitarian perspective" of Olson and others on socially structured motivation generates
"unwanted paradoxes and unnecessary resolutions of those paradoxes."
The alternative to both Olsonian organizational resolutions envisions active cultural construction of shared interests transcending and generating
particular interests in all associations.[50]

Collective Interests and "Industry" Governance

Associations' intraindustry strategies of action are usually understood as
oriented to collective economic interests of the "industry." Claims about
collective economic interest usually require assumptions about collective
identity—"our industry"—(but may occasionally be parsed as aggregated
sums of particularistic benefits accruing to members).

Such collective identities enable the pursuit of "industry" interests as
understood by scholars of industry governance and economic sociologists
like Hollingsworth and Schneiberg (above), who focus on strategic interests and outcomes at the collective, "industry" level. Viewed thus, strategic
pursuit of collective "industry" interests may be a relatively benign matter
of coordination, but is often an inherently political process of offensive or
defensive maneuvers vis-à-vis upstream and downstream "industry" partners, the state, and labor.

So far we have focused on ongoing, mundane cultural production. *Most*
cultural production is "overproduction" from a strategic point of view. But
episodes of conflict and change do emerge within stable sets of institutions, discourses, and strategies of action, and then associations' intra-
"industry" strategies of action may be influential. Associations' routine
cultural production can become important institutional resources and
cultural conditions during "unsettled times."[51]

Historical case studies are the most direct way to learn about associations' episodic influence on industry change, once we know enough about
associations to understand the general implications of specific findings.
But even the cross-sectional association stories available here provide
clear evidence of a few associations involved proactively or reactively
in episodes of industry change. Here I illustrate how some associations
used routinely developed strategies of action to address industry uncertainty and improve industry coordination, first in the face of technological
changes, then in examples in which association members' relations with

others in the industry were at issue, and, finally, in an extended analysis showing what all this industry coordination and industry politics looks like in an active group of manufacturers who make commercial kitchen equipment for buyers like McDonalds.

"Industry" Coordination and Technological Change

In some associations, education, information sharing, research, and standard setting focused on "industry" change and coordination associated with changing technologies. Collective economic benefits—stability in changing circumstances, and better performance—were sought in elaborate discussion and reflection about how to coordinate relations between different "industry" actors with new technologies.

Several atypical business associations in the focal sample were *primarily* focused on coordinating new technologies. The International Telecommunications Society (ITS) included among its four hundred members very large private corporations, government and nonprofit organizations, and academics. Its purpose was to "share information and research . . . related to the emergence of a global information society" and "forge linkages between the research, policy, and industry communities." Its conferences were sophisticated discussions of research on technical, regulatory, and economic aspects of telecommunications policies. Even though the publications and conferences of this association had a decidedly academic tone, business interests were central, and their leader emphasized that without their large business members, the association "would find it difficult to fulfill its mission."[52]

The American Society for Automation in Pharmacy also focused entirely on understanding and coordinating newer technologies. Like ITS, it included different types of members: computer companies and hospital executives as well as executives of large pharmacy companies and owners of small ones. It was interested in the "industrial and technological changes facing the pharmacy market," and its meetings covered topics like digital security, simplifying transactions, and standardizing terminology in patient medical records ("Tearing Down the Tower of Babel").[53]

Many associations focused to some degree on issues of industry coordination in the face of new technologies. Similar sorts of topics and activities were addressed more casually and intermittently in processes of certification, conference papers, technical committees, educational programs, and industry research. For instance, a regional convention of Electronics

Service Dealers led to development of an "internet vehicle for scheduling service calls"—"primarily funded and maintained by participating manufacturers and Third Party Administrators." And the Food Equipment Manufacturers actively developed templates for coordinating e-commerce (see below).[54]

The Politics of "Industry" Coordination

Governance theorists and economic sociologists would see a political dimension to all this intra-"industry" coordination. Different interests may be at stake in the negotiation of relations between suppliers and manufacturers, manufacturers and distributors, insurance firms providing "retail" life insurance and those operating as "wholesale" reinsurers, large multibranch exhibition providers and "mom and pop" firms, independent electronics retailers and major manufacturers, pension actuaries and medical insurance actuaries. The strategic discourse of associations working for the collective interests of "industries" is usually dominated by a worldview of benign coordination, and it would be naive to see conspiracy and conflict behind their every activity. Nevertheless, governance theorists and economic sociologists are certainly right to point out the intra-"industry" *politics* of coordination in the face of threats and changes.[55]

First, the politics of production can sometimes lead to the formation of new collective identities in association in relation to external threats. The Independent Bakers Association formed because of concerns about mergers and acquisitions, and the International Concrete Repair Institute because of "the proliferation of unqualified contractors entering the industry" (see chapter five). In these cases, the politics of production encouraged intraindustry coordination grounded in newly organized collective identities.[56]

Second, and most importantly, collective identities rationalizing intraindustry coordinating activities as collective goods in the face of political-economic challenges sometimes appear in routine association discourse. Some associations in the focal sample were facing what they understood as significant industry threats, which evoked strong expressions of collective interests. For instance, after significant expansion in the exhibition industry in the late twentieth century—on one account, from 2,733 exhibitions in 1986 to 7,933 in 2001—the Exhibit Designers and Producers faced retrenchment: "The exhibit and events industry has suffered through trying economic times since September 11, 2001. As the economy begins to stabilize, EDPA is eager to forge ahead to educate, to connect, promote, and to be a voice for our members." And their outgoing president invoked collective responsibility a week after September 11: "By attending this year's convention we can all rededicate ourselves to the industry that helps sustain us."[57]

Less dramatically but probably more seriously, several associations were involved in a *politics* of intraindustry coordination, not the simple functionality implied by economistic theories. For instance, big-box chains like Home Depot influenced development of the Mulch and Soil Council's elaborate certification programs. And touchy issues emerged between Electronics Service Dealers and "upstream" electronics manufacturers in a context of general industry decline.

The Mulch and Soil Council connected its standardization activities regarding types of mulch and gardening soils to the needs and interests of powerful customers. Some of this was a high-level form of collective marketing; their June 2005 newsletter reported that council president Steve Jarahian, "In addition to meetings with EPA, Lowe's Corporation and Home Depot . . . traveled to Alpharetta, GA, to introduce John Deere to the MSC Product Certification program and urge the company to buy certified products." But the association's relationship with Home Depot quickly seemed to become closer than a marketing relation. By July they had programmed a Home Depot executive as keynote speaker for their conference; the company also sponsored a conference cruise. By September, Home Depot was welcomed as an associate member (even though associate members were defined as "providing a service to bark and/or soil producers"). In their November newsletter, the keynote address was the lead story. Emphasizing "commitment to providing safe consumer products, including mulch that does not contain CCA, lead, lead paint or C&D materials," the Home Depot speaker called for extending certification efforts and developing product lot coding "as a protection for producers and retailers in the event of a regulatory, industry or corporate recall or action." He also "expressed Depot's ongoing support for the certification efforts of the Mulch & Soil Council and its members." In January 2006, the council newsletter ran a detailed story on Home Depot's report to its own annual meeting. Apparently, powerful retailers like Home Depot were something of an industry threat encouraging coordination by mulch certification.[58]

The Electronics Service Dealers frequently discussed industry threats. For instance, their newsletter reprinted an article on "Latest Attrition Figures for the Service Industry," noting that "we are losing approximately 1,000 Electronic service centers per year." Here and elsewhere, industry

decline was seen primarily as a problem between servicers and manufacturers. "Electronics Servicers need to give more consideration to those
warranty providers who support them with higher rates and good product
support . . . and allowing the warranty provider who gives poor support
and low payments to go elsewhere for their service needs. . . . Our whole
industry suffers from a lack of self-esteem and therefore we tend to sell
ourselves short on the value of our service."[59] But "lack of self-esteem"
was not the only issue between manufacturers and electronics service
dealers, as commentary showed in subsequent years. Of course, "many of
us would like to see the manufacturers raise the prices on their equipment
when it's sold, providing everyone in this discipline a chance to survive.
We all know that we would have a better chance of it snowing in Florida in
August than that ever happening." But new luxury home electronics markets were opening up, and "it is our job to help educate the people who
manufacture these products on just how important it is to provide world-
class service. . . . Profits earned by a manufacturer should include a reasonable amount to provide for quality service during warranty." Too often
this issue was ignored; for instance, at an HDTV conference attended by
the NESDA president, "the service industry was not factored into their
thought process. I felt then as I do now that it is our job to help these entities realize just how important a role we play when consumers are making
their buying decision."[60]

   In some respects "our Industry Partners" were supportive and "mutually working towards industry solutions rather than increasing the severity
of these problems has become infectious." For instance, some electronics manufacturers supported NESDA programs and sponsored members.
NESDA also had an "Industry Relations Committee" that helped particular members with routine disputes, for example, about payments for warranty claims, and the chair of that committee considered that "NESDA has
a solid relationship with . . . every member of our industry. Our industry
partners are willing and eager to listen to us." Even he admitted, though,
that on some general industry issues "we have struggled and achieved
small gains at best." At this time, the larger issues were serious, even to the
point of considering "divorce":

   Choosing people or companies to partner with is no different than choosing a
   partner to share your life with. From time to time you must ask yourself if you
   believe that you are getting what you expected from the relationship. . . . Many
   of us within NESDA need to re-evaluate whom we choose to have relation-

ships with. . . . When an impasse is reached, then we need to put an end to that relationship and move on to a more nurturing one.[61]

For businesses making mulch, downstream relations with powerful buyers were changing, and these changes generated new collective efforts toward coordination. For businesses servicing electronics, upstream manufacturers threatened their interests by weakening provisions for warranty service, which they resisted with both voice and exit. The particular configuration of relations at issue and generating collective action by business will vary by production context and historical period, and economic sociologists have provided extensive accounts of industry politics and change along these lines. But we can see here that especially in times of industry change, collective identities grounded intra-"industry" coordination attempts as collective goods. Indeed, vocabularies of motive stressing collective interests—conditioned by the construction of collective identities—can develop a strikingly heightened emotional tone ("the industry that helps sustain us," "lack of self-esteem," "nurturing"). Here the pursuit of collective interest draws on discourses that are not only foreign to economistic perspectives emphasizing particular actors' economic interests, but also distant from perspectives emphasizing strategic collective interests. In such instances, vocabularies of motive draw directly on those associated with occupational community (see chapter five).

National Business Associations and Labor

From an outsider's perspective, conflicting interests between businesses and their workers might seem the most salient political issue in intra-"industry" coordination, but in these settings, other relationships are more likely to become politically charged.

Even in the early twentieth century, only a small minority of associations provided "surveys, advice, and assistance" about collective bargaining (see chapter two). Contemporary evidence, too, shows that "coordination" with labor—as an industry "partner" or as threat—is not an important goal or activity of national business associations in the United States.

The minor exceptions, when employees are mentioned as part of association members' work worlds, can be taken to prove this rule. As already seen, some associations' intraindustry activity included forms of worker training. And nonmanagerial employees sometimes participate in business subcultures when associations systematically integrate different

actors with similar technical orientations. The International Society of
Certified Electronics Technicians ran extensive programs that addressed
employment needs of their many worker members, as well as training
needs of electronics dealers, in close collaboration with the National Electronics Service Dealers Association. The Association for Women in Aviation Maintenance mostly spoke for women aviation technicians, although
large aviation companies and some of their executives were also members
and supporters. The technical interests of employees like designers were
integrated with business interests of firms and managers in the Exhibit
Designers and Producers Association (chapter five). Similarly, the Brick
Industry Association and the North American Association of Food Equipment Manufacturers provided some information and training of more direct relevance to employees than high-level managers and owners—as did
the Envelope Manufacturers' Association and the Pellet Fuels Institute to
a lesser degree. In all these cases, technical and "industry" identities and
interests encompassed some nonmanagerial employees as well as owners
and representatives of high-level firms. Only in the Women in Aviation
Maintenance were the employees the driving force of the association, but
there was no evidence of any high social boundaries or tensions between
workers and corporate managers or small-time owners in these contexts,
but rather, shared identity and interests.

An extremely close reading of the entire realm of association discourse
finds rare occasions—mostly asides in other conversations—when business owners and managers articulate employers' points of view on labor.
Most notably, the International Society of Hospitality Consultants made
"Human Resources" one of the "Top Ten Global Issues and Challenges
in the Hospitality Industry":

> Increasing demand requires increased staffing levels at a time when the labor
> pool is shrinking. To address this issue, the industry must attempt to work with
> the unions as allies, devote more time and money to recruitment and training
> and educate politicians as to the impact of governmental economic and immi-
> gration policy on the industry.

The Exhibit Designers had a conference session on "Current Employment
Law." The winner of the Electronics Service Dealers' "Best Ideas" contest
one year was a suggestion to use GPS on technicians' trucks for more labor control. And some associations involved in national lobbying activities
attended to changes in OSHA safety regulations and other topics affecting
employees, from the point of view of reducing "regulatory impact"; the

Independent Bakers, for example, state an interest in federal labor regulation. At this time, too, many associations talked a lot about coping with health care costs, an important issue on the broader public agenda.[62]

But examples like these are hard-to-find exceptions that emphasize the relative lack of labor issues in the discourse and programs of these national business associations. Similarly, a study of national manufacturing associations in the early 1980s showed a tiny minority devoting organizational resources to the issue. Considering the long term, union foundings and union density have had little effect on association numbers.[63]

This pattern is explained by the localization and fragmentation of American labor issues, a long-standing feature of the institution, which may have been exacerbated by weakened national business regulation in the late twentieth century. In addition to this institutional decoupling, the frequent focus of associations' discourses and practices of occupational community on technical excellence would also work to silence concerns about labor issues in the politics of intra-"industry" collective identities.

The pattern of much greater concern with other business conditions — suppliers, distributors, markets, and so on—than with labor found in this study also held in the 1930s, when the last comprehensive information was collected. But as Jeffrey Haydu has shown for local groups in the nineteenth century, class formation in the course of associations' cultural production can influence indirectly the contours of labor relations, and to the extent contemporary national associations are comparable, such indirect influences on labor politics might still be possible in some industry contexts. And since business associations' varied and multifunctional cultural production is precisely suited to collective reflection on new economic circumstances, they would likely be an important site for the reconfiguration of labor regimes in any major new politics of production that emerges in the future—just as they have been a site for collective reflection on new technologies of coordination.[64]

The Politics of Industry Coordination and the North American Association of Food Equipment Manufacturers

Associations sometimes turn their mundane strategies of action to the pursuit of collective economic interests in "industry" coordination and defense in changing and contentious circumstances. We can take as an extended example the North American Association of Food Equipment Manufacturers (NAFEM), a large, active association with multiple programs spanning most of the typical association activities, which they turned to improving intraindustry coordination, responding especially to powerful downstream customers.

Founded in 1948 and located in Chicago, the North American Association of Food Equipment Manufacturers had a large staff of thirty and a membership of 625 manufacturers of commercial food equipment and supplies, as well as multiple nonmanufacturing associate and affiliate members, and claimed to account for 85 percent of the US market (a rare dominance among associations). We have already seen them "dedicated to engaging our members in moving our industry forward"; running an elaborate certification program; producing a large market-oriented biennial exhibition and several other annual meetings; publishing technical information, educational texts, and several magazines; providing research reports on the industry; and providing training for employees. They also get involved in lobbying on issues like steel prices and safety codes.[65]

Their coordination efforts address multiple "industry" relationships especially by developing, publishing, and discussing standardization of transactions. One of the resources they offer is the "NAFEM XML Transaction Standard," which includes boilerplate documents like purchase orders, invoices, and payment orders. Similar "transaction standards" are included for product service. Another document provides "Recommended Guidelines for Foodservice Equipment Catalog Specification Standards." Relations with customers were also rationalized in a "Specifier ID System" (SIS), which included around nine hundred companies; they pointed out to participants that the association covered its "ongoing administrative expenses." NAFEM also developed bar code and product identification standards in a "NAFEM-sponsored initiative involving associations, companies, and individuals . . . manufacturers, dealers, and operators" and aiming to "create efficiency within the global supply chain." They were unusually conscientious in fulfilling what they saw as the collective responsibility of "lowering transaction costs."[66]

At this time NAFEM members participated in a particularly active "Foodservice E-Commerce Group" with related associations. The group addressed the "great need for industry standards to power e-commerce" and drafted standards that "will be made available to the industry at no cost." The E-Commerce Group discussed and published "white papers" on intraindustry coordination issues, with detailed technical information and assessment of coordination issues well beyond the understanding of outsiders. One detailed assessment of benefits expected of an "All-Industry Approach" included "reduce[d] transaction costs . . . timely information . . . [and] more accurate information." But while the committee hoped for a "best of all worlds" solution, they saw "challenges" in "industry buy-in and support" of a "unified approach."[67]

Relations with distributors and manufacturers' representatives were another topic of much discussion and attempted standardization. NAFEM cooperated with the Manufacturers Agents for Foodservice Industry association (MAFSI) in multiple activities, including the Foodservice E-Commerce Group and joint training programs and conferences. One formalized coordination effort developed "Principles of Decision," a "collective attempt . . . to help define and augment the complex partnerships between independent manufacturers' representatives and the manufacturers they represent." The document included many sections of details on these relationships, like "Food Service Industry Roles," "Hiring and Evaluation Considerations," "Compensation," "Training and Education," and "Representative Councils."

But along with the specifics, it reflected extensively on principal/agent relations, including a sociologically informed analysis of "The Power of Trust in Relationships" that dealt, inter alia, with the advantages of procedural justice over distributive justice, principles of procedural justice, and jointly created performance recommendations (e.g., representatives' recommendations for manufacturers, manufacturers' recommendations for dealers, and so on).[68]

Many of these new programs arose after a 2001 reorganization. Some years later, one leader reflected that "we were coached by channel partners" in the process. They had cooperated on some projects with multiple associations representing salespeople, distributors, commercial food equipment service technicians, and with the National Restaurant Association, as well as Purdue University on training. But this leader gives special credit to a "Customer Advisory Task Force" that "helped us develop a game plan that will enhance the effectiveness of our members and channel partners." Although institutional markets in schools, hospitals, and so on also seem to have been important, this task force included mostly major restaurant chains like McDonalds, Arby's, Burger King, and Wendy's. It "meets quarterly with NAFEM officers . . . to provide feedback to the association on issues impacting operator/manufacturer relationships," topics also covered extensively in other NAFEM documents and publications.[69]

NAFEM was unusual in publishing a separate newsletter for downstream buyers ("operators"). Although it managed extensive and complex relations with multiple "channel partners" the motivation behind everything we do is our belief that the end-user—the foodservice operator—is the ultimate customer for all channel partners, thus allowing all segments of our industry to be more effective in the marketplace. Furthermore, coming to this agreement fosters NAFEM's working relationships with allied partners and their constituents, and helps our organization better focus programs and services to meet the fundamental needs of our members.[70]

Prioritizing the "end-user" gave direction to many other relationships, activities, and goals.

The direct influence of powerful and organized customers was explicit in two NAFEM standardization programs mentioned earlier, the NAFEM Data Protocol and the "Principles of Decision." The Data Protocol allowed standardized exchange of data directly between commercial food equipment and PC workstations (e.g., on times and temperatures, performance diagnostics, or energy use). It originated when "major U.S. restaurant chains, recognized the potential efficiencies associated by linking individual pieces of commercial kitchen equipment and began working with NAFEM to develop an industry-wide set of rules, or protocol, to allow the exchange of data between independent pieces of commercial equipment and a personal computer . . . working together for an all-industry solution, NAFEM and chain representatives created the NAFEM Data Protocol."[71] The "Principles of Decision" detailed guidelines in relations with sales agents. These guidelines had become necessary, they say, because of "confusion, especially among the dominate [dominant] buyers and financial analysts, as to . . . the sales, marketing and service efforts of the supplier [sic]":

> Why the confusion? . . . First, the factory and representative partner have done a poor job unilaterally and bilaterally communicating their value to the buyer and accountants. Second, the balance of power has shifted. Thanks to the rise of super chains, buying groups and a consolidating wave of mergers and acquisitions, a relative handful of customers now control an enormous amount of business. Manufacturers that had dominated their customers are now finding the customer now holds the upper hand [sic]. The customer is trying to control the supplier's sales and marketing function acting in the name of cost savings, but without an accurate understanding of their actions.

Again, powerful downstream buyers generated efforts at collective industry organization—although in this case, it is not clear to the outsider how the guidelines will really remedy the problem.

The coordination solution is analyzed and presented mostly in ethi-cal terms (before being spelled out in detailed practical recommendations with apparently little relevance to customers).

> This shift raises some important questions. Although powerful companies can, and often do, use their strength to wring concessions from their vulnerable counterparts, is the use of fear or intimidation the most effective way to manage such relationships? Or does trust produce greater benefits? And if trust is more beneficial to both sides, what policies and procedures can help it grow?

Two weighty pages of ethical analysis later, the introduction concludes:

> The guidelines you are about to review are the result of many hours of collab-orative work from MAFSI and NAFEM volunteers and staff in meeting today's marketplace realities. Without the power of trust this project never would have been completed. In the spirit in which these guidelines are being provided, use them with equal passion in the marketplace in augmenting your partnerships with the manufacturer and/or sales agency personnel.[72]

For NAFEM as a whole, the changes wrought by powerful customers' dominance were usually presented in a less critical and more upbeat way than here. But that itself was no doubt the outcome of intra-"industry" political shifts. Although at any given time coordination, standardiza-tion, and negotiation can be routine, institutionalized, and uncontentious, it often represents stable outcomes of intraindustry politics in previous episodes of change. At this time, increasing retail concentration was put-ting many manufacturers at a new disadvantage (as in the Mulch and Soil Council's work with Home Depot).

In all this industry coordination, NAFEM was much more systematic and comprehensive than most associations. But the NAFEM story shows how and why associations' established intraindustry strategies of action might matter strategically.

Conclusion

Earlier chapters have shown that American business associations are cultural institutions producing not only cognitive but also normative and expressive meaning for economic action in business. This cultural per-spective treats interests as a product of meaning-making that is reliant on disinterested solidarity and associations as an important site of that meaning-making. This perspective seems to make light of conventional assumptions that associations' core feature is simple strategic pursuit of business interests. One could treat the cultural production and the economic interests as entirely different parts of association life, but I reject that easy solution and show, instead, how the cultural account encompasses the simplistic economic account.

The idea that associations pursue business interests has been interpreted in two ways. I first examined the individual-utilitarian view that associations' actions are strategic for particular members' stability and performance because they reduce their transaction costs. Next, I discussed the more sociological view that associations promote *collective* economic interests of "industries" (however defined) by providing coordination and control.

The claim that associations improve the economic performance of either their members or their "industries" consistently and on a scale matching the scale of their activities is simply another "article of faith" of the sort Granovetter and others have identified among the claims of transaction cost economics. However, scattered evidence suggests that associations' routine programs are occasionally consequential in episodes of industry change and contention. Thus from a narrowly strategic point of view, cultural production is necessarily overproduction.

Associations operate on this article of faith when they consider economic interests; as the Concrete Repair Institute put it nicely: "the *philosophy* of the group is that if the quality of work is improved ... the demand for ... products and services will increase, and the image of the concrete repair industry will be elevated" (emphasis added).[73] Mostly, they seem fueled by the sort of unexamined faith in the general value of collective identity and collective action that is associated more with religious or political action than with economic action.

How do associations sustain this article of faith? Associations pursue economic interests with such intraindustry strategies of action as education, information sharing, research, and standard setting. Because this realm of activity is almost entirely unknown, I developed a new picture of these activities, their prevalence, and the minor variations in types of association adopting them.

I then asked how associations understand these activities as economically strategic. I illustrated the way associations sometimes claim their intraindustry strategies of action are beneficial for particular members' economic performance, but showed that this particularistic understanding was quite rare. The most common meaning attributed to intraindustry strategies of action by associations was the collective good of the "industry," and where particular and collective interests might not coincide, members could be exhorted to work for the greater good. This emphasizes the importance of the collective identity and solidarity we explored in chapter five. And such solidaristic understandings of collective economic interests were not confined to smaller or supposedly more homogeneous associations, as scholars who have problematized free riding and collective action have supposed.

Finally, I have shown that associations' tactical pursuit of economic interests can sometimes result in episodes in which associations promote or respond to industry change—for instance, by coordinating "industry" integration of technological innovations, or changing relations with upstream or downstream "partners." As economic sociologists have emphasized, their pursuit of "industry" interests in these sorts of situations is frequently politically charged, though not always. Tactics adopted in these episodes are made possible by the more fundamental but routine institutional reproduction of cognitive categories, networks, and fields discussed in chapter four. The North American Association of Food Equipment Manufacturers shows just how detailed, complicated, and thoughtful the mobilization of intraindustry strategies of action in moments of change and contention can be.

Like almost all previous accounts of business associations, this chapter has assumed that the interests meaningful in business associations must be capitalist interests in stability and profit. However, most capitalists have occupations, as well as business interests, and intra-"industry" collective action often focuses on technical issues proper to particular occupations and work processes. This suggests that association activities may be more oriented to "professional" development and to building and defending bodies of specialized expertise.

CHAPTER SEVEN

"The Highest Level of Professional Recognition"

Business Associations and Technical Excellence

"Doctor. Lawyer. Minister. Service Manager. Of course they fit together! They're all professions." So argued the North American Association of Food Equipment Manufacturers we last saw in chapter six coordinating relations with powerful downstream buyers; many other associations, too, understood their activities as oriented to their various members' presumed interests in "professionalism." Few scholars have noticed that business associations are as likely to understand their strategies of action in terms of "professionalism" as to see them more economistically in terms of industry stability and profit. Businesspeople in association are often preoccupied with issues generated by the technical, rather than the social, division of labor—the intrinsic technical features in an arena of production or line of work. They are concerned with excellence and honor on the job. The language of professionalism provides an important vocabulary of motive for associational strategies of action.[1]

So far, we have seen that American business associations present a puzzle that is best resolved if we focus first on their institutionalization of active cultural production, and—more fundamentally—the ways they articulate solidaristic disinterest in occupational community for businesspeople. On this foundation we began exploring how they understood strategies of action oriented to intra-"industry" concerns—education, information sharing, standards, and research. We saw that the particularistic economic interests of members provided only one subordinate language accounting for these activities, and that a discourse of collective "industry" interests, sometimes subordinating the particular business interests of members, provided a more common way of articulating the point of these actions. Although business associations sometimes account for their activities in terms of the direct benefits they provide for members, more often they understand activities like education, information sharing, research, and standardization as grounded in collective identity—usually the "industry"—and oriented to collective interests. Such an understanding would be impossible without the construction of solidaristic disinterest we saw earlier, in chapter five.

The larger point of this chapter is to show that a cultural account of business associations and "disinterest" in economic action is supported by associations' strong orientation to technical excellence and "professionalism" ("the highest level of professional recognition") in addition to their orientation to collective "industry" benefits ("growing the industry"). In episodes of heightened conflict and unsettled times, this orientation may be mobilized in market or occupational competition, just as chapter six showed that languages and practices of collective identity and collective good might occasionally become resources for mobilization in industry change and conflict. But a mundane and routine orientation to professional language and practices transcends and overflows any strategic value it might offer, operating as an intrinsically powerful way of understanding business.

Occupational community evokes shared experience "on the job" as much as "in the market," and for association members the technical features of their work process can attract as much interest as their market position. As they account for their various collective strategies of action, they draw on a discourse highlighting expertise and grounded in members' position in the (shifting) technical division of labor, as well as discourses related to their position as market actors in the social division of labor. A language of professionalism is important in this context because it highlights the intrinsic technical features of a line of work and the excellence and honor that can be associated with technical competence.

This observation is difficult to reconcile with standard distinctions between professionals and businesspeople, and I question the way theories of the professions treat business in the next section. I then analyze how languages of professionalism are mobilized in business associations to account for intra-"industry" strategies of action—sometimes casually, but frequently in elaborate programs. I argue that a strong theoretical distinction between "professional" and other occupational communities, including those of businesspeople, cannot be sustained. Any line between collective action by "professionals" oriented to occupational jurisdiction and collective action by businesspeople oriented to market stability and success is blurred not only by professionals' sometimes camouflaged pursuit of their economic interests but also by businesspeople's explicit interest in abstract, technical dimensions of their work.

Professional Claims and Market Interests

The institutional logic of business and the institutional logic of professional life are usually counterpoised and presumed to involve very different discourses and strategies of action. All the associations in this study are nonprofit associations of *profit-oriented* economic actors—mostly profit-oriented firms, owners, or top executives (although also sometimes employees)—because the collective organization of business in association is so little understood and sometimes seems more counterintuitive. But this distinction is slippery and hard to maintain. Magali Larson's observation that "profession" is "one of the many 'natural concepts,' fraught with ideology, that social science abstracts from everyday life" remains true today.[2]

Professions are commonly understood to be those occupations that rely on established bodies of abstract knowledge about problem solving to exercise some degree of autonomous control over their work. National associations are often active in the production and reproduction of professions, both in making claims to occupational control and in producing and policing access to bodies of abstract, specialized knowledge; licensing, examinations, specialized education, ethics codes, and journals are also typical traits. Control over work is justified with authority and prestige deriving from "general cultural legitimacy, increasingly the values of rationality, efficiency, and science."[3]

Professions and professionalization have sometimes been viewed as disinterested and functional for society, in the sense that professions' organized, independent expertise in solving social and personal problems justifies their exclusiveness, expert judgment, and legitimate control over work. In this perspective, "the meaning of the professions, both for themselves and for the public, is not that they make money, but that they make health, or safety, or knowledge, or good government, or good law"; they systematically reproduce a broader, more generalized perspective that provides a protected cultural space to mediate competing claims of individual, state, and market. Most commonly, though, sociologists see them as less disinterested than this. In this view, they are occupational groups seeking to legitimize social closure with monopolistic rules and practices protecting autonomy in the workplace, and providing control over the work process. Control over the work process may include authority over clients justified with expertise that dismisses practical experience. As Andrew Abbott points out, "a long-standing literature has seen the professions as a risk-averse upper-middle-class strategy for class reproduction," a strategy relying more directly on cultural than economic capital.[4]

While this straightforward critical view remains powerful, most scholars have also emphasized the empirical complexity of the professions as a social form. As Dietrich Rueschemeyer notes, different occupations, clients, and historical traditions "make it unlikely that we will find one modal pattern of organizing professional work in all modern societies, as much earlier work on the professions suggested." Even within one national setting, "professional power is inserted in a broad and complicated political field—more complicated than a profession's relations of authorized power with 'the public,' and broader than a profession's efforts to enlist the state in its defense." And professions' relations with a variety of other occupational groups, as well as the state and the public, generate even more empirical complexity.[5]

For these reasons, but particularly due to what he sees as their competitive relations with other occupations, Abbott challenges the tendency to see professions as discrete and enduring. Professionalization is not an independent and unilinear development; rather, professionalization is a relational and contingent historical process involving socially recognized claims to jurisdictional control over work in competition with other groups. The always-temporary resolution of these claims depends on interrelations with other professional or protoprofessional groups. Historically contingent processes of professional formation and decline may result not only in dominance (like medicine) or decline (like spiritual mediums) but various intermediate divisions of labor. Historical nuance and contingency replaced structural assumptions in theories of professions.[6]

For theorists of professions like Larson and Abbott, professional claims to jurisdictional control over work are distinctive not only for their organizational forms (accreditation, specialized training, etc.) but also for their content: professions are "carriers and creators of discursive authority." They are grounded in a specialized, formalized abstract knowledge base linked to work tasks of diagnosis, inference, and treatment. For Abbott, this attention to the substance of distinctive professional cultures is important because it distinguishes professional and protoprofessional jurisdictional claims from other forms of interoccupational claims-making:

Abstraction is the quality that sets interprofessional competition apart from competition among occupations in general. Any occupation can obtain licensure (e.g., beauticians) or develop an ethics code (e.g., real estate). But only a knowledge system governed by abstractions can redefine its problems and its tasks, defend them from interlopers, and seize new problems—as medicine has recently seized alcoholism, mental illness, hyperactivity in children, obesity, and numerous other things. . . . If auto mechanics had that kind of abstraction, if they "contained" the relevant sections of what is presently the engineering profession, and had considered taking over all repair of internal combustion engines on abstract grounds, they would, for my purposes, be a profession.

Abstract knowledge claims applied to concrete problems are important not only for the pursuit of occupational jurisdiction but also for broader cultural authority of professions with the state and the public.[7]

Well-formed professions, then, are occupational groups that successfully make jurisdictional claims *in competition with others* on the basis of *abstract knowledge.*[8]

But this emphasis on abstract knowledge claims as a core feature of professions is not straightforward. One important ambiguity emerges at the intersection of professions and capitalist markets. On one hand, scholars such as Larson and Eliot Friedson point out that professions are seen as at least "quasi-autonomous" from markets:

Professions acted in the name of a different kind of cultural authority; and they represented a different principle of allocating jobs and delivering services than the free market . . . professionalization movements brandished a meritocratic creed and ideas of collective welfare while seeking institutional shelter against the rigors of competition in protected markets. In this sense, professionalization is an accessory to the historical counter-movement in which Karl Polanyi included peasant and labor efforts to arrest or moderate the destructive advance of the capitalist market . . . the professions represent, like crafts and guilds, an *occupational* principle of order in the division of labor, opposite to the free market's fluidity and to the detailed formal hierarchies of bureaucracy.

On the other hand, professional claims are seen as advancing not only autonomy and status but also the *market* position of some occupational fields, and any separation between market-oriented action and professional work is increasingly blurred.[9]

Indicative of this ambiguity, otherwise excellent empirical studies of industries discuss professionals and professionalization in two distinct ways.

For instance, Patricia Thornton argues in a study of changes in the publishing industry that "case studies illustrate that institutional logics embodied in the professions are antithetical to the goals and means of control of corporations." In contrast, Michael Lounsbury finds that the professionalization of money managers and the rise of professional money management firms "went hand in hand with instrumental rationales—efficiency and [economic] performance" (even though the rise of money management was characterized by the development of an abstract body of financial knowledge) and suggests that we "revise the standard conceptualization of professional control of work as a form of social organization that is distinct from the organizational control of work." Similarly, Denise Bielby and Lee Harrington note that as an international market for television syndication formed, trade associations were established not only to consolidate marketing but also to establish members' "legitimacy as professionals." Overall, sociologists have no clear view on whether profit-seeking businesspeople may also be professionals. As Rakesh Khurana shows, the professionalization of business management in the United States displays an analogous, though deeper, ambivalence in its historical development.[10]

There are four initial reasons to think that an orientation to business in the associations here must be fundamentally different from a professional orientation to an occupation.

First, in broad-brush terms, we might think that since business owners and top executives control the work of others, their interests would not usually lie in pursuing greater control over their own work process. Clearly, though, such assumptions neglect more than a century of "the organizational revolution"—if profit-oriented action is located in bureaucratized and often-large organizations, we should expect that those who control the labor of others, as well as those whose labor is controlled, might develop occupational as well as market interests. Indeed, David Grusky and Gabriela Galescu have argued that class interests, identities, and collective action are *primarily* located at the occupational level, blurring any distinction between market-oriented class action and "professional" occupations. Groups of profit-oriented actors might seek control over their work process (as well as over labor and transaction costs) even if they are more often seen as market actors than workers or professionals.[11]

Second, specific historical tensions may sustain a distinction between the world of business and the occupational world of professionals. Abbott notes that although professions originated along with the expansion of capitalism in the nineteenth century, they mostly "stood outside the new commercial and industrial heart of society. . . . They were organized in a collegial manner that was distinctly anachronistic." Developmentally, professions "have tended to shed direct links with commodity sales" and their authority is sometimes challenged by the commodification of abstract knowledge. Thornton's study of book publishing, mentioned above, provides a related example. However, if we see professions as occupational groups that are (contingently) successful in their jurisdictional claims *in competition with others*, these historical tensions do not indicate that markets and professions are different institutional realms, but rather that distinctions between market-oriented and professional action are part of a broader politics of occupational distinction, as Julia Evetts has argued.[12]

But third, even if it is not generally valid, the presumed tension between market action and professional claims-making may still characterize American business associations in particular, because their claims to jurisdiction over work are legally restricted by the same legal framework that restricts other forms of overt anticompetitive action. For instance, while many business associations may provide accreditation to their members, they may not legally restrict accreditation to members only— although they generally offer discounts to members on registration and training costs. Legal limits to "jurisdiction"—or what would be explicitly labeled monopoly in such cases—mean that if we were to see their pursuit of occupational interests as the pursuit of jurisdictional claims in law, we must also see them as permanently failing. But legal arenas do not exhaust opportunities for jurisdictional claims by professions. Public opinion is also important—and as we will see in more depth in chapter nine, some business associations do court public opinion in this way. Moreover, even many organized professions do not seek or achieve *legally* enforced jurisdictional settlements in their competition with other potential professions, and, indeed, Abbott emphasizes the historical contingency and variety of outcomes of jurisdictional claims.[13]

Finally, even if professional associations are not necessarily distinguishable from business associations by the presence or absence of market orientations, another reason to doubt that most businesspeople could be "professionals" lies in the substance of their claims for jurisdictional control. For Abbott, as we saw above, professions are characterized by a particular sort of jurisdictional claim for control over work—the creation and institutionalization of abstract knowledge. However, despite the empirical breadth and historical depth of the cases of professionalization and protoprofessionalization he describes, the assumption that businesses do not attempt to develop bodies of abstract knowledge transferable to new

tasks and problems remains unexamined. Cases such as those of Lounsbury's money management firms suggest that this assumption is questionable. And Khurana's history of American business schools shows them
pursuing just such a cultural project from the late nineteenth century, even
though, he also argues, that project was distorted by short-term market
interests in the late twentieth century.

Overall, these observations suggest that although business and the professions are usually thought to differ, there is no a priori reason to make
a sharp distinction between what American business associations do and
what professional associations do: the issue requires empirical investigation. If occupational groups develop and pursue jurisdictional claims on the
basis of abstract knowledge systems in professional associations, business
associations may also pursue the interests of their members in occupational
control and distinction. Business associations' strategies of action may be
oriented to the interests of their members in control over work, rather than
their immediate market interests. Claims to abstract specialized knowledge somewhat distant from immediate market issues may be important
resources for claims to distinction and jurisdictional control. Perhaps the
Firestop Contractors understand their developing education programs as a
means of pursuing interests in jurisdictional control. Similarly, information
sharing, research, and standardization—in offerings like the Concrete Repair Institute's "clearinghouse of information," the Telecommunications
Society's research publications, or the Irrigation Association's certification
program—may be understood as "professional" activities detached from
immediate market interests and aimed at increasing occupational control
and prestige. If business associations understand their activities in this way,
we should also see evidence of jurisdictional competition with other occupations, and of the use of formalized knowledge to "seize new problems."

Professional Discourse and Strategies of Action in
Business Associations

A discourse of "professionalism" provides a pervasive vocabulary for
American business associations' intraindustry strategies of action. It allows
communication about and expression of interest in the intrinsic technical
features involved in an arena of production or line of work, along with or
beyond the business interests association members understand themselves
as sharing. Although scholars interested in professions might hesitate to

think of concrete repair contractors or exhibit designers as "profession-als," and scholars interested in business associations have usually seen them simply as oriented to their firms' and industries' stability and profit, the associations and their members have no trouble transposing languages of professionalism to market-oriented contexts. In this world, almost any-one may be a *professional* if they are serious about what they do. The term can take on some of the same floating signification that the term *com-munity* also accrues in vernacular language. Not all business associations appeal to the language of professionalism, and as we will see, associations vary in the extent to which they institutionalize "professional" practices, with only a minority pursuing the well-developed strategies of action asso-ciated with traditional professions. But as a way of articulating the nature and purpose of economic action, *professionalism* is more common than explicit appeals to particularistic economic interests.

Vernacular "Professionalism" as Honorific

In some cases and contexts, the *professional* label is used casually, as an honorific, and in ways that would be unremarkable except for our ste-reotypes of professions. For instance, the International Concrete Repair Institute is said to have "grown into a conglomerate of restoration and repair professionals" since its founding in 1988. It points out that its "peer networking" is the sort of benefit that is "the greatest value to any profes-sional organization," and the president of its Carolinas chapter writes of "this world we have selected to spend our professional lives pursuing." The Association for Women in Aviation Maintenance was "formed for the purpose of championing women's professional growth and enrichment in the aviation maintenance fields," and its information-sharing and educa-tional pursuits are understood in these terms: among the criteria for all its awards is "professionalism." And the Vacuum Dealers Trade Association offers certification seminars and classes "taught by experienced profes-sionals in the industry." In such cases, the language of professionalism evokes a claim to the status of disinterested service, but it also evokes an involvement in and commitment to specialized technical knowledge that a straightforward language of business interests cannot express.[14]

The Exhibit Designers and Producers Association mixed talk of pro-fessionalism with the other languages of particularistic interests and of collective identity in which it understood its various activities, but profes-sional talk remained a subordinate language for them, and compared to groups like the Food Equipment Manufacturers and the Electronics Technicians, its institutional apparatus for professional claims-making was only aspirational. In an article on "Training and Accreditation for Tomorrow's Designers," one writer reflected:

> The exposition industry is now finally recognized as a career profession. It was not always that way. Most of us who have succeeded in the industry have had training and attained college degrees in everything but exhibition design and trade show marketing. Our training backgrounds have ranged from degrees in Marketing and Architecture to Microbiology and Finance. In spite of this variety in training . . . we have successfully managed to grow into our career skills as "expositionologists" through on-the-job training. EDPA has worked hard over the past five years to carve paths of education that encourage exhibit design as a career profession.

At this time, four programs were cited as evidence of professionalization: (1) the creation of "UL2305 Exhibit Safety Standards," (2) the beginnings of a program in exhibit design at the University of Nevada at Las Vegas, (3) a program for introducing high school students to the exposition industry as a career opportunity, and (4) a certification program "under development." Education, standards, and accreditation were linked to professionalization. But three years later, there was no sign of an accreditation program in EDPA's lively magazine, newsletters, and web documents. In fact, one common theme of theirs—that their convention offered education—suggested little had changed: "The Trade Show and Event Marketing profession is not taught in colleges and universities. Industry leaders have gained a great deal of their knowledge from experience and from EDPA educational programming and networking opportunities."[15]

So in some associations, the label "professional" was a somewhat casual honorific. The Exhibit Designers and Producers sometimes spoke of themselves as professionals and had tried unsuccessfully to institutionalize some of the apparatus of professionalism. But in this sort of case, the discursive categories in which they understood their various programs and their collective action mixed professional talk with a stronger emphasis on collective identity and interests, particularistic interest, or occupational community (even when speaking of activities like education closely associated with "professionals").

Larson has noted that the "sense of work well done . . . is still a component of the folk concept of 'professional,'" and that this is part of the "interactional and intimate effects in everyday life" that make professionalism a "disciplinary" discourse in Michel Foucault's sense. The term works to draw distinctions between the domain of occupation and work, considered as technical and ethical practice, on the one hand, and *both* intimate and market relations, on the other. The positive effect of the boundary it draws is to identify a sphere of action associated with work life with its own independent discourse and normative practices. To take another sort of example, Abigail Saguy found that American feminist activists also drew on such a discourse of professionalism in their claims-making about sexual harassment. "American activists argued that one should be 'professional' at work. This means being productive and maintaining social distance with coworkers." She suggests that "arguments about professionalism and productivity are especially effective in legitimizing particular positions in the American context." Like those business associations using "professional" as a casual honorific, but lacking the institutionalized strategies of action and abstract knowledge base sociologists identify as features of "genuine" professions, these activists are appealing to a strong vernacular understanding of "professionalism" as normative practices in a work setting.[16]

Beyond this more casual appeal to professionalism in making sense of what they do, other associations made the language of professionalism a dominant strand in their discourse. Sometimes professional languages related to information sharing and research; more often, they were used to speak of education and accreditation activities. Different associations adopted professionalized vocabularies to different degrees in different contexts.

"Professionalism," Information, and Research

Information sharing and research are centrally important to the International Telecommunications Society (ITS), whose four hundred corporate and individual members are said to be "professionals in the information, communications, and technology sectors." Their goal is "to research and analyze issues related to the emergence of a global information society," and

> ITS achieves its goals by providing forums where academic, business, and government researchers as well as industry practitioners, policy makers, representatives of international bodies, and consultants present and discuss research results, and may interact in spontaneous ways. . . . ITS disseminates research results and news to its members and the general public via traditional and electronic means.

Although ITS members are drawn from a wide range of organizational settings, and its public officers and activities make it look more like an academic group than an industry group, the topics it deals with are predominantly business-oriented treatments of technical issues and related regulatory and industry issues; for instance, "industry structure implications of the emergence of Applications Service Providers" and "emerging entrants into telecommunications from industries such as electric, gas and water utilities or transportation companies." Newsletters and journal issues treat topics like "Bundling Strategies and Competition in ICT Industries," and the society helps publish books on topics like *Global Economy and Digital Society*.[17]

Another association that conducts informational and research activities understood primarily in terms of "professional" languages is the International Society of Hospitality Consultants we have encountered in previous chapters, a "professional society" of 175 members that provides reports to "public and private hotel owners and investors, [and] many leading financial institutions." Members are owners or directors in their firms and "recognized as leaders in their respective areas of expertise." They are active in numerous other industry-related associations and meetings, like the "American Lodging Investment Summit," and they publish articles on issues like "Financial Challenges for Indoor Waterpark Resorts." The association itself "regularly researches and reports on key industry issues," publishing reports like "New Europe and the Hotel Industry," and offers extensive informational resources in its library and bookstore; it also emphasizes the access it provides—and exposure it offers—to members' own industry publications. A sort of informal accreditation process operates because—unusually among these associations—membership is by invitation only. The association emphasizes that it provides a "worldwide pool of hospitality expertise and counsel of the highest competency, creativity and integrity. Society members are client-attested and peer-reviewed, assuring prospective clients of unassailable expertise in hospitality problem solving and trustworthy counsel."[18]

"Professionalism," Education, and Accreditation

Whereas information and research are only occasionally understood in "professional" terms, education and accreditation are frequently characterized this way. Real estate brokers, food equipment manufacturers and their associates, irrigation contractors and their associates, electronics dealers and their service technicians, vacuum cleaner dealers, and actuaries (as well as the exhibit designers mentioned above) all invoked languages associated with professionalization in at least some of their programs. These programs often involved many of the trappings of professionalization—specialized education and examinations, special letters for credentials, special publications of technical and occupational interest, and (occasionally) codes of ethics.

As we began to see with the Irrigation Association's and the Certified Electronics Technicians' education programs in chapter six, these associations devote systematic organizational attention and resources to professional accreditation. The Irrigation Association (IA), which certified over a thousand people annually, offers thirty-two courses in seven different programs, organizes tests in locations across the country, publishes a newsletter with updates on the accreditation program, rigorously details and audits requirements for certification renewal, publishes course materials, and promotes the accreditation with related associations. Their statement of purpose speaks of "uniting irrigation professionals," of the "benefits of professional irrigation services," of "professional training and certification," and they want to "raise the profile and standards of our profession."[19]

Most other accreditation programs were equally well developed. The Food Equipment Manufacturers (NAFEM) often spoke of themselves as "food service professionals," and their Certified Food Service Professional (CFSP) accreditation was developed to "enhance professionalism within the food service equipment and supplies industry and to become recognized by peers, affiliated organizations and related industries." This is oriented to "all individuals within food service . . . no matter what their level of responsibility, experience and exposure or interaction with other . . . members of the industry is." They claim 1,100 qualified CFSPs overall, with eighty-three newly accredited recruits in 2003; NAFEM's board of directors, all CEOs or other senior officers of industry corporations, all hold the qualification. Their Certification Board of Governors administers a strong formal program with seminars, exams, continuing education requirements and credits, a bulletin ("stay connected with your fellow professionals"), and a code of ethics.[20]

While the CFSP qualification was encouraged for all the various members of the "food service industry," emphatically including corporate CEOs, NAFEM also ran a separate group, an "association within an association," for service managers, aimed at "enhancing and advancing not only the Service manager's position within the Foodservice Industry, but in peripheral areas as well, i.e., improving relations with service agencies, educating future service technicians, improving general management skills, as well as interpersonal relations." (This sort of closely linked group run from another business association could also be seen within other groups, like the National Association of Real Estate Brokers.) They had their own code of ethics and emphasized that "while there is no legal requirement obligating the service executive to adopt this code, its wide acceptance can be important to the development of a true professional." They also included an article by a Purdue University economist on the rationale for professional organization.[21]

The National Association of Real Estate Brokers (NAREB) also discussed their intraindustry activities in terms of professionalism. They encouraged "all professionals in the real estate industry to become members of a local chapter," their sales division aimed to "assist in the professional development of real estate sales professionals," and their women's council president asked "that you make a professional commitment today." In several divisions of NAREB the language was not simply honorific; their sections for appraisers, and for property managers, conducted extensive education and accreditation programs. The National Society of Real Estate Appraisers, a part of NAREB, was "dedicated to promoting the highest standards of professionalism among its members" and was "recognized as one of the three top appraisal organizations in the country." For these appraisers, the standard professional apparatus of training, examinations, ethics code, and so on led to designations at three levels—RA, CRA, and MREA.[22]

Blurred Boundaries: Business or Professional Association?

In some associations in some contexts, professional identities and programs were so strong that the market orientations of member firms, or the industry, were rarely explicit. The languages and practice of the International Telecommunications Society was "professional" in this way, as was that of the appraisal division of the National Association of Real Estate Brokers. In such contexts, distinctions between professional and business associations are hard to sustain. The distinction occasionally seems to disappear completely, as it did in one of the focal associations, the Conference of Consulting Actuaries (CCA). With both discourses and strategies of action that are almost entirely "professional," the Actuaries seem at first to make a useful contrast establishing how exactly professional and business associations differ. On closer examination, however, they differ only in degree from the electronics technicians or the irrigation contractors.

These actuaries consult on pension programs and life, health, or casualty insurance, with various specialties within these fields. Their association, with over 1,100 members, operated with five staff and extensive member participation in its numerous committees, which included a disciplinary committee, a continuing education committee, and an arbitration task force, as well as the usual committees for membership, publications, conference program, nominations, and budget and finance. According to its mission statement, the CCA "strengthens both the practice of actuarial consulting and the ability of its members to better serve their clients and the public." It aims to "advance the knowledge of actuarial science," "promote and maintain high ethical standards among its members," "enable actuaries . . . to assemble to discuss common problems," "promote the interchange of information among actuaries and the various actuarial organizations," and "keep the public informed of the profession and of the responsibilities of the professional actuary in public practice."[23]

Members of the CCA were typically executives of consulting firms, which could range in size from under twenty to over fifty actuaries. They might also work in settings such as insurance companies, other corporations, government, or academic teaching. Admitted members were accredited as Enrolled Actuaries, and, depending on their experience, could become, for example, Fellows (FCA) or Associates (ACA) of the conference. All were required to "be highly proficient in the scientific and practical application of the mathematics of financial contingencies and of other techniques relating directly or indirectly thereto" and "have professional and business qualifications, moral character, and ethics that are beyond reproach." Practically speaking, the CCA specifies in formal legal detail three types of professional standards, or Actuarial Standards of Practice, developed by an independent "Actuarial Standards Board." (The standards also apply more generally to members of all "the five North American Actuarial Organizations.") Members are required to maintain continuing education credits that could be fulfilled with educational activities like seminars.[24]

The association offered many seminars on pension, health, and business topics, as well as a major annual meeting. Proceedings of the conference were published annually, along with other related informational publications and magazines. A closer look at a program for their Enrolled Actuaries meeting offers a sense of the sorts of topics that concern consulting actuaries, even if the technical dimensions are opaque to outsiders. A list of every sixth panel in the three-day meeting includes:

Practicing Professionalism
Investment in Nonliquid Assets
Recent Court Cases of Interest to Actuaries
Public Employee Retirement Benefit Workshop
Saving Private Retirement / Why We (Still) Have DB Plans
Small Plan Design and *Technical* Issues
New and Proposed Professional Standards
The Case for FAS 88—Case Studies in Pension Accounting
Paying PBGC Premiums in the 21st Century
Corporate In-House Actuaries
Contractors

Topics are indexed under headings like: "Accounting Issues," "Assumptions/Methods," "Defined Contribution Issues," "Funding and Schedule B Issues," "Health and Welfare," "Professionalism and Policy," and "Retirement/Consulting Issues."[25]

Doctors, lawyers, engineers, curators, librarians, social workers, and sociologists would all recognize the institution of the profession in the actuaries' group's language and practices. The accreditation, publications, standards of practice, and so on are all "professional." But the professional practices and discourses are also oriented to market concerns, and consulting actuaries are not interested solely in technical knowledge. Although the language and strategies of action are highly professionalized, and technical skills are emphasized for accreditation, the pursuit of business interests is integral to the Conference of Consulting Actuaries' understanding of its concerns. For instance, a seminar on Professional Standards preceding the meeting addressed questions such as, "What can I and/or my employer do to mitigate my exposure?" A roundtable on Small Consulting Firms & Practices focused on "running and marketing a small business." And a meeting on "Practicing Professionalism" addresses the following puzzle:

As actuaries, we have a professional obligation to our clients to provide the appropriate level of service for each engagement. However, for some engagements, there may be a conflict between our professional responsibilities and our business objectives. For example, our client may negotiate a fee that does not cover the scope of services you feel should be included. In a new business situation, we may try to outbid other consultants without considering the full scope of work that you would normally perform. The speakers address these and other situations and present guidelines to maintain our professionalism[26]

Actually, irrigation contractors and electronics dealers express rather similar concerns, and at about the same rate. There is little practical difference in accreditation processes of contractors like the Irrigators, or the electronics dealers and technicians of ISCET/NESDA. So is there any fundamental difference between professional and business associations?

Business as Professional, Professionals in Business

All these illustrations are typical of the adoption of professional languages and strategies of action in business-oriented groups. Sometimes this language simply articulates a sort of distinction based on occupational knowledge, purpose, and honor. Sometimes, the vocabulary of professionalism is linked with associational strategies of action only lightly, or with difficulty. Often, though, a language of "professionalism" provides a way of understanding associations' intraindustry strategies of action—information sharing, research, and especially education, and accreditation. In such cases, well-developed and well-established programs credential "professionals" in particular lines of work that are not typically considered professional occupations by outsiders. Notably, the language and strategies of action associated with professionalism are not restricted to service industries but can also be found in associations centered on manufacturing, contracting, and sales: the specific focus of the business or industry does not seem to determine whether or not it may be understood in professional terms. Occasionally, the professionalization vocabulary and programs are so fully institutionalized that the usual conceptual distinction between "business" and "professional" associations seems to disappear.

As we have seen, Abbott identifies the core features of professions as socially recognized claims to jurisdictional control over work in competition with other groups grounded in a specialized, formalized, abstract knowledge base linked to work tasks of diagnosis, inference, and treatment. Viewed historically, such claims-making by occupational groups is always a contingent and often a contested process that may result in intermediate settlements as well as full social recognition (or total decline) as professions. From one angle, the frequent adoption of professional languages and strategies of action in this focal group of business associations captures an important empirical site in this process, an "intermediate form" that is actually more likely to be the dominant form than "monopolistic" professions. Abbott notes:

> I have used the word "profession" very loosely and have largely ignored the issue of when groups can legitimately be said to have coalesced into professions: when or even how they become groups in the formal sense of acting in subjective concert.

The "professional" discourse and strategies of action we see flourishing in many business associations can be viewed (in the American context) as a vast pool from which those occupations that become widely recognized as "professions" emerge. But we can then go further and ask whether professions are really distinctive at all—whether, in fact, there is any such thing as a "profession." Perhaps socially recognized professions are only well-known instances of a more general process of involving two elements—occupational status politics and disinterested commitment to technical elaboration—seen in almost any work context.[27]

Business Associations and "Professional" Jurisdictional Claims

Many business associations articulate jurisdictional claims about control over work and adopt professional vocabularies and strategies of action to do so. Occasionally, they will do so in official settings like code hearings. For instance, the Firestop Contractors promoting their distinctive methods of fire prevention sometimes begin to resemble groups that pursue legal endorsement of monopoly, as when social workers must be licensed or lawyers accredited by state bar examinations. They were enthusiastically developing and promoting new code requirements for "Effective Compartmentation," as their president said of their work on their ASTM

2174 ("Standard Practice for On-Site Inspection of Installed Fire Stops"), "while the timetable to pass a code proposal can be years, we will continue to move this practice forward. This document is critical to the industry in that it raises the bar for installation credibility. It also places requirements on our competitors to maintain the same integrity levels. We will continue to lobby and develop this proposal." If ASTM 2174 became a widespread code requirement, their members would be well positioned to monopolize its implementation. But generally, with only a few minor exceptions—such as irrigation specialists in some states, and real estate broker licensing in some local areas—there is no legal monopoly associated with accreditation processes in business associations, and of course there could not be such a monopoly under antitrust law. Legal endorsement and official recognition is not usually possible in this context.[28]

As Abbott would point out, "professions" generally vary in their ability to enforce jurisdictional monopoly. But jurisdictional monopoly is not even mentioned or discussed in most business associations as an ideal goal. Rather, professional language and strategies of action can be used in attempts to signal comparative quality on the market. Rare discussion of the ways accreditation is in members' particularistic or collective interests refers to competition in the market. For most of these groups, interests in jurisdictional control over work are necessarily pursued in the market, and the vernacular and theoretical distinction between "professional" and "market" action is blurred.

For the Firestop Contractors, for instance, developing standards and accreditation procedures, the long haul of attempting to influence building codes was only part of their work. More immediately important was persuading their members that accreditation was worthwhile, and persuading those who hired them that their quality standards should be adopted. As they argued in one newsletter:

> Last year at this time, there were about 2–10 Projects out for bid . . . that had FM 4991 Approved Firestop Contractors as part of the specification. Today there are 67. . . . Reviewing your policies and procedures for firestopping quality is a good idea. Consider becoming FM 4991 Approved because a documented quality program is good for your business as well as fire and life safety.

They applauded qualified contractors because "FM4991 Approval means increased investment in the operations of their companies. FCIA applauds their added commitment."[29]

Most of the language and organizational apparatus of professional claims-making in business associations does not identify explicit competition with specific others; rather, and as for the Firestop Contractors, it implies a contrast to generalized, usually unnamed competitors on the market. Indeed, as a language of competitive interest grounded in claims about quality of work, professional vocabularies of motive in these associations seem rather vague and ineffectual. Theories that see professionalization as a relational process of occupational *competition* (rather than treating professions in isolation) often emphasize heightened episodes of conflict. Yet in many of these focal associations, we can see professionalization discourses and practices in a routine, mundane context. This is another illustration of the argument made in chapter four, that institutionalist perspectives need to be extended to examine routine, mundane cultural production that conditions occasional episodes of institutional change. The cultural production of professional rationales can be seen as a routine condition of occasional explicit moments of conflict, similar to the rationales based on the economic good of "the industry" seen in chapter six. The taken-for-granted institutionalization of professional vocabularies of motive and strategies of action persists to orient and account for action beneath and between such heightened episodes. As I also argue further in chapter eight, discourses operate differently in mundane contexts than they do during explicit conflict.[30]

Occasionally, as we might expect, some associations do articulate a connection between their professionalization programs and competition with explicit others. The International Concrete Repair Institute was at this time one of the most adamant of the focal groups in understanding its mostly very technically oriented activities as "professional." As we have seen, though, it was formed in 1988 out of "frustration about lack of standards and guidelines . . . [and] concern over proliferation of unqualified contractors entering the industry," who were "not properly trained . . . and were underbidding them without proper knowledge of surface preparation, equipment, materials, techniques, etc." And the president of its Rocky Mountains chapter wrote of the "competitive advantage" of "the fact that your firm is a standing member of a professional organization whose purpose is to improve the quality of repair, restoration, and protection of concrete." Such "competitive advantages are those intangible qualities your company has that make your company different then [*sic*] your competitors" because "the underlying perception was that companies that belong to such organizations are committed to on-going education, process improvement, quality and reliability." And the Irrigation Association's elaborate certification program was said to provide "nationally recognized certification" that "raises the profile and standards of our profession" with courses that "help working professionals . . . to learn and become more successful." They also provide information to the "Irrigation Consumer" on "How to Spot a Nonprofessional Contractor."[31]

In general, "professional" discourse and strategies of action in business associations are usually more oriented to claims-making in the market than to more formal—or more total—jurisdictional control. They differ from marketing, though, at least in their more elaborated forms, in one important way. They go beyond simple advertising or collective marketing in their emphatically technical grounding and often-rigorous requirements, and in the commitment to intrinsic technical quality often expressed in the discourse of professionalism.

Business Associations and Abstract Knowledge Claims

As we have seen, another core feature of typical professions besides claims for jurisdictional control is the production and organization of abstract as opposed to practical knowledge. According to Abbott, jurisdictional claims based on abstract knowledge "[enable] survival in the competitive system of professions" because they allow an occupation to "redefine its problems and its tasks, defend them from interlopers, and seize new problems." On this criterion, too, there is no clear distinction between business associations invoking professional discourses and strategies of action and more stereotypical professional associations.[32]

Certainly, they mix different forms of knowledge to different degrees. Some emphasize business knowledge, and some emphasize practical knowledge about particular products, services, and work processes. For instance, despite its strong professional discourse, the informational and research content of the International Society of Hospitality Consultants' publications mostly concerns topical business information—for example, an annual list of top ten industry issues, a report on capital expenditures— and reflections on particular products and services—for example, water parks or spring cleaning a hotel. In their case, although the research and information sharing they do is quite detailed and extensive, the content of the knowledge claims they make is concrete, oriented to very specific work processes and specific market conditions. Although their language positions them clearly as "professionals," the term signifies, primarily, status in

the market. When associations like the International Concrete Repair Institute use professional language in honorific ways, they are usually referencing recognition of members' arenas of expertise in particular types of
technical problem solving; joining their Minnesota chapter, for instance,
will provide "valuable insight for existing and potential clients as to the
level of professionalism that you and your company operate on."[33]

Usually, though, different sorts of knowledge claims are mixed. First,
it's important to note that if we consider more closely the sorts of topics
that concern the Consulting Actuaries, we see that they also hear about
rather immediate issues of business, and of developments in particular
consulting services they offer, in their annual conference (albeit in an inaccessible technical vocabulary). They do differ from the Hospitality Consultants or the Vacuum Dealers in that, for instance, they are also required
to maintain knowledge of the "mathematics of financial contingencies,"
but the difference is only in degree.

After noticing this, we can then see that other associations, too, mix
different sorts of knowledge claims, including abstract knowledge about
the diagnosis and remedy of work problems that is transferable to new
problems and becomes difficult to distinguish from more recognizably
"professional" knowledge.

The Irrigation Association's Certification Board offers numerous certification programs: Certified Irrigation Contractor (CIC), Certified Irrigation Designer (CID), Certified Agricultural Irrigation Specialist (CAIS),
Certified Golf Irrigation Auditor (CGIA), Certified Landscape Irrigation
Auditor (CLIA), and finally, also requiring a combination of the previous
credentials, Certified Landscape Irrigation Manager (CLIM). The association also provides a variety of textbooks, course materials, and courses
for each level and specialty. Applicants must have at least three years experience and sign off on an eight-point code of ethics. To be accredited at
the basic level of Certified Irrigation Contractor, they must pass a four-
hour exam. The "standard text for the industry," published by IA, treats

> water and energy conservation through design, operation and scheduling . . .
> covers system use, system planning, soil-water-plant relationships, sprinkler
> patterns, hydraulics, pumping plants, agricultural and turf systems, environ-
> mental control, chemical application with sprinklers, installation, operations
> and maintenance, economics of irrigation, piping and drip systems.

At the basic accreditation level, contractors

should have knowledge of the various soil conditions which affect the installation and operation of the irrigation system. They should be able to effectively choose and schedule the required installation equipment . . . should be able to perform the necessary cutting and joining of . . . different materials, understand the limitations of each piping system, and have knowledge of the required fittings and components of the water delivery system, including backflow prevention components. They should understand basic hydraulics . . . should have knowledge of the various types of control devices used in irrigation systems . . . have basic electrical knowledge . . . should have knowledge of the required licensing laws and codes in their respective states . . . they should know the principles of good business practices, organization, accurate bookkeeping and timely material and labor take-offs and bids.

The exam content is weighted as follows: 26 percent Water Conservation/ Irrigation Scheduling, 18 percent Irrigation Design, 15 percent Irrigation Installation, 15 percent Codes and Laws, 11 percent Equipment and Terminology, 9 percent General Business Knowledge, and 6 percent Maintenance. A two-day review course—not a substitute for studying the exam texts—aims to "help professionals in the irrigation industry understand what is expected of a competent irrigation contractor. It serves to identify areas and topics in which they should be expert, so as to be profitable and professional." Certified Irrigation Designers, who take two levels of exams, "should have working knowledge of general irrigation theory, including hydraulics, soil/water/plant relationships, plant water requirements, and the principles of electricity. They should have an understanding of related elements including grading and drainage, plant material characteristics, and site maintenance and use." The more advanced qualifications build on these general competencies for particular applications—agriculture, golf, and landscape—and focus more on water audits and planning.[34]

This accreditation program does include practical knowledge (e.g., "the limitations of each piping system") and business knowledge (e.g., "timely material and labor take-offs and bids"). But many of the learning goals are pitched at a more general level ("general irrigation theory"). There seems no reason to doubt that, over time, irrigators would apply this more abstract view of their problems and tasks to new problems and use it in defense against what Abbott labeled "interlopers." Indeed, we see this happening in their political work discussed in chapter eight. There they are positioning themselves as environmental experts—important public voices, members of the "Green Industry," stewards more expert and experienced than (ignorant if well-meaning) others in problems of water conservation (just as Abbott suggested doctors are able to position themselves as experts on new social problems such as obesity). We can also see (in a minor way at the margins of their political work), wary processes of distinction with landscape architects who might be involved in similar projects (just as we might once have seen librarians sensitive to relations with computer systems experts).[35]

Although the question of whether irrigators' discourse and strategies of action are abstract enough to enable them to survive and change as a "professional" group over time could not be decided without more detailed historical evidence, the synchronic indicators provide no reason to think they could not do so—even though, as an association, they are composed of profit-oriented firms and see themselves as an industry.

As we have seen, the North American Association of Food Equipment Manufacturers, like the Irrigation Association, also manages a complex accreditation program, the Certified Foodservice Professional Program (CFSP). To be accredited as a CFSP,

> candidates are required to successfully complete a written examination, provide documented evidence of food service industry experience, participate in continuing education programs and demonstrate leadership in industry activities. In addition to recognizing candidates for their industry and work-related efforts and experiences, the CFSP program also believes strongly in crediting individuals for outstanding non-industry related accomplishments such as community service.

Like the Irrigation Association, the Food Equipment Manufacturers publish a textbook, run seminars, and publish a newsletter for CFSPs. Applicants, who must be employed full time in the industry but otherwise may be very different (firm owners or sales managers, for instance) sign off on a twelve-point code of ethics. Although an exam is required, NAFEM places less weight than IA on the formal apparatus of courses and exams and more on points awarded by the board for experience and activities. Points are accumulated for educational accomplishments (such as a "food service industry-specific" doctoral degree, completion of the Equipment and Supplies Overview Seminar, and participation in other seminars and courses); for industry service (such as memberships and committee work with other related associations, doing an approved CFSP presentation, published articles, talks and classes on industry subjects, other volunteer/

leadership roles in business and professional organizations, honors received from other associations, or organizing a CFSP exam, seminar, or study group); and for other industry-related activities (such as years of experience, attendance at the NAFEM show and other relevant conventions, and attendance at association chapter meetings). Maintaining CFSP status requires continued point accumulation, and there are formal expulsion procedures for violating the code of ethics or "engaging in conduct not in the best interests of the CFSP program."

This accreditation process clearly selects for active industry participation rather than book knowledge. (However, talks and classes promoting the applicant's company, or particular products, are excluded.) So NAFEM rewards industry participation more than the IA, and book knowledge less. Similarly, the substantive content of its textbooks, examinations, and seminars appears, at least to the outsider, to be less abstract and generalizable. The fundamental "Equipment and Supplies Overview Seminar" treats eight areas. They include "Overview of the Foodservice Industry" (a "brief history" "macro view" "segmentation definition and review, "current trends and activities"); "Foodservice Facility Design"; "Food Preparation" (an "overview of the various . . . processes, various methods and systems for food preparation," as well as "health concerns in the food preparation process"); "Utilities Design Considerations"; "Equipment Functions and Selections"; "Cook-Chill Systems"; "The Service Area and its Primary Functions"; "The Dining Room" ("general design requirements and parameters," "table top considerations in the design process," "furniture considerations in the design process"); and "The Dish Room (including general design parameters and considerations)."

This knowledge rewarded by the CFSP credential appears to be systematized practical knowledge (or abstract empiricism) rather than anything close to abstract theory. The course description, however, suggests that abstraction is a matter of point of view, and generality in the eye of the beholder. Justifying knowledge as an essential competitive advantage helping adapt to change, NAFEM goes on:

> In responding to the challenge of "knowledge," NAFEM has developed a comprehensive, one day seminar . . . that provides the participants with a holistic view of the food service industry. It is designed to give those individuals involved a "guided tour" of the numerous and various components that make our industry the exciting, yet complicated, industry that it is. It examines many of the interrelationships and interdependencies that exist within the industry, both

at the personal level as well as with those areas and functions that traditionally are not considered "front line" in nature.

This broader perspective is "essential if we want to successfully compete on the domestic and international scene." That is, its promoters see the program as enabling the transfer of local practical knowledge to new problems and new situations—if not, exactly, as defending occupational turf from interlopers. We can also note here that it clearly works to reinforce the broad discursive category of "the industry" as a collective identity and set of collective, rather than particularistic, interests. The inculcation of this broader sense of the components of "the industry" seems important, too, for the development and success of the formal transaction models and other systematic programs of industry coordination that, as we saw in chapter six, NAFEM also emphasized. The beginning of the CFSP program, in 1986, predated the efforts to coordinate with newly powerful downstream buyers that we saw in chapter six by fifteen years. Perhaps it positioned NAFEM well for that energetic engagement.[36]

Overall, then, and even though they are composed of primarily market-oriented actors, certainly not distancing themselves from market concerns, the Irrigators' and the Food Equipment Manufacturers' professionalization discourses and strategies of action closely resemble those of occupations more typically labeled professional. They involve the routine cultural production of the grounds for competitive claims to occupational jurisdiction, grounds occasionally mobilized in episodes of explicit jurisdictional conflict. Substantively, they do not confine themselves to practical knowledge and business know-how, but also emphasize, to different degrees, sufficient abstraction to apply occupational knowledge to new problems and contexts.

The International Society of Certified Electronics Technicians

One final illustration further demonstrates the strength of "professionalism" as a discourse and strategy of action in business settings, while it challenges comfortable preconceptions about any clear distinction between professions and business. The International Society of Certified Electronics Technicians administers an even more elaborate and solidly institutionalized accreditation program than the other groups we have seen so far, like the Irrigators and the Food Equipment Manufacturers. Like some professional programs of the Real Estate Brokers and the Food

Equipment Manufacturers, ISCET was a group within another associa-tion—"the technical division of NESDA, the National Electronics Service Dealers Association." It "promotes technical certification worldwide" and "provides a place for certified technicians to band together for profes-sional advancement." Its Certified Electronics Technician (CET) Program "is designed to measure the degree of theoretical knowledge and technical proficiency of practicing technicians" . . . "enables employers to separate knowledgeable job applicants from those with less training and skills," and "protects consumers."[37]

ISCET administers detailed course work, with a national testing appa-ratus of regular examinations across the country and a cadre of hundreds of volunteer test administrators also recognized by the association. It pub-lishes a newsletter for those who qualify and requires continuing educa-tion credits. It is also a prolific publisher of study materials on electronics (and the only focal association with a substantial number of publications also issued in Spanish). Certifications are available at a basic associate level and a more advanced journeyman level, which also involves special-ization in particular applications. Lengthy lists of newly qualified techni-cians from all over the country in every newsletter make their claim of 46,000 certifications since 1965 seem plausible.[38]

Unlike the vast majority of such accreditation processes in business associations, one part of what ISCET did involved legally authoritative occupational jurisdiction: it was the official examination manager for FCC licenses, which, as they said, "in many places serves as the 'Gate Keepers' so errors are not committed by users and servicers alike when using or servicing radio signal transmitters." Among the associations examined in depth, the Consulting Actuaries were the only other group in which juris-dictional control imposed by accreditation processes came close to being a legal national monopoly. The commonsense disparity between electronics technicians and actuaries emphasizes the larger argument here that dis-tinctions between professions and other occupational groupings are hard to sustain.[39]

But the FCC license was only a very small part of the accreditation they offered, and for most of their credentials, any occupational jurisdiction involved was much more directly market related, a vague, implicit contrast with generalized, usually unnamed competitors on the market. Like other associations above, they sometimes argued that "professional" certifica-tion was good for business. As one president exhorted, "one of the best ways to prove your business is by certification and training," which "is a nationally recognized means of demonstrating your quality and professionalism." Of one certification they offered, they claimed that "NASTeC Certification Helps Business Owners . . . Increase your service income. Increase your profits. Solve employee problems . . . boost your image with customers and manufacturers." They also started a "Certified Service Center" program aimed at "raising the level of perceived professionalism to the consumer." This was only one of many ways that NESDA members were asked to "join with your professional colleagues who work together to improve themselves and their profession."[40]

What was the substantive content of ISCET accreditation? "The CET Study Guide," the basic text, "is "an overall review of basic electronics including basic math, AC/DC circuits, components, etc. . . . plus consumer electronics including digital circuits, linear circuits, televisions, VCRs, and test equipment." Topics of additional publications include "Using Mathematics in the Plant," "Making Measurements," "Understanding Basic Electricity and Electronics," "Using and Maintaining Batteries and DC Circuits," "Using and Maintaining Transformers and AC," and "Electronic Measuring Instruments." Study guides on more advanced specialties like industrial electronics were more impenetrably technical.[41]

Although they claim to be measuring both theoretical knowledge and technical proficiency, the electronics technicians and dealers interested in these qualifications see them as mostly general and theoretical, not practical knowledge (or, as other associations include in their offerings, business know-how). Certainly, the command of information they require is much more general than the industry information canvassed in newsletters, for instance, and by comparison, their *ProService Magazine* included articles on particular products and technologies like mobile phones with hard drives, high speed wireless Internet access, electronically programmable DVD home theater systems, LCD TV panel production, and game decks. Resistance to certification as merely "theoretical" knowledge was one common theme often addressed by those promoting the accreditation program. As one ISCET president argued:

"Why do I need to be a CET?"
(Or why do my employees need to be CETs).
I've heard this question many times since I've been involved with CET certification (20+ years).
Let me first address the single most common comment I hear.
"I knew a tech that was a CET, and he couldn't fix anything."

Does having a CET certification automatically make you a good technician?
Absolutely not!!

Even with all the testing and certification that doctors undergo, there are still
poor doctors practicing medicine. Does this mean we shouldn't require doctors to have a license?

His answer to those who resist certification involves technical proficiency
(become a better technician), business marketing (more and more manufacturers are supporting the program), and pride in the accomplishment.
What is significant, though, is that the knowledge involved is considered,
within this world, abstract and general. Moreover, "professional" knowledge is invoked as a defense when industry changes are considered. As one
president reflected, with some resignation, about industry change: "we in
the electronics industry are used to constantly learning new theories."[42]

Abstract Knowledge, Procedural Knowledge, and Occupational Distinction

This evidence suggests that abstract, systematized, transposable knowledge claims do not clearly or reliably mark a strong distinction between
professionals and others, because they can be found in occupational and
business settings that are not otherwise "professional." In their theory
of occupational community, John Van Maanen and Stephen Barley have
made a related but stronger argument. Like professions, they point out,
many other work groups seek occupational control "premised upon the
belief that only the membership possesses the proper knowledge, skills,
and orientations necessary to make decisions as to how the work is to
be performed and evaluated." Among the ways they might sustain claims
based on such beliefs is by preserving relatively monopolistic access to a
knowledge base. To this point, their view of occupational communities
simply generalizes features of professions. However, their approach differs because they argue that *procedural* knowledge, as well as abstract
knowledge, may preserve claims to occupational control:

The cognitive base of an occupation represents declarative sorts of knowledge
such as facts, descriptions and technologies. Since declarative knowledge is rule-
based, it can be transmitted by word of mouth or by print. Although it may be
complex, scientific in origin, and take years to master, it is, in principles, subject
to codification. In contrast, skill is fluid and, to outsiders at least, mysterious.
Skill is akin to what is called "know-how" and is represented by what acknowl-

edged experts in all fields are demonstrably able to do but are often unable or unwilling to precisely describe.

Both types of knowledge may amplify occupational control, and both may also be threatened as a basis for occupational control (the first by popular codification and diffusion, and the second by damaging public revelations of "backstage" tactics). And the two types of knowledge are not confined to mutually exclusive social locations; we may turn to recognized professional experts for their experiential know-how, as much as their book knowledge, and we may rely on savvy contractors for their codified knowledge, as much as their practical experience. Thus, Van Maanen and Barley provide a more nuanced understanding of occupationally specific knowledge than do theories of professions, a view that encompasses what we know of professions but also brings into focus—in the same picture—a much broader array of occupations, including the technical and normative dimensions of the work lives of the businesspeople here.[43]

Here, though, it is unnecessary to rely on their more differentiated understanding of knowledge as a claim to occupational control to suggest that some of business associations' discourse and strategies of action cannot be distinguished from that of professionals—despite their more direct orientation to market action. Without even considering the procedural and practical knowledge they also express and promote, we have seen that some associations develop, systematize, and accredit systematized abstract knowledge claims.

Conclusion

Despite standard distinctions between the world of professions and the world of business, we see here that professional languages and practices are well established in business associations. These provide a vocabulary of motive for associations' intraindustry activities distinct from—though often mixed with—the claims about collective industry interests and (less frequent) claims about particularistic benefits for members we saw in the last chapter. They are distinct in emphasizing interests in and claims to occupational jurisdiction, and the particularities of occupational knowledge, even in the context of market action. Sometimes this is a way of specifying means to market stability and success, and such usages illustrate a close relation between market and professional action and interests. But

the elaboration, systematization, and inculcation of occupationally specific knowledge particularly distinguish this language from a simpler language of market interests. This dimension of occupational subculture has
received little attention from scholars of either business associations or
professions.

This feature also distinguishes these national business groups from
local groups of businesspeople, like chambers of commerce, which may
otherwise share many of their solidaristic features and also share vocabularies of motive related to collective economic benefits and public good.

Theories of professions suggest they might be distinct types of occupations in two ways. First, the occupational interests they involve are
connected to jurisdictional control over a line of work, ideally by state-
sanctioned monopoly. This sort of interest supposedly differentiates them
from ordinary occupations—though the distinction is hard to maintain.[44]
It is also thought to differentiate them from the directly market-oriented
action of the business world. But, as we have seen, market interests may be
pursued with professionalization strategies too. Expertise and status are
sometimes claimed to add market value (though, like claims about the collective pursuit of economic interests more generally, discussed in chapter
six, this claim is simply an "article of faith").

The second way professions are thought to be distinct is in the nature
and amount of abstract, systematized knowledge they involve, as opposed
to practical knowledge. But the examples above suggest that some professional claims by business associations are also grounded in expertise, gen-
eralities, and abstractions beyond the practical knowledge also involved
in the lines of work they encompass, and it is difficult to clearly distinguish
the professional claims in business associations from professional claims
in occupations that are more insulated from market demands, especially
if we discount the status sensibilities of most producers of general theory
about professions.[45]

If businesspeople mobilize discourses and strategies of action usually
associated with professional occupations to make sense of their economic
action, this adds to cumulating evidence that we need to broaden our view
of what makes business meaningful in several ways.

We saw in part two that a vast infrastructure of cultural production
routinely creates and recreates not only categories, networks, and fields
that orient economic action but also solidaristic occupational communities. Now, in part three, we have examined the cultural repertoire that
provides meaningful grounds for such common intra-"industry" strate-

gies of action as education, information provision, research, and standard setting. Vocabularies of motive are not restricted to direct, particularistic economic interests but emphasize even more collective identities and interests, and the technical expertise and excellence of "professionalism." As Larson reminds us, professions are "inherently *nomic* (the opposite of anomic)," and there are "two nomic components of profession, the technical and the ethical." The irrigation contractors, actuaries, food equipment manufacturers, electronics dealers, and so on understand normative and technical dimensions of their work as ends in themselves as well as, sometimes and perhaps, maybe hopefully, economic advantages, and often see them as positive dimensions of their business worlds. Technical expertise and excellence helps make sense of putatively self-interested intraindustry strategies of action in settings putatively devoted strictly to the pursuit of market interests in industry stability and profit.[46]

But as Larson also points out, "in promoting the performance of function, the professions become central players in the constitution of a public sphere." What about the public significance of business associations' professionalization projects and professional strategies of action? To what extent are discourses and strategies of action about intraindustry matters simply part of the "legitimate construction of a seemingly autonomous knowledge field . . . indispensable for the justification of capitalism"? More generally, what about the political discourse and strategies of action we typically associate with business associations? Having explored the complex world of business associations below the radar of conventional assumptions, we are now in a better position to turn in part four to an examination of their orientation to conventional politics and the public sphere.[47]

PART IV

American Business Associations in Politics

CHAPTER EIGHT

"A Voice for the Industry"

Business Associations and Political Interests

D uring the 2004 Republican National Convention, the Distilled Spirits Council of the United States sponsored a lavish party at the New York Yacht Club. Politicians and lobbyists could "bond at open bars and buffet lines" over "the best their money did not have to buy":

> "It was great," said Frank Coleman, a senior vice president of the association, which lobbies on behalf of the liquor industry. "It had the right mix of people. It had the media folks. It had opinion leaders. It had members. It had key staff. And it had great distilled spirits products, which are the life of all responsible parties."

The Distilled Spirits party was only one of "scores of similar events" costing hundreds of thousands of dollars at the conventions in that presidential election year. Perhaps the parties were more potlatch than direct utilitarian bribe: "I honestly don't think people are going to sit there and say, 'we have a problem with H.R. 451' or whatever," Coleman continued. But potlatch or bribe, they certainly seem to confirm everyone's worst suspicions about what national business associations really do.[1]

When most people think of business associations, they think of them as lobby groups like the Distilled Spirits Council. Government policy on matters ranging from the very broad—like energy—to the very particular—like safe wood for garden mulch—can influence not only the prospects but also the very shape of firms and industries. As Neil Fligstein points out, building on a vast body of research in political and economic sociology, "modern markets defined as structured exchange are difficult to imagine without the existence of modern governments . . . their current policy domains are constituted to intervene, regulate or mediate product, capital, and labor markets." It seems obvious, then, that capitalist firms will attempt to shape policy that affects them, and business associations provide one way of doing so. Indeed, on many accounts, the *only* point of business associations is to lobby government.[2]

This chapter investigates American business associations' participation in conventional politics. After an overview of the arguments and evidence for the thesis that business associations are political interest groups, I examine orientations to lobbying and monitoring policy among contemporary American business associations and illustrate what such orientations involve by drawing on the focal sample of representative associations. I argue, overall, that although some associations' lobbying is consequential, associations that fit the "lobby group" formula do not represent most American business associations.

Moreover, the thesis that business associations are simply political interest groups pays insufficient attention to the languages in which the strategies of action oriented to the routine pursuit of industry interests are understood, and the meaning attributed to such action. It also ignores the routine in favor of the dramatic, the common in favor of the rare. Associations often express their political interests in terms of broader collective identities, ideologies of the public good, and technical reason rather than in terms of the narrow, intrinsically conflict-ridden interests of firms and industries. As Kay Schlozman and John Tierney are among the few scholars to note, "public interest groups have no monopoly on the representation of broadly shared interests: on the contrary, private interests are often animated by a concern with diffuse public interests." These broader ideologies of public good shape the claims-making of many politically active business associations and should be taken into account more fully in any understanding of the cultural construction of interests.[3]

It is important to keep in mind throughout this chapter that even taking into account the different ways in which business associations articulate "a voice for the industry," such voice is not as important to most associations as conventional wisdom suggests.[4] They focus more often on the intra-"industry" concerns we have examined at length in previous chapters. Against that background we can now investigate the element of truth in conventional wisdom about business associations as political actors, and strengthen our grasp of what exactly that means.

Business Associations as Interest Groups

Most American scholars automatically assume that business associations are political interest groups, oriented, in Max Weber's terms, to influencing the *political* order governing the group. No one disputes that—as Howard Aldrich and his colleagues suggest in their population study—"a primary focus of national trade associations is lobbying the federal government," and—as Lloyd Warner and Desmond Martin claim—"everyone knows that their influence on government is great." This assumption persists even though the same studies often include other evidence that seems to qualify the conclusion—such as the finding, noted in chapter two, that political events seem to have little effect on the long-term growth of the association population.[5]

The assumption is consistent with both political economy and pluralist theories of democratic states—theories that are otherwise competing—and often derives directly or indirectly from one or the other position. Principles of political economy suggest that powerful economic actors will successfully organize to influence state policy; pluralist theory suggests that economic actors, like others, will form interest groups. In either view, business associations are essentially political interest groups. Their political role may vary along a continuum from broad policy participation mediating a variety of interests, suggested by theories of corporatism, to narrower political advocacy.[6]

Corporatist theories cast associations as strong, cooperative interest groups. As Charles Sabel points out, they also tend to see corporatist political action by associations as "benign," an institutionalized integration of powerful economic actors in consideration of interests beyond their own, in ways that manage the potential destructiveness of pure market action for society as a whole. For corporatists, associationalism is a fourth type of social order—along with community, market, and state. It exists where there is "negotiation within and among a limited and fixed set of interest organizations that mutually recognize each other's status and entitlements and are capable of reaching and implementing relatively stable compromises (pacts) in the pursuit of their interests," pacts that may have broader social benefits. In corporatism, broad, formalized policy participation by association mediates a variety of interests—such as those between capitalists and labor, or between different types of industry. As we saw in chapter two, theories of economic governance treat formal links between state and associations in corporatism as an important feature of strong associational governance: "associations are closely consulted in the formulation of policy and are involved in its implementation. . . . In exchange, the state receives a measure of freedom to intervene . . . in the organization of the sector." For instance, Japanese associations in the 1980s took a formal role both in advising on government export ordinances, which could support standards set by associations, and in approving export applications and enforcing the ordinances.[7]

But as chapter two showed, corporatist business associations—highly integrated, possessing the authority to mediate conflicting interests within an industry, and participating in all phases of the policy process, including implementation—are most likely generated where state authorization is strong, and as we saw in chapter three, contemporary American associations are typically small and simply organized, rarely possessing any of the features of policy-capable associations. Udo Staber's study of industrial associations showed they cannot act in the way corporatist theories would suggest because they lack the necessary size, breadth, and organizational autonomy; moreover, "coordinated action by several associations was relatively rare . . . only an ad hoc arrangement . . . in relation to very specific issues." Leonard Lynn and Timothy McKeown's comparison of American and Japanese steel and machine tool industries illustrates this. They show that American associations are weak because important firms may not be members, disaffected members may create new associations, different associations within an industry may be independent or antagonistic, and peak associations like the National Association of Manufacturers are often overshadowed by issue-specific coalitions and shifting alliances. Kay Schlozman and John Tierney comment that in the American context, "the sharing of authority is more fragmented and less centralized, involving hundreds of committees in dozens of agencies and individual trade associations, corporations, unions, and other organized units rather than peak associations . . . the issues at stake are much narrower."[8]

Lynn and McKeown's reference to peak associations is a reminder of one way the general conclusion that American associations do not have "corporatist" political capacity might be qualified. William Domhoff and other elite theorists often note the political influence of American business in peak associations, including the National Association of Manufacturers, the National Federation of Independent Business, the National Small Business Association, the Business Council, the Business Roundtable, and the Committee for Economic Development. Domhoff and others unearth extensive evidence of the influence of such peak associations at key policy turning points of the twentieth century. Studies such as those of Sar Levitan and Martha Cooper, Jeffrey Berry, and Patrick Akard show peak associations organized particularly effective business unity on key policy issues in the 1970s. Mark Mizruchi, Akard, and others argue that corporate elite action in peak associations varies according to historical context, and that it was less unified and effective after the 1970s. But there is no doubt that peak associations do operate primarily as political interest groups. Unlike most of the associations discussed here, websites of groups like the Business Roundtable and the National Association of Manufacturers are dominated by stories about their work on "regulatory reform," legislative acts, court rulings, administrative nominations, voting role calls, congressional testimony, and so on. Their language appeals to the legitimacy and virtue of "voice" in democratic processes, similar to a minority of "industry" associations discussed further below. Notable examples of their pursuit of business interests appear regularly in press commentary; for instance, a study by the Business Roundtable that argued that executive pay had not kept pace with stockholder returns attracted particular attention, as did the appointment of a National Association of Manufacturers lobbyist to lead the Consumer Product Safety Commission.[9]

Little is known about the extent to which "industry"-specific associations are connected with peak associations, although Paul Burstein suggests that political sociologists should investigate these ties more because "corporatist bargaining structures may help overcome the policy fragmentation and paralysis sometimes said to characterize the United States." Corporate elite studies typically examine ties of corporations and individuals in peak associations, ties between corporations through individuals, and corporate elite ties with policy-planning institutions. Whether some "industry"-level business associations are institutional nodes in the corporate elite structure remains something of an open question.[10]

Certainly, the numerous ties between regular business associations could potentially provide fertile ground for broader corporate elite ties. But the indicators from existing corporate elite and interest group studies all point to the assessment that this fertile ground would be productive only episodically and contingently, in temporary, issue-specific alliances, and would not operate systematically. First, Lynn and McKeown observed that shifting issue alliances could overshadow peak association influence, at least some times. Second, Edward Laumann and David Knoke's study of national policy domains supports Schlozman and Tierney's argument that American interest group politics is too unsystematic to be corporatist, with cleavages on particular issues reflecting the idiosyncratic nature of organizations' interests. Third, as I note below, Laumann and Knoke found regular trade associations were minor players in the policy domains they studied. Finally, peak associations appeared only once or twice in the many links to affiliate organizations boasted by the typical business associations here.[11]

In any case, neither corporatist theories nor the power-elite perspective go far to explain the existence, activities, political languages, or potential influence of industry-level associations considered as a population, even if they sometimes play some indirect part in power-elite processes.

As we also saw in chapter three, however, some American associations developed a different type of political role, a role that was probably institutionalized nationally by the 1930s and may have expanded notably in the 1970s. According to Laumann and Knoke, "the boundaries between public and private sectors are blurred, and irrelevant, even in noncorporatist societies." So although American associations are considered politically weak by comparative and corporatist standards, encouraging some scholars to believe that the political/legal environment discourages association action, others argue, nevertheless, that they play a crucial role pursuing narrow political interests of business in what Louis Galambos calls "triocracies"— durable ties among interest groups, government agencies, and members of Congress in specific regulatory domains. In this view, the importance of regulatory agencies, government spending, and issue expertise in contemporary American politics mean that "no significant industry can afford . . . not to be represented in Washington." As Leon Lindberg and colleagues note in more reserved terms, "in some industries, associations occasionally exercise substantial influence by playing pivotal roles in both the enactment and implementation of public policies." Indeed, some argue that executive agencies are "captured" by relying on organized interests such as business associations for information, "revolving door" staffing, participation in advisory committees, and political support for agency funding. More recently, Edward Walker argues that business association foundings in the late twentieth century had a strong positive influence on foundings of grassroots lobbying firms and made up half their client base, suggesting that, increasingly, "industry activism shapes civil society."[12]

The best way to assess the political role of associations is to focus on the policy domain, "a set of actors with major concerns about a substantive area, whose preferences and actions on policy events must be taken into account by other domain participants." Problems are defined, policy alternatives formulated, and policy choices made within self-contained and relatively autonomous policy domains. Laumann and Knoke concluded from their detailed study of national energy and health policy domains that they are composed of a large and complicated mixture of public and private organizations. Despite their size and complexity, however, these domains possess a strong center-periphery structure (measured in terms of density of communication and status); as a result, many "peripheral" organizations are of little account to others except when recruited or mobilized by central actors in coalitions. In contrast to corporatist models, action in policy domains proceeds in series of shifting and idiosyncratic interorganizational coalitions. There may be around twenty such policy domains in the United States—a core group mostly concerned with economic and defense issues, and a more peripheral group mostly concerned with issues of individual rights, citizenship, and consumption.[13]

While in some policy domains interest groups "capture" government agencies, relationships between government agencies and interest groups vary more than capture theory suggests. The extent to which policy domains act as tight "iron triangles" or looser "issue networks" is not fully understood, but the "iron triangle" view is probably overgeneralized from unrepresentative domains, and most interest group politics gets done through a "more loosely defined issue network rather than the ossified subgovernment."[14]

What part do business associations play in these policy domains? In the energy and health domains Laumann and Knoke studied, business associations participated along with many other types of groups—congressional committees, federal agencies, associations of local governments, unions, research institutes, professional associations, corporations, and public interest groups. At the time of their study, a quarter of the organizations in the energy domain were trade associations, but in the health domain, where professional associations were more important, only 8 percent of the organizations were trade associations. A variety of studies now argue that business interests in these domains are promoted more by specific corporations than by business associations. Along with professional associations and specific firms and corporations, generalist trade associations "seem to mediate communication between the central authorities and the peripheral specialist actors." Some associations may focus on one policy domain, but most will be attentive to others as well: trade associations involved in energy and health domains were usually attentive to three or four other domains.[15]

Associations' work in policy domains may also vary in its strength.

Many will simply monitor legislation and policy, and this is likely the most common concern of more peripheral actors in policy domains. Beyond that, three forms of policy input can be distinguished: problem recognition or agenda setting, the formulation of policy options, and the more explicit (and better studied) politics of policy choice and change. Associations' political actions are also likely to vary according to whether their focal policy domain, if they have one, involves widely or narrowly dispersed costs and benefits.[16]

Standard perspectives on American business associations, then, emphasize their activities as interest groups in relevant policy domains. From this point of view, and building on studies of how policy domains operate, a strong business association will not only monitor policy developments for its members but will also mobilize organizational, informational, and network resources to set policy agendas according to members' interests, participate in the formulation of policy alternatives, and influence policy decisions. A good deal of this work will take place in the arcane administrative realms of particular policy domains rather than (as is sometimes assumed) in public political debate. The work may be either intermittent or routinized, and it will often involve associations' orientation to, and shifting coalitions with, a variety of other public and private organizations in policy domains.[17]

How well do American business associations conform to this picture? Typically, studies of interest group politics cast business associations as consequential political players. For example, Nicole Biggart shows how direct selling businesses formed associations to respond to restrictive state and local ordinances, and attempted to preempt Federal Trade Commission standards by creating their own code of ethics. Domhoff notes, for instance, that free trade groups active in the 1950s met resistance from campaigns of the American Textile Manufacturers Institute. Levitan and Cooper discuss the role of the American Bankers' Association, the American Society of Pension Actuaries, and the Association of Private Pension and Welfare Plans in 1970s pension politics, and the role of the American Retail Federation and the Associated Builders and Contractors in unemployment insurance politics. Schlozman and Tierney provide illustrations of numerous business associations' political activity, such as car dealers' work for a congressional veto of a new regulation about information disclosure.[18]

Such studies show consequential political action by some business associations at some times, but they are anecdotal and do not allow us to assess whether all business associations act this way and how often they might do so. How representative are politically active business associations?

Politically Active Business Associations

Late Twentieth-Century Evidence

Two systematic studies of business associations in the 1960s and 1980s (described in chapter three) begin to address this question of how well anecdotal accounts of business associations' political activities represent the entire population. Both studies take it for granted that associations' political activity is important, but their findings also raise the question of whether, looking at the issue from the point of view of associations, this role is overestimated.[19]

In Warner and Martin's study of associations in the early 1960s, just over half of their respondents reported that their officers' responsibilities included regular contact with government at some level (federal, state, or local). Contact was mostly informal rather than formal, and varied by sector. Associations in agriculture, merchandising, and finance reported regular contact more commonly than those in other sectors. More than half of associations in "finance, insurance, and real estate," and in agricultural and merchandising sectors, reported such informal contact. Of the 52 percent of associations reporting some government contact, just under a quarter reported contact with the federal government only, and 14 percent worked at both federal and state levels. A further 15 percent reported contact at all three levels of government. The sectors most involved with the federal government were merchandising, "transport, communication, and utilities," and agriculture, each with nearly a third of associations reporting federal government contact. Finance and agriculture were above average in their reports of contact with both federal and state government; services and agriculture were above average in reporting contact with government at all three levels.[20]

Later, in a 1980s survey, 58 percent of trade associations indicated in survey responses that "influencing public-policy decisions of government" was a moderate or major goal. Trade associations had greater political capacity than other types of voluntary groups, except labor unions. This was indicated by activities like policy monitoring (71 percent), public relations (65 percent), hiring outside counsel (64 percent), producing technical data (45 percent), running a Congress program (38 percent), hiring in-house counsel (23 percent), hiring lobbyists (18 percent), and organizing PACS (13 percent). Explicitly stated political goals were positively associated with political capacity, and four in ten trade associations made efforts to mobilize their members to contact government officials.[21]

The disparities of purpose, sample, and methodology in these studies make precise conclusions difficult, but (reading between the lines of the narrative implied by the interest group thesis) the information they provide raises several questions about assumptions that business associations are simply political interest groups active in policy domains. Even though larger associations were oversampled, just under half did *not* indicate *any* political interest (for Warner, contact, and for Knoke, influence). Warner and Martin's data for the 1960s show that associations in different sectors varied quite a lot in the nature and focus of their activity on political issues; in sectors "below average" on their various measures, associations reporting political activity could represent only one in ten or one in five of associations in that sector. Knoke's findings about political roles and activities indicate that policy monitoring is much more common than activities oriented to policy participation, setting policy agendas, formulating policy alternatives, and influencing policy decisions. Both studies use surveys, too, in which responses may reflect ideals as much as realities, and it is hard to assess whether the reported interest and involvement is institutionalized and routine. Combining Knoke's stricter measures—associations reporting congressional programs, in-house counsel, lobbyists, and PACs—roughly a quarter, rather than a half, of business associations were serious political interest groups. It is also important to recall that with information based on associations rather than policy domains, we have no way of knowing whether politically active associations were peripheral or central in their policy domains of interest, or of knowing whether their actions are intermittent or sustained.

All these considerations raise questions about the normal understanding of business associations as political interest groups. It is important, of course, to recognize those that are significant in policy and politics, to understand their influence, and to increase awareness of their consequences. But we cannot assume that all business associations are politically active interest groups. To understand American business associations, we also need to ask how representative politically active associations are.

Political Orientations of Contemporary Business Associations

As we saw in chapter three, American business associations are mostly small and weakly organized. Associations composed of firms had a median membership of 152, those composed of individuals averaged 950 members, and (for those reporting any staff at all) they only had a median of four staff. While this characterization is obviously partial, and there is wide variation in the population, it does begin to suggest that most business associations are "policy weak," even if they are oriented to policy issues. While many may say they do policy monitoring, for instance, this may mean something like one of three staff writing up reports for newsletters to the membership rather than a department devoted to producing arguments or writing legislation for congressional committees. As previous studies also suggest, the majority of business associations seem to lack the basic features of "policy capable" associations.[22] But leaving the issue of organizational capacity aside, do most business associations indicate an orientation to national policy domains? Evidence from the population census on national associations' headquarters location and expressed orientation to government affairs helps answer this question.

LOCATION IN DC AREA. Evidence on headquarters location of national associations also seems to qualify the political interest group picture, suggesting again that the associations with a sustained engagement as significant interest groups in national policy domains are a minority, if an important one. Only 29.5 percent of associations were headquartered in Washington, DC; Virginia; or Maryland. Warner and Martin found in the 1960s that a slightly smaller proportion—25 percent—were headquartered in DC.[23]

Are associations in the DC area distinctive compared to associations headquartered elsewhere?

- Associations in Washington do not differ very much in size from others, although they are very slightly more likely to be smaller.[24]
- DC-area associations were significantly more likely to be composed of firms than individuals. This probably accounts for the very slight tendency for DC-area associations to be smaller.[25]
- Associations in DC also had somewhat greater organizational capacity, being somewhat more likely to report four or more staff, and to indicate internal differentiation in committees, divisions, or councils.[26]
- DC location was unrelated to associations' reporting regional or national affiliates.[27]
- Sectors varied widely in the proportion of their associations located in DC. Transportation, health, finance, utilities, construction, real estate, and manufacturing ranked above the population average. Associations in agriculture and in "arts, entertainment, and recreation" were much less likely to be found in the DC area than other associations.[28]

So just under a third of associations are headquartered in the DC area. These associations tend to be composed of firms, and to have more staff and committees. Different economic sectors vary quite widely in the proportion of their associations with a DC address.

Clearly, location is not necessarily a definitive indicator of associations' political orientation, for several reasons. Associations located elsewhere may well develop political activities that provide them with a systematic engagement in national policy domains; in the focal sample, the North American Association of Food Equipment Manufacturers, located in Illinois, provides an illustration. Second, their political activities may be oriented to regional, state, or local level governments due to the nature of the economic activities they encompass; in the focal sample, the Firestop Contractors International Association was of this type. And a few associations in the DC area may not do much in political arenas, like the International Society of Hospitality Consultants, located in Virginia (although, as I note below, DC location and reports of political orientation were indeed highly correlated). In the focal sample, just under 10 percent of those coded as indicating a political orientation in the statement of purpose were not located in the DC area. Conversely, however, the same proportion was located in the DC area but did not indicate a political orientation in their statement of purpose, so at the aggregate level headquarters in Washington, DC; Virginia; or Maryland does indicate political orientation.

POLITICAL GOALS AND ACTIVITIES.   Evidence on associations' explicitly stated goals and activities also suggests that the "political interest group" characterization captures only an important minority of associations. For coding purposes, associations' orientation to goals or activities involving government, law, regulation, or public authorities was defined broadly. Some associations did explicitly state that lobbying was a goal. But associations making broader or weaker statements, such as about "concern with regulatory matters," "working with local and national governments," and "monitoring policy" were also included here among those with a political orientation. Even so, only 26 percent of associations (about 1,150) indicated any such political interest.

Associations indicating some explicit interest in their political environment were distinctive compared to associations that did not, in some of the same ways that DC-based associations were distinctive:

- Size made no significant difference to whether or not associations claimed to have political goals.[29]

- Type of membership, on the other hand, did make a big difference to claims about political goals. A third of associations composed of firms, but only 14.5 percent of associations composed of individuals, indicated such political interest or activity.[30]
- As we would expect, interest in political goals correlated with measures of organizational capacity. Associations with political goals tended to have more staff and to report internal differentiation in committees, divisions, or councils more often. Of those associations with between four and twelve staff members, 39 percent reported a political orientation, compared to 22 percent of those with fewer than four staff. Of those associations reporting some internal differentiation, 58 percent claimed some political interest, as opposed to 43 percent of those which did not report such differentiation.[31]
- As with DC location, political goals were unrelated to associations' reporting of affiliates.[32]
- Again, sectors diverged widely in proportions of associations expressing a political orientation. Sectors ranking above the population average of 26 percent were transportation, utilities, construction, real estate, mining, finance and insurance, manufacturing, and arts/entertainment/recreation. Associations in agriculture and educational services were much less likely to express a political orientation.[33]
- Predictably, DC location and political orientation were highly correlated. A half of all associations explicitly indicating a political orientation were located in Washington, compared to one in five of those that did not claim any political interest.

Overall, we see again that characterizing business associations simply as political interest groups seems to miss too much to be useful. Even using a necessarily broad measure of political interest, which includes weaker interest in monitoring the political environment as well as stronger interest in lobbying, only one in four associations express an orientation to conventional political goals and activities. Associations composed of firms, associations with larger staffs, associations reporting internally differentiated structure, and associations in Washington were all more likely to express political goals, but even in these categories, between a half and two-thirds did not do so. There was wide sectoral variation in the expression of a political orientation—but again, even at the maximum, in the transportation sector, the majority of associations did not do so. On this evidence, it is unlikely that most associations are hosting events like the well-supplied party for Republicans at the New York Yacht Club.

We can conclude that at any given time what Galambos called "policy capable" associations are an unrepresentative minority of the population. Moreover, they are not so distinct as to suggest that they should be treated as a different species of organization entirely, by dichotomizing the population. The political activities of the many associations that are composed of individuals, have small staffs, are simply organized, or are located outside Washington would not be captured if the population was partitioned in this way. On the other hand, close examination of the qualitative evidence from the focal associations shows that even associations that are politically inactive and strongly oriented to the internal industry concerns examined at length in previous chapters rarely ignore their political environment entirely. This means that their ongoing cultural production—of categories, networks, fields, boundaries, identities, norms, status, and camaraderie—is, considered over time, an institutionalized resource for possible political mobilization, and any categorical distinction between business lobby groups and other business associations would likely shift in unpredictable ways. As we saw in chapter three, any account of this population of nonprofits needs to make their *diffuse* cultural production central, and as we saw in chapter six, this diffuse but systematic cultural production may become more strategically consequential in contentious episodes and unsettled times.[34]

The data here shed little light on exactly what conditions might typically explain when and why an association would make the investment in political capacity necessary to make the change from what Galambos called "service" associations to "policy-capable" associations, if indeed such conditions could be precisely specified. The census evidence does suggest associations of firms are more likely to do so. But the cross-sectional evidence of the focal sample offers little evidence like that developed in chapter six to show episodes of associations addressing technological or other intraindustry change or conflict. Future studies could build on Galambos's account, and on McGee Young's study of small business and the way he identifies "how historical and organizational constraints on organized interests define both their character and their capacity to seek political influence." But any such study should first recognize and understand the way ongoing diffuse cultural production provides important conditions for rarer and more contingent orientations to immediate, strategic political interests.[35]

But what exactly does the pursuit of political interests mean in this world? Here, I first probe the standard, semi-institutionalized repertoire of strategies of action evident among that minority of politically engaged associations that understand themselves, at least intermittently, as political interest groups. I illustrate these routine practices because political sociologists seldom discuss them, and they help place the stereotype of collective political action by business illustrated by the Distilled Spirits Council's party for politicians in a more realistic perspective. This background on typical strategies of action then informs deeper analysis of the vocabularies of motive that make the pursuit of political interests meaningful.

Politically Oriented Strategies of Action

To learn how political interests are routinely pursued by that minority of associations oriented to conventional politics, I examined focal associations clearly oriented to the conventional political sphere—the Independent Bakers Association, Brick Industry Association, Closure Manufacturers' Association, Envelope Manufacturers' Association, North American Association of Food Equipment Manufacturers, American Council of Life Insurance, Irrigation Association, National Association of Real Estate Brokers, and International Telecommunications Society. These are unfamiliar political actors and might as well not exist in most sociologists' images of American society and politics. Nevertheless, they represent and illustrate an important part of what capitalist political action looks like on a day-to-day basis.[36]

All these associations express a conventional political orientation in their *Encyclopedia* self-description, and all but two are located in the Washington area. Their membership ranged from thirty-three—the Closure Manufacturers' Association—to 7,500—the National Association of Real Estate Brokers—with most around the population average of three or four hundred. Half are composed of firms, and half include individual members along with firms. A few have dedicated government relations or public affairs committees; for instance, the Food Equipment Manufacturers' government relations committee is "charged with monitoring legislative and regulatory issues, developing position statements and contacting legislators." Some, like the Irrigation Association, have a staff member responsible for government relations, but in others, the political work falls mostly to the association leader or to a committee of members. Their most common strategy of action in the political realm is providing updates and guidelines to members about legislative, regulatory, and environmental issues, but they are also proactive lobbyists, occasionally with legislatures but most commonly with relevant agencies like the EPA. A few proactive lobbyists also attempt to mobilize members to contact legislators. A few others emphasize their role as a site of policy discussion for members.[37]

Systematic Policy Monitoring

Legislative and regulatory updates for members—provided, in this group, by the Independent Bakers Association, the North American Association of Food Equipment Manufacturers, the Irrigation Association, the American Council of Life Insurance, the National Association of Real Estate Brokers, the Brick Industry Association, and the Closure Manufacturers' Association—may come in the form of e-mail Listservs, newsletters, or dedicated topical panels at meetings. They usually deal briefly with mundane and arcane issues—for instance, the realtors provided information on renewal procedures for Housing and Urban Development (HUD) section 8 housing qualification, and the Brick Industry Association announced new Department of Transportation regulations about loading trucks and an OSHA (Occupational Safety and Health Administration) training program. Many different sorts of associations—like the Independent Bakers, the Closure Manufacturers, and the American Council of Life Insurance—also provide information on compliance procedures along with regulatory information provided in news updates or conference panels. Only the largest and most sophisticated associations provided more extended and detailed treatment of issues: in this group, the American Council of Life Insurance provides detailed summaries, position statements, and further resources on current issues, as well as an election guide noting contested seats and key votes. Some associations, like the Food Equipment Manufacturers, have e-mail lists dedicated to local regulation as well; theirs "delivers the latest information—hot and fresh from your peers—right to your desktop. Use it to ask questions or gain advice about local food service regulation issues and to participate in peer-to-peer discussions."[38]

Intermittently Active Lobbying

More active participation in policy domains takes a range of forms. The life insurance association, by far the most policy-capable in this group, boasts a former state governor as leader, whose "Washington meetings have included key members of Congress and the Bush administration." He also spoke before the National Press Club. Members and staff of the American

Council of Life Insurance (ACLI) appear frequently before congressional committees; for instance, the ACLI chairman testified before the Senate Banking Committee on "regulatory efficiency and modernization," and particularly the industry problem of facing state rather than federal regulation. The association also lists numerous letters written to politicians as other policy activities. But these insurers, though they seem to be the ideal-typical policy-capable capitalist interest group of sociological lore, are especially unusual in the broader pool of business associations.[39]

Associations that are less resource rich and active adopt various strategies of action intermittently from the broader repertoire interest groups share. Occasionally, they will boast organized visits to members of congress; for instance, the National Association of Real Estate Brokers, composed mostly of African Americans and pursuing "democracy in housing," reports a "Day on Capitol Hill" to meet with members of Congress, and sustained work with the Congressional Black Caucus. Similarly, ACLI organized Capitol Hill visits at a meeting for a special group of "smaller" life insurers. The insurers, the black real estate brokers, and the Independent Bakers also report activities with related political action committees. The insurers and the Food Equipment Manufacturers systematically mobilized members to write to members of Congress on relevant issues. For instance, the Food Equipment Manufacturers were provided with a model letter to senators, on a steel tariff benefitting US steel producers but disadvantageous to domestic manufacturers, and thanked members who called congressional representatives to help defeat some OSHA ergonomics regulations.[40]

Coalition Formation

Confirming Laumann and Knoke's picture of fluid interest group coalitions in policy domains, these groups sometimes work with other associations on particular issues. The insurers worked with nine other groups to argue for a "level playing field" for foreign companies when Japanese life insurance was privatized. In another of many examples, they joined two other associations writing to senators on a corporate life insurance issue. The Brick Industry Association worked on standards and codes with many groups like the American Institute of Architects, the Sustainable Building Industry Council, and the National Concrete Masonry Association. The Food Equipment Manufacturers were part of a temporary coalition—the Consumer-Industry Trade Action Committee—to "advocate for the domestic users of industrial raw materials, including steel." Overall, the common practice of temporary coalition formation for proactive lobbying in the world of associations qualifies the assessment by corporatists, noted above, that politically active American business associations are weak in part because "coordinated action by several associations was relatively rare . . . only an ad hoc arrangement . . . in relation to very specific issues." Even though American industry's collective voice is not organized in a strong, hierarchical form that would enable the formal negotiation of economic issues, politically active associations amplify their "voice" in conventional politics more than corporatists would expect.[41]

However, although temporary alliances among particular groups were quite common, peak associations appeared only in the work of the Food Equipment Manufacturers at this time. They joined the American Chamber of Commerce and the National Association of Manufacturers in a suit about Occupational Health and Safety regulations. There was no evidence that the peak associations that make the pursuit of business interests their central concern usually form issue-specific alliances among politically active business associations.[42]

Federal Agencies and Technical Issues

Most of the political action associations undertake happens below this national-political radar screen, focusing on abstruse technical issues emerging within federal agencies. The black realtors worked with the Department of Housing and Urban Development; for instance, their president spoke at a HUD symposium on fair housing—"The Real Estate Industry Fights for Fair Housing"—and they also signed a Memorandum of Understanding with the lender Freddie Mac. The Food Equipment Manufacturers worked with the EPA, developing "Energy Star" certification for commercial kitchen equipment. The Brick Industry Association was also quite extensively involved with the EPA, developing a detailed strategy, including working with EPA officials, to challenge and shape their rulings. The Envelope Manufacturers claim to have worked on technical issues with the Postal Service for most of the twentieth century. Frequently, technical staff and committees—rather than dedicated "government relations" staff—do the day-to-day political work with regulatory and administrative agencies. The Brick Industry Association's engineering and research division, "attends all code meetings and analyzes each code change" and plays "an active role in advising various regulatory agencies on code changes." The

Closure Manufacturers' technical committee "works with the National Institute of Standards and Technology and state and municipal agencies in establishing closure specifications and sizes consistent with municipal, state and federal laws."[43]

Overall, for these associations, a political orientation and routine pursuit of political interests may involve systematic monitoring, intermittently active lobbying, coalition formation, and regular discussion with government on technical issues. This standard repertoire of strategies of action provides the cultural infrastructure for occasional episodes of heightened mobilization and influence in policy domains. The Irrigation Association illustrates what this routine cultural production looks like.

The Irrigation Association

Located in Falls Church, Virginia, the IA is a strong organization claiming 1,400 members, ten staff, and a budget of $2.5 million. Its members are mostly firms, especially manufacturers, wholesalers, and contractors of irrigation equipment. However, like many business associations, its membership structure crosses categorical boundaries rather than heightening them, and includes dealers, consultants, manufacturers' representatives, and "commercial end users." Members may also include "water and energy agencies" and "affiliate organizations," and individual memberships are also available, including in "student" and "retired" categories. In each category, memberships are available at three different premium levels above the regular level, an illustration of the membership stratification that other observers have noted might complicate the negotiation of interests within business associations.[44]

The IA's ten staff members work with a well-developed organizational structure of committees, "common interest groups," and councils. The association's eleven committees, composed of between fifteen and twenty-five representatives of member firms, include a Legislative Committee and a State Relations Committee. A director of State and Affiliate Relations works with both political committees; also attached to the Legislative Committee is the association's executive director and a "legislative consultant" or lobbyist from a DC firm.[45]

The IA's provision for affiliate membership—a provision it shares with many other associations—should be noted here because, like other associations, it frequently works with affiliates on particular issues. In the IA's view, this "allows both the affiliate and the IA to achieve more, faster, by taking advantage of established networks and resources." Many of its sixty affiliates are regional, state, or local associations of landscapers, or irrigation contractors, like the Associated Landscape Contractors of Colorado or the San Antonio Irrigation Association. A few are associations beyond North America—like the Irrigation Association of Australia and the "N.P.O. Japan Xeriscape Design Association." A few are associations in related fields, like the American Society of Irrigation Consultants, the North American Horticultural Supply Association, and the National Alliance of Independent Crop Consultants.[46]

This organizational background speaks to William Coleman's summary of features of "policy capable" associations—resource diversity, strong organizational structure, and organized relations with other associations. Compared to the majority of American associations, the IA is quite resource rich and organizationally strong; it also has (minimally formalized) connections with other related associations. It falls in the upper ranges of indicators of membership size and staff in the overall population of associations, especially considering it is an association mostly composed of firms, which tend to be smaller. Its DC location, goal statement, and lobbying firm all mark it as more oriented to conventional politics than the majority of associations, and it possesses at least five of the indicators Knoke used in his survey in the 1980s—policy monitoring, public relations, technical data, Congress program, and lobbyists. In American terms, then, it is among the more "policy capable" associations. But it is "policy capable" as an interest group rather than an organ of industry governance.[47]

So what does the Irrigation Association actually do when it confronts its political environment? Unlike the majority of associations, it is involved in an energetic array of over twenty topics in "government affairs," at federal, state, and local levels. Federal policy domains of particular concern are agriculture and science and environment; it is also involved in export promotion initiatives.[48] However, regulation at the local level being of most immediate concern to members, it also reports extensively on regional and local water politics, providing information and working with members and affiliates.

At the beginning of 2004, for instance, the IA was concerned with half a dozen topics at the federal level, topics mostly generated by Department of Agriculture (USDA), the National Council for Science and the Environment, and the Environmental Protection Agency (EPA). It published for members a detailed guide to a recent farm bill, especially "environmentally friendly" sections promoting the "positive use of irrigation," explaining to them how to encourage customers to get government money for irrigation projects. It reported on a recent USDA irrigation survey, the topic of a special keynote breakfast at the previous Irrigation Show. It linked to a detailed report from the Department of the Interior on "Water 2025: Preventing Crises and Conflicts in the West."[49]

Unlike most associations the IA did more than monitor policy information. In a rare example of a formal agreement with government, it signed a Memorandum of Understanding with the USDA Natural Resources Conservation Service, establishing that IA-certified irrigation designers met government standards for providing technical assistance for farm conservation programs. At a National Council for Science and the Environment conference on "Water for a Sustainable Future," their executive director chaired a session on Irrigation and Agriculture, which resulted in eight recommendations, including, first, to "research the sociological and economic impact of current technology and best management practices by the irrigation industry." It was involved in "stakeholder" meetings with the EPA about developing a labeling program for water-efficient products, claiming that its own work on the issue was "recognized as an idea that is far ahead of any other concept in the field." And it "partnered with several turf and green industry associations" to lobby for USDA funding of a "National Turfgrass Research Initiative" (because lawns and landscaping are the other irrigation market besides agriculture, and are controversial for their water usage).[50]

The IA also categorizes more than half a dozen of its own "Industry Initiatives" as related to government affairs. These are mostly technical publications. Although technical, they could be potentially useful resources in conventional politics—as the work on labeling water-efficient products (a "Smart Water Application Technology" report) turned out to be useful at the EPA stakeholder meeting mentioned above. Other publications included, for instance, a "Turf and Landscape Irrigation Best Management Practices" report, and the Water Conservation Policy. Here again there was evidence of mundane, although not routinized, cooperation with other associations; for instance, the IA called on the American Society of Civil Engineers to develop a standardized evaporation equation to "reduce the confusion caused by numerous equations," and also joined with "other green industry associations, businesses, media, and more" in "Project Evergreen," a consumer campaign promoting landscapes.[51]

Apart from work at the federal level, and a collection of informational "industry initiatives" that could be used in political contexts, the IA's third type of government affairs activity was state relations. In this arena it aimed to work through affiliates—the state and local associations mentioned above—but it also provided extensive information, including a detailed weekly report on upcoming state legislation and a bimonthly newsletter on state-level issues. It also offered some model state legislation; for instance, on contractor regulation and certification.[52]

This account shows how standard strategies of action are woven together in day-to-day cultural production and reproduction when associations are oriented to conventional political interests. We can now explore what these activities mean, and the languages in which the pursuit of political interests are understood.

Vocabularies of Motive for Political Engagement

Claims-making about political interests, like most of the claims-making about economic interests we saw in chapter six, relies on the creation and re-creation of "industry" collective identities. As we saw, intra-"industry" economic interests are sometimes understood as the particularistic interests of association members, but more often understood as collective, regardless of particular members' putative benefit. When associations turn their attention to conventional political audiences and projects, they do so almost entirely in terms of collective voice. How do they understand the collective interests they claim to represent?

Conventional wisdom assumes that routinized collective action by institutionalized actors toward established political goals needs no cultural account because it is strategic action. Meaning-making may seem transparently "rational" in mundane, instrumental social processes or arenas where the status quo is operating, in contrast to intense, expressive, episodes or realms liable to unpredictable change. But such assumptions mistake the routinization of meaning-making for the absence of meaning-making, neglecting the fact that the naturalized cultural constructions of what Ann Swidler called "settled times" can be even more consequential for action than the hot and contested meanings of "unsettled times" (or contexts).[53]

The Democratic Code and the Public Good

In contrast, Jeffrey Alexander—recognizing that action always involves meaning-making, even in "supposedly dead routines and institutions"—shows that American political culture is structured in terms of a binary code contrasting "democratic" and "counterdemocratic" features of actors, social relationships, or institutions. For instance, political debate characterizes actors as active, autonomous, rational, and reasonable, or passive, dependent, irrational, and hysterical. Relationships may be seen either as open, trusting, critical, and truthful, or as secret, suspicious, deferential, and deceitful. Institutions may be viewed as rule governed, legal, equal, and inclusive, or arbitrary, powerful, hierarchical, and exclusive. A wide variety of issues are filtered through these lenses within conventional politics, and also when social movements challenge conventional political actors. This cultural code has persisted for centuries, although, for any given issue, the typifications of what exactly is democratic or antidemocratic, and why, are shifting and contingent. Approaching American political culture in this way demonstrates a basic grammar of claims-making that is present wherever people and groups make claims oriented to a broad, differentiated public in democracy-influenced polities—including in the rhetoric of business associations. Just as Durkheim recognized the necessity of identifying shared solidarity underlying difference in modern, complex societies, we need to identify the symbols and claims that sustain political debates.[54]

However, many studies of American political culture's discursive structure treat it in circumstances of conflict or celebration, ritualized episodes of intense involvement or generalized conflict in which language is heightened, value-rational positions are highlighted, and arguments are elaborated across numerous diverse groups. Such studies often focus on the categories, narratives, norms, and frames emergent in the discourse of groups *challenging* the agendas and processes of conventional politics. In all these investigations, the unmarked background is political culture in standard, routinized, political action—such as that of conventional interest groups. This focus on heightened and conflictual contexts rather than routine politics is justified because the cultural categories, symbols, codes, and narratives operating implicitly in mundane contexts emerge more explicitly, in ways that are easier to observe, in culturally intense contexts and moments. But it leaves understudied how meaning-making happens in routine contexts like the associations here.[55]

Luc Boltanski and Laurent Thévenot have argued that "civic" rationales—understood in much the same way as the democratic code—provide one important mundane language for the justification of action in business worlds. Although their empirical evidence of civic rationales is actually based on manuals for trade unions, rather than business, it does seem likely that such rationales are indeed common in business associations, especially in claims-making oriented to conventional political settings. But if business associations, like other groups engaged in conventional political action, make claims in terms of the democratic/antidemocratic code, we need to extend analysis of the civil sphere to mundane, routine interest group politics. Extending civil sphere theory to the ordinary settings in which most routine interest group politics play out, two issues need further attention.[56]

First, what happens when "special interests"—typically characterized as antidemocratic in civil sphere discourse—are themselves institutionalized as legitimate claims-makers? "Special interests" are stigmatized in contexts of heightened, widespread national debate, but the pursuit of *particularistic* interests could also be labeled a democratic virtue in normal interest-group politics. In principle, autonomous and reasonable actors may openly pursue particularistic interests within rule-regulated institutions allowing equal access: this, of course, is the normative ideal of pluralist theories of democratic politics. While pursuit of particularistic interests may be labeled antidemocratic in heightened political debate, it could be seen as democratic in mundane politics. Do business associations avoid the stigmatizing associations of their pursuit of particularistic interests, or do they embrace this goal as a democratic virtue?

Second, how does the democratic/antidemocratic code apply to claims about *issues* worthy of broader public attention? In the cases of heightened political conflict that are usually examined, social movements carry the weight of elevating issues in the civil sphere, or issues are already considered matters of broad public concern (though typifications of actors, relationships, and institutions in terms of the democratic/antidemocratic code are contested). In mundane settings, however, we cannot assume that the agenda is already set, and an issue that concerns an industry group is considered worthy of broader attention. Issues at stake in any given debate may themselves be understood in terms of a codified contrast between particularistic interest and public good. Autonomous and reasonable actors involved in open and trusting relations within rule-regulated and equal institutions may be seen as engaging *issues* related to the public good. Passive and irrational actors involved in secret and suspicious relations within arbitrary and hierarchical institutions may be characterized as pursuing particularistic interests. The binary opposition between particularistic interest and public good can filter the ways issues at stake in any given situation are understood. This means that claims-making requires coding that counterpoises issues themselves in terms of "special interests" and broader "public good," as well as democratic/antidemocratic actors, relationships, and institutions.[57]

How would business associations claim that an issue is worthy of public interest? Rhys Williams helps refine our understanding of the ways issues may be characterized by identifying three different models of "the public good" found in political discourse in the United States. In the "contract model" of the public good, public good is a matter of equal rights, and thus political issues are understood in terms of maintaining or redressing rights of those involved. This dominant and (nationally) persuasive understanding of "public good" is usually coherent with the resolution of the public good into a constellation of particularistic interests, with political pluralism, and with claims for inclusion made by many social movements. However, Williams also identifies two other models, besides the "contract" model, regularly invoked in making claims about the public good on a variety of issues: the covenant model and the stewardship model. The former relies on appeals to transcendent authority; a position on an issue may be argued to be for "the public good" because it is consistent with higher, usually religious, authority. The latter relies on an understanding of the public good as duty to the future—to preservation for future generations, and to sustaining institutions. In both of these views, pursuit of particularistic interests is antidemocratic, and democratic claims-making will appeal to broader notions of the public good: political claims-making will encourage the attachment of heightened general significance to supposedly particularistic issues.[58]

In asking how the democratic/antidemocratic code structures political discourse in the routine settings business associations inhabit, then, we need to ask whether they understand their work as a matter of particularistic interest or public good. If they embrace their role as "special interests," how is it possible to do so without the stigma that role might carry? If they claim that apparently narrow interests are of broader public concern, in what terms do they do so?

In this group of focal associations, two languages of political engagement are mixed. Some use a clearly articulated and comfortably institutionalized language of "industry interest," which situates industries as democratic actors and understands the public good in terms of rights to political voice (a language also evident in the peak associations mentioned above). However, this language coexists with another, more abstract language—or ideology—of political engagement. In this second language, industries' collective identities are shifting and expansive; technical reason replaces political understandings drawn from the democratic/antidemocratic code, and associations are said to act not in terms of "industry interests" but for a public good that is usually understood as stewardship for the future. And just as intraindustry economic interests were more often understood as collective than particularistic, conventional political interests are more often understood in terms of public good than in terms of narrow industry interests. While some associations adopt a simple industry interest language almost entirely, most mix the two sorts of claims, and many rely mostly on the second, broader language of political engagement.

Democratic Virtue and Industry Voice

The Independent Bakers Association, of 415 "mostly family owned wholesale bakeries and allied industry trades" is, in this context, an extreme; an uncomplicated interest group that "was founded in 1968 to protect the interests of independent wholesale bakers from antitrust and anticompetitive mergers and acquisitions; pressure Congress to support market-oriented farm commodity programs, [and] seek representation to consider federal labor, tax, and environmental law." Unlike most associations, it only focuses on a few activities: a monthly newsletter "updating Washington legislative and regulatory actions and analyzing pro-business positions impacting on wholesale baking, allied industry operations," a regulatory library with compliance guides, and three member meetings a year (with parties and golfing elaborately recorded in website photos). An announcement about their winter 2005 meeting, for instance, noted that "with the Bush Administration back in power, IBA will have new opportunities for pro-business legislative and regulatory activities." Industry identity is obvious—though even here that collective identity is also extended to "business" in general. The rules of the political interest game are taken for granted, and American democratic institutions provide the infrastructure for the unabashed pursuit of industry—or "business"—interests.[59]

The larger and more sophisticated North American Food Equipment Manufacturers group (NAFEM) also speaks mostly in terms of clear industry interests. NAFEM sees its mission in terms of providing "voice," reminding its members that "your voice in government does count," and that supporting the association will "ensure your opinions on industry-related issues do not go unheard." Their more elaborated discourse represents industry interests in contrast to explicit others—such as the "domestic steel industry and unions" campaigning for import protection, or OSHA's "vague and subjective," "unreasonable and oppressive" new ergonomic health regulation. Collective identity sometimes extends beyond food equipment manufacturers to domestic manufacturers in general, an extension encouraged by NAFEM's active involvement with other associations on particular issues. But as for the Independent Bakers, a strong industry identity remains central; for instance, one report explains in detail how "Business Tax Reform Big Gain for Manufacturers" but links general manufacturing interests to "significant benefits for NAFEM members and their customers." NAFEM is unusual in its occasional explicit recognition of differing interests within "the industry," as when its newsletter publishes a debate between "manufacturers" and "operators" about whether operators should "accept higher food service equipment prices based on the current increased cost of steel." Nevertheless, "industry" identity is clear, and the pursuit of narrow industry interests is understood as legitimate.[60]

Associations like these illustrate what the democratic/antidemocratic code looks like in routine and mundane circumstances. Grounded in assumptions of the democratic code, their discourse emphasizes the legitimacy and virtue of "voice" about industry interests in government decisions. Democratic voice challenges potentially "unreasonable and oppressive" counterdemocratic actors and institutions.

Stewardship of the Public Good

But few other associations in this focal group are as unabashed as the Independent Bakers and the Food Equipment Manufacturers in their expressions of collective identity and pursuit of "industry" interest. Typically, associations mix expressions of industry interest with broader collective identities, they complicate expressions of industry interest with technocratic language, and a clear vision of particularistic industry interests is almost dissolved in claims about stewardship for the broader public good.

The sophisticated American Council of Life Insurance makes an almost seamless connection between industry interests and stewardship of the public good. Industry interests are certainly clear: ACLI provides a "unified voice" on "policy positions . . . developed through ACLI's comprehensive, member-based committee system," and "we advocate the shared interests of our member companies and their policy holders before federal and state legislators, regulators and courts." But these interests are expressed as coherent with stewardship of the public good: "the life insurance industry is the only industry uniquely focused on both the long-term financial well being of Americans and the long-term financial growth of the U.S. economy." This connection to the public good is easily articulated in terms of financial stewardship, and supported—especially in numerous meetings and panels—with detailed technical information and discussion on the nuances of various aspects of the life insurance industry.[61]

The National Association of Real Estate Brokers also mixes members' economic interests and the public good quite seamlessly. This group aims to "enhance the economic improvement of its members and the minority community it serves" on the "principle that all citizens have a right to equal housing opportunities, regardless of race, creed, or color," and is "dedicated to preserving that right for all Americans." The language of "public good" invoked here is unusual in focusing on equal rights rather than the broader notion of stewardship we see adopted by the life insurers and others.[62]

The Brick Industry Association also combines industry interests and public good. On the one hand, "the BIA's mission is to promote clay brick with the goal of increasing its market share and to safeguard the industry." On the other hand, in doing so, it has "upgraded the degree to which it invests in programs in areas of environment, health, and safety." For instance, it awards industry prizes in "Environmental Stewardship"; winners' submissions elaborate detailed, technical programs—"tools of the trade"—for "serving as a responsible steward of the environment." Industry interests are also interwoven with "public good" in reports of research that shows "adoption of a masonry ordinance" in local communities enhances "the overall fiscal health of the community" and discussions of community planning for disaster preparedness and for a "built environment that is safe, long-lasting and contributes to their community's sense of place." And for the brick industry, as for the life insurance companies, these broad claims are quickly translated into a technical language grounded in expertise, research, and information.[63]

If we take the Independent Bakers and the Food Equipment Manufacturers as illustrating the sort of strong, clear language of industry interests we might expect in an industry interest group, the Irrigation Association illustrates the other end of a continuum of political language, from narrow interest to public good, a continuum in which the insurers, the black realtors, and the brick manufacturers occupy the middle ranges. As we saw above, the Irrigation Association (IA) is broadly representative in its organization and its activities of that minority of business associations that are oriented to politics and act as conventional interest groups. The public language in which it expresses political interest, though, is inclusive, repeatedly refusing limits that potentially opposing positions might place on the collective identity grounding the interests it pursues, and failing almost entirely to explicitly construct a contrasting "other" to oppose. Sustaining this nonconflictual language is an elaborate technocratic language stressing information and expertise and eliminating almost entirely explicit opinion and argument. As a result, political actors, institutions, and relationships are only very rarely typified in terms of the democratic/ antidemocratic code. The inclusive, nonconflictual language of political action is sustained not only by a language of technical reason but also by an emphasis on the public good, understood in terms of stewardship.

The Irrigation Association and the Language of Stewardship

Among the ten benefits the IA claims to offer members is "a voice on your behalf with government." One of the ways it "protects and supports the irrigation industry" is by "providing a voice for the industry on public policy issues related to standards, conservation and water-use on local, national and international levels." The association pursues industry interests, then, by exercising democratic voice, as did the food equipment manufacturers' group. But in contrast to that group, talk of political "voice" is directly linked to a language of accountability and responsibility. Industry interests are connected to the broader collective good: "since 1949, Irrigation Association members worldwide have worked towards a shared vision—water conservation through efficient irrigation"—a vision detailed in a water conservation policy adopted by the association in 1990, which calls for "increased cooperation among all water users, agricultural and urban." The terms in which political action is understood and expressed involve democratic voice, but also protection, support, and collective good. This is a language simply deconstructed as ideology masking interests, but it should not be taken for granted and, as the examples discussed above show, it could be otherwise. Three illustrations from the IA's writings—a Best Management Practices report, a local lobbying handbook for members, and a newsletter on state and local water politics—show in more detail this important and routine dimension of political culture even among standard industry interest groups.[64]

As we saw earlier, much of what the IA characterizes as its political action comes in the form of technical "industry initiatives." Technical as most of the industry initiatives are, they are also illuminating sites for analysts of political culture. Unlikely as it may seem, the "Turf and Land-scape Irrigation Best Management Practices" report offers more intrigu-ing political rhetoric than many genres—like political speeches or news reports —more familiar to sociologists. Oriented to a variety of "stake-holders"—mostly policy makers and "industry professionals"—"who must save and extend our water supply while protecting water quality," its practical guidelines are embedded in a rhetorical context that thema-tizes "effective water stewardship"—shared responsibility and account-ability—and technologically efficient conservation.

> Water sustains every community . . . from the most basic needs of its citizens to the very lifeblood of the community's economic growth. In both urban and rural areas across the U.S., water rights, allocation, treatment, delivery, and supply issues are increasingly subject to legislation and regulation. Frequently, measures are passed in reaction to a crisis and without a comprehensive plan. As the focus on our water resources increases, so does the need for equitable policy and progressive water management practices.

Landscapes are a widely valued public—or consumer—good (presum-ably, here, not desert landscapes). The visibility of landscape irrigation "mandates accountability" so *stakeholders at every level must demon-strate their understanding of the resource and the technology that delivers it.*" Science and technology—"science-based principles," "*professionalism and expertise in water management,*" "efficient irrigation," "sensible, in-formed decisions," and "opportunities for improved efficiency"—are key, as too is "consideration of local geographic, economic, and political condi-tions" (emphasis in original).[65]

From the point of view of simple ideology critique, the underlying issue is a straightforward concern that the irrigation business would be hurt by local restrictions on water usage for landscaping. For the irrigation industry, failure in this project would bring "serious consequences," "inappropriate mandates," and inability "to control [the irrigation industry's] destiny."[66] More interesting, though, is the cultural form of the generally implicit po-litical claims. The issues are framed in terms of collective good, and the ver-sion of collective good invoked is stewardship. Just as important as themes of stewardship and the collective good are technocratic themes—techno-logical developments and professional knowledge can solve water conser-vation issues without reducing consumption inappropriately.

Because of a drought, local water politics was a highly salient issue for the IA at this time, and its efforts to shape responses extended beyond the

measured contribution of "Best Management Practices." Another "industry initiative" they made available was a "Water Action Guide" helping
"industry professionals like you" with "grassroots guidance and information you need to effectively influence decisions or restrictions that will
affect water use in your community—and your business." This mobilization "resource" was another coalition effort, developed with the American Nursery Landscape Association, Associated Landscape Contractors
of America, and Turfgrass Producers International. A "vital industry that
touches the lives of every American" was at risk from "well-intended,
knee-jerk restrictions, some of which may actually be harmful to both the
environment and the economy." Legislators needed to be educated, and
the "Action Guide" provided the tools and instructions for local mobilization. The guide outlined practical plans under headings such as "Form
a Coalition," "Get Noticed," "Lobby like a Pro . . . or Hire One," and
"Share the Facts: Water Use" (and many of the questions it raises and
strategies it suggests would easily make a model for very different groups
of activists).[67]

Even though this is explicitly mobilization in pursuit of industry interests, though, the categories and strategies of action emphasize cooperation for the collective good, and information, not self-interest and political
hardscrabble. The guide is a political etiquette manual as well as a serious
information source. "It's in your own best interests to be a team player"; "it
is more productive to engage in self-imposed restrictions . . . than to react
to someone else's restrictions"; "it is a natural instinct to have a "fend-for-
yourself" or "survival of the fittest" attitude, but that approach isn't really
in your best interests"; "remain calm"; "focus on creating and maintaining positive community relationships, while proactively working towards
permanent water management resolutions"; "we have the chance to be the
largest, number one contributor to reducing water consumption and cleaning up the water . . . our expertise and technology is going to be huge";
"your lobbying efforts are meant to inform as well as persuade"; "never
burn a bridge"; "make your points in a businesslike manner. Being overly
argumentative can hurt your case." Miss Manners might have consulted
in producing this political manual. Democratic actors, as Alexander and
Smith argued, are characterized as reasonable, calm, and controlled.[68]

The IA also publishes a newsletter that is mostly a roundup of state
political news, well presented enough to make topics like "Rain Shut-
Off Legislation Advances," "Texas Begins Revision of Chapter 344," or
"Connecticut Green Industry Associations Come Together" unexpectedly interesting to outsiders. Again, as in the federal political action and

the industry initiatives, the rhetoric is one of information, not opinion, cooperation in shared community rather than intense political conflict in the pursuit of capitalist interest.[69] The tone heightens only very occasionally. One leading story discusses new Republican Party dominance of State Houses—"Republicans Win Fifty-Year Battle"—although it also warns that "with states struggling with their worst economic outlook in a decade," legislators "may wonder what they got themselves into." Some Vermont legislation prohibiting anyone but licensed landscape architects to design irrigation draws some unusually sharp language—it will "seriously threaten" the irrigation business "under the guise of protecting public health, safety, and welfare"—but even here, peace is on the horizon because the IA will meet with the corresponding landscape association, ASLA, "in an attempt to find common ground that can be agreed upon."[70]

Notably, the only explicit argumentation, and some of the most passionate language, in the IA's *Statesman* emerges in attempts by the association's director of state and affiliate relations to persuade his readers that lobbying is legitimate. He is challenging the opinion that "there is always the faint odor of a garbage can when it comes to most people's perspective of what lobbying is all about." On the contrary, he argues, political involvement is normal and important. "Isn't your daily work a form of lobbying? . . . when you try to persuade a customer to agree to your proposal or try to sell someone your product as opposed to a competitor's you are lobbying." If salesmanship is legitimate, so too is political action. Readers may also believe that they "don't have time to spend with a bunch of politicians who know nothing about irrigation," but "that's exactly why lobbying is important. Elected officials don't know the irrigation business . . . lobbying is an effort to inform as well as persuade."[71]

The Irrigation Association's construction of its political action shows political culture not in generalized episodes of heightened political conflict or celebration, but in the unmarked context of normal political interest group activity. Although some features of heightened rhetoric occasionally make an appearance, this more routinized political discourse is significantly different in its expansive collective identities, technocratic as opposed to democratic typification and argument, and generalized versions of "public good."

With rare exceptions, there is no "other" in this routinized political discourse. Such an "other" is occasionally structurally implied—most often, as legislators who need enlightening. But a language of collective identity is flexed and extended to wrap almost any potential interaction partner or opponent. First, and as one would expect, potentially differing or conflicting positions of different types of members—manufacturers and wholesalers, agricultural businesses and landscapers, big and small companies, New York and Arizona businesses—are never expressed or discussed in these public documents. Although we might take this for granted, it could easily be otherwise, as it was in the food equipment manufacturers' group.[72]

In addition, the "we" of the Irrigation Association can extend much further than its members. It frequently encompasses related associations, and the broader identity of the "Green Industry" is repeatedly invoked. Beyond related industries, as we see above, there are "stakeholders"; beyond those active interaction partners, there is the collective identity of "shared vision," and a fact of life that confronts "every community," or "touches every American." Where opposing positions begin to threaten this flexible and all-encompassing rhetoric of shared identity, the difference is ignored or quickly defused. There is no comment or opinion in one account of a setback to passing a certification bill in New York in which opponents argued that the requirement of three years prior experience was "too discriminatory against minorities." On other issues, the irrigators "seek common ground that can be agreed upon" with the landscapers over the licensing issue. Those who promote water restrictions simply need better information, which the irrigators can supply.[73]

Very occasionally, an emotionally charged binary code of "democratic" and "antidemocratic" actors and relationships appears—as in the fear of the industry's "loss of control," the advice emphasizing reasoned and calm political involvement and the virtues of democratic "voice," and the negative characterization of opposing measures as deceitful ("under the guise of") or unrealistic and excitable ("well-intended" "knee-jerk"). On these occasions, the underlying cultural code of American civil society that emerges more clearly in dramatic political circumstances becomes part of mundane meaning-making. But, at the same time, political culture is not reducible to this underlying culture-structure. Compared to episodes of heightened drama and conflict, the discourse is flat, the tone cognitive rather than emotional, and much is simply assumed about the identities of the actors involved and their supposedly shared values and interests. Eliding these dimensions of interest-group rhetoric would miss too much. What, then, are the distinctive features of this routinized political discourse, beyond its basic civil sphere grammar?

As much of the language above illustrates, this mild-mannered expression of "political interest" is sustained in two ways. First, the dominant rhetoric is one of reason and information. It is notable that most of the discourse of the IA about "government affairs" is informational, technical, or both. Facts are presented and strategies of action are sometimes suggested, but rarely are arguments developed or interests explicitly elaborated. Government affairs and political action is, in this world, all about "sensible and informed decisions," "professionalism and expertise in water management," "technological efficiency," and so on.[74]

Second, "political interest" is understood mostly in terms of "the public good." With no identified "other" and a broad and mutable collective identity, this standard political interest group expresses itself and its purposes in terms of shared vision, cooperation, responsibility, and accountability. Such language sometimes seems clearest where, reading between the lines, issues are sharpest (as in the "Best Management Practices" document for landscape irrigation). More particularly, the IA illustrates a "stewardship" model of the public good, in which "contemporary society is charged with the careful management of its resources and gifts for future benefit as well as current advantage." Williams finds this understanding of the public good in some religious and environmental movement organizations; we see it here in mundane and conventional politics. This is notable because one might expect that in conventional politics, a "contract" model of the public good, based on shared rights and inclusion, would be most common.[75]

This standard interest group seems to share, too, another feature of American political discourse that has been identified before in less conventional political contexts. Dawne Moon found in her study of how different congregations dealt with controversies about homosexuality that opponents shared distaste for what they understood as politics. More generally, Nina Eliasoph has traced the ways a "culture of political avoidance" pervades grassroots public action in the United States. As it turns out, more mainstream political contexts also seem to show some influence of this normative demonizing of "politics"—as suggested by the argument above, directed at association members, that lobbying is legitimate. Its softened rhetoric of political engagement is not only an ideological strategy to mask, or reconfigure, the pursuit of "interest," as it certainly is, but also a necessary element in the successful communication of its interest-group work to many members.[76]

The Irrigation Association is a broadly representative example of that minority of business associations that are oriented to politics and act as conventional interest groups. As we have seen, associations mix two languages in articulating their political action, a language of "industry interest" and democratic voice, and a language of technical reason and public good. While the first is what we would expect, the second is less well known—but it is at least equally strong, and in some associations like the IA, the dominant language of political claims. The public language in which the IA and other similar associations express political interest is inclusive, repeatedly refusing limits that potentially opposing positions might place on the collective identity grounding the interests it pursues, and failing almost entirely to explicitly construct a contrasting "other" to oppose. An elaborate technocratic language stressing information and expertise, and eliminating almost entirely explicit opinion and argument, sustains this nonconflictual language. So too does an emphasis on the public good, understood in terms of stewardship. Conventional capitalist interest groups, it turns out, may speak only rarely of "interests."

Conclusion

The Distilled Spirits Council's party at the New York Yacht Club is not representative of American business associations' engagement in conventional politics. The new evidence explored in the first part of this chapter shows that most business associations are not as interested in political influence as that archetype suggests, nor as commonsense expectations and dominant theories assume. A significant minority do act as well-formed lobby groups, but the vast majority are not lobbying routinely; most address or monitor policy concerns only occasionally or rarely.

Even politically active associations are usually more attuned to monitoring policy developments than to influencing policy with proactive engagement in setting agendas, developing policy choices, and influencing policy decisions, though most politically oriented associations will occasionally be involved in more proactive ways in particular policy domains. And most politically oriented associations are involved more in abstruse political/technical issues in agencies relevant in particular policy domains, rather than in congressional politics.

The emerging picture conforms to Laumann and Knoke's analysis of American interest group politics in terms of complex, stratified policy domains involving shifting alliances and wide variation in levels of influence. The practice of making issue-specific alliances amplifies the potential voice of politically active associations, but this potential voice usually remains muted because most business associations, even those that are politically engaged to one degree or another, are minor actors in the policy domains they engage. Among the focal associations I have discussed, only the American Council of Life Insurance could be anything more than a peripheral actor.

These findings do not challenge research that demonstrates the disproportionate influence of business in American politics. Peak industry associations clearly devote themselves almost entirely to conventional lobbying for business; even their websites make a strong contrast to those analyzed here. This might suggest a field-level division of labor, in which peak associations advance business associations' political influence, and "industry" associations take care of other, more particular issues. However, any such division of labor is complicated by the evidence of other studies that also show business influence increasingly channeled through the lobbying of particular firms and by the evidence from the minority of "industry" associations examined here that address political issues particular to the enterprises of their members (so, for instance, peak associations would be unlikely to address water conservation policies important to irrigation firms). Moreover, the rare active and influential industry lobbying associations could sometimes have a big impact: policy domains routinely include such organizations representing business as well as other interests. We should also recall that less active associations may also be mobilized occasionally as peripheral actors in policy domains.

What the picture here does show is that standard theories and conventional assumptions about national business associations based on political interest—corporatist, pluralist, or elitist—cannot account for why American business associations thrive.

In the focal group of politically oriented associations, public languages of explicit political interest are mixed and diluted with a political language of flexible and broad collective identities, underpinned by claims about the public good—especially stewardship—and about technical reason and expertise. Of course, particularistic industry interests are not dissolved in ideological claims about broader identities and benefits. This ambiguity is often thought to generate puzzles about the relative mix of "self-interest" and "altruism" in the motivations and intentions of political actors, about whether political actors are opportunistic in their claims about public good. As Schlozman and Tierney suggest: "when appeals to the public good are made by those who stand to benefit selectively from a particular policy outcome, it is often difficult to assess precisely the mix of sincerity and cynicism at work." But this is a false dilemma. What is important is not the personal sincerity or guileful opportunism of the public relations director of the American Council of Life Insurance or the president of the National Association of Real Estate Brokers, but rather the vocabularies of motive in which they understand their work and communicate with their audiences. Even if one could assume that all claims about broader identities and benefits were intended as cynical manipulation, which is unlikely, the fact that conventional interest group politics often gets conducted in terms of the public good and technical reason means that "interests" cannot be taken as transparent facts by contrast to claims about collective identity and public good.[77]

The prevalence of a language of public good and technical reason might be surprising since the minority of associations engaged in conventional and routine interest group politics mostly act in policy domains and regulatory agencies that receive little attention from the public. Since there is little obvious or direct pressure from the general public, one might expect that claims about explicit industry interests would have more currency in such specialized settings. Adoption of the democratic code and ideologies of the public good are usually more associated with an orientation to participation in the broader public sphere.

To what extent and how do business associations orient themselves to influencing broader publics than bureaucrats and politicians? Answers to this question are particularly significant if, as Mark Smith has argued, the political influence of business is mediated by their influence on public opinion.[78]

CHAPTER NINE

"A Tense and Permeable Boundary"

Business Associations in the Civil Sphere

Scholars concerned with democratic governance are interested in civic engagement, civil society, and the public sphere as well as conventional political institutions. Citizens' orientations to the broader public—and the organizations, networks, and institutions that generate and articulate such orientations—are often at issue in studies of political culture, of non-profit organizations, and of "social capital." They are not often associated with economic life; indeed, they are usually defined in contrast to work, business, and industry. Because business associations are so closely associated with economic interests, no one has thought to ask whether their discourses and strategies of action ever situate their members in broader public concerns beyond their own profit and market stability. But we have already begun to see that even where they engage in conventional interest group politics, they often speak in terms of the public good. Some associations also orient themselves to the wider public sphere, beyond conventional political institutions. "Just a concern for their fellow citizens" (as one association director put it), sometimes seems to blur what Jeffrey Alexander has labeled "a tense and permeable boundary" between capitalist economic action and the civil sphere. This chapter investigates the surprisingly neglected question of how some associations participate in the public sphere, examining their attempts to influence public opinion and their engagement in civic concerns.[1]

After reviewing some scholarly assumptions about associations' interest in public opinion, I assess population evidence about their public relations work, and then narrow the focus to analyze strategies of action and discursive claims about public relations evident in the focal sample, concluding with an extended illustration from the Firestop Contractors International Association. More associations are interested in influencing public opinion than are oriented to conventional political action, and they tend to differ in major organizational features from interest-group associations. In practice, an orientation to influencing public opinion often means collective marketing of the sort discussed in chapter six. But some associations do implement programs to influence public opinion beyond the market; usually, they are concerned with opinion in small, specialist publics more than the general public. Like associations oriented to conventional politics, these associations talk in a language invoking broad-based collective identities, technical reason, and the public good.

I then sketch social scientific views of voluntary groups in the American civil sphere, especially those that emphasize substantive cultural orientations rather than formal organizational features. After analyzing orientations to "civic" goals in the business association population, I examine strategies of action and vocabularies of motive adopted by those associations in the focal sample that seem to challenge the distinction between economy and civil society, and conclude with an extended illustration from the National Association of Real Estate Brokers. Some business association discourse and action looks more like that of social movements or philanthropic groups than what one might expect of business. While we should not exaggerate the extent of this civic orientation, I argue that the blurring of boundaries between "industry" interest and broader social concerns sometimes evident in these groups warrants more attention from social scientists concerned with developing civil society than it has yet received.

Business Associations and Public Opinion

Although business associations' attempts to influence public opinion are neither well documented nor well understood by scholars and policy makers, a number of observations suggest that the topic deserves more attention. Ivar Berg and Mayer Zald argue that "in common with more organized and coherent social movements, business leaders have invested increasing amounts of resources to mobilize public opinion." Lloyd Warner and Desmond Martin assert that business associations paid increasing attention to public relations after World War II, and that general public influence is an important reason why they are significant. Richard Tedlow,

having examined public relations campaigns of the National Association
of Manufacturers (NAM) (a peak association) in the 1930s and 1940s,
claimed that NAM "was unquestionably influential in establishing public relations as a permanent fixture in the American trade association."
He also made the broader claim that associations had "been intimately
involved in a long-term program to 'sell the American way of life to
the American people,'" and speculated that this sort of political action
may be more characteristic of American associations than associations
elsewhere.[2]

Public relations activity on the part of associations could be particularly significant, politically speaking, if, as Mark Smith has argued, direct
business influence on policy outcomes is less important than "its capacity
to shape public opinion," and if, as Robert Wuthnow has noted from
another point of view, the voluntary sector shapes public discourse.[3]

On the other hand, business associations' political concerns are often
rather obscure, and many industry issues seem influenced more by arcane
regulations than by public goodwill. Most political sociologists would argue that problem definition, and the formulation of policy alternatives, are
usually more likely to happen beyond public debate than policy choice,
where public opinion is more likely to count, and that these "agenda-
setting" modes of political influence are more important than the final
step of policy choice. And even where choices are being made between
previously formulated policies, public input will not necessarily be relevant. For these reasons, efforts by ordinary business associations to "shape
public opinion" might typically be more intermittent and more focused
than earlier authors have suggested and generally less significant than
lobbying efforts.[4]

Apart from influencing their political environment, public opinion may
also be important to associations as an arena for making jurisdictional
claims to expertise and "legitimate control of a particular kind of work."
As chapter seven shows, such "professional" concerns are explicit in the
orientations of many associations. Andrew Abbott emphasizes the importance of news and fictional treatments of professional characters for
the image of professions, but certainly associations' mundane public relations work could also be oriented to informing public audiences about, or
improving the image of, particular lines of business. Abbott suggests that
public opinion formation is consequential when it "builds images to pressure the legal system" to develop institutionalized jurisdictional control,
but as we have seen, "professionalism" matters to business associations

for market position and for the status and meaning of the occupational community derived from its intrinsic technical skill.[5]

So some observers suggest public relations have become an increasingly important political function of associations, and associations may also wish to influence public opinion to strengthen claims to "professional" jurisdictional control on the market. Examples are not difficult to find. In mid-2006, for instance, the American Iron and Steel Institute began an advertising campaign in Washington to counter the steel industry's negative image and to "reposition steel-making as a vibrant and crucial part of the American economy" because "we want to be sure that Congress realizes that this industry deserves a level playing field." Similarly, as we saw briefly in chapter eight, the American Council of Life Insurance ran advertisements on their "Protecting and Investing for the Long Term" theme in Washington publications in late 2004. Smaller and more obscure associations also frequently seem to describe themselves in terms of broader public relations goals; there are groups, for instance, that aim to "promote public awareness of the self storage industry," and to "increase public interest in and awareness of the lightning protection industry." Suppliers of needlework patterns "strive to . . . promote the chartered design industry," and, in a very different economic sphere, another group "promotes and defends the use of asbestos cement building materials."[6]

Orientations to Public Opinion

In their 1960s study, Warner and Martin found that just under half of their sample (47 percent) had programs to influence general public opinion—only a slightly smaller proportion than those reporting a more direct political orientation. Later, David Knoke found that two-thirds of business associations he sampled reported having a public relations officer. However, only 13 percent of trade associations in his 1980s survey reported using media public appeals as a *tactic of political influence*, a much smaller proportion than that reporting tactics like personal contact with officials and coalitions with other groups. Kay Schlozman and John Tierney found that 31 percent of trade associations *in* Washington reported advocacy advertising, and 89 percent reported talking with the press as a technique of influence, but none saw this as consuming significant time or resources. Again, there is something of a conflict between general claims that public relations are important to associations and claims that it is not a particularly significant political tactic.[7]

Judging on contemporary associations' statements of purpose, general public relations is more important than direct concerns with monitoring or lobbying government. Associations were coded as interested in public relations if they indicated goals or activities oriented to informing, educating, or increasing the awareness of the general public, or advancing members' reputation with specific groups within the general public but beyond the association. Forty-one percent articulated public relations as a goal, compared to the one in four associations specifying an orientation to government or regulatory bodies. However, as we will see, this high proportion encompasses different sorts of "publics," not all of them political.

If associations were interested in public relations, they were also more likely to be interested in monitoring policy and lobbying.[8] But although these two types of external orientation were related, associations expressing concern with public relations did not look very much like associations expressing a direct interest in monitoring policy and lobbying. They differed in the following organizational features:

- Whereas smaller associations were more likely to be interested in monitoring and lobbying goals, larger associations were slightly more likely to express public relations goals.[9]
- Whereas associations composed of firms were more likely to be interested in policy, associations composed of both firms and individuals were more likely to express public relations goals.[10]
- Whereas reports of regional groups and association affiliates made no difference to direct expression of political goals, such connections did correlate significantly with public relations goals.[11]
- Unlike for associations interested in monitoring policy and lobbying, number of staff was *not* correlated with the expression of public relations goals.[12]

An orientation to public relations seemed more diffuse than an orientation to policy in other ways too:

- Associations expressing public relations goals also deviated from the pattern of those expressing direct political goals because public relations goals were *not* correlated with a DC location.[13]
- The proportion of associations expressing public relations goals increased markedly for those associations founded after 1960. This supports Warner and Martin's speculation that public relations became an increasingly important goal in the second half of the twentieth century. There appears to be no such

trend by decade of formation for associations expressing lobbying and monitoring goals.[14]

- Finally, sectors more inclined to express public relations goals differed markedly from those more inclined to express straightforward political goals. The five sectors with the highest proportion of associations expressing public relations goals—well above the population average—were agriculture (59 percent); utilities (56 percent); arts, entertainment, and recreation (55 percent); real estate, rental, and leasing (49 percent); and miscellaneous services (46 percent). Of these, only utilities and real estate ranked in the top five sectors expressing political goals.[15]

Overall, these patterns suggest that an interest in public relations is not simply oriented to conventional political purposes—as it was for the steel institute in the example above, and most previous observers have assumed. So what exactly does public relations mean for these associations?

Strategies of Action and the Meaning of "Public Relations"

The focal associations' documents show that some sort of interest in public relations and influencing opinion probably extends beyond the proportion captured by coding *Encyclopedia* self-descriptions; 60 percent of the focal sample, compared to 41 percent of the statements of purpose, involved some sort of significant and explicitly stated public relations interest. Even though it would not be coded with an interest in public relations from its brief self-description, the International Concrete Repair Institute includes in its strategic plan for the future,

> member representation to external audiences, message delivery about the value of quality concrete repair to customers, media, government agencies and the general public; become *the* strong voice of the concrete repair professional. Broaden the ICRI audience, reach end users (building owners, etc.), decision-makers and influences (government agencies, etc.), media and allied trade and professional organizations (emphasis in original).

And the former National Bark and Soil Producers' Association became the Mulch and Soil Council to "help build public recognition for the organization and its members."[16]

But as these examples begin to indicate, public relations often means something more, or something different, than simply tending the grounds of direct political influence. There is an important ambiguity in the ways "public relations" can be understood. Earlier claims and observations about associations' public relations activity have not distinguished public relations to influence public opinion for "political" reasons, public relations oriented to marketing, and public relations to improve members' social standing as economic actors. Given their collective identities as "industry" actors, associations are frequently oriented to—and see themselves in relation to—numerous others, and many do not sharply demarcate the boundaries between these different types of audiences. Self-descriptions often include some general claim about promotion; for instance, the Pellet Fuels Institute "promotes the increased use of pellets, briquettes, chips, and other renewable fuels," and the Equipment Service Association "improves the status and image of the equipment service industry . . . and promotes new business for the industry." In one of the lengthier statements along these lines, the United Lightning Protection Association

> works to increase public interest in and awareness of the lightning protection industry; encourage and extend the use of lightning protection; promote public education on the merits and economy of lightning protection systems; advocate members . . . in order to aid the public in securing safe, dependable, and attractive installations.[17]

Different associations will emphasize different types of public relations to different degrees. In general, public relations oriented to collective marketing is the most common orientation; public relations oriented to political issues and audiences, or to improving members' occupational status, are less commonly expressed concerns that nevertheless emerge in association with marketing issues in some associations at some times.

Associations have a standard repertoire of strategies of action for public relations, as they do for monitoring policy and lobbying. Some of their most common strategies of action are oriented more to collective marketing than to political influence. In the focal sample, over half (56 percent) develop and provide product or service information, in special website sections and in brochures. Forty percent offer membership directories, and over a quarter (28 percent) offer certification programs that are explicitly and strongly understood in terms of public relations. However, programs of press releases (52 percent) seem less necessarily tied to collective marketing and may be oriented to broader publics; so, too, do some other, less common strategies of action: offering complete media kits

(8 percent); organizing a "speaker's network" about services, products, and issues (12 percent); or writing letters to the press (8 percent).

In contrast to the implications of Tedlow and others discussed above, but as one might otherwise expect from the small size and obscurity of most associations, larger-scale public campaigns are rare. In the focal sample, only the American Council of Life Insurance (ACLI) was "advertising" in this way; the ACLI was also unusual in employing a director of media relations—with two assistants—and offering a standard press packet.[18]

Although many associations write press releases, usually up to twenty-five a year, these are often oriented to very narrow audiences, often in related industries, or even simply to members. Examples such as "Auto Lift Institute and Tire Industry Association Form Two Year Strategic Safety Alliance," "Exhibit Designers and Producers Association (EDPA) Launches Online Educational Webinars," and "EMA Releases Final Report of Intelligent Document Task Force" give a flavor of what most associations rate as newsworthy.[19]

As these examples might suggest, coverage of these focal associations in major media outlets is more the exception than the rule and seems to confirm what Ronald Jacobs and Daniel Glass found in a study of media coverage of New York nonprofits, that "media publicity is an incredibly scarce resource." Business associations highlight the rare publicity they receive. The Independent Bakers Association made much of an occasion when its director was featured on *Dateline NBC* "to talk about the Food Pyramid and the importance of Carbohydrates in the diet." The United Lightning Protection Association boasted to its members of a press release—from the Lightning Safety Alliance, of which it is a member—"which received national newswire pickup." For any given association, media recognition is a rare and notable event.[20]

But for most associations, public relations is understood more as a matter of industry business than public influence. The distinction between publics and markets, shaky at best in contemporary political culture, is especially liable to be vague for them. Some associations interested in public relations understood it almost entirely in terms of collective marketing, as discussed in chapter six. For instance, when an association aims to "promote confidence between consumer and the automotive service industry" or to "work to educate users in the uses, requirements, and security of online systems," the understanding of "public" in "public relations" is clearly more market related than political. Sometimes there are particular and explicit external audiences: the Equipment Service Association, for instance, "promotes good relations with equipment service managers." The public appears to be the audience for claims to jurisdictional control for a line of work on the market, rather than an audience for developing the legitimacy of explicit claims about an "industry's" political environment.[21]

So, overall, associations' attempts to influence public opinion take a variety of forms, commonly involving press releases; providing information for customers; reactive or proactive public statements on public issues involving the products or service of members; certification and accreditation programs; and more occasionally through techniques like speakers' bureaus, public relations campaigns, and promotional kits and brochures for members. Much of this public relations activity is directed to publics-as-markets, so it is important not to overstate associations' interest in influencing their political environment through public relations—as previous observations have implied.

However, for about a quarter of associations in the focal group, part of what good public opinion meant involved their members' connections to issues on the public agenda, and they did see their public relations efforts as directed to influencing public opinion on issues of general concern. The interests of members, potential customers, and the public at large were seen as fused. This fusion builds on a long-standing ideological tradition identified by Francis Sutton and his colleagues in the 1950s, that of considering business as sustaining the "spirit of service" and demanding "heavy social responsibilities of a business executive." Along the same lines, Arthur Lentz and Harvey Tschirgi found in the 1960s that in their annual reports, "most companies are very community conscious and attempt to project the image of 'good citizens' to their locale." In the social worlds of the business associations considered here, such issues often involved product standards, safety, or the environment.[22]

Vocabularies of Motive, Public Relations, and the Public Good

Public safety and product standards were routinely linked to public relations in many industry associations. The United Lightning Protection Association issued a press release about standards changes that they said "offers a persuasive endorsement for lightning protection systems and supports state and federal mandated lightning protection requirements." The Mulch and Soil Council, worried about publicity that woods treated with poison were making their way into mulch, made a public statement about the problem, stressing that "in an ongoing effort to protect the public, the

Council will continue its efforts to have federal and state governments prohibit the disposal of CCA-treated wood in consumer garden mulch products." The Automotive Lift Institute's press releases stress safety and standards almost entirely: "Updated Safety Materials Available for Auto Technicians," "Automotive Lift Institute Offers Updated Safety Tips," "Automotive Lift Institute Recognized by Standards Engineering Society." Whether defensive—as for the Mulch and Soil Council—or more proactive—as for the Lightning Protection group—public relations for these associations meant addressing the public, and sometimes regulatory agencies, on issues of public safety.[23]

In addition to product safety, public relations efforts were sometimes couched in terms of supposed environmentalist virtues, as we also saw in the conventional political engagement of the Irrigation Association in chapter eight. The Pellet Fuels Institute, for instance, which sees itself in part as a "trade association dedicated to the advancement and promotion of densified fuel technology that will help solve global ecological issues," put out press releases on topics like "Wood Pellets for Home Heating Can Help Reduce Poor Air Quality," and "Pellet Fuel Can Help Reduce Global Warming." While not as engaged in routine political monitoring as the Irrigation Association, it fused industry interest and public good in the same way in its public relations. The wide diffusion and apparent legitimacy of environmentalist language (diffused in part by regulatory agencies like the EPA) is worth noting as an unacknowledged if incomplete success of environmental advocates, and business associations should be added to the range of actors considered in organizational fields generating environmental policy outcomes.[24]

A few associations address social issues when they link their public relations and public good. This was evident in one project of the Association for Women in Aviation Maintenance, which organizes a speakers' network intended to "expand public awareness of women in aviation maintenance, to encourage young people to explore aviation as a career option and to inspire women of all ages to pursue their dreams." And the Investment Division of the historically black National Association of Real Estate Brokers issued a press release about how "Answering President's Call to Increase Minority Home Ownership Minority Real Estate Agents Nationwide Deliver Free Real Estate Advice to Consumers." However, this connotation was more typical of associations and strategies of action oriented to civic goals, discussed below, than to those oriented to public relations.[25]

Typically, associations oriented to public opinion see themselves as bringing their distinctive technical expertise to bear on creating public standards for the common good—understood as product safety or environmental benefits. As we have seen, business associations often create, disseminate, and reward technical standards. Standard setting can be understood as a strategy of action oriented to the pursuit of market interests; standards may be developed in an attempt to signal market quality. Beyond that, chapter seven showed that this sort of strategy of action is also understood as expressing an occupational community's disinterested technical excellence, and discussed in a language of professionalism. But there is a third discourse in which standard setting as a strategy of action may be understood: in politics and the public sphere, standard setting becomes stewardship of the public good. This is evident in some of the work of associations in conventional politics, described in chapter eight, and it is very explicit in associations' understanding of their work to influence public opinion.

We can take as an extended example the Firestop Contractors International Association (FCIA). Often sounding more like a social movement than a conventional interest group, this association is more focused on its public relations work than most associations. It is not strictly representative, but rather it provides a particularly sharp illustration of strategies of action and vocabularies of motive that are evident more intermittently in other associations.

The Firestop Contractors International Association

The FCIA was formed in 1998 and within five years boasted a membership of a hundred firms. Voting members are "specialty building construction contractors with a specific interest in the installation of firestop materials and systems," but manufacturers, distributors, code officials, architects, building owners, and other interested parties may join as associates. Officially located in the Chicago area, the association has an executive director but no other staff. Most of its extensive work is done by the active membership in eight committees—accreditation, codes, technical, standards, marketing, education, membership, and program. Through their "professional commitment" members are said to "bring considerable value to their customers and help promote life safety."[26]

The big issue for this group is competing methods of fire prevention. On their account, established methods—like sprinklers—are inadequate.

They promote the use of "passive" fire prevention, or "effective compartmentation" that will prevent fire and smoke from spreading from one part of a building to another. For example, a 2003 press release on the occasion of a fatal fire recommended that "we shouldn't limit the conclusion to a single solution of sprinkler suppression systems. . . . Passive fire protection features can limit the spread of both fire and smoke."[27]

The group tells a prehistory of fire disasters in the 1980s and 1990s due to "lack of or improper use of 'Firestop Systems.'" A passionate "Charter Member Group" formed at a 1999 meeting of a standards organization, and growth was rapid from then. As their newsletter said in June 2004, "It's hard to believe that just 5 years ago, there were only 7 founding members thinking about an association for Firestopping Contractors." They quickly developed the industry standards we saw in chapter seven—FM 4991 "Standard for the Approval of Firestop Contractors," and ASTM E 2174 "Standard for the Inspection of Through Penetration Firestop Systems"—as well as an FCIA Manual of Practice and accreditation procedures. They were soon issuing newsletters and press releases and organizing annual conventions. Unlike the Irrigation Association, the FCIA is not particularly strong in organizational resources, and it is not routinely active in conventional politics. It is, however, extremely proactive in its efforts "promoting Fire and Life Safety through the Specialty Firestop Contractor Concept."[28]

STRATEGIES OF ACTION FOR INFLUENCING PUBLIC OPINION. Reflecting on the rapid development of programs and documents in the first five years of the association, its 2003 president, Scott Rankin, foreshadowed increasingly energetic public relations: "as our organization continues to grow, we need to focus on increasing FCIA's stature in the construction environment and becoming synonymous with 'the hub of firestop system knowledge.'" A new president, Ray Usher, proclaimed in August 2004 that "FCIA continues to move forward through the efforts of volunteers who believe in our industry, believe in Fire and Life Safety through the Specialty Firestop Contractor Concept and the quality process for Firestopping. We've been telling our story nationally through magazines, presentations at major conventions, our Enewsletter and Website." He provided detailed evidence in a "PR Results Summary":

- Magazine Articles/Exposure—4 published—Engineering News Record, Association of Licensed Architects, The Construction Specifier, 4specs.com.

- Webcast Participation—2 FCIA Exposures—Consulting Specifying Engineer and BOMA were sites for FCIA to speak about Effective Compartmentation.
- Testimony—2—International Code Council and City of Chicago audiences
- Major FCIA Presentations—7 for over 300 architects like Skidmore Owings and Merrill, RTKL, BWBR, and many others.
- Enews Circulation—Our Enews list is over 550, with a forwarding average of 7, plus 165 visits to newsletter on www.fcia.org about 4,000 circulation.

Also mentioned were a campaign for new members and a detailed analysis of website visitors and visits. Among the points made about the website visits was the popularity of the membership directory and its value as a "marketing tool" for members. At the same time, the Education Committee reported drafting an education program "used to train architects, engineers, contractors and installers nationwide," and the Marketing Committee was "forming relationships with the National Association of State Fire Marshals Conference . . . submitting for 2005's speaking engagements and reviewing trade shows for FCIA to display the FCIA Trade Show Booth." An equally energetic list of promotional activities took place during 2003, especially at trade shows, trade magazines, and presentations by "FCIA members passionate about their industry."[29]

Newsletters frequently described many of these activities in more detail; they also provided a variety of updates on more technical code and standards issues and association business like membership, committees, and conventions. Members were lauded for bringing the "Firestopping Message" to other audiences; for instance, "RectorSeal National Sales Manager, Jim Park was quoted in the Consulting Specifying Engineer E-News about Firestopping and maintenance. . . . Way to go Jim . . . keep up the good work publicizing the Firestopping industry . . . and promoting the need to maintain effective compartmentation." And they were provided with an "elevator pitch": "Now that you have someone on the phone, what do you say about FCIA? Here's our FCIA 'Elevator Pitch,' the 15 second speech to tell someone about FCIA, in between floors on an elevator ride."[30]

In such public relations activities the FCIA is oriented to—indeed, may be said to be in the process of constituting—a "public" consisting of private, nonprofit, and public actors in construction as the central audience. As critical theorists have argued and research such as that of Jacobs has shown, the public sphere is better understood as composed of multiple publics and interpretive communities. As many of the examples in this chapter illustrate, economic actors sometimes orient themselves to their own "publics," like the African American communities Jacobs examined and other groups more conventionally interesting to sociologists and critical theorists—although, of course, they do not usually perform the counterhegemonic functions Jacobs and others emphasize.[31]

As for a number of other groups in the focal sample of associations, the main public audience for FCIA is constituted in trade journals, related associations, and other trade shows. Fifteen other associations are listed among the "useful links" FCIA provides, associations like the Association of Licensed Architects, the International Firestop Council, the National Fire Protection Association, and the Society for Fire Protection Engineers. FCIA officers or members were sometimes active in these other associations; FCIA's executive director received a Certificate of Merit for his service in the Construction Specifications Institute, a former president was a member of a National Fire Prevention Association committee, and members were encouraged to take the FCIA trade show booth to any show they attended. Reports in 2004 newsletters mentioned news and activities of these associations and others: a list of associations mentioned in 2004 gives a sense of the nature and depth of the firestoppers' core public. It included the National Association of Fire Safety Marshals (whose president was awarded honorary membership in FCIA), the Construction Specifications Institute and two of its local chapters, Specification Consultants in International Practice, the Total Facility Management Show, the Chicago Board of Realtors, the Building Owners and Managers Association, the National Fire Sprinkler Association, and the Northern Illinois Fire Sprinkler Association. FCIA was also a member of the Alliance for Fire and Smoke Containment and Control (AFSCC), which consisted of members from all "Passive Fire and Life Safety Systems Industries; Fire Walls/Floors, Fire Dampers, Fire Doors, Firestopping, and others . . . major firestopping manufacturers are also members, and have supported AFSCC with personnel and funding." Codes groups like Underwriter Laboratories, the National Safety Council, FM Approvals, and the International Code Council were also important in this "public" sphere.[32]

Although FCIA's promotional activities are unusually intense, most other associations also situate themselves in such a field. We have seen that associations active in conventional politics often operated in issue-based alliances with other associations; such affiliations and alliances activated in conventional politics are a tiny part of the complex web linking trade associations with one another and with other private, nonprofit, and public organizations. This complex web creates the conditions for some of their conventional political engagement, and it can also form the core "public" to which many associations address their attempts to influence public opinion.[33]

But FCIA's efforts are not restricted to this core, specialized public. As for other associations, their attempts at public influence intermittently extend out more broadly from this base: on the one hand to more conventional political settings, like code hearings (or, for other associations, state legislatures or federal regulatory agencies), and on the other, to the mainstream media. For instance, a fatal fire in October 2003 quickly generated a press release from the FCIA board. FCIA "was saddened with the rest of the country to hear about the loss of life at the high rise County Building in Chicago recently" and suggests "some fire protection features the expert fire investigation panel should consider to prevent future tragedy." A few months later, the FCIA executive director testified at a City of Chicago hearing—arguing, of course, that sprinklers were not the magic bullet solution and "compartmentation" was also a necessary requirement in effective fire codes. (His testimony was posted so that association members could use it in other contexts.) They emphasized the importance of these hearings because "nationally and worldwide, major cities look to Chicago for High Rise Building Safety benchmarks . . . as Chicago goes, so goes the country with fire and life safety in high rise buildings." As a result of the testimony, the Building Owners and Managers Association planned to "educate BOMA Members about effective compartmentation through firestopping." The newsletter boasted: "FCIA Chicago Testimony Opens Doors for National Discussion." Here, efforts at public influence through the mainstream media and in conventional political settings channeled back to public relations with FCIA's core audience.[34]

FCIA's public orientation also extended beyond its core specialist audience to the mainstream media. Although like most associations its press releases were often targeted at very specialized audiences, it also addressed the general public after fire disasters that might provide a receptive climate for their concerns. Just as they were quick to comment in a press release on the Chicago County Building fire, they wrote a letter to the editors of major southeast newspapers on the occasion of a fatal fire at a hotel in Greenville, South Carolina. They also promoted the speeches and press articles by the leader of the World Trade Center Building Performance Study, who shared their view that fire barriers and fire-resistant construction, as well as sprinklers, were necessary for safe buildings.[35]

The Firestoppers illustrate what influencing public opinion means for those business associations that do not confine themselves simply to collective marketing. They mobilize a variety of strategies of action like writing press releases, doing presentations, and creating standards to influence audiences that are primarily composed of specialist nonprofit, private, and public organizations and constituted in associations, meetings, and trade publications. However, they also make occasional efforts directed to mainstream media and occasional forays into the sort of conventional political lobbying of the sort discussed in chapter eight.

VOCABULARIES OF MOTIVE FOR INFLUENCING PUBLIC OPINION. We have seen that associations with conventional political lobbying programs formulated their efforts as much in terms of expansive collective identities, technical reason, and stewardship of the public good as in more predictable terms of clearly articulated industry or member interests—and frequently, the former vocabulary of motive dominated the latter. I noted that ideologies of collective good might seem more oriented to attempts to influence broader public opinion beyond conventional political settings than to conventional interest group politics. As we have already begun to see here, the meaning-making involved in associations' efforts to influence public opinion does indeed fuse members' and industry interests with broader, more expansive collective identities in language that emphasizes technical reason and stewardship of the public good.

Certainly, member interests are occasionally mentioned in rationales and explanations of public relations, but this is a very minor thread in the discourse. Hours of combing FCIA documents turn up only a few references to direct business advantages that might flow to members from FCIA work. For instance, among the objectives of the Codes Committee is to "defend our position against proposals submitted that would adversely affect our trade." But it needs a very close reading of the extensive FCIA archive to find these hints that members might have business interests in passive fire protection methods.[36]

A somewhat more explicit language of interest surrounds the collective identity of the "industry." Again, though, this is not expressed in terms of business interest but in terms of recognition. The FCIA's "mission is for member organizations to be recognized throughout the construction industry as preferred quality contractors of life safety firestop systems . . . members contribute to the advancement of the firestop industry and maintain exceptional knowledge of this specialized service." A "Key Initiative" in 2002 is to gain recognition: "We will strive to be recognized for the work we are doing within the industry. We will make people aware that firestopping is not a trade that can be installed by anybody who creates a condition. It is a fire safety issue and has to be installed by a single source contractor with the knowledge of what they are doing." Talk of benefits of accreditation for members, above, quickly shifts to talk of members' helping the industry—"we need you to help make it [accreditation] a success—let's get dressed up and go to the party by getting FM 4991 Approved." As with intraindustry economic interests examined in chapter six, collective industry interests often trump—or at least fuse with—members' particular business interests in association identities.[37]

Overall, industry interests were hard to find in the firestop contractors' discourse. Instead, their public relations languages were formulated mostly in terms of collective good, like some of the associations engaged in more conventional lobbying we saw in chapter eight.

The discourse of the Irrigation Association in their conventional interest group activities usually left potential opponents unmarked and uncharacterized, except, occasionally, as needing better information that the IA could provide. Although FCIA is clearly challenging what they see as a dominant tendency—"active fire protection" such as sprinklers—they too almost always avoid demonizing, and their rhetoric blurs the boundaries between themselves and their opponents. A strong and repeated theme—almost a cliché—of their writing is "Why Not Have Both?" As the press release on the Chicago fire concluded: "maybe our call to action as a result of this tragedy should be 'why not have both?'" Press releases, trade journal articles, and presentations promoting the FCIA cause invariably recognize the value of sprinklers first; as they argued to the Association of Licensed Architects, "while the association fully endorses . . . the use of sprinkler systems, fire history suggests that there is no single way to make buildings safe when fire breaks out . . . experience shows that active and passive firestopping systems play distinct, complementary roles." The testimony on the Chicago fire also took this line: there is no "single solution," the executive director told the inquiry, and a combination of prevention methods "should be your standard to protect people." So even though they were against reliance on sprinklers, the firestoppers blurred the potentially charged distinction between supporters of such "active" fire prevention and themselves. Another issue with a potential political charge in this world—that between accredited and unaccredited contractors—is blurred in an interview with the FCIA director in *Daily Commercial News*: "Contractors who have chosen, for whatever reason, not to obtain certification can be high-quality contractors as well," he said. "It's just that the FM 4991 contractor has taken it one step further and quantified that."[38]

Like the Irrigation Association, the firestoppers mobilize a discourse of technical reason in their attempts at influence. The theme of comprehensive technical knowledge and education dominates their claims and is backed up by technical analyses that quickly lose the nonspecialist reader. Even the press release on the Chicago fire uses some technical vocabulary in its recommendations; other articles and reports make measured, informational cases for passive fire prevention with elaborate evidence. For instance, a "White Paper" of 2001 arguing against proposed code changes ("Maintaining Life Safety Effectiveness in the New Building Codes") provides an engineer's assessment of the deficiencies of sprinkler systems backed up with detailed evidence. Similarly, the firestoppers critique their opposition with a barrage of evidence in a paper on "Reliability of Automatic Sprinkler Systems." Technical information makes up the bulk of articles in trade journals and informational presentations. To impress a contractor with knowledge of these issues, ask about interior perimeter joint fire ratings, or the "W" rating of firestop sealants.[39]

Beyond technical expertise, and, as many of the examples already provided show, the public good—understood in terms of stewardship, safety, and protection—is the central discursive grounding for the firestoppers' claims. "It is a fire safety issue" and "FCIA will continue as a leading construction life safety force for many years." "We at FCIA are passionate that Passive Fire and Life Safety systems are an integral part of people protection in buildings . . . buildings can be safer for all our citizens, and more important, our families." An explicit benefit for members is to "help promote life safety." Quality should be maintained because

> when a firm intentionally or unintentionally misapplies firestopping materials, or varies from the tested and listed system design, the system may not work and put life safety and property protection in jeopardy . . . [but] . . . [o]nce the crews, estimators and office staff understood an unauthorized variance could possibly hurt or kill someone, they fell into step quickly.[40]

So like the irrigators, FCIA uses a promotional language that blurs identity boundaries, usually refusing the expressed perception of opposing interests. As for the irrigators, languages of technical reason and stewardship of the collective good support their claims. Industry interests exist, of course, but they are rhetorically fused with the broader public good. As the FCIA president said in summer 2003, "we must not lose sight of our long term goal as we fight our daily battles, together we will enhance building and occupant safety, effect change within our industry, and increase our business opportunities." More typically, FCIA rhetoric leaves the impression that it would be vulgar and trivial to talk about building one's business, even though that is an obvious consequence of their project. Ultimately, and although much of their work is a matter of technical reason, their project of influencing opinion is expressed—in Weber's terms—as *wertrational* rather than *zweckrational*, a value in itself, rather than a means to an end. Obviously, we cannot assess here how members understand such formulations, and certainly their commitment is likely to vary, as I have noted repeatedly in these chapters. What is more important is the language in which their orientation to the public is expressed.[41]

In one passionate essay by an FCIA director, the usual discourse of measured technical reason is dropped for persuasion based entirely on collective good and ultimate ends. He begins by testifying to his commitment to quality in his business:

> When I first got into the construction industry, I had a desire to create a company that acknowledged and accepted that our scope of work needed to be done correctly, according to code, whether we were told to or not! I set out to "raise the bar higher" so that other contractors who wanted to perform this Life Safety work that I had chosen, did it right, or they would be forced to get out of the business.

But "I've seen changes that concern me and should concern anybody who has concern for their friends, relatives, loved ones or just a concern for their fellow citizens." He is referring to code changes that weaken requirements for passive fire protection in favor of sprinkler systems.

> They're betting that we don't have to worry about the possibility of a fire happening below us and the smoke rising up from floor to floor to our floor. . . . The room, where we may be sleeping. The office where we may be working. The floors, the offices, the rooms where our friends our family or our fellow citizens will be!
>
>   . . . So who's willing to gamble! You're on top of a high rise building. It's been built to today's codes and it is completely covered by sprinklers. There's a fire on the first floor. It starts to put out a lot of smoke. That's what fires do, put out a lot of smoke! By the way, more people die of smoke inhalation than they do

from the fire. That's a fact nobody disputes! All those nasty toxic gases the fire
is putting off. So you're on the top floor. The sprinklers fail. Can you get down
in time? Will you be able to see or breathe if there's dark smoke in the halls?
Will the smoke be toxic, poisonous? Will you get out? Who knows? So are you
ready to gamble with your life? How much money can "they" save to make it
worth it to you?

    . . . I think some things are priceless. A life any life, is one of those!

    . . . So my question is simple. WHY NOT HAVE BOTH? Did we eliminate
seat belts when airbags were created. Of course not! We got the benefit of both.
Did it, does it cost more money? Without a doubt! So why is it that an industry
that has suffered so many tragedies is trying to cut corners to save money? How
much is a single life worth? How much is 84 of them worth. How much is the
life of the 16 elderly occupants who died in their nursing home from smoke
inhalation worth. They were in a single story building that didn't require even
sprinklers. But they died from smoke . . . not fire!

    . . . So all said and done, WHY NOT HAVE BOTH?

This essay is not typical FCIA talk, because there's nothing technical
about it. It does, however, distill the firestoppers' understanding of their
promotional project as value-rational activity for the collective good, not
simply a matter of business interest. Another way it deviates from typical
firestopper discourse is in its clear identification of an enemy. "There are
a lot of special interest groups who have their own agenda and in order to
achieve their goals, they're willing to cut corners . . . Save Money!" They
make tradeoffs between safety requirements and cost that "saved money,
no doubt! But will they save lives? Experts admit that sprinklers do fail
occasionally. . . .What's a life or two worth? What's yours worth?" Ironically, considering social scientists' standard views of business associations,
the enemies of this contractor's promotional project are "special interest
groups" only interested in the bottom line. And in efforts to cut costs, they
fail in their stewardship of the future: "We need the people who put the
codes together to start thinking long term."[42]

It is hard to imagine that committed members of FCIA are entirely
cynical in their promotional claims about the public good, with group
etiquette enforcing the expression of self-interest in camouflaged terms
as such a passionate concern with safety. On the other hand, simple ideology critique suggests that what groups like this are "really" interested
in is improving their business opportunities. What is important, though,
is not what firestoppers "really" believe in their promotional projects,

but the vocabularies of motive that make their claims meaningful—vocabularies that themselves, no doubt, shape their interpretation of their actions. Although industry interests are a minor theme in many associations' promotional projects, a language of technical reason and collective good dominates, even more than for associations involved in conventional political action.

Taken-for-granted languages seem obvious and unavoidable. Many political analysts would take it for granted that business associations must speak in a language of industry interest. This evidence of languages of collective good and technical reason challenges that assumption. Now, having seen the language of collective good and technical reason in operation, they, too, may seem obvious and transparent. Naturally, and perhaps even persuasively, businesspeople in fire prevention would promote their work as a contribution to public safety. How could it be otherwise? Indeed, fire is a special danger that might evoke a primal response beyond "special interests." But one isolated example shows that it would be perfectly possible for the Firestop Contractors to speak in a language of industry interest: their claims to stewardship of the public good are a matter of active meaning-making, not the transparent expression of reality. The newsletter of the Alliance for Fire and Smoke Containment and Control speaks almost entirely in terms of industry interest. "Dear fellow AFSCC members," their president writes, "all of us are part of this organization for one major reason. The commercial interests we represent are going to be negatively affected in some way as jurisdictions around the country reduce the level of fire safety in buildings." He goes on to argue for collective as well as individual responses to "the realities of a shrinking market," and details research and lobbying efforts toward such a response. The firestop contractors do not talk in this way, even in their own newsletters.[43]

The Firestop Contractors have led us into an obscure world, but their story reveals how public relations may work as associations address their external environments. Previous observers have suggested that public relations is an important means by which associations provide political "voice for the industry," but there has been little evidence so far to adjudicate or explore those claims. The overall picture suggests that public relations *in general* is more important to associations than lobbying or monitoring policy, and that its importance grew in the late twentieth century. Although the two sorts of "industry voice" are correlated, associations interested in public relations differ in important ways from those interested in lobbying and monitoring policy; for instance, they tend to be larger, less formally organized, and less concentrated in DC. Closer examination shows that when public relations oriented to publics-as-markets is excluded, about the same proportion of associations seem to express an interest in political public relations as those expressing an interest in conventional political participation.

Focusing on associations interested in promoting their causes with political publics, we see a strong emphasis on multiple specialized publics, in part through extensive work with related associations, and an even stronger tendency to articulate their claims in languages of public good and technical expertise than we saw earlier among lobbying associations.

Business Associations and Civil Society

Of that minority of business associations involved in conventional politics, most mix languages of explicit industry interest with broader claims based on technical reason and public good, and associations attempting to address broader issues with public relations strategies mobilize a language of public good and technical reason even more than those involved in more conventional lobbying. This cultural fusion of industry interest and public good—and the way languages of interest are elided in this fusion—seems to blur the conventional distinction between "interest group politics" and "civil society." This suggests that we need to reconsider contemporary understandings of civil society and challenge business associations' marginalization in debates about the civil sphere.

As Walter Powell and Elisabeth Clemens point out, nonprofit, voluntary associations play "a critical role in almost every conception of civil society." They have long been valued as social infrastructure generating solidarity and collective efficacy apart from, and counterbalancing, state and market, and as important indicators of the strength of "civil society." But the parameters and core features of the nonprofit sector present a "terminological tangle." Many definitions attempt to characterize institutions, organizations, and actions that are in some way distinct from both state and market. Wuthnow, for instance, distinguishes principles of association characterizing the three sectors; in contradistinction to state and market, he suggests, nonprofits involve "freedom of association for purposes of mutuality, camaraderie, or services rendered free of obligation or remuneration." David Watt notes that in practical terms the core of the US nonprofit sector is usually understood legally as "all 501 c(3) and 501 c(4) tax-exempt organizations as defined by the Internal Revenue Service," but is better defined substantively as "all those organizations in which membership is neither mandatory nor acquired by birth, which are not part of the state, and which are not primarily concerned with making a financial profit." Drawing on their comparative work and assessment of alternative definitions, Lester Salamon and Helmut Anheier identify five characteristic features of nonprofits: they are "(a) formally constituted; (b) organizationally separate from government; (c) non-profit-seeking; (d) self-governing; and (e) voluntary to some significant degree."[44]

Business associations fit all these definitions well. Nevertheless, they have been neglected by those who study the nonprofit sector, who generally focus more on philanthropic than "mutual-benefit" associations. As Salamon and Anheier point out, business and professional organizations are "not what most people have in mind when they think of nonprofit organizations in the U.S." Despite their resemblances to other voluntary associations, business associations have seemed too embedded in markets, tainted with narrow market interests, and unconcerned with collective purposes to be categorized along with neighborhood improvement associations, bowling leagues, museums, or charities—or even the educational and medical institutions that, in fact, dominate the nonprofit sector. But while it certainly seems theoretically and normatively crucial to distinguish between the pursuit of market interest and an orientation to collective purposes, a closer examination suggests that this distinction does not work in any simple or stereotypical way.[45]

As Russell Faeges has argued, such definitional confusion happens when the purposes of definition are not clearly articulated, and especially when definition is not theoretically driven. One important conceptual ambiguity that is often blurred in discussions of nonprofits is that between organizational features and cultural orientation. Although scholars' theoretical interest in nonprofits often derives from a Tocquevillian interest in their potential as sites of a collective, public *orientation* free of the imperatives of state (or market), definitions based on *organizational features* capture many organizations with little overt "public" orientation. In fact, Jason Kaufman makes the stronger case that, historically, voluntary organizations in the United States actually encouraged self-segregation and sectarianism. At the least, nonprofit organizations may not generate public orientation—and vice versa. Potential contradictions between orientation and organization lie behind many debates in the field: discussion about the extent to which nonprofits mimic for-profit organizations despite the fact that financial gains are not distributed to owners or shareholders, discussion about the extent to which they collaborate with or fulfill the purposes of government, and debates about the extent to which members' participation is routinely engaged or merely nominal. Defined organizationally, nonprofits seem to include many groups that don't seem to fulfill scholars' underlying theoretical interests.[46]

As a result, other discussions emphasize nonprofits' public actions and orientation more than their organization. In a historical overview, for instance, Peter Hall stresses public orientation. He sees a nonprofit organization as "a body of individuals who associate for any of three purposes: (1) to perform public tasks that have been delegated to them by the state; (2) to perform public tasks for which there is a demand that neither the state nor for-profit organizations are willing to fulfill; or (3) to influence the direction of policy in the state, the for-profit sector, or other nonprofit organizations." Scholars influenced by Habermasian concerns with the strength of the public sphere think of nonprofit organizations as groups that will "sustain critical-rational public discourse" and function as "voices in society wide discussion." For Wuthnow, the real importance of the voluntary sector lies not so much in organization or actions but in the way it "contributes to the shaping of public discourse," direct or indirect debate about or concern with "relationships among individuals, between individuals and communities, and among communities." Watt considers the extent to which American voluntary associations contribute to "a vital public sphere," but concludes, pessimistically, that they illustrate, rather, the state and market pressures that "eat away at the public sphere in advanced capitalist societies."[47]

By emphasizing that the normative and theoretical interest of nonprofit organizations lies in their potentially public orientation, scholars impose a stronger criterion for the relevance of voluntary association for civil society. Their orientation becomes the crucial defining feature of organized actors in civil society. From this more cultural perspective, recent theories of civil society refine questions about voluntary organizations' role in the public sphere by emphasizing that they could only be a merely formal—and very rough—indicator of a public realm counterbalancing state and market. A definition of nonprofits—or voluntary organizations—driven by a theory of civil society emphasizes that while organizational form and democratic procedure are necessary, they are not sufficient, and organizations that possess the organizational form without the cultural orientations are not distinct from both state and market as an object of theoretical inquiry.

So Alexander criticizes "merely formal understandings of democracy ... and of narrowly Tocquevillian (recently Putnamesque) concerns" with voluntaristic associations: "there are many different kinds of voluntary public associations. While their mode of expression—uncoerced communication—may be democratic, the content of their message, and the kind of society they envision, may very well not be." What is key is not organization but a discourse of universalistic solidarity based on categories of inclusion and exclusion, a cultural form with inherent contradictions that is analytically independent of state and market but may be weakened or strengthened in relations with other spheres:

> Civil society should be conceived as a solidary sphere in which a certain kind of universalising community comes gradually to be defined and to some degree enforced. To the degree this solidary community exists, it is exhibited by "public opinion," possesses its own cultural codes and narratives in a democratic idiom, is patterned by a set of peculiar institutions, most notably legal and journalistic ones, and is visible in historically distinctive sets of interactional practices like civility, equality, criticism and respect. This kind of civil community can never exist as such; it can exist only "to one degree or another."

Making a similar point about voluntary group interaction, Paul Lichterman argues that many contemporary voluntary groups often seen as strengthening civil society do not in fact do so, because they are not settings in which such meaningful public orientations are customarily enacted. Robert Fishman also emphasizes such cultural differences in otherwise similar settings.[48]

So while nonprofit voluntary associations may be potentially important institutions of civil society, they are not necessarily so: it depends on whether they sustain and generate universalizing discourses and routine practices that articulate the cultural orientations that define the civil sphere. It would be easy to assume, as many have, that this stronger criterion of the relevance of voluntary groups to civil society would make business associations even more irrelevant to civil society than the weaker criterion of nonprofit organization. Conversely, though—and this is less often noticed—defining voluntary organizations' contribution to civil society in terms of their public orientations and actions may also sometimes include some of the actions of nonprofits that superficially seem grounded in the market. While the principles of the capitalist market and the principles of civil society should not be conflated, the possibility that civil society discourses and practices are generated in voluntary associations for business should not be excluded, but rather treated as an empirical question. We can ask whether voluntary associations of capitalist businesses sometimes generate the routine practices and universalizing discourses characteristic of the civil sphere.

As we have already seen, lobbying and public relations activities of associations are sometimes understood in terms that seem to invoke solidary community; in terms that demonstrate norms of civility, equality, criticism, and respect; in terms that show an expansive understanding of the meanings of (economic) relations that could be viewed more narrowly; and in terms that routinize and cultivate mutual responsibility in organizing social relations. To the extent that they do so, associations are neglected institutional sites where the "tense and permeable boundary relationships" between civil society and capitalist markets are routinely negotiated. Broadly speaking, even lobby groups—as well as associations oriented to public relations—may be considered institutions of civil society because "in making their case for the particular, functional interests they represent, these associations are compelled to make an appeal to the entire civil community or those mandated to represent it." As Alexander would predict, the translation of particular interests into universalizing languages of public good is routine even for lobby groups (though the conventions of "interest group politics" also allow some to avoid broader considerations even in addressing political interests). This does not negate the fact that some business associations operate as interest groups against public good and in violation of civil society norms. Rather, it suggests that there is a civic potential in these groups that needs more attention for a better understanding, not only of collective action by business, but also of the possibilities of a strengthened civil sphere in market societies.[49]

In this regard the debate generated by Robert Putnam about whether Americans' participation in civil society has declined in recent generations has generally not taken into account participation in work-related voluntary associations. On straightforward measures like time devoted to voluntary group participation, it is entirely possible that Americans' voluntary energies have shifted to occupational groups from geographically based "community" groups or other philanthropic groups, but inattention to business associations in the nonprofit literature means that this possibility has been neglected. For instance, Robert Anderson, James Curtis, and Edward Grabb suggest that time spent on voluntary activities in the United States has indeed declined, and most of that decline is attributable to a decline in voluntary participation among working women. If voluntary activity in business associations, as well as "community" groups, were to be measured, perhaps that decline would disappear. In addition to the question of shifting voluntary group participation by women, another question that needs investigating is how participation in geographically organized business groups like Rotary is related to participation in "industry"-based business groups like those studied here.[50]

Here, though, we are concerned with the groups themselves, and whether they are oriented to civil society. In Alexander's view, all American interest groups would necessarily be "civil associations" because they would be compelled to articulate their pursuit of interests in relation to the languages of the broader public sphere. But there is a more particular sense in which we can examine whether some business associations are civically oriented, resembling voluntary associations more typically thought to contribute to the civil sphere. To ask in this narrower sense whether some business associations should be considered along with other voluntary nonprofit groups in broader scholarly and policy discussions about civil society, we can examine their stated goals, the practices, skills and information for civic engagement they offer, and the substantive issues their members may sometimes engage.[51]

"Civic" Orientations and "Business" Identities

As we saw in chapter three, business associations are an unruly population of organizations when viewed through the lens of theories of comparative economic governance, which equate strong associational governance with systematic, one-to-one relationships between "industries" and their associations. "Industries" will often generate a variety of associations; conversely, associations often encompass members in a number of related industries and frequently cross even sectoral boundaries. Contrary to the idea that associations simply represent objectively defined "industries," there is no one-to-one correspondence between industries and associations. Indeed, associations often produce "industries" as cultural categories.

One entirely unrecognized aspect of this disconnection between official industry categories and the more vernacular generation of collective action by business is the surprisingly frequent formation of business associations around goals and activities oriented to civic issues beyond, or not strictly related to, the industry, profession, or business of members. Profit-oriented actors sometimes bring extraeconomic identities, and noneconomic concerns beyond their productive activities, to the associations they form.

This observation—counterintuitive against the background of extant theories—emerged from preliminary investigations of the association population and was later examined by coding whether or not associations indicated goals or activities oriented to civic issues not necessarily related to the economic interests of an industry, profession, or business, strictly defined. Some associations note or highlight public safety concerns, like the Research Institute for Fragrance Materials, or the International District Energy Association; others indicate an environmental focus, like the International Ecotourism Society, which worked "to make tourism a viable tool to conserve natural environments and sustain the well-being of local people." A substantial number of associations are formed around minority or women's identities and issues, like the National Association of Black Accountants, the Black Broadcasters Alliance, the Latin Business Association, Women Construction Owners and Executives U.S.A., and the Organization of Women in International Trade.[52]

Associations that form at the intersection of economic and other identities—for African Americans, Asian Americans, and especially women—drew on the models provided by larger twentieth-century movements for civic inclusion for collective action in the economic sphere. Over a hundred associations in the census—3 percent—included such identity labels in their titles. Others with more neutral titles might also form around non-"industry" identities. Of course, the simple presence of women, or minorities, in the public sphere does not mean full participation in civil society, and may block it. But on the other hand, an organization of Women in International Trade is unlikely to be encouraging the restriction of women's civil society participation or acting as a "Ladies Auxiliary" supporting the real civic participation of men.[53]

For instance, the Women in Aviation Maintenance (AWAM) are an intriguing borderline case. A comparatively simple organization that mostly uses informal, support-group language, its officers include, along with experienced aircraft mechanics, directors and executives of industry corporations. AWAM has seven local chapters, and its members meet at the conventions of other related associations, like the Professional Aviation Maintenance Association. It makes awards and scholarships, and offers detailed career-related information, including convention calendars, newsletters, and discussion groups covering topics ranging from worries about responsibilities to customers, to pregnancy and maintenance, to convention trip arrangements—along with themed merchandise like "Rosie the Riveter" business card holders. AWAM is mostly concerned with topics, programs, and issues internal to the group, but their understanding of their mission and activities easily fuses with a broader civic orientation to community service and "inspiring all women to pursue their dreams." Although certainly exceptions, a significant number of associations in the population draw on gender, ethnic, and racial identities in similar ways—like the Black Broadcasters Alliance, or the Women in International Trade.[54]

"Civic" Orientations in Business Associations

Even on the superficial evidence of name and goal statement, 13 percent, or 568 of the 4,465 associations in the population, indicated some orientation to civic issues not strictly intrinsic to the economic realm—if not minority or women's issues, then issues like safety or environment. If associations expressed such an orientation, they were also more likely to express an interest in public relations goals, but the relationship between policy monitoring and lobbying goals and orientation to broader social issues was *not* significant.[55]

These one in eight business associations that overtly expressed some general "civic" orientation were more similar in their organizational features to associations expressing an orientation to public relations than to those explicitly expressing policy monitoring and lobbying goals:

- Associations expressing a civic orientation were more likely to be larger associations. This relationship was similar but more pronounced than that for associations expressing public relations goals, and contrasted with the tendency for associations expressing policy monitoring and lobbying goals to be smaller.[56]
- A civic orientation was positively related to associations' reporting of state groups and other organizational affiliates; in this, such groups were similar to groups expressing public relations goals but unlike groups with policy monitoring and lobbying goals.[57]
- Unlike associations expressing lobbying goals, but similar to those with public relations goals, the founding decades of associations with a civic orientation were distinctive. Larger proportions of associations with civic orientations than associations with a narrower industry focus were formed in the 1970s, 1980s, and 1990s. Prior to the 1970s, there was no such pattern.[58]

In the aggregate, though, associations expressing more generalized "civic" goals also differed from public-relations-oriented associations in a couple of significant ways:

- Associations expressing a civic orientation were more likely to be composed of individuals than firms or both types of members. Thus they differed, in the aggregate, from associations interested in lobbying—more likely to have firms as members—but also from associations interested in public relations—more likely to include both firm and individual members.[59]
- A civic orientation and DC location were positively related. In this, such associations resembled those interested in lobbying more than those interested in public relations.[60]
- A civic orientation was *not* correlated with many other organizational features and activities: full-time leader, staff numbers, committee structures, various sorts of publications, and various sorts of conventions and meetings. In contrast, an orientation to public relations was correlated with activities like publications, committees, and meetings, and an orientation to policy monitoring and lobbying was positively related to most measures of organizational structure and activities. Unlike associations with less generalized orientations, organizational features were irrelevant to an association's civic focus.[61]
- Associations with civic goals differed markedly in their overall sectoral location from associations with either public relations or policy-monitoring/lobbying goals. Sectors with associations expressing civic goals at comparatively high rates were public administration (24 percent); associations crossing many sectors, which were often formed around non-industry-based identities (23 percent); utilities (17 percent); and accommodation and food services (17 percent). Of these, only utilities rank in the top five on other measures of political orientation like lobbying or public relations. Mining; construction; transportation; real estate; professional services; arts, entertainment, and recreation; and other services also ranked above the population average in the proportion of associations expressing some civic orientation. Manufacturing and wholesale were very low.[62]

Overall, these aggregate patterns suggest that an expression of "civic" goals is not simply a covert language for an interest in conventional political lobbying, although like lobby groups they tend to be located in DC. Associations with civic concerns resemble associations with public relations goals on dimensions like size, affiliate groups, and founding decade. They reflect the population as a whole in organizational features and activities, but they are distinctive in their tendency to individual memberships and in their sectoral locations.

These indications of civic orientation are superficial, but they are theoretically important because they have previously been ignored. We can turn to the focal associations to explore in a little more depth whether business associations sometimes sustain the routine practices and universalizing discourses commonly associated with the civil sphere.

Civic Practices in Business Associations

Some business associations are settings that encourage routine skills and information for civic engagement often associated only with other voluntary associations. Andrew Perrin shows that membership in business associations (broadly defined) encourages civic participation indirectly by instilling political efficacy and civic skills. Even associations with no overt civic interest are often sites where routine "civic" practices and occasionally universalizing discourses can be seen. Sometimes these common practices are understood in terms restricted to industry or occupational identities, but they are also frequently detached from immediate interests and are represented as public virtues. But regardless of whether they are understood in universalizing terms, members may be oriented to the civil sphere when associations support civic practices.[63]

First, associations may offer general information, encouragement, and education in conventional political participation for their members. At least a third of the associations in the focal sample did so in the period preceding the 2004 national election. A few of these associations offered elaborated and specific information on ways to contact elected officials and their challengers, "general election facts," and "tips about communicating with Members and general information about Hill staffers, the legislative process, and more"—information that members (and others) might turn to a variety of purposes besides lobbying about industry concerns. Other associations, like the Aluminum Anodizers Council, Automation in Pharmacy, and the International Concrete Repair Institute, touched on political participation less elaborately, for instance, by including an "Election Overview" or simple exhortations in newsletters and presentations—"Vote!!"; "Be informed . . . be cautious—VOTE your convictions."[64]

Second, discussion in newsletters, e-mail lists, and conference panels sometimes covered topics on the contemporary public agenda, and if such discussion is counted along with more formal promotion of public participation as a civic virtue, over half of the focal associations provided settings for occasional civic reflection. For instance, general health care policy, trade with China and India, science education, international communications policy, and the aftermath of 9/11 were all public topics business association members engaged in associational settings.

Apart from the ways in which business associations sometimes provide settings in which members are oriented to consideration of and involvement in issues of broader public concern, another way they can be considered occasional actors in civil society, like other nonprofit organizations, is in their programs for volunteering, community service, or charity, and in programs for mentoring and education. One in three of the focal associations included some such program—intended to benefit people beyond the association—among their strategies of action (although such programs are usually a minor and peripheral part of their overall activities).

Third, many business associations explicitly promote the virtues and rewards of volunteering, often in nonstrategic terms. Of course, they usually rely on member volunteers, not only paid staff, to get real work done—to do public relations, develop industry standards, and so on—as did the Firestop Contractors. But some also extend their encouragement of volunteering as a strategy of action to social contexts beyond the association or industry group and understand volunteering and community service as a general civic orientation valuable in its own right. The Baltimore chapter of the International Concrete Repair Institute asked members to sign up for an "Industry Outreach Committee" that would "make contact with other industries with the same interests (i.e., ACI, PCI, ABC, etc.) and try to foster joint activities and provide services to our community (i.e., Christmas in April)." Similarly, ICRI's San Diego chapter devoted many of its 2004 efforts—like talks on repairing fire-damaged concrete and fundraising auctions and tournaments—"to help rebuild families and structures devastated by the October 2003 wildfires." A group associated with the International Association of Floor Care & Sewing Professionals (composed of independent dealers of vacuum cleaners and sewing machines) had its members participate in "National Make a Difference Day" with its "Pillow Patrol" program; "Make a Difference in YOUR community"; "Rally your friends to help make PILLOW CASES for hospital pediatric wards, homeless shelters, domestic abuse safe houses and victims of natural disasters." A student chapter of the International Society of Certified Electronic Technicians visited middle schools, tutored peers, and was "still looking for ways to be more involved with the community."[65]

Fourth, industry awards and accreditation sometimes included community service beyond the industry in their criteria. Nominees for awards from the Association for Women in Aviation Maintenance "must have demonstrated, among other qualities, their commitment to community . . . service." Such concerns were not only evident among lower-status, small-capital associations. The 2004 winner of the International Society of Hospitality Consultants' Pioneer Award, in addition to being "a catalytic force propelling the timeshare industry from a fledging start [*sic*] to the fastest growing segment of the travel and tourism industry" had also "established Christel House, a public charity with a mission to help impoverished children around the world break the cycle of poverty and become self-sufficient and contributing members of their respective societies." The North American Association of Food Equipment Manufacturers included community service in its rigorous accreditation program. The Certified Food Service Professional program "believes strongly in crediting individuals for outstanding non-industry related accomplishments such as community service." Only time, not monetary contributions, was counted as community service toward the CFSP accreditation.[66]

Fifth, some business associations—at least one in five of the focal associations—were involved in promoting education and mentoring efforts that extended outward from the basis of industry skills and concerns. The Conference of Consulting Actuaries invited members to "get involved with a program in your area that could be the most rewarding volunteer opportunity of your career." Their program "combines actuaries' expertise in math with a sense of community spirit, creating a vehicle to work as volunteer math-mentors in public and private schools. When business professionals and educators join in voluntary partnerships that increase student achievement in math, everybody wins." And the Envelope Manufacturers' Association Foundation runs a "learning and literacy" program that "targets at risk elementary students and emphasizes reading and writing skills." (Of course, students are taught "the importance of good letter writing" and why greeting cards "are important forms of correspondence.") The Delta, Atlanta chapter of the Association for Women in Aviation Maintenance "participated in Delta's annual Girl Scout day . . . for Girl Scouts in the southeastern region ranging in ages from 13 through 16 to visit Delta and learn about careers in aviation . . . the girls were educated on the wide variety of jobs available just in the maintenance operations side of Delta." AWAM also encouraged members to join their Speakers' Network "designed to expand public awareness of women in aviation maintenance, to encourage all young people to explore aviation as a career option and to inspire women of all ages to pursue their dreams."[67]

In sum, business associations sometimes encouraged various forms of political participation, public discussion, volunteering, community service, and mentoring that are typically considered civic practices.

Civically Oriented Vocabularies of Motive

Industry identities certainly provided a basis for the initial relevance of these practices, and sometimes they were understood purely in terms of industry interests. The discussion group of the Independent Bakers Association, for instance, treated topics like "Opening of Trade between U.S. and China" from the point of view of how the baking industry would be affected (though they usually focused on more compelling issues like "Steamed vs boiled bagels—which is better?"). The Irrigation Association commented on the trade implications of the fact that "China's Ag Economy [is] at Crossroads." Issues like health care policy and pension reform were extensively discussed during meetings of the Conference of Consulting Actuaries and the American Society for Automation in Pharmacy in terms restricted to technical and business concerns of members.[68]

But sometimes discussion extended easily beyond specific industry interests to broader considerations. An actuaries' pension symposium, for instance, dealt with the issue that "five years ago, the United States' private pension system was the envy of the world. Today, that very same system is in a state of uncertainty. . . . While we can all come up with band-aid remedies to immediate concerns, we need to determine what is best in the long run? . . . presenters address these four key areas: 1. Solvency . . . 2. Predictability . . . 3. Transparency . . . 4. Promises." The Mulch and Soil Council, asking "Is Affordable Health Care Coming?," discussed health care issues for employees of small business in the course of a report on legislation "that would reduce the surging cost of health care for small employers and help provide affordable access to health care for 45 million uninsured Americans."[69]

The boundary between business interest and civic concern was tested in other contexts too. For instance, technology policy, which in one light might affect the business interests of some associations' members, also attracted consideration as a broader social issue. Newsletters of the International Society of Certified Electronics Technicians included general commentary on issues like the recycling of electronic goods: "besides the obvious, education of consumers and ourselves, we need to make wiser choices about our purchases. . . . Hopefully I've given you some insight into the issues and enough to allow you to wade your way thru the maze of questions and ideas. I only ask that you get involved! [*sic*]" They sometimes ranged quite widely, beyond the immediate interests of their members, to consider topics like the long-term value of the American space program and US science education. In a more academic language, discussion about technology and society was also the central interest of the International Telecommunications Society, which had about four hundred members from for-profit corporations, nonprofit and government agencies, and research settings. It aimed, according to one chair, to "encourage informed debate among the community of industry leaders, research scholars, government officials, and consultants who want to remain at the forefront of telecommunication economics and policy. That interplay goes to the heart of the ITS mission—an open, free debate, a meeting place for interchange, a symbiosis among these groups which is increasingly important." Their conference schedules treat topics like "Spectrum Policy," "Junk Mail," and "Avoiding a Tragedy of the Telecommons," as well as many more technically inaccessible topics. Business associations' concerns with questions of safety and technology may not meet Michael Schudson's ideal criteria for the way expertise should contribute to the democratic process, but they do suggest a reassessment of the part they could play.[70]

Occasionally, too, business associations became settings where members could make sense of public issues from the point of view of their industry and occupational identities. For instance, discussion of the aftermath of the events of 9/11 filtered through these settings (and its effects should be considered along with public reactions in the media, conventional political institutions, and local groups that come to mind more easily). For the firestoppers discussed above, a keynote speaker at their 2004 Education and Committee Action Conference in Toronto "kept us at the edge of our seats" when he spoke on "Lessons Learned from the World Trade Center." At their 2002 meeting in Florida, actuaries could hear about the "Aftermath of 9/11/01," and a presentation at the 2004 meeting of the American Society for Automation in Pharmacy noted that "we have no nationwide monitoring system to identify bio-terrorism in a timely manner." Members of the Exhibit Designers and Producers Association joined with twenty-nine other associations in the "convention industry" to make a public statement on the topic, because of the way it affected their business, but their president also reflected more broadly that "while we go about the business of repairing our lives, our businesses and our country I want to remind you that none of us are alone and, in fact, our fellow members of EDPA share a special bond that I believe can provide us with strength in the challenging days ahead." In their chat room, members of the Association for Women in Aviation Maintenance briefly considered ripples of the event in the airline industry, although for them, civility imposed obvious limits on their discussion: "Does anyone out there have an opinion on the Presidential Emergency Board's recommendations?" "I have heard some opinions but the are not repeatable in polite company [sic]." And 9/11 was not the only public disaster to evoke such widespread attention.[71]

Encouragement of political participation could also take on a universalizing tone about the intrinsic public value of civic practices. Members of the Pellet Fuels Institute, for instance, heard an impassioned call to generalized political participation at their 2004 conference. Elizabeth McRoberts, manager of government affairs at the (related) Hearth, Patio, and Barbeque Association, began her presentation by citing a Supreme Court ruling that "the opportunity for free political discussion to the end that government may be responsive to the will of the people . . . is fundamental to our constitutional system." Her talk on "Advocacy Essentials" was brought to a stirring conclusion with a quote from Margaret Mead: "never doubt that a small group of thoughtful citizens can change the world. Indeed, it is the only thing that ever has." And in a letter to the *Engineering News Record* commenting on an article on fire protection, the leader of the Firestop Contractors praised their "provocative articles" that "improve our construction industry, through the discussion that's allowed in our free society."[72]

So at the margins of American business associations' political engagement, beyond lobbying, policy monitoring, and attempts to influence public opinion, we find routinized activities and discourses that situate economic actors as actors in civil society. These associations are occasionally settings that encourage conventional political participation as a public virtue; settings for generalized discussion of issues of broader public concern; and settings encouraging volunteering, mentoring, and community service. Consideration of members' business interests in the public sphere could sometimes expand to more generalized civic interest. Civic orientations could be attached to industry or occupational identities—not only the generalized identities as citizens, or localized identifications with communities, which the vast majority of discussions of civil society emphasize.

Overall, these discourses and strategies of action situating members' activities and concerns in a wider public context—evident in stated goals, in the cultivation of information, skills and programs for civic engagement, and in the discourses in which such activities are understood—are confined to the margins of the business association world. But while the extent and centrality of the broadening of such "civil society moments" should not be overstated, they do suggest a neglected civic potential to which most social scientists have been blinded by the strong categorical distinction between economy and civil society.

These illustrations demonstrate that when analysis goes beyond nominal categorizations to look at the substance of their work, voluntary associations for business sometimes provide settings for the universalizing discourses and routine practices necessary to civic engagement, even setting aside the fact that their own claims are often framed in universalizing terms. Industry identities—and not only local communities or generalized identities as citizens—may generate broader social engagement. Durkheim predicted this long ago, of course, but his insight has been neglected in the face of the conflicts of interest, illegitimate powers, and violations of civil society norms that also characterize collective action by business. But while any large-scale civic potential in collective action around industry identities remains incipient, normative theories of civil society are naive and ultimately self-defeating if they neglect this possibility entirely.

For obvious historical reasons, such blurring of industry identity and civic action emerged most strongly, among the focal associations here, in the historically black association of real estate businesses and salespeople, the National Association of Real Estate Brokers (NAREB). Whereas most associations' civic practices and discourses were somewhat peripheral to their main activities, the business concerns and activities of African American realtors (or, as they called themselves, "REALTISTS") were often difficult to distinguish from civically oriented languages and activities. They offer a particularly sharp illustration, and historically innovative model, of the blurring of economic and civic claims.

The National Association of Real Estate Brokers

Formed in 1947, NAREB is large, with 7,500 members (though the better-known National Association of Realtors claims 710,000), and it claims to be the "oldest minority trade association," "whose mission is to enhance the economic improvement of its members and the minority community it serves." It includes real estate brokers and sales agents, and their businesses, but also people and businesses in "allied professions" such as appraisers, developers, property managers, and mortgage brokers/bankers. Its head office is located in Maryland with a staff of three, but, with an elaborate volunteer-run organizational structure of chapters, state groups, affiliates, and partners, its organizational capacities and activities extend much further than a staff of three would suggest. Members are organized in seventy-eight chapters—such as the Greater Kansas City Chapter, and the Fort Worth Real Estate Association—and the national board of directors includes, in addition to nine standard offices (treasurer, secretary, and so on), eighteen regional vice presidents. This federal structure was not merely nominal. As NAREB's president wrote in June 2004 of "REALTIST© week activities":

> Many local board presidents around the nation wrote and advised me of the activities that their chapters were involved [sic] . . . Some included the Dearborn REALTIST© Board's attendance at the grand memorial African Methodist Episcopal Church in Chicago, IL; The Associated Real Property Brokers (ARPB) of Oakland, CA held a membership drive breakfast. . . . the Columbus REALTIST© Association sponsored several activities including promoting the NAREB© mission and history on an urban talk radio show which generated great response and the New Jersey Association of Real Estate Brokers held a successful blood drive and networking mixer.

A "Parade of States," a "colorful and impressive event" with "light and humorous" skits by members, was planned for NAREB's 2004 convention. NAREB was "counting on the support of each local board in conjunction with your state and/or regional association to make this a successful event." Although it was founded in 1947, NAREB models to some extent the classic picture of American associationalism developed by Theda Skocpol and her colleagues—"translocal as well as local efforts connected to broad movements and federal organizational frameworks."[73]

NAREB's national board also included ten voting members "by virtue of office"—the leaders of NAREB's extensive and active system of affiliate organizations. Specializations in Sales, Appraisal, or Property Management each have their own divisions: other affiliates included the Young REALTIST division, the NAREB Investment Division, and the Women's Council of NAREB. Affiliates were often, though not always, active associations in their own right, with their own formal organization and programs. For instance, the Sales Division was "the largest sub group within the National Association of real estate brokers" with "over 5,000 members

representing agents and brokers who are principally involved in real estate sales"; it was mostly involved in training courses, certification, and
referrals. To take another example, the Women's Council of NAREB resembles the Association for Women in Aviation Maintenance and aims to
"evaluate the standards of women in the real estate industry by encouraging leadership, education and the exchange of information through group
learning techniques"; among its activities were a retreat and a detailed
survey of members (e.g., "What automated underwriting system do you
use?" "Please estimate the percentage of your total business that is conducted in Spanish," "Please list the 5 mortgage lenders/brokers that your
company originates the most loans for," "How do you counsel to improve
credit scores?"). It also ran an Annual Scholarships and Awards Luncheon
and sold Women's Council promotional items at the NAREB convention.
In 2004, the luncheon theme was "Connecting People to Make a World of
Difference In Real Estate."[74]

NAREB draws on many standard associational strategies of action in
its programs and activities. Its numerous publications include a newsletter and membership directory; its sales, appraisal, and property management affiliates each offer elaborate training and certification programs; it
licenses all members to use the Realtist© symbol; it organizes an annual
convention with exhibits, and a fall meeting of boards and committees in
DC; it surveys its members about existing and possible future benefits;
it offers "business opportunities," such as programs in partnership with
private firms to offer free alarm systems to clients, and a "gateway" to the
secondary mortgage market; and it offers NAREB merchandise such as
mouse pads. Some of its affiliates and subdivisions, like the National Society of Real Estate Appraisers, focus almost entirely on professional issues
of education, accreditation, ethics, and exchange of information (sounding like the Conference of Consulting Actuaries).[75]

NAREB is among that minority of associations that take a proactive
lobbying stance, and it also does some public relations. One of the benefits
NAREB claims to offer members is "Input on National Housing Policy
Issues." Its public affairs committee reported ongoing meetings and programs with the Congressional Black Caucus, the Department of Housing
and Urban Development (HUD), and the government lenders Fanny Mae
and Freddie Mac. In 2004, for instance, they had a three-day gathering during which they met with members of congress, attended a Policy Briefing
Luncheon about some HUD programs and "urban and rural housing and
development issues," and reported "working closely" with Fannie Mae

and HUD on topics like the primary and secondary mortgage industry and title companies. And in one of the sort of informal coalitions characteristic of the policy fields Laumann and Knoke describe, "REALTISTS have joined with the Congressional Black Caucus and our lender partners: Fannie Mae, Freddie Mac, Chase Manhattan Mortgage, and Bank of America in a National Alliance for Homeownership. Through our industry Alliance, the caucus will be convening homeownership events in every CBC congressional district." And some of NAREB's activities, like occasional press releases, their membership directory, and their accreditation program, can be seen as the sort of industry public relations discussed above.[76]

But to focus only on NAREB's many standard associational activities would be to allow theoretical blinders to filter out its central meaning and stretch ideology critique to its limit. Not only does it blur members' identities as economic actors and African Americans, it also situates its members as actors in civil society on the basis of their industry identities, providing settings for generalized discussion of issues of broader public concern and fusing what might be understood as industry interest with numerous programs for industry-related community service.

The key public issue for NAREB is equal housing opportunities "regardless of race, creed, or color":

> Our mission is to serve the un-served, and develop creative and effective methods of doing so . . . the REALTIST organization is an integrated entity open to all qualified practitioners who are committed to achieving the ideals of the REALTIST theme—Democracy in Housing.

One incoming president claimed in his inaugural address:

> For 56 years NAREB has stood and continues to stand as a beacon of hope for minorities and the underserved. To that end, we will continue to serve as that hope for many Americans—more than that we will make that hope a reality. We will challenge the status quo and insist on greater access and availability of funds for minority home purchasers. Our theme for the next two years will be "REALTISTS: African Americans Showing the Way Home."[77]

A number of established and elaborated programs, "strategic partnerships," and affiliate activities follow up on this mission. Among the regular education and certification programs offered by the Sales Division, for instance, is a course on Faith Based Community Development "de-signed to build congregations through homeownership . . . it educates church leadership on how to form a community development corpora-tion and how to purchase projects with no money." Another affiliate of NAREB, the Real Estate Management Brokers Institute (REMBI), a group of "approximately 200 of real estate professionals whose day-to-day focus is property management," was initiated in Chicago in Novem-ber 1968 by "members [who] felt it essential to integrate the training for ethical and social responsibilities, good tenant management relationship and proper maintenance of the product." They were concerned that "in nearly all of our larger cities, more housing units were being lost through abandonment and mismanagement than those being added through new construction and rehabilitation." REMBI is responsible for an extensive training and accreditation program in property management. But among the standard course announcements and photos of recent graduates in their newsletter run stories like that about collaborative seminars and partnerships with churches and banks to address low-income home financ-ing topics, and about the historical origins of public housing high-rises.[78]

The national president also spoke in 2003 of the importance of mentor-ing, again blurring industry and community identities: "we must also serve as positive role models for the real estate industry and for our youth . . . develop, expand and nurture our youth because they are our future." At this time NAREB supported a "Teens on the Green" program using golf to "provide a professional attitude among it's [sic] participating youth" and open opportunities to a "scholarship to the college of their choice due to the education and experience they will receive."[79]

Another affiliate of NAREB is almost entirely devoted to issues of public concern beyond the industry, in both its discourse and its strategies of action—though, certainly, NAREB's members might stand to benefit from any successes it might record. NID-HCA (NAREB–Investment Division–Housing Counseling Agency) ran a number of programs ori-ented to outreach, information, and assistance for minority home owner-ship. Broadly speaking, its mission was

> to improve the quality of life in America's cities. We will accomplish this as partners, working together with our friends and neighbors. We will help our communities become places where families can live in safety, prosperity and harmony; places where the American dream of home ownership can flourish; places where fair, decent and affordable housing is a reality for all people.

To do so, it aims to "provide financial literacy and economic empower-
ment to inner city communities." It works in a number of partnerships
with HUD, other associations, and mortgage providers of various sorts,
and it claimed to have "counseled over 15,000 persons/entities nationwide" since 1995.[80]

This group published educational brochures for first-time home buyers
(e.g., "how to address credit issues," and "find affordable housing units
available in your area"); for homeowners (e.g., "steps to protect your investment from foreclosure," and "municipal housing repair assistance");
and for "Faith-Based Organizations and Community Groups" ("on the
process of effectively and efficiently developing affordable housing and
affordable housing programs in their local communities"). It also provided
the opportunity of online consultations direct with consumers and counselors (or "local advocates") in twenty-four offices in thirteen states:

> NID-HCA Certified Counselors receive extensive training in housing counsel-
> ing and community development. Transferring the training and experience into
> productivity is a difficult proposition and takes exemplary skills and dedication
> of the NID-HCA counselor and their support staff. Whether the task is sim-
> ple homebuyer education or complex predatory lending workouts or assisting
> FBO'S (faith-based orgs.) [sic] in affordable housing development, the NID-
> HCA Certified Counselor must provide the multitude of services that we offer
> in a professional and cost effective manner that leads to actual results.

Newsletters also provide information on such issues as predatory lending.[81]

As for many other of the business associations discussed above, the
discourse in which these programs is understood is one of expertise and
public good:

> Counselors work to level the information playing field for minority homebuyers
> and homeowners. The absence of sound and rational financial decisions cripple
> minority and immigrant populations and communities, and increases cost to
> government.

> Lack of information and access to reliable information is a major barrier im-
> pacting minority homeownership, wealth building and community building.
> The capitalistic system is based on the citizenry making informed, sound and
> rationale financial decisions [sic]. The absence of rationality and correct and vi-
> able information exacerbates economic uncertainty and social instability which

disproportionately plague urban and minority populations and communities. Homeownership and small and minority business development is the corner-stone of minority and urban community self-sufficiency. It is imperative and economically opportunistic to create an effective mechanism of impartial, un-biased, non-predatory information and communication sources to effectively reach and service minority markets.[82]

Conclusion

The rich and neglected social worlds of the real estate brokers, firestop contractors, women in aviation maintenance, and other business groups we have seen in this chapter challenge sociologists to reexamine their as-sumptions about what business associations do, and why. The standard view of business associations' orientation to their external political envi-ronments assumes they act as interest groups in conventional politics. This conventional view has inhibited investigation of associations' orientation to the public sphere and civil society. Scholarly distinctions between civil society and economic life have also inhibited inquiry into business asso-ciations' orientation to the public. This chapter shows that neglect of this question is unjustified.

As well as lobbying and monitoring policy, politically oriented asso-ciations may seek to influence public opinion, or to contribute to public sphere discussion of issues in which they claim some expertise. In fact, as-sociations are more commonly oriented to influencing public opinion than to engaging in conventional interest group politics, and they mobilize a standard repertoire of strategies of action to that end. Around half do so, slightly less or slightly more depending on the data source. However, many do not distinguish publics-as-markets from civil publics. On the basis of the focal sample, about one in four direct their public relations efforts to public opinion on issues of general concern, most frequently environmen-tal and product standards. Their attempts to influence public opinion are mostly oriented to specialized publics.

A previously unrecognized minority of associations—perhaps one in eight—orient themselves to civic issues (e.g., public safety or minority inclusion) that are not intrinsic to their economic activities—in ways more characteristic of other voluntary groups in civil society than of the stereo-typical industry interest group.

Attempts to influence public opinion and to participate in civil society are usually understood in languages of public good, especially stewardship of the public good through technical expertise. Moreover, politically engaged associations' extensive use of languages of technical expertise and public good, rather than strategic industry interest, and their occasional appearance here as specialized little social movements in civil society, both suggest that interest group theory is not only empirically inadequate but also theoretically naive. Collective action by business sometimes attempts functional contributions, and occasionally attempts "civil repair." Such civic engagement may be dismissed as "blowing smoke" to conceal narrower and perhaps more sinister self-interest, but even if this cynical view were entirely plausible, the social fact of languages and practices oriented to "the public good" needs an account, especially considering that the language of "industry voice" we saw in chapter eight is easily available and would be perfectly virtuous from the point of view of pluralist theory and commonsense views of politics.

The assumption that members of business associations are simply self-interested actors is naive because it takes interests as transparent and immutable facts of life, curiously detached from and uninfluenced by the languages in which they are constructed. This is true not only of the political interests we have been exploring in part four, but also of the economic interests we examined in part three. To get beyond the opposition between solidarity and strategy ultimately requires a reformulation of our understanding of "interests."

Conclusion

CHAPTER TEN

The Power of Business Culture

What makes self-interested action for profit make sense? This question challenges a widely shared article of faith: that self-interested economic action in the pursuit of profit is both natural and essential these days, and other, more anomalous orientations—such as reciprocity in long-standing networks—need to be explained as some complicated variant of self-interest. The meaning-making we have explored shows that naïveté lies in assuming that businesspeople always see what they are doing as profit-seeking, not in wondering how profit-seeking makes sense to them.

To explore the question of what the pursuit of business interests means, this study focuses on American business associations. These are, prima facie, leading cases of business "interest groups," and Adam Smith's famous observation about trade conspiracies in association seems like a truism. If this truism were a theory, it would predict that business associations would demonstrate a highly distilled and unashamed discourse of economic self-interest. Most of the few writers who have examined business associations take this assumption as an article of faith.

Partly as a result of this unexamined assumption, very little is actually known about American business associations, so the first task of this study has been to begin to redress that scholarly neglect. I have analyzed the basic parameters of the American business association population—their political and organizational history, some of their organizational features, and their main goals and activities. The first main conclusion of this study is that the American business association population cannot be explained except as an institution of cultural production for economic action.

I then build on that investigation to learn more about business culture, and especially the cultural construction of norms of self-interested exchange. First, developing suggestions implicit in neoinstitutionalist theories of industries, and drawing out their implications for other more recent developments in economic sociology, I have shown how business associations produce cognitive categories, networks, and fields that create collective cognitive goods for economic action. I then argued that this indirectly instrumental function is only made possible by normative and expressive languages and practices creating disinterested solidarity in occupational subcultures. These are evident in the ways "industry" boundaries are set, in the ways collective identities are characterized, in normative and status orders, and in occupational camaraderie. The second main conclusion of this study is that business associations are more active than neoinstitutionalists have suggested, not only in producing indirectly strategic cultural goods but also in the infrastructure they provide for occupational solidarity. The well-established scale of this activity shows that they should be more fully recognized as an important part of American economic life, and that they should be included more routinely in research that examines how cognitive categories, networks, and fields influence economic action.

Next, I explored the symbolic repertoire or vocabulary of motive with which meaning is assigned to associations' supposedly self-interested strategies of action, both those activities that seem more oriented to intraindustry coordination problems and those that seem more oriented to external influence. The third main conclusion of this study is that reductionist assumptions about economic orientations are inadequate even for capitalist economic activity in business, just as Viviana Zelizer has argued for other sorts of economic relations.

Investigating what economic action in business actually means is important because both critics and celebrants of the power of business usually naturalize interest-oriented action with ungrounded assumptions about *normative models of exchange* contrasting self-interest and altruism. The cultural construction of self-interested norms of exchange in capitalist markets has only rarely been questioned—by critics, celebrants, or scholars—since Weber suggested that the iron cage had closed. (By contrast, the cultural constructions of objects of exchange in commodification, and the cultural construction of partners to exchange in market formation, are widely understood as contingent, mutable, and often contestable.)[1]

What are the theoretical and normative implications of taking business culture seriously and recognizing that it cannot be reduced simply to pursuit of profit and industry stability? The vocabulary of motives that make business meaningful is frequently disinterested. The fourth important conclusion of this study is that economic action in markets and industries is oriented by a *discursive field* structured not only by strategic interest but also by disinterested solidarity. This fundamental culture-structure generates the many ways of understanding economic action available in the symbolic repertoires I have analyzed here, as well as in other sites of economic culture. We should no longer take for granted that business action is oriented by self-interested profit-seeking, but rather understand discourses orienting business action as formed in the semiotic opposition between self-interested profit-seeking and disinterested solidarity.

Recognizing this cultural structure helps understand the ideological power of business better than simplistic assumptions about economic self-interest. The many ways that business is understood as disinterested that we have seen in these pages are not trivial exceptions or odd anomalies; they explain why and how self-interested, profit-oriented action can be sustained. In fact, they suggest that capitalist relations of production and exchange are much more psychically powerful than analyses based on normative self-interest might suggest. But they also offer a normative basis for imagining how the profound inequalities, conflicts, and inefficiencies of the social division of labor in capitalism might be more effectively challenged.

This concluding chapter provides an overview of what we have learned about business culture and American business associations, and what that means for our understanding of contemporary economic life.

A Primer on American Business Associations

Weberian-inspired theories of comparative economic governance suggest that business associations do not flourish in the American political climate because their political authorization to legitimately pursue and coordinate economic interests is restricted compared to elsewhere. What Gerald Berk and Marc Schneiberg have termed the "conventional narrative"—more often, scholarly silence—assumes that national associations began to form as a means of coordinating industries after the Civil War, but failed after antitrust law was imposed in the late nineteenth century and strengthened a few decades later. But as I argued in chapter two, and further discussed in chapter three, their shifting political context has been rather inconsequential for the strength and stability of the institution. Moreover, the available evidence of associations' organization and orientations presents serious challenges to this episodic view and suggests more continuity. This continuity can be explained if we recognize that associations were *never* oriented solely to the short-term promotion of economic interests through price-and-production agreements (which were, in any case, difficult to sustain), but *always* much more multifunctional— producing, for instance, information, education, and occupational camara- derie. Reexamining neglected evidence from a variety of case studies and reassessing the trajectory of the organizational population, we saw that, through the late nineteenth century and into the early twentieth century associations developed a standard portfolio of strategies of action all in- volving the systematic, collective production of information for economic action. By the time of the first comprehensive overview of national business associations in the 1930s, we see them long- and well-established as a robust institution for cultural production.[2]

So the history of American business associations presents an anomaly and a puzzle for theories of comparative economic governance that sug- gest they must be ineffective. This puzzle is resolved if we recognize that the pursuit of economic interests requires cultural production. American business associations are not permanently failing institutions for economic governance in the way Weberian theory suggests, but successful institu- tions for cultural production, as Durkheimian theory implies. American associations should not be seen as "unstable, redundant, and limited" economic organizations but rather as stable, diverse, and minimal cultural organizations.

This stability, diversity, and minimal organization is further confirmed in chapter three, which shows the persistence of the institution relatively unchanged through the second half of the twentieth century. Business asso- ciations resemble other voluntary organizations in their governance struc- ture, and have done so at least since the early twentieth century. Numbers of business associations increased steadily throughout the twentieth century, with at least a hundred forming each decade before 1940, and at least two hundred forming in each subsequent decade: in the late twentieth century, the average was likely around four hundred. They are long lasting. Even in the early twenty-first century, almost 40 percent of associations had been founded before 1960, and as we saw earlier in chapter two, some had even persisted from the nineteenth century. This persistence is an important feature of minimalist organizations.

The vast majority of business associations hold various types of meet- ings for their members and produce various types of publications. As was also evident by the 1930s, the central shared feature of business associations is their cultural production. This meaning-making is distinctive for its context specificity and resonance with what are, from a scholarly point of view, very specific and variable economic orientations. Like associations' longevity, this is a substantively important feature characteristic of minimalist organization. Although previous accounts have taken this feature entirely for granted, I argue that it explains the stability, diversity, and organizational minimalism of the business association population much better than assumptions about their pursuit of political or economic "interests."

The comprehensive census analyzed here, along with the spotlights provided by surveys from the 1960s and 1980s, show organizations that remain remarkably similar in their main features to those of the early twentieth century. These voluntary organizations challenge conventional understandings not only of American economic organization but also of occupational culture, professional organization, interest groups, and civil society.

They are typically small organizations; overall, their median membership is around 350, almost a quarter operate with fewer than a hundred members, and two-thirds with fewer than a thousand. They report a median staff of four (and, as noted in chapter three, only around a third explicitly report internal organization in the form of committees or affiliated groups). However, they vary widely; for instance, 7 percent (more than three hundred) have over ten thousand members, and 23 percent (over a thousand) have more than twelve staff.

One reason for this wide variation is the nature of business association membership. Unlike many other types of voluntary organizations, members may be firms, individuals, or both. While the typical and stereotypical association is composed of firms, a third of them are composed of individuals, and there is some indication that this proportion was slowly increasing in the late twentieth century. Associations including individuals tend to be larger, and they report committees and affiliations more frequently, but they do not differ from others in reported staff.

For most of the twentieth century, and into the twenty-first, American business associations seem to have clustered in three cities—Washington, DC; New York; and Chicago, with the many associations outside these cities widely scattered. Insofar as this information is comparable to information from the 1960s, there may have been less clustering later, and more associations were forming at a greater rate in the west and south at the expense of New York and Chicago. However, the basic pattern remains remarkably stable.

Scholars of economic governance often assume that characteristics of economic sectors influence the importance of associations. However, a substantial minority of associations—two in five—include members from more than one sector (broadly defined), and there is some indication that many associations include members in more than two sectors and in more than one industry within a sector. There are many types of sectoral mixes: a combination of manufacturers and wholesalers was the most common, but even that included only 7.5 percent of the population. For this and other reasons noted in chapter three, the economic demands specific to different economic sectors provide little purchase in accounting for associations' importance. Moreover, although business associations are conventionally assumed to be composed of manufacturers, manufacturing was the main focus of only a quarter of associations. Another quarter involved various types of services, and the rest were widely distributed across other economic arenas.

As an institution, business associations are characterized by a standard repertoire of goals and activities (what I treat in later chapters as "strategies of action," as distinct from the symbolic repertoires or vocabulary of motives that make them meaningful). Some of these strategies of action are mostly oriented to internal audiences and to issues internal to the field of economic activity—education, sharing information, research, and standards and accreditation. Others mediate between the economic orientations of members and the broader public—public relations, lobbying or monitoring policy, and civic goals. Overall, internally oriented goals and activities are probably more common than externally oriented concerns, an observation that casts doubt on typical stereotypes of business associations but helps explain why many of these groups and the issues that preoccupy them seem arcane. Although these sorts of activities fall below the radar of most social scientists, they constitute an absorbing arena of collective action to business, represent a significant volume of cultural production by business, and typically engage more associational energy than more well recognized public activities. To the extent this portfolio of goals and activities is comparable to findings from surveys in the 1930s and 1980s it confirms that the range of orientations associations may adopt has remained as stable as their organization.

Because almost nothing is known of what associations are actually doing when they claim to be providing education, for example, or when they express an interest in public relations, later chapters have included more detailed explanation of each orientation, drawing on the qualitative information provided by the representative focal associations to illustrate typical activities and assessing broader variation in attachment to these goals in the population as a whole. These illustrative overviews provide a more concrete sense of business association life. They demonstrate, for example, that associational strategies of action usually address technical as well as business-related issues, and they may be implemented in more or less formal and resource-intensive ways by different associations. For instance, education programs vary in their formality, shared information is frequently technical rather than business related, research is typically intermittent, certification and accreditation are highly technical and resource intensive, an orientation to conventional politics typically involves passive monitoring, public relations is often understood as collective marketing but sometimes is concerned with issues on the public agenda, and associations sometimes encourage routine civic engagement such as political participation and community service. The focal groups also suggest that the frequency of each of these goals and activities is understated in the population data drawn from statements of purpose. This underscores the multifunctionality of associations.

The population data suggest some broad ways in which different types of associations sometimes vary in their goals and activities. For instance, and very generally speaking, younger associations of individuals in service industries are more likely to claim internally oriented goals, especially education and information sharing. Associations oriented to public relations or expressing civic goals were also more likely to be larger, younger, and to include individual members. Conversely, an older association of manufacturing firms would more likely be interested in research, but less likely claim an orientation to education and sharing information. Associations located in Washington, smaller associations, and associations composed of firms were also somewhat less likely to express an intraindustry orientation than others, but more likely to express an orientation to conventional political goals and activities.

But these are all marginal differences that do not sharply differentiate the population into conveniently distinct and substantively important categories, and there are too many exceptions to all these marginal tendencies for minor correlations to be illuminating. Rather, all these goals and activities make up a repertoire of organizational practices or strategies of action that is best seen as a cultural attribute of business associations as an institution.

Louis Galambos long ago suggested a better general typology of associations; he distinguished "dinner-club" associations (which offer relatively few services but provide a meeting ground for members), "service" associations (which have more systematic organization and an array of longer-range programs for members), and "policy-shaping" associations (which add intermittently effective powers of industry governance and public influence). Galambos assumed that these different types made a historical and developmental series, but, taking a population view, they serve better as contemporaneous ideal types. In reality, their features can overlap, and associations do not necessarily strengthen their coordinating capacities and influence over time; indeed, they may "regress." And at any given time, examples of all three types are easily seen, as the focal sample investigated demonstrates. However, this typology conveys a valid thumbnail sketch summarizing the wide variation among business associations in their organization and orientations, while at the same time avoiding misleading assumptions about types and purposes of association that ignore the characteristic variability, minimalism, and multifunctionality of culture-producing organizations.[3]

Business Associations, Cultural Production, and Occupational Community

Business associations provide a whole new wealth of evidence to expand on economic sociologists' arguments that economic action is socially embedded, and these arguments in turn can help explore what business associations do in more depth.

Many economic sociologists have been drawing renewed attention to cultural embeddedness—the ways culture influences economic action. Although they do so in disparate theoretical vocabularies and at different levels of analysis, these arguments take one of three forms: they address how surrounding social context influences economic meaning-making; they examine varied meaning-making in interaction; and they analyze economic discourse for its fundamental and generative categories, often moral categories. This study has shown how these different approaches may be combined: first, by examining an important institution for the production of American economic culture; second, by exploring extensive evidence of highly context-bound and varied practical meaning-making; and third, by showing the way those varied meanings are generated within the discursive opposition between interest and disinterest. In my view, the different theoretical voices making claims about economic culture should be harmonized by recognizing that no study of economic culture is complete without attending to all three dimensions—organizational, practical-hermeneutic, and discursive—and this study models that injunction.[4]

I have explored exactly how business associations are cultural producers by drawing on suggestions from neoinstitutionalist organizational theorists. Apart from scholars investigating comparative economic governance, discussed in chapter two, and those examining populations of organizations, mentioned in chapter three, they are the only economic sociologists who have provided any theoretically informed treatment of business associations. Because of their focus on the significance of interorganizational cultural production for organizations' orientations, Paul DiMaggio and Walter Powell briefly proposed that business associations might be sites generating mimetic and normative isomorphism within fields of organizations. Excepting a few case studies, this proposal was never followed up, but as I argued in chapter four, isolated examples of associations' role in industry change rely on unexamined assumptions about their routine constitution of identities and interests in settled times.[5]

And as it turns out, routine cultural production of this sort contributes to three other aspects of embedded economic action that have interested economic sociologists—cognitive categories, networks, and fields. First, business associations routinely articulate and promote cognitive categories and practices. These categories and practices are distinctive for their special resonance and resolution compared to other more generic sources like the business press and business education. Second, business associations institutionalize opportunities for producing networks with upstream and downstream exchange partners, peers, and other industry actors (and as I noted, how networks are generated has been an understudied problem for economic sociologists). Third, business associations generate organizational fields, creating "mutual awareness among participants . . . that they are involved in a common enterprise." Business associations are often more about lowering boundaries than heightening them, and they articulate orientations to, and sometimes establish interactive links with, upstream and downstream market partners, standards organizations, academic researchers, other related associations, and regulatory agencies, among other groups. Business associations routinely produce and reproduce cognitive categories, networks, and fields.[6]

This analysis extends neoinstitutionalist arguments in several ways—by examining institutionalized, routine, field-level cultural production in associations, and by showing how that field-level cultural production speaks to other themes in economic sociologists' examination of embeddedness.

But business associations also do much more than this indirectly strategic work of producing collective cultural goods, and I go beyond standard neoinstitutionalist arguments about cultural production for economic action in another way too.

As chapter five shows, associations generate solidarity in normative and expressive ways characteristic of occupational communities. Solidarity is an end in itself, evident in collective identities, normative and status orders, and camaraderie that are hard to understand from a strictly strategic point of view. It is important to note, first, that contrary to the assumptions of previous investigators, the collective identities articulated in association bear little relation to objectively defined industries and are set by the members themselves. These more "vernacular" collective identities are expressed in occupationally specific interactional engagement, insider complaints, perspectives on public matters, collective memory, and collective symbols. Beyond that, subculturally specific normative and status orders are evident in standards, ethics codes, awards for both technical achievements and for "industry" contributions, and an informal language of "industry" standing. And sociability and occupational camaraderie are evident in meeting reports, insider jokes, charity, provision for the young, and memorials.

So when we examine business associations' cultural production systematically and in depth, we see that the neoinstitutionalist intuition that associations might help generate mimetic and normative isomorphism in fields of economic action is extended by the new analysis here of their routine reproduction of cognitive categories, networking opportunities, and fields. This indirectly strategic cultural production is only possible because they also produce nonstrategic solidarity—collective identities, normative and status orders, and camaraderie. Normative and expressive culture—discourse and action that is primarily nonstrategic—is fundamental to associational life.

Vocabularies of Motive for Economic Action

This examination of how "the movers and shakers of the industry" experience "a special camaraderie with colleagues" shows what business associations do. But to conclude the analysis with an account of cultural production would leave mostly unexplored the ways meaning-making operates in action. Many scholars have challenged neoinstitutionalists attending to cultural production for underemphasizing the particularities of meaning-making in practice and overstating isomorphism and homogeneity—ignoring variation among and within organizations and industries in the agentic enactment of cultural repertoires that are themselves local, multivocal, and fluid. Generally speaking, analyses of cultural production can only provide preliminary background context for the close hermeneutic analysis of meaning-making in practice.

Such close hermeneutic analysis of meaning-making in practice is usually conducted with more interactional and ideographic research strategies than those adopted in this study. Research on economic culture in practice typically examines particular organizations or markets with fieldwork or interviews that allow an analytic focus on thick description of meaning-making processes. Because this study takes a wider angle of vision, I do not examine meaning-making in its particular interactional context in this way. Until now, so little has been known and so much has been wrongly presumed about what happens in business associations that such isolated studies could have only limited value. Certainly, however, another important contribution of this research should be to open many new possibilities for theoretically driven fieldwork in associations that can offer a deeper understanding of economic meaning-making in practice.[7]

What I do instead is an extended and comprehensive analysis of the various meanings available in association discourse, the cultural repertoire in terms of which they can account for and make sense of their typical strategies of action. In place of a thick local account of meaning-making in practice limited to one or two settings, I develop a thick hermeneutic analysis of the vocabulary of motives associations use to communicate their strategies of action. Because the analysis is based on a systematically developed and comprehensive archive of documents generated by a focal sample of associations representative of the national association population, it is possible to show the more-or-less complete repertoire of meaning-making practices that are available and typically mobilized in particular associational settings.

To the extent all this varied meaning-making in business association practice can be summarized beyond its context, table 10.1 provides an overview of what we have seen.

Vocabularies of Motive for Intraindustry Strategies of Action

The analysis of vocabularies of motive for economic action begins in chapter six by focusing on typical strategies of action mostly related to intra-"industry" concerns—education, sharing information, research, and

TABLE 10.1 **Vocabularies of motive in American business associations**

Members' Particularistic Interests	• "Invaluable marketing support tools to help maintain your competitive edge" • "saves you time and money"
Collective "Intraindustry" Interests	• "ensures a healthy and strong industry for everyone" • "illustrates a commitment to the industry" • "programs designed to improve the industry"
Professionalism and Technical Expertise	• "experienced professionals in the industry" • "expertise and counsel of the highest competence, creativity, and integrity" • "stay connected to your fellow professionals"
Collective "Public" Interests	• "seek representation to consider federal . . . law" • "providing a voice for the industry"
Stewardship of the Public Good	• "serving as a responsible steward" • "an ongoing effort to protect the public" • "just a concern for their fellow citizens"

standards and accreditation. As I noted earlier, these strategies of action make up a large part of the cultural repertoire that characterizes the business association as an institution.

But what is the point of all this energetic economic activity? In principle, strategies of action can be understood in many different ways. But strong conventional assumptions suggest an easy answer to this question. These strategies of action are oriented to promoting members' economic interests in the efficiency and performance, and thus the profitability and stability, of their firms.

Of course, institutionalized cooperation in business associations contradicts the stereotype of isolated, competitive economic actors under capitalism. The obvious point that the very existence of these associations challenges the simplistic individualism of popular economistic models and supports instead economic sociology's extensive evidence of "embeddedness" does bear repeating here.

In chapter six I sketched a more sophisticated economic answer to the "what's the point" question: associations are strategic for particular members because they reduce transaction costs, for example, by helping reduce potential costs of gathering information about new markets, or of trying to sell unstandardized products. There is almost no concrete evidence that associations benefit their members in this way, and as I pointed out, such evidence is difficult to develop because associational boundaries are political-cultural creations, not usually economically functional categories mapping on to objectively defined industries. The idea that associations reduce transaction costs for members is simply another instance of what Mark Granovetter and others have argued is an economistic "article of faith." But the more important question is whether these strategies are generally *understood* as promoting such particularistic economic interests of members.[8]

And as it turns out, education, information sharing, research, and standard setting are rather rarely understood as promoting members' particular economic interests. Certainly, we saw evidence of occasional appeals to the direct interests of members in some accounts of these activities, as well as in the occasional promotion of networking, marketing, and member discounts as selective benefits for members, especially for very small business. But overall, members' particularistic economic interests rarely seem to offer good reasons for engagement in intraindustry strategies of action, and, in practice, such accounts were deeply fused with stronger discourses concerning collective business interests and professional commitments.

Economic sociologists like Granovetter, Marc Schneiberg, William Roy, and Rogers Hollingsworth who are critical of the "just-so" functionalist explanations of firms' economic interests in lowering transaction costs adopt a more collective and political understanding of economic interests and generally focus on "industry"-level, collective interests and outcomes. From this perspective, answers to the "why bother" question about associations' intra-"industry" strategies of action are framed in terms of collective interests and collective goods—and the political battles they generate. As we saw, associations do, indeed, often understand what they are doing— such as their educational programs, information sharing, research, and standard setting—as promoting collective interests of the (self-defined) group or industry. And while such work is understood as oriented to collective interests on a routine basis, we can also see, by digging deep into evidence offered by the focal sample of associations, instances in which their routine work accrues immediate tactical significance as associations and their members face new contingencies and challenges of intra-"industry" coordination and control. We saw examples of associations mobilizing their collective identities and routine strategies of action to respond to technological change, and other instances in which associations were using intraindustry strategies of action to address growing power of channel partners, such as big-box retailers. These episodes were not routine, but associations' routine cultural production is a condition of such episodic responses to problems of industry coordination and control. As I noted, cultural production is necessarily overproduction from a strategic point of view. Overall, associations' accounts of their intraindustry strategies of action in terms of collective interests further emphasize the importance of their routine production of collective identity and solidarity.

It also invites the question of how beliefs about the promotion of particularistic interests of members are reconciled with claims about collective industry benefits, since—as the Olsonian problem of "free riding" also suggests—there is no logical reason to assume that collective promotion of the "industry" will naturally "trickle down" to every particular member, and it is quite possible that the particular interests of different members or different sorts of members may actually conflict. Sometimes the presence of both particularistic and collective accounts creates glaring textual tensions in association discourse. Sometimes, more logically, collective interests are specified as those particularistic interests members share. And sometimes members are explicitly exhorted to make sacrifices for the collective good. But mostly, the ambivalence is left unexplored, a silence that, again, shows why associations' creation of collective identities cannot be trivialized or ignored.[9]

And claims about particular members' and collective "industry" interests in profitability and economic stability do not exhaust vocabularies of motive that answer the "why bother" question about associations' intraindustry strategies of action. In this language, "the highest level of professional recognition" is as important as "growing the industry." Chapter seven showed that members' occupational community makes a language of professionalism another important way of accounting for intraindustry strategies of action like education, information sharing, research, and standards and accreditation. In fact, although theories of professions have usually distinguished professions from business, many businesspeople do not recognize this distinction and attribute professional honor and distinction to their lines of work. And as I showed with extended examples from the focal associations, if professionalism is defined by claims to occupational jurisdiction on the basis of abstract knowledge, they have plausible grounds for doing so.

So part three analyzes in comprehensive detail multifarious examples of associations' meaning-making about intra-"industry" strategies of action and shows that their meaning cannot be reduced to the pursuit of particularistic economic interests. Vocabularies of motive providing accounts in all these innumerable practical instances do include rare appeals to members' own business interests, but much more frequently stress vaguely specified collective interests and appeal to the technical excellence and honor of professionalism.

Vocabularies of Motive for Publicly Oriented Strategies of Action

Similarly, part four explores vocabularies of motive for strategies of action primarily oriented to external audiences—lobbying and monitoring policy, public relations, and civic practices. These externally oriented strategies of action are less prevalent and weaker in national business associations than scholarly stereotypes influenced by political economy, pluralism, and corporatism presume, but they do engage the energies of a significant minority of associations. They involve such practices as systematic monitoring, intermittent lobbying, coalition formation, regular technical discussions with government, providing public information, certification, discussing public issues, and volunteering. Against scholarly stereotypes, but as with intra-"industry" strategies of action, there is little evidence that associations are routinely consequential political players. Rather, a politically engaged minority is composed of peripheral players in relevant policy domains, and their voice may be heard occasionally, especially in coalitions or on abstruse technical matters.

Again, the important question here is, why bother? Challenging conventional wisdom, that what is assumed to be routine strategic action needs no cultural analysis, I ask how these strategies of action are understood and how associations account for them. What vocabularies of motive make sense of associations' routine public engagement? I answer this question by exploring the ways those focal associations oriented to the public sphere account for many, various, and specific instances of public strategies of action they adopt, and with extended illustrations drawn from what Galambos would call more "policy capable" associations.

As with intra-"industry" strategies of action, two general languages of public engagement are mixed. A minority of associations account for their public engagement, especially their attention to policy, as the pursuit of (collective) "industry" interests (demonstrating once again the importance of associations' collective identity formation). In doing so, they adopt the "democratic code" prevalent in American public life. They show how that code is elaborated in "settled" times, rather than unsettled times of heightened political engagement during social movements or national ritual. Whereas the "democratic code" in unsettled times stigmatizes "special interests," in favor of broader claims about the public good, associations using a clearly articulated and comfortably institutionalized language of "industry interest" appeal to the public virtue of "democratic voice" to avoid that stigma. But this interest-based language is not common and is mostly mixed with or superseded by a language appealing to stewardship of the public good. This inclusive language avoids boundary drawing and is typically based on technocratic appeals to information and expertise, appeals that stigmatize "special interests." They also reinforce the significance of "professional" understandings of intraindustry strategies of action.[10]

Claims-making about stewardship of the public good is even more resonant when associations attempt to influence public opinion than when they act in conventional political settings. Although much of what associations see as public relations is oriented to the market rather than broader publics, some see public relations as a matter of influencing public opinion on matters of general concern, especially when involving issues of standards, safety, and the environment, but occasionally, too, issues of social inclusion. Again, associations fuse industry identities with broader, more expansive collective identities and emphasize technical expertise they might contribute to the public good. Languages of interest almost disappear in claims-making about associations' strategies of action oriented to public opinion; "interest group politics" is reimagined as benign participation in civil society. And as we saw, some few associations take this sort of account of their participation in civil society to its logical conclusion, with routine strategies of action and universalizing discourses characteristic of the nonprofit groups usually considered to be more typical civic actors.

This extended investigation of meanings associated with business association practices shows that the cultural repertoire providing a vocabulary of motives to account for associational strategies of action is extensive and varied. It shows that economic orientations cannot be understood with simple and reductionist assumptions about the pursuit of interests, even in business and even in organizations that are supposedly quintessential interest groups. Just as Zelizer argues of economic action generally, business relies on far richer (and less disciplined) meaning-making than a simple separation between "expressive cultural" and "instrumental economic" action allows.

Strategy and Solidarity in Economic Life

Overall, this examination of how business associations seek to "grow the industry," to offer "the highest level of professional recognition," to provide "a voice for the industry," and to express "concern for their fellow citizens" shows how, in practice, business associations account for their strategies of action. What can we learn more generally about economic culture from this investigation?

To conclude the analysis here, with investigation of cultural production and culture in practice, would leave only implicit the grammar of economic culture, the structure of the discursive field within which these claims are made. Just as analysis of business associations' cultural production provides a foundation for closely analyzing meaning-making in practice, so too, the preceding analysis of meaning-making in practice is a basis for drawing out the implications of business association discourse for economic culture more generally. Only by identifying the underlying structure of discourse about business interests can we make a theoretical and normative generalization beyond what Laurent Thévenot has called "purely contextual stories" about economic culture.[11]

Whereas conventional and scholarly wisdom alike mostly presume that business must be conducted as strategic action in pursuit of particular, strategic interests in profitability and stability, this study shows that business culture is not so simplistic. Rather, meaning-making about business happens and claims about strategies of action are made within a discursive field structured by the semiotic opposition between strategy and solidarity, interest and disinterest. This semiotic opposition forms a deep cultural structure generating, like a grammar, all the many various sorts of claims that give meaning to economic action.

Because this is a foundational cultural grammar for economic action, it can be seen across many different fields of action, at different levels of analysis. The evidence in this study is both fractal and cumulative.

First, we saw that theories assuming business associations were simply interest groups, and that the meaning-making they do is secondary, cannot account for American business associations as a robust and long-lasting institution. We need Durkheim, more than Weber, to explain them. The inadequacies of historical accounts in terms of strategic economic interest are redressed with a theory of American associations as cultural producers for economic action.

Second, we saw that the cultural production business associations do was as much about elaborate and sometimes emotional occupational solidarity as about the indirectly strategic cultural production of cognitive categories, networks, and fields for economic action. The neoinstitutionalist insight that associations supply strategic value in the shape of collective goods—like shared categories essential to market action—is deepened to examine the ways they treat solidarity in occupational community as an end in itself.

Third, we saw that business association discourse rarely explains strategies of action like education, information sharing, standards, and research as directly promoting members' interests. Rather, the collective interests of the (self-defined) "industry" are at stake, interests that presume solidarity, even to the extent of calling for sacrifice for the common good. Intra-"industry" strategies of action are also understood in terms of the expertise and honor of (occupational) "professionalism." Languages invoking the pursuit of collective economic interests are balanced against languages that emphasize the intrinsic professional virtue of technical excellence.

Fourth, we saw that associations' orientations to public life are understood not only in terms of the presumed democratic virtues of publicly voicing (collective) "industry" interests but also, and more often, in terms of stewardship of the public good. And associations' framing of their conventional political activities in terms of the public good and technical expertise is elaborated in their previously unrecognized participation in civil society.

So this study shows in four different ways that meaning-making about economic action involves solidarity as well as strategy. This picture of the underlying cultural grammar of meaning-making about economic action is fractal: the same elements recur in the same relations at different levels of analysis and in different settings. At each step in the argument, assumptions and claims about associations and their members as strategic actors are challenged and modified with neglected evidence of the significance of disinterested solidarity. The four different dimensions of the argument also make a cumulative case for the general significance of the "strategy/solidarity" binary code as a basic structure of economic meaning-making. It applies to business culture in general as well as to different variants of business orientations usually considered purely strategic or instrumental.

If the "strategy/solidarity" binary code provides a fundamental grammar for economic culture, we need to rethink our deeply grounded assumptions that the normative basis of economic action in business is strategic self-interest.

Both critics and celebrants of modern capitalist economic organization and business culture assume that a straightforward orientation to economic action in terms of self-interest is fundamental. This assumption strangely ignores the obvious but neglected fact that, as Karl Polanyi argued in a different way, pure competitive self-interested production and exchange is culturally unsustainable. Of course, it is briefly possible in highly structured settings in which presocialized actors play by preestablished rules toward predetermined ends that are socially defined in terms of individual benefits and zero-sum outcomes, as in the Monopoly board game. In such settings, the necessity of solidarity is externalized to the social institutions producing the settings and the actors involved. But both critics and celebrants of capitalist production and exchange tend to treat all economic action as this sort of game. While it is indeed possible to orient economic action to competitive self-interested exchange in such isolated and highly structured circumstances—and sometimes to structure settings and institutions for this purpose—it is not possible that this singular orientation could be sustained on a broader scale.

The typical response to recognition of this unsustainability is splitting, assuming that strategy and solidarity orient action in different settings, "separate spheres" or "hostile worlds." This splitting preserves faith in the fundamentally strategic orientation of business (as well as some faith in more solidaristic orientations in other spheres of action). In contrast, the argument that the strategy/solidarity binary code generates meaning-making in business settings refuses such splitting and embraces instead a potentially more dangerous recognition of ambiguity.[12]

Recognizing this fundamental ambiguity in business culture is difficult and dangerous both empirically and normatively. First, and obviously, solidaristic cultural production and solidaristic claims-making may be undertaken with cynical and strategic purposes and thus seem reducible to strategic self-interest. Anyone tutored in Ideology Critique 101 can recognize, for example, that claims to contribute to the public good can mask devious and destructive intent, and even if well intended, they may be short-sighted and exclusionary. Similarly, solidaristic claims about the pursuit of self-defined collective interests (rather than particularistic interests) may be deconstructed as either insincere or inherently exclusionary, ignoring important stakeholders in systematic ways (as we saw in chapter six was mostly true of labor). Along the same lines, claims about technical excellence and professionalism may simply be camouflaged claims to exclusive occupational jurisdiction, as scholars of professions mostly argue. And occupational community may be performed with strategic purposes in mind. Overall, we have many ways of dismissing expressions of solidaristic and nonstrategic orientations of business action as simply "blowing smoke," and depending on the context these critical interpretations may often be valid. As Marx put it memorably, "every shopkeeper is very well able to distinguish between what somebody professes to be and what he really is." Ideology critique rightly takes to heart his challenge to the scholars of his time who had "not yet won even this trivial insight."[13]

Nevertheless, it is impossible to dismiss all solidaristic interpretations of economic action as vacuous for two reasons, one empirical and one theoretical. First, it is hard to imagine that all the many, varied, and often emotionally intense claims made in disinterested ways that we have seen in these pages are entirely disingenuous, even though they might violate our commonsense, cynical faith in strategic, self-interested orientations to economic action. In some contexts, as we have seen, claims about strategic interest even come close to seeming an ideological fig leaf for association members' "real" orientation to solidarity.

Second, and much more theoretically important, even if it were possible that the solidaristic orientation expressed in all this wide-ranging discourse was fake, a matter of strategic and self-conscious performance, the adoption of this vocabulary in claims-making shows even more strongly that business culture requires an orientation to solidarity as much as an orientation to strategy. What is important for our general understanding of economic culture is that plausible claims-making demands language referencing considerations beyond particularistic strategy. Even if it were actually true that strategic motivations were all there was to the subjective experience of economic actors, this would mean that it is even more significant that solidarity is an essential element of economic culture.

In any case, generalizable cultural analysis should bracket individual motivations and the many ways in which people might inflect shared cultural forms in the course of their active meaning-making. Of course, tendencies to solidaristic or strategic accounts of strategies of action will vary along many dimensions, not only by psychological predisposition but also by historical context, organizational setting, training, and experience. But what is important here is the generative grammar, or culture-structure, that makes various accounts of economic action meaningful.[14]

This analytical focus on the grammar of economic culture carries with it an important corollary about altruism. Many social scientists and psychologists share the view that reducing human action to strategic self-interested action is overly restrictive, both empirically and normatively, and so they study the nature and social ecology of altruism. But altruism is only relevant where actors' self-interest is viewed as primordial. By treating the solidarity/strategy binary code as a fundamental and general-

izable grammar of economic culture, we are not only setting aside Ideology Critique 101 concerns that all business is essentially and suspiciously
strategic. We should also bracket the mirroring scholarly interest in altruism, because if strategic self-interest is a secondary issue when we want to
understand the fundamentals of economic culture, so too is altruism. The
argument that economic culture is founded on the "solidarity/strategy"
binary code, and the evidence of solidaristic claims in this study, are not
arguments for altruism. The same goes for Tocqueville's observations
about "self-interest rightly understood."[15]

Rather, identifying the solidarity/strategy binary code as a fundamental culture-structure generating symbolic repertoires of meaning for economic action provides a basis for cultural generalization and comparison
across different contexts. This culture-structure is a more flexible and finer
analytic tool than the main alternative approach to understanding the fundamentals of economic culture—as self-interested strategy. Rather than
assuming self-interested strategic action (and then analyzing how surrounding social relations shape, direct, and limit self-interest), scholars interested in how economic culture works in particular settings—Thévenot's
"contextual stories"—should examine the ways in which meaning-making
variously draws on solidaristic and strategic language, and how the two
themes are counterpoised or interwoven. The ways in which they are expressed will vary according to context, of course, and so too will the extent
to which each is emphasized as a normative basis for economic relations.
But a theory of economic culture as founded on the semiotic opposition
between solidarity and strategy offers a comparative basis for exploring
such variation in a more systematic and cumulative way.

But surely meaning-making about economic action in business associations is systematically different from economic meaning-making in
other settings, in ways that seriously undermine the generalizability of
this conclusion about the significance of solidarity in economic culture.
How can general conclusions based on an investigation of business associations apply more broadly to economic culture in different sorts of
firms or different sorts of markets, at levels of resolution ranging from the
small struggling challenger firm in an established local service economy to
the global giant operating in multiple markets on a scale larger than many
nation-states? Perhaps business associations make too distinctive a setting
to examine economic culture. Even though the Smithian stereotype casts
them as a distillation, to the point of distortion, of capitalist culture, other
observers have leaned in a more Durkheimian direction (though without

acknowledging Durkheimian precedents). Corporatism, for instance, sometimes casts them as a coordinating institution above and beyond the normal workings of markets and industries, as we saw in chapter two, so perhaps any solidaristic language in these settings is a deviant exception to economic culture considered more broadly.[16]

I argue that economic culture in these business associations represents economic culture in other business settings in its fundamental discursive structure, and that the association discourse I have explored offers naturalistic evidence of business culture that is otherwise hard to observe. Economic sociologists have been accumulating for some time findings that are anomalous for the paradigm of fundamentally interest-oriented economic action in modern capitalism, qualifying to the point of erasure the assumption that self-interested strategy is all there is to capitalist economic culture. In many different ways, there is increasing attention to the morality in market exchange, and all these findings are better accommodated by the perspective developed here.[17]

So far, these cumulating arguments and the detailed evidence that economic action means much more than self-interested strategic action have seriously undermined the foundations of our understanding of the normative basis of economic action—yet much of the facade built on those foundations remains standing. This is because the idea of "economic interests" remains fundamental and mostly unanalyzed. In economic sociology, for example, theories of markets, neoinstitutionalist theories of industry change, network and field theory, political economy, and organizational theory all take for granted Weber's axiom that "all economic activity in a market economy is undertaken and carried out by individuals acting to provide for their own ideal or material interests"—even as Weberian questions about how those interests are specified have driven economic sociology's flourishing research program. We now know much more and we can think much more precisely about the social construction of *objects* of exchange—as in the politics of standardization, or niche positioning in consumer markets—and about the social construction of *partners* to exchange—such as in the formation and change of markets, or organizational cognition. But the many observed complexities in cultural understandings of the *normative basis* of market action have yet to undermine our presumption that strategic interests are fundamental in modern economic life and solidarity is not. Even though the rule is hard to see for the accretion of exceptions these days, it has not been rescinded.[18]

By arguing that we replace the (psychological) axiom of strategic interests with the (cultural) postulate of a solidarity/strategy binary code as the general foundation of meaning-making in business, I am challenging economic sociologists to have the courage of their convictions and explicitly embrace the full implications of economic embeddedness. This should not mean that we simply turn existing assumptions on their head and treat capitalist business as altruistically oriented public good. Just as physicists finally came to accept the idea in quantum mechanics that "everything has both particlelike and wavelike attributes," we need to come to terms with the empirical fact that business culture is necessarily structured by an orientation to disinterested solidarity as much as an orientation to strategic interest in competitive profit-seeking.[19]

The Power of Business Culture

If recognizing this fundamental ambiguity in a theoretically serious way seems, on the face of it, empirically dangerous, apparently ignoring the way solidaristic claims may be strategically mobilized, the normative dangers it seems to present are even more threatening. This issue may not be so apparent among economic sociologists who simply aim to promote the relevance of sociological perspectives for understanding business. But from a broader critical perspective more sensitive to power and inequality, the normative dangers are immediately clear. To claim that meaning-making in capitalist business is as solidaristic as it is strategic seems like conservative, sentimental, and dangerous business ideology. The argument seems to ignore the many destructive and stratifying powers unleashed by capitalist business, the inevitable political conflicts it generates, and its human costs.

In caricature, capitalist economic actors will do everything they can to pursue narrow and exploitative interests in shameless ways at the expense of others. They promote unjust ideologies and they shape state policy to protect their profits and the stability of their industries. The evidence for this common sense seems to be in every headline and media narrative, especially in times of crisis such as recession, and in times of heightened political gamesmanship, as when new regulations are introduced. We know that Wall Street financiers strategize to reap superprofits from risky financial products, regardless of their dangers to ordinary debtors, smaller creditors, and the global economy. We know that manufacturers risk known environmental damage and cut jobs to protect their bottom line. We know that millions of service and care workers in the United States receive compensation and benefits so minimal as to make a secure life impossible. We know that companies larger than nation-states manage their economies so as to protect their power over workers, states, and markets in the global south. We know that businesses everywhere routinely attempt to shape their political environments and to resist public regulation. We know that life in advanced capitalism is unavoidably saturated with manipulative consumerist messages, to the extent that much of the meaning of sociability and social relations is now expressed through profit-driven consumption, and many historically strong distinctions between commercial and noncommercial social relations are becoming anachronistic. And these are only the scandalous truisms of critique, obvious and available to all. Digging a little deeper inevitably exposes scandals that never reach beyond activist publics, as well as past losses and alternative futures that never become public because of the power of business.[20]

So the normative risks of questioning the idea that action in capitalist economies is simply strategic and self-interested might seem high. But naturalizing interested-oriented action in capitalist market relations is ultimately riskier, for two reasons.

First, it underestimates the contemporary normative power of business, which runs much deeper than the norm of competitive self-interested strategy would suggest.

Critical perspectives on business power too often rest on outdated and one-dimensional assumptions about how power operates. In Steven Lukes's classic formulation, power works in three ways. Most obviously, the exercise of power may be intentional and overt, when one party to an observable conflict imposes its preferences on a well-defined issue on another weaker party. More insidiously, one party may exercise agenda-setting power, so well-recognized conflicts of interest are not engaged and remain unexpressed due to procedural exclusion, fear of reprisals, hopelessness, or cynicism that silences subordinate parties. But power is not always consciously exercised and need not be a matter of conflicting intentions. On this view, "real interests" may be masked, and subordinate parties may see powerlessness as legitimate, defining problems in ways that avoid addressing their real causes, or choosing apathy or fatalism. Taken-for-granted symbols, codes, categories, boundaries, narratives, and practices mediate power relations in this way.[21]

Strangely, business power is still usually understood as overt or more subtly agenda-setting, with differing and competing interests seemingly clear and explicit to businesspeople, if not to subordinate parties. Recognizably differing and competing interests are often attributed to relations between firms, between industries and sectors, between firms and employees, between public and private interests, and so on, even if subordinate parties like workers or consumers may misunderstand the issues at stake because of more subtly exercised cultural power. We tend to think of businesspeople as well aware of what is at stake in their pursuit of market interests against others. But as this study has shown, stereotyping business in this way misses a great deal of what business means to businesspeople, and when we miss those meanings, we underestimate the taken-for-granted power of business. Only if we see disinterested solidarity as fundamental to the pursuit of business interests—as constitutive of business orientations as is the widely recognized idea of the competitive pursuit of self-interest—can we begin to understand the contemporary power of business culture and how it is sustained. A sophisticated critical perspective on how businesspeople make sense of what they are doing will recognize their disinterested commitments, even as it challenges their sometimes unintended destructive human consequences.

Second, and, in the longer term, it is ultimately futile and self-defeating to adopt even a sophisticated critical perspective on contemporary economic action if, at the same time, strategic self-interest in economic action is thought to be the sole, natural, and unavoidable normative basis for production and exchange in a complex society. Despite every battle won, the war is inevitably lost.

If real critical potential exists only outside the everyday workings of our economy, and contemporary society only accomplishes its astoundingly rich production and complex exchange with a normative model of economic action as naturally and eternally self-interested, the possibility of critique remains confined to a morally "separate sphere." As a result, a critique assuming normative self-interest in business throws the baby out with the bath water. Accomplishments only possible in a highly complex technical division of labor are unavoidably tainted by the moral failures of a highly stratified social division of labor.

As we have seen in these pages, business is often understood as sociable, absorbing, honorable, and helpful because of the specialized knowledge and technical expertise embedded in "industry" practice. This is not in some fictional utopian universe but in ordinary, routine, and often eye-glazing corners of contemporary business and industry that are also necessarily strategic. And whether expertise concerns annuities, garden mulch, commercial ovens, auto lifts, fire prevention, or any of the many other obscure objects of exchange that make a focus for the worlds businesspeople inhabit, it is impossible to imagine modern society without it. Such solidarity and expertise must be a necessary element of any "real utopia."[22]

Forms of disinterested solidarity, as well as self-interest, are intrinsic in orientations to economic action even of capitalist business. Solidarity grounded in the technical division of labor exists as a critical potential within capitalist economic activity. This is what critical theorists used to call a "cultural surplus," a shared normative grounding for claims-making in favor of institutions of production and exchange that might turn self-interested strategy to more encompassing solidarity. In view of this cultural surplus, assuming that economic action grounded on a norm of strategic, self-interested exchange is a transparent and immutable fact of life is ultimately more dangerous than investigating disinterest and exploring the conditions of its creation in solidaristic institutions.

Appendix

Methodological Overview

This study began when fundamental questions about economic culture piqued my interest. As I wondered how people really understood "economic interests"—an idea that was especially unquestionable before the economic crisis beginning in 2008—I was puzzled by the fact that while "the cultural turn" in the social sciences had brought significant advances in our understanding of political meaning-making, both as discourse and practice, meaning-making about economic action was often treated as natural and unproblematic. From my perspective at the time, broad assumptions about political "ideology" or "values" had been investigated and refined in many ways, but our understanding of how people thought about their economic action remained superficial. I thought advances in cultural sociology could help develop better understanding of economic action, even though many cultural sociologists at the time also tended to view it as what Viviana Zelizer labeled a "separate sphere," and distant from the field of cultural sociology.[1]

I explored a wide variety of foundational works and innovative research in economic sociology, familiarizing myself with the ways that economic sociologists were also beginning to examine questions about economic culture more intensively. With the support of a Guggenheim Memorial Fellowship, I further developed my questions about the cultural construction of economic exchange and investigated a list of possible empirical settings in which I might productively investigate them. "Business associations" made it onto that list toward the end; at that time, I was not aware of any sociological treatments of them, except perhaps for some work on power elites, but I thought of them because their listings in the *Encyclopedia of Associations* had once caught my attention and sparked my sociological imagination. Much later, I remembered that I had done research for a business association during my student days, which probably primed my attention subconsciously.

As I reviewed the list of potential research sites for my questions, and as I learned more of the little that was known about them, American business associations seemed more and more intriguing. They seemed to be an important economic institution that economic sociologists should know more about and include more routinely in their research (which typically tended to focus mostly on firm-level data, in part because of the influence of the sociology of organizations in recent economic sociology's origins). My curiosity also grew because many people I spoke with in a wide variety of settings had stories to tell of personal connections and experiences with one business association or another, even though we rarely hear of them in everyday conversation.[2] Methodologically, I realized that they fulfilled my main criteria for an empirical setting that would help answer my questions about economic culture.

My questions required a research site that offered access to naturally occurring meaning-making by people in business about their economic action. Because of the nature of my research questions, I wanted to avoid potential limitations imposed by research methods that unavoidably influence the meaning-making of respondents, for instance, by the categories implied in the way survey questions are framed, or by the distinctive interactional context of interviewing. As voluntary groups routinely communicating in public about business among members and to external audiences, business associations offered a rich source of the sort of naturally occurring meaning-making I sought.

I also wanted to avoid limiting the investigation to a few specific groups, as would be necessary if I were to explore my questions about economic meaning-making in extended fieldwork. Although meaning-making in interactional practice in specific contexts is important, as many ethnographically inclined cultural sociologists emphasize, I was more interested in establishing the language within which specific meaning-making practices could make sense. And while I agree that it is possible to make theoretical generalization from case studies, and it is notable that many economic sociologists draw very general conclusions from case studies of particular organizations or industries, broad generalization from particular cases should rely, at least implicitly, on a well-established and deep knowledge of the population from which the cases are selected, or the realm of action to which the generalization applies (as is more true of fieldwork on social movement groups or religious congregations). When that broader picture is not well understood, general conclusions based on case studies are difficult to interpret, as I have noted of the few case studies of American business associations discussed in these pages. So I wanted a research site that offered wide-ranging, as well as naturally occurring, evidence of discourse about economic action.[3]

My training and experience in comparative historical methods suggested that rich, broad-based evidence of cultural processes was available in the routinely produced documents of ordinary groups many sociologists ignore. For this reason, too, I chose to investigate my questions about economic meaning-making by investigating American business associations.

Despite these methodological advantages, so little was known of American business associations that the research required considerable spadework before I could begin to answer my core questions about meaning-making for economic action. I use three types of evidence in this study, collected in three somewhat overlapping phases of research. A comprehensive review of published studies of business associations supplements a census of national business associations including data on organizational features and goals, and, most importantly, a full archive of public documents from the websites of twenty-five representative associations.

Published Studies

Published studies of American business associations are scattered in obscure corners of several disciplines. They focus at different levels of analysis and examine very disparate and mostly unrelated research questions. As noted above, they are mostly case studies of limited generalizability, but I have also drawn extensively on reports of three original surveys, discussed in chapters two and three, and a report on a longitudinal population study. The basis of these studies, and their advantages and limitations, are discussed in chapters two and three. The work of "manufacturing a literature" in this way was especially important for the reassessment of American business associations' historical trajectory in chapter two. I have also used and assessed evidence from the later surveys and other published studies where relevant in later chapters that discuss basic features of contemporary associations and explore associations' strategies of action. The published literature provides only indirect evidence for my argument that business associations are cultural producers, because it is almost entirely based on the unexamined commonsense assumption that they are primarily interest groups. However, it does help lay the foundation for my argument, and I also hope that the secondary literature assembled here makes an accessible basis for future studies of business associations.[4]

Census of American National Business Associations

The census of contemporary national business associations, created in collaboration with Rui Gao, Xiaohong Xu, Brian Miller, and Georgian Schiopu, was supported by ASA/NSF Fund for the Advancement of the Discipline No. 6848 and the Institute for Scholarship in the Liberal Arts, University of Notre Dame.[5] The aim of this part of the project was to provide a new overview of contemporary, national American business associations that would not only map this little-known institution for the purposes of this study but also provide a sampling frame for future research and set benchmarks for the assessment of the representativeness of case studies. The data set includes information on basic organizational features, activities and goals, and industry sector, and is publicly available at the Inter-University Consortium for Political and Social Research (ICPSR), University of Michigan (No. 4333; www.icpsr.umich.edu).

Data Sources and Case Inclusion

Data were collected and coded between December 2003 and June 2005. The unit of analysis is the national American business association, defined as a *mutual-benefit non-profit association composed of members primarily engaged in for-profit activity drawn from more than one locality or state who share a common orientation to some sector of trade, business or commercial activities.*[6]

Public directories of associations in the United States provided the starting point for data collection. Review of the *Encyclopedia of Associations* was supplemented with the *National Trade and Professional Associations Directory*. We also reviewed the *Associations Yellowbook*, but no additional listings appeared in that source. The total number of cases is 4,465. The nature of the sources and unit of analysis, the size of the data set, and extrapolation of population trends identified elsewhere encourage confidence that the data set includes close to the universe of national business associations as of 2002–3. For this reason, sampling issues are not relevant here.

Rui Gao wrote the codebook and provided a large part of the original data collection, with some contributions by Georgian Schiopu. Xiaohong Xu and Brian Miller completed the later data collection and industry coding. Xiaohong Xu completed the data analysis.

Data from these sources was extensively modified and developed for the purposes of this research. An important part of the work of construction of the data set was the development and implementation of criteria for case inclusion and exclusion.

First, data collection was not restricted to associations categorized in the *Encyclopedia of Associations* as "Trade, Professional and Commercial Organizations," since preliminary analysis soon showed that a significant number of business associations were also included in other categories, such as "environmental and agricultural" and "health and medical" associations. The *National Trade and Professional Associations Directory* also listed some business associations not found in the *Encyclopedia*. Overall, 25 percent of the associations in the census were found in sources other than the *Encyclopedia*'s listing of trade associations.

Second, even those listings included many associations irrelevant to our theoretical interests and definition of the unit of analysis. Associations in the following categories were excluded in the process of coding:

- Professional and scholarly associations. The basic criterion here was whether most members were primarily engaged directly in for-profit activity or were "social and cultural specialists."[7]
- Associations with a local membership and orientation (e.g., chambers of commerce). However, rarely, a regionally based association strongly oriented to national marketing was included, for example, an association of Napa Valley wineries.
- Associations composed of other associations, or federations of associations (e.g., a national federation of paralegal associations).
- Associations that are part of other associations, where this could be determined.
- Associations that are primarily representatives of foreign governments or businesses (e.g., some trade or tourism associations).
- Branches of foreign-based associations.
- Inactive associations, with no known address.

The following issues and resulting decisions about case inclusion should be noted:

BUSINESS AND PROFESSIONAL ASSOCIATIONS.   As discussed at length in chapter seven, the distinction between business and professional associations is often blurred. For instance, a medical association focused on a particular medical issue, such as a society for women's health research, may include researchers, doctors, and industry actors like drug firms or equipment manufacturers. Such associations were excluded if the overall description of the association was in terms of research/professional language, and for-profit actors were presented as peripheral to the main focus, but included if the explicit focus was primarily market oriented. As a result, for example, a small minority of medical associations was included but the majority excluded. In another type of example of this gray area, an association might be predominantly "professional" but include more market-oriented divisions, for example, the Institute of Electrical and Electronics Engineers; such associations too were excluded. However, by contrast, an association that looked like a professional research group but related directly and specifically to a particular industry, such as the American Society of Brewing Chemists, was included. Similarly, we felt it reasonable to include an association of hospital administrators.

HOBBY AND AVOCATIONAL ASSOCIATIONS.   Hobby, avocational, and some agricultural categories also generated a number of ambiguous cases. Associations composed of hobbyists or collectors alone were excluded, but some groups with an explicit and strong inclusion of dealers or other profit-oriented economic actors were included. For instance, gardening groups interested in particular flowers could include commercial growers or sellers; animal breeders' associations often included commercially oriented stores or dealers; horse-related associations could be primarily hobbyist, or primarily market-oriented; computer or software users' groups could sometimes include primarily profit-oriented actors such as retailers of a product, or businesses doing desktop publishing.

A general note on blurring between for-profit and professional or avocational activity is appropriate here. As the qualitative investigation demonstrates, an important activity of business associations is providing the organizational and cultural infrastructure to make connections and cross boundaries between different types of business and, more broadly, different arenas of social activity. Thus, the problematic coding issues associated with distinguishing avocational or professional associations from business associations are an indicator of the substantive nature of the phenomenon.[8]

Informational Genre and Inference

Information about associations was coded from self-descriptions provided by associations themselves, usually involving mission statements and other information on features like conventions and committees (according to reference source format). The information collected pertains to organization, activities, stated purposes or goals, and "industry" sector of the national business associations, as summarized in table A.1. Final variable definitions included in the codebook by Gao were developed in iterative stages of pretesting.

This approach has important advantages in its unobtrusiveness and relative comprehensiveness. In contrast to the earlier studies mentioned above based on surveys, this information is nonreactive. For example, when association officers answer investigators' questions about how and to what extent they are actively oriented to their industry's political environment, they may be inclined to overstate their interest, or to exaggerate their activity, because the question itself focuses their attention on political concerns without also asking about the relative importance of political concerns compared to others. This is especially true if the iconic image of an ideal association is that of a political interest group, as it tends to be. By contrast, self-descriptions allow association officials to articulate their own point of view on why they exist and what they are doing. Methodologically, then, the approach here has the important advantage of enhancing the validity of measures of goals and activities.

One disadvantage is the absence of some general-interest information that might be better assessed in a well-designed survey, such as operating budget. Some information like this was missing, or what was provided was highly ambiguous and not usable. However, this methodological trade-off was worthwhile because some of this general-interest information was not particularly relevant to my theoretical questions, and because enough alternative information was available to make some theoretically meaningful inferences about the organizational population.

The other important issue to be assessed about this data is the question of how it is shaped by the genre constraints of the statement of purpose. As cultural and historical sociologists are especially aware, no source of information is transparent, and every source is shaped by the constraints of its process of production and the specific categories and genres of its cultural form. This is as true of drier and more "objective" sources like statistics and directories as it is of novels, speeches, or blogs. And certainly, the "statement of purpose" as a genre is a widespread and semiformalized discourse that itself may shape what is said. Association officials can draw on established and familiar rhetorics of organizational purposes that, as neoinstitutionalists would argue, are part of their very constitution as organizations related to others in a field. Many will use statements of purpose already developed for members and the general public, repeating, for example, what might also be said on a website homepage. Does this rhetorical form of the mission statement unduly restrict the types of claims associations might make about their purposes? Do they all say basically the same thing, as writers of grant proposals, course descriptions, real estate advertisements, or acceptance speeches must do?[9]

One important general question about how the rhetorical form might influence the information is whether it encourages an emphasis on collective goods rather than selective incentives, or vice versa (this issue is discussed at more length with respect to the information from focal associations in chapter six). On one hand, as Diane Barthel argues, mission statements are "fictions" that "recapture the sense of moral purpose and . . . achieve forms of legitimacy," implying that there would be a bias to expressive purposes and solidarity at the expense of the pursuit of interests. On the other hand, legitimacy for these associations is usually presumed to derive from their strategic activities. So for business associations, the potential impact of this sort of genre constraint is ambiguous: association self-descriptions could be biased in quite opposite ways in relation to the questions examined.[10]

Moreover, extensive variation in content, tone, and style among the thousands of self-descriptions coded here provides some reason to believe that this sort of evidence is not seriously biased in one way or the other. Associations differed a great deal in the sorts of purposes they claimed and the ways they articulated them, even in these short and semiformalized paragraphs. This is at least partly because the genre invites, though it does not require, a list format. In this way, it contrasts with genres that are structured narratively (which would involve articulated connections between claims). So even though this sort of organizational statement of purpose is a semiformalized genre, it is structured to allow "elaborated" rather than "restricted code." Elaboration of a number of somewhat disconnected goals and activities was typical. Moreover, as discussed below, we ultimately coded more specifically rather than more generally framed goals and activities. Overall, this wide variation in association self-descriptions generates confidence that the data capture a valid picture of the overall purposes of business associations, if not the whole truth about each association.

A second way the generic statement of purpose may be consequential for inference in this study is in its selectivity. Associations may work on goals they don't articulate, or state goals they don't seriously pursue (not to mention there is no way of knowing whether their actions are in any way effective). In addition, statements of purpose are written in terms that are sufficiently general to apply over the medium term, so particular goals and activities may shift. Some indication of the extent of this possible selectivity was discussed in chapters six and eight, in which the census data on internal and external goals was compared with the detailed analysis of the focal sample, described below. The evidence of this comparison can only be suggestive, and the comparison depends partly on whether more casual and intermittent attention to a goal or activity is included along with more systematic, resource intensive programs. Nevertheless, it does suggest that, for many associations, the self-descriptions coded for the census typically omitted at least some of each association's activities. The direction of difference was similar for all goals and activities measured; whether internally or externally oriented, they may be understated in the census by up to 20 percent. The significance of this potential undercounting for conclusions about particular goals and activities is explored at more length in chapters six and eight. Generally speaking, what it means is that we should see the census data as identifying *relative* rather than absolute proportions of associations committed to particular activities. More theoretically relevant, this emphasizes the point I have made that these goals and activities constitute an institutional repertoire that flexible and multifunctional groups draw on according to context.

So the information in the sources on which the "census" coding is based offers two important and hitherto unexploited advantages. It is comprehensive, and it is naturalistic, providing extensive and unobtrusive measures not shaped and directed by the research questions or setting.

The trade-off is that the genre of the sources could influence the information available in several ways (as would any research source, although the genre influences are too often neglected). Two of the three potential influences I have examined are relatively inconsequential, but the third should be recognized as potentially significant for inference from these data. First, some information of general but not significant theoretical interest, like budgets, is omitted or is too unreliable to be useful. Second, the genre could demand an emphasis on solidarity to the exclusion of strategy, or vice versa, but these potential demands cancel each other out, and there is sufficient variation in the associational statements of purpose to deduce that neither is a rigid requirement of the genre. Third, however, the comparison with the focal sample suggests that these sources omit some goals and activities of interest, and the proportions of each goal and activity among associations in the census should be treated as relative rather than absolute. In the end, and even considering this genre constraint, there is so little relevant information on the population, and so much of what we know is based on case or industry studies, that even the basic information drawn from self-descriptions is valuable.

Coding Development and Implementation

The coding scheme was developed in several stages. After a thorough immersion in theoretical questions suggested by scholarship in economic and cultural sociology, and a close investigation of surveys used in previous studies (especially in David Knoke's *Collective Action*), I drafted a code sheet for pretesting. Data on a random sample of 231 associations from the *Encyclopedia of Associations* was collected and analyzed, preliminary observations were made about the population (e.g., relationship between DC location and type of membership), and limitations of information provided by the sources were identified. On the basis of this pretest, the coding scheme was further revised by (a) specifying variable definitions and examples and (b) simplifying and combining variables, for example, variables coding different sorts of publications. Gao then drafted the codebook. Gao and Schiopu tested the revised coding scheme jointly by beginning the coding of all relevant cases. For three months, intercoder reliability was assessed and possible ambiguities in the variables and their values discussed among Spillman, Gao, and Schiopu. Further simplification and reduction in the variables was implemented as data collection proceeded, and intercoder reliability and problematic cases were reviewed weekly. Data was checked and cleaned of blanks and inconsistencies twice during this process and at its conclusion.

Overall, few coding ambiguities emerged in coding variables for *organization and cultural production*—leader, location, founding date, size, membership type, staff, committees, regional or national groups, newsletter, directory, other publications, library, other information, convention, exhibits, and other meetings.

However, the process led to several further revisions in the coding scheme for goals and activities, most notably the combinations of some

TABLE A.1 **National business associations, 2003: Measures**

Variable Coded	Brief Description*
Organizational Features	
Leader	Full-time leader reported
Location	State of association address
Year	Year founded
Membership	Number of members reported
Membership type	Firms, individuals or both
Staff	Number of staff reported
Committees	Reported organizational differentiation in committees, etc.
Groups	Reported regional subgroups and affiliates
Cultural Production	
Newsletter	Reports published newsletter
Directory	Reports published directory of members
Other publications	Reports other publications, e.g., journals, brochures
Library	Reports library, online database, etc.
Other information	Reports other information services, e.g., speakers' bureaus.
Convention	Reports convention, conference, annual meetings, etc.
Exhibitions	Reports trade shows etc.
Other meetings	Reports additional meetings e.g. monthly dinners, etc.
Goals and Activities	
Standards	Standardization, accreditation goals and activities
Share information	Sharing management and other information among members
Statistics	Research goals, surveys, forecasts, etc.
Education	Educational and training programs and projects
Public relations	Informing public, improving public reputation, etc.
Lobbying	Lobbying, monitoring policy, regulatory concerns, etc.
General social issues	Civic activities and goals, nonbusiness interests
Industry Sector	
Sector one	Major industry sector of members
Sector two	Other industry sector of members
Other sector	Includes more than two sectors, or nonindustry members

*See "National Business Associations, United States, 2003: Codebook" for detailed technical descriptions.

variables coding goals that had previously been distinguished. Most often, distinctions in the original coding scheme between more general and more particular goals were collapsed—for instance, the general goal of informing, educating, or increasing the awareness of the public was combined with the more specific goal of public relations. Similarly, variables originally intended to code very general statements of goals, like "representing, promoting, serving members," were eliminated as too vague or unnecessary.[11]

Another general development in the iterative process of revising the coding scheme was the elimination of variables for which information in sources was extremely rare (though the variable measured something of theoretical interest). Examples are the goals of "ethics" and "labor relations." Of course, as discussed above, associations may still be involved, if peripherally, in activities toward these goals but not see them as relevant to a statement of purpose. In our judgment, supported by later qualitative analysis, associations with codes of ethics see this as more routine than central to their purposes. Perhaps surprisingly, "labor relations" were not relevant in the activities of most associations, although a very small minority address labor issues: this assessment is also based on qualitative work with a smaller sample (as discussed in chapter six).

The most regrettable revision of the coding scheme was the elimination of a variable originally coding "networking, support, cooperation, and discussion." This was intended to capture the numerous statements of goals that were framed in terms that went beyond strategic purposes to emphasize the association's aim of providing a general context for collective sociability and help: in a pretest sample, this goal was somewhat more frequently stated by associations with individual members than associations with firm members. However, intercoder reliability was always low for this variable, and it was eliminated.

As discussed in chapter four and illustrated further in chapter five, "industry" coding was significantly more complex than is usually assumed, because many associations cross formal industry boundaries in one way or another. The possibility of detailed industry coding was explored with "industry" coding to the six-digit NAICS level of the pretest random sample of 231 associations, but because of the frequently imprecise and complex nature of association membership, a more limited sectoral (two-digit) coding for all associations in the census was completed by Xu and Miller after other coding was done. Sectoral codes slightly simplify the NAICS scheme, for example, by combining different types of manufacturing. The NAICS coding is only approximate in another way, since strict NAICS codes apply to the productive activity of economic establishments, whereas associations were coded based on the directly stated or inferred sectoral location of members. Where an association drew its members from two industry sectors, the second sector was also coded. If an association included members from more than two sectors, or included consumers or users, we coded that fact but did not code more than two specific sectoral locations. If an association included members of more than one sector, manufacturing was usually coded first, because this was usually the first sector emphasized in association self-descriptions. For this reason, the data may slightly understate the sectoral presence of, for example, finance and insurance, or administrative services, because some members in these sectors might be included in other, more diffuse associations.[12]

After publication of the data set, Xiaohong Xu developed answers to a full range of questions about features of the population, introduced here where relevant to the analyses discussed in chapter three, six, eight, and nine. This information is important for providing an overall portrait of this little-known American institution, for identifying some of the dimensions of variation within the association population, and for selecting cases for qualitative analysis. While it would have been possible to develop more detailed and less descriptive statistical analysis of patterns and relationships between association features, and I hope other scholars follow up on the possibilities opened up with this census (e.g., Walker, "Privatizing Participation"), I did not pursue further analysis of differentiation within the population because that sort of investigation would be of limited value for understanding processes of meaning-making. In my view, beginning with the sort of descriptive overview a quantitative analysis can provide strengthens cultural analysis, but this is only a beginning.

In contrast to standard methodological injunctions, I do not believe that the main purpose of qualitative analysis is developing *exploratory* knowledge that can generate ideas for more "scientific" quantitative investigation. Instead, I believe quantitative description should be preliminary to the *explanation* provided by qualitative analysis.[13]

Thus, the argument requires the qualitative evidence provided by the focal sample of twenty-five business associations.

Focal Sample of American National Business Associations

The evidence from the focal sample of associations was developed with the central purpose of obtaining representative, extensive, rich, and naturalistic discourse about economic action by businesspeople.

Charles Ragin distinguishes what he terms "qualitative" from "comparative" research design by suggesting that the former investigates commonalities with thick description of a single case study or group of similar case studies, while the latter structures comparison to account for difference. In my view, most significant studies of meaning-making should combine these research strategies in different ways, but it is true that the relative emphasis will vary according to the central research question. In these pages I have noted many comparative observations: most importantly, in chapter two, the puzzling strength of American business associations when set in comparative perspective, but also numerous comparative questions associated with associations' change over time, and some intrapopulation comparisons between, for example, associations composed of firms or individuals. However, these comparisons are subsidiary to the central questions about meaning-making for economic action—about vocabularies of motive and discursive field—so, in Ragin's terms, the "comparative" questions are subordinated to the "qualitative" questions in this study although both are addressed. Epistemologically, my findings here about (a) American business associations as an institution of cultural production, and (b) a discursive field for economic action (binary code, vocabularies of motive, and strategies of action) are new *colligations* that help understand conditions and mechanisms of economic processes.[14]

For this reason (1) the focal cases are purposively selected, as representative of the population; (2) the data collection was based on archival models that presume analysis of all available documents (though availability is necessarily incomplete); and (3) the qualitative analysis of this data was developed in an iterative process of close reading that refined step by step the process of drawing tighter the inferential chain between ideas and evidence.

Case Selection

The purposive selection of the representative sample of twenty-five associations involved a painstaking iterative process of refinement to bring the selection as close as possible to typical on three basic benchmarks—membership size, membership type, and "industry" representation.[15]

My practical aim was the selection of a manageable but representative "slice" of business association discourse. I first compared the census data with the data in the "pretest" sample of 231 associations on key variables; although there were a few differences, they were mostly very similar. Since I had more information on the random sample of 231 associations I had used to pretest the data collection for the association census, I decided to select associations from that sample. I aimed to select twenty-five to thirty associations to examine in depth, because I knew that it was feasible to develop close familiarity and recall about the "character"—for example, the name, background, purposes, capabilities, distinguishing features, and so on—of each member of a group of that size.

I set benchmark targets for numbers of associations in each size range, with each membership type, and industry representation (for instance, with about 50 percent of all national associations reporting that members were firms, I aimed for a similar proportion of the focal sample). I repeatedly filtered the sample to develop lists of associations in each targeted category (for instance, associations with fewer than a hundred members and including both firms and individuals as members). With these lists, which typically included fifteen to forty cases, I selected every fifth case for closer examination. After several iterations of this process, adjustments for closer approximation, and a few necessary revisions that reduced the sample from twenty-eight to twenty-five, I reached the fairly close though obviously not perfect representation reported in table 1.2 (chapter one). As one would expect, the most difficult was the final stage of adding industry type to the constraints on the three-variable representative sample. I further reviewed the draft sample for its relative representativeness on other descriptive variables like location, founding date, and such, checking that the focal group was not egregiously different on any of these measures.[16]

As I noted in chapter one, the focal sample of associations resulting from this process is obscure, unfamiliar, and, at first, intuitively puzzling. Even the list itself begins to challenge standard presuppositions about these associations, because the associations we mostly hear about and the few studies available are not representative. In case the obscurity of this purposive sample seems somewhat biased in the other direction, I will note just a few of the many associations removed in the process of filtering and development of the sample. They included, for instance, associations devoted to the Wall and Ceiling Industry, Industrial Glove Distributors, Petroleum Equipment, Associated Sales and Marketing Companies, Pipe Tobacco, Business Communication, Theater Equipment, Church Food Services, Juvenile Products, Airforwarders, Hispanic Advertising Agencies, Farm Managers, Boarding Kennels, Media Brokers, Consumer Healthcare, Security Hardware, Cosmetic Toiletries and Fragrance, and Wall Coverings. Moreover, the sampling frame for the focal sample was randomly selected from the population of 4,465 national associations, and even that category excludes a multitude of local, state, and regional business associations. As I have repeatedly noted, the scale, persistence, and diversity of all this little-known collective action in the economy should be intrinsically intriguing to the sociological imagination. Certainly, they convinced me that there was something important about economic action going on here that sociologists had almost completely ignored.

Although this sample represents the business association population, it may not seem to capture what we often think of—from public sphere discussion and stereotype—as the business world, because "big business" seems underrepresented. Some commentators have suggested that the vocabularies of motive I find here are unrepresentative because they are characteristic of small business settings and would not be found in "big business"—for example, Vacuum Cleaner Dealers would be less focused on strategic interests and more focused on expressive disinterest than Walmart. Certainly, as I have argued, it is true that different settings would generate different selections from the cultural repertoire I have examined. However, it is important to recognize that big, well-known corporations are also members of many of these associations (e.g., Home Depot in the Mulch and Soil Council, Pratt and Whitney in the Women in Aviation Maintenance group, McDonald's in the Food Equipment Manufacturers). And executives of large corporations are often members of several associations as individuals. Overall, it is unlikely that disinterested vocabularies of motive are restricted to small business settings; indeed, there are some indications that the reverse is sometimes the case (see chapter six). Moreover, disinterested vocabularies of motive may be mobilized to make sense of economic action in large corporations as well as in these associations. And in any case, as Gerald Davis summarizes: "The few hundred behemoths in the right tail of the size distribution were hardly representative of the 4.3 million corporations in the United States in 1994, and nearly 40 percent of employees worked for firms with fewer than 100 employees." For these various reasons, and because of the representativeness of the cases, the scope of the argument about the meaning of business is wide ranging and intended to apply to American business generally.[17]

Data Collection

The websites of this focal sample generated a vast, representative body of routine and publicly available discourse about economic action in business.[18] Because websites are ephemeral, I transformed them into associational "archives" in late 2004 and early 2005. (Some additional data collection on a few associations, like those that had been undergoing reconstruction in the earlier period, was completed in July 2006.) I did so simply by printing all publicly available "pages" in sequence and organizing them by association. As with the data collection for the association census, I was not treading well-trodden methodological pathways in this process, and although I explored some of the literature on social science use of web sources that was then beginning to emerge, I found little direct methodological guidance. However, I knew that my basic aim was to create a comprehensive and systematic collection of all available documents. At this stage, I did not want to select those documents that might seem more intrinsically interesting to an outsider, or richer for my theoretical questions.[19]

Because Internet information search is designed more for idiosyncratic customization rather than systematic overview, data collection from each website usually involved at least a three-stage process. In order to ensure that all available documents had been accessed, I first collected all those documents linked to the home page in one step, then all those documents accessible from first-order documents, then all documents accessible from second-order pages, and so on. I did not include in this data collection pages accessible to association members only.

Two minor ambiguities demanded commonsense resolution in this process—how to treat links to "off-site" sources, and how to treat repetitions, or redundant cross-links within the site. First, I did not collect documents from most "off-site" sources, such as government or commercial sites the association considered relevant to their members, although I did note them. However, I did collect documents from "affiliated" regional groups similar to the focal organization where they existed, such as the newsletters of the chapters of the International Concrete Repair Institute. Second, where "drilling down" in the site generated redundancies, I simply noted that on the "origin" document. As an aside, this data collection process suggested one measure that would be informative if attached to available documents: a degree measure of minimum access distance from the association's home page (for instance, how deep in the site it would be necessary to click to find mention of standards or policy monitoring). However, this question was peripheral to my main concerns, and I did not pursue it.

Collected systematically in this way, the websites of the focal sample of associations generated an enormous number of documents. At that time, a detailed website of this sort could run to more than a thousand pages, and even the most amateurish and minimal was rarely less than fifty.

The timing of this data collection fairly early in the diffusion of web-based communication probably favored my research project. At this time, association websites did not yet conform to any strict rhetorical formula, and many sites were not simply dedicated to public relations or marketing. Most were oriented to members, and some were in what now appears as a somewhat awkward transition phase, with ordinary organizational documents and communications uploaded to the site. There were few so-phisticated images (so I included few images from the sites in this analysis). My impression is that styles have since converged and are more restricted in the ways they are formatted and what they include. Certainly, the twenty-five sites showed family resemblances and common features, but at this time they varied a great deal, each showing what might be thought of as a distinctly different "personality." They varied not only in their size but also in their degree of technical sophistication and the transparency and lucidity of their organization. More substantively, they varied in the de-gree to which they were oriented to the public, or to potential consumers, or to members or prospective members. A surprisingly large proportion of the sampled discourse was oriented to the knowledgeable in-group audi-ence, mostly to the members. The majority of the documents I collected were written for insiders; they would be of no interest to the public and were not simply marketing or public relations efforts. More specifically, "documents" available in these archives included, but were not restricted to, some selection of the following:

- statements of purpose, staff lists and contacts, by-laws, reasons to join, mem-bership criteria, membership categories, application forms, directories of members
- letters from leaders, detailed information about sections and committees, re-ports of committee meetings, strategic plans
- information about future meetings, meeting programs, descriptions of past meetings, photographs from past meetings, occasional full-text or slide versions of meeting presentations, information about awards and award winners
- archives of newsletters, typically extending back to around 2000; information about other publications available; various publications; archives of press re-leases; industry or association histories
- various technical information, elaborate specifications of technical standards, elaborate specifications of accreditation types and procedures
- information about related associations, information on industry "partners" such as standards bodies or suppliers, "state-of-the-industry" analyses and prognoses, discussion of relevant issues from other sources
- promotional materials directed at consumers or the public, safety guides, infor-mation about scholarships and charity programs

It should be unnecessary to emphasize that I am not suggesting or assuming that this discourse gives a complete picture of any given associations' subculture, much less that it provides any valid insight into the attitude and opinions of members. Clearly there are many systematic forces limiting the availability of materials, and thus the nature of the discourse examined here—antitrust law, organizational pressures, and so on. However, even given these many inevitable constraints, there is rich evidence of public languages about economic action that has hitherto been mostly neglected, and that is particularly valuable because it is nonreactive.

Analysis

As Michael Mann argues, "socio-logic is a habit of mind which pulls tightest the chain which links the two extremes of all research programmes: an initial idea in the head and an eventual body of research data, created by the sociologist's intervention in the world." This process is iterative, not simply sequential; the links between problem, operationalization, evidence, and conclusions must be reviewed and revised again and again as the research and writing proceeds. While this is true of all sociological research, it is especially evident in qualitative research. And while it characterizes the entire research process I have been summarizing, it is especially pertinent to the process of what is often too cursorily summarized as "data analysis."[20]

Most qualitative researchers summarize this process with hardly less dispatch: for example, "all the interviews were transcribed and coded by topic. I developed files on each topic so that I could compare individual responses to a particular question." Many do not mention it at all. And indeed, further elaboration does seem unnecessary, at least for readers with any background in literature, history, philosophy, or other humanities disciplines. The process is intuitive, building on skills of reading and interpretation that are not particularly specialized, even if they are demanding. Reading, rereading, developing preliminary categories to organize the material, detailed note taking, returning to the evidence with new questions in mind, testing the evidence for newly observed connections, eliminating appealing ideas unfounded in the evidence, and so on and so on—these processes do not need a manual, and the quality of the process should be evident in the depth and range of the interpretation. (In sociological projects, all these generic processes are further disciplined by a distinctive disciplinary sensibility that demands some sort of generalizability, and clear, well-grounded connections to what real people are doing with their lives.)[21]

In the process of analyzing the archives of documents from business associations, I read, reread, transcribed, coded, categorized, organized, took detailed notes, returned to them again and again, tested ideas about connections, eliminated appealing but unfounded ideas, and did all this several times over in relation to different topics treated in the each chapter. For many readers, I am sure there is no need to know more, and this list is already tedious.

But I have been surprised that this process seems like a black box to many who haven't done it themselves. Some assume that there is little analytic work involved, and that using qualitative evidence is simply a matter of cherry-picking supporting quotations while writing a theoretical argument. Others, especially students I have encountered, seem to feel baffled, as though they are missing out on some magical secret manual about how to do qualitative work (I think this explains the common fallacy that software will improve qualitative work—since software does, at least, have a manual). I hope the following account helps open that black box and reveal that while there are no hidden secrets about qualitative data analysis, it is also a highly disciplined and involving process.

In this project, that iterative analytic process took the following steps:

1. I drew up a detailed draft "questionnaire" for my archives based on my theoretical questions and taking into account the implications of different theories in economic sociology for business associations, and of the existing studies.
2. I did a quick analysis of all documents from the focal associations according to that "questionnaire." I also took extensive additional notes. Part of what I learned was that many of my preliminary categories and questions were too abstract to relate directly to the data. In Mann's terms, I needed to develop my thinking to make a tighter connection between sociological idea and real-world evidence. But I also saw many more precise connections between sociological ideas and real-world evidence in this process, and my detailed notes became the basis for proceeding.
3. I wrote a paper based on this preliminary analysis, as a quick and superficial synthesis of what I had learned so far and a framework for further development of the work.[22] This preliminary statement also enabled me to speak on my research to a variety of sociological audiences, and to take their feedback into account.
4. Working with this preliminary background, along with detailed findings from the census, and often returning to various relevant literatures, I sketched the broader argument and a potential chapter outline (later significantly expanded) with subtopics. This work, a process of beginning to see the wood apart from its

constitutive trees, required the detachment and extended concentration only made possible with a semester's leave from other academic obligations. My ability to begin to focus on the bigger picture at this point was also directly encouraged by the intellectual stimulation and pleasure of that semester's visit to the Center for Cultural Sociology at Yale.

5. With the framework of the analysis further developed in this way, I began a close reading focusing specifically on evidence about external orientation—the analysis mostly embedded here in chapters eight and nine. I made detailed notes of specific claims, events, people, programs, and such, related to politics, public relations, and the civil sphere in each of the focal associations.

6. Continuing with the analysis of meaning-making related to external orientations, I then organized notes according to different topics, rather than associations: for example, various indicators (from existing literature) of "policy capable" associations; public relations programs; charity programs; and such. I also analyzed the focal associations in terms of the relevant variables used in the census. I then began drafting an "external orientations" chapter, which later became chapters eight and nine.

7. Later I returned to the full archive and examined documents of each association to consider a second set of questions, questions about their internally oriented goals and activities, and the ways they made these strategies of action meaningful. Again, I took detailed notes on activities and languages and reviewed those notes repeatedly to flag examples of categories of interest.

8. As with the examination of external orientations, there was a second iteration of this analysis. I organized the new notes by topics like "awards," "obituaries," "education," and by vocabulary of motives.

9. All these various notes provided the basis for writing draft chapters. The process of redesigning, writing, and revising draft chapters led to further questions and tests. An additional level of checking of both evidence and inference came with the necessary but grueling and time-consuming completion of endnotes citing sources of all quotations.

For many scholars this extended, detailed process, both systematic and intuitive, needs no description. But even if it is obvious to some, it remains mysterious to others, and as a result the work involved in "data analysis" for a project of this sort can be either mystified or underestimated. No doubt the iterative steps I took to analyze the qualitative data of the focal business associations could have been further rationalized, and perhaps simplified, and different scholars would take different paths. But any qualitative data analysis will demand this sort of careful, iterative, detailed application of simple skills to tighten the chain between theoretical idea and fresh evidence. Although reading and writing about it can be tedious, the process can and should be so deeply involving that doing the research means entering, exploring, and inhabiting, for a time, a complex alternative universe.

Conclusion

I have sketched the research process generating the findings reported and the argument developed in this study. I began by touching on how my underlying questions emerged and how and why I came to pursue them by studying business associations. I noted that scattered published studies provide supplementary evidence, and that the work of "manufacturing" this literature from very disparate and mostly unrelated corners of the social sciences was the first important part of the research process. I then summarized the methodological decisions and processes involved in creating the census of national business associations, including data sources, case inclusion, genre constraints on inference, and coding development and implementation. Finally, I described the selection of the focal sample for qualitative analysis, the process of assembling an archive of the focal associations' public documents, and the iterative analysis of this qualitative data.

Apart from attempting to answer methodological questions that may arise for readers of this study, part of the point of this overview has been to provide a foundation for other scholars to pursue questions about American business associations, about economic governance, and about economic culture. One hope is that the literature I have assembled and the census of national business associations now available will enable the explicit and routine integration of these associations into economic sociology's understanding of the institutions and processes constituting American economic life. Another hope is that the approach to studying economic culture I use—combining background quantitative description with a focus on thick description and cultural explanation, and (more theoretically, as discussed in chapter ten) setting a hermeneutic analysis of broad themes in economic discourse against a background understanding of institutional processes of cultural production—can be replicated and improved as we learn more about the significance of culture for economic action.

Notes

All dates associated with URLs cited are dates accessed.

Chapter One

1. Dickens, *Christmas Carol*; Zelizer, *Purchase of Intimacy*, chap. 1; Spillman, "Enriching Exchange."

2. Spillman, "Enriching Exchange"; Polanyi, *Great Transformation*.

3. However, the necessity of cultivating the propensity to "truck, barter and exchange" is itself, for Smith, a social phenomenon. As this passage continues, "in civilized society he stands at all times in need of the co-operation and assistance of great multitudes" (*Wealth of Nations*, 14–15). Smith does not distinguish the social from the economic in ways that were later institutionalized, and a stereotypically optimistic view of self-interested exchange is qualified even in later books of *Wealth of Nations*. See also Smith, *Moral Sentiments*, 235–37; Copley and Sutherland, *Wealth of Nations*; Fry, *Adam Smith's Legacy*.

4. Marx challenged early political economists for naturalizing (and individualizing) interests in "Economic and Philosophical Manuscripts": "political economy proceeds from the fact of private property, but it does not explain it to us. . . . When, for example, it defines the relationship of wages to profit, it takes the interest of the capitalists to be the ultimate cause; i.e., it takes for granted what it is supposed to evolve [*sic*] . . . exchange itself appears to be a fortuitous fact . . . the only wheels which political economy sets in motion are *avarice* and the *war amongst the avaricious—competition*" (70–71, emphasis in original). But his response was to make a life's work of analyzing the historical constitution of those economic interests, their structural force, and the power relations and dynamics they generated. See also Marx, "German Ideology," *Grundrisse*, "Buying and Selling of Labour Power," "Capitalistic Character of Manufacture"; and Marx and Engels, "Manifesto."

5. Weber, *Economy and Society*, 1: 41. See also 1: 63–212; 2: 311–55; Weber, *Protestant Ethic*; Swedberg, *Max Weber*; Collins, "Weber's Last Theory"; Hung,

"Agricultural Revolution." For more on Weber's theory of economic associations see chapter two.

6. See Durkheim, *Division of Labor*, especially "Organic Solidarity and Contractual Solidarity" (149–65), and Muller, "Social Differentiation and Organic Solidarity." For a useful modern interpretation of Durkheim's potential contributions to economic sociology, especially on themes of cooperation and uncertainty, see Beckert, *Beyond the Market*, chap. 2. See also note 16 herein.

7. During the twentieth century, the murmur of dissent to the naturalization of economic interests was evident in economic history and economic anthropology, and, to a lesser degree, in social theory and comparative political science. Among the works most well known to sociologists are Polanyi, *Great Transformation*; Polanyi, Arensberg, and Pearson, *Trade and Market*; Sahlins, *Stone Age Economics* and *Culture and Practical Reason*; and Douglas and Isherwood, *World of Goods*. Also challenging economists' assumptions at a fundamental level, and building on the sociological classics, Parsons and Smelser develop a sustained analysis of what would later be called "embeddedness" in *Economy and Society*, chap. 3. They argue that what economists would call market "imperfections" are better understood by situating economic theory within a broader social theory. See also Parsons's treatment of Durkheim, Pareto, and Weber in "Sociological Elements in Economic Thought," and "The Motivation of Economic Activities"; Smelser, *Sociology of Economic Life*, "Economic Rationality as a Religious System"; and Barber, "Absolutization of the Market," 15–31, in Dworkin, Bermant, and Brown, *Markets and Morals* (a collection in which philosophers also dissent from the dominance of mainstream economics). Stinchcombe's *Economic Sociology* makes a somewhat different critique that foreshadows later economic sociology's focus on embedded economic action at the level of the firm. Swedberg, "Major Traditions"; and Lie, "Sociology of Markets," provide useful overviews of thinking about economic matters in sociology in the twentieth century.

8. Zelizer, "Beyond the Polemics."

9. Geertz, "Bazaar Economy," 28; Swedberg and Granovetter, "Introduction," in Granovetter and Swedberg, *Sociology of Economic Life*, 8. This revival showed the value of Paul Hirsch's early recommendation to focus on mesolevel problems: see "Study of Industries," 285. A number of useful surveys now recapitulate the intellectual history of economic sociology. See Smelser and Swedberg, *Handbook*; Swedberg, *Principles* and "New Economic Sociology"; Dobbin, *New Economic Sociology*; Guillén et al., *New Economic Sociology*; Granovetter and Swedberg, *Sociology of Economic Life*; Biggart, *Readings*; Carruthers and Babb *Economy/Society*; Carruthers, "Historical Sociology and the Economy"; Trigilia, *Economic Sociology*; and Beckert, *Beyond the Market*. Smelser provides an early overview in *Sociology of Economic Life*, and other earlier agenda-setting statements that remain useful include Friedland and Robertson, "Beyond the Marketplace"; Martinelli and Smelser, *Economy and Society*; and Zelizer, "Beyond the Polemics."

For sympathetically critical views of the field, see Barber, "All Economies are 'Embedded' "; Krier, "Assessing the New Synthesis"; and Krippner, "Elusive Market." Bourdieu restates economic sociology's theories of embeddedness in terms of his field theory in *Social Structures of the Economy*, arguing, for example, that Granovetter's focus on networks is "reminiscent of the painstaking constructions with which Tycho Brahe sought to rescue Ptolemy's geocentric model from the Copernican revolution" (233). Peter Abell challenges economic sociology for lacking rigor and parsimony compared to the modified rational choice models of economics in "Prospects for a Unified Social Science."

10. Granovetter, "Economic Action and Social Structure," 495. For more on each of these influences on economic action, see the reviews collected in Smelser and Swedberg, *Handbook*, 2nd ed. On national capitalisms, and on industry variation, see also the discussion of economic governance in chapter two, and of neoinstitutionalism in chapter four.

11. Key sources on these approaches are Powell and DiMaggio, eds., *New Institutionalism in Organizational Analysis*; White, *Markets from Networks*; Fligstein, *Architecture of Markets*; and Biggart and Beamish, "Economic Sociology of Convention." See also Spillman, "Culture and Economic Life" for a more extended overview. For arguments suggesting that economic sociology still makes too strong a distinction between "economy" and "culture," see Krippner, "Elusive Market"; and Fourcade and Healy, "Moral Views of Market Society." For reflections attending to ambivalence and ambiguity in economic orientations, see Wuthnow, *Rethinking Materialism*.

12. Zelizer, *Social Meaning of Money*, "Human Values and the Market," *Morals and Markets*, more broadly, see especially *Purchase of Intimacy*, "Enter Culture," "Multiple Markets: Multiple Cultures," and "Beyond the Polemics." See also Berezin, "Emotions and the Economy"; and Illouz, *Cold Intimacies*.

13. Indeed, as Paul Lazarsfeld pointed out long ago, "most sociologists have tended to ignore many aspects of the business world" ("Reflections on Business," 1), and as Francis Sutton and colleagues comment, in what remains one of the most extensive and sophisticated studies of American business culture, "to many persons, often of acute and sophisticated intellect, the business ideology was so obviously a reflection of businessmen's interests that they could conceive no problem in accounting for its content" (*American Business Creed*, 303). Certainly, the economic sociologists noted above, and others discussed in the chapters that follow, have begun to explore the complex sociological dynamics operating in business worlds, but for many sociologists, they still seem distant compared to social worlds like those of schools, congregations, gangs, social movements, or families, and as a result simplistic stereotypes about self-interested action remain powerful. This social distance has occasionally been bridged: in addition to Sutton et al.'s study, Jackall (*Moral Mazes*) and Morrill (*Executive Way*) provide valuable analyses and often gripping pictures of how people in business think, and a number of others

also begin to probe business worlds more deeply (e.g., Kunda, *Engineering Culture*; Blair-Loy, *Competing Devotions*; Miller, *Reluctant Capitalists*; Boltanski and Thévenot, *On Justification*; Boltanski and Chiapello, *New Spirit of Capitalism*; Illouz, "From *Homo economicus* to *Homo communicans*"; and Bandelj, *From Communists to Foreign Capitalists*, chap. 6). Haydu compares business organization in Cincinnati and San Francisco in the late nineteenth and early twentieth centuries and how the forms it took shaped understandings of class interests in *Citizen Employers*. All these works suggest in various ways that the self-interested pursuit of economic interests in business is rarely single minded or simple, and most of them also illustrate, at least in passing, disinterested understandings of business action. However, they do not directly raise the question here of what the pursuit of interests actually means in business worlds, and most still presume that, in principle at least, self-interest must be the primary way of understanding action in business.

14. On the conceptual framework with which I approach the cultural analysis here, see Spillman, "Culture, Social Structure, and Discursive Fields"; for its broad application to research in economic sociology, see Spillman, "Culture and Economic Life"; and for its application to understanding national identities, see Spillman, *Nation and Commemoration*, especially 7–11 and 136–50. This framework synthesizes several sorts of cultural analysis that are usually treated as distinct, and several implications of my approach should be noted here. For instance, neoinstitutionalism typically examines processes of cultural production, but quite rarely elaborates a thick description of the meanings produced, treating culture as an "external environment of action" rather than "lived text" (Alexander, *Meanings of Social Life*, 23). Here, however, I develop the argument that business associations are institutions of cultural production, but I go on to explore specifically and in depth the meanings they produce. Similarly, while I examine in detail the variable and extensive cultural repertoires evident in the meaning-making work of these associations, I also conclude that all the very variable meaning-making is structured by a discursive field constituted by the binary opposition between interest and disinterest. Analyzing discursive structure at this level of generality is uncommon in recent economic sociology (Spillman, "Culture and Economic Life"), but exploring the underlying discursive grounding of economic action is ultimately essential for generalizing about the particular accounts of variation, conflict, and change in cultural repertoires developed in specific contexts. In my view, economic sociologists need no longer hesitate to analyze broad cultural patterns in economic action as well as particular cultural processes in particular cases.

15. Most observers assume that disinterested language must be adopted cynically; however, as we will see most explicitly in chapter five, it is also possible that a language of self-interest is invoked as a cover for solidarity in public contexts (see also Eliasoph, *Avoiding Politics*). I am not saying businesspeople do not act to further particularistic economic interests; rather, that economic culture cannot be reduced to self-interest (see Mills, "Situated Actions and Vocabularies of Motive"; and Miller, "Norm of Self-Interest.")

I use the notion of interests in a conventional way, as when a manufacturer aims to "increase sales, market share, and profit," or when an industry group promises to "bring significant bottom line returns for your business" (see chapter six). I do so because, as Swedberg suggests, "interest is seen as having only one meaning today, and that is as economic interest in the sense of economic self-interest" (*Interest*, 79), and my primary concern here is not how sociologists have viewed interested-oriented action, but how it is understood by presumably interested-oriented actors themselves.

Swedberg also suggests that the idea of interests tends to be what Robert Merton called an unexamined "proto-concept" in sociology, and sociologists have varied in the weight they have given to interests in their explanations (*Interest*, 48). While some have seen interests as crucial, the majority has understood interested-oriented action as one important basis of social life among others, as we will see in chapter two that Weber did. Even when they see interest-oriented action as an important element of social life, most also place it in broader context: subject to normative regulation, specified in relation to fields, and mixed with other action orientations (e.g., DiMaggio, "Culture and Economy," 37–39; Friedland and Robertson, "Beyond the Marketplace"; Illouz, "*Homo economicus*"; Prasad, "Morality of Market Exchange"; Campbell, "Institutional Analysis"; Bourdieu, *Economy*). Others, especially those who focus on cultural processes, are cautious about giving "interests" any analytical weight in sociological explanation, investigating instead how interests are constructed (see Swedberg, *Interest*, 73–74; Spillman, "Culture and Interests"; and the economic sociologists discussed above). Some also show how intentions explicitly grounding interest-oriented action might be almost dissolved by the way contingent practical action reshapes goals and means (e.g., Bandelj, *Communists to Foreign Capitalists*, chap. 5; Dobbin, *Forging Industrial Policy*). In my view, the most productive direction for future sociological inquiry is to theorize, specify, and investigate the social conditions under which interested-oriented action is generated rather than naturalizing the existence of at least some interested-oriented action, or investigating how particular interests are constructed (see Friedland and Robertson, *Beyond the Marketplace*; Smelser, "The Rational and the Ambivalent"; Hirschman, *The Passions and the Interests*; Mansbridge, "Contested Nature"; Spillman and Strand, "Interest-Oriented Action").

16. Smith, *Wealth of Nations*, 148; Durkheim, *Professional Ethics and Civic Morals*, 12–13. Durkheim elaborates on his theory of the moral importance of "professional" associations, and their role in history, chaps. I–III. See also Durkheim, *Division of Labor*, "Some Notes on Occupational Groups" (preface to the 2nd edition), 1–31; Durkheim, *Suicide*, 378–84; Beckert, *Beyond the Market*, 119–22; and Hawkins, "Durkheim on Occupational Corporations." Tocqueville also famously observed and theorized the importance of associations, especially given the perceived equality of the United States: "Americans of all ages, all conditions and all dispositions constantly form associations. They have not only commercial and manufacturing companies, in which all take part, but associations of a thousand

other kinds." He thought associations were necessary in part for cooperation in "the vast multitude of lesser undertakings" generated with the increasingly complex division of labor: "it is easy to foresee that the time is drawing near when man will be less and less able to produce, by himself alone, the commonest necessaries of life." He does not clearly distinguish companies and business associations, but he does suggest that "the idea of industrial associations [linking owners and workers] will be fruitful but I do not believe it is ripe" (*Tocqueville Reader*, 181, 182, 150).

17. Warner and Martin, "Big Trade and Business Associations," 314. Zuckerman and Sgourev, in "Peer Capitalism," investigate a related phenomenon, what they call "industry peer networks," small groups of parallel peers in business that meet to share information and generate motivation for higher performance. They distinguish these networks from trade associations because they assume the latter are simply groups of competitors or exchange partners pursuing shared interests. Despite this distinction, their analysis of what industry peer networks do also applies to many business associations, which differ mostly in their average size and institutionalized multifunctionality. Here I open to investigation their assumption that some particularistic self-interest, such as motivation to perform better, must explain the existence of such groups.

18. These examples are drawn from the *Encyclopedia of Associations* (EA), the *National Trade and Professional Associations Directory* (NTPA), and the *Associations Yellowbook* (AY), and can be found (in the sequence given) in NTPA, 7; AY, 715; EA, 3623; EA, 3623; AY, 1118; AY, 904; AY, 208; AY, 1067; AY, 5. Of the roughly 4,400 national business associations in the United States, over one thousand had annual budgets of at least $2 million in 2002; these leading associations engaged the energies of 41,000 officers, executives, staff, and board members (AY, v). As we will see in chapter three, however, the more intriguing and ultimately consequential feature of these organizations is their typically small scale, so to focus on their financial or human capital is to miss their real significance.

19. International Concrete Repair Institute, http://www.icri.org/membership/benefits.asp; http://www.icri.org/committees/index.asp (accessed 12/10/2004). See also chapter five.

20. See Chaves, *Congregations in America*, on congregational activities.

21. These examples are explored further in chapter five, and discursive resolutions of potential contradictions between members' particularistic interests and collective "industry" interests are discussed in chapter six.

22. See Lamont, *Money, Morals, and Manners* on this distinction.

23. As noted earlier, and as we will see in the following chapters, most of the few studies of American business associations make no claim to be representative. Cases are usually chosen opportunistically, according to unexamined assumptions about what associations do. And, to my knowledge, the few broader surveys available are out of date, biased to larger associations, and fail to include more than a tiny fraction of the population (see Warner and Martin, "Big Trade and Business

Associations"; and Knoke, *Organizing for Collective Action*). The most rigorous study available was conducted in the 1930s (Pearce, *Trade Association Survey*). All this means that our census opens new territory for researchers interested in economic sociology, political sociology, nonprofit organizations, and civil society. However, it is important to emphasize that because the research questions that generated this study emerged from cultural sociology, I treat the census data as preliminary to a more hermeneutic project (see appendix). On one hand, I was dissatisfied that thick interpretive description of meaning-making in economic life remained rare, and on the other, that even some exemplary thick description in cultural sociology failed to situate the evidence in the universe from which it was drawn. This research design is intended to model a way of situating cultural sociology's claims about meaning-making while focusing on what I view to be absolutely central to cultural sociology's project, the thick description of processes of meaning-making and their discursive analysis.

24. For more on both the census and archive data, see the appendix. Slight biases were unavoidable in the purposive sample—toward smaller associations, and associations with members in more than one sector—but they do compensate for strong biases in the opposite direction in previous studies (see chapter three). And because smaller associations are more likely composed of firms, and associations encompassing several sectors are more likely, in principle, to offer selective incentives to mobilize members, we should expect more, not less, interest-oriented vocabularies of motive in this sample. See also discussion of problems with the "two-track" solution to Olsonian problems of "free riding" in chapter six.

25. Abolafia, *Making Markets*; Domhoff, *Power Elite*; Besser, *Conscience of Capitalism*; Haydu, *Citizen Employers*. I discuss peak associations like the National Association of Manufacturers and the Business Roundtable in chapter eight, where I note that they are likely to use explicit languages of strategic interest similar to— though likely more well developed than—the minority of explicitly political associations in the focal sample. See also the detailed discussion of peak association lobbying in Levitan and Cooper, *Business Lobbies*. (Interestingly, though, a study of business discourse from the 1950s by Sutton et al., *American Business Creed*, seems to show less emphasis on strategic languages in peak associations.) Local business groups likely use solidarity language more, judging by Besser's detailed study of business social responsibility in communities, though her evidence shows that the meaning of business in local settings, too, must be seen as filtered through a solidarity/strategy binary code: see *Conscience of Capitalism*, "Enlightened Self-Interest," "Business Networks," and "Good Corporation." Local business groups would not share vocabularies of motive related to shared technical features of work worlds, discussed here in chapters five and seven. I discuss countries with stronger formal governance by association in chapter two; there, too, one would expect an emphasis on solidarity languages, although to the extent that industry fields are highly structured by government, particularistic interests would also be

legitimately expressed in some contexts. Finally, the national associations I examine here can change their orientation according to historical contingency and episodic demand; as I discuss in chapter three, Louis Galambos's typology capturing this sort of differentiation (in *Competition and Cooperation*; see also Haydu, *Citizen Employers*). I provide suggestive evidence of such an episodic shift in an extended discussion of the North American Association of Food Equipment Manufacturers in chapter six. I note in chapters six, seven, and eight that solidaristic cultural production is occasionally turned to the pursuit of collective interests in heightened episodes of change or conflict. So the argument about solidaristic languages and orientations is certainly not intended to suggest that business groups (or firms or businesspeople) do not *also* understand their action in terms of interests. Rather, solidarity and strategy are both important in making economic action meaningful. The evidence from these national business associations demonstrates solidaristic language that is usually ignored.

26. My central research questions here focus on business culture as a condition of economic action, and I do not take it for granted that interest-oriented action in business is natural. The task of analyzing cultural conditions is distinct from, and prior to, the task of examining the direct causal effects of business associations in any particular context. However, this study also makes business associations more accessible to future investigation by scholars concerned with questions about particular and contingent causal consequences. I hope that scholars interested in other lines of inquiry in economic sociology besides the cultural are now better able to take account of this arena of American economic life.

Chapter Two

1. Spillman et al., *National Business Associations*. Elizabeth Blakey Martinez and Michael Strand contributed research to this chapter.

2. I use case studies to support or illustrate generalizations based on a broader reading of associational history, and to suggest aspects of their politics, organization, and purposes that have been elided in conventional accounts. Future research should close important gaps in historical knowledge of American trade associations by relaxing assumptions that corporate hierarchy and associationalism are mutually exclusive, and by replacing the case study with the organizational field as the unit of analysis.

3. Weber, *Economy and Society*, 1: 74 (ibid. for the following Weber quotes). In optics, "heteronymous" is applied to "two images of one object seen in looking at a point beyond it." (*Oxford English Dictionary*, vol. 1). So here, economic actors are oriented simultaneously to their own market interests and to shared interests with competitors in that field in the social order structuring their shared field of action. The quotation in the following paragraph on self-interested economic action is in

Weber, *Economy and Society*, 1: 202, and pure, rationalized exchange is discussed ibid., 43. See also Swedberg, *Max Weber.*

4. Hamilton, "Organization of Economies," 190–91; Swedberg, *Max Weber*; Martinelli and Smelser, *Economy and Society*; Collins, "Weber's Last Theory"; Hollingsworth, "Doing Institutional Analysis."

5. Weber, *Economy and Society*, 1: 50, 41, 42. For cooperative associations of competitive, profit-oriented economic actors, the "free riding" problem can seem particularly acute, since members are supposedly competitive businesses (Olson, *Collective Action*; see also chapter six, this volume). Some scholars investigate organizational dimensions of associations like size and governance to explain how they manage the tension between self-interested and cooperative action (Knoke, "Associations and Interest Groups"). Since Weber recognizes that communal and associative relations are usually mixed, he avoids problems generated by rational-utilitarian approaches such as Olson's, even though economic action is, in principle, self-interested.

6. Weber, *Economy and Society*, 1: 41.

7. Ibid., 75, 65, cf. 38–46.

8. Parts of the following passages are included in Spillman, "Culture and Economic Life." Like Weber, scholars of economic governance assume that rational self-interested economic action is shaped by the historically and comparatively variable political-institutional contexts within which it is undertaken, and bounded by institution-level "norms, rules, conventions, habits, and values" (Hollingsworth, "Institutional Analysis, 601; Hollingsworth and Boyer, *Contemporary Capitalism*). Industrial or sectoral governance should be distinguished from corporate governance (e.g., Aguilera and Jackson, "Corporate Governance"), and international economic governance (e.g., Gereffi, "Global Economy," 3). See also Fligstein and Freeland, "Corporate Organization."

9. Staber, "Population Perspective," 216n1, 186. On different frameworks of coordination, see also Staber and Aldrich "Trade Association Stability," 176n1; and Lindberg, Campbell, and Hollingsworth "Economic Governance," 14. Schmitter and Streeck ("Associative Action") also develop a comprehensive theoretical overview of factors that might influence business to organize in association.

10. Hollingsworth, Schmitter, and Streeck, *Governing Capitalist Economies*; Hollingsworth and Boyer, *Contemporary Capitalism*; Biggart and Guillén, "Developing Differences." For an introduction to "comparative capitalism" perspectives on the German and Japanese cases discussed below, see O'Sullivan et al., "Symposium on the 'Origins of Non-Liberal Capitalism'"; and Fligstein and Freeland, "Corporate Organization," 32–39.

11. Hollingsworth, Schmitter, and Streeck, *Governing Capitalist Economies*, 5; Hollingsworth and Lindberg, "Governance of the American Economy, 221–22. See also Hollingsworth, "Institutional Analysis," 605; Chung, "Networks and Governance," 62; and Lindberg, Campbell, and Hollingsworth, "Economic Governance," 6.

12. Hollingsworth and Boyer, *Contemporary Capitalism,* 8–11.

13. Hollingsworth, "Institutional Analysis," 613 (see also 608–9). On hybrids of market and corporate hierarchy, see Williamson, "Comparative Economic Organization." On different governance forms, see Hollingsworth and Lindberg, "Governance of the American Economy," 222–23; and Hollingsworth, Schmitter, and Streeck, *Governing Capitalist Economies,* 6. On mixes with dominant forms, see also Hollingsworth and Streeck, "Countries and Sectors," 270–71. As Hollingsworth notes, this literature is fragmented; much of the empirical evidence is contained in limited comparisons and case studies, and different sources include different governance forms.

14. Lindberg, Campbell, and Hollingsworth, "Economic Governance," 26–27; Hollingsworth and Lindberg, "Governance of the American Economy," 223.

15. Hollingsworth and Boyer, *Contemporary Capitalism,* 12, 16; Streeck and Schmitter, "Community, Market, State," 27; Coleman, "Associational Governance," 147.

16. Streeck and Schmitter, "Community, Market, State," 25. On the importance of the state for governance theory, see Lindberg, Campbell, and Hollingsworth, "Economic Governance," 7–8; Hollingsworth, "Institutional Analysis"; Hollingsworth and Boyer, *Contemporary Capitalism*; and Fligstein, *Architecture of Markets.* On associations' need for state authorization, see Schneiberg, "Governance by Associations"; Schneiberg and Hollingsworth, "Transaction Cost Economics"; Staber, "Corporatism"; and Lindberg, Campbell, and Hollingsworth, "Economic Governance." On cross-national variation, see Hollingsworth and Streeck, "Countries and Sectors," 274.

17. Gao, "State and Associational Order," 418; Coleman, "Associational Governance," 134; Schneiberg and Hollingsworth, "Transaction Cost Economics," 324–25. See also Chandler, "Scale and Scope," 501, "Large Industrial Corporation, 421; Streeck and Schmitter "Community, Market, State"; Yamazaki and Miyamoto, "Trade Associations"; and Staber, "Corporatism." Discussions of cross-national differences in economic governance from other points of view include Biggart and Guillén, "Developing Differences"; Hamilton and Biggart, "Market, Culture, and Authority"; Dobbin, "Comparative and Historical Approaches"; and Fourcade, *Economists and Societies.*

18. Chandler also traces the larger role played by associations in Germany than in the United States to legal traditions: "Legally permitted interfirm cooperation in Germany . . . reflected a fundamental legal difference between continental and Anglo-Saxon law. . . . German firms had less incentive than those in the United States to attempt to control markets through mergers and acquisitions . . . [and] it led to a more complex set of formal ties between companies than those that had developed in either Britain or the United States" (*Scale and Scope,* 395).

19. Herrigel, *Industrial Constructions,* 52, 57, 64; Chandler, *Scale and Scope,* 395. Herrigel also discusses sectors of German industry in which large firms and

corporate hierarchy dominated due to regional histories: national development was regionally differentiated.

20. Herrigel, *Industrial Constructions*, 168; Coleman, "Associational Governance," 141. See also, for example, Herrigel, "Machine Tool Industries"; Dankbaar, "Sectoral Governance"; Strath, "Modes of Governance"; Lynn and McKeown, *Organizing Business*; Schneiberg and Hollingsworth, "Transaction Cost Economics," 330, 338.

21. Gao argues that "private ordering remained dominant in Japanese economic governance before the Great Depression" (*Associational Order*, 424), but neglects the earlier, locally based associational order described by Fujita in "Local Trade Associations." Notably, both German and Japanese associational orders appear to have emerged on the basis of strong local associations existing early in the industrialization process—a process that, as I argue below, has also been neglected in accounts of American associations.

22. Fujita, "Local Trade Associations," 99, 88–91; Sako, "Circuit Board Industry," 31; Witt, *Changing Japanese Capitalism*, 42. See also Miyamato, "Prewar Japan," on more national and cross-sectoral associations in the early twentieth century, and Gao, "Associational Order," on government policy in the 1930s. On postwar associations generally, see Procassini, *Competitors in Alliance*, 21–41; Lynn and McKeown, *Organizing Business*, 13–14, 24–28; and Schneiberg and Hollingsworth, "Transaction Cost Economics," 330, 339. On the Circuit Board Association, see also Coleman, "Associational Governance," 142; and on the steel industry see Lynn and McKeown, *Organizing Business,* 65–69. Witt, in *Changing Japanese Capitalism*, includes associations in the micromachine, semiconductor, and apparel industries in the 1990s.

23. Schneider and Doner, "New Institutional Economics," 55; Procassini, *Competitors in Alliance*, 70; Schneiberg and Hollingsworth, "Transaction Cost Economics," 324–25. Berk and Schneiberg critique the "conventional narrative" on US associational governance in "Varieties *in* Capitalism" (see also discussion of uniform cost accounting, below). On American associational governance as weak, see also, for example, Streeck and Schmitter, "Community, Market, State"; Yamazaki and Miyamoto, *Trade Associations*; and Staber, "Corporatism." Fewer than 10 percent of articles on business associations appearing between 1995 and 2005 and listed in *Sociological Abstracts* treated American associations. The contrast with German and Japanese governance structures was a recurring theme of American advocates of industrial reform for greater international competitiveness (e.g., Lynn and McKeown, *Organizing Business*; and Procassini, *Competitors in Alliance*).

24. Tedlow, "Trade Associations and Public Relations," 139; Roy and Parker-Gwin, "Logics of Collective Action," 229 (229–39). See also Warner and Martin, "Big Trade and Business Association," 318–19; Hollingsworth, "Logic of Coordinating," 38–45; Dobbin and Dowd, "Anti-Trust"; and Chandler, "Large Industrial Corporation," 421. Exceptional periods include the First World War, when the

state encouraged industrial governance by association; a growth period after 1925, when trade associations were acquitted of antitrust violations; and a brief period of state encouragement under the National Industrial Recovery Act between 1933 and 1935 (Staber, "Population Perspective," 198; Warner and Martin, "Big Trade and Business Associations, 320–23; Aldrich et al., "Minimalism, Mutualism, and Maturity," 212). Sectoral exceptions have influenced, for example, insurance, agriculture, and professional sports (Schneiberg and Hollingsworth, "Transaction Cost Economics, 337; Schneiberg, "Governance by Associations").

25. On the Rhode Island candle makers, the New York Chamber of Commerce, and the Marine Underwriters, see Bradley, *Role of Trade Associations*, 19, 42, 20–21. On "club associations," see Procassini, *Competitors in Alliance*, 52; and Galambos, "American Trade Association Movement," and *Competition and Cooperation*.

26. Chandler, *Visible Hand*, 317. Examples of Civil War–era manufacturing associations can be found, along with others, in Bradley, *Role of Trade Associations*, 21–22; Procassini, *Competitors in Alliance*, 49–50; Warner and Martin, "Big Trade and Business Associations," 318; and Becker, "Hardware Trade Associations." Consistent with the argument in this chapter, Gamm and Putnam note a steady increase in density of (local, not national) business groups from 1840 to 1920 (see "Growth of Voluntary Associations," 526). The formation of translocal business associations in the late nineteenth century is also part of a larger story: the "post–Civil War era brought a broader flourishing of social organizations and voluntary associations" (Clemens, *People's Lobby*, 36; see also Skocpol, "Membership to Advocacy"). The connections have yet to be fully explored. Kaufman (*American Civic Life*, 85–91) argues that business associations were one of several types of interest groups adopting the more secretive and populist fraternal association model in the late nineteenth century. (He shows that commercial, mercantile, and trade organizations in Boston increased steadily in the late nineteenth century and leveled off from 1920 to 1940.) Business associations should certainly be reintegrated in to the story and assessment of American associationalism (see chapter nine). However, it would be important to include consideration of the issues of economic governance discussed here, which also account for late nineteenth-century associationalism, independent of the fraternal models. Kaufman and Clemens are mostly concerned with associations' political role, at the expense of their other strategies of action.

27. Aldrich and Staber, "Organizing Business Interests," 115; Roy and Parker-Gwin, "Collective Action," 215; Becker, "Hardware Trade Associations," 195–97.

28. On association disbandings, see Chandler, "Large Industrial Corporation," 231–31; and Becker, "Hardware Trade Association"; on dinner club associations, see Galambos, *Competition and Cooperation*, 33–35; and on earlier local "club associations," Haydu, "Business Citizenship." If it is true that associations managing price and production were volatile, rates of disbanding would have been much higher than the very low rates Aldrich and colleagues report of twentieth-century

associations in "Minimalism, Mutualism, and Maturity" (230), but there is no more than anecdotal evidence on this question.

29. On the federation of local chambers of commerce, see Bradley, *Role of Trade Associations*, 42; and on the printers, see Jucius, "Uniform Cost Accounting." On the milk producers, see Young, "Dairy Industry," 244, 247; on direct selling companies, see Biggart, *Charismatic Capitalism*, 32; and on cotton manufacturers, see Galambos, *Competition and Cooperation*, 101–6. On Germany, see Herrigel, *Industrial Constructions*; and on Japan, Miyamoto, "Prewar Japan." Procassini, in *Competitors in Alliance*, 49, also notes that American associations began locally and became national, but his contrast with Japan's "central government impetus" is questionable.

30. Becker, "Hardware Trade Associations," 325.

31. Schneiberg and Hollingsworth, "Transaction Cost Economics," 325; Becker, "Hardware Trade Associations."

32. Hollingsworth, "Logic of Coordinating," 39; Chandler, "Large Industrial Corporation," 232; Becker, "Hardware Trade Associations," 184, 182.

33. Chandler, "Large Industrial Corporation"; Procassini, *Competitors in Alliance,* 51. On the Bankers' and Lumber Dealers Associations see Bradley, *Role of Trade Associations*, 22; on the Transit Association, Procassini, *Competitors in Alliance*, 49; and on other associations see note 1.

34. Bradley, *Trade Associations*, 21–22; Roy and Parker-Gwin, "Collective Action," 223, 224; see also Haydu, "Business Citizenship" and *Citizen Employers.*

35. Lindberg and Campbell, "Economic Activity"; Roy, *Socializing Capital.*

36. Roy, *Socializing Capital*, 180.

37. Ibid.; Roy and Parker-Gwin, "Collective Action," 215; Lynn and McKeown, *Organizing Business*, 8.

38. Roy and Parker-Gwin also propose that "communal" relations became more important after price and production agreements were outlawed: one trade journal "suggested that it discontinue its poorly attended reports on technical and political questions and focus instead on the banquet" ("Logics of Collective Action," 231).

39. Sanders, "Antitrust Politics," 152–53, 155; Lindberg and Campbell, "Organization of Economic Activity," 359. Sanders argues convincingly that economic differentiation and political conflict between northeastern states at the industrial core and the extensive agrarian periphery has been a strong and persistent force in antitrust politics. However, a comparative perspective also suggests that proponents of antitrust "had an invincible rhetorical weapon in a central precept of political culture" and followed a history of anticorporate critique (Dobbin, *Forging Industrial Policy*, 221; Roy, *Socializing Capital*, 51–55).

40. "Mr. Dooley" (Finley Peter Dunne) is quoted in Cashman, *Age of Titans*, 65. On the broader context of antitrust politics in this period, see Fligstein, *Corporate Control*, 33–74, and Sklar, *Corporate Reconstruction*; and on the consequences of

antitrust, see Dobbin and Dowd, "Anti-Trust," and Sanders, "Antitrust Politics," 155–58.

41. Hollingsworth, "Logic of Coordinating," 41 (40–45). Roy discusses consequences of innovations in corporate law in *Socializing Capital*, and argues (against Chandler's account) that these legal innovations rather than (the relatively weak) antitrust law were responsible for the wave of corporate mergers around the turn of the century and the emergence of corporate hierarchy as a dominant governance form. See also Chandler, *Scale and Scope*, 71–89 and part two); Dobbin and Dowd, "Anti-Trust"; Sanders, "Antitrust Politics," 153; and Scranton, *Endless Novelty*, 4–6. On the oil industry and government in this period, see Laumann and Knoke, *Organizational State*, 51–57.

42. Chandler, "Large Industrial Corporation," 234.

43. Bradley, *Role of Trade Associations*, 27; Young, "Dairy Industry," 242–43. On associations' agreements, see Roy and Parker-Gwin, "Logics of Collective Action," 230, and Tedlow, "Trade Associations," 139. As Scranton points out, small firms dominated industry at this time: "it was the giants who were peculiar and unrepresentative, and the 'others' who constituted the bulk of American production" (*Endless Novelty*, 7; see also Berk and Schneiberg, "Varieties *in* Capitalism, 48; Haydu, "Business Citizenship"). Moreover, as noted above, the antitrust-and-corporate-hierarchy story underemphasizes sectors other than manufacturing, which also remains Scranton's focus. Therefore, consequences of antitrust for smaller business are important. Organized labor also suffered, because antitrust law was used against it (Roy and Parker-Gwin, "Logics of Collective Action," 218–19; Sanders, "Antitrust," 160).

44. Tedlow, "Trade Associations and Public Relation," 140.

45. Warner and Martin, "Big Trade and Business Associations," 320. On the Hotel Association and the Investment Bankers, see Bradley, *Role of Trade Associations*, 22. Laumann and Knoke discuss associations in energy and health in *Organizational State*, chap. 2. Pearce found that "the period from 1890 to 1915 witnessed a rapid growth of trade association" (*Trade Association Survey*, 12). Aldrich and colleagues find roughly 150 associations formed between 1900 and 1910, and more than two hundred in each of the following decades. After 1930 foundings per decade consistently rose above four hundred ("Minimalism, Mutualism, and Maturity," 225); the new data here suggest this is probably an underestimate.

46. Chung, "Networks and Governance," 63; Becker, "Hardware Trade Associations," 198–99; Berk and Schneiberg, "Varieties *in* Capitalism," 73; see also Berk, "Communities of Competitors," 376; and Scranton, *Endless Novelty*. Yakubovich, Granovetter, and McGuire ("Electric Charges"), analyze more of the intraindustry politics in electrical supply associations. As I have also argued above about the formation of national price and production associations from local ones, it is unlikely that new associational functions blossomed with no antecedents.

47. Bradley, *Role of Trade Associations*, 32. Emphasizing the importance of organizational antecedents of nineteenth-century associations noted earlier, they

emerged from a precursor group, the National Trade Organization Secretaries. In 1956 they became the American Society of Association Executives.

48. Galambos, *Competition and Cooperation*, 50, 50, 51, 55.

49. Pearce, *Trade Association Survey*, 2–3, 465. Of the estimated population of 1,505 regional and national associations, more than 1,300 responded, and the authors classify two-thirds of these (898) as "national," rather than regional, in scope (a thousand, including nonrespondents). This careful and detailed report deserves more attention from scholars. On the Temporary National Economic Commission, which generated this report, see Fligstein, *Corporate Control*, 29, 164–67.

50. Pearce, *Trade Association Survey*, 5, 360, 359. Like other previous studies, individual and firm memberships are not distinguished, and this probably explains some of the wide range in membership size. See chapter three.

51. Pearce, *Trade Association Survey*, 35–36. Twenty percent of associations sometimes hired lawyers, 17 percent accountants, 12 percent engineers or scientists, and 10 percent economists or statisticians. On the wide range of staff sizes, see ibid., 8, 365. Insurance associations were distinctively large, with 6.4 percent reporting more than a hundred staff.

52. Ibid., 37–38; Galambos, *Competition and Cooperation*, 108–11.

53. On activities of staff, committees, and contractors, see Pearce, *Trade Association Survey*, 384; on management firms, 38–41; on federating, 40–42, 389. Federating was more common among state and local associations. Only just over half of associations were legally incorporated, though incorporation varied widely across sectors (9).

54. Even though they emphasize the weakness of American associations, governance theorists occasionally note this multifunctionality, and associations "many coordinating functions" (Hollingsworth, "Logic of Coordinating," 40).

55. Pearce, *Trade Association Survey,* 373–75. The survey of activities excludes insurance associations, perhaps for reasons associated with their unusual size (n. 51). This report also analyzes relations between types of activities and features such as staff, size, and industry group.

56. Overall, trade promotion activities were minor rather than major activities for 20 percent of associations, and the careful authors of the report also cautioned that there was likely "a tendency to overstate" these activities (ibid., 23, 373). A somewhat lower estimate is indicated in another contemporaneous survey (Warner and Martin, "Big Trade and Business Associations," 322).

57. Pearce, *Trade Association Survey*, 373, 326–33; Haydu, "Business Citizenship." On anecdotal evidence about labor challenges and national business associations, see Procassini, *Competitors in Alliance*, 56; Warner and Martin, "Big Trade and Business Associations," 315; and Laumann and Knoke, *Organizational State*, 50. Less anecdotally, Aldrich and colleagues did find that strike rates had a modestly significant effect on association foundings over the twentieth century, but union foundings and union density had no significant effect on national trade association foundings or disbandings (though density had a slight effect on merger

rates). They attribute this to the United States' decentralized "system" of industrial relations ("Minimalism, Mutualism, and Maturity," 234–35). As an illustration, emerging national associations among cotton manufacturers in the 1920s
were unsuccessful in "efforts to counter union activity" because these issues were
considered local, and "in later years . . . most labor matters reverted to the hands
of local trade organizations" (Galambos, *Competition and Cooperation*, 71; see
Pearce, *Trade Association Survey*, 331–32 for another local example, from New
York). A better account of associations oriented to labor relations would require
investigation of regional and local associations: see the valuable overview in "Types
of State and Local Associations of Businessmen," appendix D in Pearce, ibid. On
associations and labor before 1900, see Bonnett, *History of Employers' Associations*. For a detailed study of national lobbying on labor issues by peak associations
like the National Association of Manufacturers, mostly in the 1870s, see Levitan
and Cooper, *Business Lobbies*.

58. Pearce, *Trade Association Survey*, 25, 373.

59. Ibid., 23, 373; Procassini, *Competitors in Alliance*, 56.

60. Pearce, *Trade Association Survey*, 23–24, 373.

61. Ibid., 25.

62. Ibid., 43; Roy and Parker-Gwin, "Logics of Collective Action."

63. Pearce, *Trade Association Survey*, 22–23.

64. Berk and Schneiberg, "Collaborative Learning," 48, 68; Jucius, "Uniform
Cost Accounting," 223–24. See also Ahmed and Scapens, "Cost-Based Pricing
Rules"; and Berk, "Discursive Cartels." For survey evidence on uniform cost accounting, see Pearce, *Trade Association Survey*, 373–74; on more general attention
to cost information, and overreporting, see page 24 and chapter VI. Berk expands
on implications of developmental associations for institutional theory and for historical interpretation of the New Deal in *Regulated Competition*, and "National
Recovery Administration Reconsidered."

65. Lynn and McKeown, *Organizing Business*, 155; Pearce, *Trade Association
Survey*, 373, 374; Yates, *Life Insurance and Technology*, 21, 80–84.

66. Sutton et al., *American Business Creed*, 289.

67. Berk, "Communities of *Competitors*," 380; Sanders, "Antitrust Politics."

68. Berk, "Communities of Competitors," 381; Sanders, "Antitrust Politics,"
184; Fligstein, *Corporate Control*, 89–98.

69. Bradley, *Role of Trade Associations*, 27, 23, 28; Hollingsworth, "Logic of
Coordinating," 40–41; Aldrich et al., "Minimalism, Mutualism, and Maturity." See
also Staber, "Population Perspective," 197–98; and Warner and Martin, "Big Trade
and Business Associations," 321. On Hoover, see Lynn and McKeown, *Organizing Business*, 100–101; and Himmelberg's important study of associationalism and
antitrust politics in the 1920s, *National Recovery Administration*. For an example
of Hoover's early support of associations, see Young, "Dairy Industry," 244; and
on Brandeis's more consistent defense, see Berk, "Communities of Competitors,"

376–77. On the Webb-Pomerene Act, see Bradley, *Role of Trade Associations*, 28; and Lynn and McKeown, *Organizing Business*, 125–26. Hawley, "Antitrust and the Association Movement," provides a useful overview of association politics in this period, and Berk, in *Regulated Competition*, an important reassessment.

70. Jucius, "Uniform Cost Accounting," 225; Berk, "Communities of Competitors," 391. See also Carrott, "Supreme Court and American Trade Associations." For a broader view of associations' part in the political debates of this period, see Berk, *Regulated Competition*, especially 60–65, and "National Recovery Administration Reconsidered."

71. Bradley, *Role of Trade Associations*, 28, and on government encouragement of associations' statistical activities, see Pearce, *Trade Association Survey*, 147–51. On the Court's actions and effects, see also Berk, "Communities of Competitors," 392; and Galambos, *Competition and Cooperation*, 99–100. On Hoover and the late 1920s, see Himmelberg, *National Recovery Administration*, and Staber, "Population Perspective."

72. Bradley, *Role of Trade Associations*, 24; Pearce, *Trade Association Survey*, 12. On differing reactions to the Swope Plan, see Procassini, *Competitors in Alliance*, 58; on NIRA's context and impact, see Dobbin, "Great Depression," 11–15, and Bradley, *Role of Trade Associations*, 25; and on the direct selling companies, see Biggart, *Charismatic Capitalism*, 33–40. Himmelberg, in *National Recovery Administration* (181–222), shows how "business planning" advocates came to influence NIRA's formulation, arguing that it privileged business interests at the expense of arguments for political "responsibility and accountability" also in play at the time. See also Berk, *Regulated Competition*, and "National Recovery Administration Reconsidered."

73. Aldrich et al., "Minimalism, Mutualism, and Maturity," 233; Pearce *Trade Association Survey*, 12. On opposition to NIRA, see, for example, Bradley, *Role of Trade Associations*, 25–26; on labor provisions and code enforcement, see Dobbin, "Great Depression," 16–17; on NRA's actions from 1934, Dobbin, "Great Depression," 15 and Jucius, "Uniform Cost Accounting," 228–29; on the late 1930s antitrust enforcement, see Dobbin, "Great Depression," 17–18 and Sanders, "Antitrust Politics," 191–94. On the judicial politics of antitrust from the 1930s to the 1950s, arguing for stronger application to corporations than associations, see Adams, "Rule of Reason."

74. Warner and Martin, "Big Trade and Business Associations," 323; Bradley, *Role of Trade Associations*, 26; Aldrich et al., "Minimalism, Mutualism, and Maturity"; Galambos, "Trade Association Movement," 123. One study identified fifty types of association projects as part of the war effort (Bradley, *Role of Trade Associations*, 27). A detailed directory of associations published after Pearl Harbor was subtitled "A Directory of 3,100 National and Interstate Associations *Available for National Mobilization Activities* in 1942" (emphasis added). See Judkins, *Trade and Professional Associations*.

75. Pearce, *Trade Association Survey*, 374, 333.

76. Ibid., 338, 336, 373.

77. Ibid., 333–34.

78. Galambos, *Competition and Cooperation*, 293.

79. Pearce, *Trade Association Survey*, 147–51.

80. Aldrich and Staber, "Organizing Business Interests," 124.

81. Durkheim, *Division of Labor*, 25. Yet business association theory and history is almost entirely innocent of Durkheimian insights (except, implicitly, in Warner and Martin, "Big Trade and Business Associations"). Skocpol ("Membership to Advocacy," 122) challenges Durkheimian accounts of late nineteenth-century associational growth in general, but does not address trade associations specifically.

Chapter Three

1. This overview has benefited substantially from research and analysis by Michael Strand and Elizabeth Blakey Martinez.

2. As Fligstein discusses in *Corporate Control*, the varying politics of antitrust law and enforcement also influences the strategies and structure of firms. The question of how changes in firms as organizations relate to business association organization and orientations remains open, but on the evidence of this study, the multifunctional, flexible, minimal form of the business association has been much more stable than dominant forms of firm organization. This suggests that changes in firms attributable to state influences like antitrust are somewhat decoupled from associational life.

3. Freyer, *Antitrust*, 130, 134; Williamson, *Antitrust Economics*. In this view, as Freyer continues, "concentrated markets fostered anti-competitive conduct . . . stimulating inflation, encouraging 'inefficient' . . . mergers, facilitating needless product multiplication . . . and accentuating wealth inequalities." See also Fligstein, *Corporate Control*, 197–212 on this period.

4. (FTC and trade associations), American Bar Association, *Antitrust Law*, 1: 645–46; (enforcement procedures), ibid., 2: 1054–55; ("agitation"), Freyer, *Antitrust*, 146.

5. Sanders, "Antitrust Politics," 211, 195–212; Williamson, *Antitrust Economics*, 325, 328; Lindberg and Campbell, "Economic Activity," 383–84.

6. Holman, "Regulatory Flexibility Act"; Freyer, *Antitrust*, 147. See Campbell, Hollingsworth, and Lindberg, *Governance of the American Economy*, on antitrust politics in telecommunications, nuclear energy, rail, steel, auto, dairy, meatpacking, and health care, and Laumann and Knoke, *Organizational State*, chap. 2 (with Elisabeth Clemens) on nuclear and health care industries.

7. Lynn and McKeown, *Organizing Business*, 45–49.

8. (Exporting, research consortia), Lynn and McKeown, *Organizing Business*, 126–28, 161–64; Procassini, *Competitors in Alliance*, 63–65; (consortia growth), Barnett, Mischke, and Ocasio, "Collective Strategies," 345.

9. "Automotive Lift Institute Recognized by Standards Engineering Society," Press Release 3/21/2006, at http://www.autolift.org (6/14/2006). The impact of this law encouraging privatized standard setting needs more investigation, but as chapters two and six show, standard setting was long established in associations. The act also encouraged product development, innovation, and research design by providing private sector access to public research facilities.

10. Lynn and McKeown, *Organizing Business*, 48–49; Martinez, personal communication. Among the rare public references to antitrust constraints among the focal associations here were some specifications of rules by the Closure Manufacturers' Association and a notice by the American Council of Life Insurance about a retreat they were sponsoring.

11. Knoke, *Collective Action*, 19, 188; Smith, "Industrial Associations," 9. See also, for example, Berry, *Interest Group Society* and Galambos, "Trade Association Movement," 127–32. Laumann and Knoke, *Organizational State*, 7, and Walker, "Privatizing Participation" provide more evidence of how associations could become established actors in "issue networks." See also chapter eight.

12. On earlier "policy-shaping" associations, see Galambos, *Competition and Cooperation*, and Pearce, *Trade Association Survey*. On general arguments against the "advocacy explosion" thesis, highlighting problems in earlier data, see Tichenor and Harris, "Conceits of Modern Times," and "American Political Development." Political scientists also argue that any "advocacy explosion" in the 1970s changed "the balance between firms and business associations in the national interest organization population," and while earlier scholars "could reasonably equate pressure groups with business associations," "that equation is now obsolete" because individual firms now dominate the roster of interest organizations and clients of lobbying firms (Hart, " 'Business' Is Not an Interest Group," 49). Many firms do their own lobbying but are also association members (Hansen, Mitchell, and Drope, "Corporate Activity or Inactivity"; Hansen and Mitchell, "Corporate Political Activity").

Another mode of political participation by business that grew in the late twentieth century is "outsourcing" to the grassroots lobbying firm. Walker, in "Privatizing Participation," summarizes support for the "advocacy explosion" thesis and argues that business association foundings in the late twentieth century had a strong influence on the founding of lobbying firms.

However, this argument should be qualified. First, there is no evidence that business *association* mobilization in politics increased compared to previous decades (although other forms of business mobilization might have done so). Associations in the census founded in decades before the 1960s expressed conventional political goals at around the same rate as associations formed in the 1960s, '70s and '80s (25–30 percent of associations founded each decade). Second, *public affairs associations* had a greater impact on grassroots lobbying firm foundings than trade associations. The impact of trade associations on lobbying firm foundings was slight if DC associations were removed from the analysis (p ≤ 0.001 shrinks to p < 0.2). This seems to indicate that business associations already inclined to political lobbying might have changed their tactics, rather than that business associations in general were newly mobilized.

13. On estimated foundings per decade, see Aldrich et al., "Minimalism, Mutualism, and Maturity," 225; cf. Aldrich and Staber, "Organizing Business Interests," 123; Spillman et al., "National Business Associations." Knoke (*Collective Action*, 71) estimated 3,505 national business associations in 1983; our data suggest that at least 3,146 currently existing national associations formed by 1980. Dissolutions and mergers between 1980 and 2002 likely explain Knoke's higher estimate. Aldrich et al. suggest at least 2,100 national associations existed in the early 1980s, but this is probably an underestimate, because they probably rely mostly on the somewhat ad hoc "Trade Associations" classification by the *Encyclopedia of Associations* (see the appendix).

14. Warner and Martin, "Big Trade and Business Associations," 316–17; Knoke, *Collective Action*. On "minimalist" organizations, see Aldrich et al., "Minimalism, Mutualism, and Maturity," 224; Rao, "Nonprofit Watchdog Associations," 914–15n3. Lloyd Warner and his colleagues were interested in the significance of large-scale organization (corporations, government, churches, and voluntary associations) in "the emergence of national society" and analyzed voluntary associations in terms of size, complexity, and activities. Their sample was biased to larger organizations and also included groups like the Rotary Club not included here; nor did they include business associations appearing in other *Encyclopedia of Association* categories beyond the category of "trade, business, and commercial" associations (see the appendix). So although their study is more systematic than the more typical anecdotal accounts, their picture is only suggestive. Knoke defined large associations as those with budgets over $250,000 (*Collective Action*, 69). His study of how associations mobilized collective action also included professional societies, labor unions, recreational, and other associations.

15. Warner and Martin, "Big Trade and Business Associations," 326–27; Knoke, *Collective Action*, 74–76. Actual membership means from both studies are dubious because of problems in sampling, skewed distributions, and ambiguities in membership criteria.

Information on association finances is also murky. Finances are not reported in our study because there is too much missing data (52 percent of associations) and available figures are not reliable or comparable. Warner and Martin find about three-quarters of business association revenue deriving from members, more than for other types of associations (296; cf. Salamon and Anheier, *Emerging Nonprofit Sector*, 73). Knoke reports 62 percent of association income from member dues, with a further 23 percent from sales. Unlike Warner and Martin, Knoke finds that business associations are not very different from other types of associations in their revenue sources (76), except that they are more dependent on a small number of large contributors (94). It is unclear whether either study includes income from conventions and trade shows; a number of commentators point out that this can be important for business associations (Smith, "Industrial Associations"; Staber, "Population Perspective," 187).

16. Warner and Martin, "Big Trade and Business Associations," 331–32, 306; Knoke, *Collective Action*, 79, 150. The staffing difference between these two studies may reflect trends in staffing between the 1960s and 1980s, but could be due to sampling differences. Our data support the more minimal staffing of Knoke's study.

17. Warner and Martin, "Big Trade and Business Associations," 306.

18. Ibid., 325–26, 329–39; subcontracting is discussed in Pearce, *Trade Association Survey*, and Walker, "Privatizing Participation."

19. Warner and Martin, "Big Trade and Business Associations," 304, 299, 302, 303; Knoke, *Collective Action*, 150, 160–61.

20. Warner and Martin, "Big Trade and Business Associations," 291, 334.

21. Hollingsworth and Lindberg, "Markets, Clans, Hierarchies," 223.

22. On mutual-benefit associations' philanthropy, see O'Neill, "Mutual Benefit Associations"; on sector expenditures, see Salamon and Anheier, *Defining the Nonprofit Sector,* 47, 51, 100. The distinction between business associations and other voluntary organizations is examined in more detail in chapter nine.

Salamon counts 140,000 business and professional nonprofits in the United States in 1990, 35.9 percent of all "member-serving" nonprofits but only 12.4 percent of all nonprofit organizations ("United States," 299, 301). And this category of business and professional organizations refers to a significantly broader array of groups than those considered here; it would also include local and regional organizations, business leagues, chambers of commerce, boards of trade, labor unions, agricultural groups, and local associations of employees, all of which "exist to promote some common business or professional interest of their members." Defining business associations more narrowly, the 4,465 associations in our census would be only 3 percent of all business and professional associations, 1.1 percent of all member-serving nonprofits, and 0.4 percent of all organizations in the nonprofit sector. Even these rough estimates may overstate the proportion, because the numerator is from 2003 data and the denominator is from 1990 data.

Salomon and Anheier recognize the problematic theoretical status of business associations considered as voluntary organizations discussed in chapter nine (*Emerging Nonprofit Sector*, 46). See also Abzug and Webb, "Stakeholder Perspective"; Lampkin, Romero, and Finnin, "Taxonomy"; Smith, "Nonprofit, Voluntary Associations"; Quarter et al., "Social Economy Framework"; and, more generally, Powell, *Nonprofit Sector*; Powell and Clemens, *Private Action and Public Good*; and Wuthnow, *States and Markets*.

23. This data set is more comprehensive, and its composition more conceptually driven, than information in previous studies, because we did not rely on an existing list composed with different purposes and principles in mind (see the appendix). Compared to previous surveys, a disadvantage is the absence of some more detailed information about organizational structure, activities, and finances; compared to the population census in Aldrich et al. ('Minimalism, Mutualism, and Maturity"), a disadvantage is the lack of historical depth to assess trends.

24. While unobtrusive and comprehensive, this information on association goals and activities omits some details captured in older surveys, and it is shaped by the genre requirements of the "statement of purpose" discussed in the appendix. As subsequent chapters show, frequencies of goals and activities here are typically underestimates.

25. All information in this section is summarized from Spillman et al., "National Business Associations." Percentages are rounded. In the 1930s, the "average" membership was 362 (Pearce, *Trade Association Survey*, 5). Mean membership reported in the 1980s survey was 1,216 (Knoke, *Collective Action*, 74–76).

26. Knoke, *Collective Action*, 74; Coleman, *Business and Politics*, 33. By contrast, 56 percent of associations surveyed in the late 1930s had fewer than fifty members, 71.5 percent fewer than a hundred members, 24.5 percent between 100 and 1,000 members, and 4 percent more than a thousand members (Pearce, *Trade Association Survey*, 360). Although memberships remained small, they had, overall, increased markedly.

27. Warner and Martin, "Big Trade and Business Associations," 329 (cf. 325–26.) They set aside the issue of different types of members, as does Knoke, though for different reasons (*Collective Action*, 74). Aldrich et al. ("Minimalism, Mutualism, and Maturity") and Pearce (*Trade Association Survey*) do not appear to address the topic. Arguably, whatever associations might do for firms is, in any case, accomplished by individual representatives of those firms in association, and, conversely, individual members of business associations are members to the extent that their interests are mostly understood to overlap with those of the firms they own or manage (cf. Coleman, *Business and Politics*, 15). In the focal associations here, individual members were typically identified by their firms, as we see in many illustrations in later chapters. Very occasionally, associations with both individual and firm members would spell out how the relationship was to be understood (for example, in some committee voting rules of the Food Equipment Manufacturers, and in some of the Exhibit Designers procedures).

However, no one has actually investigated whether associations composed of firms differ in any significant way from associations composed of individual businesspeople. Since our new data allow empirical investigation of these questions, they are explored in more detail below and where relevant in subsequent chapters. In general, business associations with different types of memberships are not categorically different, but differ significantly on some particular features of interest.

There are more differences than previously recognized, but they are not so absolute as to suggest that associations with different membership types are actually different organizational populations; even on features where measures of central tendency differ significantly, similar distributions remain.

28. Roughly the same proportion of associations of each type fell into the modal category of 100–999 members: 45 percent (firm members), 43 percent (individual members), and 47 percent (both). But associations of firms were much more likely than others to report fewer than a hundred members, and of individuals to report more than a thousand. Nevertheless, exceptions—such as very large associations composed of firms—are too frequent and empirically significant to ignore. Variation in size by type of membership does not appear to reflect a categorical distinction: these are not two or three completely distinct organizational populations.

29. Coleman, *Business and Politics*, 42–43. Two conflicting observations could qualify this data. It probably overestimates average staff because over 27 percent of (likely simple) associations did not report staff size. Alternatively, staff size may underestimate organizational capacity should associations contract out services, an anecdotal possibility about which there is little systematic information. In the 1930s, 10–20 percent of associations sometimes contracted experts or hired management firms (see chapter two). Coleman found that 14 percent of Canadian business associations outsourced staff services. On staff size as a simplistic measure of organizational complexity, see Kimberley, "Organizational Size," 592.

30. Of those reporting any staff, 42–44 percent of associations had fewer than four staff and 20–23 percent more than twelve, regardless of membership type.

31. Associations providing terse rather than expansive self-descriptions often omitted committees. Even among that minority of associations with more than 10,000 members, 46 percent did *not* report committees, divisions, or councils, so underreporting seems likely.

32. Skocpol et al., "How Americans Became Civic." A third of mixed-membership associations reported affiliates or subgroups. On many measures like this one such associations fell somewhere between the two pure types.

33. New York and Chicago seem to have lost a greater proportion of associations than Washington, DC, since the 1960s. Warner and Martin suggest that DC associations (25 percent) were increasing, and the 30 percent in the contemporary census may support this claim. However, it is unclear whether they included Virginia and Maryland associations along with DC associations, as does the later data, nor whether it would have been valid to do so at the time (cf. chapter eight on DC associations). Minor shifts in the population periphery can be inferred because while overall 21 percent of associations were formed in the 1980s, the rate was 30 percent in California and 26 percent in Florida. In the 1990s, 11 percent of the overall association population formed, but rates were notably higher (14–16 percent) for associations in California, Florida, Texas, and Colorado. More generally, the comparison with the 1960s data is inexact and should be treated with caution

because of Warner and Martin's bias to larger associations (exaggerating declining concentration in larger cities), and because the contemporary data code state rather than city, possibly exaggerating inference about larger city concentrations.

34. Associations that disbanded or merged before 2002 are not included, so foundings per decade are underestimates. However, Aldrich et al. found that disbanding and merger rates were extremely low among trade associations—for example, the odds of disbanding in any given year were 0.0033 to 1—a feature they take to be "characteristic of minimalist organizations" ("Minimalism, Mutualism, and Maturity," 230, 235).

35. Many scholars assume that the best unit of analysis for investigating associations empirically is the industry or sector, with different industry or sectoral conditions influencing the prevalence of associations. These theoretical intuitions are difficult if not impossible to test, for several reasons. What constitutes a sector or industry is often ambiguous (for instance, among different governance theorists); criteria for formal industry categories do not apply directly to associations; and, as we see here, many associations are not simply categorized at an industry or sectoral level. These observations suggest skepticism about the generalizability of sectoral explanations and support the theory of associations as cultural producers.

Rough comparisons between sectoral locations of associations in the 1930s, the 1960s, and in the contemporary data show roughly predictable trends, with increases in finance-related, communications-related, and service-related associations between the 1930s and the contemporary data; declines in proportions of manufacturing, agricultural, and wholesale and retail associations between the 1960s and the contemporary data; and increases in services and information-related associations between the 1960s and the present. There are no clear-cut patterns in relations between sectoral proportion of associations and GDP, and sectoral proportion of associations and the labor force, or in the trends in each of these relationships.

36. Lindberg, Campbell, and Hollingsworth, "Economic Governance," 26–27; Hollingsworth and Lindberg, "Markets, Clans, Hierarchies, 223.

37. Galambos, *Competition and Cooperation*. Examining national manufacturing associations and developing Weberian organizational theory, Leblebici and Salancik, in "Rules of Organizing," offer a similar account of business associations as "communal" or "organizational."

38. Galambos, *Competition and Cooperation*, 291; Independent Bakers Association, http://www.mindspring.com/~independentbaker/ (12/9/2004); Hunt, *Encyclopedia of Associations*, 60.

39. Galambos, *Competition and Cooperation*, 291–92; International Concrete Repair Institute, http://www.icri.org/ (12/10/2004); Hunt, *Encyclopedia of Associations*, 99.

40. Galambos, *Competition and Cooperation*, 297; American Council of Life Insurance, http://www.acli.com/ (12/23/2004); Hunt, *Encyclopedia of Associations*, 225.

41. For other cases that illustrate associations' changing organizational capacity over time, see Haydu, "Business Citizenship," and *Citizen Employers*; Berk and Schneiberg, "Collaborative Learning."

42. ("Influenced by milieux"), Peterson, "Progress and Prospects," 165; see also Hirsch, "Cultural Industries Revisited"; Griswold, *Cultures and Societies*, chap. 4; (early development), Peterson, "Revitalizing"; Hirsch, "Culture Industry Systems"; Crane, *Production of Culture*; DiMaggio, "Mass Culture Theory"; (ideological innovation), Wuthnow, *Communities of Discourse*, 548–54; (Billboard charts), Anand and Peterson, "Commercial Music Industry"; (stock coverage), Zuckerman, "Stock Market Activity"; (industry media), Lounsbury and Rao, "Product Categories."

43. Hirsch, "Culture Industry Systems"; see also "Cultural Industries Revisited."

44. Pearce, *Trade Association Survey*, 373, 384; Sutton et al., *American Business Creed*, 89; Bielby and Harrington, *Global TV*, 2–10.

45. Thirty-nine percent of associations specifically report meetings that are exhibitions or trade shows rather than conventions. The rate at which associations report conventions or trade shows varies slightly by founding decade, size, and organizational differentiation, but not membership type, and typically remained above 75 percent for almost all categories of association. Reports of other types of meetings (from four in ten associations) did not vary by association size: for smaller associations these other meetings could replace the convention or trade show, and larger associations often held interim or committee meetings in addition to conventions. As for conventions and trade shows, reports of other meetings varied slightly by founding decade and organizational differentiation. None of this minor shading in the population distribution of meetings detracts from their absolute centrality to the institution of the business association; even in the lower ranges, reports of meetings are higher than those for most other association features and activities.

46. As for meetings, the rate at which associations reported publications varied slightly by organizational size and differentiation, with larger and more differentiated associations reporting more. Unlike for meetings, membership type made a slight difference, with slightly fewer associations of firms reporting publications than those with other membership types. Also in contrast to reports of meetings, founding decade generally made little difference to reports of publications. As with meetings, none of this minor shading changes the main point that publications are a central feature of business associations as an institution.

47. On the limits of theories of cultural production, see, for example, Spillman, "Discursive Fields"; Alexander, *Cultural Sociology*; and Alexander and Smith, "New Proposal."

48. Knoke, *Collective Action*, 80–81. Notable here are the one in five associations concerned with members' social lives. Compared to other sorts of associations, more trade associations ranked influencing public policy, raising members' status, and improving members' economic position as important. Knoke also analyzed

incentives offered to association members—normative, utilitarian, and affective. Three-quarters of associations offered normative incentives of some sort, often in combination with utilitarian and affective incentives, more than the 50 percent offering utilitarian incentives in some combination, and 53 percent offering social incentives in some combination (calculated from ibid., 119). Knoke challenges Olsonian accounts of group membership with his incentives data, but does not include trade association members in this data. See also chapter six.

49. Pearce, *Trade Association Survey*, 22–25.

50. Yates, in *Structuring the Information Age*, shows how insurance associations were important for developing and sharing technological information even before their member firms adopted computers from the 1940s—a finding that likely applies to other industries and other associations, perhaps especially in the last decades of the twentieth century (see chapter six).

51. On the increasing importance of public relations, see Warner and Martin, "Big Trade and Business Associations," 323–24; Tedlow, "Public Relations." See also chapter nine.

52. Relative proportions for "internal" and "external" goals reported are influenced by the number of possible goals—four internal and three external goals. However, this comparison retains some substantive significance because the coding scheme emerged from extensive pretesting.

53. Variable definitions for goals coded were created by Rui Gao. See the appendix on coding.

54. Variable descriptions are drawn from Spillman and Gao, "Codebook," and associations' statements from Hunt, *Encyclopedia of Associations*, 187, 1245, 886, 1466, 1452, 3153, 3379, 1153, 276, 3088, and 3287.

55. Spillman and Gao, "Codebook"; Hunt, *Encyclopedia of Associations*, 907, 1153, 1542, 1579, and 2047.

56. Spillman and Gao, "Codebook"; Hunt, *Encyclopedia of Associations*, 584, 812, 1254, 1542, 3153, 276, 186.

57. Spillman and Gao, "Codebook"; Hunt, *Encyclopedia of Associations*, 365, 926, 886–87, 187, 1153, 1466, 3153.

58. Spillman and Gao, "Codebook"; Hunt, *Encyclopedia of Associations*, 3287, 1542, 3088, 812, 926, 1153, 1579, 3379, 584, 1466, 365.

59. Spillman and Gao, "Codebook"; Hunt, *Encyclopedia of Associations*, 434, 926, 1579, 2027, 3586, 187, 3153, 584, 1466.

60. Spillman and Gao, "Codebook"; Hunt, *Encyclopedia of Associations*, 3863–64, 907.

Chapter Four

1. Michael Strand contributed to this chapter, and some passages have been adapted from Spillman, "Special Camaraderie." The view of associational strate-

gies of action adopted here, which generalizes across contingent case-level variation, parallels the ideas of organizational repertoires (Clemens, *People's Lobby*, 44), and tactical repertoires of social movements.

2. Fligstein and Freeland, "Corporate Organization," 32; DiMaggio and Powell, "Introduction," 14; Meyer and Rowan, "Institutionalized Organizations"; Friedland and Alford, "Bringing Society Back In," 243.

3. DiMaggio and Powell, "Iron Cage Revisited," 69, 71, 71.

4. Becker, *Art Worlds*.

5. International Concrete Repair Institute, http://www.icri.org/membership/index.asp (12/10/2004); North American Association of Food Equipment Manufacturers, "NAFEM and CAT create The NAFEM Show Technology Pavilion," *NAFEM in print* (Spring 2003), 13, http://www.nafem.org/publications/inprint/ (12/23/2004); Firestop Contractors International Association, http://www.fcia.org/articles/flameout.htm (12/20/2004); Spillman, "Enriching Exchange."

6. Change is a puzzle "if institutions exert such a powerful influence over ways in which people can formulate their desires and work to attain them" (DiMaggio and Powell, "Introduction," 29). In 1991 they wrote that "up until now, it is fair to say the new institutionalism has been most attentive to processes of legitimation and social reproduction" ("Introduction," 27; see also, for example, Dacin, Goodstein, and Scott, "Institutional Theory"). Yet scholars from the 1990s onward commented approvingly that institutional approaches to organizations were focusing on change: even in 1991, DiMaggio and Powell aimed to "address head on the issues of change, power and efficiency" (27). A decade later, Scott ("Organizations and New Institutionalism") commented approvingly that institutional theory had shifted its primary focus from stability to change (and suggested that focusing on intermediaries, including associations, was a promising direction for future enquiry). On exogenous forces for change, see, for instance, Leblebici et al., "Institutional Change," 335. On sources of endogenous change, see Friedland and Alford, "Bringing Society Back In"; Schneiberg and Clemens, "Institutional Analysis"; Clemens and Cook, "Politics and Institutionalism"; Meyer and Rowan, "Institutionalized Organizations"; and Leblebici et al., "Institutional Change." On cultural production and institutional diffusion, see Strang and Meyer, "Diffusion"; Hirsch, "Corporate Takeovers"; and Davis, "Firms and Environments," 490–91. Nee, in "New Institutionalism," develops a model of institutional causes and effects that incorporates resistance and change as well as stability.

7. Lounsbury, Ventresca, and Hirsch, "U.S. Recycling; Greenwood, Suddaby, and Hinings, "Theorizing Change"; Fligstein, *Architecture of Markets*, 76. On "industry recipes," see Porac, Ventresca, and Mishina, "Interorganizational Cognition." Business associations are also mentioned in accounts of industry change, provided in Hirsch, "Organizational Effectiveness," 327; Chung, "Networks and Governance"; Boczkowski, *Digitizing the News*, 25; Thornton, "Logics of Control," 296; Schneiberg and Clemens, "Institutional Analysis," 203; Baker, Faulkner, and Fisher, "Interorganizational Market Relationships," 151; Bielby and Harrington,

Global TV, 9; Miller, *Reluctant Capitalists*, 169; and Weber, Heinze, and DeSoucy, "Mobilizing Codes," 547.

8. International Telecommunications Society, http://www.itsworld.org/about/abo.htm (12/28/2004); American Society for Automation in Pharmacy, http://www.asapnet.org/ (12/27/2004); North American Association of Food Equipment Manufacturers, http://www.nafem.org/resources/DataProtocol/History/ (12/23/2004); Independent Bakers Association, http://www.mindspring.com/~independentbaker/ (12/9/2004); International Concrete Repair Institute, http://www.icri.org/about.asp (12/10/2004); Exhibit Designers and Producers Association, "Our Industry Will Not Succumb to Terrorist Activities," http://www.edpa.com/archivelatestnews_01.html (12/22/2004); Brian Gibson, "NESDA's Position on National Service," *ProService Magazine: A Journal of NESDA and ISCET*, August 2004, 11, 13, http://www.iscet.org/proservice/index.html (12/20/2004); North American Association of Food Equipment Manufacturers, http://www.nafem.org/resources/pod (12/22/2004); Mulch and Soil Council, *News, Notes and Quotes*, November 2005, 1, http:www.mulchandsoilcouncil.org/Inforesorce/Industry/News.html (7/6/2006); Larry Kulchawik, "New World Economy Requires Knowledge and Partnerships," *EDPA today* XI (2) Spring 2002, 2, at Exhibit Designers and Producers Association, http://www.edpa.com/archivelatestnews_01.html (12/22/2004); Automotive Lift Institute, http://www.autolift.org/history.html (6/14/2006); Conference of Consulting Actuaries, http://www.ccactuaries.org/about/strategicplan.html (12/27/2004).

9. Friedland and Alford, "Bringing Society Back In," 245; Lawrence, Suddaby, and Leca, "Institutional Work," 8; Lawrence and Suddaby, "Institutions and Institutional Work," 234.

10. (Cognitive homogeneity and legitimacy), DiMaggio and Powell, "Iron Cage Revisited"; Meyer and Rowan, "Institutionalized Organizations." (Microlevel account), Zucker, "Role of Institutionalization," 83 (cf. Spillman, "Culture, Social Structure, and Discursive Fields"; Goffman, "Felicity's Condition"). Investigations of "competing logics" in industries do examine stability in institutional fields and emphasize the cognitive, categorical work of associations, discussed below; see Marquis and Lounsbury, "Competing Logics and the Consolidation"; Lounsbury, "Competing Logics and Practice Variation." In another promising return to the question of institutional continuity that moves beyond microlevel processes, Lawrence and Suddaby suggest six types of processes maintaining institutions: enabling, policing, deterring, valorizing and demonizing, mythologizing, and embedding and routinizing ("Institutions and Institutional Work," 229–34). These suggestions should be explored further, but they also need to be connected to explicit recognition of persistent field-level players devoted to institutional maintenance as well as change.

11. Sabel, "Learning by Monitoring," 149; cf. Farrell and Saloner, "Coordination"; Berk, "Communities of Competitors," "Discursive Cartels," *Regulated Competition*.

12. Schneiberg, "Conditions for Governance," 92; Berk and Schneiberg, "Collaborative Learning," 40.

13. Roy and Parker-Gwin, "Collective Action," 216, 232.

14. Saxenian, "Business Interests," 28–29, 59. See also Sine, Havemann, and Tolbert, "Risky Business," for an example of an association playing a conservative role in industry change.

15. DiMaggio and Powell, "Introduction," 22, 24; Fligstein, "Social Skill," 108. See also Douglas, *How Institutions Think*, 8; Bourdieu, *Language and Symbolic Power*; DiMaggio, "Culture and Cognition"; Zerubavel, *Social Mindscapes*; Cerulo, *Culture in Mind*.

16. Thornton, "Institutional Logics," 83; White, *Markets from Networks*, 103; Davis, "Firms and Environments, 485; Zuckerman, "Stock Market Activity." See also Ocasio, "Attention-Based View," 193; and Vaughn, "Signals and Interpretive Work."

17. Irrigation Association, http://www.irrigation.org/about/default.aspx?pg= cig.htm&id=21 (12/11/2004); Conference of Consulting Actuaries, http://www .ccactuaries.org/resourcecenter/yearbook.html (12/27/2004); Closure Manufacturers' Association, http://www.cmadc.org/closmater.tpl?page=6000 (12/20/2004); Independent Bakers Association, "BakingNetwork.com: A Trading Exchange for the Baking Industry," http://www.mindspring.com/~independentbaker/id11.html 12/9/2004; International Society of Certified Electronics Technicians, http://www .iscet.org/certification/journeyman.html (12/20/2004).

18. International Concrete Repair Institute, http://www.icri.org/membership/ index.asp (12/10/2004); Exhibit Designers and Producers Association, http://www .edpa.com/membershipinfo.html (12/21/2004); Independent Bakers Association, http://www.mindspring.com/~independentbaker/id11.html (12/9/2004); Conference of Consulting Actuaries, http://www.ccactuaries.org/membership/membersurvey form.html (12/27/2004).

19. National Association of Real Estate Brokers, http://www.nsrea.org/education .htm and http://www.nareb.com/NAREB/benefits.shtml (12/28/2004); Envelope Manufacturers' Association, http://www.envelope.org/index.v3page;jsessionid= 44igmcnu2dcqs?p=230 (12/28/2004); American Council of Life Insurance, http://www .acli.com/ACLI/Events/CatalogSearch.htm?EventType=past (12/23/2004).

20. International Concrete Repair Institute, http://www.icri.org/advertising 2005/2005editorial.asp and http:/www.icri.org/bulletin/index.asp (12/19/2004); International Society of Hospitality Consultants, http://www.ishc.com/articles.html (12/20/2004).

21. Exhibit Designers and Producers Association, "There Is No Educational Programming Like This in the Exhibit Industry," *edpa today* XIII (3) Fall 2003, 3, http://www.edpa.com/currentpublications.html (12/21/2004); Aluminum Anodizers Council, http://www.anodizing.org/membership_info.html (12/9/2004); Closure Manufacturers' Association, http://www.cmadc.org/reg10reasons.tpl (12/20/2004).

22. Schudson, "How Culture Works," 171, 167–74; Biggart and Beamish, "Economic Sociology of Convention"; Firestop Contractors International Association, http://www.fcia.org/articles/firestopsystems.htm (12/20/2004); Mulch and Soil Council, *News, Notes & Quotes*, June 2005, 7, http://www.mulchandsoilcouncil.org/Inforesorce/Industry/News.html (7/6/2006); Pellet Fuels Institute, http://pelletheat.org/3/2004conference/index.html (12/23/2004); Brick Industry Association, http://bia.org/html/brickuniversity.html (6/21/2006); Vacuum Dealers Trade Association, http://www.vdta.com/LV06-Sems-thursday.htm (6/14/2006). For an extended example of industry-specific cultural resonance, see Bielby and Harrington, *Global TV*, 115–20.

23. Schneiberg and Clemens, "Institutional Analysis," 203; Smith-Doerr and Powell, "Networks and Economic Life," 379; Nee, "New Institutionalisms," 53. On the general significance of networks for economic action, see also Powell, "Network Forms of Organization." On the specific influence of network ties on financing, strategic alliance formation, and such, see Baker, "Market Networks"; Garud and Kumaraswamy, "Technological and Organizational Designs"; Geletkanycz and Hambrick, "External Ties"; Davis, "Firms and Environments"; Gulati, "Alliances and Networks"; Uzzi, "Network Effect" and "Social Relations and Networks"; Ingram and Roberts, "Friendships among Competitors"; Podolny, "Pipes and Prisms"; and Mizruchi and Stearns, "Getting Deals Done." For questions about what produces and sustains networks, see also Galaskiewicz, "Interorganizational Relations," 285–86; Gulati, "Alliances and Networks," 296; Zuckerman and Sgourev, "Peer Capitalism," 1328; and Powell, "Network Forms of Organization," 323–26.

24. Walker, Kogut, and Shan, "Social Capital, Structural Holes"; Gulati and Gargiulo, "Interorganizational Networks"; Uzzi, "Interfirm Networks," 48. On third-party referrals and previous personal ties, see also Gulati's finding that prior strategic relationships between firms generate new ones ("Alliance Formation," 645), and Sorenson and Stuart's evidence for the influence of geographic propinquity in venture capital markets—though they also argue that prior relationships, or the "evolution of interfirm relations," can erode geographic boundaries in funding ("Syndication Networks," 1584). The possibility that business associations encourage interorganizational ties is mentioned by Walker, Kogut, and Shan ("Social Capital, Structural Holes," 110); Gulati and Gargiulo ("Interorganizational Networks," 1445); and Smith-Doerr and Powell, ("Networks and Economic Life," 393). More generally, Smith-Doerr and Powell, "Networks and Economic Life," 384–88; and Davis, "Firms and Environments," 492, suggest that networks may originate from formal and informal organizational structures, prior task-related contingencies, or regional propinquity.

25. Smith-Doerr and Powell, "Networks and Economic Life," 387; Hollingsworth and Streeck, "Countries and Sectors," 276; Galaskiewicz, "Interorganizational Relations," 285. On institutional infrastructure, legitimacy, and network

formation, see, for example, Human and Provan, "Legitimacy Building"; and Baker, Faulkner, and Fisher, "Interorganizational Market Relationships," 151. On regional economies, see, for example, Saxenian, "Organization of Business Interests"; Herrigel, "Form of Order"; Powell, Koput, and Smith-Doerr, "Interorganizational Collaboration"; and Powell, "Network Forms of Organization."

26. Galaskiewicz, "Professional Networks," 640; Bielby and Harrington, *Global TV*, 63.

27. For an example of particularistic networking, see Darr, "Obligational Networks," 48-49.

28. Envelope Manufacturers Association, http://www.envelope.org/index .v3page?p=9460 (12/28/2004); Exhibit Designers and Producers Association, http://www.edpa.com/membershipinfo.html and *edpa today* XII (3) Fall 2002, 1, http://www.edpa.com/currentpublications/html (12/21/2004); Closure Manufacturers' Association, http://www.cmadc.org/reg10reasons.tpl (12/20/2004); Firestop Contractors International Association, http://www.fcia.org/articles/newsletter-6-01 .htm (12/19/2004); International Concrete Repair Institute, http://www.icri.org/ membership/benefits.asp (12/10/2004); "President's Message," *International Concrete Repair Northern California Chapter Newsletter*, April 2004, 4, http://www.icri .org/chapters/chap_details.asp?id=NCA (12/19/2004).

29. Aluminum Anodizers Council, http://www.anodizing.org/htm/body_ networking.html (12/9/2004); American Council of Life Insurance, http://www.acli .com/ACLI/Events/Upcoming+Events/Insurance+and+Law_ConferenceDetails... and http://www.acli.com/ACLI/Events/CatalogSearch.htm?EventType=featured (12/23/2004); Pellet Fuels Institute, http://www.pelletheat.org/3/2004conference/ index.html (12/23/2004); Small Publishers Association of North America, http:// www.spannet.org/directory.htm (12/27/2004); National Association of Food Equipment Manufacturers, conference program at http://www.nafem.org/events/ NAFEM-MAFSI/2005/index.cfm (12/22/2004); International Concrete Repair Institute, *New England Chapter . . . October 19th*, 2004 *Newsletter*, 1, http://www .ne-icri.org/PastNewsletters.htm (12/19/2004).

30. Independent Bakers Association, http://www.mindspring.com/~independent baker/id1.html (12/9/2004).

31. National Association of Food Equipment Manufacturers, http://www.nafem .org/about/benefits (12/22/2004); National Electronics Service Dealers Association, *ProService Magazine*, June 2004, 10, http://www.iscet.org/proservice/index.html (12/20/2004); Mulch and Soil Council, http://www.mulchandsoilcoucil.org/About/ HowToJoin.html (7/6/2006); Vacuum Dealers Trade Association, http://www.vdta .com/conventions.htm and *Floor Care Professional*, October 2004, http://www.vdta .com/oct04/fc-toc.htm (6/14/2006); Irrigation Association, "Exhibitor Prospectus, 25th Annual International Irrigation Show," 3, http://www.irrigation.org/show/ default.aspx?pg=exhibit.htm&id=35 (12/30/2004); Zuckerman and Sgourev, "Peer Capitalism."

32. International Telecommunications Society, http://www.itsworld.org/about/
abo_1.htm (12/28/2004); Aluminum Anodizers Council, http://www.anodizing.org/
anodizing_conference.html (12/9/2004); International Concrete Repair Institute,
Rocky Mountain Chapter . . . Newsletter, May 2003 Issue 1, 4, http://www.icri.org/
chapters/chap_details.asp??id=RM (12/19/2004).

33. See note 24. The institutional conditions for network ties are better understood in the extensive literature on East Asian business groups: see, for example,
Gerlach, "Japanese Corporate Network"; and Granovetter, "Business Groups and
Social Organization." Witt, *Changing Japanese Capitalism*, examines in detail the
interpenetration of networks and associations in three Japanese industries. On
the limits of using closer thick description from fieldwork for this sort of question
(compared to the archival analysis here), see the appendix.

34. DiMaggio and Powell, "Iron Cage Revisited," 64–65; Fligstein, "Theory of
Fields," 108; Breiger and Mohr, "Institutional Logics," 20. On the important but
neglected issue of whether field relations are inherently agonistic, see Breiger and
Mohr, "Institutional Logics"; Martin, "Field Theory," 31–33; and Benson, "Field
Theory," 482.

35. White, *Markets from Networks*, 7; Davis, "Firms and Environments," 486;
Zuckerman, "Stock Market Activity."

36. (Field formation), DiMaggio and Powell, "Iron Cage Revisited," 65; (external influences), Fligstein, *Architecture of Markets*; Lounsbury, Ventresca, and
Hirsch, "Industry Emergence"; Zuckerman, "Stock Market Activity"; (templates),
Davis, "Firms and Environments," 487; see also Fligstein, *Architecture of Markets*,
chap. 4; Sewell, "Theory of Structure."

37. Fligstein, "Social Skill"; Davis, "Firms and Environments," 489.

38. Aldrich and Staber, "Organizing Business Interests," 120. In the focal sample
with more extensive qualitative evidence, only a quarter of associations restricted
membership to one or more industries within a single sector; the census evidence
likely understates associations' construction of relational fields for industries.

39. Aldrich et al., "Minimalism, Mutualism, and Maturity," 236; Geletkanycz
and Hambrick, "External Ties."

40. Brick Industry Association, http://www.bia.org; http://www.gobrick.com/
html/HBawardwinner.html (6/14/2006); http://www.bia.org/html/BENEFITS.html;
http://www.bia.org/html/brickuntiversity.html (6/21/2006).

41. Closure Manufacturers' Association, http://www.cmadc.org/membershipcma
.tpl (12/20/2004); American Council of Life Insurance, http:www.acli.com/ACLI/
E-Marketplace/Partners.htm (12/27/2004); Pellet Fuels Institute, http://www.pellet
heat.org/3/institute/mission.html (12/23/2004); United Lightning Protection Association, http://www.ulpa.org/info.htm (12/28/2004).

42. International Concrete Repair Institute, http://icri.org/membership/index
.asp; http://www.icri.org/about.asp (12/10/2004).

43. North American Food Equipment Manufacturers, *NAFEM in print* (Summer 2004), 11, http://www.nafem.org/publications/; 2003 *Year End Report*, http://

www.icex.com/namfemiq/default.asp?12=home&id=guest (12/22/2004); Exhibit Designers and Producers Association, *edpa today* XIII (3) (Fall 2003), 3, http:// www.edpa.com/currentpublications.html (12/21/2004).

44. Aluminum Anodizers Council, http://www.anodizing.org/membership_info .html (12/9/2004); International Society of Hospitality Consultants, http://www.ishc .com/what_is/about/cfm (12/20/2004); American Council of Life Insurance, http:// www.acli.com/ACLI/Newsroom/News+Releases/default.htm (12/27/2004); Exhibit Designers and Producers Association, "International Focus Drives 2001 EDPA Convention," *EDPA today* X (2) (Spring 2001), 2, http://www.edpa.com/current publications.html (12/21/2004). See also chapter six on collective marketing.

45. Exhibit Designers and Producers Association, *EDPA today* X (3) (Summer 2001), 8, http://www.edpa.com/currentpublications.html (12/21/2004).

46. North American Association of Food Equipment Manufacturers, http:// www.nafem.org/resources (12/22/2004); Brick Industry Association, http://www .bia.org/html/Shelter_from_the_Storm.html (6/14/2006); http:www.gobrick.com/ planning/UM_Synopsis.html (6/21/2006); Irrigation Association, http://www.iaef .org/academy.htm (12/31/2004); Association for Women in Aviation Maintenance, http://www.awam.org/edulinks.htm (12/28/2004); American Council of Life Insurance, http://www.acli.com/Events/CatalogSearch.htm?EventType=past (12/23/2004).

47. Warner and Martin, "Big Trade and Business Associations," 325–26; Conference of Consulting Actuaries, http://www.ccactuaries.org/membership/reasons .html (12/27/2004). This CCA quotation emphasizes in bold type "liaisons," "Represent the consultants' viewpoint," "Keep Conference members informed," and "Have strategic alliances." North American Association of Food Equipment Manufacturers, http://www.nafem.org/about/committee_descriptions.cfm (12/22/ 2004); Irrigation Association, *E-Times*, November 2004, 2, http://www.irrigation .org (12/30/2004); Association for Women in Aviation Maintenance, http://www .awam.org/events.htm (12/28/2004); Firestop Contractors International Association, http://www.fcia.org/links.php and http://www.fcia.org/articles/newsletter-03-03.htm (12/19/2004); International Concrete Repair Institute, http://www.icri .org/neews/fixconcrete.asp (12/19/2004); Closure Manufacturers' Association, http://www.cmadc.org/membershipcma.tpl (12/20/2004).

48. Brick Industry Association, http://bia.org/html/codeissues.html/codissues. html (6/21/2006); North American Association of Food Equipment Manufacturers, http://www.nafem.org/resources/local_regulations.cfm and http://www.nafem .org/resources/gov/stoposha.cfm (12/23/2004); American Society for Automation in Pharmacy, http://www.asapnet.org/presentations.html (12/27/2004); Mulch and Soil Council, *News, Notes & Quotes* (January 2006), 1, http://www.mulchandsoil council.org/new.html (7/6/2006); International Concrete Repair Institute, http:// www.icri.org/publications/memapply.htm (12/10/2004); Firestop Contractors International Association, http://www.fcia.org/membership.htm (12/19/2004).

49. Galaskiewicz, "Interorganizational Relations," 295; Uzzi, "Social Relations and Networks," 501. See also Berezin, "Emotions and the Economy."

Chapter Five

1. Perry Garfinkel, "Cupid Takes to the Road, Too," *New York Times*, February 13, 2007, C8; Cyndia Zwahlen, "Nurturing Female Entrepreneurs," *LA Times*, September 20, 2007. John Davis argues that "camaraderies of market-places are universal and reported from every study" ("Anthropologist's View of Exchange," 221). Some passages in this chapter rely on Spillman, "Special Camaraderie."

2. Streeck and Schmitter, "Community, Market, State," 27. Similarly, Gerald Berk sees "economic agents as sociable beings, whose identities are shaped by the language or conventions they share with others" ("Discursive Cartels," 230).

3. Friedland and Alford, "Bringing Society Back In"; Alexander, *Meanings of Social Life*, chap. 1. Campbell ("Role of Ideas") notes that organizational institutionalism mostly examines implicit cognitions. I analyze here implicitly normative dimensions of associational subcultures. See also Goodstein, Blair-Loy, and Wharton, "Organization-Based Legitimacy," on moving beyond neoinstitutionalism's cognitive focus.

Nonstrategic meaning in occupational community may also be important in processes by which a market's "conception of control" is established to "erect social understandings whereby firms can avoid direct price competition and can solve their internal political problems" (Fligstein, *Architecture of Markets*, 70), and the analysis here expands on the cultural processes in Fligstein's "political-cultural" theory of markets. This application is likely fruitful: see the discussion of the North American Association of Food Equipment Manufacturers in chapter six. But this sort of indirectly strategic purpose of expressive and normative meaning-making does not exhaust its significance, for several reasons. Since there is no one-to-one correspondence between association and industry, most associations are not well positioned to provide the sort of strategic insulation Fligstein's theory implies. More importantly, explaining associations' normative and expressive meaning-making as indirectly strategic insulation assumes firm and industry "interests" are primordial, an assumption challenged in the studies discussed in chapter four.

4. Van Maanen and Barley, "Occupational Communities." Part of the value of Van Maanen and Barley's argument is their clear distinction between work identities associated with occupations and with organizations. Similarly, Mary Blair-Loy (*Competing Devotions*, chap. 1) analyzes gendered "work devotion schemas" and Abbott ("Sociology of Work, 322) points out that occupations involve "particular and enduring groups of people" who may form specialized organizations. See also Trice and Beyer, *Cultures of Work Organizations*, 174–225; Pettinger, "Blurred Boundaries"; Harper and Lawson, *Cultural Study of Work*; and more generally, Beamish and Biggart, "Economic Worlds of Work," and Korczynski, Hodson, and Edwards, *Social Theory at Work*. But, as Hirsch noted, research on work culture fails to ask, "how the world is experienced by persons occupying superordinate positions in organizations" ("Study of Industries," 277), like most of the association members here.

5. Van Maanen and Barley, "Occupational Communities," 290, 295; Grusky and Galescu, "Class Analyst." See also Lincoln and Guillot, "Organizational Culture."

6. Van Maanen and Barley, "Occupational Communities," 292–95, 348.

7. Ibid., 293–94, 297.

8. Ibid., 299, 302.

9. Ibid., 303.

10. Ibid., 305, 307.

11. Ibid., 331.

12. United States, Office of Management and Budget, *Industry Classification System*, 3.

13. International Concrete Repair Institute, http://www.icri.org/ (12/10/2004); Aluminum Anodizers Council, http://www.anodizing.org/ (12/9/2004); Closure Manufacturers' Association, http://www.cmadc.org/reg10reasons.tpl (12/20/2004); (brewing), Staber and Aldrich, "Trade Association Stability"; (printing), Berk and Schneiberg, "Collaborative Learning."

14. Van Maanen and Barley, "Occupational Communities," 293–94; Eliasoph and Lichterman, "Culture in Interaction," 739. On formally defined industries including numerous associations, see also Staber and Aldrich, "Trade Association Stability." On associations including different industries and the resulting difficulties of correlating industry and association change, see Aldrich and Staber, "Organizing Business Interests," 120, and chap. 4. Zuckerman and Sgourev, "Peer Capitalism," emphasize member definition of group boundaries in their study of small peer networks sampled within formally defined industries.

15. Fligstein, *Architecture of Markets*.

16. International Concrete Repair Institute, http://www.icri.org/about.asp (12/10/2004); Aluminum Anodizers Council, "Industry Leader Donn W. Sanford, CAE, 1940-2004," https://www.anodizing.org/documents.html (12/9/2004); Closure Manufacturers' Association, http://www.cmadc.org/history_cma.tpl?page=page1 and http://www.cmadc.org/regcode.tpl (12/20/2004). See also Fligstein, *Architecture of Markets*, chap. 4.

17. Aldrich and Staber, "Business Interests," 119, 121–22; Aldrich et al., "Minimalism, Mutualism, and Maturity," 235.

18. Small Publishers Association of North America, http://www.spannet.org/about%20span.htm; http://www.spannet.org/FAQ.htm (12/27/2004).

19. North American Association of Food Equipment Manufacturers, "Membership Requirements," http://www.nafem.org/about/requirements.cfm (12/22/2004); "Introduction to the Certified Foodservice Professional Program," http://www.nafem.org/cfsp/index.cfm?print=yes (12/23/2004).

20. Association for Women in Aviation Maintenance leaders and members included at least seventeen large, publicly recognizable corporate members such as United UPS, Boeing, Lockheed, Delta, and Pratt and Whitney: http://www.awam.org/leaders.htm; http://www.awam.org/memlinks.htm (12/28/2004). The

American Society for Automation in Pharmacy included not only independent and hospital pharmacies but also members from colleges, regulatory agencies, other associations, software companies, health insurance, and medical billing corporations: http://www.asapnet.org/member1.html (12/27/2004).

21. Independent Bakers Association, http://www.mindspring.com/~independent baker/ (12/9/2004); Association for Women in Aviation Maintenance, "Wellman Award to Mary Feik," http//www.awam.org/news.htm (12/28/2004); International Society of Hospitality Consultants, "Top Ten Issues 2005," 3, http://www.ishc.com .html (12/20/2004); National Association of Real Estate Brokers, http://www.nareb .com/NAREB/president_message_2.shtml (12/28/2004).

22. International Society of Certified Electronics Technicians, http://www .nastec.org/certify.html (12/21/2004); http://www.iscetstore.org/about/index.html; *ProService Magazine*, October 2004, 3, http://www.iscet.org/proservice/index.html (12/20/2004); Irrigation Association, http://www.irrigation.org/about/default.aspx? pg=default.htm&id=5 and http://www.irrigation.org/gov.default.aspx?pg=project_ EverGreen.htm&id=107 (12/30/2004); Exhibit Designers and Producers Association, "Our Industry Will Not Succumb to Terrorist Activities," http://www.edpa .com/archivelatestnews_01.html (12/22/2004), and *EDPA today*, X (3) Fall 2001, http://www.edpa.com/currentpublications.html (12/21/2004); Firestop Contractors International Association, http://www.fcia.org/articles/newsletter-03-03.htm (12/19/2004).

23. Van Maanen and Barley, "Occupational Communities," 298, 303.

24. Exhibit Designers and Producers Association, http://www.edpa.com/ membershipinfo.html (12/21/2004); EDPA.COMmunications 5 (11) November 2004, 2, http://www.edpa.com/newsletter/2004_november.html (12/22/2004); *edpa today* XII (4) Winter 2002, 4, http://www.edpa.com/currentpublications.html (12/21/2004); Closure Manufacturers' Association, http://www.cmadc.org/reg10 reasons.tpl and http://www.cmadc.org/membercma.tpl (12/20/2004). The CMA's claim about collective identity as an incentive for joining is in bold type, unlike other incentives on their list.

25. International Concrete Repair Institute, http://icri.org/membership/benefits .asp; http://www.icri.org/committees/index.asp (12/10/2004); Aluminum Anodizers Council, http://www.anodizing.org/html/regulatory_advocacy.html; http://www .anodizing.org/membership_info.html (12/9/2004); Firestop Contractors International Association, http://fcia.org/membership.htm and http://www.fcia.org/ articles/message-1-04b.htm (12/19/2004); North American Association of Food Equipment Manufacturers, *NAFEM in print* 3 (2) Summer 2004, 4, 7, http://www .nafem.org/publications/inprint (12/23/2004).

26. American Council of Life Insurance, http://www.acli.com/ACLI/Events/ Annual2003_ProgramatGlance?EventURL=ACLI%2FEvent (12/27/2004); International Concrete Repair Institute, "Northern California Chapter Newsletter," July 2003, 1, http://www.icri.org/chapters/chap_details.asp?id=NCA (12/19/2004); Fire-

stop Contractors International Association, http://www.fcia.org/articles/newsletter-
12-03.htm (12/19/2004). For another example of interactional engagement in an occupationally specific work world, see Bielby and Harrington, *Global TV*, 144–45.

27. National Electronics Service Dealers Association, "2003 NESDA Best Ideas
Contest," *ProService Magazine*, August 2003, 10, 16, http://www.iscet.org/proservice/
index.html (12/20/2004). Similarly, the Vacuum Dealers Trade Association held
"45 Tips in 45 Minutes," a "fast-paced, action packed seminar" of tips from others "just like yourself," Vacuum Dealers Trade Association, http://www.vdta.com/
LV06-Sems-Wednesday.htm (6/14/2006). See also Zuckerman and Sgourev, "Peer
Capitalism," 1344.

28. International Concrete Repair Institute, *The Aggregate*, 4th Quarter 2004,
2, http://www.icri.org/chapters/chap_details.asp?id=BWC (12/19/2004).

29. Brick Industry Association, "WSPCA Rho Max Summit Transcript March
3, 2002," 2, 5, 11, 11, 47, http://www.brick-wscpa.org/reports.htm (6/21/2006).

30. Exhibit Designers and Producers Association, http://www.edpa.com/
newsletter/2004_september.html (12/22/2004); International Concrete Repair
Institute, http://www.icri.org/chapters/topics.asp (12/10/2004), and "Northern
California Chapter Newsletter," http://icri.org/chapters/chap_details.asp?id=NCA
(12/19/2004). A quarter of focal associations had regional or local chapters or close
organizational analogues, differing widely in industry type, membership type, geographic coverage, and level of activity.

31. Exhibit Designers and Producers Association, *edpa today* XIII (3) Fall 2003,
4, http://www.edpa.com/currentpublications.html (12/21/2004); EDPA.COMmu-
nications October 2004, 1, http://www.edpa.com/newsletter/2004_October.html
(12/22/2004); North American Association of Food Equipment Manufacturers,
NAFEM in print 3 (3) Fall 2004, 16, http://www.nafem.org/publications/inprint/
(12/23/2004).

32. North American Association of Food Equipment Manufacturers, *NAFEM
in print* 3 (4) Winter 2004, 11, http://www.nafem.org/publications/inprint/ (12/
23/2004); International Society of Certified Electronics Technicians, *ProService
Magazine*, August 2002, 12, http://www.iscet.org/proservice/index.html (12/20/
2004).

33. Firestop Contractors International Association, http://www.fcia.org/articles/
newsletter-12-03.htm (12/19/2004); "President's Message," International Concrete
Repair Institute, Northern California Chapter Newsletter, July 2003, 2, http://www
.icri.org/chapters/chap_details.asp?id=NCA (12/19/2004). Other examples ranged
from commentary on ancient "quake proof cement" in an Istanbul cathedral to
fears for the US space program.

34. Aluminum Anodizers Council, Sanford obituary, http://www.anodizing
.org/documents.html (12/9/2004); Firestop Contractors International Association,
http://www.fcia.org/articles/message-1-04a.htm (12/19/2004); Vacuum Dealers
Trade Association, *Central Vac Professional*, November 2005, http://www.vdta

.com/NOV05/CV-toc-Nov05.htm and *Floor Care Professional*, March 2006, http://
www.vdta.com/MAR06/fc-toc-mar06.htm (6/14/2006). On collective identity and
imagined past and future, see Anderson, *Imagined Communities*, and Spillman,
Nation and Commemoration.

35. Automotive Lift Institute, http://www.autolift.org/history.html (6/14/2006);
Exhibit Designers and Producers Association, EDPA.COMmunications 5 (2) February 2004, 1, http://www.edpa.com/newsletter/nl_february_04.html (12/22/2004).
The actuaries tell another postwar founding story: "the roots of the conference of
Consulting Actuaries can be traced to the Fall of 1949, when six consulting actuaries met for lunch in Chicago to discuss the need for an organization to set standards and exchange information." Conference of Consulting Actuaries, http://www
.ccactuaries.org/about/history.html (12/27/2004).

36. International Society of Certified Electronics Technicians, *ProService Magazine*, October 2004, 17, http://www.iscet.org/proservice/index.html (12/20/2004).

37. International Concrete Repair Institute, http://www.icri.org/chapters/chap-
details.asp?id=FWC (12/19/2004); International Society of Certified Electronics
Technicians, http://www.iscet.org/store/index.html (12/20/2004); Firestop Contractors International Association, http://www.fcia.org/merchandise.htm (12/19/2004);
National Association of Real Estate Brokers, http://www.nareb.com/events/realtist%
20store.shtml (12/28/2004); Association for Women in Aviation Maintenance,
http://www.awam.org/products_details.htm (12/28/2004).

38. DiMaggio and Powell, "Iron Cage Revisited," 71–72; Zuckerman and
Sgourev, "Peer Capitalism," 1346. For economic sociology's analysis of norma-
tive and status orders, see, for example, Podolny, "Status-Based Model"; Dobbin,
"Cultural Models of Organization"; DiMaggio, "Culture and Economy"; Abolafia,
Making Markets; Porac, Ventresca, and Mishina, "Interorganizational Cognition";
Phillips and Zuckerman, "Middle-Status Conformity"; and Strang and Macy, "Ex-
cellence."

39. International Society of Certified Electronics Technicians, http://www.nastec
.org/certify.html (12/21/2004); North American Association of Food Equipment
Manufacturers, "Certified Foodservice Professional Program," http://www.nafem
.org/cfsp/index.cfm?print=yes (12/23/2004); Conference of Consulting Actuaries,
membership application, http://www.ccactuaries.org/membership/ce-requirement
.html (12/27/2004). For an overview of work on economic standards, see Biggart
and Beamish, "Economic Sociology of Convention," 453–54.

40. Abbott, "Professional Ethics," 871; cf. Lentz and Tschirgi, "Ethical Content."

41. Irrigation Association, "Certified Irrigation Contractor Program Application," http://www.irrigation.org/certification/default.aspx?pg=programs.htm&
id=93 (12/31/2004). On ethics and intraprofessional status, see Abbott, "Professional Ethics," 871; he also argues that status threats generate attention to formal
ethics (875–77; see also Lentz and Tschirgi, "Ethical Content," 387). The observation that most focal associations with ethics codes were in sales or service supports

this argument, which is also consistent with more general neoinstitutionalist claims about normative isomorphism, especially the less cognitive formulations in Meyer and Rowan, "Institutionalized Organizations."

42. North American Association of Food Equipment Manufacturers, http://www.nafem.org/serv_mgr/ten_commandments.cfm?print=yes and http://www.nafem.org/serv_mgr/ethics.cfm?pring=yes (12/23/2004.) The Food Equipment Manufacturers compare service managers to more standard professions when discussing ethics; see chapter seven.

43. Vacuum Dealers Trade Association, http://www.vdta.com/code_of_ethics.htm (6/14/2006); Equipment Service Association, http://www.2esa.org/bylaws.html (12/28/2004).

44. International Society of Hospitality Consultants, http://www.ishc.com/what_is/about.cfm (9/29/2007); Conference of Consulting Actuaries, http://www.ccactuaries.org/about/bylaws.html (12/27/2004); North American Association of Food Equipment Manufacturers, http://www.nafem.org/cfsp/ (12/22/2004).

45. Abbott, "Professional Ethics," 859–60. Thanks to Lisa McCormick for this point: see also chapter eight on differences between mundane and heightened discourse.

46. Two exceptions oriented awards to external audiences. The Brick Industry Association organized an extensive awards program for clients—"Brick in Architecture," etc., http://www.bia.org/html_public/winners_commercial.htm, 6/21/2006. The Envelope Manufacturers' Association was developing an awards program for suppliers' innovations (*on paper* VI [II] Second Quarter 2004, 4, http://www.emafoundation.org/index.v3page?p=47767 [12/28/2004]).

47. International Concrete Repair Institute, http://www.icri.org/news/2004projectawards.asp and http://www.icri.org/nes/2003awards.asp; *Concrete Connection*, June 2003, 5, http://icri.org/chapters/chap_details.asp?id=CAR (12/19/2004).

48. Irrigation Association, http://www.irrigation.org/about/default.aspx?pg=committees.htm&id=20 and http://www.irrigation.org/press_releases/default.aspex?r=1&pg=2004-11-23-2.htm (12/31/2004); Exhibit Designers and Producers Association, *edpa today* XII (3) Fall 2002, 4, http://www.edpa.com/currentpublications.html (12/21/2004).

49. Aluminum Anodizers Council, http://www.anodizing.org/html/awards_of_excellence.html (12/9/2004); Conference of Consulting Actuaries, http://ccactuaries.org/news/hansonprize.html (12/27/2004).

50. Exhibit Designers and Producers Association, *edpa today* XII (4) Winter 2002, 3, http://www.edpa.com/currentpublications.html and http://www.edpa.com/awardsprogram.html (12/21/2004). The International Society of Hospitality Consultants resembles the Exhibition Designers and Producers in its emphasis on rewarding "industry" contributions; for instance, their Pioneer Award recognizes "involvement in the industry, contribution to the industry and personal attributes and qualities," http:www.ishc.com/new.html (12/20/2004).

51. North American Association of Food Equipment Manufacturers, "2003 Year End Report," 11, http://www.icex.com/nafmeiq/default.asp?12=home&id=guest (12/23/2004); Association for Women in Aviation Maintenance, http://www.awam .org/Awards.htm (12/28/2004); Irrigation Association, http://www.irrigation.org/ news/default.aspx?pg=press_releases_2004.htm&id=146 (12/31/2004); International Society of Certified Electronics Technicians, *ProService Magazine*, August 2002, 3, http://www.iscet.org/proservice/index.html (12/20/2004).

52. International Society of Certified Electronics Technicians, *ProService Magazine*, August 2002, 9, http://www.iscet.org/proservice/index.html (12/20/2004); Vacuum Dealers Trade Association, Hall of Fame nomination form, http://www .vdta.com/membership_info.htm (6/14/2006).

53. International Concrete Repair Institute, http://www.icri.org/membership/ benefits.asp (12/10/2004); Closure Manufacturers' Association, http://www.cmadc .org/reg10reasons.tpl (12/20/2004).

54. Independent Bakers Association, http://www.mindspring.com/ ~independentbaker/id1.html (12/9/2004); Mulch and Soil Council, *News, Notes & Quotes*, November 2005, 6, http://www.mulchandsoilcouncil.org/Inforesource/ Industry/News.html (7/6/2006); International Concrete Repair Institute, *Chicago Tri-States Chapter Newsletter*, vol. 22, March 2004, 2, http://www.icri.org/chapters/ chap_details.asp?id=TRI (12/19/2004).

55. Association for Women in Aviation Maintenance, http://www.awam.org/ scholarships%202001.htm (12/28/2004); International Concrete Repair Institute, http://www.icri.org/supporting.index.asp (12/10/2004), and *The Aggregate*, 4th Quarter 2004, 8–9, http://www.icri.org/chapters/chap_details.asp?id=BWC (12/19/2004). Recognition of industry standing from sponsorships was evident in many other ways, too, such as in acknowledgments for a Firestop Contractors' conference, http://www.fcia.org/articles/newsletter.htm (12/19/2004), and for donors to the Irrigation Association's Education Foundation, http://www.iaef.org/donors .htm (12/31/2004).

56. International Concrete Repair Institute, http://www.icri.org/membership/ benefits.asp (12/10/2004). For the banker's "call for better acquaintance" in the previous paragraph, see Bradley, *Trade Associations*, 21–22. Abbott also suggests the work/leisure boundary is blurred, but because leisure involves productive work ("Work and Occupations," 308–9). See also chapter nine on voluntary sector features of business associations.

57. American Council of Life Insurance, http://www.acli.com/ACLI/Events/ CatalogSearch.htm?EventType=past (12/23/2004); North American Association of Food Equipment Manufacturers, events, http://www.nafem.org/events (12/22/2004); Association for Women in Aviation Maintenance, http://awam.org/ events.htm (12/28/2004). For some large associations with trade shows, meetings are an important revenue source. The Food Equipment Manufacturers reported that their major biennial trade show generated 86 percent of revenue but only 74

percent of expenses, http://www.icex.com/nafemiq/default.asp?12=home&id=guest (12/22/2004).

58. Pellet Fuels Institute, http://www.pelletheat.org/3/2004conference/index .html (12/23/2004); American Society for Automation in Pharmacy, http://www .asapnet.org/meeting.html (12/27/2004); Vacuum Dealers Trade Association, http://www.vdta.com/LV06-Sems-Thursday.htm (6/14/2006). See also Zuckerman and Sgourev, "Peer Capitalism, 1337–38.

59. Pellet Fuels Institute, http://www.pelletheat.org/3/2004conference/index .html (12/23/2004); American Society for Automation in Pharmacy, http://www .asapnet.org/meeting.html (12/27/2004); Vacuum Dealers Trade Association, http://www.vdta.com/MB06.htm (6/14/2006); Irrigation Association, 25th International Irrigation Show Attendee Brochure, http://www.irrigation.org/show/default .aspx?pg=attend.htm&id=14 (12/30/2004); Conference of Consulting Actuaries, http://www.ccactuaries.org/news/index.html (12/27/2004).

60. Independent Bakers Association, http://www.mindspring.com/~independent baker/id1.html (12/9/2004); Firestop Contractors International Association, http:// www.fcia.org/articles/newsletter-08-04.htm and http://www.fcia.org/articles/news letter-07093.htm (12/19/2004); Exhibit Designers and Producers Association, *edpa today* XII (3) Fall 2002, 1, http://www.edpa.com/currentpublications.html (12/21/2004).

61. North American Association of Food Equipment Manufacturers, http:www .nafem.org/events/NAFEM-MAFSI/2005/index.cfm (12/22/2004).

62. North American Association of Food Equipment Manufacturers, http://www .thenafemshow.org/registration_05.cfm (12/22/2004); Mulch and Soil Council, http:// www.mulchandsoilcouncil.org/About/CouncilGoals.html (7/3/2006); Exhibit Designers and Producers Association, http://www.edpa.com/04meetings/networking .html (12/21/2004); Firestop Contractors International Association, http://www .fcia.org/articles/newsletter-05-03.htm (12/19/2004). On socializing as business, see Darr, "Gifting Practices," and on peer socializing, see Zuckerman and Sgourev, "Peer Capitalism," 1350–51.

63. International Concrete Repair Institute, New England Chapter Newsletter, February 2004, 2, and October 2003, 2, http://www.icri.org/chapters/chap_details .asp?id=NE (12/19/2004).

64. Aluminum Anodizers Council, http://www.anodizing.org/anodizing_conference .html and http://www.anodizing.org/html/body_networking.html (12/9/2004); Conference of Consulting Actuaries, http://www.ccactuaries.org/news/index.html (12/ 27/2004); Exhibit Designers and Producers Association, http://www.edpa.com/ 04meetings/networking.html and *edpa today* XIII (3) Fall 2003, 2, http://www.edpa .com/currentpublications.html (12/21/2004).

65. International Society of Certified Electronics Technicians / National Electronics Service Dealers Association, *ProService Magazine*, August 2004, 14, and August 2003, 14, 17, http://www.iscet.org/proservice/index.html (12/20/2004).

66. Firestop Contractors International Association, http://www.fcia.org/articles/newsletter-08-04.htm; http://www.fcia.org.articles/newsletter.htm; http://www.fcia.org/articles/newsletter-08-03.htm; http://www.fcia.org/articles/newsletter-12-03.htm; http://www.fcia.org/articles/newsletter-10-01.htm (12/19/2004).

67. International Concrete Repair Institute, Rocky Mountains Chapter Newsletter, May 2003, 4, http://www.icri.org/chapters/chap_details.asp?id=RM (12/19/2004); Association for Women in Aviation Maintenance, http://www.awam.org/forum_and_chatroom.htm (12/28/2004) and http://www.awam.org/Chapters.dir/Vannuys_Chapter.htm (12/30/2004).

68. International Concrete Repair Institute, Western New York Chapter, *Repair Reporter*, November 2004, http://www.icri.org/chapters/chap_details.asp?id=WNY (12/19/2004).

69. Charles Potts, "The 'Every-Day' Rituals of Sociability," personal communication, March 28, 2006; Craig, "Sociability," 8. See also Simmel, "Sociability"; Aldrich, "Sociable Organization"; Arnirou, "Sociality"; Hansen, *Social Time*, 7; and Berezin, "Festival State," 72–73. Of course, some latent functions of such nonstrategic sociability might include (in unpredictable circumstances) motivation (Zuckerman and Sgourev, "Peer Capitalism"), or more generally, "economic confidence" (see DiMaggio, "Animal Spirits").

70. International Concrete Repair Institute, http://www.icrisd.org/nes.php and http://www.icrisd.org/events.php?&Eid=60 (12/19/2004); *The Aggregate*, 4th Quarter 2004, 8, http://www.icri.org/chapters/chap_details.asp?id=BWC (12/19/2004); Firestop Contractors International Association, http://www.fcia.org/articles/lasvegas/index.htm and http://www.fcia.org/articles/nashville/index.htm (12/20/2004); United Lightning Protection Association, *More Static*, Spring 2004, 2, http://www.ulpa.org/tech.htm (12/28/2004).

71. MAFSI Conference brochure, http://www.nafem.org/events/NAFEM-MAFSI/2005/index.cfm (12/22/2004); Irrigation Association Educational Foundation, http://www.irrigation.org/about/defaoult.aspx?pg=iaef.htm&id=25 (12/30/2004).

72. Exhibit Designers and Producers Association, http://www.edpa.com/article_rsmgc9th.html; *edpa today* XII (3), Fall 2002, 1, 6, http://www.edpa.com/current publications.html (12/21/2004); http://www.edpa.com/newsletter/nl_august_02.html (12/22/2004), and http://www.edpa.com/article_rsmgc_triumph.html (12/21/2004).

73. Exhibit Designers and Producers Association, http://www.edpa.com/newsletter/2004_september.html (12/22/2004), and http://www.edpa.com/article_five-imaginative.html (12/21/2004).

74. International Concrete Repair Institute, scholarship application, http://www.icri.org/chapters/chap_details.asp?id=RM 12/19/2004, and Northern California Chapter Newsletter, November 2003, http://www.icri.org/chapters/chap_details.asp?id=NCA (12/19/2004); North American Association of Food Equipment Manufacturers, Year End Report, http://www.icex.com/nafemiq/default.asp?12=home&id=guest (12/22/2004); Irrigation Association, http://www.irrigation.org/

about/default.aspx?pg=iaef.htm&id=25 (12/30/2004); International Society of Certified Electronics Technicians, *ProService Magazine*, April 2004, 7, http://www .iscet.org/proservice/index.html (12/20/2004). A few small-business groups, like the Vacuum Dealers Trade Association, understood their occupational community to contribute to intergenerational transmission in even more direct terms, sponsoring scholarships for dependants of members and their employees.

75. International Telecommunications Society, *Communications and Strategies* #54, Second Quarter 2004, n.p., http://www.itsworld.org/its.htm (12/28/2004); Mulch and Soil Council, *News, Notes & Quotes*, February 2005, 3, http://www .mulchandsoilcouncil.org/Inforesorce/Industry/News.html (7/6/2006); Exhibit Designers and Producers Association, EDPA.COMmunications 4 (3) March 2003, 4, http://www.edpa.com/newsletter/nl_march_03.html (12/21/2004).

76. International Society of Certified Electronics Technicians, *ProService Magazine*, June 2004, 15, 6, http://www.iscet.org/proservice/index.html (12/20/2004).

77. International Concrete Repair Institute, Northern California Chapter Newsletter, May 2003, 4, and November 2003, 4, http://www.icri.org/chapters/chap_details.asp?id=NCA (12/19/2004); International Society of Certified Electronics Technicians, *ProService Magazine*, August 2003, 5, http://www.iscet.org/proservice/index.html (12/20/2004).

78. Friedland and Robertson, "Beyond the Marketplace," 26. As I point out in chapter ten and elsewhere, articulation of solidarity in normative and expressive discourse will vary according to setting, experience, and such. This is entirely predictable if we are analyzing a vocabulary of motive or cultural repertoire. If some association members are oriented to the strategic pursuit of particularistic interests in joining associations—which will vary—they will likely learn to adjust their perceptions and language to the more solidaristic norms of groups they join. This socialization process is suggested by attempts to reconcile particularistic and collective interests discussed at length in chapter six, where I note that members are sometimes called to "give something back to the industry" or "ensure a healthy and strong industry for everyone." The socialization process is also suggested by rare comments like this exhibit designer commenting on a very successful charity golf tournament:

> Our first year was a smashing success . . . I think we had 80 golfers! It was like Christmas day during wartime—both sides would come out of their respective foxholes, share a meal together and then go back to their foxholes . . . seeing labor companies side by side, shops side by side, shipping companies side by side, was an immensely gratifying sight.

But members will vary in the extent to which they see their association membership as self-interested (see also chapter six), and in any case not all associations are composed of members who are direct competitors. Exhibit Designers and

Producers Association, *edpa today* XIII (2) Summer 2003, 1, http://www.edpa.com/currentpublications.html (12/21/2004). For another similar example, see Mack, *Executive's Handbook*, 4.

79. The norm that economic action is necessarily and universally oriented to the competitive pursuit of particularistic interests is obviously destructive to competitors in industry fields and to labor. It is also more broadly destructive in the many ways identified by critics of capitalism over generations. I am not retracing these well-known arguments in this analysis, but I take them as given. Here, I challenge as unrealistic as well as normatively dangerous the assumption of critics as well as supporters of capitalism that production and exchange are necessarily oriented by competitive self-interest; see chapter ten.

Chapter Six

1. Small Publishers Association of North America, http://www.spannet.org; *SPAN Connection*, July 2004, http://www.spannet.org/view%20-july_2004.htm; *SPAN Connection*, June 2004, http://www.spannet.org/view_june_2004.htm; http://www.spannet.org/benefits_update.htm; http://www.spannet.org/kudos.htm (12/27/2004). Russell Faeges made significant contributions to work on this chapter.

2. Pellet Fuels Institute, http://www.pelletheat.org/3/2004conference/index.html (12/23/3004); North American Association of Food Equipment Manufacturers, http://www.nafem.org/events/NAFEM-MAFSI/2005/index (12/22/2004).

3. See chapter one on economic sociologists' challenge to the neoclassical stereotype of anonymous, uncooperative market action. To take one example, Fligstein makes cultural politics crucial in accounts of industry stability and change; as I show later in this chapter, associations can be important sites of such cultural politics and can work explicitly to coordinate the stability he sees as firms' main goal. I am adding to this and other accounts of economic sociologists by focusing on the cultural conditions for collective coordination of market action.

4. Williamson, "Nexus of Treaties," "Comparative Economic Organization," "Transaction Cost Economics"; Nee, "New Institutionalism"; Fligstein and Freeland, "Corporate Organization"; Granovetter, "Business Groups," 459; Macher and Richman, "Transaction Cost Economics." As Williamson notes, "although the study of economic organization deals principally with markets and market mechanisms, it is haunted by a troublesome fact: a great deal of economic activity takes place within firms" ("Comparative Economic Organization," 270). Business historian Alfred Chandler showed how large firms came to dominate many industries from the late nineteenth century, because, he argued, they were more efficient than the "heroic" small businessman of early capitalist lore given American legal conditions and national markets (*Scale and Scope*, chap. 2; "Large Industrial Corporation," chap. 2; see also chapter two herein). Whether transactions are organized in

markets, according to the price mechanism, or within firms, relying on administrative control, depends upon factors like their frequency, uncertainty, and asset specificity, which affect the difficulty and uncertainty of making transactions and thus the costs of "doing business." If transactions are costly in these ways, they might be internalized in firm "hierarchies"—where information may be thicker and more authoritatively controlled—rather than externalized in markets.

5. Williamson, "Comparative Economic Organization," 281–83; Schneider and Doner, "New Institutional Economics," 40. Granovetter has also suggested that the cooperation of firms in "business groups" raises theoretical questions analogous to Ronald Coase's about the cooperation of individual economic actors, but he rejects transaction cost theory's solution to that problem. He asks "why it is that in every known capitalist economy, firms do not conduct business as isolated units, but rather form cooperative relations with other firms, with legal and social boundaries of variable clarity around such relations" (Granovetter, "Business Groups," 453–54). Just as Coase suggested firms are illogical in an economic picture of isolated individual actors, Granovetter suggests that business groups could pose a problem for an economic picture counterpoising markets and firm hierarchy.

6. For economic sociologists drawing on transaction cost principles, see Schneiberg, "Governance by Associations," 95; Pfeffer and Salancik, *Resource Dependence*, 179; and Weeden, "Social Closure and Earnings Inequality," 65–69. Schneiberg and Hollingsworth claim that "structural features connected with the development of the association [like information gathering, and full-time staff] constitute devices whereby members manage interfirm agreements, subject intraindustry transactions to administrative controls, and regulate directly the exchange relations they have created amongst themselves" ("Transaction Cost Economics," 332). Thus many economic sociologists investigating business associations seem to concede that the day-to-day operations of business associations are largely focused and organized around intraindustry economic goals associated with improving the efficiency and performance of their members on the market.

7. Mack, *Government Relations,* 168–69, 170. One rare exception to the scholarly silence on association memberships' effects for members is Geletkanycz and Hambrick's finding that top executives' active participation in business association leadership had no significant effect on a firm's average return on assets ("Strategic Choice and Performance," 672). See also the discussion on lack of evidence of collective "industry" benefits, below.

8. Granovetter, "Economic Action and Social Structure," 503. Similarly, as chapter eight shows, associations' political effects are an article of faith for sociologists.

9. For Granovetter's critique of Williamson's argument about markets and hierarchies, see "Embeddedness"; for his critique of transaction cost accounts of business groups, see "Business Groups," 454–55, 457–58 and "Social Organization," 431–38. His scope limitation excluding associations seems to derive more from the principles of transaction cost economics than from economic

sociology; but see "Theoretical Agenda" for a discussion that includes broader cultural and institutional considerations. For related arguments, see Hollingsworth and Boyer, *Contemporary Capitalism*, chap. 1, and Roy, "Functional and Historical Logics."

10. Schneiberg and Hollingsworth, "Transaction Cost Economics," 340. Even price competition may be addressed indirectly: after the 1890 antitrust restrictions, some associations "sought to stabilize competitive relations indirectly by eliminating 'waste,' by restricting competition to price, and by providing firms with the data needed to make independently price and output decisions that would reduce overcapacity and the likelihood of price warfare" (Schneiberg and Hollingsworth, "Transaction Cost Economics, 337; Warner and Martin, "Big Trade and Business Associations," 320; McGahan, "Cooperation in Prices"). And as we saw in chapter two, even pre-Sherman associations provided channels of technical and market information, capacities that expanded after 1890, as in the 1920s and 1940s, when associations developed mass promotional campaigns and market research, effectively organizing cooperative marketing for industries.

11. Berk and Schneiberg, "Collaborative Learning"; (interorganizational networks), Powell, Koput, and Smith-Doerr, "Interorganizational Collaboration"; DiMaggio, *Changing Economic Organization*, 211–15; (encouraging consortia), Barnett, Mischke, and Ocasio, "Collective Strategies, 345; (technical committees), Rosenkopf, Meitiu, and George, "Technical Committee Activity"; (standardization committees), Farrell and Saloner, "Coordination through Committees."

Scholars interested in how far American associations might provide significant economic benefits for either their individual members or for the "industry" have collectively faced serious conceptual and empirical hurdles. First, antitrust law prevents associations from substantiating vague claims about economic returns. Second, Berk and Schneiberg's approach is difficult to generalize because it assumes a clear correspondence between industries and associations, which is rarely the case (see also Geletkanycz and Hambrick, "External Ties"). Third, until now there has been no general picture of the association population with which to assess the representativeness of industries or associations studied, a lack this study helps fill. To solve these problems requires better theoretical understanding of associations and a more comprehensive picture of the association population.

I conclude here that in any given case at any time the concrete economic benefits provided by associations or association membership are marginal at best, and they cannot explain the enormous variety and energy we see in association activity, but that associations will occasionally have successes and long-term strategic impacts.

12. Lounsbury, Ventresca, and Hirsch, "U.S. Recycling"; Chung, "Networks and Governance"; Yakubovich, Granovetter, and McGuire, "Electric Charges"; Boczkowski, *Digitizing the News*, 25; Thornton, "Logics of Control," 296; Schneiberg and Clemens, "Institutional Analysis," 203; Baker, Faulkner, and Fisher, "In-

terorganizational Market Relationships," 151; Yates, *Information Age*; Bielby and Harrington, *Global TV*, 9; Miller, *Reluctant Capitalists*, 169; and Weber, Heinze, and DeSoucy, "Mobilizing Codes," 547.

13. Hirsch, "Culture Industry Systems."

14. Firestop Contractors International Association, http://www.fcia.org/committehome.php?selection=Education (12/19/2004).

15. Conference of Consulting Actuaries, http://www.ccactuaries.org/about/strategicplan.html (12/27/2004); Aluminum Anodizers Council, http://www.anodizing.org/membership_info.html (12/9/2004); Mulch and Soil Council, http://www.mulchandsoilcouncil.org/Meetings/workshops.html (7/6/2006); Brick Industry Association, http://www.BIA,bia.org/otc/brickotc.htm and http://www.bia.org/html/brickuniversity.html (6/21/2006). All these educational activities occur in associations that would not be coded as educationally oriented in the more superficial census data.

16. Hunt, *Encyclopedia of Associations*, 370; "AWAM Annual Honors," press release 4/14/2004, http://www.awam.org/news/htm (12/28/2004); International Concrete Repair Institute, http://www.icri.org/membership/benefits.asp (12/21/2004); Irrigation Association, http://www.irrigation.org/about/default.aspx?pg=default.htm&id=5 (12/30/2004); Vacuum Dealers Trade Association, http://www.vdta.com/magazines.htm (6/14/2006).

17. North American Association of Food Equipment Manufacturers, magazine description, http://www.nafem.org/resources/inprint (12/23/2004); International Concrete Repair Institute, http://www.icri.org/chapters/chap_details.asp?id=WNY (12/19/2004); Brick Industry Association, http://www.bia.org/omnisam/product_custom/search.cfm (6/21/2006); Aluminum Anodizers Council, http://www.anodizing.org/membership_info.html (12/9/2004).

18. International Society of Hospitality Consultants, http://www.ishc.com/feature_articles.html (12/20/2004); North American Association of Food Equipment Manufacturers, http://www.nafem.org/secure/forms/study_form.cfm; *NAFEM in print* 2 (1) Spring 2003, 16–20, http://www.nafem.org/publications/inprint/; http://www.nafem.org/about/committee_descriptions.cfm; http://www.nafem.org/about/benefits.cfm (12/22/2004); Mulch and Soil Council, *News, Notes & Quotes*, August 2005, 3, http://www.mulchandsoilcouncil.org/Inforesorce/Industry/News.html (7/6/2006).

19. Firestop Contractors International Association, http://www.fcia.org/articles/message-1-04.htm (12/19/2004). Commensuration "structures attention and judgment concerning matters for which a large and diffuse body of information is available," creates a means of transferring information to external audiences, and subsequently orients action reactively and as "self-fulfilling prophecy" (Michael Strand, "Commensuration," personal communication, June 18, 2008); see also Biggart and Beamish, "Convention," 453–54; Espeland, "Commensuration and Cognition"; Espeland and Stevens, "Commensuration"; Espeland and Sauder,

"Rankings and Reactivity"; Zerubavel, "Lumping and Splitting"). Standards and accreditation are also important ways associations create constitutive cognitive infrastructure for their members' economic action; see chapter four.

20. Mulch and Soil Council, http://www.mulchandsoilcouncil.org/ProductCert/ Industry/Why.html (7/6/2006). The Irrigation Association's development of their Smart Water Application Technology (SWAT) Protocols was similarly complex, involving work by several committees with other associations and with ASTM; see http://www.irrigation.org/gov/default.aspx?pg=inudstry_standards.htm&id=174 [sic] (12/31/2004). Important independent standards organizations frequently encountered in the association world include the American National Standards Institute (ANSI), Underwriters' Laboratory (UL), and ASTM. American associations occasionally refer to the International Organization for Standardization (ISO), too, but ISO seems much less important than the plethora of national-level standards bodies. The Irrigation Association had an ISO connection: http://www .irrigation.org/gov/default.aspx?pg=industry_standards.htm&id=174 (12/31/2004).

21. Irrigation Association, http://www.irrigation.org/about/default.apx?pg= certification_board.htm&id=24 (12/30/2004). The International Society of Certified Electronics Technicians, a division of the National Electronics Service Dealers Association, claims 46,000 "Certified Electronic Technicians" since 1965, a large administrative apparatus, extensive development of course materials and examinations in multiple subfields at several levels, a program for examination administrators, a continuing education program, and student chapters; http://www.nastec.org/ and http://www.iscetstore.org/about/index.html (12/20/2004).

22. Around 54 percent of associations reporting interests in standards, research, and sharing information were larger than median size. The impact of size was more marked for associations interested in education, 64 percent of which were larger than median size, whereas only 40 percent of associations without interest in education were larger. The small associations, with fewer than a hundred members, were much less likely to have an interest in education.

Two-thirds, or 68 percent, of associations below median size expressed at least one internally oriented goal, compared to 82 percent of associations above median size, and compared to the population average of 74 percent (Pearson chi-square = 0.000). The difference was most marked among associations of fewer than a hundred members.

23. The difference between associations reporting committees compared to those not doing so in the degree to which they expressed all four "internally oriented" goals—research, standards, education, and sharing information—was pronounced. For example, 18 percent of associations without committees reported an interest in standards and accreditation compared to 33 percent of those reporting committees; for research goals the relevant contrast is 28 and 48 percent; for education goals the contrast is 34 and 51 percent; and for sharing information, 35 compared to 41 percent. Associations reporting state and regional groups and other

affiliations were similarly much more likely to report an interest in standards and accreditation, research, and education; however, there was no correlation between reports of groups and affiliations and an interest in "sharing information" (Pearson chi-square = 0.101).

24. Around a third of associations reporting fewer than four staff members also reported an interest in research, compared to just over half of associations with over thirteen staff. An interest in education was reported by around a third of associations with one or two staff, by 43 percent of associations with three staff, and by just over half of associations with more than thirteen staff.

Of more interest here is the absence of any correlation between staff numbers and an interest in standards and accreditation and sharing information. For standards and accreditation, 23 percent of associations reporting only one staff member compared to 28 percent of associations reporting thirteen or more staff expressed an interest (Pearson chi-square = 0.222). For sharing information, 35 percent of associations with one staff member and 39 percent of associations with thirteen or more reported this goal (Pearson chi-square = 0.162). Since interests in standards and accreditation and sharing information do not seem to call for more staff, though one might expect otherwise, this suggests that these interests are related more to shared occupational community than the interested pursuit of market growth or professional interests in expanding jurisdictions.

25. See chapter eight; headquarters located in Washington, DC, and its environs is taken here as a simple, though imperfect, indicator of an orientation to political influence. The same proportions of associations reporting an interest in sharing information and in research were located in DC (29 percent and 30 percent respectively) as in the general population (29.5 percent). The absence of any statistical difference is unusual given the size of the data set. Associations reporting an interest in standards and accreditation were slightly less likely to be located in the DC area: 26 percent compared to 29.5 percent in the general population (Pearson chi-square = 0.003). Associations reporting an interest in education were also slightly less likely to be located in the DC area; 27 percent (Pearson chi-square = 0.005).

Of that minority of associations located in the DC area, 70 percent expressed some internally oriented goal, compared to 75 percent of those outside DC, and compared to the population average of 74 percent (Pearson chi-square = 0.001).

26. Twenty-one percent of associations composed of firm members reported an interest in standards and accreditation, compared to 26 percent of associations composed of individuals and 28 percent of associations with both types of members. For "sharing information," the proportions were 34 percent, 39 percent, and 47 percent for firms, individuals, and both respectively. The correlation between individual membership and education goals was particularly strong: whereas 33 percent of associations composed of firms expressed such an interest, 48 percent of associations composed of individuals did so, as did 48 percent of associations composed of both.

The tendency for associations of individual members to express intraindustry goals was reversed for research. For research, the respective proportions were 37 percent of associations composed of firms compared to 33 percent of associations of individuals and 39 percent of associations composed of both. However, this relation between firm membership and research goals was weaker than usual for this data (Pearson chi-square = 0.018).

Note again that associations composed of both firms and individuals made up 16 percent of the population. As seen here, they take on features of both other types of association.

Sixty-nine percent of associations composed of firms expressed at least one internally oriented goal, compared to 78 percent of associations composed of individuals, 82 percent of those with both individual and firm members, and the population average of 73.6 percent (Pearson chi-square = 0.000).

27. Forty-five percent of associations formed in the 1970s and 1980s expressed an orientation to "sharing information," a notably higher rate than the overall population average at 37.5 percent and also compared to the average for the 1950s and 1960s of 36 percent. The pattern was similar, although not as marked, for associations indicating an orientation to education: for the 1970s–1980s an average of 45 percent were coded for this goal, compared to the population average of 40.5 percent and an average of 40 percent for the preceding decades. There was no such increase in the proportion oriented to standardization and certification or to research.

28. Fifty-seven percent of associations primarily located in agriculture and related industries and 42 percent of associations primarily located in manufacturing articulated research-related goals; these proportions were well above the population average of 35 percent. But associations in agriculture and manufacturing fell well below population averages of 40.5 percent for education and 37 percent for sharing information, and were among the lowest of all sectors for these goals. Only 25 percent of associations primarily located in agriculture and 33 percent of associations primarily located in manufacturing were interested in education. Twenty-nine percent of associations in agriculture, and 31 percent of associations in manufacturing articulated sharing information as a goal.

Associations primarily located in the administrative support services sector, and in professional, scientific, and technical services, were close to the population average in their expression of research goals, with both at 35 percent. For educational goals, they exceeded the population average of 40.5 percent notably, with 55 percent of administrative support associations and 53 percent of professional and technical associations expressing educational goals. For standardization and certification, 30 percent of administrative support associations and 27 percent of professional associations articulated this goal, somewhat above the population average of 24 percent. For sharing information, professional and technical associations were at 45 percent, and administrative support associations at 42 percent, compared to a population average of 37.5 percent.

29. Future research should investigate further the organizational or sectoral features encouraging particular intra-"industry" strategies of action, but we need to understand business associations better before examining their minor variations.

30. These questions become more puzzling because associations are weakly differentiated in their attachment to particular strategies of action. If strategic effects in different "industry" contexts were transparent, there should be stronger and more systematic differences between the strategies adopted in very different arenas of economic action. Manufacturers such as the Irrigators would have little need for an education program as extensive as the Actuaries, and the Hospitality Consultants would not do as much research as the Aluminum Anodizers. As objectively defined economic demands of different "industries" or sectors would differ substantially in systematic ways, so too would the collective strategies of action they adopt to address them.

31. Irrigation Association, http://www.irrigation.org/membership/default .aspx?pg=benefits.htm&id=128 (12/30/2004).

32. Vacuum Dealers Trade Association, http://www.vdta.com/membership_info .htm; http://www.vdta.com/conventions1.htm; http://www.vdta.com/LV06-Sems Wednesday.html (6/14/2006); North American Association of Food Equipment Manufacturers, "*NAFEM in print* Media Kit," http://www.nafem.org/resources/ inprint/ (12/23/2004). The Envelope Manufacturers' Association also touted education as a direct economic benefit to members and offered a variety of technical and management workshops and publications and in-plant training for both management and employees (http://www.envelope.org [12/28/2004]). Others claiming information as a direct member benefit included the Closure Manufacturers, the National Association of Real Estate Brokers, the Envelope Manufacturers, and the Exhibit Designers and Producers.

33. North American Association of Food Equipment Manufacturers, *NAFEM in print*, Spring 2003, 5, http://www.nafem.org/publications/inprint (12/23/2004); Mulch and Soil Council, http://www.mulchandsoilcouncil.org/ProductCert/Industry/ Why.html (7/6/2006). Other associations sometimes tying research to members' particularistic interests were the Exhibit Designers and the Brick Industry Association. The Firestop Contractors and the Irrigation Association sometimes labeled their standards and accreditation programs as member benefits, though more often as a professional matter; see chapter seven.

34. North American Association of Food Equipment Manufacturers, http:// www.thenafemshow.org/show05/ and http://www.thenafemshow.org/exhibitor.cfm (12/22/2004). The Irrigators and the Vacuum Dealers were others who highlighted strategic benefits of networking.

35. International Concrete Repair Institute, http://www.icri.org/advertising 2004/membermarket.asp and *Newsletter*, May 2003, Issue 1, 3, http://www.icri .org/chapters/chap_details.asp?id=RM (12/19/2004). The Aluminum Anodizers, the Brick Industry Association, and the Exhibit Designers were other groups that pitched particularistic benefits of collective marketing. On associations and

collective marketing, see Weeden, "Social Closure and Earnings Inequality," 67. Occasionally, too, associations that do employee training—such as the Food Equipment Manufacturers and the Brick Industry Association—list employment openings.

36. Vacuum Dealers Trade Association, http://www.vdta.com/benefits.htm (6/14/2006); Hunt, *Encyclopedia of Associations*, 380; Equipment Service Association, http://www.2esa.org/credit_card.htm (12/28/2004). See Knoke, *Organizing for Collective Action*, 128–29, on the relative insignificance of utilitarian incentives like discounts to members of the associations he studied.

37. See chapter one on the cultural grammar of capitalist business in different sorts of settings like local business groups, and chapter nine on business associations compared to other nonprofit groups.

38. Closure Manufacturers' Association, http://www.cmadc.org/reg10reasons .tpl (12/20/2004); Brick Industry Association, http://www.bia.org/html/BENEFITS .html (6/21/2006). The Closure Manufacturers' claim about collective identity is emphasized in bold type.

39. Brick Industry Association, http://www.bia.org/html/BENEFITS.html (6/21/2008); International Concrete Repair Institute, http://www.icri.org/chapters/chap_details.asp?id=LAO and Rocky Mountain Chapter *Newsletter*, May 2003, Issue 1, 4, http://icri.org/chapters/chap_details.asp?id=RM (12/19/2004); Envelope Manufacturers' Association, http://www.emafoundation.org/inde .v3page?p=4694 and "Prospectus 2003," 2, http://www.emafoundation.org/index .v.3page?p=4694 (12/28/2004); Exhibit Designers and Producers Association, "Message from the President," http://www.edpa.com/edpaataglance.html (12/21/2004); North American Association of Food Equipment Manufacturers, http://www .nafem.org/about/mission.cfm (12/22/2004); Irrigation Association, http://www .irrigation.org/about/default.aspx?pg=awards.htm&id=126, and http://www.irrigation .org/about/default.aspx?pg=default.htm&id=5 (12/30/2004); United Lightning Protection Association, http://www.ulpa.org/info.htm (12/28/2004); Pellet Fuels Institute, http://www.pelletheat.org/3/institute/index.html (12/23/2004); Mulch and Soil Council, http://www.mulchandsoilcouncil.org/About/CouncilGoals.html (7/3/2006) and *News, Notes & Quotes*, February 2006, 1, http://www.mulchandsoilcouncil.org/ Inforesorce/Industry/News.html (7/6/2006); Vacuum Dealers Trade Association, http://www.vdta.com/membership_info.htm (6/14/2006).

40. North American Association of Food Equipment Manufacturers, *NAFEM in print* 3 (2) Summer 2004, 5, http://www.nafem.org/publications/ inprint/ (12/23/2004).

41. Aluminum Anodizers Council, http://www.anodizing.org/membership_info .html (12/9/2004); Independent Bakers Association, http://www.mindspring.com/ ~independentbaker/ (12/9/2004); Exhibit Designers and Producers Association, http://www.edpa.com/newsletter/2004_september.html (12/22/2004) and *EDPA today* XI (2) Spring 2002, 2, http://www.edpa.com (12/21/2004); Closure Manufacturers' Association, http://www.cmadc.org/membercma.tpl (12/20/2004).

42. Brick Industry Association, http://www.bia.org/html/BENEFITS
.html (6/21/2006); Closure Manufacturers' Association, http://www.cmadc.org/
reg10reasons.tpl (12/20/2004); International Concrete Repair Institute, http://www
.icri.org/committees/index.asp (12/10/2004); Exhibit Designers and Producers Association, EDPA.COMmunications 5 (8) August 2004, 3, http://www.edpa.com/
newsletter/2004_august.html (12/22/2004); International Concrete Repair Institute, http://www.icri.org/membership/benefits.asp (12/10/2004); Firestop Contractors International Association, http://www.fcia.org/membership.htm and fcia.
org/articles/newsletter-01-03.htm (12/19/2004).

43. Willer, "Collective Action Problem."

44. Knoke, *Organizing for Collective Action*, 139, 140. Mack reports a 1980s
survey suggesting executives were "complimentary if not effusive" about their associations, with three-quarters reporting moderate or great benefits for their companies (*Executive's Handbook*, 220–21). Elsewhere, he develops a guide, "Evaluating
Association Effectiveness," because he believes many executives confuse business
associations with "care-giving" nonprofits and should be more rigorous in assessing benefits for their companies. His exhortations suggest that few members really
think consistently about particularistic benefits of membership (*Practice of Government Relations*, 168–76).

45. Olson, *Collective Action.*

46. Schlozman and Tierney, *Organized Interests*, 123–31; Schneider and Doner,
"New Institutional Economics"; Jordan and Halperin, "Olson Triumphant?"; and
Roy and Parker-Gwin, "Logics of Collective Action," 207, who distinguish between
organizations which are "mere aggregations of individuals" and corporate bodies.
Jordan and Halperin's case study suggests that Olsonian selective incentives may
matter at some times in a group's history, but not others; that smaller business may
be more susceptible to Olsonian incentives, as seems to be confirmed by the exceptional cases here; and that organization leaders sometimes use Olsonian ideas in a
sort of performative application of theory.

47. Leblebici and Salancik, "Rules of Organizing," 317; Staber, "Governance
Structure," 287; see also Knoke, *Organizing for Collective Action*, 32, 107–22;
Knoke and Adams, "Incentive System," 305. Aldrich et al. ("Minimalism, Mutualism, and Maturity," 236) find, against Olsonian assumptions, that internal diversity
was an advantage for associations.

48. On associations' reliance on member contributions, see also Staber, "Governance Structure, 285; Knoke, *Organizing for Collective Action*, 94; Jordan and
Halperin, "Olson Triumphant?," 446.

49. National Electronics Service Dealers Association, http://www.iscetstore
.org/join/index.html (12/20/2004); North American Association of Food Equipment Manufacturers, http://www.nafem.org/about/benefits.cfm (12/22/2004).

50. Smelser, *Problematics*, 33, and "Rational and Ambivalent."

51. See Swidler, "Culture in Action," on culture in settled and unsettled times.
Campbell ("Role of Ideas") makes a similar distinction. Of course, the routine

practices and languages of collective coordination we have seen above are some-times settled regimes resulting from earlier "unsettled times."

52. International Telecommunications Society, http://www.itsworld.org/about/ ab01.htm; "Bylaws," http://www.itsworld.org/about/ab3.htm; membership infor-mation, http://www.itsworld.org/about/ab8_1.htm (12/28/2004); *Interconnect* 1 (8) April 2006, 4, http://www.itsworld.org/newsletter/news0.htm (7/11/2006).

53. American Society for Automation in Pharmacy, http://www.asapnet.org/ meeting1.html; http://www.asapnet.org/presentations.html (12/27/2004).

54. National Electronics Service Dealers Association, *ProService Magazine*, December 2002, 12, http://www.iscet.org/proservice/index.html (12/20/2004).

55. While the focus here is intraindustry politics, industry coordination and industry collective identities may also be politically charged by larger political environments. As Schneiberg and Hollingsworth point out, such *political* condi-tions as hostile publics, organized consumers, or state autonomy may intrinsically shape "economic" interests in association, as we see when the Automotive Lift Institute cited the 1995 National Technology Transfer and Advancement Act as encouraging privatization of standard setting (chapter three); and when the Brick Industry Association links its serious technical research program to its participa-tion in code hearings (chapter eight). Although this general point can only be fully demonstrated in detailed case studies, the history of American business associa-tions outlined in chapter two reminds us that national politics set the parameters of their activities, and we will see in chapter eight many instances of associations re-sponding to or attempting to shape the influence of external audiences on their col-lective economic interests. See Schneiberg and Hollingsworth, "Transaction Cost Economics"; Schneiberg, "Governance by Association," 93; and on the relation among market coordination, political contexts, and cultural institutions, Bartley and Schneiberg, "Rationality and Institutional Contingency."

56. Independent Bakers Association, http://www.mindspring.com/independent baker/ (12/9/2004); International Concrete Repair Institute, http://www.icri.org/ about.asp (12/10/2004).

57. Exhibit Designers and Producers Association, *EDPA.COMmunications* 5 (3) March 2004, n.p., http://www.edpa.com.newsletter/nl_march_04.html; *EDPA. COMmunications* 5(8) August 2004, n.p., http://www.edpa.com/newsletter/2004_ august.htm; *EDPA today* X (3) Fall 2001, 1 (12/22/2004).

58. Mulch and Soil Council, *News, Notes & Quotes*, June 2005, 2; November 2005, 1, http://www.mulchandsoilcouncil.org/Inforesorce/Industry/News.html (7/6/2006); (associate membership), http://www.mulchandsoilcouncil.org/About/ HowToJoin.html (7/6/2006).

59. National Electronics Service Dealers Association, *ProService Magazine*, April 2002, 11, http://www.iscet.org/proservice/index.html (12/20/2004).

60. National Electronics Service Dealers Association, *ProService Magazine*, August 2003, 16; December 2003, 10; February 2004, 10; http://www.iscet.org/ proservice/index.html (12/20/2004).

61. National Electronics Service Dealers Association, *ProService Magazine*, December 2002, 12, 14; August 2003, 21; October 2003, 8, http://www.iscet.org/proservice/index.html (12/20/2004).

62. International Society of Hospitality Consultants, "Top Ten Global Issues," http://www.ishc.com/new.html; they also made available a member's article on "Savvy Arbitrators, Mediators Needed to Settle Hotel Disputes," http://www.ishc .com/articles.html (12/20/2004). Exhibit Designers and Producers Association; (current employment law), "Annual Meeting 2004 Educational Program Highlights," http://www.edpa.com/04meetings/educational.html (12/21/2004); National Electronics Service Dealers Association, "Best Ideas Contest," *ProService Magazine*, October 2004, 5–6, http://www.iscet.org/proservice/inde.html (12/20/2004); Independent Bakers Association, http://www.mindspring.com/~independentbaker/ (12/9/2004).

63. Staber and Aldrich, "Trade Association Stability"; Aldrich et al., "Minimalism, Mutualism, and Maturity." See also chapter two.

64. Haydu, "Business Citizenship." Students of labor politics in firms and labor politics in conventional political institutions typically ignore another important level of collective action by business in association. If labor had a stronger voice, and better ways of improving labor conditions became institutionalized in the United States, associations would need to be recognized, addressed, and integrated into new strategies of collective action by workers. But languages structured in terms of binary oppositions and heightened boundaries between capital and labor would make little cultural sense in this context; rather, collective identities based on shared technical orientations are more important.

65. North American Association of Food Equipment Manufacturers, http://www .nafem.org/about/mission (12/22/2004); Hunt, *Encyclopedia of Associations*, 163.

66. North American Association of Food Equipment Manufacturers; (XML standards), http://www.nafem.org/resources/nafem_xml.cfm and "Recommended Guidelines," http://www.nafem.org/resources/ (12/22/2004); "Specifier ID System," http://www.nafem.org/resources/sis_faq.cfm (12/23/2004); participating firms estimated from listing, http://www.nafem.org/neo_apps/sis_db/; bar code and product id projects, http://www.nafem.org/resources/bar_code.cfm (12/22/2004); "efficiency," http://www.nafem.org/resources/fegbarcodefaq/cfm (12/23/2004).

67. North American Association of Food Equipment Manufacturers, "Groundbreaking Foodservice E-Commerce Group Formed," http://www.nafem.org/resources/_feg/. The numerous other associations involved included, for instance, the Food Equipment Distributors Association and the Commercial Food Equipment Service Association. Other comment in "Introductory information, draft of XML Standards," http://www.nafem.org/resources/intro_info.cfm; benefits and challenges, "Charting the Course for Our Industry's Future," http://www.nafem .org/resources/_feg (12/23/2004).

68. North American Association of Food Equipment Manufacturers, http:// www.nafem.org/resources/pod (12/22/2004).

69. North American Association of Food Equipment Manufacturers, *NAFEM in print*, Spring 2004, 4, http://www.nafem.org/publications/inprint/ (12/23/2004); *Annual Report* 2003, http://www.icex.com/nafemiq/default.asp?12=home&id=guest (12/22/2004).

70. North American Association of Food Equipment Manufacturers, *Annual Report* 2003, http://www.icex.com/nafemiq/default.asp?12=home&id=guest (12/22/2004).

71. North American Association of Food Equipment Manufacturers, http://www.nafem.org/resources/DataProtocol/History/ (12/23/2004). Although powerful downstream customers instigated the Data Protocol, NAFEM argued somewhat less convincingly that manufacturer members would benefit too.

72. North American Association of Food Equipment Manufacturers, http://www.nafem.org/resources/pod (12/22/2004).

73. International Concrete Repair Institute, http://www.icri.org/about.asp (12/10/2004).

Chapter Seven

1. North American Association of Food Equipment Manufacturers, http://www.nafem.org/serv_mgr/ethics.cfm?pring=yes (12/23/2004).

2. Larson, *Professionalism*, xi. Michael Strand contributed significantly to the research and analysis in this section.

3. Abbott, *Professions*, 16, 84; see also Friedson, *Professionalism*; Evetts, "Professionalism"; Macdonald, "Professional Work."

4. R. H. Tawney, quoted in Larson, "Disciplinary Cultures," 327; Abbott, "Work and Occupations," 323. On professions as disinterested, see also Parsons, "Professions"; Goode, "Community within Community"; Schudson, "Trouble with Experts"; and Friedson, *Professionalism*. On professions and social closure, see also Lo, "Prodigal Daughters"; Larson, "Disciplinary Cultures," 321, and *Professionalism*.

5. Rueschemeyer, *Division of Labor*, 119; Larson, "Disciplinary Cultures," 318.

6. Abbott, *Professions*, 69–79.

7. Larson, "Disciplinary Cultures," 320; Abbott, *Professionalism*, 8–9. See also Evetts, "Professionalism."

8. Abbott, *Professions*, 19.

9. Larson, "Disciplinary Cultures," 321, see also *Professionalism*, chap. 5, and Friedson, *Professionalism*. For Larson, "the old and proven strategy of seeking ordered jurisdictions or sheltered markets . . . does not seem able to insure stable elite status for even the length of one professional's worklife [*sic*]" ("Disciplinary Cultures, 329). And for Abbot, there is "increasing involvement of the . . .

commercial sector in professional life" ("Work and Occupations, 323). Implicitly, here, theorists of professions draw an important conceptual distinction between professional and market-oriented action, while the empirical connection of the two thickens.

In addition to ambiguities of the relation between professions and markets, Lo suggests another limitation of viewing abstract knowledge claims as characteristic of standard professions. She argues that the modernity and rationality of professional expertise is often combined with less abstract, more traditional racial, ethnic, and gendered forms of knowledge and collective identity claims ("Prodigal Daughters," 392–98), emphasizing the intersection of the modern and premodern, or primordial, in professional distinction.

10. Thornton, "Craft Industry," 83; Lounsbury, "Competing Logics," 303; Bielby and Harrington, *Global TV*, 32; Khurana, *Business Schools*.

11. Grusky and Galescu, "Is Durkheim a Class Analyst?" In their view, conventional class analysis has been limited by a focus on nominal categories that ignore the technical division of labor and neglect "Durkheim's fundamental insight that the site of production is structured around rather smaller functional niches (i.e., occupations)" (323). Focusing on labor, rather than capital, they suggest that while Durkheim's predictions about the modern division of labor must be qualified in several ways, his central ideas could help improve class analysis: "In many ways the labor market has become increasingly 'Durkheimianized,' not merely because industrial conflict at the macro-class level has come to be regulated and contained, but also because occupational groupings have emerged as the elementary building blocks of modern and postmodern labor markets" (331–32). "Class-like" behavior emerges at the level of the occupation. Identities are routinely understood and discussed in terms of occupation rather than class; social closure processes (such as credentialing) are occupation-based rather than generically class-based; more generally so too is collective action in pursuit of economic interests. Although the aggregated class category they are challenging here is "labor," their "realist" account of class in terms of occupations could apply equally to the category of "capital." Capitalists too may pursue interests in control over work, not only—or perhaps even primarily—the narrower economic interests in profitability and efficiency.

12. Abbott, *Professions*, 3, 342n47; Thornton, "Craft Industry." See also Larson, "Disciplinary Cultures," 321, and *Professionalism*; and Friedson, *Professionalism*. Abbott suggests a long-standing historical tension between the "professional" and the "commercial." Commodification of "esoteric professional activity" threatens professional jurisdiction, and "the gradual loss of administrative work to commercial organizations" and "the increasing dominance of physical capital in professional life" further undermine "professional" control of work life. He recognizes that jurisdictional claims about professional work may be made in the market (as in advertising) but suggests that this is not the main arena for the pursuit of professional distinction (*Professions*, 146, 155, 64–65). Evetts, in "Occupational Change,"

suggests a broader view of professions not as distinct groups but as languages expressing normative and ideological aspects of work worlds and facilitating occupational change. The argument and evidence here provides further support for her perspective (see also Van Maanen and Barley, "Occupational Communities").

13. Associational certification and accreditation cannot be denied to nonmembers, foreign competitors, or those unable to pay fees (Lynn and McKeown, *Organizing Business*, 48). Business associations thus differ from bar associations, which achieved monopoly control over legal credentialing. The impact of a strict criterion of legal monopoly on the concept of professions is clear in this contrast, but so too are its ambiguities: see Aldrich et al., "Minimalism, Mutualism, and Maturity."

14. International Concrete Repair Institute, http://www.icri.org/membership/index.asp; http://www.icri.org/membership/benefits.asp (12/10/2004); http://www.icri.org/chapters/chap_details.asp?id=CAR (12/19/2004); Association for Women in Aviation Maintenance, press release, June 2 2004, http://www.awam.org/news.htm and http://www.awam.org/awards.htm (12/28/2004); Vacuum Dealers Trade Association, http://www.vdta.com/conventions.htm (6/14/2006). Abbott discusses professional status claims about disinterested service, but pays less attention to the commitment to specialized technical knowledge they evoke (*Professions*, 867).

15. Exhibit Designers and Producers Association, *EDPA today* X (2) Spring 2001, 3, http://www.edpa.com/currentpublications.html (12/21/2004); EDPA. COMmunications 5 (9) September 2004, 4, http://www.edpa.com/newsletter/2004_september.html (12/22/2004). The International Concrete Repair Institute also demonstrated this sort of "weak" professionalization.

16. Larson, "Disciplinary Cultures," 322; Saguy, *Sexual Harassment*, 119. Sennett also reflects on this vernacular sense of a normatively independent work sphere in *The Craftsman*.

17. International Telecommunications Society; (membership, goals), http://www.itsworld.org/about/abo_1.htm; (typical issues), http://www.itsworld.org/about/ab)_1b.htm (12/28/2004); *Interconnect: Publication of the International Telecommunications Society* 8 (1) April 2006, 11, http://www.itsworld.org/newsletter/newso.htm; (book) http://www.itsworld.org/about/ab6.htm (7/11/2006).

18. International Society of Hospitality Consultants ("professional society," "public and private"), ISHC's TOP TEN ISSUES & CHALLENGERS [*sic*], 2004, 1, http://www.ishc.com/members_news.html; ("recognized as leaders," "Lodging Investment Summit"), "TOP TEN ISSUES 2005," http://www.ishc.com/new.html; (Indoor Waterpark), http://www.ishc.com/articles.html; ("regularly researches," "peer reviewed"), "Order Form for Cap Ex Report 2000," http://www.ishc.com/feature_articles.html; ("New Europe and the Hotel Industry"), http://www.ishc.com/feature_articles.html (12/20/2004).

19. Irrigation Association (certification numbers, categories, and testing locations), *Certification News*, Spring 2004, 3, 5, 9, http://www.irrigation.org/certification/default.asp?pg=news.htm&id=92; (courses and programs), http://www.irrigation

.org/certifiction/default.aspx?pg=programs.htm&id=93; (renewals and auditing), http://www.irrigation.org/certification/default.aspx?pg=renewal.htm&id= 94; (course materials), http://www.irrigation.org/certification/default.aspx?pg= references.htm&id=95; (other associations), "IA Education: Course Sponsor Program for Associations," http://www.irrigation.org ("Education"); (professional language), http://www.irrigation.org/about/default.aspx?pg=default.htm&id=5 and http://www.irrigation.org/membership/default.aspx?pg=benefits.htm&id=128 (12/30/2004).

20. North American Association of Food Equipment Manufacturers ("foodservice professionals"), http://www.nafem.org (12/22/2004); ("enhance professionalism") in "An Introduction to the Certified Foodservice Professional Program," http://www.nafem.org/cfsp/index.cfm?print=yes; ("all individuals"), http://www.nafem.org/events/es/who.cfm (12/23/2004); (CFSP numbers) in "2003 Annual Report," http://www.ice.com/nafemiq/default.asp?12=home&id=guest; (board members), http://www.nafem.org/about/boardroster.cfm (12/22/2004); (CFSP Program, "stay connected"), http://www.nafem.org/cfsp/index.cfm?print=yes; ("CFSP Code of Ethics"), http://www.nafem.org/cfsp/inde.cfm?print=yes (12/23/2004).

21. North American Association of Food Equipment Manufacturers ("association within, "enhancing and advancing"), http://www.nafem.org/serv_mgr/ what_is_it.cfm; ("no legal requirement"), http://www.nafem.org/serv_mgr/ten_ commandments.cfm?print=yes; ("Code of Ethics for the Service Manager"), http://www.nafem.org/serv_mgr/ethics.cfm?print=yes (12/23/2004).

22. North American Association of Real Estate Brokers ("all professionals"), http://www.nareb.com/NAREB/benefits.shtml; ("professional development"), http://www.nareb.com.affiliates.sales_division.shtml; ("make a professional commitment"), http://www.nareb.com/events/WCN2.shtml; (property managers group certification), http://www.rembi.org/about.htm; (appraisers group), http://www.nareb.com/affiliates/society_appraisers.shtml; ("dedicated to promoting"), http://www.nsrea.org/; ("three top appraisal organizations"), http://www.nsrea.org/ presprofile.htm; (three levels of accreditation), http://www.nsrea.org/designations .htm (12/28/2004).

23. Conference of Consulting Actuaries (members), Hunt, *Encyclopedia of Associations*, 228; (mission), http://www.ccactuaries.org/about/mission.html; (committees), http://www.ccactuaries.org/about/committees/; (objectives), http://www.ccactuaries.org/about/bylaws.html (12/27/2004). Minor CCA activities included awards, mentoring program, clearinghouse for peer review, directory of members, model engagement letter guidelines, and endorsed "errors and omissions" insurance.

24. Conference of Consulting Actuaries; (member employment), http://www.ccactuaries.org/membership/membersurveyform.html; ("highly proficient"), http://www.ccactuaries.org/about/bylaws.html; (Standards of Practice), http://www.ccactuaries.org/resourcecenter/standards/asops.html; (board and actuarial

organizations), http://www.ccactuaries.org/resourcecenter/standards/dailyguide
.html (12/27/2004).

25. Conference of Consulting Actuaries, http://www.ccactuaries.org/events/
ea2005/programschedule/ (12/27/2004).

26. Conference of Consulting Actuaries, http://www.ccactuaries.org/events/
ea2005/programschedule/ and http://www.ccatuaries.org/events/seminars/
(12/27/2007).

27. Abbott, *Professions*, 315.

28. Firestop Contractors International Association (code proposal discussion),
http://www.fcia.org/articles/message-5-02.htm (12/19/2004). The Irrigation Association lists five states with licensing requirements, but disparages the requirements as weaker than their own elaborate certification (http://www.irrigation.org/
certification/default.aspx?pg=faq.htm&id=90 [12/30/2004]). The National Association of Real Estate Brokers links to an off-site commercial service offering courses
with "content coverage guided by state licensing requirements," http://www.career
webschool.com/about-us.html/?erid=641 (12/28/2004.) See also the Electronics
Technicians, below.

29. Firestop Contractors International Association, http://www.fcia.org/articles/
newsletter-09-04.htm and http://www.fcia.org/articles/newsletter-02-04.htm (12/19/
2004).

30. Abbott, *Professions*, xii, 112.

31. International Concrete Repair Institute; ("frustration"), http://www.icri
.org/about.asp (12/10/2004); ("competitive advantage"), "ICRI Rocky Mountain Chapter Newsletter," May 2003, no. 1, 3, http://www.icri.org/chapters/chap_
details.asp?id=RM (12/19/2004); Irrigation Association ("nationally recognized
certification"), http://www.irrigation.org/membership/default.asp?pg=benefits
.aspx?pg=benefits.htm&id=128; ("How to Spot"), http://www.irrigation.org/Rsrcs/
default.aspx?pg=consumer_info.htm&id=140 (12/30/2004).

32. Abbott, *Professions*, 9.

33. International Society of Hospitality Consultants, "ISHC's TOP TEN IS-
SUES," 1, http://www.ishc.com/members_news.html; (ordering Cap Ex Report),
http://www.ishc.com/feature_articles.html; (water parks), http://www.ishc.com/
articles.html (12/20/2004); International Concrete Repair Institute ("valuable insight"), http://www.icri.org/chapters/chap_details.asp?id=MIN (12/19/2004).

34. Irrigation Association (standard text), http://www.irrigation.org/bookstore/
default.aspx?pg=bookstore.ascx&id=49&bkid=64; (various certification programs),
http://www.irrigation.org/certification/default.aspx?pg=cic_program.htm&id=
122 (12/31/2004).

35. See chapter eight on the Irrigation Association's claims to environmental
expertise and its dispute with landscape architects over some Vermont licensing
legislation. On librarians and computer technicians, see Abbott, *Professions*, 224.

36. All quotations in preceding paragraphs at North American Association

of Food Equipment Manufacturers, "An Introduction to the Certified Foodservice Professional Program," "CFSP Personal Data Form and Application," and "Equipment and Supplies Overview Seminar," and other documents, http://www.nafem.org/cfsp/index.cfm?print=yes (12/22/2004).

37. International Society of Certified Electronics Technicians, "About ISCET," http://www.iscetstore.org/about/index.html (12/20/2004).

38. Ibid.; (levels of accreditation and other activities), http://www.iscetstore.org/certification/index.html (12/20/2004).

39. International Society of Certified Electronics Technicians (gatekeeper), (http://www.iscet.org/certification/fccquick.html (12/20/2004).

40. National Electronics Service Dealers Association ("best ways"), *ProService Magazine*, April 2004, 9, http://www.iscet.org/proservice/index.html (12/20/2004); ("NASTeC Certification"), http://www.nastec.org/certify.html (12/21/2004); ("perceived professionalism" and "professional colleagues"), *ProService Magazine*, April 2002, 11, http://www.iscet.org/proservice/index.html (2/20/2004).

41. International Society of Certified Electronics Technicians, Study Guide topics in catalog, iscetore/org/store/index.html (12/20/2004).

42. International Society of Certified Electronics Technicians (magazine topics and "Why Certification?—Again!"), *ProService Magazine*, October 2004; ("Facing New Technologies"), *ProService Magazine*, December 2003, 10, http://www.iscet.org/proservice/index.html (12/20/2004).

43. Van Maanen and Barley, "Occupational Communities," 309, 311 (see also Evetts, "Professionalism"). Flyvbjerg, in *Making Social Science Matter*, develops a strong theoretical basis for distinguishing abstract, codified and practical, context-based knowledge, but mistakenly assumes that they are not usually mixed (see also Spillman, "Causal Reasoning"). Friedson (*Professionalism*, 24–35, chap. 7) develops a nuanced overview of types of knowledge involved in work, but also contrasts abstract formal learning in professions with market-based work worlds.

44. Van Maanen and Barley argue strongly that "there are no fundamental distinctions to be found between a profession and an occupation which are inherent in the work itself" ("Occupational Communities," 318). The evidence from business associations supports this position, but I focus on the putative differentiation between professional and market orientations rather than that between professions and other occupations.

45. Typical professions and the business groups do generally differ in the relative importance of professional discourses compared to discourses about collective economic interests in the broader cultural repertoire they use to articulate the meaning of intra-"industry" strategies of action. They would also differ in the rate at which accreditation programs are institutionalized in the respective populations of the groups involved. These are differences in degree, rather than kind.

46. Larson, "Disciplinary Cultures," 321, 330.

47. Ibid., 327.

Chapter Eight

1. Hulse, "Reining in Lobbyists." Since this is a long-standing theme in American political commentary it is curious, but not surprising, that Schlozman and Tierney cite a report from the early 1980s of the very same council's gift of luxurious trips to a House committee chair (*Organized Interests*, 267).

2. Fligstein, *Architecture of Markets*, 65.

3. Schlozman and Tierney, *Organized Interests*, 34.

4. Associations expressing lobbying, public relations, or civic goals comprised 58 percent of the population. This is likely an overestimate (see chapter nine on public relations). As a loose comparison, 74 percent of associations expressed at least one intraindustry goal. However, see also chapter three, note 52.

5. Aldrich et al., "Minimalism, Mutualism, and Maturity," 227; Warner and Martin, "Big Trade and Business Associations," 340.

6. Coleman, *Business and Politics*, 47–65; Laumann and Knoke, *Organizational State*, 6–8. Berg and Zald ("Business and Society," 137, 121) and Smith (*American Business*) both challenge standard assumptions and emphasize instead how business mobilizes public opinion.

7. Sabel, "Learning by Monitoring," 149; Streeck and Schmitter, "Community, Market, State," 10; Coleman, "Associational Governance," 147; Lynn and McKeown, *Organizing Business*, 130–31. See also Schmitter and Streeck, "Business Interests," and Grant, *Business Interests*.

8. Staber and Aldrich, "Trade Association Stability," 175; Lynn and McKeown, *Organizing Business*, 82–83; Schlozman and Tierney, *Organized Interests*, 335n32. See also Coleman, *Business and Politics*, 77; Lindberg and Campbell, "Economic Activity," 380; Hollingsworth and Lindberg, "Governance of the American Economy"; Streeck and Schmitter, "Community, Market, State," 19; Schneiberg, "Governance by Associations"; Schneiberg and Hollingsworth, "Transaction Cost Economics," 337–39; and Gao, "Associational Order." Schmitter and Streeck provide a comprehensive theoretical overview in "Business Interests."

9. Domhoff, *Power Elite*, 266–67; Lynn and McKeown, *Organizing Business*, 81–82; Mizruchi, "American Corporate Elite"; Laumann and Knoke, *Organizational State*, 386; Levitan and Cooper, *Business Lobbies*; Berry, *Interest Group Society*; Akard, "Corporate Mobilization"; Business Roundtable, http://www.businessroundtable.org/; National Association of Manufacturers, http://www.nam.org/ (6/23/2011); Morgenson, "Total Pay"; New York Times, "Appointed Hobblers of Government." See also Young ("Small Business Identity") on how historical context influences the organization of small business interests.

10. Burstein, "Policy Domains," 345.

11. If peak associations are disconnected from "industry"-specific associations, this may give them more license to speak in the name of business without "corporatist" accountability. See also Young, "Small Business Identity."

12. Laumann and Knoke, *Organizational State*, 381; Galambos, "Trade Association Movement," 130; Lindberg, Campbell, and Hollingsworth, "Economic Governance," 27; Walker, "Privatizing Participation," 100. In contrast, Yamazaki and Miyamoto (*Trade Associations*, 306) suggest the American political environment discourages association action. For other comments on the supposed "advocacy explosion," see Berry, *Interest Group Society*; Knoke, *Organizing for Collective Action*, 187–95; Burstein, "Policy Domains," 332, 334, 343; Lynn and McKeown, *Organizing Business*, 102–4; Levitan and Cooper, *Business Lobbies*, 50–52; and Schlozman and Tierney, *Organized Interests*, 75–82, 152–57, 387–98. Skocpol summarizes specifics of the "advocacy explosion" thesis for post–civil rights and "public interest" groups ("Membership to Advocacy, 131–32). Schlozman and Tierney find that the percentage of organized groups representing business interests in Washington increased even controlling for parallel increase of public interest groups. However, Tichenor and Harris argue that "advocacy explosion" claims ignore the importance of interest groups in earlier periods: see "Organized Interests" and "Interest Group Politics." See also chapter three, note 12, for reasons to think claims about a direct "advocacy explosion" of business associations are overstated. But as chapter nine shows (notes 14, 58), business associations' interest in participation in the *public sphere* did increase after the 1960s, if not their participation in conventional national politics. For a nineteenth-century example of associations' local political influence, see Kaufman, "Municipal Social Spending." On the origins of "interest group politics," see Clemens, *People's Lobby*.

13. Laumann and Knoke, *Organizational State*, 10. On features of policy domains, see ibid., 375–77, 379, 386, 393–95; Burstein, "Policy Domains," 330; and Knoke, *Organizing for Collective Action*, 188.

14. Schlozman and Tierney, *Organized Interests*, 277 (cf. 39–46, 82–85). Burstein ("Policy Domains," 341–42) analyzes factors like cost/benefit concentration that might affect the composition and typical strategies of different policy domains. See also Coleman, *Business and Politics*, 67–77.

15. Laumann and Knoke, *Organizational State*, 104–5, 377, 106. Strong evidence suggests that firms are more important than associations for business interests in Washington (Hart, "'Business' Is Not an Interest Group," 47; Hansen, Mitchell, and Drope, "Corporate Activity"; Hansen and Mitchell, "Corporate Political Activity"; cf. Schlozman and Tierney, *Organized Interests*, 82, 49–50).

16. Laumann and Knoke, *Organizational State*, 284, 15; Burstein, "Policy Domains."

17. On associational strategies in different political arenas, see Schlozman and Tierney, *Organized Interests*, especially chap. 7.

18. Biggart, *Charismatic Capitalism*, 27–40; Domhoff, *Power Elite*, 234; Levitan and Cooper, *Business Lobbies*, 70, 92; Schlozman and Tierney, *Organized Interests*, 339, 41, 194, 219, 229.

19. See chapter two, and Pearce, *Trade Association Survey*, for 1938 findings remarkably similar to those here, emphasizing the stability of the population.

20. Warner and Martin, "Big Trade and Business Associations," 340–42. They found agriculture associations to be much more integrated with the state than others, further inflating overall sample averages. See note 28 below.

21. Knoke, *Collective Action*, 80, 197–99; Schlozman and Tierney, *Organized Interests*.

22. The hypothetical consequences of small size are ambiguous, but I lean to the conclusion that small size is more likely to weaken than strengthen associations' political action. Large memberships seem important because they provide more resources and legitimize political demands (Schlozman and Tierney, *Organized Interests*, 101–2, 123–28) but could create more organizational problems and "free riders" (Olson, *Collective Action*; see also chapter six).

23. Warner and Martin, *Big Trade and Business Associations*, 335. They do not indicate whether they included surrounding Virginia and Maryland suburbs, or whether it would have been appropriate to do so at the time.

24. In the DC area, 52.5 percent of associations were less than median size, compared to 49 percent outside DC (Pearson chi-square = 0.04).

25. Of associations composed of firms, 37 percent were located in the DC area, compared to 20 percent of associations composed of individuals and 31 percent of those including both firms and individuals.

26. Of those associations reporting any staff, 69 percent of associations in the DC area reported four or more staff, compared to 52 percent of associations elsewhere. Forty-three percent reported committees, and such, compared to 34 percent of those outside the DC area.

27. Regardless of whether or not they were located in the DC area, just over a quarter of associations (27 and 28 percent respectively) reported affiliate groups.

28. Sectors ranking above the population average of 29.5 percent in DC included, most notably, transportation (54.5 percent), health (39 percent), finance (37 percent), and utilities (36.5 percent). Associations in agriculture (15 percent) and in "arts, entertainment, and recreation" (11 percent) were much less likely to be found in the DC area than other associations. Somewhat similarly, Warner and Martin found that "Transportation, Communication and Utilities" ranked highest by far in the proportion of associations with a DC location, but for them, "Finance, Insurance, and Real Estate" (13 percent) ranked lowest ("Big Trade and Business Associations," 335).

29. Associations reporting a political orientation and associations with no such interest were almost indistinguishable in size; for instance, 68 percent of associations with each orientation had fewer than a thousand members. Very small and very large associations both indicate political goals very slightly more often than the majority of associations.

30. For associations with both types of members, 29 percent indicated a political orientation. Generally speaking, associations with both types of members fell between those composed of individuals and those composed of firms on many indicators, but resembled associations composed of firms more.

31. For that minority of associations with more than twelve staff, the proportion indicating a political orientation was closer to the population average, at 28 percent. Some of the correlation between reports of organizational differentiation and political orientation may be an artifact of coding (e.g., "political affairs committee"), but the correlation is also consistent with that between staff and DC location, and with Knoke's earlier findings.

32. Of associations reporting affiliates, 27 percent indicated political orientations, and the population average was 26 percent.

33. Sectors expressing a political orientation at notably higher rates than the population average of 26 percent were transportation (45 percent), utilities (38 percent), construction (37 percent), real estate (37 percent), mining (33 percent), finance and insurance (32 percent), and manufacturing (30 percent). Associations in agriculture (15 percent) and educational services (13 percent) were much less likely to express a political orientation. With the exception of health care/social provision, and arts/entertainment/recreation, this sectoral pattern is roughly the same as that for associations with a DC location.

34. Conversely, of course, most politically active groups typically do much more than lobby.

35. Galambos, *Competition and Cooperation*, 291-92; Young, "Small Business Identity," 462.

36. For more detail on tactics of political influence among politically active associations, see also Knoke, *Organizing for Collective Action*, 193, 208; Schlozman and Tierney, *Organized Interests*, 211, 291; Mack, *Practice of Government Relations*.

37. North American Association of Food Equipment Manufacturers, http://www.nafem.org/about/committe_descriptions.cfm (12/22/2004); Hunt, *Encyclopedia of Associations*, 50, 67, 104, 163, 225, 354, 402.

38. North American Association of Food Equipment Manufacturers, http://www.nafem.org/resources/local_regulations.cfm (12/22/2004); (monitoring), National Association of Real Estate Brokers, *REMBI, Inc. Management News*, 4th Quarter 2000, 3-4, http://www.nareb.com/affiliates/REMBI.shtml (12/28/2004); Brick Industry Association, http://www.bia.org (6/14/2006) and http://www.bia.org/html/ehmain.html (6/21/2006); (compliance procedures), American Council of Life Insurance, http://www.acli.com/ACLI/Events/CatalogSearch.htm?EventType=past (12/23/2004); Closure Manufacturers' Association, http://www.cmadc.org/history_cma.tpl?page=page4 (12/20/2004); Independent Bakers Association, http://www.mindspring.com/~independentbaker/ (12/9/2004); (detailed issue updates), American Council of Life Insurance, http://www.acli.com/ACLI/Issues+nonmembers/Default.htm (12/23/2004).

39. American Council of Life Insurance; (leader), http://www.acli.com/ACLI/About+ACLI+nonmember/Frank+Keating's+Biography.htm; (senate testimony), http://www.acli.com/ACLI/Issues+nonmembers/Corporate-Owned+Life+Insurance/Default.htm; (regulatory efficiency and letters to politicians), http://www.acli.com/acli/Issues+nonmembers/Regulatory+Efficiency+and+

Modernization/ and http://www.acli.com/ACLI/Issues+nonmembers/Corporate-Owned+Life+Insurance/Default.htm (12/23/2004).

40. National Association of Real Estate Brokers; (slogan), http://www.nareb .com/NAREB/history.shtml; (Capitol Hill visit), http://www.nareb.com/NAREB/ president_message_5.shtml; (PAC and Congressional Black Caucus), http:/www .nareb.com/events/events_1.shtml (12/28/2004). American Council of Life Insurance (smaller members meeting), "Forum 500 Leadership Retreat," program, http://www .acli.com/ACLI/Events/Event+Detail.htm?cs_id=FORUM%5F2004&cs_catalog; (PAC), "ACLI PAC Appreciation Dinner," in annual conference program, http:// www.acli.com/Events/Event+Detail.htm?cs_id=Ann%5F2004&cs_catalog=Event (12/27/2004); (member mobilization), http://www.citizenaction.acli.com/ (12/23/ 2004). Independent Bakers Association (PAC), in "2005 Winter Membership Meeting," http://www.mindspring.com/~independentbaker/id1.html (12/9/2004). North American Association of Food Equipment Manufacturers (tariff letters), http://www.nafem.org/resources/gov/ww599.cfm; (calls to OSHA), http://www .nafem.org/resources/gov/stoposha.cfm (12/23/2004).

41. Laumann and Knoke, *Organizational State*; ("coordinated action"), Staber and Aldrich, "Trade Association Stability," 175. American Council of Life Insurance, "ACLI JOINS Global Industry," press release, December 9, 2004, http:// www.acli.com/ACLI/Newsroom/News+Releases/Text+Releases/NR04-067 .htm, and "Joint ACLI, AALU, NAIFA LETTERS," http:/www.acli.com/ACLI/ Issues+nonmembers/Corporate-Ownded+Life+Insurance/Default.htm (12/23/ 2004). Brick Industry Association collaborations, http://www.bia.org/html/pr1010 primer.html (6/21/2006). North American Association of Food Equipment Manu-facturers collaborations, http://www.nafem.org/resources/gov/steeltrade.cfm and http://www.nafem.org/resources/gov/steeltrade.cfm (12/23/2004). Schlozman and Tierney found that only 20 percent of the Washington lobby groups they studied devoted significant time and resources to coalitions, though all groups used them sometimes (*Organized Interests*, 48, 150–51, 280–82).

42. North American Association of Food Equipment Manufacturers, http:// www.nafem.org/resources/gov/steeltrade.cfm (12/23/2004).

43. National Association of Real Estate Brokers; (HUD), http://www.nareb .com/NAREB/president_message_6.shtml and http://www.nareb.com/events/ events_1.shtml; (memorandum of understanding), http://www.nareb.com/NAREB/ president_message4.shtml (12/28/2004); North American Association of Food Equipment Manufacturers; (EPA), *NAFEM in print* 3 (1) Spring 2004, 22–24, http://www.nafem.org/publications/ (12/22/2004); Brick Industry Association; (EPA), http://www.bia.org/html/ehsmain.html and http://www.bia.org/html/ pr.html; ("attends all code meetings"), http://www.bia.org/html/codeissues.html (6/21/2006); Envelope Manufacturers' Association, http://www.envelope.org/ index.v3;jsessionid=44igmcnu2dcqs?p=230 (12/28/2004); Closure Manufacturers' Association, http://www.cmadc.org/history_cma.tpl?page=page4 (12/20/2004).

Schlozman and Tierney show that providing technical information was much more important than direct lobbying efforts (*Organized Interests*, 263; see also 95–97, 150–51, 155, 291, 297–98, 331–35).

44. Hunt, *Encyclopedia of Associations*, 23; Irrigation Association, membership application form, http://www.irrigation.org/membership/default.aspx?pg=benefits .htm&id=128 (12/30/2004).

45. Irrigation Association, http://www.irrigation.org/about/default .aspx?pg=committees.htm&id=20 (12/31/2004). A "legislative consultant" is typically a lobbyist hired on retainer from a DC firm; see Mack, *Government Relations*, chap. 7.

46. Irrigation Association, "Government Affairs: State Relations," http://www .irrigation.org/gov/default.aspx?pg-IA_Affiliates.htm&id=114 (12/30/2004); "All Affiliates," http://www.irrigation.org/directories (6/18/06).

47. For Coleman (*Business and Politics*) and even more for governance theorists, indicators of strong policy capability that the Irrigation Association and most American associations lack include significant financial sources besides members, state privilege, vertical integration of committees, and monopoly of industry membership.

48. The Irrigation Association describes "Export Promotions" as a member benefit, and its "Irrigation Show" was part of the Department of Commerce International Buyer Program, http://www.irrigation.gov/membership (12/30/2004) and http://www.irrigation.org/press releases (12/31/2004).

49. Irrigation Association, http://www.irrigation.org/gov/default.aspx?pg= Farm_Bill.htm&id=98; http://www.irrigation.org/gov/default.aspx?pg=Farm-Ranch_ Surveh.htm &id=99; and http://www.irrigation.org/gov/default.aspx?pg=Water_ 2025.htm&id=101 (12/30/2004).

50. Irrigation Association (Memorandum of Understanding), http://www .irrigation.org/gov/default.aspx?pg=Farm_Bill.htm&id=98; (conference), http:// www.irrigation.org/gov/default.aspx?pg=ncse.htm&id=139; (EPA), http://www .irrigation.org/gov/default.aspx?pg=EPA_Labeling.htm&id=97; (turfgrass), http:// www.irrigation.org/gov/default.aspx?pg=Turfgrass_Study.htm&id=100 (12/30/2004).

51. Irrigation Association; (labeling), http://www.irrigation.org/gov/default .aspx?pg=swat_intro.htm&id=105; (Management Practices), http://www.irrigation .org/gov/default.aspx?pg=BMPs.htm&id=104; (conservation policy), http://www .irrigation.org/about/default.aspx?pg=conservation.htm&id=23; (equation), http://www.irrigation.org/gov/default.aspx?pg=ET_Connection.htm&id=103; (Project Evergreen), http://www.irrigation.org/gov/default.aspx?pg=project_Ever Green.htm&id=107 (12/30/2004).

52. Irrigation Association; (weekly report), http://www.irrigation.org/gov/ default.aspx?pg=legis_regul.ascx&id=130; (model legislation), http://www.irrigation .org/gov/default.aspx?pg=Model_Legislation.htm&id=113 (12/30/2004).

53. Swidler, "Culture in Action."

54. Cordero, Carballo, and Ossandón, "Performing Cultural Sociology," 508; Alexander, *Civil Sphere*, 105; "Central Problems"; Alexander and Smith, "American Civil Society."

55. See Alexander, *Civil Sphere*, 62 and "Central Problems," and Spillman, "Strong Program," on the methodological rationale for examining heightened contexts. Eliasoph and Lichterman ("Culture in Interaction," 745) and Swidler (*Talk of Love*, 20) are also concerned about how meaning-making works in mundane rather than heightened contexts. Unlike the focus here, their solutions call for attention to interactional context. On the sociological tendency to foreground "marked" categories, see Breckhus, "Unmarked." Other studies of American political discourse in heightened contexts include Smith, *Why War*; Jacobs, *Crisis of Civil Society*; Kane, *Irish National Identity*; and Spillman, *Nation and Commemoration*.

56. Boltanski and Thévenot, *Justification*, 105–17, 185–93, 155.

57. In heightened episodes of public debate, issue entrepreneurs can be criticized as having elevated them for irrational or deceitful reasons, but by then they have already succeeded in agenda setting. Part of what interest groups do in routine politics is try to elevate particularistic issues to the public agenda.

58. Williams, "Public Good"; cf. Boltanski and Thévenot, *Justification*, 159–64, 81. Boltanski and Thévenot's understanding of "industrial" (or functional) justifications seems to come closest to Williams's understanding of "stewardship."

59. Independent Bakers Association, http://www.mindspring.com/~independent baker/ and http://www.mindspring.com/~independentbaker/id1.html (12/09/2004).

60. North American Association of Food Equipment Manufacturers; ("voice"), http://www.nafem.org/about/benefits.cfm (12/24/2004); (steel industry), http://www.nafem.org/resources/gov/steeltrade.cfm; (OSHA), http://www.nafem.org/resources/gov/osha.cfm (12/23/2004); (tax reform), *NAFEM in print* 3 (4) Winter 2004, 10–11; "internal debate" *NAFEM in print* 3(2) Summer 2004, 9, http://www.nafem.org/publications/ (12/22/2004).

61. American Council of Life Insurance, http://www.acli.com/ACLI/About+ACLI+nonmember/Default.htm; http://www.acli.com/ACLI/DefaultINotLoggedIn.htm (12/23/2004). On the insurers' stewardship theme, see also Zelizer, "Human Values."

62. National Association of Real Estate Brokers, http://www.nareb.com/NAREB/mission.shtml and http://www.nareb.com/NAREB/history.shtml (12/28/2004).

63. Brick Industry Association, http://www.bia.org/html/ehsmain.html (6/21/2006); http://www.bia.org/html_public/2004_EHS_Winners.html; http://www.bia.org/ (6/14/2006); http://www.bia.org/planning/planning.html (6/21/2006).

64. Irrigation Association, http://www.irrigation.org/membership and http://www.irrigation.org/about (12/30/2004). "Providing a voice" is emphasized in bold type.

65. Irrigation Association, "An Overview: Turf and Landscape Irrigation Best Management Practices," http://www.irrigation.org/gov/default.aspx?pg=BMPs .htm&id=104 (1/26/2005). "Stakeholders at every level . . ." and "professionalism and expertise" are emphasized in bold type.

66. Ibid.

67. Irrigation Association, http://www.irrigation.org/gov/default.aspx?pg=Water_ Action_Guide.htm&id=108 (12/30/2004). See also Schlozman and Tierney (*Organized Interests*, 144–45) for similar examples of interest groups educating members in political strategy.

68. Irrigation Association, http://www.irrigation.org/gov/default.aspx?pg= Water_Action_Guide.htm&id=108 (12/30/2004); Alexander and Smith, "American Civil Society."

69. Irrigation Association, *Statesman*, December/January 2003, 2; August 2004, 4; March 2003, 2, http://irrigation.org/news (1/26/2005).

70. Irrigation Association, *Statesman*, December/January 2003, 1; February 2004, 3, http://www.irrigation.org/news (1/26/2005).

71. Irrigation Association, *Statesman*, December 2004, 1, http://www.irrigation .org/news (12/30/04).

72. In a similar cultural process, rhetorics of "diversity" emerged to encompass conflict and difference in national identity (Spillman, *Nation and Commemoration*).

73. Irrigation Association, *Statesman*, July 2003, 1, and February 2004, 3, http:// www.irrigation.org/news (1/26/2005).

74. See Schudson, "Trouble with Experts," for a general assessment of the role of expert knowledge in democratic governance. Associations like the IA do not fulfill the criteria he sets out for productive and controlled use of expertise in the democratic process, especially the criterion of normal mechanisms of expert accountability. However, they do challenge scholars to be less partial in their normative visions of the potential role of economic actors in democratic processes. See also chapter nine.

75. Williams, "Public Good," 137.

76. Moon, *God, Sex, and Politics*; Eliasoph, *Avoiding Politics*.

77. Schlozman and Tierney, *Organized Interests*, 34n34.

78. Smith, *American Business*; Berg and Zald, "Business and Society."

Chapter Nine

1. Alexander, "Civil Society," 23.

2. Berg and Zald, "Business and Society," 121; Warner and Martin, "Big Trade and Business Associations," 324; Tedlow, "Trade Associations and Public Relations," 146–47. See also Sutton et al., *American Business Creed*. On Tedlow's evidence, public relations by industry-specific associations (e.g., 164n16 and *Corporate Image*, 89,

98) is rare compared to public relations by corporations and peak associations; cf. chapter eight.

3. Smith, *American Business and Political Power*, 11; Wuthnow, "Voluntary Sector," 22.

4. See Burstein, "Policy Domains," for a typology of policy domains involving broader or narrower mobilization. Arguably, generic public opinion is usually less important than proactive mobilization of members to lobby decision-makers (cf. Schlozman and Tierney, *Organized Interests*, chap. 8).

5. Abbott, *Professions*, 60, 59.

6. *New York Times*, June 27, 2006, C10; American Council of Life Insurance, http://www.acli.com/ACLI/Issues+nonmembers/Default.htm (12/23/2004); Hunt, *Encyclopedia of Associations*, 428, 370, 301, 35.

7. Warner and Martin, "Big Trade and Business Associations," 344–45; Knoke, *Organizing for Collective Action*, 194, 208; Schlozman and Tierney, *Organized Interests*, 173. See chapter two on associations' public relations activities in the 1930s.

8. One in three associations interested in public relations was also interested in policy, compared to one in five associations not interested in public relations and also interested in policy.

9. Compared to 47.5 percent of associations smaller than median size, 52.5 percent of associations with greater than median size stated a public relations goal. But this difference is not marked (Pearson chi-square = 0.008).

10. Associations with both types of members were more likely to express public relations goals than associations with one type of member. Of associations including both firms and individuals, 47 percent reported public relations goals; associations with individual members were close to the population average of 41 percent in interest in public relations, and 39 percent of associations with firm members did so (Pearson chi-square = 0.003).

11. Of associations with related affiliates such as state groups, 49 percent expressed public relations as a goal, compared to 38 percent of associations not reporting such affiliates. This difference was not evident for lobbying goals. However, associations reporting public relations goals and lobbying goals were similar in their higher tendency to report committee structure. Almost half (49 percent) of those associations reporting committees were also interested in public relations, compared to 37 percent of those without reported committees.

12. Pearson chi-square = 0.386.

13. Pearson chi-square = 0.356.

14. Before 1960, an average of 36 percent of associations formed each decade expressed public relations goals, compared to an average of 46 percent for decades after 1960. The earlier figure is inflated, too, by the 1930s, when an atypically high 48 percent of associations included public relations among their goals (cf. Tedlow, *Corporate Image*). The higher averages later in the century were especially marked in the 1960s and the 1980s. By contrast, conventional lobbying goals averaged 26 percent throughout the century.

15. In the 1960s, Warner and Martin found that agricultural, manufacturing, and financial sectors were above average in the proportion of associations indicating interest in public relations ("Big Trade and Business Associations," 344–45). Manufacturing and financial sectors were not distinctive in this later census, probably because of the earlier sample's bias to larger associations.

16. International Concrete Repair Institute, http://www.icri.org/misc/strategic plan.asp (12/10/2004); Mulch and Soil Council, htto://www.mulchandsoilcouncil .org/Inforesorce/Pressrelease1.html (7/6/2006). The simple existence of a website is not a sufficient indicator of a public relations orientation. Forty percent of focal associations did not show an interest in public relations on their website. As noted in the appendix, websites at this time were often oriented to members more than to the public. See also Spillman and Gao, "Codebook."

17. Hunt, *Encyclopedia of Associations*, 175, 380, 370.

18. American Council of Life Insurance, http://www.acli.com/ACLI/Newsroom/ Contacts%20Nonmember.htm (12/23/2004).

19. Automotive Lift Institute, http://www.autolift.org/ (6/14/2006); Exhibit Designers and Producers Association, http://www.edpa.com/latestnews.html (12/21/2004); Envelope Manufacturers' Association, http://www.emafoundation .org/index.v#page?p=229 (12/28/2004). Press releases often seem oriented only to association members.

20. Jacobs and Glass, "Media Publicity," 245; Independent Bakers Association, http://www.mindspring.com/~independentbaker/id14.html (12/9/2004); United Lightning Protection Association, *More Static*, Spring 2004, 3, http://www.ulpa .org/tech.htm (12/28/2004).

21. Hunt, *Encyclopedia of Associations*, 46, 402, 380.

22. Sutton et al., *American Business Creed*; Lentz and Tschirgi, "Ethical Content," 389.

23. United Lightning Protection Association, http://www.ulpa.org/tech.htm (12/28/2004); Mulch and Soil Council, http://www.mulchandsoilcouncil.org/ (7/6/2006); Automotive Lift Institute, http://www.autolift.org (6/14/2006).

24. Pellet Fuels Institute, http://www.pelletheat.org/3/institute/mission.html; press releases at http://www.pelletheat.org/3/news/index.cfm (12/23/2004). See also Hoffman and Ventresca, *Natural Environment*.

25. Association for Women in Aviation Maintenance, http://www.awam.org/ speakersnet.htm; National Association of Real Estate Brokers, http://www.nidonline .org/html/press_releases_frame.htm (12/28/2004).

26. Firestop Contractors International Association, http://www.fcia.org/ membership.htm; http://www.fcia.or/committees.php; http://www.fcia.org/ membership.htm (12/19/2004).

27. Firestop Contractors International Association, http://www.fcia.org/ articles/press-10-03.htm (12/19/2004).

28. Firestop Contractors International Association; (pre-history), http://www .fcia.or/articles/firestopsystems.htm (12/20/2004); (charter group), http://www.fcia

.org/articles/message-1-04a.htm; (first five years), http://www.fcia.org/articles/
newsletter-06-04b.htm; (standards development), http://www.fcia.or/articles/
message-8-03.htm; (promoting safety), http://www.fcia.org/articles/message.htm
(12/19/2004).

29. Firestop Contractors International Association; (foreshadowing public relations), http://www.fcia.org/articles/message-8-03.htm; ("PR Results Summary"),
http://www.fcia.org/articles/message.htm; (2003 activities), http://www.fcia.org/
articles/message-1-04c.htm (12/19/2004).

30. Firestop Contractors International Association; ("firestopping message"),
http://www.fcia.org/articles/newsletter-06-04.htm; ("elevator pitch"), http://www
.fcia.org/articles/newsletter-02-04b.htm (12/19/2004).

31. Jacobs, *Civil Society*, chap. 1; Fraser, "Actually Existing Democracy"; Calhoun, *Public Sphere*.

32. Firestop Contractors International Association; ("useful links"), http://www
.fcia.org/links.php; (Certificate of Merit), http://www.fcia.org/articles/newsletter-
04-04b.htm; (committee membership), http://www.fcia.org/articles/nfpaletter1
.htm; (trade show booth), http://www.fcia.org/articles/newsletter-02-04b.htm; other
associations compiled from newsletters, http://www.fcia.org; (Alliance), *AFSCC
Newsletter* 2 (2) May 16 2003, 4, http://www.fcia.org/articles.htm; (code groups),
http://www.fcia.org/links.php (12/19/2004).

33. See also chapter four and chapter eight.

34. Firestop Contractors International Association; (Chicago fire), http://www
.fcia.org/articles/press-10-03.htm (12/19/2004); (testimony), http://www.fcia.org/
articles/chicagotestimony.htm (12/20/2004); (importance of hearings), http://www
.fcia.org/articles/newsletters-03-04; http://www.fcia.org/articles/newsletter-02-04b
.htm; http://www.fcia.org/articles/newsletter-02-04b.htm (12/19/2004).

35. Firestop Contractors International Association; (Greenville fire), http://
www.fcia.org/articles/socarolinafire.htm; (World Trade Center), http://www.fcia
.org/articles/corleysprinklers.htm (12/20/2004).

36. Firestop Contractors International Association; (Codes Committee), http://
www.fcia.org/committeehome.php?selection=Codes (12/19/2004).

37. Firestop Contractors International Association; (mission), http://www
.fcia.org/; ("Key Initiative"), http://www.fcia.org/articles/message-5-02.htm; (accreditation), http://www.fcia.org/committeehome.php?selection=Accreditation
(12/19/2004).

38. Firestop Contractors International Association; (Chicago fire), http://www
.fcia.org/articles/press-10-03.htm; (architects), http://www.fcia.org/articles/press-
4-03.htm (12/19/2004); (testimony), http://www.fcia.org/articles/chicagotestimony
.htm (12/20/2004); (interview), at http://www.fcia.org/articles/dailycommercial.gif
(12/19/2004).

39. Firestop Contractors International Association, Richard Licht, "Maintaining Life Safety Effectiveness in the New Building Codes," http://www.fcia.org/

articles.htm; William E. Koffel, P.E. "Reliability of Automatic Sprinkler Systems," http://www.fcia.org/articles.htm; technical reason is also evident in archived presentations, fcia.org/articles/presentations.htm (12/19/2004).

40. Firestop Contractors International Association; (fire safety issue), http://www.fcia.org/articles/message-5-02.htm; (people protection), http://www.fcia.org/articles/messages-12-01.htm; (promote life safety), http://www.fcia.org/articles/message-1-04b.htm; ("intentionally or unintentionally"), Bill McHugh, "Ending the 'He Who Pokes It, Fills It' Mentality: Firestopping for the 21st Century," *Construction Specifier*, July 2003, fcia.org/articles.htm (12/19/2004).

41. Firestop Contractors International Association, http://www.fcia.org/articles/message-8-03.htm (12/19/2004); Weber, *Economy and Society*, I: 24–25.

42. Firestop Contractors International Association, http://www.fcia.org/articles/whynotboth.htm (12/20/2004). Bielby and Harrington report a similar comment from a syndication seminar on Latino TV markets: one audience member "asked somewhat incredulously, 'Is this all about money for you guys?'" (*Global TV*, 170–71).

43. Alliance for Fire and Smoke Containment and Control, "AFSCC Newsletter" 2 (2) May 16 2003, 4, http://www.fcia.org/articles.htm (12/19/2004).

44. Powell and Clemens, *Public Good*, xvi; Wuthnow, "Voluntary Sector," 8; Watt, "Cultural Challenges," 270; Salamon and Anheier, *Emerging Nonprofit Sector*, xvii–xviii, 13–16. See also Salamon and Anheier, *Cross-National Analysis*, part 1, chap. 3.

45. Salamon, "United States," 312. But as Alexander noted long ago, "independent sector theory reveals romantic and distorted ideas about the egotistical nature of capitalist markets" ("Altruism and Voluntarism," 170). Clemens and Guthrie address blurred boundaries between state, market, and civil society in *Politics and Partnerships*. See also chapter three, note 22, on business associations considered as part of the nonprofit sector. As noted there, the distinction between philanthropic and "mutual benefit" associations is occasionally challenged because mutual benefit associations sometimes engage in philanthropic activities (O'Neill, "Mutual Benefit Organizations"). Some argue that nonprofits should be classified at the level of their particular programs and activities, rather than the general purposes indicated by their titles (Lampkin, Romero, and Finnin, "Taxonomy"). Moreover, some views of nonprofit/for-profit organizational relations are potentially fruitful for analyzing business associations (Abzug and Webb, "Stakeholder Perspective"). Other relevant discussions include Smith, "Some Parameters," and Quarter et al., "Social Economy Framework."

46. Faeges, "Theory-Driven Concept Definition"; (definitional issues), Salamon, "United States," 301–3; (sectarianism), Kaufman, *Common Good*. For discussion about whether nonprofits mimic for-profit organizations, see, for instance, Skloot, "Enterprise and Commerce," 387–90; Steinberg, "Nonprofit Organizations and the Market"; and Gronjberg, "Markets, Politics, and Charity," 138–42. On the extent

to which they act for the state, see, for example, Salamon, "Government-Nonprofit Relations"; Jenkins, "Policy Advocacy," 312–14; Gronjberg, "Markets, Politics, and Charity," 142–47; Salamon and Anheier, *Emerging Nonprofit Sector*, 160; Watt, "Voluntary Sector," 277–78; Wuthnow, "Voluntary Sector," 10–19; and Skocpol et al., "How Americans Became Civic," 33–37. On engaged or nominal participation by members see, for example, Skocpol and Fiorina, *Civic Engagement*, 491–504; Skocpol, "United States"; Wuthnow, "Privileged and Marginalized," 64; and Schudson, "Trouble with Experts."

47. Hall, "Private Nonprofit Sector," 3; Veugelers and Lamont, "France," 150; Wuthnow, "Voluntary Sector," 22; Watt, "Cultural Challenges," 279. See also Powell and Clemens, *Public Good*, xv–xvi.

48. Alexander, "Civil Repair," 374, 387; "Prospects," 20; see also *Civil Sphere*, 96–103; 31–36; Lichterman, "Rescuing Tocqueville," *Elusive Togetherness*; Fishman, *Democracy's Voices*.

49. Alexander, *Civil Sphere*, 93.

50. Putnam, *Democracies in Flux* (see also Fishman, *Democracy's Voices* and Lichterman, "Tocqueville's Insights"); Anderson, Curtis, and Grabb, "Trends in Civic Association." Wuthnow also makes the more general point that many studies have omitted newly important types of voluntary groups ("United States," 88–95). See also Dumenil, *Freemasonry and American Culture*, for geographically based business groups with some striking parallels.

51. Of course, evidence of broad patterns in the population and in public documents does not capture microinteractional customs (see Lichterman, "Tocqueville's Insights"). But the broader patterns need examination to remedy the neglect of business associations in discussions about civil society.

52. Hunt, *Encyclopedia of Associations*, 172, 198, 412, 6, 61, 81, 115, and 244.

53. Alexander, "Civil Repair, 384–88; *Civil Sphere*, chap. 10.

54. Association for Women in Aviation Maintenance; (association officers), http://www.awam.org/leaders.htm; (chapters), http://www.awam.org/Chapters .dir/Chapters_Main.htm; (awards), http://www.awam.org/Awards.htm; (scholarships), http://www.awam.org/scholarships.htm; (conventions), http://www.awam .org/events.htm; (newsletters), http://www.awamnews.htm; (discussion groups), http://www.awam.org/forum_and%20_chatroom.htm; (merchandise), http://www .awam.org/product_details.htm; ("inspiring all women"), http://www.awam.org/ speakersnet.htm (12/28/2004).

55. For lobbying goals and civic goals, Fisher's Exact (two sided) = 0.181. For public relations and civic goals, Fisher's Exact (two sided) = 0.006. This one in eight of associations with some civic orientation beyond purely economic identities is likely an underestimate. Notably, the focal association of African American real estate brokers discussed at length below would have been missed in the population coding of civic orientations in title and self-description. And as I discuss below, one in three associations in the focal sample are peripherally involved in mentor-

ing, community service, and such, and over half may be counted as peripherally involved in providing members with information or skills for political involvement (beyond lobbying for industry interests).

56. Sixty percent of associations expressing a civic orientation were larger than median size.

57. Over a third of associations (37 percent) expressing a civic orientation also reported associate state groups and affiliates, compared to 26 percent of those with no civic orientation, close to the population average. Associations with some civic goals and numerous affiliates resemble the translocal organizational networks Skocpol and colleagues view as characteristic of the "classic" American voluntary groups of the past ("How Americans Became Civic," 33). However, unlike those groups they are less likely to involve cross-class memberships. And unlike networks of geographically based business groups, they are organized around particular work worlds or "industries."

58. The proportion of associations stating civic orientations increased significantly in decades after 1970, with the most notable change in the 1980s. This increase seems related to the cultural innovations of the 1960s and 1970s, especially the creation of new political languages of diversity and environmental protection, and suggests a previously unrecognized feature of the "interest group explosion" of the late twentieth century. (Associations with civic orientations formed before the 1970s were more likely expressing orientations to safety or charity.)

59. Fifty-four percent of associations expressing a civic orientation were composed of individuals, compared to a third of associations that did not express any civic orientation. The pattern was reversed considering associations composed of firms.

60. Over a third of associations (37 percent) expressing a civic orientation were located in the DC area, compared to 28 percent of those with no civic orientation.

61. As noted earlier, the absence of a relationship is particularly informative in these data.

62. "Health care and social assistance" was an outlier, for obvious reasons, with 70 percent of associations coded with some civic orientation. The population average of 13 percent of associations expressing civic goals would be much higher if manufacturing and wholesale sectors were excluded. These sectors are numerically dominant in the association population but expressed civic goals very rarely (6 and 3 percent respectively). Manufacturing and wholesale aside, it is notable that expression of a civic orientation is not limited to service sectors.

63. Perrin, *Citizen Speak*, 29–31.

64. (Contacting officials), American Council of Life Insurance, http://www.citizenaction.acli.com/acli/e4/ and http://www.citizenaction.acli.com/acli/issues/ (12/23/2004); Envelope Manufacturers' Association, http://www.bipac.net/lookup.asp?g=ENVELOPE (12/28/2004); (election overview), Aluminum Anodizers Council, "AAC's View from Washington," http://www.anodizing.org/anodizing_

conference.html (12/9/2004); (exhortations to vote), American Society for Automation in Pharmacy, "New and Improved Medicare," http://www.asapnet.org/ presentations.html (12/27/2004); International Concrete Repair Institute, Baltimore–Washington, DC, Chapter, "The Aggregate," 4th Quarter 2004, 1, http://www.icri.org/chapters/chap_details.asp?id=BWC (12/19/2004); and National Electronics Service Dealers Association, *ProService Magazine*, April 2004, 8, http://www.iscet.org/proservice/index.html (12/20/2004). See also Verba, Schlozman, and Brady (*Voice and Equality*, 312) on developing basic civic skills in the workplace, and Fung for an analysis of potentially conflicting effects of associations on democracy ("Associations and Democracy," 519–24).

65. International Concrete Repair Institute, "Committee Sign-up Sheet," http://www.icri.org/chapters/chap_details.asp?id=BWC and http://www.icrisd.org/events.php?stat=Past%20Event (12/19/2004); Vacuum Dealers Trade Association; ("Pillow Patrol"), http://www.vdta.com/ (6/14/2006); International Society of Certified Electronics Technicians; (student chapter), *ProService Magazine*, April 2003, 12, http://www.iscet.org/proservice/index.html (12/20/2004).

66. Association for Women in Aviation Maintenance, http://www.awam.org/Awards.htm (12/28/2004); International Society of Hospitality Consultants, http://www.ishc.com/new.html (12/20/2004); North American Association of Food Equipment Manufacturers, http://www.nafem.org/cfsp/index.cfm?print=yes (12/23/2004). See also chapter five on charity and chapter six on intra-association volunteering.

67. Conference of Consulting Actuaries, http://www.ccactuaries.org/nes/mentors.html (12/27/2004); Envelope Manufacturers' Association, http://www.emafoundation.org/index.v3page?p=2375 (12/28/2004); Association for Women in Aviation Maintenance, http://www.awam.org/Chapters.dir/Delta_Atlanta_Chapter.htm and http://www.awam.org/speakersnet.htm (12/28/2004).

68. Independent Bakers Association, http://www.bakingnetwork.com/apps/Discussion/Tree.asp?ID=86 (11/26/2004); Irrigation Association, *E-Times*, November 2004, 4, http://www.irrigation.org (12/30/2004).

69. Conference of Consulting Actuaries, http://www.ccactuaries.org/events/seminars/2005pensionsymposium.html (12/27/2004); Mulch and Soil Council, *News, Notes & Quotes*, August 2005, 1, http://www.mulchandsoilcouncil.org/Inforesorce/Industry/News.html (7/6/2006).

70. International Society of Certified Electronics Technicians, *ProService Magazine*, April 2002, 1, 15; April 2003, 6; June 2004, 13, http://www.iscet.org/proservice/index.html (12/20/2004); International Telecommunications Society; (aim), http://www.itsworld.org/news/message.htm; (conference topics), *Interconnect* 6 (2) July 2004, 5, 9, http://www.itsworld.org/newsletter/news0.htm (12/28/2004); Schudson, "Trouble with Experts."

71. Firestop Contractors International Association, http://www.fcia.org/articles/newsletter-06-04.htm (12/19/2004); Conference of Consulting Actuaries, "2002 An-

nual Meeting Cassette Order Form," http://www.ccactuaries.org/resourcecenter/ am-meetingmaterials.htm (12/27/2004); American Society for Automation in Pharmacy, "The Healthcare Collaborative Network," (Annual Meeting presentation, 2004), http://www.asapnet.org/presentations.html (12/27/2004); Exhibit Designers and Producers Association, *EDPA TODAY* X (3) Fall 2001, 1, "Special Issue: Our Industry Reacts to Tragedy," http://www.edpa.com/currentpublications.html (12/21/2004); Association for Women in Aviation Maintenance, http://www.pub28 .bravenet.com/forum/2345150732/fetch/7720/ (12/28/2004).

72. Pellet Fuels Institute, http://www.pelletheat.org/3/2004conference (12/23/2004); Firestop Contractors International Association, "Letter to the Editor," http://www.fcia.org/articles.htm (12/29/2004).

73. On the National Association of Real Estate Brokers' founding date, membership size, and comparison with National Association of Realtors, see Hunt, *Encyclopedia of Associations*, 354 (#3156 and #3161); (oldest minority trade association), http://www.nareb.com/NAREB/history.shtml; (mission), http://www.nareb .com/NAREB/mission.shtml; (members), http://www.directory-online.com/nareb/ register.cfm; (chapters), http://www.directory-online.com/NAREB/public/index .cfm?PageNum_getChapters=3; (board members), http://www.nareb.com/NAREB/ directors.html; (regional directors), http://www.nareb.com/NAREB/directors_RVP .shtml; (regional activities), http://www.nareb.com/NAREB/president_message_5 .shtml; (parade of states), http://www.nareb.com/NAREB/president_message.shtml (12/28/2004); Skocpol et al., "How Americans Became Civic," 37.

74. National Association of Real Estate Brokers; ("virtue of office"), http:// www.nareb.com/NAREB/directors_Virtue_Of_Office_Held.shtml; (affiliates), http://www.nareb.com/NAREB/affiliates/sales_division.shtml; (sales division), http://www.nareb.com/affiliates/sales_divisions.shtml; (women's council goals), http://www.nareb.com/affiliates/Women's%20Council%20of%20NAREB.shtml; (survey), at nareb.com/events/events_wcn1.shtml; (luncheon), http://www.nareb .com/events/WCN2.shtml (12/28/2004).

75. National Association of Real Estate Brokers; (newsletters, directories, REALTIST symbol), Hunt, *Encyclopedia of Associations*, 354; (sales division training and certification), http://www.nareb.com/affiliates/sales_divisions.shtml; (property management training and certification), http://www.nareb.com/affiliates/ REMBI.shtml; (appraiser training and certification), http://www.nareb.com/affiliates/ society_appraisers.shtml; (convention), http://www.nareb.com/NAREB/president_ message.shtml; (fall meeting), http://www.nareb.com/events/events/shtml; (member survey), http://www.nareb.com/NAREB/feedback.shtml; (business opportunities), http://www.nareb.com/partners.shtml; (merchandise), http://www.nareb.com/ events/realtist%20store.shtml; (appraisers), http://www.nareb.com/affiliates/society_ appraisers.shtml (12/28/2004).

76. National Association of Real Estate Brokers; (policy input), http://www.nareb .com/NAREB/feedback.shtml; (Washington meeting), http://www.nareb.comevents/

events_1.shtml; (alliance), http://www.nareb.com/partners/partners.shtml; (membership directory), http://www.nareb.com/members/search.shtml; (appraisal certification), http://www.nsrea.org/ (12/28/2004).

77. National Association of Real Estate Brokers; (mission), http://www.nareb .com/NAREB/history.shtml; (president's address), http://www.nareb.com/NAREB/ president_message_2.shtml (12/28/2004).

78. National Association of Real Estate Brokers; (Faith Based Community Development), http://www.maxx-technologies.com/narebsales/whatweoffer.htm; (ethical and social responsibilities), http://www.nareb.com/affiliates/affiliates .shtml and http://www.rembi.org/about.htm; (newsletters), rembi.org/news.htm (12/28/2004).

79. National Association of Real Estate Brokers; (role models), http://www.nareb .com/NAREB/president_message_1.shtml; (golf mentoring program), http://www .nareb.com/partners/partners.shtml (12/28/2004).

80. National Association of Real Estate Brokers; (NID-HCA's goals), http:// www.nidonline.org/html/header_frame.htm; (financial literacy and numbers counseled), http://www.nidonline.org/html/history_frame.htm; (programs and affiliations), http://www.nidonline.org/html/programs_frame.htm and http://www .nidonline.org/html/affiliations_frame.htm (12/28/2004).

81. National Association of Real Estate Brokers; (brochures), http://www.nid online.org/html/homepage_frame.htm; (online consultation), http://www.nidonline .org/html/free_advice_frame.htm; (counselors' offices), http://www.nidonline.org/ html/local_advocate_frame.htm; (counselors' training), *NID HouseCall*, vol. 2, Summer 2004, 3, http://www.nidonline.org/html/newsletter_frame.htm (12/28/ 2004).

82. National Association of Real Estate Brokers; (expertise and public good), http://www.nidonline.org/html/free_advice_frame.htm (12/28/2004).

Chapter Ten

1. Zelizer, *Purchase of Intimacy*; Spillman, "Enriching Exchange."

2. Berk and Schneiberg, "Collaborative Learning"; Pearce, *Trade Association Survey*. This argument makes the weak functionalist assumption that humans need meaning to orient their actions, which I do not view as controversial. It does not assume that associations are the only ways the meaning of business is produced and reproduced, that they are usually functional for society as a whole, or that they do not express or generate conflict.

3. Galambos, *Competition and Cooperation*.

4. Spillman, "Culture and Economic Life."

5. DiMaggio and Powell, "Introduction." For governance theory, this evidence suggests that associations might be intermittently influential sites of institutional-

ized interfirm coordination and control *even* where corporate hierarchy is considered the dominant form of governance, and other institutionalized social relations between economic actors seem sparse (see chapter two). For population ecology, the historically stable institutionalization of the national business association population supports the idea that organizational populations are composed of classes of organizations defined by historically embedded identities and codes (Carroll and Hannan, *Corporations and Industries*, chap. 5; cf. Mohr, "Implicit Terrains").

6. DiMaggio and Powell, "Iron Cage Revisited," 65.

7. See also chapter five and, for example, Zelizer, *Purchase of Intimacy*.

8. Berk and Schneiberg, "Collaborative Learning," offer a rare examination of the collective economic benefits of associations, but the problem of generalizability due to loose coupling of industries and associations remains.

9. See also chapter six on problems with other resolutions of Olson's paradox.

10. Alexander, *Civil Sphere*; Swidler, *Talk of Love*.

11. Thévenot, "Organized Complexity," 419.

12. Zelizer, *Purchase of Intimacy*; Smelser, "The Rational and the Ambivalent." See also Wuthnow, *Poor Richard's Principle*. By identifying a binary code in meaning-making about economic action in business associations, I am applying neo-Durkheimian theoretical insights (developing Durkheim's *Elementary Forms*) about how codes help create shared symbols and rituals to the problems and solutions in his earlier work in *Division of Labor*.

13. Marx, "German Ideology," 175.

14. Businesspeople using solidaristic vocabularies of motive in these pages are likely also speaking in terms of particularistic interests in other business settings. Different organizational settings—peak associations, local business groups, associations in other countries, and such—will evoke different "dialects" too. Overall, settings are likely a stronger factor influencing languages adopted than, for example, seniority of association members, size of business, or structure of industry (see also chapter five). Beginning with the postulate of a solidarity/strategy binary code, we can develop accounts of setting features that encourage more solidaristic or more strategic orientations. This is an important direction for future research. We have seen here that shared technical expertise provides one basis for solidarity, as Durkheim suggested. See also chapter one, note 25.

15. For Tocqueville, "the inhabitants of the United States . . . maintain that virtue is useful and prove it every day" ("How the Americans Combat Individualism by the Principle of Self-Interest Rightly Understood," *Reader*, 191). The argument here is stronger—that regardless of presumed psychological motivation, economic action is oriented by solidarity as well as self-interested strategy. See also Spillman and Strand, "Interest-Oriented Action."

16. Streeck and Schmitter, "Community, Market, State," 16, 17; Coleman, "Associational Governance," 147. However, these theories assume that associations aggregate *private* business interests, which may then be managed for the *public*

good. But in fact the opposite seems to be happening in American associations: sometimes associations are aggregating collective experiences associated with an economic activity and occasionally turning them to the pursuit of private interests. Most theorists of political-economic governance display a striking amnesia about Durkheimian theory, even where they are articulating proto-Durkheimian ideas (but see Grusky and Galescu, "Is Durkheim a Class Analyst?"). However, the proto-coordinating and proto-civic potential of American business associations have very occasionally been noticed by commentators who sometimes propose associational governance to improve American industry (Procassini, *Competitors in Alliance*; Lynn and McKeown, *Organizing Business*). Bruyn (*Civil Economy*, 165–78) explicitly argues for the importance of business associations in his blueprint for a new "civil economy."

17. See, for example, Bandelj, *Communists to Foreign Capitalists*; Miller, *Reluctant Capitalists*; Zelizer, *Purchase of Intimacy*; Boltanski and Thévenot, *Justification*; Fourcade and Healy, "Moral Views"; and Spillman, "Culture and Economic Life." See also Sutton et al., *American Business Creed*, for a rare and impressive analysis of American business culture in the 1950s, which explicitly challenges assumptions about interest-oriented action in ways that support the argument here.

18. Weber, *Economy and Society*, 1: 202. See also Swedberg, *Interest*; Spillman, "Enriching Exchange."

19. Greene, *Fabric of the Cosmos*, 90; Gregory, *Inventing Reality*.

20. Or, as Pierre Bourdieu puts it in a classic polemic, "the immediately visible effects of the implementation of the great neo-liberal utopia" are

> not only the poverty and suffering of a growing proportion of the population of the economically most advanced societies . . . the progressive disappearance of the autonomous worlds of cultural production . . . but also and above all the destruction of all the collective institutions capable of standing up to the effects of the infernal machine . . . and the imposition, everywhere . . . of that kind of moral Darwinism which . . . establishes the struggle of all against all and *cynicism* as the norm of all practices.

And he notes that "corporate discourse has never spoken so much about trust, cooperation, loyalty, and corporate culture" and "even the dominant themselves" are "led into compensatory actions inspired by the very logic they want to neutralize, as with the benefactions of Bill Gates" (*Acts of Resistance*, 102, 98, 100). On economic scandal and its routinization, see Jacobs, "No-Fault Society."

21. Lukes argues—as would most social theorists now—that cultural and ideological power is important for understanding subordinate groups (*Power: A Radical View*). But dominant groups are unlikely to be clear-sighted about their own

powers; moreover, as Stewart Clegg argues, the idea of dominant ideology takes fixed, objective interests for granted (*Frameworks of Power*). In any case, it is clear that business power is reinforced by dominant groups' lack of awareness of their domination, belief that they represent a consensus, act in the general interest, and so on.

22. Wright, *Real Utopias*; see also Bruyn, *Civil Economy*.

Appendix

1. Zelizer, "Beyond the Polemics"; Spillman, "Enriching Exchange."

2. As I was working on this project I was surprised by how many people had stories to tell of some personal connection to the sorts of associations I was studying. One friend recalled her father's association leadership and her childhood experience at convention hotels; another remembered his brief job with an association mostly preoccupied with organizing its annual dinner. Relatives and (more predictably) fellow plane passengers recounted with pleasure their recent industry conventions in fields from airlines to orchards. One fellow party guest counted up his membership in five or six different associations in the health care industry. Many colleagues and students had stories of friends and relations deeply involved in their various business associations. All these stories interested me because association involvement is so rarely discussed otherwise, perhaps especially in the academic circles I frequent but not only there. I did conclude that social scientists in particular prefer to keep closeted their contacts with the social world of business—as one appalled colleague responded when I told him of my research, "But that's business school stuff!" Needless to say, such distinctions, and the blinkers they encourage, cannot be theoretically justified.

3. See, for example, Eliasoph and Lichterman, "Culture in Interaction," on the importance of interactional practice in specific contexts, and Burawoy, "Extended Case Method," on theorizing with cases. As discussed in chapter five and elsewhere, I develop a thick hermeneutic analysis of associations' vocabularies of motive for their strategies of action instead of a series of local accounts of meaning-making in copresent interaction. During the research, I also designed a phase of ethnographic and interview work with four representative associations, but decided not to implement it because the association census and the qualitative analysis of documents from the focal sample of twenty-five associations already generated far more data than I could reasonably use. I think the broader understanding of business associations I develop can provide a basis for future, theoretically driven ethnographic case studies, with better-informed case selection and research questions.

Some scholars who explicitly argue for the significance of textual evidence include Smith, Texts, Facts, and Femininity; Marcus, "Economic and Cultural Analysis"; Illouz, Glamour of Misery; and Mohr and Lee, "Discourse Shifts." Thévenot

("Organized Complexity") shares my concern that case studies too often turn into "purely contextual stories."

4. Pearce, *Trade Association Survey*; Warner and Martin, "Big Trade and Business Associations"; Knoke, *Collective Action*; Aldrich et al., "Minimalism, Mutualism, and Maturity."

5. The discussion in this section includes passages from "Project Description" and "Codebook" for the data set; "National Business Associations, United States, 2003" available at www.icpsr.umich.edu.

6. See Salamon, "United States," 297, on official classifications of nonprofit organizations, and a useful overview of the US nonprofit sector as of the 1990s.

7. Lamont, *Money, Morals, and Manners*.

8. See Spillman and Gao, "Codebook," appendix A for discussion of other issues of case inclusion.

9. See Spillman, "Culture and Interests," for a short comment on the associational subgenre of the "Chair's Message."

10. Barthel, "Redefinition of Mission," 417.

11. Initially two new variables—"other internally oriented goals" and "other externally oriented goals"—were introduced to replace such cases where goal statements went beyond specific goals such as public relations; in the end, these variables too caused significant intercoder reliability problems and were eliminated.

12. See also Spillman and Gao, "Codebook" and, for more detailed sectoral distributions, Spillman et al., "National Business Associations." For further information on classification, subcategories, and examples, see United States, Office of Management and Budget, *Industry Classification Scheme*. NAICS sectors 12–19 are combined for the overall proportion of associations in the service sector (24 percent); sectors 01–02 for primary industry (10 percent); sectors 06–07 for wholesale and retail trade (10 percent); and sectors 10–11 for finance and real estate (8 percent).

13. See also Spillman, "Causal Reasoning"; Perrin, *Citizen Speak*.

14. Ragin, *Constructing Social Research*; Spillman, "Causal Reasoning."

15. See chapter one, tables 1.1 and 1.2, and for a similar but smaller scale procedure, see, for example, Biggart, *Charismatic Capitalism*, 175–76. I spent some time considering a wide range of alternative selection criteria, taking into account both the economic sociology of industry governance and other features of the population. Of course, I did not want to select on types of association goals, since they were related to what in other research designs might be my "dependent variable." Some alternatives included, for instance, developing a sample including both stable industries and industries in transition (Fligstein, *Architecture of Markets*), or industries under threat (Smelser, personal communication); or comparing industries in sectors with small firms, low technology, and undifferentiated goods—where Hollingsworth and Lindberg ("Governance of the American Economy," 249) expect more association governance—with other sectors. But this sort of theoretically

driven comparison took for granted much that was coming into question about the nature of business associations as the study developed, and ultimately seemed neither viable nor useful. As I ultimately concluded and have argued here, the business association should be considered a multifunctional institution of cultural production and limited, contingent functional needs in particular industry circumstances—like "industry" change or threat, or small scale industry organization—do not begin to capture their well-institutionalized multifunctionality.

16. Small associations are slightly overrepresented in the purposive sample, and large associations are underrepresented to the same degree. Associations including both firms and individuals are overrepresented at the expense of associations of individuals. These differences are probably not consequential, but as the more detailed analysis in chapter six and eight shows, they would, if anything, bias the findings to more interest-oriented and less solidaristic subcultural expressions.

17. Davis, "Firms and Environments," 481. See Geletkanycz and Hambrick, "External Ties," and Galaskiewicz, "Professional Networks" for examples in which executives of large corporations are members of several associations as individuals.

18. Some passages in this section rely on Spillman, "Special Camaraderie."

19. Some of the earlier reflections on scholarly uses of web sources were Harker, "World Wide Web"; Ho, Baber, and Khonder, "Alternative Websites"; and Bainbridge, "Cyberspace." More recent resources not available when I was designing the project are Hine, "Internet Research," and Hewson, "Internet-Mediated Research."

20. Mann, "Socio-Logic," 545.

21. The example is from Biggart, *Charismatic Capitalism*, 177. I do not discuss the process at all in *Nation and Commemoration*.

22. Spillman, "A Special Camaraderie with Colleagues."

Bibliography

Abbott, Andrew. "Professional Ethics." *American Journal of Sociology* 88, no. 5 (1983): 855–85.

———. "Sociology of Work and Occupations." In Smelser and Swedberg, *Handbook of Economic Sociology*, 2nd ed., 307–30.

———. *The System of Professions: An Essay on the Division of Expert Labor*. Chicago: University of Chicago Press, 1988.

Abell, Peter. "On the Prospects for a Unified Social Science: Economics and Sociology." *Socioeconomic Review* 1 (2003): 1–26.

Abolafia, Mitchell. *Making Markets: Opportunism and Restraint on Wall Street*. Cambridge, MA: Harvard University Press, 1996.

Abzug, Rikki, and Natalie Webb. "Relations between Nonprofit and For-Profit Organizations: A Stakeholder Perspective." *Nonprofit and Voluntary Sector Quarterly* 28, no. 4 (1999): 416–31.

Adams, Julia, Elisabeth Clemens, and Ann Orloff, eds. *Remaking Modernity: Politics, History, and Sociology*. Durham, NC: Duke University Press, 2005.

Adams, Walter. "The 'Rule of Reason': Workable Competition or Workable Monopoly?" *Yale Law Journal* 63, no. 3 (1954): 348–70.

Aguilera, Ruth, and Gregory Jackson. "Hybridization and Heterogeneity across National Models of Corporate Governance." *Economic Sociology: European Electronic Newsletter* 3, no. 2 (2002): 1–7, at http://www.siswo.uva.nl/ES/esfeb02art2.html (accessed 2/21/2002).

Ahmed, Mirghani, and Robert Scapens. "The Evolution of Cost-Based Pricing Rules in Britain: An Institutionalist Perspective." *Review of Political Economy* 15, no. 2 (2003): 173–91.

Akard, Patrick. "Corporate Mobilization and Political Power: The Transformation of U.S. Economic Policy in the 1970s." *American Sociological Review* 57, no. 5 (1992): 597–615.

Aldrich, Howard. "The Sociable Organization: A Case Study of Mensa and Some Propositions." *Sociology and Social Research* 55, no. 4 (1971): 429–41.

Aldrich, Howard, and Udo Staber. "Organizing Business Interests: Patterns of Trade Association Foundings, Transformations, and Deaths." In *Ecological Models of Organizations*, edited by Glenn Carroll, 111–26. Cambridge MA: Ballinger, 1988.

Aldrich, Howard, Catherine Zimmer, Udo Staber, and John Beggs. "Minimalism, Mutualism, and Maturity: The Evolution of the American Trade Association Population in the 20th Century." In *Evolutionary Dynamics of Organizations*, edited by Joel Baum and Jitendra Singh, 223–39. New York: Oxford University Press, 1994.

Alexander, Jeffrey. "Central Problems in Cultural Sociology: A Reply to My (Friendly) Critics." *Culture* 19, no. 2 (2005): 8–12.

———. *The Civil Sphere*. Oxford: Oxford University Press, 2006.

———. "The Long and Winding Road: Civil Repair of Intimate Injustice." *Sociological Theory* 19, no. 3 (2001): 371–400.

———. *The Meanings of Social Life: A Cultural Sociology*. Oxford: Oxford University Press, 2004.

———. "The Past, Present, and Future Prospects of Civil Society." In *Civil Society, Citizenship, and Learning*, edited by A. Bron and M. Schemmann, 15–25. Hamburg and Münster: Lit Verlag, 2001.

———. "The Social Requisites for Altruism and Voluntarism: Some Notes on What Makes a Sector Independent." *Sociological Theory* 5, no. 2 (1987): 165–71.

Alexander, Jeffrey, and Philip Smith. "The Discourse of American Civil Society: A New Proposal for Cultural Studies." *Theory and Society* 22 (1993): 151–207.

American Bar Association. *Antitrust Law Developments*, 6th ed. Chicago: American Bar Association, 2007.

Anand, N., and Richard Peterson. "When Market Information Constitutes Fields: Sensemaking of Markets in the Commercial Music Industry." *Organization Science* 11, no. 3 (2000): 270–84.

Anderson, Benedict. *Imagined Communities: Reflections on the Origin and Spread of Nationalism*. Rev. ed. London: Verso, 1991.

Anderson, Robert, James Curtis, and Edward Grabb. "Trends in Civic Association Activity in Four Democracies: The Special Case of Women in the United States." *American Sociological Review* 71, no. 3 (2006): 376–400.

Aoki, Masahiko, Bo Gustafsson, and Oliver Williamson, eds. *The Firm as a Nexus of Treaties*. Newbury Park, CA: Sage, 1990.

Arnirou, Rachid. "Sociability/'Sociality.'" *Current Sociology* 37, no. 1 (1989): 115–20.

Associations Yellowbook: Who's Who at the Leading U.S. Trade and Professional Associations. Vol. 12, no. 1. New York: Leadership Directories, 2002.

Bainbridge, William. "Cyberspace: Sociology's Natural Domain." *Contemporary Sociology* 28, no. 6 (1999): 664–67.

Baker, Wayne. *America's Crisis of Values: Reality and Perception*. Princeton, NJ: Princeton University Press, 2005.

———. "Market Networks and Corporate Behavior." *American Journal of Sociology* 96, no. 3 (1990): 589–625.

Baker, Wayne, Robert Faulkner, and Gene Fisher. "Hazards of the Market: The Continuity and Dissolution of Interorganizational Market Relationships." *American Sociological Review* 63 (1998): 147–77.

Bandelj, Nina. *From Communists to Foreign Capitalists: The Social Foundations of Foreign Direct Investment in Postsocialist Europe.* Princeton, NJ: Princeton University Press, 2008.

Barber, Bernard. "Absolutization of the Market: Some Notes on How We Got from There to Here." In *Markets and Morals*, edited by Gerald Dworkin, Gordon Bermant, and Peter Brown, 15–31. Washington, DC: Hemisphere Publishing Corporation, 1977.

———. "All Economies Are 'Embedded': The Career of a Concept, and Beyond." *Social Research* 62, no. 2 (1995): 387–413.

Barnett, William, Gary Mischke, and William Ocasio. "The Evolution of Collective Strategies among Organizations." *Organization Studies* 21, no. 2 (2000): 325–54.

Barthel, Diane. "The Role of 'Fictions' in Redefinition of Mission." *Nonprofit and Voluntary Sector Quarterly* 26, no. 4 (1997): 399–420.

Bartley, Tim, and Marc Schneiberg. "Rationality and Institutional Contingency: The Varying Politics of Economic Regulation in the Fire Insurance Industry." *Sociological Perspectives* 45, no. 1 (2002): 47–79.

Beamish, Thomas, and Nicole Biggart. "Economic Worlds of Work: Uniting Economic Sociology with the Sociology of Work." In *Social Theory at Work*, edited by Marek Korczynski, Randy Hodson, and Paul Edwards, 233–71. Oxford: Oxford University Press, 2006.

Becker, Howard. *Art Worlds.* Berkeley: University of California Press, 1982.

Becker, W. H. "American Wholesale Hardware Trade Associations, 1870–1900." *Business History Review* 45, no. 2 (1971): 179–200.

Beckert, Jens. *Beyond the Market: The Social Foundations of Economic Efficiency.* Translated by Barbara Harshav. Princeton, NJ: Princeton University Press, 2002.

Benson, Rodney. "Field Theory in Comparative Context: A New Paradigm for Media Studies." *Theory and Society* 28, no. 3 (1999): 463–98.

Berezin, Mabel. "Exploring Emotions and the Economy: New Contributions from Social Theory." *Theory and Society* 38, no. 4 (2009): 335–46.

———. "The Festival State: Celebration and Commemoration in Fascist Italy." *Journal of Modern European History* 3, no. 1S (2006): 60–74.

Berg, Ivar, and Mayer Zald. "Business and Society." *Annual Review of Sociology* 4 (1978): 115–43.

Berk, Gerald. "Communities of Competitors: Open Price Associations and the American State, 1911–1929." *Social Science History* 20 (1996): 372–400.

———. "Discursive Cartels: Uniform Cost Accounting among American Manufacturers before the New Deal." *Business and Economic History* 26 (1997): 229–51.

———. *Louis D. Brandeis and the Making of Regulated Competition, 1900–1932.* Cambridge: Cambridge University Press, 2009.

———. "The National Recovery Administration Reconsidered: Or Why the Corrugated and Solid Fiber Shipping Container Code Succeeded." *Studies in American Political Development* 25, no. 1 (2011): 56–85.

Berk, Gerald, and Marc Schneiberg. "Varieties *in* Capitalism, Varieties *of* Association: Collaborative Learning in American Industry, 1900–1925." *Politics and Society* 33, no. 1 (2005): 46–87.

Berry, Jeffrey. *The Interest Group Society.* Boston: Little, Brown, 1984.

Besser, Terry. *The Conscience of Capitalism: Business Social Responsibility to Communities.* Westport, CT: Praeger, 2002.

Besser, Terry, and Nancy Miller. "Is the Good Corporation Dead? The Community Social Responsibility of Small Business Operators." *Journal of Socio-Economics* 33 (2001): 221–41.

———. "The Risks of Enlightened Self-Interest: Small Business and Support for the Community." *Business and Society* 43, no. 4 (2004): 398–425.

Besser, Terry, Nancy Miller, and Robert Perkins. "For the Greater Good: Business Networks and Business Social Responsibility to Communities." *Entrepreneurship and Regional Development* 18 (2006): 321–39.

Bielby, Denise, and C. Lee Harrington. *Global TV: Exporting Television and Culture in the World Market.* New York: New York University Press, 2008.

Biggart, Nicole. *Charismatic Capitalism: Direct Selling Organizations in America.* Chicago: University of Chicago Press, 1989.

Biggart, Nicole, ed. *Readings in Economic Sociology.* Malden, MA: Blackwell, 2002.

Biggart, Nicole, and Thomas Beamish. "The Economic Sociology of Convention: Habit, Custom, Practice, and Routine in Market Order." *Annual Review of Sociology* 29 (2003): 443–64.

Biggart, Nicole, and Mauro Guillén. "Developing Differences: Social Organization and the Rise of the Auto Industries of South Korea, Taiwan, Spain, and Argentina." *American Sociological Review* 64 (1999): 722–47.

Blair-Loy, Mary. *Competing Devotions: Career and Family among Women Executives.* Cambridge, MA: Harvard University Press, 2003.

Boczkowski, Pablo. *Digitizing the News: Innovation in Online Newspapers.* Cambridge, MA: MIT Press, 2004.

Boltanski, Luc, and Eve Chiapello. *The New Spirit of Capitalism.* Translated by Gregory Elliott. London: Verso, 2005.

Boltanski, Luc, and Laurent Thévenot. *On Justification: Economies of Worth.* Translated by Catherine Porter. Princeton, NJ: Princeton University Press, 2006.

Bonnett, Clarence. *History of Employers' Associations in the United States*. New York: Vantage Press, 1956.

Bourdieu, Pierre. *Acts of Resistance: Against the Tyranny of the Market*. Translated by Richard Nice. New York: New Press, 1999.

———. *Language and Symbolic Power*. Edited by John Thompson. Cambridge, MA: Harvard University Press, 1991.

———. "Neo-Liberalism, the Utopia (Becoming a Reality) of Unlimited Exploitation." In *Acts of Resistance: Against the Tyranny of the Market*, 94–105.

———. *The Social Structures of the Economy*. Translated by Chris Turner. Cambridge: Polity, 2005.

Bradley, Joseph. *The Role of Trade Associations and Professional Business Societies in America*. University Park, PA: Pennsylvania State University Press, 1965.

Breckhus, Wayne. "A Sociology of the Unmarked: Redirecting Our Focus." *Sociological Theory* 16 (1998): 34–51.

Breiger, Ronald, and John Mohr. "Institutional Logics from the Aggregation of Organizational Networks: Operational Procedures for the Analysis of Counted Data." *Computational and Mathematical Organization Theory* 10 (2004): 17–43.

Bruyn, Severyn. *A Civil Economy: Transforming the Market in the Twenty-First Century*. Ann Arbor: University of Michigan Press, 2000.

Burawoy, Michael. "The Extended Case Method." *Sociological Theory* 16 (1998): 4–33.

Burstein, Paul. "Policy Domains: Organization, Culture, and Policy Outcomes." *Annual Review of Sociology* 17 (1991): 327–50.

Calhoun, Craig, ed. *Habermas and the Public Sphere*. Cambridge, MA: MIT Press, 1992.

Campbell, John. "Institutional Analysis and the Role of Ideas in Political Economy." In *The Rise of Neoliberalism and Institutional Analysis*, edited by John Campbell and Ove Pedersen, 159–89. Princeton, NJ: Princeton University Press, 2001.

Campbell, John, J. Rogers Hollingsworth, and Leon Lindberg, eds. *Governance of the American Economy*. New York: Cambridge University Press, 1991.

Campbell, John, and Leon Lindberg. "The Evolution of Governance Regimes." In Campbell, Hollingsworth, and Lindberg, *Governance of the American Economy*, 319–55.

Carroll, Glenn, and Michael Hannan. *The Demography of Corporations and Industries*. Princeton, NJ: Princeton University Press, 2000.

Carrott, Browning. "The Supreme Court and American Trade Associations, 1921–1925." *Business History Review* 44, no. 3 (1970): 320–38.

Carruthers, Bruce. "Historical Sociology and the Economy: Actors, Networks, and Context." In Adams, Clemens, and Orloff, *Remaking Modernity*, 333–54.

Carruthers, Bruce, and Sarah Babb. *Economy/Society: Markets, Meanings, and Social Structure*. Thousand Oaks, CA: Pine Forge Press, 2000.

Cashman, Sean. *America in the Age of Titans: The Progressive Era and World War I*. New York: New York University Press, 1988.

Cerulo, Karen, ed. *Culture in Mind: Toward a Sociology of Culture and Cognition*. New York: Routledge, 2002.

Chandler, Alfred. "The Large Industrial Corporation and the Making of the Modern Economy." In *The Essential Alfred Chandler: Essays toward a Historical Theory of Big Business*, edited by Thomas McCraw, 225–46. Boston: Harvard Business School Press, 1988.

———. *The Visible Hand: The Managerial Revolution in American Business*. Cambridge, MA: Belknap Press of Harvard University Press, 1977.

Chandler, Alfred, with Takashi Hikino. *Scale and Scope: The Dynamics of Industrial Capitalism*. Cambridge, MA: Belknap Press of Harvard University Press, 1990.

Chaves, Mark. *Congregations in America*. Cambridge, MA: Harvard University Press, 2004.

Chung, Chi-nien. "Networks and Governance in Trade Associations: AEIC and NELA in the Development of the American Electricity Industry, 1885–1910." *International Journal of Sociology and Social Policy* 17, no. 7/8 (1997): 57–110.

Clegg, Stewart. *Frameworks of Power*. Newbury Park, CA: Sage, 1989.

Clemens, Elisabeth. *The People's Lobby: Organizational Innovation and the Rise of Interest Group Politics in the United States, 1890–1925*. Chicago: University of Chicago Press, 1997.

Clemens, Elisabeth, and James Cook. "Politics and Institutionalism: Explaining Durability and Change." *Annual Review of Sociology* 25 (1999): 441–66.

Clemens, Elisabeth, and Doug Guthrie. eds. *Politics and Partnerships: The Role of Voluntary Associations in America's Political Past and Present*. Chicago: University of Chicago Press, 2010.

Coleman, William. "Associational Governance in a Globalizing Era: Weathering the Storm." In Hollingsworth and Boyer, *Contemporary Capitalism*, 127–88.

———. *Business and Politics: A Study of Collective Action*. Kingston and Montreal: McGill-Queen's University Press, 1988.

Collins, Randall. "Weber's Last Theory of Capitalism." *American Sociological Review* 45 (1980): 925–42.

Copley, Stephen, and Kathryn Sutherland, eds. *Adam Smith's Wealth of Nations: New Interdisciplinary Essays*. Manchester: Manchester University Press, 1995.

Cordero, Rodrigo, Francisco Carballo, and José Ossandón. "Performing Cultural Sociology: A Conversation with Jeffrey Alexander." *European Journal of Social Theory* 11, no. 4 (2008): 501–20.

Craig, Ailsa. "Sociability and the Transliterative Practices of Occupational Subculture." *Culture* 20, no. 3 (2006): 1, 7–9.

Crane, Diana. *The Production of Culture: Media and the Urban Arts*. Newbury Park, CA: Sage, 1992.

Crane, Diana, ed. *The Sociology of Culture.* Oxford: Blackwell, 1994.

Dacin, M. Tina, Jerry Goodstein, and W. Richard Scott. "Institutional Theory and Institutional Change." *Academy of Management Journal* 45 (2002): 45–57.

Dankbaar, Ben. "Sectoral Governance in the Automobile Industries of Germany, Great Britain, and France." In Hollingsworth, Schmitter, and Streeck, *Governing Capitalist Economies*, 156–82.

Darr, Asaf. "Gifting Practices and Interorganizational Relations: Constructing Obligational Networks in the Electronics Sector." *Sociological Forum* 18, no. 1 (2003): 31–51.

Davis, John. "An Anthropologist's View of Exchange." *Social Anthropology* 4 (1996): 213–26.

Davis, Gerald. "Firms and Environments." In Smelser and Swedberg, *Handbook of Economic Sociology*, 2nd ed., 478–502.

Dickens, Charles. *A Christmas Carol.* Edited by John Irving. New York: Modern Library, 2001.

DiMaggio, Paul. "Culture and Cognition." *Annual Review of Sociology* 23 (1997): 263–83.

———. "Culture and Economy." In Smelser and Swedberg, *Handbook of Economic Sociology*, 1st ed., 27–57.

———. "Endogenizing 'Animal Spirits': Toward a Sociology of Collective Response to Uncertainty and Risk." In Guillén et al., *The New Economic Sociology*, 79–100.

———. "Market Structure, the Creative Process and Popular Culture: Toward an Organizational Reinterpretation of Mass Culture Theory." *Journal of Popular Culture* 11, no. 2 (1977): 436–52.

DiMaggio, Paul, ed. *The Twenty-First Century Firm: Changing Economic Organization in International Perspective.* Princeton, NJ: Princeton University Press, 2001.

DiMaggio, Paul, and Hugh Louch. "Socially Embedded Consumer Transactions: For What Kinds of Purchases Do People Most Often Use Networks?" *American Sociological Review* 63 (1998): 619–37.

DiMaggio, Paul, and Walter Powell. "Introduction." In Powell and DiMaggio, *The New Institutionalism in Organizational Analysis*, 1–38.

———. "The Iron Cage Revisited: Institutional Isomorphism and Collective Rationality in Organizational Fields." In Powell and DiMaggio, *The New Institutionalism in Organizational Analysis*, 63–82.

Dobbin, Frank. "Comparative and Historical Approaches to Economic Sociology." In Smelser and Swedberg, *Handbook of Economic Sociology*, 2nd ed., 26–48.

———. "Cultural Models of Organization: The Social Construction of Rational Organizing Principles." In Crane, *Sociology of Culture*, 117–41.

———. *Forging Industrial Policy: The United States, Britain, and France in the Railway Age.* Cambridge: Cambridge University Press, 1994.

———. "The Social Construction of the Great Depression: Industrial Policy during the 1930s in the United States, Britain, and France." *Theory and Society* 22 (1993): 1–56.

Dobbin, Frank, ed. *The New Economic Sociology: A Reader*. Princeton, NJ: Princeton University Press, 2004.

Dobbin, Frank, and Timothy Dowd. "The Market That Anti-Trust Built." *American Sociological Review* 65 (2000): 631–57.

Domhoff, William. *The Power Elite and the State: How Policy Is Made in America*. New York: Aldine de Gruyter, 1990.

Domhoff, William, and Thomas Dye, eds. *Power Elites and Organizations*. Newbury Park, CA: Sage, 1987.

Douglas, Mary. *How Institutions Think*. Syracuse, NY: Syracuse University Press, 1986.

Douglas, Mary, and Baron Isherwood. *The World of Goods*. New York: Basic Books, 1979.

Dumenil, Lynn. *Freemasonry and American Culture, 1880–1930*. Princeton, NJ: Princeton University Press, 1984.

Durkheim, Émile. *The Division of Labor in Society*. Translated by W. D. Halls. New York: Free Press, 1984.

———. *The Elementary Forms of Religious Life*. Translated by Karen Fields. New York: Free Press, 1995.

———. *Professional Ethics and Civic Morals*. Translated by Cornelia Brookfield. Glencoe, IL: Free Press, 1958.

———. *Suicide*. Edited by George Simpson. Translated by John Spaulding and George Simpson. New York: Free Press, 1951.

Eliasoph, Nina. *Avoiding Politics: How Americans Create Apathy in Everyday Life*. Cambridge: Cambridge University Press, 1998.

Eliasoph, Nina, and Paul Lichterman. "Culture in Interaction." *American Journal of Sociology* 108, no. 4 (2003): 735–94.

Espeland, Wendy. "Commensuration and Cognition." In Cerulo, *Culture in Mind*, 63–89.

Espeland, Wendy, and Michael Sauder. "Rankings and Reactivity: How Public Measures Recreate Social Worlds." *American Journal of Sociology* 113 (2007): 1–40.

Espeland, Wendy, and Mitchell Stevens. "Commensuration as a Social Process." *Annual Review of Sociology* 24 (1998): 313–43.

Evetts, Julia. "A Sociological Analysis of Professionalism: Occupational Change in the Modern World." *International Sociology* 18, no. 2 (2003): 395–415.

Faeges, Russell. "Theory-Driven Concept Definition: The Challenge of Perverse Cases." Paper presented at the Annual Meeting of the American Political Science Association, Atlanta, 1999.

Farrell, Joseph, and Garth Saloner. "Coordination through Committees and Markets," *Rand Journal of Economics* 19, no. 2 (1988): 235–52.

Fishman, Robert. *Democracy's Voices: Social Ties and the Quality of Public Life in Spain*. Ithaca, NY: Cornell University Press, 2004.

Fligstein, Neil. *The Architecture of Markets: An Economic Sociology of Twenty-First Century Capitalist Societies*. Princeton, NJ: Princeton University Press, 2001.

———. "Social Skill and the Theory of Fields." *Sociological Theory* 18 (2001): 105–25.

———. *The Transformation of Corporate Control*. Cambridge, MA: Harvard University Press, 1990.

Fligstein, Neil, and Robert Freeland. "Theoretical and Comparative Perspectives on Corporate Organization." *Annual Review of Sociology* 21 (1995): 21–43.

Flyvbjerg, Bent. *Making Social Science Matter: Why Social Inquiry Fails and How It Can Succeed Again*. Cambridge: Cambridge University Press, 2001.

Fourcade, Marion. *Economists and Societies: Discipline and Profession in the United States, Britain, and France, 1890s to 1990s*. Princeton, NJ: Princeton University Press, 2009.

Fourcade, Marion, and Kieran Healy. "Moral Views of Market Society." *Annual Review of Sociology* 33 (2007): 285–311.

Fraser, Nancy. "Rethinking the Public Sphere: A Contribution to the Critique of Actually Existing Democracy." *Social Text* 25/26 (1990): 56–80.

Freyer, Tony. *Antitrust and Global Capitalism, 1930–2004*. Cambridge: Cambridge University Press, 2006.

Friedland, Roger, and Robert Alford. "Bringing Society Back In: Symbols, Practices, and Institutional Contradictions." In Powell and DiMaggio, *The New Institutionalism in Organizational Analysis*, 232–63.

Friedland, Roger, and A. F. Robertson, eds. *Beyond the Marketplace: Rethinking Economy and Society*. New York: Aldine de Gruyter, 1990.

———. "Beyond the Marketplace." In Friedland and Robertson, *Beyond the Marketplace*, 3–49.

Friedson, Eliot. *Professionalism: The Third Logic*. Chicago: University of Chicago Press, 2001.

Fry, Michael, ed. *Adam Smith's Legacy: His Place in the Development of Modern Economics*. London: Routledge, 1992.

Fujita, Teiichiro. "Local Trade Associations (*Dogyo Kumiai*) in Prewar Japan." In Yamazaki and Miyamoto, *Trade Associations in Business History*, 87–113.

Fung, Archon. "Associations and Democracy: Between Theories, Hopes, and Realities." *Annual Review of Sociology* 29 (2003): 515–39.

Galambos, Louis. "The American Trade Association Movement Revisited." In Yamazaki and Miyamoto, *Trade Associations in Business History*, 121–35.

———. *Competition and Cooperation: The Emergence of a National Trade Association*. Baltimore: Johns Hopkins University Press, 1965.

Galaskiewicz, Joseph. "Interorganizational Relations." *Annual Review of Sociology* 11 (1985): 281–304.

———. "Professional Networks and the Institutionalization of a Single Mind Set." *American Sociological Review* 50 (1985): 639–58.

Gamm, Gerald, and Robert Putnam. "The Growth of Voluntary Associations in America, 1840–1940." *Journal of Interdisciplinary History* 29, no. 4 (1999): 511–57.

Gao, Bai. "The State and the Associational Order of the Economy: The Institutionalization of Cartels and Trade Associations in 1931–1945 Japan." *Sociological Forum* 16, no. 3 (2001): 409–43.

Garfinkel, Perry. "Cupid Takes to the Road, Too." *New York Times*, February 13, 2007, C8.

Garud, Raghu, and Arun Kumaraswamy. "Technological and Organizational Designs for Realizing Economies of Substitution." *Strategic Management Journal* 16 (1995): 93–109.

Geertz, Clifford. 1978. "The Bazaar Economy: Information and Search in Peasant Marketing." *American Economic Review* 68 (2): 28–32.

Geletkanycz, Marta, and Donald Hambrick. "The External Ties of Top Executives: Implications for Strategic Choice and Performance." *Administrative Science Quarterly* 42 (1997): 654–81.

Gereffi, Gary. "Merging Economic Sociology, Public Sociology, and the Global Economy." *Accounts* 5, no. 2 (2006): 3–4.

Gerlach, Michael. "The Japanese Corporate Network: A Blockmodel Analysis." *Administrative Science Quarterly* 37 (1992): 105–39.

Goffman, Erving. "Felicity's Condition." *American Journal of Sociology* 89 (1983): 1–53.

Goode, William. "Community within Community: The Professions." *American Sociological Review* 22 (1957): 194–200.

Goodstein, Jerry, Mary Blair-Loy, and Amy Wharton. "Organization-Based Legitimacy: Core Ideologies and Moral Action." In Reed and Alexander, *Meaning and Method*, 44–62.

Granovetter, Mark. "Business Groups." In Smelser and Swedberg, *Handbook of Economic Sociology*, 1st ed., 453–75.

———. "Business Groups and Social Organization." In Smelser and Swedberg, *The Handbook of Economic Sociology*, 2nd ed., 429–50.

———. "Coase Revisited: Business Groups in the Modern Economy." In Granovetter and Swedberg, *The Sociology of Economic Life*, 2nd ed., 327–36.

———. "Economic Action and Social Structure: The Problem of Embeddedness." *American Journal of Sociology* 91, no. 3 (1985): 481–510.

———. "A Theoretical Agenda for Economic Sociology." In Guillén et al., *The New Economic Sociology*, 35–60.

Granovetter, Mark, and Richard Swedberg, eds. *The Sociology of Economic Life*. 2nd ed. Boulder, CO: Westview Press, 2001.

Grant, Wyn. *Business Interests, Organizational Development, and Private Interest Government: An International Comparative Study of the Food Processing Industry*. New York: Aldine de Gruyter, 1987.

———. "Private Organizations as Agents of Public Policy: The Case of Milk Marketing in Britain." In Streeck and Schmitter, *Private Interest Government*, 182–96.

Greene, Brian. *The Fabric of the Cosmos: Space, Time, and the Texture of Reality.* New York: Knopf, 2004.

Greenwood, Royston, Roy Suddaby, and C. R. Hinings. "Theorizing Change: The Role of Professional Associations in the Transformation of Institutionalized Fields." *Academy of Management Journal* 45, no. 1 (2002): 56–80.

Gregory, Bruce. *Inventing Reality: Physics as Language.* New York: Wiley, 1988.

Griswold, Wendy. *Cultures and Societies in a Changing World.* 3rd ed. Los Angeles: Pine Forge Press, 2008.

Gronjberg, Kirsten. "Markets, Politics, and Charity: Nonprofits in the Political Economy." In Powell and Clemens, *Private Action and the Public Good*, 137–50.

Grusky, David, and Gabriela Galescu. "Is Durkheim a Class Analyst?" In *The Cambridge Companion to Durkheim*, edited by Jeffrey Alexander and Philip Smith, 322–59. Cambridge: Cambridge University Press, 2005.

Guillén, Mauro, Randall Collins, Paula England, and Marshall Meyer, eds. *The New Economic Sociology: Developments in an Emerging Field.* New York: Russell Sage Foundation, 2002.

Gulati, Ranjay. "Alliances and Networks." *Strategic Management Journal* 19 (1998): 293–317.

———. "Social Structure and Alliance Formation Patterns: A Longitudinal Analysis." *Administrative Science Quarterly* 40 (1995): 619–52.

Gulati, Ranjay, and Martin Gargiulo. "Where Do Interorganizational Networks Come From?" *American Journal of Sociology* 104, no. 5 (1999): 1439–93.

Hage, Jerald, and Catherine Alter. "A Typology of Interorganizational Relationships and Networks." In Hollingsworth and Boyer, *Contemporary Capitalism*, 94–126.

Hall, Peter. "A Historical Overview of the Private Nonprofit Sector." In Powell, *The Nonprofit Sector: A Research Handbook*, 3–26.

———. *Inventing the Nonprofit Sector and Other Essays on Philanthropy, Voluntarism, and Nonprofit Organizations.* Baltimore: Johns Hopkins University Press, 1992.

Hamilton, Gary. "Civilizations and the Organization of Economies." In Smelser and Swedberg, *The Handbook of Economic Sociology*, 1st ed., 183–205.

Hamilton, Gary, and Nicole Biggart. "Market, Culture, and Authority: A Comparative Analysis of Management and Organization in the Far East." *American Journal of Sociology* (Supplement) 94 (1988): S52–S94.

Hansen, Karen. *A Very Social Time: Crafting Community in Antebellum New England.* Berkeley: University of California Press, 1994.

Hansen, Wendy, and Neil Mitchell. "Disaggregating and Explaining Corporate Political Activity: Domestic and Foreign Corporations in National Politics." *American Political Science Review* 94, no. 4 (2000): 891–903.

Hansen, Wendy, Neil Mitchell, and Jeffrey Drope. "Collective Action, Pluralism, and the Legitimacy Tariff: Corporate Activity or Inactivity in Politics." *Political Research Quarterly* 57, no. 3 (2004): 421–29.

Harker, Kathryn. "Data Resources on the World Wide Web." In *Blackwell Companion to Sociology*, edited by Judith Blau, 464–525. Malden, MA: Blackwell, 2001.

Harper, Douglas, and Helene Lawson, eds. *The Cultural Study of Work*. Lanham, MD: Rowman and Littlefield, 2003.

Hart, David. " 'Business' Is Not an Interest Group: On the Study of Companies in American National Politics." *Annual Review of Political Science* 7 (2004): 47–69.

Hawkins, Hugh. *Banding Together: The Rise of National Associations in American Higher Education, 1887–1950*. Baltimore: Johns Hopkins University Press, 1992.

Hawkins, M. J. "Durkheim on Occupational Corporations: An Exegesis and Interpretation." *Journal of the History of Ideas* 55 (1994): 461–81.

Hawley, Ellis. "Antitrust and the Association Movement, 1920–1940." In *National Competition Policy: Historians' Perspectives on Antitrust and Government-Business Relationships in the United States*, 97–141. Washington, DC: Office of Special Projects, Bureau of Competition, Federal Trade Commission, 1981.

Haydu, Jeffrey. "Business Citizenship at Work: Cultural Transposition and Class Formation in Cincinnati, 1870–1910." *American Journal of Sociology* 107, no. 6 (2002): 1424–67.

———. *Citizen Employers: Business Communities and Labor in Cincinnati and San Francisco, 1870–1916*. Ithaca, NY: Cornell University Press, 2008.

Herrigel, Gary. *Industrial Constructions: The Sources of German Industrial Power*. Cambridge: Cambridge University Press, 1996.

———. "Industry as a Form of Order: A Comparison of the Historical Development of the Machine Tool Industries in the United States and Germany." In Hollingsworth, Schmitter and Streeck, *Governing Capitalist Economies*, 97–128.

Hewson, Clare. "Internet-Mediated Research as an Emergent Method and Its Potential in Facilitating Mixed Methods Research." In *Handbook of Emergent Methods*, edited by Sharlene Nagy Hesse-Biber and Patricia Leavy, 543–70. New York: Guilford Press, 2008.

Himmelberg, Robert. *The Origins of the National Recovery Administration: Business, Government, and the Trade Association Issue, 1921–33*. New York: Fordham University Press, 1993.

Hine, Christine. "Internet Research as Emergent Practice." In *Handbook of Emergent Methods*, edited by Sharlene Nagy Hesse-Biber and Patricia Leavy, 525–41. New York: Guilford Press, 2008.

Hirsch, Paul. "Cultural Industries Revisited." *Organization Science* 11, no. 3 (2000): 356–61.

——. "From Ambushes to Golden Parachutes: Corporate Takeovers as an Instance of Cultural Framing and Institutional Integration." *American Journal of Sociology* 91 (1986): 800–837.

——. "Organizational Effectiveness and the Institutional Environment." *Administrative Science Quarterly* 20 (1975): 327–44.

——. "Processing Fads and Fashions: An Organization-Set Analysis of Culture Industry Systems." *American Journal of Sociology* 77 (1972): 639–59.

——. "The Study of Industries." *Research in the Sociology of Organizations* 4 (1985): 271–309.

Hirschman, Albert. *The Passions and the Interests: Political Arguments for Capitalism before Its Triumph.* Princeton, NJ: Princeton University Press, 1977.

Hirst, Paul, and Jonathan Zeitlin. "Flexible Specialization: Theory and Evidence in the Analysis of Industrial Change." In Hollingsworth and Boyer, *Contemporary Capitalism*, 220–39.

Ho, K. C., Zaheer Baber, and Habibul Khonder. "'Sites' of Resistance: Alternative Websites and State-Society Relations." *British Journal of Sociology* 53, no. 1 (2002): 127–48.

Hoffman, Andrew, and Marc Ventresca, eds. *Organizations, Policy, and the Natural Environment: Institutional and Strategic Perspectives.* Stanford, CA: Stanford University Press, 2002.

Hollingsworth, J. Rogers. "Continuities and Changes in Social Systems of Production: The Cases of Japan, Germany, and the United States." In Hollingsworth and Boyer, *Contemporary Capitalism*, 265–310.

——. "Doing Institutional Analysis: Implications for the Study of Innovations." *Review of International Political Economy* 7, no. 4 (2000): 595–644.

——. "The Logic of Coordinating American Manufacturing Sectors." In Campbell, Hollingsworth, and Lindberg, *Governance of the American Economy*, 35–73.

Hollingsworth, J. Rogers, and Robert Boyer. *Contemporary Capitalism: The Embeddedness of Institutions.* Cambridge: Cambridge University Press, 1997.

Hollingsworth, J. Rogers, and Leon Lindberg. "The Governance of the American Economy: The Role of Markets, Clans, Hierarchies, and Associative Behaviors." In Streeck and Schmitter, *Private Interest Government*, 221–54.

Hollingsworth, J. Rogers, Philippe Schmitter, and Wolfgang Streeck, eds. *Governing Capitalist Economies.* Oxford: Oxford University Press, 1994.

Hollingsworth, J. Rogers, and Wolfgang Streeck. "Counties and Sectors." In Hollingsworth, Schmitter, and Streeck, *Governing Capitalist Economies*, 270–300.

Holman, Keith. "The Regulatory Flexibility Act at 25: Is the Law Achieving Its Goal?" *Fordham Urban Law Journal* 33 (2006): 1119–37.

Hulse, Carl. "As Congress Weights Reining in Lobbyists, Will the Hidden Perks Be Overlooked?" *New York Times*, January 22, 2006, 19.

Human, Sherrie, and Keith Provan. "Legitimacy Building in the Evolution of Small-Firm Multilateral Networks: A Comparative Study of Success and Demise." *Administrative Science Quarterly* 45 (2000): 327–65.

Hung, Ho-fung. "Agricultural Revolution and Elite Reproduction in Qing China: The Transition to Capitalism Debate Revisited." *American Sociological Review* 73 (2008): 569–88.

Hunt, Kimberly, ed. *Encyclopedia of Associations*. 39th ed. Farmington Hills, MI: Gale Group, 2003.

Illouz, Eva. *Cold Intimacies: The Making of Emotional Capitalism*. London: Polity, 2007.

———. "From *Homo economicus* to *Homo communicans*." In *Saving the Modern Soul: Therapy, Emotions, and The Culture of Self-Help*, 58–104. Berkeley: University of California Press, 2008.

———. *Oprah Winfrey and the Glamour of Misery*. New York: Columbia University Press, 2003.

Ingram, Paul, and Peter Roberts. "Friendships among Competitors in the Sydney Hotel Industry." *American Journal of Sociology* 106, no. 2 (2000): 387–423.

Jackall, Robert. *Moral Mazes: The World of Corporate Managers*. Oxford: Oxford University Press, 1988.

Jacobs, Mark D. "The Culture of Savings and Loan Scandal in the No-Fault Society." In *The Blackwell Companion to the Sociology of Culture*, edited by Mark D. Jacobs and Nancy Weiss Hanrahan, 362–80. Malden, MA: Blackwell, 2005.

Jacobs, Ronald. *Race, Media, and the Crisis of Civil Society: From Watts to Rodney King*. Cambridge: Cambridge University Press, 2000.

Jacobs, Ronald, and Daniel Glass. "Media Publicity and the Voluntary Sector: The Case of Nonprofit Organizations in New York City." *Voluntas: International Journal of Voluntary and Nonprofit Organizations* 13, no. 3 (2002): 235–52.

Jenkins, J. Craig. "Nonprofit Organizations and Policy Advocacy." In Powell, *The Nonprofit Sector: A Research Handbook*, 296–319.

Jordan, Grant, and Darren Halperin. "Olson Triumphant? Recruitment Strategies and the Growth of a Small Business Organisation." *Political Studies* 52 (2004): 431–49.

Jucius, M. J. "Historical Development of Uniform Cost Accounting." *Journal of Business of the University of Chicago* 16, no. 4 (1943): 219–29.

Judkins, C. J. *Trade and Professional Associations of the United States*. US Department of Commerce, Industrial Series No. 3. Washington, DC: Government Printing Office, 1942.

Kane, Anne. *Constructing Irish National Identity: Discourse and Ritual during the Land War, 1879–1882*. New York: Palgrave MacMillan, 2011.

Kaufman, Jason. *For the Common Good? American Civic Life and the Golden Age of Fraternity*. Oxford: Oxford University Press, 2002.

———. "Rent-Seeking and Municipal Social Spending." *Urban Affairs Review* 39, no. 5 (2004): 552–88.

Khurana, Rakesh. *From Higher Aims to Hired Hands: The Social Transformation of American Business Schools and the Unfulfilled Promise of Management as a Profession.* Princeton, NJ: Princeton University Press, 2007.

Kikkawa, Takeo. "Functions of Japanese Trade Associations before World War II: The Case of Cartel Organizations." In Yamazaki and Miyamoto, *Trade Associations in Business History,* 53–83.

Kimberly, John. "Organizational Size and the Structuralist Perspective: A Review, Critique and Proposal." *Administrative Science Quarterly* 21, no. 4 (1976): 571–97.

Knoke David. "Associations and Interest Groups." *Annual Review of Sociology* 12 (1986): 1–21.

———. *Organizing for Collective Action: The Political Economies of Associations.* New York: Aldine de Gruyter, 1990.

Knoke, David, and Richard Adams. "The Incentive Systems of Associations." *Research in the Sociology of Organizations* 5 (1987): 285–309.

Korczynski, Marek, Randy Hodson, and Paul Edwards, eds. *Social Theory at Work.* Oxford: Oxford University Press, 2006.

Krier, Dan. "Assessing the New Synthesis of Economics and Sociology: Promising Themes for Contemporary Analysis of Economic Life." *American Journal of Economics and Sociology* 58, no. 4 (1999): 669–96.

Krippner, Greta. "The Elusive Market: Embeddedness and the Paradigm of Economic Sociology." *Theory and Society* 30 (2001): 775–810.

Kunda, Gideon. *Engineering Culture: Control and Commitment in a High-Tech Corporation.* Philadelphia: Temple University Press, 1992.

Lamont, Michele. *Money, Morals, and Manners: The Culture of the French and the American Upper-Middle Class.* Chicago: University of Chicago Press, 1992.

Lampkin, Lynda, Sheryl Romero, and Emily Finnin. "Introducing the Nonprofit Program Classification System: The Taxonomy We've Been Waiting For." *Nonprofit and Voluntary Sector Quarterly* 30, no. 4 (2001): 781–93.

Larson, Magali. "Professions as Disciplinary Cultures." In *Blackwell Companion to the Sociology of Culture,* edited by Mark Jacobs and Nancy Weiss Hanrahan, 318–31. Malden, MA: Blackwell, 2005.

———. *The Rise of Professionalism: A Sociological Analysis.* Berkeley: University of California Press, 1977.

Laumann, Edward, and David Knoke. *The Organizational State.* Madison: University of Wisconsin Press, 1987.

Lawrence, Thomas, and Roy Suddaby. "Institutions and Institutional Work." In *Sage Handbook of Organization Studies,* 2nd ed., edited by Stewart Clegg, Cynthia Hay, Tom Lawrence, and Walter Nord, 218–34. Thousand Oaks, CA: Sage, 2006.

Lawrence, Thomas, Roy Suddaby, and Bernard Leca. "Introduction: Theorizing and Studying Institutional Work." In *Institutional Work: Actors and Agency in Institutional Studies of Organizations*, edited by Lawrence, Suddaby, and Leca, 1–27. Cambridge: Cambridge University Press, 2009.

Lazarsfeld, Paul. "Reflections on Business." *American Journal of Sociology* 65, no. 1 (1959): 1–31.

Leblebici, Huseyn, and Gerald Salancik. "The Rules of Organizing and the Managerial Role." *Organization Studies* 10, no. 3 (1989): 301–25.

Leblebici, Huseyn, Gerald Salancik, Anne Copay, and Tom King. "Institutional Change and the Transformation of Interorganizational Fields: An Organizational History of the US Radio Broadcasting Industry." *Administrative Science Quarterly* 36 (1991): 333–63.

Lentz, Arthur, and Harvey Tschirgi. "The Ethical Content of Annual Reports." *Journal of Business* 36, no. 4 (1963): 387–93.

Levitan, Sar, and Martha Cooper. *Business Lobbies: The Public Good and the Bottom Line*. Baltimore: Johns Hopkins University Press, 1984.

Lichterman, Paul. *Elusive Togetherness: Church Groups Trying to Bridge America's Divisions*. Princeton, NJ: Princeton University Press, 2005.

———. *The Search for Political Community: American Activists Reinventing Commitment*. Cambridge: Cambridge University Press, 1996.

———. "Social Capital or Group Style? Rescuing Tocqueville's Insights on Civic Engagement." *Theory and Society* 35, no. 5/6 (2006): 529–63.

Lie, John. "Sociology of Markets." *Annual Review of Sociology* 23 (1997): 341–60.

Lincoln, James, and Didier Guillot. "A Durkheimian View of Organizational Culture." In *Social Theory at Work*, edited by Marek Korczynski, Randy Hodson, and Paul Edwards, 88–120. Oxford: Oxford University Press, 2006.

Lindberg, Leon, and John Campbell. "The State and the Organization of Economic Activity." In Campbell, Hollingsworth and Lindberg, *Governance of the American Economy*, 356–95.

Lindberg, Leon, John Campbell, and J. Rogers Hollingsworth. "Economic Governance and the Analysis of Structural Change in the American Economy." In Campbell, Hollingsworth, and Lindberg, *Governance of the American Economy*, 3–34.

Lo, Ming-Cheng. "The Professions: Prodigal Daughters of Modernity." In Adams, Clemens, and Orloff, *Remaking Modernity*, 381–406.

Lounsbury, Michael. "A Tale of Two Cities: Competing Logics and Practice Variation in the Professionalizing of Mutual Funds." *Academy of Management Journal* 50, no. 2 (2007): 289–307.

Lounsbury, Michael, and Hayagreeva Rao. "Sources of Durability and Change in Market Classifications: A Study of the Reconstitution of Product Categories in the American Mutual Fund Industry, 1944–1985." *Social Forces* 82, no. 3 (2004): 969–99.

Lounsbury, Michael, Marc Ventresca, and Paul Hirsch. "Social Movements, Field Frames, and Industry Emergence: A Cultural-Political Perspective on U.S. Recycling." *Socio-Economic Review* 1, no. 1 (2003): 71–104.

Lukes, Steven. *Power: A Radical View*. London: Macmillan, 1974.

Lynn, Leonard, and Timothy McKeown. *Organizing Business: Trade Associations in America and Japan*. Washington, DC: American Enterprise Institute for Public Policy Research, 1988.

Macdonald, Keith. "Professional Work." In *Social Theory at Work*, edited by Marek Korczynski, Randy Hodson, and Paul Edwards, 356–87. Oxford: Oxford University Press, 2006.

Macher, Jeffrey, and Barak Richman. "Transaction Cost Economics: An Assessment of Empirical Research in the Social Sciences." *Business and Politics* 10, no. 1 (2008): 1–63.

Mack, Charles. *Business, Politics, and the Practice of Government Relations*. Westport, CT: Quorum Books, 1997.

———. *The Executive's Handbook of Trade and Business Associations: How They Work—and How to Make Them Work Effectively for You*. Westport, CT: Quorum Books, 1991.

Mann, Michael. "Socio-Logic." *Sociology* 15, no. 4 (1981): 544–30.

Mansbridge, Jane. "On the Contested Nature of the Public Good." In Powell and Clemens, *Private Action and the Public Good*, 3–19.

Marcus, George. "Once More into the Breach between Economic and Cultural Analysis." In Friedland and Robertson, *Beyond the Marketplace*, 331–52.

Marquis, Christopher, and Michael Lounsbury. "Vive la Résistance: Competing Logics and the Consolidation of U.S. Community Banking." *Academy of Management Journal* 50, no. 4 (2007): 799–820.

Martin, John L. "What Is Field Theory?" *American Journal of Sociology* 109 (2003): 1–49.

Martinelli, Alberto, and Neil Smelser, eds. *Economy and Society: Overviews in Economic Sociology*. London: Sage, 1990.

Marx, Karl. "The Buying and Selling of Labour Power." From *Capital*, vol. 1. In Tucker, *The Marx-Engels Reader*, 336–43.

———. "The Capitalistic Character of Manufacture." In Tucker, *The Marx-Engels Reader*, 397–403.

———. "Economic and Philosophical Manuscripts of 1844." In Tucker, *The Marx-Engels Reader*, 66–125.

———. "The German Ideology: Part One." In Tucker, *Marx-Engels Reader*, 147–200.

———. "The *Grundrisse*." In Tucker, *The Marx-Engels Reader*, 221–93.

Marx, Karl, and Friedrich Engels. "Manifesto of the Communist Party." In Tucker, *The Marx-Engels Reader*, 469–500.

McGahan, A. M. "Cooperation in Prices and Capacities: Trade Associations in Brewing after Repeal." *Journal of Law and Economics* 38, no. 2 (1995): 521–58.

McGraw, Thomas, ed. *The Essential Alfred Chandler: Essays toward a Historical Theory of Big Business*. Boston: Harvard Business School Press, 1988.

McIntire, Mike, and Jennifer Medina. "Lieberman's Donors Include Many Who Favor Republicans." *New York Times*, July 20, 2006, A20.

Meyer, John, and Brian Rowan. "Institutionalized Organizations: Formal Structure as Myth and Ceremony." *American Journal of Sociology* 83, no. 2 (1977): 340–63.

Miller, Dale. "The Norm of Self-Interest." *American Psychologist* 54, no. 12 (1999): 1053–60.

Miller, Laura. *Reluctant Capitalists: Bookselling and the Culture of Consumption*. Chicago: University of Chicago Press, 2006.

Mills, C. Wright. "Situated Actions and Vocabularies of Motive." *American Sociological Review* 5 (1940): 904–13.

Miyamato, Matao. "The Development of Business Associations in Prewar Japan." In Yamazaki and Miyamoto, *Trade Associations in Business History*, 1–45.

Mizruchi, Mark. "The American Corporate Elite and the Historical Roots of the Financial Crisis of 2008." In *Markets on Trial: The Economic Sociology of the U.S. Financial Crisis*, edited by Michael Lounsbury. *Research in the Sociology of Organizations* 30B (2010): 103–39.

Mizruchi, Mark, and Linda Stearns. "Getting Deals Done: The Use of Social Networks in Bank Decision-Making." *American Sociological Review* 66 (2001): 647–71.

Mohr, John. "Implicit Terrains: Meaning, Measurement, and Spatial Metaphors in Organizational Theory." In *The Economic Sociology of Markets and Industries*, edited by Marc Ventresca, Karnal Munir, and Michael Lounsbury. Cambridge: Cambridge University Press, forthcoming.

Mohr, John, and Helene Lee. "From Affirmative Action to Outreach: Discourse Shifts at the University of California." *Poetics* 28, no. 1 (2000): 47–71.

Moon, Dawne. *God, Sex, and Politics: Homosexuality and Everyday Theologies*. Chicago: University of Chicago Press, 2004.

Morgenson, Gretchen. "Is 'Total Pay' That Tough to Grasp?" *New York Times*, July 9, 2006, Section 3: 1, 7.

Morrill, Calvin. *The Executive Way: Conflict Management in Corporations*. Chicago: University of Chicago Press, 1995.

Muller, Hans-Peter. "Social Differentiation and Organic Solidarity: The *Division of Labor* Revisited." *Sociological Forum* 9 (1994): 73–92.

National Trade and Professional Associations Directory. Washington, DC: Columbia Books, 1999.

Nee, Victor. "The New Institutionalisms in Economics and Sociology." In Smelser and Swedberg, *Handbook of Economic Sociology*, 2nd ed., 49–74.

New York Times. "Appointed Hobblers of Government." Editorial. May 18, 2007, A26.

O'Brien, Patricia. "Governance Systems in Steel: The American and Japanese Experience." In Hollingsworth, Schmitter, and Streeck, *Governing Capitalist Economies*, 43–71.

Ocasio, William. "Towards an Attention-Based View of the Firm." *Strategic Management Journal* 18 (1997): 187–206.

Olson, Mancur. *The Logic of Collective Action: Public Goods and the Theory of Groups*. Cambridge, MA: Harvard University Press, 1965.

O'Neill, Michael. "Philanthropic Dimensions of Mutual Benefit Organizations." *Nonprofit and Voluntary Sector Quarterly* 23 (1994): 3–20.

O'Sullivan, Mary, Gary Herrigel, T. J. Pempel, and Wolfgang Streeck. "Symposium on the 'Origins of Non-Liberal Capitalism.'" *Socio-Economic Review* 3 (2005): 545–87.

Oxford English Dictionary. Compact edition. Vol. 1. Oxford: Oxford University Press, 1971.

Parsons, Talcott. "The Motivation of Economic Activities." *Canadian Journal of Economics and Political Science* 6, no. 2 (1940): 197–202.

———. "The Professions and Social Structure." *Social Forces* 17, no. 4 (1939): 457–67.

———. "Sociological Elements in Economic Thought: II, The Analytical Factor View." *Quarterly Journal of Economics* 49, no. 4 (1935): 646–67.

Parsons, Talcott, and Neil Smelser. *Economy and Society: A Study of the Integration of Economic and Social Theory*. New York: Free Press of Glencoe, 1964.

Pearce, Charles. *Trade Association Survey*. Monograph No. 18, Investigation of Concentration of Economic Power. A Study Made under the Auspices of the Department of Commerce for the United States Senate, Temporary National Economic Committee, Seventy-Sixth Congress, Third Session. Washington, DC: Government Printing Office, 1941.

Perrin, Andrew. *Citizen Speak: The Democratic Imagination in American Life*. Chicago: University of Chicago Press, 2006.

Peterson, Richard. "Cultural Studies through the Production Perspective: Progress and Possibilities." In Crane, *The Sociology of Culture*, 163–90.

———. "Revitalizing the Culture Concept." *Annual Review of Sociology* 5 (1979): 137–66.

Pettinger, Lynne. "Friends, Relations, and Colleagues: The Blurred Boundaries of the Workplace." In *A New Sociology of Work?*, edited by Lynne Pettinger, Jane Parry, Rebecca Taylor and Miriam Glucksmann, 39–55. Malden, MA: Blackwell Publishing/The Sociological Review, 2005.

Pfeffer, Jeffrey, and Gerald Salancik. *The External Control of Organizations: A Resource Dependence Perspective*. New York: Harper and Row, 1978.

Phillips, Damon, and Ezra Zuckerman. "Middle-Status Conformity: Theoretical Restatement and Empirical Demonstration in Two Markets." *American Journal of Sociology* 107 (2001): 379–429.

Podolny, Joel. "Networks as Pipes and Prisms of the Market." *American Journal of Sociology* 107 (2001): 33–60.

———. "A Status-Based Model of Market Competition." *American Journal of Sociology* 98 (1993): 829–72.

Polanyi, Karl. *The Great Transformation*. Boston: Beacon Press, 1957.

Polanyi, Karl, Conrad Arensberg, and Harry Pearson, eds. *Trade and Market in the Early Empires*. New York: Free Press, 1957.

Porac, Joseph, Marc Ventresca, and Yuri Mishina. "Interorganizational Cognition and Interpretation." In *Blackwell Companion to Organizations*, edited by J. A. C. Baum, 579–98. New York: Blackwell, 2002.

Portes, Alejandro. "The Informal Economy and Its Paradoxes." In Smelser and Swedberg, *Handbook of Economic Sociology*, 1st ed., 426–49.

Powell, Walter. "Neither Market nor Hierarchy: Network Forms of Organization." *Research in Organizational Behavior* 12 (1990): 295–336.

Powell, Walter, ed. *The Nonprofit Sector: A Research Handbook*. New Haven, CT: Yale University Press, 1987.

Powell, Walter, and Elisabeth Clemens, eds. *Private Action and the Public Good*. New Haven, CT: Yale University Press, 1998.

Powell, Walter, and Paul DiMaggio, eds. *The New Institutionalism in Organizational Analysis*. Chicago: University of Chicago Press, 1991.

Powell, Walter, Kenneth Koput, and Laurel Smith-Doerr. "Interorganizational Collaboration and the Locus of Innovation: Networks of Learning in Biotechnology." *Administrative Science Quarterly* 41 (1996): 116–45.

Powell, Walter, and Laurel Smith-Doerr. "Networks and Economic Life." In Smelser and Swedberg, *Handbook of Economic Sociology*, 1st ed., 368–402.

Prasad, Monica. "The Morality of Market Exchange: Love, Money, and Contractual Justice." *Sociological Perspectives* 42, no. 2 (1999): 181–214.

Procassini, Andrew. *Competitors in Alliance: Industry Associations, Global Rivalries, and Business-Government Relations*. Westport, CT: Quorum Books, 1995.

Putnam, Robert, ed. *Democracies in Flux: The Evolution of Social Capital in Contemporary Society*. Oxford: Oxford University Press, 2002.

Quarter, J., J. Sousa, B. J. Richmond, and I. Carmichael. "Comparing Member-Based Organizations within a Social Economy Framework." *Nonprofit and Voluntary Sector Quarterly* 30 (2001): 351–75.

Ragin, Charles. *Constructing Social Research: The Unity and Diversity of Method*. Thousand Oaks, CA: Pine Forge Press, 1994.

Rao, Hayagreeva. "Caveat Emptor: The Construction of Nonprofit Watchdog Associations." *American Journal of Sociology* 103 (1998): 902–61.

Reed, Isaac, and Jeffrey Alexander, eds. *Meaning and Method: The Cultural Approach to Sociology*. Boulder, CO: Paradigm, 2009.

Rosenkopf, Lori, Ance Meitiu, and Varghese George. "From the Bottom Up? Technical Committee Activity and Alliance Formation." *Administrative Science Quarterly* 46 (2001): 748–72.

Roy, William. "Functional and Historical Logics in Explaining the Rise of the American Industrial Corporation." *Comparative Social Research* 12 (1990): 19–44.

———. *Socializing Capital: The Rise of the Large Industrial Corporation in America.* Princeton, NJ: Princeton University Press, 1997.

Roy, William, and Rachel Parker-Gwin. "How Many Logics of Collective Action?" *Theory and Society* 28 (1999): 203–37.

Rueschemeyer, Dietrich. *Power and the Division of Labor.* Stanford, CA: Stanford University Press, 1986.

Sabel, Charles. "Learning by Monitoring: The Institutions of Economic Development." In Smelser and Swedberg, *Handbook of Economic Sociology*, 1st ed., 137–65.

Saguy, Abigail. *What Is Sexual Harassment? From Capitol Hill to the Sorbonne.* Berkeley: University of California Press, 2003.

Sahlins, Marshall. *Culture and Practical Reason.* Chicago: University of Chicago Press, 1976.

———. *Stone Age Economics.* Chicago: Aldine-Atherton, 1972.

Sako, Mari. "Neither Markets nor Hierarchies: A Comparative Study of the Printed Circuit Board Industry in Britain and Japan." In Hollingsworth, Schmitter, and Streeck, *Governing Capitalist Economies*, 17–42.

Salamon, Lester. "Partners in Public Service: The Scope and Theory of Government-Nonprofit Relations." In Powell, *The Nonprofit Sector: A Research Handbook*, 99–117.

———. "The United States." In Salamon and Anheier, *Defining the Nonprofit Sector*, 280–319.

Salamon, Lester, and Helmut Anheier. *Defining the Nonprofit Sector: A Cross-National Analysis.* Manchester: Manchester University Press, 1997.

———. *The Emerging Nonprofit Sector: An Overview.* Manchester: Manchester University Press, 1996.

Sanders, Elizabeth. "Industrial Concentration, Sectional Competition, and Antitrust Politics in America, 1880–1980." In *Studies in American Political Development*, vol. 1, edited by Karen Orren and Stephen Skowrenak, 142–214. New Haven, CT: Yale University Press, 1986.

Saxenian, Anna Lee. "In Search of Power: The Organization of Business Interests in Silicon Valley and Route 128." *Economy and Society* 18 (1989): 25–70.

Schlozman, Kay, and John Tierney. *Organized Interests and American Democracy.* New York: Harper and Row, 1986.

Schmitter, Philippe, and Wolfgang Streeck. "The Organization of Business Interests: Studying the Associative Action of Business in Advanced Industrial Societies." MPIfG Discussion Paper 99/1. Max-Planck-Institut für Gesellschaftsforschung, 1999.

Schneiberg, Marc. "Political and Institutional Conditions for Governance by Associations: Private Order and Price Controls in American Fire Insurance." *Politics and Society* 27 (1999): 67–103.

Schneiberg, Marc, and Tim Bartley. "Regulating American Industries: Markets, Politics, and the Institutional Determinants of Fire Insurance Regulation." *American Journal of Sociology* 107, no. 1 (2001): 101–46.

Schneiberg, Marc, and Elisabeth Clemens. "The Typical Tools for the Job: Research Strategies in Institutional Analysis." *Sociological Theory* 24, no. 3 (2006): 195–227.

Schneiberg, Marc, and J. Rogers Hollingsworth. "Can Transaction Cost Economics Explain Trade Associations?" In Aoki, Gustafsson, and Williamson, *The Firm as a Nexus of Treaties*, 320–46.

Schneider, Ben, and Richard Doner. "The New Institutional Economics, Business Associations, and Development." *Brazilian Journal of Political Economy* 20, no. 3 (2000): 39–62.

Schudson, Michael. "How Culture Works: Perspectives from Media Studies on the Efficacy of Symbols." *Theory and Society* 18, no. 2 (1989): 153–80.

———. "The Trouble with Experts and Why Democracies Need Them." *Theory and Society* 35, no. 5/6 (2006): 491–506.

Scott, Richard. "Organizations and New Institutionalism." Paper presented at "The Cultural Turn Conference IV." University of California, Santa Barbara, March 2003.

Scranton, Philip. *Endless Novelty: Specialty Production and American Industrialization, 1865–1925*. Princeton, NJ: Princeton University Press, 1997.

Sennett, Richard. *The Craftsman*. New Haven, CT: Yale University Press, 2008.

Sewell, William. "A Theory of Structure: Duality, Agency, and Transformation." *American Journal of Sociology* 98 (1992): 1–29.

Simmel, Georg. "The Sociology of Sociability." Translated by Everett C. Hughes. *American Journal of Sociology* 55, no. 3 (1949): 254–61.

Sine, Wesley, Heather Havemann, and Pamela Tolbert. "Risky Business: Entrepreneurship in the New Independent Power Sector." *Administrative Science Quarterly* 50 (2005): 200–232.

Sklar, Martin. *The Corporate Reconstruction of American Capitalism, 1890–1916: The Market, the Law, and Politics*. Cambridge: Cambridge University Press, 1988.

Skloot, Edward. "Enterprise and Commerce in Nonprofit Organizations." In Powell, *The Nonprofit Sector: A Research Handbook*, 380–96.

Skocpol, Theda. "United States: From Membership to Advocacy." In Putnam, *Democracies in Flux*, 103–36.

Skocpol, Theda, and Morris Fiorina. "Making Sense of the Civic Engagement Debate." In Skocpol and Fiorina, *Civic Engagement in American Democracy*, 1–23.

Skocpol, Theda, and Morris Fiorina, eds. *Civic Engagement in American Democracy*. Washington, DC, and New York: Brookings Institution Press and Russell Sage Foundation, 1999.

Skocpol, Theda, with Marshall Ganz, Ziad Munson, Bayliss Camp, Michele Swers, and Jennifer Oser. "How Americans Became Civic." In Skocpol and Fiorina, *Civic Engagement in American Democracy*, 27–80.

Smelser, Neil. "Economic Rationality as a Religious System." In Wuthnow, *Rethinking Materialism*, 73–92.

———. *Problematics of Sociology: The Georg Simmel Lectures, 1995*. Berkeley: University of California Press, 1997.

———. "The Rational and the Ambivalent in the Social Sciences," *American Sociological Review* 63 (1998): 1–16.

———. *The Sociology of Economic Life*. Englewood Cliffs, NJ: Prentice Hall, 1976.

Smelser, Neil, and Richard Swedberg, eds. *The Handbook of Economic Sociology*. Princeton, NJ: Princeton University Press; New York: Russell Sage Foundation, 1994.

———. *The Handbook of Economic Sociology*. 2nd ed. Princeton, NJ: Princeton University Press; New York: Russell Sage Foundation, 2005.

Smith, Adam. *The Theory of Moral Sentiments*. Edited by D. D. Raphael and A. L. Macfie. New York: Oxford University Press, 1976.

———. *The Wealth of Nations*. Introduction by Robert Reich. Edited by Edwin Cannan. New York: Modern Library, 2000.

Smith, David Horton. "National Nonprofit, Voluntary Associations: Some Parameters." *Nonprofit and Voluntary Sector Quarterly* 21, no. 1 (1992): 81–94.

Smith, Dorothy. *Texts, Facts, and Femininity: Exploring the Relations of Ruling*. New York: Routledge, 1990.

Smith, Mark. *American Business and Political Power: Public Opinion, Elections, and Democracy*. Chicago: University of Chicago Press, 2000.

Smith, Philip. *Why War? The Cultural Logic of Iraq, the Gulf War, and Suez*. Chicago: University of Chicago Press, 2005.

Smith, Theodore. "Industrial Associations: Reflections of an Insider." *Journal of Voluntary Action Research* 1, no. 2 (1972): 8–12.

Smith-Doerr, Laurel, and Walter Powell. "Networks and Economic Life." In Smelser and Swedberg, *The Handbook of Economic Sociology*, 2nd ed., 379–402.

Sorenson, Olav, and Toby Stuart. "Syndication Networks and the Spatial Distribution of Capital Investments." *American Journal of Sociology* 106, no. 6 (2001): 1546–88.

Spillman, Lyn. "'As We Look Ahead to the New Year': Culture and Interests." *Culture* 22, no. 1 (2007): 1–5.

———. "Causal Reasoning, Historical Logic, and Sociological Explanation." In *Self, Social Structure, and Beliefs: Explorations in the Sociological Thought of Neil J. Smelser*, edited by Jeffrey Alexander, Gary Marx, and Christine Williams, 216–34. Berkeley: University of California Press, 2004.

———. "Culture and Economic Life." In Jeffrey Alexander, Philip Smith, and Ron Jacobs, *Oxford Handbook of Cultural Sociology*, 2011.

———. "Culture, Social Structure, and Discursive Fields." *Current Perspectives in Social Theory* 15 (1995): 129–54.

———. "Enriching Exchange: Cultural Dimensions of Markets." *American Journal of Economics and Sociology* 58 (1999): 1041–71.

———. "Is the Strong Program Strong Enough?" *Culture* 19, no. 2 (2005): 1, 4–6.

———. *Nation and Commemoration: Creating National Identities in the United States and Australia.* Cambridge: Cambridge University Press, 1997.

———. "A Special Camaraderie with Colleagues: Business Associations and Cultural Production for Economic Action." In Reed and Alexander, *Meaning and Method*, 17–43.

Spillman, Lyn, and Rui Gao. "Codebook." In "National Business Associations, United States, 2003." Inter-University Consortium for Political and Social Research (ICPSR), University of Michigan. No. 4333, 2005.

Spillman, Lyn, Rui Gao, Xiaohong Xu, Brian Miller, and Georgian Schiopu. "National Business Associations, United States, 2003." Inter-University Consortium for Political and Social Research (ICPSR), University of Michigan, No. 4333, 2005

Spillman, Lyn, and Michael Strand. "Interest-Oriented Action." *Annual Review of Sociology*, forthcoming.

Staber, Udo. "Corporatism and the Governance Structure of American Trade Associations." *Political Studies* 35 (1987): 278–88.

———. "A Population Perspective on Collective Action as an Organizational Form: The Case of Trade Associations." *Research in the Sociology of Organizations* 4 (1985): 181–219.

Staber, Udo, and Howard Aldrich. "Trade Association Stability and Public Policy." In *Organizational Theory and Public Policy*, edited by Richard Hall and Robert Quinn, 163–78. Beverley Hills, CA: Sage, 1983.

Steinberg, Richard. "Nonprofit Organizations and the Market." In Powell, *The Nonprofit Sector*, 118–40.

Stinchcombe, Arthur. *Economic Sociology.* New York: Academic Press, 1983.

Strang, David, and Michael Macy. "In Search of Excellence: Fads, Success Stories, and Adaptive Emulation." *American Journal of Sociology* 107 (2001): 147–82.

Strang, David, and John Meyer. "Institutional Conditions for Diffusion." *Theory and Society* 22 (1993): 487–511.

Strath, Bo. "Modes of Governance in the Shipbuilding Sector in Germany, Sweden, and Japan." In Hollingsworth, Schmitter, and Streeck, *Governing Capitalist Economies*, 72–96.

Streeck, Wolfgang, and Philippe Schmitter. "Community, Market, State—and Association? The Prospective Contribution of Interest Governance to Social Order." In Streeck and Schmitter, *Private Interest Government*, 1–29.

Streeck, Wolfgang, and Philippe Schmitter, eds. *Private Interest Government: Beyond Market and State.* London: Sage, 1985.

Sutton, Francis, Seymour Harris, Carl Kaysen, and James Tobin. *The American Business Creed*. Cambridge, MA: Harvard University Press, 1956.

Swedberg, Richard. *Interest*. Maidenhead, UK: Open University Press, 2005.

———. "Major Traditions of Economic Sociology." *Annual Review of Sociology* 17 (1991): 251–76.

———. *Max Weber and the Idea of Economic Sociology*. Princeton, NJ: Princeton University Press, 1998.

———. *Principles of Economic Sociology*. Princeton, NJ: Princeton University Press, 2003.

———. "What Has Been Accomplished in New Economic Sociology and Where Is It Heading?" *European Journal of Sociology* 45, no. 3 (2004): 317–30.

Swedberg, Richard, and Mark Granovetter. "Introduction to the Second Edition." In Granovetter and Swedberg, *The Sociology of Economic Life*, 2nd ed., 1–28.

Swidler, Ann. "Culture in Action: Symbols and Strategies." *American Sociological Review* 51, no. 2 (1986): 273–66.

———. *Talk of Love*. Chicago: University of Chicago Press, 2001.

Tedlow, Richard. *Keeping the Corporate Image: Public Relations and American Business, 1900–1950*. Greenwich, CT: JAI Press, 1979.

———. "Trade Associations and Public Relations." In Yamazaki and Miyamoto, *Trade Associations in Business History*, 139–67.

Thévenot, Laurent. "Organized Complexity: Conventions of Coordination and the Composition of Economic Arrangements." *European Journal of Social Theory* 4 (2001): 405–25.

Thornton, Patricia. *Markets from Culture: Institutional Logics and Organizational Decisions in Higher Education Publishing*. Stanford, CA: Stanford University Press, 2004.

———. "Personal versus Market Logics of Control: A Historically Contingent Theory of the Risks of Acquisition." *Organization Science* 12 (2001): 294–311.

———. "The Rise of the Corporation in a Craft Industry: Conflict and Conformity in Institutional Logics." *Academy of Management Journal* 45, no. 1 (2002): 81–101.

Tichenor, Daniel, and Richard Harris. "The Development of Interest Group Politics in America: Beyond the Conceits of Modern Times." *Annual Review of Political Science* 8 (2005): 251–70.

———. "Organized Interests and American Political Development." *Political Science Quarterly* 117, no. 4 (2002): 587–612.

Tocqueville, Alexis de. *The Tocqueville Reader: A Life in Letters and Politics*. Edited by Olivier Zunz and Alan Kahan. Oxford: Blackwell, 2002.

Trice, Harrison, and Janice Beyer. *The Cultures of Work Organizations*. Englewood Cliffs, NJ: Prentice Hall, 1993.

Trigilia, Carlo. *Economic Sociology: State, Market, and Society in Modern Capitalism*. Translated by Nicola Owtram. Malden, MA: Blackwell, 2002.

Tucker, Robert, ed. *The Marx-Engels Reader*. 2nd ed. New York: W. W. Norton, 1978.

United States. Executive Office of the President. Office of Management and Budget. *North American Industry Classification System: United States, 2002*. Lanham, MD: Bernan, 2002.

United States Department of Commerce, Temporary National Economic Committee. See Pearce.

U.S. Statistical Abstract. Online edition, http://www.census.gov/compendia/statab.

Uzzi, Brian. "Embeddedness in the Making of Financial Capital: How Social Relations and Networks Benefit Firms Seeking Finance." *American Sociological Review* 64 (1999): 481–505.

———. "Social Structure and Competition in Interfirm Networks: The Paradox of Embeddedness." *Administrative Science Quarterly* 42 (1997): 35–67.

———. "The Sources and Consequences of Embeddedness for the Economic Performance of Organizations: The Network Effect." *American Sociological Review*, 61 (1996): 674–98.

Van Maanen, John, and Stephen Barley. "Occupational Communities: Culture and Control in Organizations." *Research in Organizational Behavior* 6 (1984): 287–365.

Vaughn, Diane. "Signals and Interpretive Work: The Role of Culture in a Theory of Practical Action." In Cerulo, *Culture in Mind*, 21–54.

Verba, Sidney, Kay Schlozman, and Henry Brady. *Voice and Equality: Civic Voluntarism in American Politics*. Cambridge, MA: Harvard University Press, 1995.

Veugelers, Jack, and Michèle Lamont. "France: Alternative Locations for Public Debate." In Wuthnow, *Between States and Markets*, 125–37.

Walker, Edward. "Privatizing Participation: Civic Change and Organizational Dynamics of Grassroots Lobbying Firms." *American Sociological Review* 74, no. 1 (2009): 83–105.

Walker, Gordon, Bruce Kogut, and Weijiean Shan. "Social Capital, Structural Holes, and the Formation of an Industry Network." *Organization Science* 8, no. 2 (1997): 109–25.

Warner, W. Lloyd, and Desmond Martin. "Big Trade and Business Associations." In *The Emergent American Society*, vol. 1, edited by W. Lloyd Warner, 314–46. New Haven, CT: Yale University Press, 1967.

Watt, David Harrington. "United States: Cultural Challenges to the Voluntary Sector." In Wuthnow, *Between States and Markets*, 243–87.

Weber, Klaus, Kathryn Heinze, and Michaela DeSoucy. "Forage for Thought: Mobilizing Codes in the Movement for Grass-Fed Meat and Dairy Products." *Administrative Science Quarterly* 53 (2008): 529–67.

Weber, Max. *Economy and Society: An Outline of Interpretive Sociology*. 2 vols. Edited by Guenther Roth and Claus Wittich. Berkeley: University of California Press, 1978.

———. *The Protestant Ethic and the Spirit of Capitalism*. 2nd ed. Los Angeles: Roxbury, 1998.

Weeden, Kim. "Why Do Some Occupations Pay More Than Others? Social Closure and Earnings Inequality in the United States." *American Journal of Sociology* 108, no. 1 (2002): 55–101.

White, Harrison. "Cognition in Social Constructions: Market Rivalry Profile versus Cost Schedule." In Cerulo, *Culture in Mind*, 101–21.

———. *Markets from Networks: Socioeconomic Models of Production*. Princeton, NJ: Princeton University Press, 2002.

Willer, Robb. "Groups Reward Individual Sacrifice: The Status Solution to the Collective Action Problem." *American Sociological Review* 74 (2009): 23–43.

Williams, Rhys. "Constructing the Public Good: Cultural Resources and Social Movements." *Social Problems* 42, no. 1 (1995): 124–44.

Williamson, Oliver. *Antitrust Economics: Mergers, Contracting, and Strategic Behavior*. Oxford: Basil Blackwell, 1987.

———. "Comparative Economic Organization: The Analysis of Discrete Structural Alternatives." *Administrative Science Quarterly* 36, no. 2 (1991): 269–96.

———. "The Firm as a Nexus of Treaties: An Introduction." In Aoki, Gustafsson, and Williamson, *The Firm as a Nexus of Treaties*, 1–25.

———. "Transaction Cost Economics and Organization Theory." In Smelser and Swedberg, *Handbook of Economic Sociology*, 1st ed., 77–107.

Witt, Michael. *Changing Japanese Capitalism: Societal Coordination and Institutional Adjustment*. Cambridge: Cambridge University Press, 2006.

Wright, Erik Olin. *Envisioning Real Utopias*. New York: Verso, 2010.

Wuthnow, Robert. *Communities of Discourse: Ideology and Social Structure in the Reformation, the Enlightenment, and European Socialism*. Cambridge, MA: Harvard University Press, 1989.

———. *Poor Richard's Principle: Recovering the American Dream through the Moral Dimension of Work, Business, and Money*. Princeton, NJ: Princeton University Press, 1996.

———. "Tocqueville's Question Reconsidered: Voluntarism and Public Discourse in Advanced Industrial Societies." In Wuthnow, *Between States and Markets*, 288–308.

———. "The United States: Bridging the Privileged and Marginalized?" In Putnam, *Democracies in Flux*, 59–102.

———. "The Voluntary Sector: Legacy of the Past, Hope for the Future?" In Wuthnow, *Between States and Markets*, 3–29.

Wuthnow, Robert, ed. *Between States and Markets: The Voluntary Sector in Comparative Perspective*. Princeton, NJ: Princeton University Press, 1991.

———. *Rethinking Materialism: Perspectives on the Spiritual Dimension of Economic Behavior*. Grand Rapids, MI: Eerdmans, 1995.

Yakubovich, Valery, Mark Granovetter, and Patrick McGuire. "Electric Charges: The Social Construction of Rate Systems." *Theory and Society* 34, no. 1 (2005): 570–612.

Yamazaki, Hiroaki, and Matao Miyamoto, eds. *Trade Associations in Business History*. Tokyo: University of Tokyo Press, 1988.

Yates, JoAnne. "The Structuring of Early Computer Use in Life Insurance." *Journal of Design History* 12, no. 1 (1999): 5–24.

———. *Structuring the Information Age: Life Insurance and Technology in the Twentieth Century*. Baltimore: Johns Hopkins University Press, 2005.

Young, Birgitte. "The Dairy Industry: From Yeomanry to the Institutionalization of Multilateral Governance." In Campbell, Hollingsworth, and Lindberg, *Governance of the American Economy*, 236–58.

Young, McGee. "The Political Roots of Small Business Identity." *Polity* 40, no. 4 (2008): 436–63.

Zeitlin, Jonathan, and Charles Sabel. "Historical Alternatives to Mass Production." *Past and Present* 108 (1985): 133–76.

Zelizer, Viviana. "Beyond the Polemics on the Market: Establishing a Theoretical and Empirical Agenda." *Sociological Forum* 3 (1988): 614–34.

———. "Enter Culture." In Guillén et al., *The New Economic Sociology*, 101–25.

———. "Human Values and the Market: The Case of Life Insurance and Death in 19th-Century America." *American Journal of Sociology* 84 (1978): 591–610.

———. *Morals and Markets: The Development of Life Insurance in the United States*. New Brunswick, NJ: Transaction, 1983.

———. "Multiple Markets: Multiple Cultures." In *Diversity and Its Discontents: Cultural Conflict and Common Ground in Contemporary American Society*, edited by Neil Smelser and Jeffrey Alexander, 193–212. Princeton, NJ: Princeton University Press, 1999.

———. *The Purchase of Intimacy*. Princeton, NJ: Princeton University Press, 2005.

———. *The Social Meaning of Money*. New York: Basic Books, 1994.

Zerubavel, Eviatar. "Lumping and Splitting: Notes on Social Classification." *Sociological Forum* 11 (1996): 421–33.

———. *Social Mindscapes: An Invitation to Cognitive Sociology*. Cambridge, MA: Harvard University Press, 1997.

Zucker, Lynne. "The Role of Institutionalization in Cultural Persistence." In Powell and DiMaggio, *The New Institutionalism in Organizational Analysis*, 83–108.

Zuckerman, Ezra. "Structural Incoherence and Stock Market Activity." *American Sociological Review* 69 (2004): 405–32.

Zuckerman, Ezra, and Stoyan Sgourev. "Peer Capitalism: Parallel Relationships in the U.S. Economy." *American Journal of Sociology* 111, no. 5 (2006): 1327–66.

Zwahlen, Cyndia. "Nurturing Female Entrepreneurs." *Los Angeles Times*, September 20, 2007.

Index